THE HISPANIC PRESENCE

◆ IN NORTH AMERICA ◆

FROM 1492 TO TODAY

UPDATED EDITION

Carlos M. Fernández-Shaw

Updated Appendixes by Gerardo Piña Rosales

Translated by Alfonso Bertodano Stourton
and others

Facts On File, Inc.

The Hispanic Presence in North America from 1492 to Today, Updated Edition

Facts On File, Inc.
11 Penn Plaza
New York NY 10001

Library of Congress Cataloging-in-Publication Data

Fernández-Shaw, Carlos M.
[Presencia española en los Estados Unidos. English]
The Hispanic presence in North America from 1492 to today / Carlos M. Fernández-Shaw ; updated
appendixes by Gerardo Piña Rosales ; translated by Alfonso Bertodano Stourton and others.
— Updated ed.
p.   cm.
Includes bibliographical references (p.   ) and index.
ISBN 0-8160-4010-9
1. United States—Civilization—Spanish influences. 2. Spaniards—United States—History. 3. Spanish
Americans—History. 4. Hispanic Americans—History. I. Title.
E169.1.F375   1999
973'.0468—dc21   98-50718

Text design by Donna Sinisgalli
Cover design by Cathy Rincon

Printed in the United States of America

VB Hermitage 10 9 8 7 6 5 4 3 2 1

This book is printed on acid-free paper.

To my parents
To my wife
To my daughters

"A Queen of Castilla, Isabela, with her profound feminine instincts, named an unknown but expert navigator, Cristóbal Colón, as Admiral of the Spanish Fleet so that he could turn his dreams into reality. The ships of Spain found America, which was waiting for them, waiting to enter fully into History and to become in a few centuries an extraordinary protagonist of human destiny."

—King Juan Carlos I of Spain
Address to Congress, June 2, 1976

"In our international relations, Hispanic Americans also contribute to our nation's identity, our own perception of who we are and our role in the world, as well as others' perception of us. The strong family and cultural ties which bind Hispanics in the United States with our nearest neighbors and with Spain are an important element of the strength of the Western Hemisphere and the world."

—President Ronald Reagan
April 1985

CONTENTS

PREFACE TO THE UPDATED EDITION

I face with great joy this updated edition of my *Hispanic Presence in North America*. During my stay in Washington, D.C., in the 1960s, when I decided to undertake the difficult task of offering the public a summary of the Spanish and Hispanic influence on the United States, past and present, I would never have thought that such a topic would arouse such a broad interest in the Hispanic countries and in North America. I hope that this new edition of my work will also receive a broad reception and that it will contribute to bringing closer together the peoples of different origins.

I acknowledge my gratitude to Ms. Nicole Bowen, senior editor of Facts On File; to Mr. Gerardo Piña Rosales and Ms. Pamela Wicksel-Zayer for their cooperation in the updating of the appendixes; and to the Documentation Service of the American Embassy in Madrid for providing some present data.

Madrid, 1999

PREFACE TO THE FIRST EDITION

W hen planning to study this huge country, the United States, I chose as my guideline how it has been influenced by Spain and the Spanish across its length and breadth, and through the centuries. It would be impossible to cover every aspect of the country's history, and while I have highlighted the Spanish presence, readers should remember that many things must go unmentioned. Moreover, the country of Washington, Jefferson and Lincoln cannot help but be seen in the perspective of my own experience, with the advantages and disadvantages that this implies, but at least with the authentic voice of one who has had the opportunity of coming into personal contact with considerable sectors of the country, thousands of miles apart. Instead of writing a scholarly history, I have chosen to combine historical data with present-day events and anecdotes.

The book comprises an introduction and state-by-state study of the Spanish presence in the United States. In the Introduction, I have not tried to be exhaustive, but to emphasize some aspects of this general history and to summarize facts, exploits or events in order to give a broad basic understanding of the subject. Following the Introduction, the book traces the history and influence of the Spanish in each state. I have found no other book like this one, which is intended not only to provide a portrait of the culture but also to serve as a useful resource for those desiring to delve in greater detail into the Hispanic presence in a specific place or region.

I have chosen to approach the subject by geographic region but have, of course, adapted it to the purpose in mind by giving greater attention to the states with a significant Hispanic community. Thus, separate chapters have been devoted to Florida, Louisiana, Missouri, Texas, New Mexico, Arizona, Colorado and California.

A general history is given in Part I. Part II encompasses the Atlantic states, some of which were introduced to Western civilization through Spanish colonization, while others were settled by the English to become the original thirteen colonies. Part III covers those states lying between the East Coast and the banks of the Mississippi, which were also partly settled by the French and came into British hands through the peace settlement of 1763. The fourth part highlights the territories of Louisiana that Spain inherited from France, stretching westward from the banks of the big river as far as the Rocky Mountains. In Part V can be found the states of the Southwest, Texas, New Mexico and Arizona. Sharing a border with Mexico greatly influenced the development of these states. Part VI covers the Rocky Mountain states, and Part VII details the Pacific Coast states as well as Alaska and Hawaii.

The appendixes that follow have been included to serve as a résumé of the main points of the text and as an auxiliary tool for those who wish to learn more about Hispanic America. The first deal mainly with the historical presence of Spain, while the latter include contemporary people and organizations. A bibliography includes books and works which I have consulted, mainly in North American libraries; the index aims to facilitate the search for those topics that might be of particular interest to readers.

The text of this work, originally published and reprinted by Ediciones de Cultura Hispánica, in Madrid, is now published in English to reach non-Spanish-speaking readers and find a broader audience. This slightly abridged edition does not elaborate on some of the points of the history and life in the United States, which will already be familiar to American readers. Most Americans are proud of their country's past, comprising the story of so many ethnic groups. My aspiration is for the American reader to consider the facts in this book as something that belongs to him: the history of his own country. It is also my hope that this book will prompt English-speaking readers, whatever their nationality, to take an interest in the Hispanic contribution to the history of the United States. King Juan Carlos I of Spain, being welcomed to the White House in June 1976 by President Gerald Ford, stated: "Our two countries are bound by so many ties that it may well be said that in a certain way your history and geography have been, [a] large extent, ours too."

I would like to give special thanks, both for the English and third Spanish editions, to Facts On File, and Ms. Deirdre Mullane, for her enthusiasm and friendly attitude; Mr. Luis Zalamea, for establishing contact with her; my adviser in many respects, Dr. Rafael Peñalver; my colleagues, the Consuls of Spain in the United States; the Minister of Cultural Affairs of the Spanish Embassy, José Ramón Remacha, and the colleagues in the OID and in the Office of Treaties in the Ministry of Foreign Affairs; and my daughter Carla, who was charged with the laborious task of updating the original text and appendixes. For preparation of the indexes, I must also acknowledge *The Directory of Historical Societies and Agencies in the United States and Canada*, published by the American Association for State and Local History; the *Guide to Departments of History*, from the American Historical Association; the list of Universities and Schools where Spanish is taught, provided by the American Association of Teachers of Spanish and Portuguese; the chapters of the Sociedad Nacional Hispánica, Sigma Delta Pi, supplied by its Board of Directors; the information on Spanish Associations facilitated by Carta de España of the Instituto Español de Emigración and by the Casa de España in New York; the *Hispanic Resource Directory* from Denali Press; the *Directory of the Hispanic Community of the County of Los Angeles*; an article on Hispanic magazines in the United States since 1932, provided by Mr. Hensley C. Woodbridge; the publication *Caminos, National Hispanic Media Directory*; the volume *Hispanic Media, USA* by Ana Veciana; and the quarterly publication *Hispanic Media and Markets, SRDS*.

October 12, 1989, on the Anniversary of the Spanish Discovery
of America by Cristóbal Colón (Christopher Columbus)

INTRODUCTION

As the Renaissance exploded in Spain, its blast scattered Don Quixotes far and wide all over America. A sturdy handful of these bearded explorers burst upon the scene, heralding the arrival of European civilization. Their adventures began as soon as Columbus made his landfall on the shores of Guanahani and ended when their own homeland eventually ceased to exercise her sovereignty.

This epic unfolded in three stages. The initial one concluded when Captain John Smith succeeded in establishing the first Anglo-Saxon colony on the American mainland, at the beginning of the 17th century; meanwhile, Spain had for an entire century persevered in the discovery of new horizons as her *conquistadores* and missionaries roamed over immense territories and explored uncharted seas and coastlines.

The second stage lasted until the 1760s, when the first sparks of revolution flared in the thirteen colonies, and the Spanish monarch's governors arrived in Louisiana. Material and spiritual gains continued to be the keynote of this second phase, in which the colonist himself began to play the leading role.

The third stage was to endure for as long as the red and golden flag fluttered over Spanish territory and marked a greater contrast between the goals of Spanish policy on the American continent and the weakness of the central power in the Iberian Peninsula. Two more features can be highlighted in this period: Spain's approach to these new lands, the native Indians and rival European powers, and her attitude toward the newborn nation that—partly thanks to Spain herself—had wrested its independence from Britain.

The years that have elapsed since the independence of the United States, and, in particular, the nation as it is today, have been no less remarkable.

Throughout the first period, Spain had a free hand north of the Rio Grande and (except for the brief French interlude in Florida) met with no European resistance, though some conflict was sustained with the natives. In the second phase, she had to fight—not always successfully—to retain her conquests and defend her claims against Britain and France. In the course of the third stage, Anglo-Spanish rivalry waxed fierce (the other enemy having been defeated) and eventually resulted in Charles III's armies siding with the revolutionaries in their struggle against Great Britain.

For 20-odd years, relations between the United States and Spain were marked by growth and cooperation, but inevitable setbacks arose with the advent of peace. A period of friction ensued owing to the growing expansionism of the Anglo-Saxon settlers and the differences of opinion that the Treaty of Paris, in 1763, caused between Britain's successors and the representatives of Spain, whose rights were founded upon history and conquest. Three areas were the subject of controversy: the boundaries of Louisiana, the lands lying west of the Appalachians as far as the east bank of the Mississippi and certain territories in southern Georgia.

These differences did not give way to armed conflict but were settled peacefully: the 1795 Treaty of San Lorenzo de El Escorial, which as its full name indicates (Treaty of Friendship, Limits, Trade and Navigation), laid the foundations for friendship between the two countries and established normal, reciprocal diplomatic relations. The treaty solved the problems of boundaries, which were defined by the 31° north latitude and the Mississippi River; it permitted freedom of navigation up that great waterway and recognized New Orleans as a free port for American merchandise. The transfer of Louisiana to France, and subsequently to the United States, put an end to the incidents that its possession by Spain had caused.

The "Treaty of Friendship, transfer of the Floridas and limits," signed in Washington, D.C., in 1819, by John Quincy Adams and Luis de Onis, repeated the desire for "firm and inviolable peace" and "sincere friendship" between the two countries and their citizens already formulated in the 1795 treaty. It established Spain's relinquishment of all territories east of the Mississippi and defined the new nation's western frontier with the Spanish dominions. These limits followed a line that ran from the mouth of the Sabine River on the Gulf of Mexico, up the western bank of the river as far as 32° north latitude to meet the Red River at Natchitoches and follow its course as far as longitude 100° west. From this point the boundary ran to the Arkansas River, and then along its southern bank until it reached the parallel 42° north latitude, which it followed as far as the South Sea or Pacific Ocean.

While the treaty of 1819, ratified by King Ferdinand VII in 1820, signaled Spain's disappearance from the eastern half of the United States, it was the independence of Mexico and the fact that she inherited the remaining Spanish territories situated in the other half of the United States that caused the descendants of the *conquistadores* finally to abandon in 1822, the North American continent.

The differences between the Spaniards and the Americans in the last few years of the century of Enlightenment were not only due to problems over frontiers, but also to the attempts at secession on the part of the erstwhile State of Franklin, which straddled the boundaries between the Carolinas, Georgia and Tennessee, and also the territories of Cumberland and Kentucky. These communities repeatedly petitioned the Spanish authorities to send them aid so that they might separate from the new nation and, as independent entities within the orbit of Spanish influence, swear loyalty to the king of Spain. Some historians have criticized Spain for entertaining their requests and her reluctance to abandon her western territories for the benefit of the settlers from the east. It is certainly true that these separatist tendencies threatened the very existence of the Union, which had been achieved by dint of so much effort. But, it is no less true that it was the petitioners themselves who took the initiative in seeking separation; the Spanish authorities simply gave them a fair hearing. Their wishes might well have come to fruition if the court at Madrid had shown more determination and less fear of the possible repercussions. It should also be kept in mind that, in those early years, the leaders of the young country were unable to plan with much forethought, but were largely confined themselves to solving the problems of the present and to obtaining a period of peace, primarily to the west of the Appalachians. It was the land-hungry settlers seeking wealth who, on the one hand, caused the frontier conflicts and, on the other, felt inclined to separate from the 13 states. Spain, who had a long-standing vested interest in her North American possessions, clung to her territories and strove to consolidate them by taking advantage of the creation of a number of buffer states within her own sphere of influence. Spain's attachment to her territories, which now form part of the United States, and her determination to keep them even at the cost of bloodshed, if need be, should be readily understood by those who now proudly consider them as an inseparable part of the national wealth. It would have been quite a different history if the Spaniards, like Napoléon with his sale of Louisiana, had simply disposed of those territories as if they were mere chattels.

During the ensuing period, the United States and Spain went their separate ways, and the only significant development was the Settlement of the Claims, so thoroughly studied by the historian French Ensor Chadwick; it was signed in Madrid, on February 17, 1834, during the regency of Queen María Cristina, the signatories being Delegate C. P. Van Ness and José de Heredia.

So we come to the start of the revolutionary movements in Cuba and the aid given to the rebel leaders by their northern neighbor. The outcome was the bloody year of 1898, when the sun finally set on the Spanish Empire as her army and navy were defeated by the might of the United States. (In 1998, many commemorations, of varying types, of such a sad chapter in Spanish history took place in Spain.) Much anti-Spanish sentiment was spread by William Randolph Hearst and Joseph Pulitzer, through the influence of their newspapers. (In fact, a growing number of historians argue that Spain did not sink the battleship *Maine*, a source of much controversy.) An enormous print campaign was launched at the average citizen to rally support for the invasion of Cuba, the attacks on Manila and the Philippine Islands, and the occupation of Puerto Rico. As a result of the annexation of these possessions, the Anti-Imperialist League was founded in Boston by such well-known figures as Grover Cleveland and Andrew Carnegie and succeeded in enrolling 500,000 members.

It is curious to note the impact that the armed conflict with Spain had on the American public, who, probably impressed by the past greatness of Spain, believed in the enduring power of their rival's armed forces. In articles published on the subject subsequently. Theodore Roosevelt, himself one of the promoters of the conflict, related how one state governor would not allow the state militia to join the national army for fear of a Spanish invasion and how well-to-do inhabitants of Boston fled inland as far as Worcester with their belongings for the same reason. On Long Island, people signed contracts with additional clauses pertaining to the destruction of their properties by the Spaniards. Roosevelt commented that congressmen asked him for battleships to defend their constituencies, as did some states' chambers of commerce.

This unfortunate war ended with the peace treaty signed in Paris, on December 10, 1898, by the U.S. and Spanish delegations, the latter presided over by Eugenio Montero Ríos. Among other things, Spain handed over Cuba, Puerto Rico, the Philippine Islands and Guam. By the Treaty of Washington of 1900,

Spain further relinquished any islands in the Philippines archipelago situated outside the limits described in the treaty of 1898. The curtain fell on this episode when a Treaty of Friendship and General Relations was signed in Madrid, July 3, 1902. At least one historian has claimed that, politically speaking, this war situated the United States among the great world powers.

In the 20th century, the Spanish Civil War (1936–1939) had a considerable impact on American public opinion. Spain's own postwar period was followed by the post–World War II years, when Spain was isolated from much of Europe.

A fresh chapter in relations between the United States and Spain began in the 1950s, with agreements regarding defense and economic aid. In 1970, an Agreement of Friendship and Cooperation was signed, covering not only military matters but developments in the fields of education, agriculture, environment, space, science and technology. Further treaties were signed in the 1970s, including one in which Spain joined NATO. The U.S. Department of State has published a "List of the Treaties and Other International Agreements" in force in January 1, 1997, with Spain.

The Spanish monarchs have paid visits to the United States in 1976, 1983, 1984, 1993 and 1997. The heir to the Spanish Crown has had the opportunity to visit a large part of the United States as well. In return, some American presidents, such as Dwight D. Eisenhower, Richard Nixon, Gerald Ford, Jimmy Carter and Ronald Reagan have also traveled to Madrid. To improve Spanish-U.S. relations, a "Forum Spain–United States" was founded with annual meetings alternating at each country. The second forum in Toledo (Spain) was chaired by the Prince of Asturias. In such a spirit, the foundation MAPFRE AMERICA printed in 1992 a 15-volume account of the relations between Spain and the United States.

On October 24, 1961, John F. Kennedy invited a group of Spanish dignitaries to the White House. Welcoming them he said: "I have always felt that one of the great lacks among Americans of this country, in their knowledge of the past, has been their knowledge of the whole Spanish influence and exploration and development in the sixteenth century in the Southwest United States, which is a tremendous story. Unfortunately, too many Americans think that America was discovered in 1620 when the Pilgrims came to my own State, and they forget the tremendous adventure of the sixteenth century and the early seventeenth century in the Southern and Southwest United States."

Two years later, on March 12, 1963, Vice President Lyndon B. Johnson commented at the end of a gala banquet held by the city of St. Augustine, Florida to commemorate the 450th anniversary of the discovery of those lands by Juan Ponce de León:

> Much of my life has been spent in contact with the living vestiges of that Spanish heritage. My first job after college was as teacher and principal in a Spanish-speaking school. My association with descendants of our Spanish heritage has been intimate and my friendship for them and affection toward them has been warm and rewarding all my life. Under these personal circumstances, it is specially gratifying to me to have this part in your efforts here to remind the nation of the rich endowment our culture has received, and the great debt our history owes, to the explorers and settlers from Spain, who opened the New World . . . If we of this country have taken our language, our law, and other components of our life from the Anglo-Saxon heritage, we have also taken into our culture and our values and our national characteristics much that is important to us from virtually all the cultures from Europe.

Referring to St. Augustine he said: ". . . no American can come here and see the restoration of the first city on the North American mainland without appreciating anew how great was the faith of the men who landed on these shores 450 years ago."

Similar sentiments had been expressed by others. Walt Whitman wrote as follows on July 20, 1883:

> We Americans have yet to really learn our own antecedents, and sort them, to unify them. They will be found ampler than has been supposed and in widely different sources. Thus far, impress'd by New England writers and schoolmasters, we tacitly abandon ourselves to the notion that our United States have been fashion'd from the British Islands only, and essentially from a second England only—which is a very great mistake . . . To that composite American identity of the future, Spanish character will supply some of the most needed parts. No stock shows grander historic retrospect—grander in religiousness and loyalty, or for patriotism, courage, decorum, gravity and honor . . . It is time to realize—for it is certainly true—that there will not be found any more cruelty, tyranny, superstition, and, in the résumé of Spanish history than in the corresponding résumé of Anglo-Norman history. Nay, I think there will not be found so much.

Finally, the historian Charles F. Lummis has commented, "the honor of giving America to the world belongs to Spain."

By a joint resolution passed on September 17, 1968, Congress approved the proclamation of a National Hispanic Heritage Week, a proclamation that was repeated annually under President Nixon and his successors. The week of October 12 has also been named Hispanic Heritage Week by Dade County, Florida. These important testimonials indicate a growing tendency to acknowledge the Hispanic contribution to events in North America.

Many historians have overlooked the Spanish contribution to the history of the United States. Here, certainly, many examples could be quoted. The well-known historians Allan Nevins and Henry Steele Commager, in *A Pocket History of the United States*, make no reference whatsoever to Spain in the chapters dealing with the first colonies, the colonial heritage or the southern colonies, and it is only in the chapter on the "French Wars" that they devote two pages to Spanish activity. In *The Birth of the United States*, Isaac Asimov begins his account in 1763 and only mentions the Spaniards in the chronology, in regard to California and the Treaties of Transfer. The same author, in his work *The Shaping of North America*, mentions Columbus and his ships without stressing Spanish participation in the discovery. However, he does devote a chapter to the expansion of Spain in the other areas of the American continent. And yet, there is no denying what Henry Adams describes as the immense, but intermittent, influence of Spain upon the United States, in the different stages of exploration, the settling of various areas, the occupation of Louisiana and the American Revolution. Regarding Spanish influence on the indigenous populations, the historian Dean Snow, among others, has concluded that the Spanish expeditions in the early days did not kill as many Indians as it has been supposed; Snow believed that the existing Indian population may have been nine times smaller than what some historians have stated.

What would have happened without Spanish influence? The whole history of the South, Southwest and West would have been substantially different, and so, to a lesser extent, would the history of the rest of the country. What would have been the effect if success had crowned the efforts of Vázques de Ayllón to settle at San Miguel de Gualdape (the Carolinas), or Menéndez de Avilés at Santa Elena (Port Royal, South Carolina), for example. And what if Spain's 18th-century rulers, who had to contend with the nation's decline at home, had harkened to the separatist intentions of Kentucky or Cumberland, or had not agreed to the return of Louisiana to France?

Let us now indeed consider the stamp left by Spain and her civilization in states like New Mexico, Colorado, Florida, California, Arizona and Louisiana. This influence is found in some states more than in others and is witnessed by elegant architectural works that speak for themselves, including San Marcos Castle at St. Augustine, the Vieux Carré in New Orleans, the Palace of the Governors of Santa Fe, or the missions in Texas, New Mexico, Arizona and California. To these can be added the thousands of Spanish names borne by states, cities and towns, streets, rivers, mountains; the numerous Spanish words that have been assimilated into the English language; the modern buildings whose style shows Spanish artistic traits; the hallmark left upon customs, festivities and folklore; and the land whose title deeds are based on grants made in the name of the king of Spain.

The most interesting part of Spain's contribution to the United States is to be found in the years before the Anglo-Saxon population came to dominate certain areas of the country. Spain entered American history prior to the period that American historians often choose as the real starting point of the nation's history. The frequent exclusion of the Hispanic presence in North America from history books is not easily explained in the light of the abundant historical sources available. It is known that the Spaniards were at pains to given their conquests the proper legal status, and that is why any expedition bent on conquest or exploration was accompanied by a scrivener, who bore witness to and would draft the record of any historic events they had seen. Bureaucracy, which played such an important part in the decline of Spain by slowing down the processes of urgent decision making, was at the same time responsible for the abundance of sources of information.

The missionaries also wrote about their work in their periodic reports to their superiors. Moreover, whenever differences arose between the civil and religious authorities, the ensuing spate of letters and reports from both sides provides a magnificent source of historical information. In this respect, the historian Ralph P. Wright has noted in *California's Missions* that the Spanish occupation of California is one of the best-documented colonizing efforts carried out by any nation: the number of registers, accounts, liens, diaries and reports written up by the first Californians is truly astounding.

The first known reports on the geography and native peoples of the United States are written in Spanish. A complete list would be too long to include here, but a few examples will serve to illustrate this activity: *Naufragios (Shipwrecks)*, written by Cabeza de Vaca and published in 1542; the writings of Hidalgo de Elvas, Biedma and Secretary Ranjel on the Hernando de Soto expedition (1539–1542); Pedro de Castañeda's report on Vázquez de Coronado's march through the Southwest (1540–1542); *Florida del Inca*, by Garcilaso de la Vega; the chronicle of the travels of Juan Rodriguez Cabrillo up the Pacific coast, in 1542; the statement given by Pedro de Bustamante on the Rodriguez y Chamuscado expedition in 1582; the poem *La Florida* by Father Escobedo (1578); Antonio Espejo's chronicle of his entry into New Mexico in 1583; Juan de Oñate's letter to the viceroy, written from New Mexico on March 2, 1599; Sebastián de Vizcaíno's log book relating his explorations on the West coast in 1602; the two chronicles of that expedition written by Father Antonio de la Ascensión; the diary of Fernando del Bosque recounting his entry into Texas in 1675; the letter written by Father Damián Massanet to Carlos de Sigüenza in 1690; and many more texts of this sort, which must go unmentioned here.

How long did the Spanish flag fly over the territory of what is now the United States? On April 2, 1513, Juan Ponce de León sighted the coast of Florida, went ashore and claimed it in the name of King Ferdinand and Queen Isabella of Spain. On December 26, 1821, news of Mexico's independence from Spain reached Santa Fe, but it was not until well into 1822 that the Spanish flag was lowered in California. Thus, the Spanish colors flew for 309 years north of the Rio Grande.

By contrast, let's see how long other sovereign flags have flown over these territories. The Stars and Stripes was established by Congress on June 14, 1777, therefore existing for a little more than 200 years. If we take the first date for the reign of the British flag to be 1586, when Sir Walter Raleigh established his colony on Roanoke Island in Virginia (whose mysterious demise would earn it the name "Lost Colony"), then it only flew for 197 years in the land on which it had such a lasting effect. The French presence began in 1672 with the explorations of Father Jacques Marquette and Louis Joliet; they left in 1763, when Louisiana was ceded to Britain under the Treaty of Paris, so they were here for less than a century. If the starting point is taken as the sporadic presence of Jean Ribault and his men on the east coast, in 1563, even though no other Frenchman returned until 1672, at the very most the French were here for two centuries. Mexico succeeded Spain in the western territories of the United States in 1821 and left after the Treaty of Guadalupe Hidalgo of 1848, when New Mexico and California were handed over to the United States, a total of 27 years. The periods of Swedish and Dutch domination were even shorter.

The Spaniards withdrew their permanent settlement from South Carolina in 1587, and the last mission disappeared from Georgia in 1703. They held Florida until July 17, 1821, when General Andrew Jackson took possession of the western sector. They left Alabama on April 13, 1813, when Jackson himself took Mobile. In Mississippi, they ruled until that same date, when Biloxi and Gulfport became part of the United States. Spain held the far-flung territories of Louisiana from 1763 until 1803. In all the territories of Lower Louisiana, the end of Spanish sovereignty came on November 30, 1803. In what was known as Upper Louisiana, namely Missouri, Iowa, Minnesota and all the lands to the west, except those mentioned below, Spanish rule lasted until March 9, 1804. Spain remained in Arizona, Colorado, Utah and New Mexico until 1821, although Mexico did not assume sovereignty until January 6, 1822. The Spanish flag was not lowered in California until November 1822, when the first Mexican governor took possession. In Texas, Spanish rule ended on July 1, 1821. Thus, Spain played a significant role in American history until only a little over a century and a half ago.

PART I:
A GENERAL HISTORY

◆ *DISCOVERY AND EXPLORATION* ◆

Christopher Columbus

The man who claimed the New World for Spain was Christopher Columbus (Cristóbal Colón), a native of Genoa, Italy. However, it was as a subject of Spain's Queen Isabella of Castile and King Ferdinand of Aragon and while sailing on the Spanish caravels *Santa María, Pinta* and *Niña* with a largely Spanish crew that he discovered the New World on October 12, 1492, and he was rewarded with the title Admiral of the Ocean Sea. To this day, his direct Spanish descendants in the male line still bear his other titles of dukes of Veragua and marquesses of Jamaica.

Columbus introduced the American continent to the Old World. He landed on an island named San Salvador. Historians are now undecided as to whether this was what the British later called Watling Island—named after the pirate Watling—or Cat Island (Isla del Gato), or the Samana Cay. At any rate, Columbus landed on one of the islands in the Bahamas archipelago, which belongs geographically to North America, and claimed it for Spain.

Of this event the historian Charles F. Lummis has declared: "It was, indeed, a man of Genoa who gave us America; but he came as a Spaniard from Spain, on Spanish faith and Spanish money, in Spanish ships and with Spanish crews; and what he found he took possession of in the name of Spain." Historian Michael Kraus

describes the travels of Columbus and Vespucci as Spanish voyages. In fact, most Americans attribute the discovery of America to Spain.

The United States has been generous in honoring Columbus. October 12 is called Columbus Day, and in 1971 President Richard Nixon proclaimed the second Monday in October a national holiday. Nine states (Arkansas, Florida, Georgia, New York, North Carolina, Oregon, Pennsylvania, Washington and Wisconsin) have

Two representations of Spain's oceanic fleet, circa 1490. The illustration on the right is taken from a Latin version of a letter from Columbus to King Ferdinand, written in May 1493.

1

Coat of arms granted Christopher Columbus by Queen Isabella of Spain. Foto Bourbon.

A painting of Christopher Columbus, known as the "Talleyrand portrait," attributed to Sebastiano del Piombo.

counties named for Columbus. There are towns named after Columbus in 27 states, and in some cases there are two or three different variants; towns of a certain size usually have at least one street dedicated to Columbus; Columbia is the name of the largest river flowing into the Pacific Ocean and of one of the country's most prestigious universities; the Knights of Columbus is the largest Catholic men's society in the country; and statues to the memory of Christopher Columbus abound. The District of Columbia is the administrative name for the nation's capital, and a lasting reminder of early suggestions to name the country Columbia.

Queen Isabella has been less heralded, though statues have been erected in her honor in Washington, D.C., Sacramento and St. Louis. Queen Isabella Day is celebrated in some states on April 22, and the Daughters of Isabella, based on the Catholic University in Washington, grant annual scholarships in her honor. Her image has also appeared on various U.S. stamps and coins.

Let us look briefly at the Spanish explorers, *conquistadores* and *adelantados,* or governors, who gave their hopes, blood and efforts to North America. In a nation where progress is a keynote today, it is easy to forget the part played by the men who first opened up the country. The early Spanish governors found themselves in a largely inhospitable land, uncultivated, uninhabited over wide areas, often extreme in climatic conditions and peopled by fierce Indians. This was a difficult land to travel on horseback, let alone on foot, and the speed of travel was invariably hampered by the need to take livestock and merchandise to ensure survival in the unknown vastness ahead. In less than two centuries, 92 Spanish expeditions are estimated to have crisscrossed the United States.

The Years Before 1607

The first group of Spanish expeditions that made history took place prior to 1607, the year in which Captain John Smith set up the first British colony at Jamestown. Juan Ponce de León reached the coast of Florida in 1513 and visited its western shores again in 1521. In 1526, the lawyer Lucas Vázquez de Ayllón established a colony at San Miguel de Gualdape, now in the state of South Carolina. In the spring of 1528, Pánfilo de Narváez disembarked with an expedition of 300 from Tampa, Florida, and explored north and western Florida before reembarking in the Gulf of Mexico and voyaging, in boats the expeditionaries built themselves, along the coast as far as the shores of Texas. There, they were shipwrecked and, with the exception of Alvar Núñez Cabeza de Vaca and several others, most of them lost their lives. Cabeza de Vaca survived enslavement and great hardship and eventually made his way on foot with three of his companions to New Spain (now Mexico), which they reached in 1536.

In 1539, Hernando de Soto left Cuba with an imposing expedition of 570 men and 223 horses. They disembarked at Tampa Bay, Florida, and their explorations took them through parts of what are now the states of Florida, Georgia, the Carolinas, Tennessee, Alabama, Mississippi, Arkansas and Louisiana. Following de Soto's death in 1542, the expedition proceeded under the command of Luis de Moscoso, crossed Texas and eventually found its way back to Mexico by following the Mississippi downstream to the sea. Their journey has been characterized as "the most remarkable expedition in the history of North America" by the historian E. G. Bourne. (These states are now cooperating in a project to reconstruct the De Soto Trail, placing trailside markers at five-mile intervals and locating roadside exhibits along the way.) In 1549, the Dominicans tried to found a mission at Tampa. Ten years later, Tristán de Luna established a Spanish settlement at Pensacola, Florida. In 1565 St. Augustine was founded by Menéndez de Avilés, and this was the beginning of Spanish colonization in Florida and the lands to the north. Between 1539 and 1542, Francisco Vázquez de Coronado led an expedition through what are now New Mexico, Oklahoma, Kansas and, perhaps, Nebraska, and stopped little more than 300 miles short of Moscoso's position. In 1566 and 1567, Juan Pardo and Hernando Boyano explored the present states of Georgia, South Carolina and, possibly, North Carolina and Alabama. Jesuits founded a mission at Chesapeake Bay in 1570, having already done so at several other points in Florida and Georgia, which were later take over by Franciscans. In 1581, Brother Agustín Rodríguez and Francisco Sánchez Chamuscado ventured into Texas and New Mexico. The following year, Antonio Espejo led an expedition through Arizona and New Mexico. In 1598, Juan de Oñate entered New Mexico with a large contingent of settlers and soldiers, and explored the territories of Texas, Oklahoma and Kansas. Santa Fe was founded in 1610.

Spain had a great hand in establishing the geography of the United States. Lummis writes, "One nation had the glory of discovering and exploring America, of chang-ing the whole world's ideas of geography . . . And Spain was that nation." While working at Puerto de Santa María in 1500, Juan de la Cosa, a Spaniard from Santander, completed the first general map of America, in which the lands discovered up to that date were shown as a separate landmass. The Spanish map drawn by Alberto Cantino in 1502 includes the peninsula of Florida, which was to be visited in 1513 and 1521 by Ponce de León. In 1521, Francisco Gordillo and Pedro Quexos reached and took possession of Chicora, in what is now North Carolina. Four years later, Quexos again explore the coast of North America to a point north of Cape Hatteras.

In that same year, 1525, another Spanish navigator, Esteban Gómez, spent 10 months sailing up the east coast as far as what are now New Brunswick and Nova Scotia, in Canada. He then sailed south to Cuba, sighting along the way Cape Cod, Nantucket Island, the mouths of the Connecticut, Hudson and Delaware Rivers, and also, perhaps, the Chesapeake Bay. (The World Almanac names the discoverer of Chesapeake Bay as Pedro [Menéndez] Marqués.) His reports were used by Diego Ribeiro, cartographer to the Holy Roman Emperor and king of Spain Charles V, as a basis for his famous map of 1529, the first ever to show the east coast of the United States almost perfectly outlined.

Another exceptionally important map was to appear in 1562, drawn by Diego Gutiérrez. Apart from the map's artistic merit, it showed a number of geographical features that had not until then been charted so thoroughly; it was to be the most detailed map of the New World of its day and included the name California for the first time. Apart from his association in exploratory ventures with Sebastian Cabot, Gutiérrez was pilot major and examiner of pilots to the Spanish Crown from 1518 to 1547.

Spain's contribution to the discovery and cartography of the Atlantic seaboard of North America prior to 1607 was certainly important, but so was the charting of the coast of the Gulf of Mexico. In the first two decades of the 16th century, these shores had been visited and explored in an erratic fashion by a number of Spanish navigators, but no one had plotted a chart of the coastline until Alonso de Alvarez de Pineda did so in 1519 on the orders of the Governor of Cuba, Francisco de Garay. His chart was the first ever to include what is now the state of Texas. Therefore, by the mid-16th century, the Spaniards had provided the world with fairly accurate information about the New World, the Atlantic coast and the Caribbean.

The 1542 expedition of Juan Rodriguez Cabrillo and Bartolomé Ferrelo was the first to explore the coast of California. The former man sailed as far as the 38th parallel, to a spot just north of San Francisco Bay. On Rodriguez Cabrillo's death, Ferrelo succeeded him in the command of the expedition. Setting sail once more, he reached Cape Mendocino at the 40th parallel and then proceeded northward until, in March 1543, he arrived at 44° north latitude in southern Oregon. Francisco de Ulloa, in 1539, was the first navigator to realize that lower California was a peninsula. The first man to draw the coast of California was Sebastián Vizcaíno, who also sailed as far as 43° north latitude, reaching southern Oregon in 1602. In the last quarter of the 18th century, Spanish seamen completed their reconnaissance of the western coast, including the coast of Alaska.

Spanish explorers also contributed to the knowledge of geography of the interior of the country. The Appalachians and their southern ranges, the Great Smokies, were seen and crossed for the first time, in 1540, by Hernando de Soto and his party, who gave this mountain chain its present name. Having been told by Indians that there was a town north of Florida called Apalachee (present-day Tallahassee), they gave the name to the whole region and, subsequently, to the nearby mountains through which they passed. Pedro de Castañeda, the chronicler on Francisco Vázquez de Coronado's expedition, was the first European to mention the Rocky Mountains in his *Relación,* or "account." Two centuries later, in 1761, another Spaniard, Juan de Rivera, was the first European ever to cross the Rockies.

The Rio Grande separating the United States from Mexico was originally called Río de las Palmas (River of the Palms) by Alvarez de Pineda in 1519. It was thus the first river on the continent to receive a European name. Juan de Oñate, in 1598, like Castaño de Sosa before him in 1590, called it Río Bravo, the name by which it is still known in Mexico. The lay brother Agustín Rodríguez had named it Río Guadalquivir in 1581. The historian Paul Horgan lists 13 other names by which the river has been known over the centuries.

The mouth of the Mississippi was sighted in 1519 by Alonso Alvarez de Pineda, who called it Río del Espíritu Santo (River of the Holy Spirit). The first explorers to encounter it while trekking overland were Hernando de Soto and his expedition in 1541 in the vicinity of Memphis. It was in this river that the great *conquistador's* body was laid to rest in 1542. De Soto also discovered the Tennessee River and many others.

Indians reported to Coronado in 1540 that there was a great river some distance away with very muddy waters—the Missouri River. Hernando de Alarcón discovered the Colorado River in 1540. Its lower reaches were first named Buena Guía (Good Guide), and also Tizona, but these names did not last. It received its present name from Oñate in 1604 because, as Father Salmerón pointed out, "its waters flow red."

The Arkansas River was crossed by Coronado in Kansas on June 29, 1541, the feast day of St. Peter and St. Paul, from which it got the name Río de San Pedro y San Pablo. Some claim that Juan de Zaldívar, Juan de Oñate's nephew, reached Denver, Colorado, about 1600 and called the nearby river Chato (flat), this characterization preserved in its present name Platte. The Columbia River was first seen by members of the expedition led by Bruno de Heceta and Juan Pérez on August 17, 1775.

The Years After 1607

These were the exploits of the Spaniards before the first Englishman settled permanently in North America. The Atlantic seaboard abounded in Franciscan missions and *presidios* (forts) during the 17th century. Florida was coveted by Britain from 1763 to 1783, when she finally succeeded in wresting it from Spain through diplomacy rather than the force of arms. Between 1763 and 1803, Mobile, Alabama, New Orleans and the territories of Louisiana were governed by Spain.

Texas became the objective for many Spanish expeditions, in the 17th and 18th centuries, from that of Fernando Bosque, accompanied by Father Larios, to those of Alonso de León, the marquess of San Miguel de Aguayo and Martín de Alarcón. Many missions, *presidios* and a considerable number of towns were founded, chiefly on the initiative of José de Escandón. The great endeavor of colonizing New Mexico took place after its reconquest by Diego de Vargas, when this territory experienced a period of prosperity. A similar task was undertaken in Arizona thanks to Father Eusebio Francisco Kino and his fellow Jesuits, who were later succeeded by the Franciscans.

Colorado was the scene of a series of exploratory expeditions that opened the way for subsequent settlements. The route linking Utah with Arizona was discovered by Father Francisco Hermenegildo Garcés in 1776 and later came to be known as the Vado de los Padres, or Crossing of the Fathers; for many years it was the only known ford

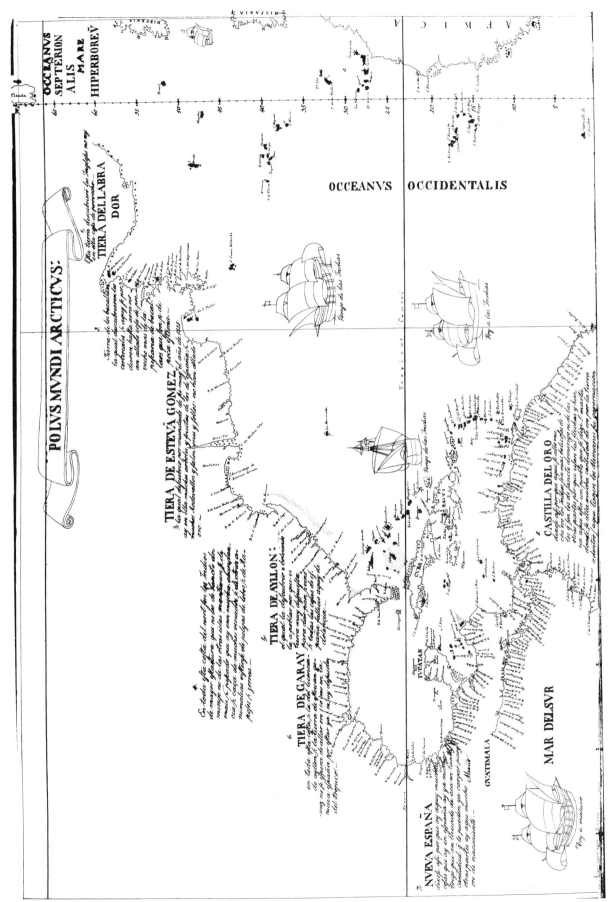

Spanish territories in the New World at the end of the 16th century.

leading west. Fathers Silvestre Vélez de Escalante and Atanasio Domínguez appeared at the same spot a few days later, after being the first to see Lake Utah. In 1769, Spaniards from the south, under the command of Gaspar de Portolá and the spiritual guidance of Father Junípero Serra, disembarked in California.

The Spaniards were the first Europeans to explore the west coast of North America. In 1774, Juan Pérez, aboard the *Santiago,* sighted the coast of Alaska and cast anchor at Nootka. In 1775, with the expedition of Bruno Heceta, Juan Francisco de la Bodega y Cuadra sailed as far as 58° north latitude and plotted the geographical chart of the coastline between Monterey (California) and 50° north latitude. In 1779, a third expedition commanded by Ignacio de Arteaga, with Bodega y Cuadra as his second-in-command, reached Bucarelli Cove, north of California, where they disembarked and took possession of the land on May 13. Prince of Wales Island was explored during that expedition. A fourth expedition, led by Ensign Esteban José Martínez, reached Prince William sound (above 60° north latitude) in 1788 and took possession of the northernmost tip of Unalaska Island, the remotest and westernmost of the major Aleutian Islands at 167° longitude. Alejandro Malaspina reached Alaska in 1791. The Spaniards also visited the Hawaiian Islands during the 16th, 17th and 18th centuries.

The two oldest cities in the United States were founded by the Spaniards. The first was St. Augustine, founded by Admiral Pedro Menéndez de Avilés, who called it San Agustín, on August 28, 1565. The second was Santa Fe, whose full name was La Villa Real de la Santa Fe de San Francisco de Asís. It was founded by Governor Pedro de Peralta in 1610. It should be remembered that the oldest city in North America, Santo Domingo, was likewise founded by the Spaniards in 1498; San Juan, in Puerto Rico, dates back to 1510.

The Spaniards founded many other towns and cities, such as Pensacola, Florida; New Iberia and Lake Charles, Louisiana; San Antonio, Texas; Albuquerque, Bernalillo and Los Lunas, New Mexico; Tucson, Arizona; and Los Angeles, San Diego, Santa Barbara, Monterey and San Francisco, California. Galveston, Texas, takes its name from Governor Bernardo de Gálvez. A large number of other townships came into being by special charter of the king of Spain. Examples are Dubuque, Iowa; and New Madrid, New Bourbon, Carondelet and Florissant (San Fernando de Florissant), Missouri. In addition to those mentioned, a multitude of other smaller towns and villages bear Spanish names. (A list of these cities appears at the end of the chapter dedicated to each state. The Hispanic place-names have been mostly respected; however, there have been cases—as Professor Emilio Lorenzo points out—where these have been added more with the imagination than with command of the language: for example Buena Park, Mount Alta, Arroyo Creek, etc.).

The Extent of the Hispanic Influence

Having seen Spain's achievements through the centuries, it is worth looking at the area of her influence. In the year of independence, 1783, the newborn United States consisted of the 13 provinces, with some small territories dominated de facto by unorganized groups of United States citizens. The modest area covered by the new nation at that time contrasts with Spain's possessions: all of the territories west of the Mississippi, as well as those east of the Mississippi below the 31st parallel, including Florida. Spain also claimed sovereignty over the land between the great river and the Appalachians. These possessions amounted to well over two-thirds of the country.

Few states in the Union have not been influenced by Spain in one way or another. Those where Spain's presence is most obvious are, of course, Florida, Louisiana, Texas, New Mexico, Arizona and California. Nevertheless, some of the Spanish exploits in the other states were truly outstanding. The coastline from Maine to the South was visited by Esteban Gómez in 1525. Exercising an act of sovereignty in the name of the king of Spain, he named many landmarks, and some of those names survive to this day. It is hardly surprising that the neighboring regions shown on maps of the day bear the legend Tierras de Gómez (Lands of Gómez). Esteban Gómez himself or another navigator in the service of the Emperor Charles V is known to have sought refuge ashore in what is now Maryland in that very year and was probably the first European to set foot on that soil.

The first to disembark in Virginia were Angel Villafañe's men, in 1561, while the first to settle were the Jesuits, at Axacán (near Jamestown), in 1570. The first settlers in the Carolinas founded San Miguel de Gualdape, in 1526; the eastern seaboard from Chesapeake Bay southward was called Tierras de Ayllón, or Ayllón's Land (on Ribeiro's map, for instance).

In 1539, de Soto's expeditionaries, and later, in 1566–1567, members of Juan Pardo and Hernando Boyano's party, were the first white men to explore the eastern states overland. By 1565, the Spaniards had a permanent settlement at Santa Elena, South Carolina, near what is now Port Royal. The Spanish presence in Georgia dates back to de Soto, in 1539, and to the Jesuit and Franciscan missionaries from 1565 onward.

De Soto trekked through the states of Florida, Georgia, the Carolinas, Tennessee, Alabama, Mississippi, Arkansas and Louisiana (some claim that his route also passed through Oklahoma, Missouri and Kansas) between 1539 and 1542. The following year, his men traveled through Texas, already visited by Cabeza de Vaca and his companions after they were shipwrecked in 1528, in the vicinity of present-day Galveston. The coastline of the Gulf of Mexico was shown on maps such as that drawn by Ribeiro as Tierras de Garay, or Garay's Land.

This small band of men was also the first to roam through the states of New Mexico and Arizona, while it was Father Marcos de Niza who took possession of these territories in the name of the king of Spain, in 1539. The states of Oklahoma, Kansas and Nebraska were visited by Vázquez de Coronado in 1541 and by Juan Oñate and his party in 1601. It was in what is now the state of Michigan that the Spaniards won a victory over the British at San José (present-day Niles) in 1780; to do this, they had to pass through Indiana and Illinois, where their march went unchecked. The state of Wisconsin likewise saw Spanish military success in 1796, during the war against Britain.

Over the centuries, 71 Spanish military forts were built in North and South Carolina, Georgia, Florida, Tennessee, Alabama, Mississippi, Louisiana, Arkansas, Missouri, Colorado, Texas, Arizona and California. The city of Dubuque was founded by a grant of the king of Spain with the name of Minas de España (Mines of Spain). Several states belonging to the Upper Louisiana territory—such as the Dakotas, Iowa and Nebraska—were visited by the popular Spanish pioneer Manuel Lisa, particularly in the years between 1800 and 1820. St. Louis, Missouri, was the seat of the Spanish lieutenant governor for almost 40 years, while several of his subordinate commanders resided in the territory, and many localities were founded during the Spanish period.

Colorado was the objective for frequent expeditions after the visit of Juan de Zaldívar in about 1600, and its colonization was directly linked to that of New Mexico. Father Silvestre Escalante reached Lake Utah in 1776, long before the Mormon pioneers. California was traversed by Rodríguez Cabrillo and his men in 1542, and his successor, Ferrelo, explored the coasts of Oregon in the following year.

Spain's Role in the War of Independence

On the occasion of the bicentennial of the United States, Spain made a special effort to take part and emphasize her role in the battle for independence. When proclaiming National Hispanic Heritage Week, President Ford declared that "America's Hispanic Heritage was strong even before we achieved our independence. Men and women of Hispanic origin fought in the Revolutionary War and in subsequent conflicts." On their first official visit abroad, King Juan Carlos I and Queen Sofía of Spain traveled to Washington, D.C., and New York. In Washington they unveiled a monument to Bernardo de Gálvez and a statue of Don Quixote, presented by the Spanish government; they also opened an exhibition on Christopher Columbus and his times. In New York they unveiled a plaque at the foot of the monument to the Spanish soldiers who fell in the War of Independence.

King Juan Carlos was received by Congress on June 2, 1976, and in his address said: "Today we render homage to the birth of the United States of America, to the Independence you proclaimed in the Congress of Philadelphia two hundred years ago. This homage cannot be limited to a few ceremonial phrases, for it has profound historic roots which rest on the common experience in which our nations have participated."

President Ford welcomed the king of Spain at the White House saying: "The people of Spain and America can recall with pride a group of brave Spaniards led by Bernardo de Gálvez, who helped 200 years ago in our struggle for national independence." (In Spain, four postage stamps were issued to commemorate the occasion, bearing the effigy of Gálvez, the taking of Pensacola, a dollar bill and one of the Spanish rifles supplied to the rebels.)

Spain's contribution to the struggle of the thirteen colonies indeed deserves closer attention. The American historian Buchanan Parker Thomson writes: "The story of the contribution of France has often been told. But what of the contribution of Spain? That story has been sadly and inexplicably neglected. It is my purpose to reveal that story dispassionately and objectively as it was unrolled in Spain itself and on the continent of North America. It is a story revealed in the actions and the testimony of Americans and Spaniards—traders, soldiers, diplomats, as well as simple citizens, both Spanish and American, who played their heroic roles and who are until this day forgotten heroes of a forgotten ally." Spanish author Manuel Conrotte states: "The role played by Spain in the independence of the United

States is not so negligible that it can be disregarded when recounting this event of such undeniable importance in the history of modern people." While some historians have minimized Spain's role, the Resolution of the Philadelphia Congress in 1783 is meaningful: the king of Spain was bestowed the title of Powerful Protector and Defender of the Independence of the United States of America.

The abundant documentation on the War of Independence shows how essential the Spanish alliance was for the victory of the rebels. This is clear from the correspondence between the first representative in Europe, Silas Deane, and Robert Morris; from the letters that the Committee of Secret Correspondence sent its envoys (describing the help of France and Spain as "indispensably necessary"); from the statements of John Adams in Amsterdam; from the instructions given on several occasions by Congress to Franklin and his colleagues; and from statements made by Washington himself, to mention but a few sources.

France and Spain were the only countries to harken to the rebel appeals and to assist them in their enterprise. Russia and Prussia were less generous; they remained neutral or, at most, offered to mediate in the conflict. It is true that the respective policies pursued by France and by King Charles III's ministers, first Grimaldi and then Floridablanca, were on different planes. But, so, too, were the positions of the two countries: France had relinquished all interest in America by the peace of 1763; Spain, on the other hand, had a vast American empire that would inevitably be affected by the outcome of the war.

Two periods can be distinguished here: the period between the start of the Revolution and Spain's declaration of war on Britain in 1779; and the period from 1779 until Britain's recognition of independence. If Spain's open military role in the war came during the latter period, her assistance during the first period was no less considerable.

As early as 1776, Charles III provided the rebels with a loan of 1 million *livres tournoises*, equivalent to 4 million *reales de vellón*, the same sum granted by France. This sum was sent to the count of Aranda, Spain's anti-British ambassador in Paris, who handed it over to the French treasury in exchange for a receipt signed by M. Vergennes. This significant loan was noteworthy in itself; but what makes it more significant is the fact that the loan was made available in foreign currency at a time when the Spanish treasury was impoverished and the country was preparing the expedition led by Pedro Antonio de Cevallos to the Río de la Plata.

All matters concerning loans to the Americans were cloaked in secrecy to prevent British agents from catching wind of them. These funds and those furnished by France were channeled through the Spanish firm Rodríguez, Hortalez y Compañía, which was run by the famous dramatist Caron de Beaumarchais, author of *The Marriage of Figaro, The Barber of Seville* and other works with Spanish settings. This company paid for the journey of the renowned Baron von Steuben, who disembarked at Portsmouth, New Hampshire, on December 1, 1772, and contributed so greatly to eventual victory by the training methods and discipline that he introduced in Washington's armies. Lafayette himself embarked for America at the Spanish port of Pasajes, because he did not think it safe to leave from France.

Spanish ports were opened to American privateers seeking refuge along the Spanish coast. These Spanish facilities caused the first clash with Britain over the uprising in her colonies. When the British ambassador asked that the rebel ships be denied refuge, the Spanish answer was that they were British ships, that it was hard to tell the difference between loyalists and rebels; and, secondly, that a refusal of Spanish port facilities might induce them to capture Spanish shipping, in which case a threat of reprisals by Spain would be useless owing to the small volume of American trade. The activities of these privateers undoubtedly caused serious harm to British trade, and they benefited considerably from the benevolence of both France and Spain. The taking of prizes by rebel privateers gave rise to new problems in international law, since the colonies were not a belligerent power and their independence had not been recognized.

As a result of her benevolent attitude, Spanish shipping was harassed by British vessels, and the complaints of the Spanish government went unanswered. This was the case, for instance, with the packet boat *Santa Barbara*. British policy caused Count Floridablanca to draft a "summary of the harm done by the Navy of Great Britain to the ships and territories of Spain so far, of which we have delivered complaint." This summary met with silence, which contributed to the severance of relations between the two countries.

In Spain, newspapers such as the *Gaceta de Madrid* and *El Mercurio Histórico* published pro-rebel propaganda foretelling their victory before there was any real basis for doing so (the January 1776 issue of *El Mercurio* reads: "everything seems to make their resistance sacred and respectable, and their claims, just"). Meanwhile, on the North American continent, the Spanish authorities acted accordingly. One night in the spring of 1776, a small vessel arrived at New Orleans from the upper Mississippi. On board was Captain George Gibson, accompanied by "his lambs," as his band of 15 men were nicknamed, and Lieutenant William Linn. Gibson was the bearer of a message from Virginia, from General Charles Lee (Washington's second-in-command) requesting urgent aid for the rebel provinces in the form of weapons, munitions and medical supplies, to be set up the Mississippi in exchange for regular trade relations between the colonies and the Spanish provinces of America. Lee advocated the success of his request by posing the dilemma that, if the colonies were victorious, Spain would always be able to rely on a friendly power, whereas if they were defeated, a victorious Britain would take the first opportunity of wresting Mexico and Cuba from her.

Governor Luis de Unzaga received the emissary late at night, so as not to raise suspicions, and heard Gibson out. The Spanish governor perceived the danger to the western provinces, and, in order to safeguard his officially neutral position while helping the rebels at the same time, he resorted to the ingenious stratagem of imprisoning Gibson but letting Linn depart upriver with his group, warning the Spanish detachments of their approach and ordering them to cooperate with the travelers. Later, in October, Gibson was set free and took with him invaluable reports as to the favorable attitude of the Spanish governor—together with 1,000 pounds of gunpowder from the Spanish arsenals.

Unzaga's assistance went even farther. Apart from his report to the Secretariat of the Indies, he decided on his own initiative to provide Linn with 9,000 pounds of gunpowder from the Spanish magazines, which reached Fort Pitt on May 2, at a critical moment. The wealthy merchant Oliver Pollock played an important part in this operation and in the payment of $2,400 for the food and supplies made available to the expeditionaries at Fort Arkansas. In his reply to Lee, Unzaga expressed his willingness to meet his requests as discreetly as possible and his own personal sympathy for the colonists' cause.

Linn's party reached Whealing on May 2, 1777. It was a critical moment, argues the historian Thomson, in the defense of Fort Pitt. The 9,000 pounds of powder saved that fort, a circumstance of vast significance for the course of the Revolution in the West. The gunpowder provided by Gibson to the Committee of Congress gave Washington a respite at a time of desperate need.

As a result of Unzaga's report, Charles III did not hesitate to agree to Lee's petitions and announced the dispatch from Havana of all possible war and medical supplies; to avoid raising suspicion, a merchant in the Cuban capital, Eduardo Miguel, would act as a front. In spite of the precautions taken, on his arrival the supplies were discovered by the British, who protested. Likewise, at the beginning of 1777, the Havana mail boat sailed from Corunna with provisions for the rebels.

In the diplomatic field, Congress appointed a committee to draw up a plan for treaties with European nations; as a result, Benjamin Franklin left for Paris, where he was joined by Silas Deane and Arthur Lee. Calling themselves "Plenipotentiaries of the Congress of the United Provinces of North America," they held an interview with the Spanish Ambassador in Paris, the count of Aranda, on January 4, 1777. Four days later, Aranda received from Franklin an official petition addressed to the king of Spain. On receiving it, Charles III called a meeting of the Council of State at which it was decided to adopt a policy of assisting the rebels and to put preparations in hand in case war broke out with Britain. Franklin drew up another petition in 1777, with a fresh request for aid from France and Spain: 2 million pesos, to be spent on war supplies and other provisions, together with six frigates of not less than 24 guns. To Spain he proposed an alliance with the colonies, and promised their support for the conquest of Pensacola. To support his project he arranged that Arthur Lee should travel to Madrid.

To avoid any possible leaks of news, it was considered wiser for the American envoy not to reach Madrid, and it was arranged that he and Grimaldi should meet at Burgos. Grimaldi was accompanied by the merchant Diego de Gardoqui, whose firm Gardoqui e Hijos had been dealing for some time with Willing, Morris & Co.

The interview took place on March 4, 1777, and has been described as of outstanding importance by various historians. Lee's urgent request that Spain establish an alliance with the new nation was heard out, but he was told that it was not feasible at that time. When he insisted, he received Grimaldi's well-known answer: "You have considered your own situation, but not ours. The time has not yet come . . . These reasons possibly will cease to be within a year, and then it will be time."

The outcome of this conference was that Lee received considerable funds to buy supplies, not only in Spain, but anywhere in Europe; they were spent chiefly to procure blankets, shoes, tents, medical supplies, bronze cannon, etc. In May 1777, Lee sent Gardoqui an acknowledgment of receipt of 187,500 *livres tournoises* sent to him on two previous occasions. In April he had been provided with 50,000 pesos in bills. In the course of 1778 he was to receive a further 50,000 pesos.

Franklin gratefully reported to Aranda the arrival of 12,000 rifles in Boston. Meanwhile, at New Orleans, the American agent Oliver Pollock received a variety of invaluable aid from the Spanish governor. This will be seen in greater detail later in the chapter on Louisiana, but an outstanding example was that aid given to Captain James Willing. At Havana, the commander of the Squadron of South Carolina also received help in meeting the expenditure incurred in two emergencies.

The victory of American general Horatio Gates at Saratoga, with the surrender of the British commander, General Burgoyne, changed the course of the war and led to the recognition of the new country by France when the Treaty of Versailles was signed on February 6, 1778. Spain was not informed in advance of this important step, and relations between the two Bourbon courts cooled for a time. Charles III called a meeting of his cabinet and drew up the 36 conclusions, which were to become known as "The Catechism," laying down Spain's international position.

Spain's attempts at mediation failed because they took recognition of independence of the colonies as their starting point. In April 1779, Spain sent the British government an ultimatum and, on April 12, signed a private treaty with France at Aranjuez, clause 4 of which reads as follows: ". . . the two contracting Powers undertake not to lay down their arms until such independence [of the thirteen colonies] has been recognized by the British Crown." The wording of this clause was subsequently amended slightly. On June 21, 1779, Charles III made it known that Spain was at war with Great Britain. The decision caused great joy in the United States.

This declaration signaled the beginning of a new stage in Spain's cooperation with the rebel provinces and served the latter's cause even more usefully, for it was now that the Spanish navy and army intervened, quite apart from other forms of aid received by the fighters for independence. In the ensuing years, Oliver Pollock received no less than 67,610 gold pesos from the royal treasury in Louisiana. Similarly, the new North American envoy in Spain, John Jay, obtained from the Spanish government the promise that it would guarantee bills to a value of £100,000, which Congress could obtain through Jay, this being a means of obtaining financial resources without having to resort to new issues of bills.

The Spanish navy's contribution to the eventual victory in the War of Independence has often been overlooked. Nevertheless, the historian George Stimpson admits that dozens of engagements took place between the ships of Great Britain, Spain and France and had a marked influence on the course of the conflict. It is important to remember what it must have meant for the British fleet to fight against the other two fleets together, with only 72 ships of the line against their 90 ships. Britain had to withdraw a number of units from the American coast to defend her own seaboard against the unsuccessful Spanish-French project to invade the British Isles in the summer of 1779 and to defend the Rock of Gibraltar. This withdrawal was a boon to American maritime trade, which was thus relieved from British pressure and from the convoys that sailed from French and Spanish ports bound for the New World. In a letter of October 4, 1778, Washington revealed that he was well aware of the importance of the collaboration between the two foreign fleets.

Mention should also be made of the powerful naval expedition, commanded by José Solano, which sailed from Cadiz, Spain, on April 5, 1780, bound for Cuba. This expedition, recruited enthusiastically all over Spain, had twice the number of men than that of the French one commanded by Count Rochambeau, and was largely responsible for the conquest of Pensacola. The Spanish fleet likewise played a major part in the taking of Mobile and actions in Louisiana.

The assistance given by the Spanish armies throughout two years of hostilities is perhaps even more impressive, though it too has not been recognized by historians of the War of Independence. The Spanish army, as such, commanded entirely by Spanish officers, acted as the strong arm of an ally in coming to the aid of the rebels from its own bases. The key figure in this strategy was the governor of Louisiana, Bernardo de Gálvez, who, as soon as he heard of the outbreak of hostilities, took steps to strike the first blow at his enemy. Thus, in a matter of months, he took the British strongholds at Baton Rouge, Fort Manchac and Fort Panmure without giving the occupants time to react. In the ensuing years he proceeded to conquer Mobile and Pensacola and was completely successful in spite of all the difficulties and dangers encountered.

Gálvez thus contributed to the cause of independence a handful of victories, achieved control of the Mississippi, thwarted the British plan to conquer the Mississippi basin and outflank Washington's armies from the West, gained the friendship of the Indians and gave effective aid to Generals George Rogers Clark and John Montgomery. Historian Buchanan Parker Thomson noted that had it not been for Gálvez's successes, the King's Mountain Battle would never have taken place, the shift of the war in the South due to Cornwallis's defeat would never have been produced and the Carolinas and Georgia would have been lost.

"The conquest of the port of Mobile and, above all, the assault and taking of Pensacola, in May 1781," said King Juan Carlos of Spain in his address to Congress on June 3, 1976, "marked the triumph of the North Americans in Florida and in the Gulf of Mexico." Thomson reminds us: ". . . this young Spaniard had given the most vital aid contributed by any one man to the struggling American colonies. In winning this triumphant victory over the last great British outpost, he had not only served his King to the limit of his strength but had made to the United States the most important gift an ally could offer: the security of their southeastern and western frontiers."

Spanish military successes in aid of the 13 provinces did not end with Gálvez. In 1780, the lieutenant governor of St. Louis, Missouri, repulsed a major British attack with the cooperation of 1,000 Indian allies. Thanks to the bravery of the garrison, the British did not succeed in gaining command of the Mississippi valley in order to encircle the rebels from the west; their failure left them with their own flank exposed, and British forces, which would undoubtedly have been essential in the struggle elsewhere, were pinned down in that theater.

Yet another victory was won by Spanish troops over the British at the taking of Fort San José, in the present-day state of Michigan (near Niles). This exploit was undertaken by an expeditionary force commanded by Eugenio Purré in February 1781. On November 22, 1780, a Spanish officer, Baltasar de Villiers, crossed the Mississippi from Arkansas and formally took possession of the lands east of the Big River in the name of the king of Spain.

While these feats of arms deserve acknowledgment of Spain's role as an ally and coauthor of independence, there were many other less important contributions that, nevertheless, well deserve mention. News of Spain's declaration of war against Great Britain took some time to reach California. But, when Father Junípero Serra heard the news, he sent his religious brethren a letter dated June 15, 1780, informing them of the news. Reminding the friars of the generosity shown by King Charles III's government toward the missions, he exhorted them to offer prayers for the victory of the arms of Spain and her allies over Britain. The historian John Tracy Ellis notes how far the rebels on the East Coast were from realizing that, 3,000 miles away, on the other side of the continent, Spanish friars were praying for the defeat of the common enemy! Later on, a collection was ordered at the missions to gather funds for help in the struggle against Britain: the contribution made was two pesos for every Spaniard and one peso for every Indian. So it was that the mission at San Luis Obispo, for instance, contributed $107.

Likewise, when General Rochambeau's troops went south, in 1781, to prepare the final blow against the British, they found the fields laid waste and a dearth of financial resources. Needing money to continue the struggle and prevent the settlers from being easily won over by the British, the French admiral François-Joseph-Paul de Grasse tried in vain to obtain the necessary funds from the French colonists on the island of Santo Domingo. It was then that the city of Havana opened a public subscription to which the well-known Ladies of Havana contributed their jewels. The collection reached a figure of 1.5 million *livres tournoises,* and Rochambeau was thus enabled to continue the fighting until the final victory at Yorktown on October 17, 1781.

Also noteworthy is the fact that the American Revolution was financed with the Spanish monetary system and that the dollar was the standard currency, not only during that critical time, but for almost a century after that. (This topic will be explored in greater depth in the account of Spain's contributions in the economic and legal fields.) And it is said that a tower is missing from Málaga Cathedral because the money for its construction was sent to help the colonial rebels.

On September 3, 1783, the count of Aranda, acting as plenipotentiary of King Charles III, signed the peace treaty with Britain at Versailles. The king wrote an affectionate letter to his ambassador in France and a document in the Library of Congress in Washington, D.C., is signed by the Spanish king Charles III on September 27, 1784, "To our great and well beloved friend, the United States of America." It was Aranda who, that same year, submitted to the king his famous "Exposition . . . on the advisability of creating independent kingdoms in America," in which he stated, with regard to the new federal republic: ". . . it has needed the support and forces of two such powerful States as Spain and France to achieve independence. A day will come when it will grow and become gigantic, and even a fearsome colossus in those regions. Then, it will forget the benefits which it has received from the two powers, and will only think of its enlargement . . ."

According to José A. Armillas, the overall volume of Spanish aid can be estimated at 611,328 *pesos fuertes* (397,230 not subject to repayment). Spain profited by the recovery of the Floridas and Minorca; but, not only did she not regain Gibraltar, but she also mortgaged possession of her colonies and provided funds that she could not recover. The gratitude of the rebel colonists was soon forgotten as they thereafter sought their own expansion on the American continent.

◆ THE MISSIONARIES ◆

From Queen Isabella onward the Spanish monarchs took a close interest in the Christianization of the native peoples in North America and, consequently, in the presence of missionaries as an essential factor in attaining that end.

The Dominicans made two attempts to evangelize in the New World with Father Luis Cáncer's activities in Florida in 1549 and the venture of San Miguel de Guadalpe, in the Carolinas, in 1526. Having failed, the Dominicans gave up spiritual conquest in that area and concentrated their efforts on other parts of America.

The Jesuits worked on three fronts, although not simultaneously. In the latter half of the 16th century, following the foundation of St. Augustine by Menéndez de Avilés, they spent a number of years in Florida, Georgia and Virginia. Then, throughout the 17th century, they were active in the Mississippi valley (supervising French priests from Canada as well). Finally, after the initial work done by Father Eusebio Francisco Kino and Father Juan María Salvatierra, they worked in the Sonora and Arizona areas until their expulsion from those lands.

But it was to the Franciscans that the greatest task fell of converting the native tribes north of the Rio Grande to Christianity. They also had the difficult task of replacing the Jesuits, both when the latter abandoned their enterprises along the east coast and, following their expulsion, in the area of Pimería Alta. They strove to keep a foothold in Georgia and West Florida and accompanied the *conquistadores* of New Mexico both before and after the 1680 Indian uprising. The Franciscans were responsible for evangelizing Texas, and under the dynamic lead of Father Junípero Serra, California.

The National Conference of Catholic Bishops published in November 1987 a "National Pastoral Plan for Hispanic Ministry" outlining the church's history:

The Hispanic presence in the Americas began immediately with Christopher Columbus' first voyage of discovery in 1492, and the first Christian evangelization began in 1493 with the Spanish settlements on Hispaniola. The event was more encounter than discovery because Europeans rapidly intermingled with native Americans of high and sophisticated cultures, thus launching a new age and a new people—a true mestizaje.

In search of land and labor, Spaniards soon encountered the region that would one day become the United States. In 1513 Ponce de Leon probed the coasts of La Florida; then, Panfilo de Narvaez attempted the settlement of Florida in 1527 while Nuno de Guzman at the same time pressed overland north of Mexico. Survivors of Narvaez' failed expedition brought word of many tribes and great wealth. Fray Marcos de Niza responded in 1539 by preceding the great expedition of Francisco Vasquez de Coronado into the flanks of the Rockies. A year later Fray Juan Padilla gave his life as a martyr on the Kansas plains. Padre Luis Cancer, a Dominican missionary, poured out his life in Florida in 1549. Despite the setbacks in conversion Pedro Menendez de Aviles forged ahead by founding the city of San Agustin in 1565. Jesuit missionaries moved into Chesapeake Bay only to vanish long before Roanoke. A map of 1529 illustrated by the royal Spanish cartographer, Diego Ribero, shows that missionaries and explorers arrived as far north as present day Maryland, New York, and New England, and gave Spanish names to the rivers and mountains they saw. Far to the west, adventurers probed into New Mexico where missionaries lost their lives in futile attempts at evangelization; not until Juan de Onate arrived in 1598 with scores of new settlers did stability finally come. Generations before the Pilgrims tenuously built their colonies, Spanish missionaries struggled to bring the Americas into the fold of Christ.

In the 17th century Franciscan missionaries raised elegant churches in the Pueblo towns of New Mexico; Jesuits along the western slopes of New Spain wove scattered Indian rancherias into efficient social systems that raised the standard of living in arid America. But the primacy of evangelization as a cornerstone of Spanish royal policy was swept away by political ambitions in the 18th century; the missions fell victim to secularism. First, the Jesuits were exiled and the order suppressed; Franciscans and Dominicans tried valiantly to stem the tide of absolutism, but their numbers dwindled rapidly and the Church's service to the poor crumpled.

Nowadays, some Spanish-speaking bishops belong to such a conference. Among those bishops is the writer David Arias from Spain.

By 1675, when the missionary effort reached its peak, there were 66 Franciscan missions along the coasts of Florida and Georgia, and westward around Tallahassee. From the late 17th to the early 19th centuries, a total of 44 Franciscan mission stations sprang up in Texas. The first foundation in New Mexico, built at Paraguay in 1581, was followed by a further 51 missions, while those in Arizona reached a total of 19. The chain set up by Father Serra, in California, after laying the foundations of San Diego de Alcalá on July 16, 1769, eventually totaled 23. All in all, apart from other buildings for worship, such as those erected in Louisiana, the Spanish missionaries built no less than 203 missions. Some of them are extraordinarily beautiful places such as San Xavier del Bac in Arizona, San José in Texas and Santa Barbara in California.

Father Juan de Padilla is considered to be the first martyr in North America, killed during his apostolic work on the plains of Kansas, in 1542. He was followed by the Dominican father Luis Cáncer on the western coast in 1549 and by the Jesuit father Pedro Martínez, on the coast of Georgia, in 1566. A total of 80 missionaries—not all of them Spaniards—are reckoned to have suffered martyrdom during the colonial period.

The Spanish missionaries were concerned with the physical health of the Indians, their religious and moral conversion to Christianity, and their economic encompassment within Spanish society; their motives were humanity, justice, education and moral persuasion. Inevitably, abuses occurred but were not the norm and should be considered alongside the more positive aspects of Spanish colonial policy.

Although Governor Gonzalo Méndez Canzo yielded to the temptation to take revenge by ordering the enslavement of the Indian rebels after the massacres perpetrated by Juanillo and his followers in 1597, a subse-quent royal command nullified his orders and forbade such steps in future. Those Indians who had begun their punishment were returned to their homes. In 1521, when Pedro Quexós and Francisco Gordillo took Indians as slaves on the East Coast, in the course of the exploratory expedition entrusted to them by Licenciado Vázquez de Ayllón, they were punished for their conduct and ordered to return the prisoners to their homelands.

The predominant objective in New Mexico throughout the 17th century was to maintain the missions there, in order to protect the converts and spread the Christian faith. From a purely material standpoint, Spain gained nothing by remaining in that area, where no wealth was to be found and nature was hardly hospitable; nor was her presence necessary in order to counter any dangers of invasion. Maintaining these missions from 1609 to 1680 cost the royal coffers 1 million pesos, a very large sum in those days. Likewise St. Augustine was not abandoned during the reign of King Philip III, in the early 17th century, among other reasons, because of the Indian converts.

The civil authorities remained involved in the missionary effort. The king of Spain's right of patronage gave him a decisive say in the appointment of ecclesiastical posts and dignities, and he decided which order, or even which individual, would do missionary work in a particular sector. The evangelizing of the Indians and the work of the missionaries were included in the scheme of conquest and colonization so that one is unthinkable without the other. Rivalry arose at times between the civil and religious authorities, and there were even differences of opinion over the policy to be pursued, but these incidents sprang from Spain's ceaseless activity in the New World. No other colonizing country gave its religious authorities comparable power. This policy even resulted in the (not always just) imprisonment of some governors, which shows the influence of the missionary or his superior's opinion in government circles.

All missions were provided with a military force for their protection. Its members sometimes provoked the missionaries (generally on account of their relations with the Indian women at the missions), but the soldiers did not waver in their support. The missions also received an annual grant from the Crown, and the missionaries were paid wages out of the royal coffers. These contributions came to an end upon the independence of New Spain, and the lack of aid had a marked influence on the rapid decadence of the missions in areas such as New Mexico, Arizona and California.

Under Mexican rule, the Spanish missionaries were forced to leave and were replaced by their native or Mexican brethren. The result was a complete decline of the missions, the loss of support by many previously converted Indians and the crumbling of most of the mission buildings and churches. Many works of art were lost, and the Catholic faith—spread by so much effort in the preceding centuries—was in jeopardy of disappearing. Only 13 priests were left in New Mexico when the Spanish missionaries withdrew.

Spain, the historian C. Lummis argues, did not leave the Indians homeless, nor did she crush them or corner them as she advanced; on the contrary, they were protected by special laws and ensured possession of their lands. Spanish legislation on the Indians was the broadest, most comprehensive, systematic and humanitarian of its day. Because of the laws introduced by Spain three centuries ago, the Pueblo Indians of New Mexico today enjoy the ownership of their land.

From a cultural standpoint, there were schools for Indians in America from 1524 onward. By 1575—almost a century before there was a printing press in Anglo-America—many books had already been published in Mexico in 12 different Indian dialects, and three Spanish universities were almost a century old when Harvard was founded.

The desire for wealth certainly contributed, at times, to successful conquests and exploration, but this is no discredit. In the 16th and 17th centuries, when industry had not developed, the wealth of a nation depended on mining for precious metals. Spain sought them from her need to carry on wars for her defense and the defense of spiritual principles, which she considered herself duty-bound to defend. She did not seek them to improve her own land and people.

The search for gold and silver did play a part in the boom and subsequent progress by other Europeans and their descendants in states like Colorado, Nevada, California and Alaska, though the often ruthless gold-crazed prospectors are rarely mentioned.

Much has also been said about Spanish cruelty to the Indians. Understandably, the natives fiercely resisted the Spanish encroachment and resorted to all sorts of stratagems, from voluntary acceptance of the standards introduced by the Spaniards to blind resistance, from hair-raising slaughters to honorable acts. Spaniards paid dearly for their trust in the sincere conversion and honest friendship toward Spain of such Indians as Don Luis, in the case of the Jesuits of Axacán; Francisco Chicora, in the case of Vázquez de Ayllón's colony;

Luisillo, at the Franciscan missions in Georgia; Magdalena, in the attempted evangelization of Florida by Friar Luis Cáncer; Luis Saric, who led the uprising of the Pimas in Arizona; or Estanislao, a convert at San José Mission, in California.

Nevertheless, when Francisco Vázquez de Coronado, for example, withdrew to New Spain after his failure to colonize New Mexico, his last act as governor of the province was to order the release of captive Indians. Before Oñate ordered the assault on the rock at Acoma, New Mexico, in 1599, in order to avenge the murder of a group of Spaniards led by Zaldívar, he first asked the missionaries accompanying him if there was just cause for war; it was only after he obtained their reassurance on that point that he gave the orders that resulted in the bloody defeat of the Zuni Indians responsible for the deaths.

In 1779, Juan Bautista de Anza defeated the dreaded Comanche leader Cuerno Verde (Green Horn) to punish his followers for murdering some Spanish settlers. But a short time later he overlooked past hostilities and came to the aid of those same Indians when they were striving to settle on the banks of the Arkansas River. He provided the Comanche with considerable Spanish funds to enable them to build the township of San Carlos de los Jupes under the guidance of Spanish experts. The instructions issued in this respect by the general commander of the Inland Provinces, Jacobo Ugarte y Loyola, give an enlightening insight into Spanish policy.

It is curious how often Spanish policy with respect to the Indians comes under attack, while excesses committed by Anglo-Saxon frontiersmen against Indians in those regions are ignored. In fact, the Indians of New Mexico and Arizona are the only Indians in the United States who inhabit the same lands as their forefathers. They live in towns established by the Spaniards (even the place-names show that influence) and still bear their Spanish names and speak Spanish. For instance, the Indian governor of Taos in 1965 was Teófilo Romero (his predecessor was called Ceferino Martínez) who spoke very correct Spanish. The Spanish Embassy in Washington, D.C., receives fairly frequent visits from Indians belonging to tribes with whom Spain once signed peace treaties or alliances.

At the same time it was the Spaniards who first took an interest in Indian languages, not only from the practical standpoint of learning to speak them themselves, but with a systematic approach that included familiarity with their grammar and compiling dictionaries, thereby making it easier for anyone who wished to learn them later. The first Indian grammar compiled in the United States was the work of Brother Domingo Agustín Báez, on the Georgia missions, while Father Francisco Pareja was the author of the first grammar and vocabulary of the Timucua Indians. At the Mission of San Juan Bautista, in California, where he worked from 1808 to 1823, Father Arroyo de la Cuesta wrote two major works on the Mutsumi language. This missionary came to master 12 native languages and preached in seven of them. Needless to say, the Spanish missionaries invariably had to learn the dialects of the Indians entrusted to their spiritual care, as did many of the *conquistadores*. Cabeza de Vaca spoke six Indian tongues, while his colleague, Estebanico, knew even more.

COLONIZATION

The Spanish Colonists

The role of the Spanish people in colonizing North America started in the very early days, not with army officers and soldiers, or even the missionaries, but due to the presence of groups of men, women and children of all ages, who brought with them cattle, farm implements and seed, and tools of all kinds. They came to the New World with a view to settling permanently, prepared to fight against any adversities, leaving their own homes behind.

On the eve of his visit to Madrid in the spring of 1985, President Reagan remarked that "Hispanic Americans were among the first settlers in the New World, some arriving in America long before the United States became an independent nation. They came in search of a better life for themselves and their children and they have helped to create a richer life for all of us."

There were no women on Ponce de León's expeditions, or any missionaries either. Nor did women accompany Hernando de Soto, although male colonists did join him in 1539. On the other hand, Vázquez de Ayllón's expedition of 1526 to Chicora (in the Carolinas) was a well-prepared enterprise composed of colonists of different sexes and ages and a variety of professions.

Pánfilo de Narváez's endeavor in 1528 included the wives of various members of the expedition, as well as many men selected because of their trades. Fortunately, the women did not meet the disastrous end that was in store for the men in their hapless wanderings through Apalachee and, subsequently, in the dangerous waters of the Gulf of Mexico. They voted against Pánfilo's plan and chose to board the expeditionary ships and set sail from Tampa in search of a safe bay to the north. Before their departure, the most enterprising of these women told their leader that his efforts were doomed to complete and tragic failure.

Tristán de Luna made a concerted effort at colonization at Pensacola in 1559 and Pedro Menéndez de Avilés was, of course, successful in founding St. Augustine in 1565 with the help of female colonists, their husbands and children. Permanent settlement was likewise a purpose of the expedition that Vázquez de Coronado led northward from New Spain in 1540; the armed contingent was accompanied by colonists and the wives of three soldiers. In 1598, Juan de Oñate laid the foundations of the new Kingdom of New Mexico with 130 families and 270 men without wives.

In California, the expedition led by Portolá in 1769 opened up the West Coast to European civilization. A few years later in 1776 Juan Bautista de Anza's expedition traveled overland through Arizona and, after many trials, achieved its goal: the foundation of San Francisco.

On several occasions, such as in the cases of the colonists accompanying Juan de Oñate, or the Canary Islanders who settled at San Antonio, they were granted *hidalgo* rank (lower nobility), and some Spaniards, or their descendants, were bestowed titles of nobility.

Many Spanish colonists came directly from peninsular Spain, as was the case in Florida and San Antonio, but the majority spread over North America from New Spain. A fair number had been born in Europe, but as time went on, a growing number were from the Americas themselves. In any case, the outcome and their motives were the same.

In some areas they arrived in groups following in the footsteps of the *conquistadores* and missionaries; in others, they settled separately of their own accord. Often enough, the very soldiers comprising an expeditionary party volunteered to form the first settlement afterward. On some occasions, they even stayed behind in the areas they had explored, amid Indians in unfamiliar country, while the expedition marched onward. That was the case with the soldier Feriada on Hernando de Soto's expedition; accompanied by a black man called Robles, he settled at Coosa and thus became the first European settler in Alabama.

While the colonization of some areas was improvised and somewhat haphazard, effected by all comers, in other parts it was the result of greater planning, with provisions made for all necessary material, personal and organizational means.

Following those early efforts at foundation, it was from Spain's two island provinces, the Balearic Islands and the Canary Islands, that many of the Spaniards came to North America on organized settlement schemes. The Canary Islanders came mainly to four places: San Antonio and San Saba in Texas; Nueva Iberia in Louisiana; and Florida. The governor of New Orleans, Bernardo de Gálvez, was responsible for bringing a group of islanders over at royal expense. Having settled in the Teche area, they called their main township New Iberia after the distant peninsula and made a livelihood by raising cattle and growing flax and hemp. Later, they spread out to other parts of Louisiana, and groups of the descendants of those pioneers can still be found in certain localities, for instance Delacroix, Louisiana.

A contingent of Canary Islanders reached San Antonio on the morning of March 9, 1731, after a 13-month journey from Veracruz, in Mexico, and after a long wait at Tenerife until the fleet that was to carry them to Havana could be formed. In the meantime, many had died, others had married, and offspring had been born. The Royal Treasury had not only defrayed their travel expenses and guaranteed the necessary funds and materials to build their homes, sow their fields and live for a year, but had also granted the rank of *hidalgo* to the head of each family so that the decision to join the expedition was rewarded with social betterment.

In July, they started building the town (initially called San Fernando de Béjar in honor of the then-prince of Asturias, who was later to become King Ferdinand VI); it was the only civilian settlement built with such extensive planning along the Camino Real. Six months after their arrival, the settlers came under a violent Apache attack but repelled the invasion with the help of the garrison of the *presidio* of San Antonio. From that base a group was to set out northward in April 1757 under the command of Colonel Diego Ortiz y Parrilla, to settle around the *presidio* of San Luis de las Amarillas, not far from the Mission of Santa Cruz (now called Menard). As many as 400 civilians, mostly Canary Islanders, had joined the venture, attracted by tales of the discovery of important mines.

The transport of Canary Island families to Florida was entrusted to the Real Sociedad de Comercio at Havana. About 200 families are estimated to have arrived by 1763.

The largest contingent of Balearic Islanders who came to North America were from the island of Minorca and settled in Florida. This colonization effort was undertaken not by a Spaniard, but by a Scotsman, Dr. Andrew Turnbull, who sought permission from the British Crown—during the British occupation of Florida—to bring a party of colonists from Greece, Italy and Spain. Settling around New Smyrna, they did not stay there long but, before Spanish domination in Florida had ended, moved to St. Augustine, where they formed the main Spanish population in the second period of Spanish rule there. Descendants of theirs still live in that part of Florida; the well-known American writer Stephen Vincent Benét was descended from Esteban Benét, one of the original Minorcan settlers. There also appear to have been Minorcan colonists in other British settlements in America.

Another Spanish contingent deserving mention due to their number are the Basques, although they arrived long after independence, from the mid-19th century onward. The first party arrived at the time of the 1850 California gold rush, among them Pedro Altube and Segundo Ugariza. In 1860, a group went to Nevada, where, since they could not speak English, they made a living as shepherds. They soon spread through Idaho and Oregon. (A story goes that a newly arrived Basque traveling by rail thought that his three fellow travelers were continuously and devoutly muttering the Rosary, until he was told they were chewing gum!)

As soon as they could, the Basques turned to other trades, and only 10% continued to work as shepherds. Between 1903 and 1910, more Basques arrived constantly. A contingent of 500 Basques arrived in the United States in 1917, aboard the steamship *Alfonso XII*. Immigration continued until the laws of 1921 and 1924 introduced the quota system in the United States.

The popularity of jai alai, in Florida, started in 1924, at the Hialeah (Miami) *pelota* court. As a result, the other Basque immigrant group arrived in the United States to compete with the shepherds, the *pelotaris* of *pelota*-players. In 1926, the Miami Jai-Alai opened, while one in Chicago opened in 1927, and the popularity of the game has grown ever since. Dania is another court, near Hollywood, Florida. The game can be seen in West Palm Beach, Daytona, Orlando, Tampa, Miami, Quincy, Melbourne, Ocala and Fort Pierce (Florida); Bridgeport, Hartford and Milford (Connecticut); and Newport (Rhode Island). About 200 *pelotaris* are reckoned to play at these courts.

Basque Americans fought, and many gave their lives, for their country in World War II. On the home front, they formed a completely Basque company within the Idaho Volunteer Reserve. In 1952, Nevada senator Pat McCarran spurred Congress to pass a law permitting the immigration of a special quota of 250 Basques every year. As a result, in 1950, the California Ranger Association was formed, its named changed to Western Ranger Association when the other western states also joined. Since then, Spanish Basques have settled chiefly in Nevada, Idaho and Oregon. (French Basques usually immigrate to California, Colorado, Wyoming and Montana.) About 3,000 Basques from the Spanish provinces of Vizcaya, Guipúzcoa and Alava are estimated to work as shepherds, together with a considerable number of Navarrese (as many as 400 have settled in California). Even shepherds from the neighboring Spanish provinces of Burgos and Palencia have immigrated.

Some Basques have become leading personalities, such as Nevada senator Peter Echevarria and language teacher Emilia Doyaga.

In his book *Memorias Exteriores,* José María de Areilza gives an interesting account of his attendance at the Basque Festival at Reno. Fresno, California, is the headquarters of the Basque American Foundation, which promoted the Second International Basque Conference in North America, at Santa Barbara, in August 1986, and publishes the review *The Journal of Basque Studies.* The president of the Basque government, the *lendakari* José Antonio Ardanza, visited Basques living in California, Nevada and Idaho in March 1988.

Tampa is the city with the largest number of Spaniards in the United States, with many other inhabitants from various parts of the Spanish-speaking world, particularly Cuba. The city was founded when a Spaniard from Cuba, Vicente Martínez Ybor, settled in Tampa Bay in 1886. Today, one of the districts of Tampa is named after him. He founded a tobacco factory where many Spaniards from Asturias and Galicia came to work, some directly from Spain others via Cuba. (Former governor of Florida Bob Martinez is the grandson of an Asturian.) Because of these Spanish and Cuban immigrants and their second- and third-generation descendants, Ybor City is a place where Spanish is heard on the streets, and signboards are written in Spanish.

More than 500 people from Málaga, Andalusia, contributed to the foundation of Nueva Iberia, Louisiana, under the settlement scheme organized by Bernardo de Gálvez. About 100 Catalonian *miqueletes* reached Florida in 1761. The Catalonians made an active contribution to the discovery and settlement of California.

In this list of Spain's descendants in the United States, one needs also to include the Sephardim, the descendants of the Jews whose expulsion from Spain was decreed by Isabella and Ferdinand the Catholic in 1492. Some settled in New Amsterdam in 1654—before it became New York—when the ship *St. Catherine* was driven off course by a storm, carrying at total of 23 men and women who had sailed from Recife bound for Amsterdam. (An exhibition, "The Jewish Community in Early New York, 1654–1800," held in New York in 1980, listed, among others, two individuals named Gómez, and one called Rodriguez Pacheco.) A member of this community, Mendes Seixas, fought with distinction in the War of Independence. During this period, the Shearit Israel Congregation was the only Jewish one in New York.

In his book *A Nation of Immigrants,* John F. Kennedy recalls: "Over two thousand Jews came to this country in pre-Revolutionary days. Most were from Spain and Portugal. Some established themselves in the Dutch Colony of Nieuw Amsterdam, after winning recognition of their right to trade, travel and live in the colony of Peter Stuyvesant. Others settled in Newport, Rhode Island, then a thriving center of the maritime trade. Many prospered in the West India trade, which included sugar, rum and molasses. The oldest synagogue in the United States built in 1763, is located in Newport, Rhode Island."

Sephardim were to be found in Oglethorpe's Georgia in the mid-18th century, and they were influential in New England, while still a colony and after independence. As a result of the failure of the Liberal movements in Europe in 1848, German jews or Ashkenazim began to arrive in the United States in large numbers, and the Sephardim became a minority, boosted somewhat by the arrival of their Hispano-Levantine brethren in the early 20th century. New York, Cincinnati, Rochester, Indianapolis, Los Angeles, Atlanta, Montgomery and Seattle (with the greatest number after New York) became Sephardi centers, although New York is home to far more than these other cities. About 200,000 Sephardim are estimated to live in the United States, 40,000 of whom are in New York.

Due to their Spanish origins and many years living under the Turkish Empire, the Sephardim have maintained their Spanish language and their own customs and culinary habits; wherever they go, they re-create an atmosphere similar to that which they left behind. In this way, each regional group forms a small private world of its own, alien to its surroundings. Leading members of the Sephardic community include the U.S. Supreme Court judge Benjamin Cardozo and the writers Mair Jose Bernadette and Henry Besso. The Jewish-Hispanic weekly *La Vara (The American Sephardi)* by the Yeshiva University (since 1978) and *The Sephardic Scholar* (since 1982) are no longer published, but the monthlies *Sephardic Highlights, Sephardic Views International, The Sephardic Home News, Boletín de FESELA* and the quarterly *Bulletin* of the Yeshiva University are all active.

Sephardic studies are promoted through the annual conventions of the MLA (Modern Language Association) and AATSP (American Association of Teachers of Spanish and Portuguese), international congresses such as the Third International Congress on the Sephardic Heritage celebrated in Jerusalem in July 1988, and conferences held at SUNY–Binghamton. The FESELA (Federación Sefardi Norteamericana) meets annually, as does the American-Sephardic Federation.

The Present Hispanic Population

According to the U.S. Department of Commerce's *Statistical Abstracts,* of the 1996 U.S. population, 28.269 million people were of Hispanic extraction. Due to underreporting, however, the actual number may be much higher. Population projections for the year 2050 expect the Hispanic population to reach as high as 96.508 million. Of the current Hispanic population, 11 million people speak Spanish at home. That figure makes the Spanish-speaking population in the United States the fifth largest in the world (after Mexico, Spain, Argentina and Colombia). Hispanics are the second largest ethnic minority in the United States and are growing. Their annual purchasing power exceeds

$170,000, according to the Strategy Research Corporation, and that figure has increased by 20% in only two years. The growing interest in Hispanic culture in the United States can be seen through such activities as the Congresos Internacionales de Culturas Hispanas en los Estados Unidos (International Congresses of Hispanic Cultures in the United States) held in 1984, 1986 and 1988.

From census data it is clear that Hispanics are most concentrated in California, Texas, New York, Florida, Arizona, New Mexico and Colorado. Cities with a large Hispanic population include Miami, New York, Chicago, Newark, Brownsville, Laredo, El Paso, San Antonio, Corpus Christi, Albuquerque, Phoenix, Los Angeles, Denver, San Diego and San Francisco–Oakland. About 60% of the U.S. Hispanic population is Mexican; 11%, Puerto Rican; 4.1%, Cuban; 1.3%, Dominican; 1.2%, Colombian; .8%, Spaniard; .7%, Ecuadoran; .7%, Salvadoran; and 20.2%, other groups. From 1988 data, it is clear that the Hispanic population has increased 34% over the past decade, which might help explain that among the 100 most common names in the United States, Martinez, Rodriguez, Gonzales and Garcia rank in the top half. The Census Bureau predicts that the Hispanic population in the year 2020 will be 36.5 million and in 2046 will reach 51 million. In 2080 it will represent 19% of the population (in 1980, Hispanics comprised 6.4% of the total).

Much of the Hispanic community arrived as immigrants. While laws in the 1920s assigned a quota to the number of émigrés allowed, an immigration law that came into effect December 1, 1965, more accurately reflected what President John F. Kennedy described, in his volume *A Nation of Immigrants,* as "the principles of equality and human dignity to which our nation subscribes." In his State of the Union address in January 1965, President Lyndon Johnson declared, "Let a just nation throw open its doors . . . to those in other lands who are seeing the promise of America, through an immigration law based on the work a man can do and not where he was born or how he spells his name." In more recent times the Mexican author Octavio Paz wrote that "the activity of the Hispanic community could mark the beginning of another historical change: the coexistence of a plurality of cultures within a democratic society. It would represent the dawn of a true universal civilization." And President Ronald Reagan stated, "We Americans seek economic progress and justice for mutual benefit throughout the hemisphere and the world, and we look to Americans of Hispanic heritage for leadership as we work together toward these goals."

Coexistence of this population of Spanish and Hispanic origin within the dominant Anglo-Saxon culture gives rise to a number of problems. (The differences between these groups have been the topic of a series of clarifying articles by Paz.) If an individual wants to make progress in the whirl of everyday life, he must adapt and allow himself to be absorbed as quickly as possible. The same is not always the case when it is a matter of a large group of immigrants who, for one reason or another, focus in a particular area or locality: Puerto Ricans in New York, exiled Cubans in Miami, Mexican workers in California, Texas, New Mexico or Colorado. Their long-term adaptation is inevitable, as with other large national groups, but the process depends on whether they are potential voters, are in the majority (as in areas near the Mexican border) or whether they have certain cultural advantages.

In the case of Spanish-speaking descendants of settlers who arrived in colonial times, or even just afterward, the problem is somewhat different: they are United States citizens, but in their way of life, speech, etc., they differ from their Anglo-Saxon neighbors.

Of whatever origin, it is clear that Hispanics will play an ever-increasing role. The National Conference of American Catholic Bishops published a pastoral letter in 1983 called "The Hispanic Presence: Challenge and Commitment," which stressed the growing influence of Hispanics. Two paragraphs of the pastoral letter were very specific: "No other European culture has been in this country longer than the Hispanic. Spaniards and their descendants were already in the Southeast and Southwest by the late sixteenth century. In other regions of our country a steady influx of Hispanic immigrants has increased their visibility in more recent times. Plainly, the Hispanic population will loom larger in the future of both the wider society and the Church in the United States."

Unfortunately, whether longtime citizen or new immigrant, Hispanics have faced discrimination. The problems still experienced by Mexican workers in California form just one example: the authorities do not give them residence permits and only allow them to sign annual contracts, which place them at a disadvantage with respect to their employers, who pay them low wages, in spite of the protests of the trade unions, citing the competition this introduces for American workers. In a cover story of *Time* magazine, César Chávez, the unquestionable leader of Californian Chicanos, claimed in an interview that "the

discrimination experienced by the Hispanic minority is increasingly economic and less social."

The problems facing Puerto Rican immigrants in New York have also been voiced in the media and in public demonstrations: housing, schools and employment. The position with the anti-Castro Cubans is quite different, for most of them have received effective, substantial aid from federal and local authorities since the start of their exile.

This discrimination has diminished somewhat over the years, particularly since World War II, but the financial situation of the Hispanic community continues in general to be precarious, and some claim that it has deteriorated. In 1987, a Hispanic family earned an annual income of approximately $20,310, compared to that of a non-Hispanic family's $32,270. The Hispanic poverty rate was 28.2%, reaching a figure of 5.5 million.

However, increasingly aware of their influence in elections, in spite of their lack of cohesiveness, the Hispanic community has become more active. Various organizations have been formed for legal defense or political action: Liga de Ciudadanos Hispanos, LULAC (Latinos Unidos) and La Raza, Organization for the Defense of Mexican-Americans and Spanish Speaking United States Citizens, Fuerza Hispana 84, Asociación de Educación para el Votante Hispano en USA, MALDEF (in San Francisco), the Cruzada por la Justicia (Denver), the Alianza de los Pueblos Libres (New Mexico), the Southwest Voter Registration and the Coalición Hispanoamericana (Latin-American Coalition), whose origin can be traced to the Colombian CANCO, as well as about 160 women's associations.

In 1971, the First Conference of Americans of Hispanic Origin was held in Washington, D.C., drawing almost 1,000 people. In April 1984, the Third National Conference of Hispanic Leaders (Tercera Conferencia Nacional de Líderes Hispanos) convened in Washington, D.C., and about 100 of them were received at the White House by President Reagan. Since the conference is convoked every four years, it met again in April 1988, heralding a Hispanic swing vote for the then-coming elections. Conference leaders stated that "Hispanic issues are America's issues." The Hispanic Chamber of Commerce in the United States has become very powerful and currently holds annual conventions, which are attended by approximately 10,000 people. It represents about 400,000 Hispanic companies established in the country. The CAMACOL (Latin Chamber of Commerce) stands out in Miami because of its large influence.

Like their Democratic opponents, the last two Republican presidents, Reagan and George Bush, duly took the Hispanic vote into account in the elections that brought them to office, as did President Jimmy Carter. In 1980, 9 million Hispanics were eligible to vote, and by 1984 there were 12 million. It was estimated that in the elections of November 1988, approximately 5 million Hispanics could vote. In 1989, FEDLMN, the Fondo Educacional y de Defensa Legal Mexicano Norteamericano (Mexican–North American Educational and Legal Defense Fund), initiated a campaign to encourage a greater Hispanic participation in the 1990 census, in order to achieve increased representation in Congress. If they were to vote, it would be a decisive factor in obtaining 40 electoral districts in Congress (one-tenth of the House of Representatives).

The number of elected Hispanic officials has risen to a total of 3,360, according to the head of the National Association of Latino Elected and Appointed Officials. In recent years, a growing number of Hispanics have played a significant role in government or important community posts: in the federal Congress, Senators Joseph M. Montoya and Richard G. Lugar, and Representatives Robert Garcia and Herman Badillo (New York), Eduardo Roybal, Esteban Torres and Matthew Martinez (California), Ileana Ros-Lehtinen (Florida), Manuel Luján (New Mexico), Albert G. Bustamante, Solomon Ortiz, Henry B. Gonzalez and E. (Kika) de la Garza (Texas); members of the president's cabinet; Laura F. Cavazos (Education) and Manuel Luján (Interior); the Chicano leaders César Chávez (California) and Reyes López Tijerina (New Mexico); Ambassadors Frank Ortiz, John Jova, John Gavin, Phillip V. Sánchez, and Alberto Martinez Piedra; successive Undersecretaries of the Interior (Office of Territories) Pedro Sanjuán and Richard T. Montoya; Governors Tony Anaya (New Mexico), Bob Martinez (Florida), Richard F. Celeste (Ohio), Ricardo Bordallo (Guam) and Juan Luis (Virgin Islands); the mayors of more than 20 towns, such as Henry Cisneros (San Antonio), Mauricio Ferré and Xavier Suárez (Miami), Alfonso J. Cervantes (St. Louis), Raúl Martínez (Hialeah), Federico Peña (Denver), and Bob Martínez (Tampa); the Democratic politician Amalia Betanzos; as treasurer of the United States, Katherine Davalos Ortega and Catalina Vázquez Villalpando; the president of the Florida International University, Modesto Maidique; the chief of staff, U.S. Air Force, General Charles A. Gabriel; the director of the Academy of West Point, General James S. Medina; the actress Rita Cansinos (Rita Hayworth); the president of Coca-Cola, Robert Goizueta; the president of Texas Air, Frank Lorenzo; etc.

In 1976, a Hispanic caucus in the House was formed and the number of its members reached more than 20 (some visited Spain in 1998).

Among other difficulties, attempts by Hispanic citizens to join together may be thwarted by differences among themselves, between the relatively recent immigrants and those of European descent whose families have lived in the United States for generations (who may identify more with Spain). Many are now firmly established in their own country and have a good command of the English language, although they have not always enjoyed the same educational opportunities as their fellow Anglo-Saxon citizens. In recent postwar years, many Hispanic Americans have married non-Hispanics and have settled in other parts of the country, and the new generations risk losing their command of the Spanish language.

Some Outstanding Americans of Spanish Origin

Many descendants of Spaniards in America have been outstanding for their contributions to the culture of the country and have achieved well-deserved acknowledgment. In the Civil War, Admiral David Glasgow Farragut, the son of a Minorcan, Jorge Farragut, was the victor at Mobile and New Orleans; he was promoted to become the first admiral in the history of the U.S. navy. He had a good command of Spanish, and when paying an official visit to Queen Isabella II of Spain, a well-known sonnet was dedicated to him by the Spanish poetess Carolina Coronado. When he returned to his country, one newspaper even went so far as to propose him as a possible candidate for the Spanish throne, after Queen Isabella II had been overthrown.

Jorge de Santayana is considered to be an American philosopher. In fact, however, he was born in Madrid in 1863 and never gave up his Spanish nationality. He went to Harvard as a student and was later a professor there. He wrote many works in English and was justly renowned in the world of philosophy and poetry.

Dr. Walter C. Alvarez was the son of Dr. Luis Fernández Alvarez, a native of La Puerta, in Asturias (he used his paternal grandmother's maiden name instead of his father's last name, which, in Spain, always precedes the maternal last name; as a result, even his father became known by the name Alvarez, instead of Fernández!).

Orphaned when he was 13, Luis immigrated to Cuba, where he was educated. When he was 20, he traveled to New York and continued his studies there. Later, he went to Los Angeles and Hawaii, where he concentrated his efforts on fighting leprosy. He even became Spanish vice-consul in Hawaii. Walter C. Alvarez graduated in medicine from Stanford University and, in a lifetime devoted to medical practice and research, published a number of books and a thousand articles, worked for 25 years at the Mayo Clinic and was professor at the University of Minnesota, from which he received the title of professor emeritus. At age 80, he was still running two medical reviews and had a medical consultancy column in a press syndicate controlling 100 newspapers. The most famous member of the family was Walter's son Luis W. Alvarez, one of the most distinguished physicists in the United States, a consultant to the president of the United States, Codirector of the laboratory of the University of California and a Nobel Prize winner. He played a decisive part in the preparation of the atom bomb and invented the ground control approach, which has saved the lives of thousands of aviators. He was also vice president of the National Space Commission. A cousin of Luis W. Alvarez, Richard, is actively engaged in the construction of the world's largest accelerator, a mile from Stanford University.

Rear-Admiral Luis de Florez, the son of a Spaniard, was born in New York, organized a naval aviation instruments division during World War I and, in World War II, played an active part in the "synthetic" training of pilots under a revolutionary program that won him the Collier Trophy in 1943. He was largely responsible for the introduction of instruments on board airplanes, the installation of safety belts and the application of some 30 other inventions in aviation. Another important figure in this field was General Elwood Richard Quesada, who for a time was director of the American Civil Aviation Agency.

There are said to be some 500 descendants of El Cid in the United States, who planned to form The Society of Sons and Daughters of El Cid. Other bearers of Spanish names include Dr. Worrall Mayo, the father of Dr. W. J. and Dr. C. H. Mayo, who founded the Mayo Clinic at Rochester, Minnesota, and Juan Ortega, who was the first person with a Spanish name to be decorated with the Congressional Medal of Honor for his courage aboard the *Saratoga* in 1864. Marcelino Serna received the Distinguished Service Cross during World War I. A total of 31 Hispanics received the Medal of Honor during World War II and the Korean and Vietnam Wars.

There is a long list of eminent men born in Spain but with U.S. citizenship, who have made contributions to the progress of science and the arts: Dr. Severo Ochoa, the director of the Department of Biochemistry of New York University and a Nobel Prize winner in 1959; Dr. Ramon Castroviejo, an ophthalmologist, and the first to perfect the transplant of a cornea, as well as his nephew, Pedro Ramon Escobal, a mathematician on the Apollo Space Project; Dr. Rafael Lorente de No, a member of the Rockefeller Institute for Medical Research, and a world authority in neurophysiology; Dr. Miguel Maria-Padilla, winner of the Jacob Javits prize in neurosurgery in 1988; and the botanist José Cuatrecases; Dr. Santiago Grisolía, director of the Department of Biochemistry of the University of Kansas; Dr. José Rodriguez Delgado, a professor of neurophysiology at Yale University; Dr. Francisco Grande Covián, an expert in the field of nutrition at the University of Minnesota; Dr. José Luis Sert and Dr. Rafael Moneo, successive deans of the faculty of Architecture at Harvard University; and Dr. Emilio Nuñez, a judge of the Superior Court of the state of New York.

Recent scientific accomplishments have been made by oncologists Mariano Barbacid, Angel Pellicer, Juan Massegué, José Costa and Enrique Gómez Lahoz; biologists Francisco Javier Castillo and Rubén Moreno-Palenque; cardiologists Roque Pifarré and Valentín Fuster; nutritionists José M. Ordovás and Carlos Iribarren; neurologists Antonio Culebras, José Masdeu and José de León; virologist Alejo Erice; physicists Alberto Fernandez Soto and Carlos Lasheras; astronauts Miguel Lopez Alegría and Pedro Duque; and Raúl Cano, the discoverer of prehistoric bacteria.

Other Spaniards whose presence has been noteworthy in American affairs include a native of Lerida, Professor Juan Oró, a biochemist at Houston; the painter Salvador Dalí; the pianist and conductor José Iturbe; musician Xavier Cugat; the master guitarist Andrés Segovia; Carlos Montoya, a popular flamenco guitarist; sculptor José Creeft; painter Adolfo Estrada; singers Julio Iglesias and Raphael; philosopher Ferrater Mora; historians Javier Malagó and Guillermo Céspedes; mathematician Aguilar; architect Martín Domínguez; the head of the Department of Space Photography at NASA, Suárez Estevez; scientist Cardús; geneticist and president of the American Association for the Advancement of Sciences (AAAS) Francisco Ayala; and others. Other prominent Hispanics are mentioned in the books *Cerebros Españoles en USA (Spanish Minds in the USA)* by Alfredo Gomez Gil and

Contributions of Hispanic Scientists in the United States by Alfredo Giner-Sorolla. The ALDEEU foundation (Asociación de Licenciados y Doctores Españoles en los Estados Unidos [Association of Spanish Graduates and Doctors in the United States]) is also a source of names of prominent Hispanics.

There has been a certain amount of speculation as to the ethnic origin of film director Walt Disney. Some authorities on the subject claim that his father, José Guirao, and his mother, Isabel Zamora, were born in Spain and that one of their sons, José Luis, may have been born at Mojacar, in the Spanish province of Almería. Apparently these immigrant parents died prematurely in Chicago, and the two orphaned brothers were adopted by Elias Disney, who gave them his name. Later José Luis Guirao Zamora changed his first name to Walter and eventually became known as Walt Disney.

A native of Madrid, Antonio Moreno, was well known in Hollywood in its heyday and acted with such leading stars as Greta Garbo, Mary Pickford and others. With Rodolfo Valentino and Ramón Novarro, he was a member of the trio of so-called Latin lovers who became so popular in the days of silent movies. He died in 1967, at the age of 80. Spanish actor Duncan Renaldo played the part of the famous Californian hero Cisco Kid; he died in Los Angeles in 1980.

In the entertainment world, many prominent Hispanic figures come to mind, including Ruben Blades, Los Lobos, Gloria Estefan, and other groups, and such actors as Rita Moreno, Jose Ferrer, Eddie Olmos and Anthony Quinn.

The Role of Spanish Women

In discussions of the part played by missionaries, *conquistadores* and later Spanish immigrants in U.S. history, the role of Spanish women is sometimes overlooked. But the part they played was vitally important; it was nearly always exemplary and often astonishing.

In fact, the present territory of the United States first became known to the Western world, in 1513, through the efforts of Ponce de León—on account of a Spanish woman. Then governor of Puerto Rico, he had achieved everything that a Renaissance man could have wished for: glory, power and wealth. But, one thing was missing—love—and he aspired to find it in the person of Beatriz de Córdova, the daughter of a former lover of the governor, and therefore much younger than himself.

While bitterly complaining of his lack of the youthful zest needed in order to press his suit, Ponce de León was told by some Indians about an island to the north called Bimini, where there was a spring whose waters rejuvenated those who drank from them. With the excitement worthy of a youth, he let himself be carried away by the story and, abandoning everything he possessed, set off on his venture into the unknown. As a result, Florida was discovered, and Ponce de León himself met his death from wounds sustained during his second expedition, as an elderly man enamored of a pretty Spanish lass.

While the history of the East Coast thus boasts this romantic tale, it is thanks to the pretty eyes of another Spanish woman that the West Coast did not fall to Russia's possession. Conchita Argüello, the sister of the governor of the *presidio* at San Francisco, had seemingly hypnotized Russian count Rezanov, who arrived on the coast of California in 1805 on a mission of territorial expansion entrusted to him by the tsar. The Russian fell in love, and instead of expansion, he devoted his efforts to obtaining leave to marry her from his own sovereign and from the king of Spain. He hurriedly left for the Russian court to seek permission, and with him disappeared the likelihood of Russians becoming entrenched in California. The story in fact ended on a tragic note, for the Russian count died on his journey through Siberia, and Conchita Argüello entered a convent quite some years later. It is curious to think that the future of this important territory should have been affected by such a romantic episode!

Another figure who should not be neglected is María de Agreda, a nun who had an enormous impact on the destiny of Spain through her correspondence on matters of government with the monarch reigning in her day, King Philip IV of Spain. On July 22, 1629, 50 Humano Indians arrived at the Isleta Mission, near El Paso, requesting that missionaries come to their territory to baptize them; the preceding summers they had come to the mission with a similar request, but it had never been granted owing to the shortage of missionaries.

Shortly afterward, news reached the mission of the arrival in Mexico of a new archbishop, Francisco Manso y Zúñiga, who had come from Spain to investigate rumors of visits by Sister María de Agreda to the territories north of the Rio Grande. The nun—who had not in fact left her convent in the province of Soria, in Spain—had given a detailed description of the territory and of the Indians to whom she had preached the Christian religion. When questioned, the Indians confirmed that they had received the visit of "a lady dressed in blue" (like a nun of the same order, Mother Luisa de Carrión, whose portrait hung in the home of the missionary at Isleta). The lady in blue was young and had preached Christianity to them. When asked why they had not mentioned this before, they replied that they had never been asked; moreover, they assumed that the missionaries must know about the lady and her activities.

Faced with this surprising news Friar Juan de Salas and Friar Diego López departed at once with the Humano Indians. On reaching their territory, they were received enthusiastically by the populace, who had gathered to welcome them carrying a garlanded cross in procession, on the advice given by the "lady in blue," who had visited them only recently. Shortly afterward, Indians from other tribes likewise asked to be baptized on the advice of the mysterious "lady," who used to visit them with all the appearances of a flesh-and-blood human being.

On hearing these reports, the superior of the Franciscan province, Friar Alonso de Benavides, traveled to Mexico, and then to Spain, to ask the nun from Agreda to confirm the account given by his missionaries. On April 30, 1631, he held an interview with Sister María at her convent. She admitted that she had been carried to New Mexico by her guardian angels and that she had visited New Mexico in this way for the first time in 1620 and on many occasions since then. She recognized Friar Alonso himself from the occasion on which he had come to baptize the Piro people, a ceremony which she had attended, and she gave a detailed description of the visit of Friar Juan and Friar Diego to the Humano Indians. She also described Friar Cristobal Quirós, a missionary who was well known in New Mexico. Her astonished visitor reported to his superiors, and for years afterward, in the territories around the Rio Grande—including large areas of Texas—the visits of the "lady" left their mark.

Many other Spanish women played a noteworthy part in events in the new territory. They include such figures as Eufemia de Sosa Peñalosa, the wife of the ensign, or standard-bearer, of the expedition lead by Juan de Oñate. She took command of the defense of San Juan against rebel Indians at a time when most of the Spanish forces were absent on the expedition to Acoma in 1599. Luisa de Trujillo, Damiana Domínguez de Men-doza, Petronilla de Salas, and Lucia, María and Juana de Leiva all met heroic deaths, the first three accompanied by their children, in the rebellion of the Pueblo Indians in 1680. The wives of three soldiers on the expedition led by Vàzquez de Coronado loyally accompanied their husbands and rode on horseback for over 6,000 miles under difficult circumstances, yet all the while bravely helping and encouraging the expeditionaries. María Dolores Valencia de Grijalva with her two daughters, Josefa and María del Carmen, accompanied her husband, Juan Pablo de Grijalva, on the rough trek from Sonora to California when Anza led his expedition to found San Francisco. In the spring of 1716, Manuela Ramón, the daughter of the governor of San Antonio, Texas, married the well-known French explorer Louis Jucherau de St. Denis, helping soften Spanish-French tensions, which at the time, were rather strained as a result of French encroachment on territories that the Spaniards considered to be theirs.

Also worth mentioning was the love that sparked between Teresa de Leyba, a sister of the Spanish governor of St. Louis, and George Rogers Clark, one of the independence leaders. It did not end in marriage because Teresa de Leyba entered a convent. When Clark left for the war, she mistakenly thought that he had no intention of marrying her.

Indian women also contributed to the Spanish colonization effort in North America. When Hernando de Soto disembarked in Florida in 1539 he was pleasantly surprised to meet a fellow countryman called Ortiz, who had accompanied Pánfilo de Narváez on his unsuccessful expedition 10 years earlier. Captured and imprisoned, he had almost been put to death on orders from a local chief but had been saved from a tragic early end by the chief's enamored daughter. This circumstance was to have important consequences for the expedition led by Hernando de Soto because the assistance given by Ortiz as an interpreter (he had learned the native dialects during his years of captivity) proved invaluable to the Spanish leader until his death at the Battle of Mobile. This romantic adventure took place almost 90 years before that of Captain John Smith, likewise saved from a sure death in Virginia through the love of Pocahontas. Indian women also rendered important assistance to Cabeza de Vaca and his three surviving companions when they approached what is now the area of El Paso, Texas, in November 1535.

HISTORIC CULTURE

The end of Spanish sovereignty in the territory of the United States did not signal an end to Spanish influence on American culture, to the mutual benefit of both.

Literature

A nearly exhaustive work on the Spanish influence in literature is the thoroughly documented study by Professor Stanley Williams, references to which appear throughout this volume. Readers interested in the subject would be well advised to refer to that source, in which ample bibliography can be found. Among the famous American writers discussed are George Ticknor, the historian of Spanish literature; William Prescott, the biographer of Queen Isabella; James Russell Lowell, author of *Impressions of Spain*; Washington Irving, creator of *Tales of the Alhambra*, biographer of Christopher Columbus and a man whose interest in and love for things Spanish had great influence in his own country; Farris Bryant; Irving Babbit, author of *Light and Shades of the Spanish Character*; Henry Wadsworth Longfellow, who translated the Spanish poet Jorge Manrique; Bret Harte, with his romantic tales about Spanish California; William Dean Howells, who knew Spanish authors Benito Pérez Galdós and Armando Palacio Valdes; Mark Twain, whose characters Tom Sawyer and Huckleberry Finn are so reminiscent of Don Quixote and Sancho Panza; Gertrude Stein, the author of *Tender Buttons*; Maxwell Anderson, who wrote *Night Over Taos*, dramatizing the tension caused by the arrival of settlers in Spanish New Mexico between 1840 and 1850; John Dos Passos, for *Rosinante to the Road Again*; Eugene O'Neill, in whose play *The Fountain* Ponce de León is the leading character; Ernest Hemingway, a self-proclaimed disciple of Pío Baroja and author of *For Whom the Bell Tolls*, *The Sun Also Rises* and *Death in the Afternoon*; John Steinbeck, who set his novel *Cup of Gold* in colonial Spanish America; Tennessee Williams, whose works include *Camino Real*, a criticism of modern society in which Don Quixote makes a symbolic appearance; Thornton Wilder, the novelist whose work *The Bridge of San Luis Rey* reveals a Spanish influence; Archibald MacLeish, the author of the poem "El Conquistador"; Waldo Frank

and his volume *España Virgen*; James Michener, author of *Iberia*; and many more individuals.

The first theatrical work in what is now the United States was performed in Spanish, and the script was written by Marcos Farfán de los Godos, one of the captains accompanying Juan de Oñate on his travels in the West. It was performed in the vicinity of El Paso on April 30, 1598, to celebrate a historic occasion: the fact that Oñate had taken possession of the Kingdom of New Mexico. Its subject was the arrival of the Franciscans in the region, their long journeys overland, their initial contacts with the natives, how they preached the Gospel and their conversion of the Indians. A comedy—the name of the author is unknown—was performed by members of the same expedition at San Juan, New Mexico, on September 8 of that year. It ended with a mock battle between Moors and Christians. Others plays written in the early days include *Adán y Eva (Adam and Eve)* at Atrisco, near Albuquerque; *El Niño perdido (The Lost Boy)* at Taos: *Los Pastores (The Shepherds)* and *Los Reyes Magos (The Magi)* at San Antonio and Sante Fe. All of these plays are customarily performed in Spanish, and sometimes, in a recent English translation.

Similarly, the first book authored in what is now the United States was by Brother Domingo Agustín Báez, a Jesuit with the missions in Georgia, in 1569. It was a grammar of the language of the Indians at Guale, Georgia. Of course, the first description of the territory of the Union is to be found in the work *Naufragios (Shipwrecks)* by Alvar Núñez Cabeza de Vaca, published in 1542.

To move quickly to the present day, we should mention a number of fine Spanish writers in the United States, who have made it possible to establish the Academy of the Spanish Language, with its headquarters in New York (and with a branch in Miami). In 1986 the University of Miami launched a literary contest called Letras de Oro (in five fields: novel, poetry, theater, essay and short stories) for Spanish-language writers, which has achieved an enormous success. Also, the Latin Festivals of Literature promote a continuing dialogue between Spanish authors and American editors.

Likewise, it is worth noting the developments in literature, cultivated along different genres by a growing number of writers using an evolved form of Spanish, mixed occasionally with English—as spoken by the Mexican-American community. A Chicano publishing house, Tonatiuh International, was formed in 1976 and awards literary prizes. In the summer of 1983, Menéndez Pelayo University at Santander held a seminar on Chicano theater. In this same field, Luis Valdés founded the Teatro Campesino in 1965, and has put on performances of such works as *Los Vendidos* and *El soldado Razo.* The film *El Norte,* about illegal immigrants from Central America, was a critical success, and *La Bamba,* about the Chicano Singer Richie Valens, was a hit in the United States and abroad. Chicano literature has received an increasing amount of interest in the media, in seminars, and in other academic and intellectual circles. Of particular interest are works by authors such as Rolando Hinojosa, Oscar Hijuelos and others.

Music

North American composers of both symphonic and folk music show the impact of Spanish influence, particularly in the regions once under Spanish rule. Quite apart from the enormous popularity of songs from countries south of the Rio Grande that have a Spanish flavor, some songs that the *conquistadores* brought with them have survived in the Southwest and in the West. These songs are revived especially at certain times of the year, as in the case of Christmas carols and the dance of the Matachines performed at Christmas time, or the so-called *alabados,* or "praises," during Holy Week. They can be heard in Texas, New Mexico, Arizona and Colorado and can now be found on CD. Basque folklore and music is thriving today in the main Basque population areas, such as Idaho, Nevada, Oregon and California. In some cases, the history and stories of Spanish exploration and Christianization inspired musicians' works. The subject of the missions, for example, inspired composer Harl McDonald's two nocturnes, called "San Juan de Capistrano" and "Mission," as well as his second symphony, subtitled "Rumba." In his own symphony "The California Missions," Meredith Willson dedicated the third movement to a Franciscan legend. "Hymn of the Union" attributed to Louis Gottschalk, was actually by Tomás Genovés from Aragón. Gottschalk was in Saragossa in 1852 and directed one of Genovés's symphonies, "Los Sitios de Zaragoza." Upon his return to the States, he adapted it and presented it without indicating his source. A patriotic hymn sung by the Aragonese against Napoléon forms part of the symphony and was inter-preted thousands of times during the U.S. Civil War, thus becoming the "Hymn of the Union."

For a closer look at Spanish music in the United States and Spanish influences in American music, the reader should consult Professor Gilbert Chase's *The Music of Spain.* The Spanish composers Isaac Albéniz, Enrique Granados and Carlos Surinach have been prominent influences among musicians in the United States, as have been the guitar players Los Romeros (several members of which are from the same family) and pianist José Iturbe. Spanish writer Federico García Lorca has been the inspiration for many American choreographers and composers, such as Ruth Page, Norman Lloyd, Leo Smith and George Crumb.

Architecture and Other Arts

In October 1987, Colombia was the host country of the conference on Tradiciones Hispanas en Arquitectura y Urbanismo Americanos (Hispanic Traditions in American Architecture and Urbanism). Representatives from 11 counties clarified the similarities of the colonial work in the hemisphere and the disparities that the history of each country has imposed. According to the Argentinian architect Ramón Gutiérrez, "the history of the Spanish colonization is the history of the cities. The Spaniards moved on across the American continent building cities." In the United States the history is interrupted with the end of the Spanish sovereignty, but at the beginning of the 20th century the maintenance of its spirit is revived, with individual or planned constructions such as in Coral Gables. For Charles Moore, architect of the University of Texas, the Spanish architecture in the New World looked "impossibly romantic and filled with unbridled enthusiasm," or in the words of Colombian architect Germán Tellez, "like a flamenco song, with no beginning and no end, its rhythms haphazard rather than fixed."

Spanish art has had specific influence on some aspects of American artists. The oldest buildings standing in the United States are Spanish; in some cases their value may be chiefly their age, but most of them also boast aesthetic features that give them a high place in the history of U.S. art. As far as military architecture is concerned, no building in the United States can rival San Marcos Castle, at St. Augustine, Florida. It can proudly claim to have fulfilled the purposes for which it was built proving impregnable to the many British and pirate attacks it endured. Not only is it beautifully proportioned, but it stands out artistically against the urban and coastal scenery around it.

In religious architecture there are well-known examples of the California missions and the less popular, but more artistic, missions at San Xavier del Bac, in Arizona, and San Jose, in San Antonio, Texas, which combine European and Indian artistic themes. Traces of Spanish influence in architecture can be found all over the country: houses in St. Augustine, La Villita in San Antonio, Avila Adoba in Los Angeles, the buildings in Calle de España in Santa Barbara, the Vieux Carré in New Orleans, the palaces of the governors at San Antonio and Santa Fe, the *presidio* in Monterey, and many other masterpieces.

In the course of the 20th century, Spanish architecture has had an influence on many architects throughout the country, particularly in Florida and California, where the so-called Spanish colonial style became the fashion in the 1920s. (Addison Mizner stands out among them.) The book by R. W. Sexton on the subject is sufficient as a source of information through which that influence can be seen in the layout of exteriors and interiors, materials used (such as roofing tiles, decorative tiles, wrought iron work, etc.) and in the choice of furniture. The Spanish colonial style is particularly suitable in areas with a semitropical climate where much of daily life is spent outdoors, and this style of building takes advantage of light, air and sunshine while preserving a certain intimacy. The Spanish word *patio* has become commonplace in America.

The Spanish eschew symmetry and therefore greatly favor inspiration and variety. Colors also play a part, and the whitewash or red brick used for walls, black wrought iron grilles and pink or gray roofing tiles lend an overall Spanish impression to the architecture.

A large number of major residences at Palm Beach, Coral Gables, Santa Barbara, San Diego, Beverly Hills, Denver, Washington, D.C., and elsewhere are exponents of the Spanish style. But, a more formal kind of building has also been influenced by Spanish architecture. This is true of the splendid Palacio de Justicia, or Court House, at Santa Barbara, and the buildings on several university campuses. At the University of Texas in Austin a sort of Spanish Renaissance style is predominant. At Stanford University near San Francisco the keynote is Romanesque art, while the University of California at Los Angeles is unmistakably Mudejar in style. The University of Colorado is a modest version of Spanish rural architecture. Rice University at Houston shows Spanish Renaissance influence. The Alhambra at Granada was taken—albeit not very successfully—as the model for the building that now houses part of the University of Tampa. The unmistakable style of Catalan architect Antonio Gaudí can be seen in the Watts Towers in California where a number of mosaics by Simon Rodia with his rich decorative art adorn the outer cement walls, reminiscent of the Güell Park in Barcelona.

The Valencian architect Rafael Guastavino (1842–1908) who immigrated to the United States brought with him his familiarity with the Catalonian vault. Once in America, he perfected the form and patented it as the Guastavino system, on which he wrote two books. He was assisted in his work by his son, Rafael, who died in 1950. From 1880 until World War II, the popularity of this system became enormous, and hundreds of buildings all over the country have vaulting constructed along these lines. Examples include subway stations in New York, the chapel of Columbia University and the Boston Public Library.

The Spanish contribution to United States architecture is being studied in depth by Professor R. Collins of Columbia University.

Important works of art, including sculptures, paintings and murals, were created during the Spanish period at the different missions that are still standing in the United States; a comprehensive study of the paintings in California has been undertaken by Norman Neuerburg. Spanish art and civilization had an impact on the works of John Singer Sargent, for example, who was deeply impressed by the *Dolorosas*, or statues of Our Lady of Sorrow. One of his best works is *El Jaleo*, a remarkably expressive painting that vividly captures the flamenco atmosphere. Another admirer of Spain was Thomas Eakins, who painted *Carmelita Requena* (1869).

State Flags, Coats of Arms and Other Symbols

The Spanish heritage is recalled in various emblems or symbols of many states of the Union. The flag of Alabama is a red St. Andrew's Cross on a white background, similar to the banners that the Spaniards brought to America and used after the Duchy of Burgundy was inherited by the emperor Charles V and subsequently by his successors, the kings of Spain. The coat of arms of Alabama has four quarterings, in addition to a central one flanked by eagles as supporters, and a sailing ship as a crest; the upper right-hand quartering consists of two castles and two lions, the oldest quarterings on the Spanish coat of arms. The flag of Arizona is divided in two halves horizontally, with the upper sector showing the setting sun in the form of alternating red and yellow stripes spreading out fanwise from a centrally situated five-pointed star. The flag of Arkansas, in red, white and blue, includes three stars beneath the word Arkansas, symbolizing France, Spain and the United States, the three powers that have ruled there in the course of its history. (Curiously enough, there is nothing to recall the past presence of Spain in any of the state insignia of California.)

The New World as depicted by the Old. A map from 1562.

The flag of Colorado consists of three horizontal stripes, a white one between two blues; on the left-hand side, occupying the central stripe and partly overlapping onto the other two, there is a large red letter C with its central space in yellow; these colors honor the Spanish background of Colorado.

The flag of Florida resembles that of Alabama, but in the center of the St. Andrew's Cross is a circle containing the official seal. The red cross of Burgundy on a white background flutters over San Marcos Castle at St. Augustine in recognition of its past history. The present flag of Louisiana does not contain any such symbols, but when the state declared its independence from the Union in 1861, a flag was prepared with a red background, a golden star at the top, and 13 blue and white stripes below: the first two colors were an acknowledgement to Spain "for her gentle and paternal government," according to the statement made by Representative Elgée at the convention held on February 11, 1861.

The motto of the state of Montana is Oro y Plata, or "gold and silver" in Spanish. The state tree of Nevada is the single-leaf piñon, a variety of the pine family, which has retained its Spanish name. The flag of New Mexico shows the red symbolic sun of the Zia Indians on a gold background, the color a tribute to the original mother country. The state bird is the chaparral cock, or roadrunner; the state flower is the yucca, and the state tree, the piñon—all words of Spanish origin. Oregon bears a caravel on its coat of arms in memory of the Spanish navigators.

There are also many cities and institutions with coats of arms evoking a Spanish past. The seal of Los Angeles includes in one of its quarters a castle and a lion from the Spanish coat of arms. The coat of arms of Mobile, Alabama, includes the castles and lions, while those of St. Augustine are a copy of the imperial arms of Charles V. The University at Toledo, Ohio, has adopted the imperial coat of arms as its own, with a Spanish motto: Coadyuvando el presente, formando el porvenir, meaning "Helping the present, forming the future."

The Spanish Language

Use of the Spanish language is becoming increasingly common in the United States, and there are several facets in any discussion of this subject: Spanish as a learned language, Spanish as a mother tongue, Spanish as an official language and Spanish influence on English usage. It is interesting to note that while more and more people are learning Spanish, those who speak it as a mother tongue in the United States have also begun to abandon it. Since World War II, and particularly as a result of many young people traveling throughout the United States and other countries, the younger generations of Hispanic Americans have come to master English at the expense of their knowledge of Spanish. However, more Spanish-speaking citizens born in the United States now feel encouraged to retain the Spanish language when they realize that knowledge of Spanish is becoming more and more important among their fellow citizens. New large-scale immigration from Cuba and Central America and the Bilingual Education Act passed in 1978 may help preserve use of Spanish.

In recent years, though, many politicians have resisted bilingual education and instituted as ESL (English as a Second Language) program as an alternate system. A wave of "English-only" movements has met with some success. Many states have already voted favorably for these movements. In a referendum in California in 1986, English was proclaimed the state's official language; in another referendum in 1998, California passed Proposal 227, thereby unifying all teaching methods throughout the state to be taught solely in English. In Arizona, the English-only referendum was rejected in 1989. In this matter there has been a struggle between those who consider that English must be equally mastered by all citizens (Hispanics included) and those who favor the knowledge and ability for all to be able to use more than one language.

Other groups recognize the place of Spanish in the United States today. In 1973 the Liga Nacional Defensora del Idioma Español was founded, and the Academia de la Lengua Española en Estados Unidos, with its headquarters in New York, is now more than 20 years old and is comprised of members of diverse national origins. According to its director, Odón Betanzos, common features can be perceived in the Spanish used in Florida, the Southeast, the East and the Midwest. Spanish as spoken in the States has been altered due to the number of anglicized Spanish speakers, the improper syntax and inaccurate usage in the media, and badly written advertisements.

Even though Spanish may not be an official language, it remains the second most frequently used language in the United States. According to Professor John Gutierrez from the University of Pennsylvania, Spanish is not really a language of immigrants as others have been; it has become a permanent language, spoken in certain Southeastern areas since 1598. "The Hispanics will assimilate and will learn English," he says, "because they need it in order to progress. But this does not mean they will forget their Spanish. On the contrary, they might become the first group of immigrants who will not abandon the use of their language in the third generation as is usually the case."

In a visit to the University of California at Berkeley in 1987, King Juan Carlos I of Spain commented: ". . . the English and Spanish languages have never clashed in linguistic struggles or spoken or written rivalry. Each of our powerful languages has spread over the five continents, spurred on by its own vigorous proof of its long-standing inner strength; its very phonetic simplicity has imbued it with great resilience and firmness. . . Spanish and English. . . must coexist in a perfect symbiosis of mutually compatible and harmonious spheres of influence."

From the early days of the Spanish colony, an elite group practiced Spanish. This small group underwent considerable growth when trade relations with the West Indies developed. In the different provinces and especially in New England, Virginia and Philadelphia could be found outstanding Spanish scholars and teachers and many libraries containing books in Spanish. Great interest was shown in Spanish studies by such prominent individuals as Ben Franklin and Thomas Jefferson, and the progress of Spanish studies continued in the 19th century, the leading centers being Harvard University—with the Smith chair in Spanish studies, held by George Ticknor, Henry Wadsworth Longfellow and James Russell Lowell—and the University of Virginia. At the beginning of the 20th century, Spanish studies had lost some influence, and there was far more interest in French and German. (At the Philadelphia founding conventions the possibility of making German the official language of the new nation instead of English was discussed, and in states such as Colorado, for many years German was used as an official language together with English and Spanish.) With the outbreak of World War I, German studies declined enormously, whereas Spanish underwent a very substantial increase.

Following World War II, renewed U.S. interest in Spanish America, a growing national awareness of the need to master foreign languages if political domination was to be maintained and, in the specific case of Spain herself, the development of a growing tourist trade and U.S.-Spain agreements are factors that have led to a marked increase in the teaching of Spanish at the primary, secondary and university levels. The growth in the number of students has brought with it an increase in the number of teachers. This need has partly been met by youths who fought in the war, and, having been abroad, realized the need for a knowledge of languages. In recent years the establishment of the Institutes of Languages by the National Defense Education Act, proved helpful in this respect; these institutes mostly functioned during the summer in the United States, although some of them could be found in foreign countries, including Mexico, Ecuador, Argentina and Spain. Besides these courses funded by the federal government, many universities organized specialized language courses on their own account. Middlebury College, one of the first, founded the Spanish School with native teachers in 1917. The 1966 International Education Act partly amended the National Defense Education Act by increasing the possibilities of federal aid for foreign language teaching.

The number of Spanish courses and, in many cases Spanish departments, at colleges and universities has risen to more than a thousand in the last few years.

Similar growth is true of independent institutes and associations offering Spanish, and the same favorable trend can be seen in primary or secondary education, where Spanish is the most widely taught language after English. In 1974, pupils at public secondary schools enrolling for Spanish studies numbered 2,064,361, while the figure at private schools was about 10% of the total student force. In 1980, at colleges and universities (including junior colleges) Spanish students totaled 379,379 and had overtaken the number of French students (248,361). At that time, in the states of New Mexico, Texas, Arizona, Florida, Nevada, California and Oklahoma, 50% of the students in grades nine through 12 at public schools were studying Spanish.

By an order of July 1, 1965, the California legislation made it compulsory to teach a foreign language at elementary schools in that state. As a result, Spanish, which had been taught at many schools for six or seven years, with few exceptions became the first choice among students. In some places, the students of Spanish represent a very high percentage of the total number of pupils enrolled; for instance, at La Cumbre the figure stood at 76.3%; at La Colina, 66%; and at Goleta Valley, 54.6%.

In 1967, the press gave wide coverage of various bills discussed before the House of Representatives to make the teaching of the Spanish language at public schools compulsory. Since 1975, bilingual teaching in Spanish and English has been available in New Jersey, provided 20% of the students have a limited knowledge of English. The South East Pastoral Institute (SEPI) has been offering in Miami for the last eight years an intensive course, called Inmersión en el Idioma Español.

The competition Letras de Oro, sponsored by the University of Miami, with support in its beginning from American Express, and aimed at the writers-in-Spanish residents in the United States, is an interesting initiative that began in 1986. The competition, in its various summons, has attained both qualitative and quantitative success and has worked its way up to a federal level. According to Professor Joaquin Roy, the writers-in-Spanish live in Florida, New York, California, Texas, Puerto Rico, New Jersey and Illinois. They come from Cuba (35%), Colombia (14.3%), Puerto Rico (8.2%), Argentina (6.4%), Mexico (6.2%), Spain (6.0%), Chile (3.8%) and Peru (3.8%). The young Spanish organization Instituto Cervantes plans to develop stronger efforts to promote the Spanish language and culture by opening more branch offices in the main U.S. cities, such as the one already operating in New York City.

Cultural Exchanges

A major effort has been promoted by the federal government, a number of important educational institutions and by the Spanish government and various organizations that are active in this field, to encourage crosscultural exchange. This policy of encouraging linguistic studies focused from the start on the granting of scholarships to study abroad, both for teachers and for students. As of 1998, Spanish authorities had set up "A Strategic Plan for the Teaching of the Spanish Language in the United States." Some U.S. states, including New York, Florida, California and New Mexico, have already signed agreements with this plan.

Under the Friendship and Cooperation Agreement of August 6, 1970, the two governments recognized the importance of the program and undertook to boost it. In addition to these agreements, the U.S. Information and Educational Act (Smith-Mundt) of 1948 and the Foreign Economic Assistance Act of 1950 provided resources to assist in this educational drive. Soon after, several Spanish private institutions, such as the Banco de Bilbao and the Caixa de Catalunya, and a number of ministries, such as Health and Consumption, and Economy and Finance, have contributed to the program. On January 24, 1976, the Treaty of Friendship and Cooperation was signed between the United States and Spain providing for cultural and educational cooperation. Under this agreement and others, including $5 million available under the Fulbright program, these allocations sometimes bring the total budget up to a figure in excess of $17 million, a sum that Spain has never spent under an agreement on the exchange of people and knowledge with any other country in the world.

American institutions that have granted, and continue to grant, scholarships to study Spanish in Spain include, among others, the Department of State, the Agency for International Development (AID), the American Field Service, the Experiment on International Living, and the Good Samaritan and Del Amo Foundations. Spanish agencies cooperating in this work include the Division of Cultural Relations at the Ministry of Foreign Affairs and sporadically the Consejo Superior de Investigaciones Científicas, the Agencia de Cooperación Iberoamericana and the March Foundation.

The U.S. State Department has been active in distributing scholarships through its Bureau of Educational and Cultural Affairs, with cooperation from the Associated Research Councils, for scholarships for lecturers, research workers and university professors; the Institute of International Education (with its headquarters in New York) for postgraduates; and the Office of Education of the Federal Department of Health, Education and Welfare for primary and secondary education teachers. Subsequently, the program was handed over to the USIA (United States Information Agency), which acts in cooperation with the Cooperation General Institute and the CIES. The American Field Service and the Experiment on International Living were private institutions that concerned themselves with secondary education students and have given them, not only an opportunity of studying, but also of living in a Spanish family atmosphere. Herencia Española and the Foreign Study League have also been active in this area.

The Good Samaritan program was founded by the Spaniard Elías Ahuja, who came to the United States in 1880 and made a considerable fortune. After a spell in his native country he returned to the United States in 1937 and set up his foundation to help the youths of both countries become exchange students. The Del Amo Foundation was established by Dr. Gregorio del Amo in California in 1929, its main purpose being to promote cultural relations between Spain and southern California. Needless to say, these organizations have, not only granted scholarships for Americans to study in Spain, but also provided facilities for Spaniards who wish to widen their knowledge in the United States.

In addition, many American universities have established study abroad programs of various kinds and durations in Spain. An exhaustive list cannot be given here, but it is worth mentioning the winter courses run by the following universities: New York, California,

Standford, Vanderbilt, Pennsylvania State, Michigan, Purdue, Indiana, Bowling Green, Georgetown, Tulane, St. Lawrence and Marquette. Courses are also run by Middlebury College, Colgate, Cornell, Tufts and Rutgers, as well as by many other colleges and universities. Summer courses are established by the Institute of European Studies, Academic Year Abroad, Syracuse University and the University Studies Abroad Consortium.

Some Spanish universities, such as Salamanca, have summer courses for foreigners, with a considerable American student attendance. The Association of North American University Programs in Spain includes more than 60 institutions of higher education. The International Institute, founded in 1877, also deserves special praise.

A number of programs are designed for international students seeking an American degree or the opportunity to study part of their studies in an American university. Examples of these programs are the Center for International Studies, St. Louis University and Schiller International University in Madrid, and Saint Thomas and San Diego State in El Escorial. The Instituto de Estudios Norteamericanos in Spain's Alcalá de Henares University is also very active and influential.

The University of New York has established the Center of Hispanic Studies Juan Carlos I, and Harvard University has the Real Colegio Complutense, opened by King Juan Carlos in 1993.

Associations and Institutions

One of the most active associations to promote Hispanic language and literature is the Modern Language Association of America (MLA). The association was founded in 1883, and the following year it began publishing a magnificent review called *PMLA*, with five issues a year, containing articles in all modern languages. The list of its presidents includes such notable Spanish scholars as James Russell Lowell, Charles Carroll Marden, Rudolph Schevill, S. G. Morley and Hayward Keniston. The association holds an annual meeting and publishes a very useful list of the deans and heads of the departments of languages at U.S. colleges and universities; the list also includes the members of the association, who must necessarily be professors of higher education.

Another active body is the American Association of Teachers of Spanish and Portuguese (AATSP), which was founded in 1915. It is made up of Spanish teachers at all levels, and its members at present number more than 40,000. (Not all Spanish teachers necessarily belong

to the association.) The association publishes a very good quarterly review called *Hispania*.

The National Federation of Modern Language Teachers was created to encompass all regional associations of language teachers (it subsequently added "Associations" to its name). The Association of Spanish Teachers was admitted to this federation, which brought out the *Modern Language Journal,* whose editor was for a long time the Spanish scholar Henry Grattan Doyle.

The Sociedad Nacional Hispánica Sigma Delta Pi enthusiastically promotes Hispanic culture. Founded at the University of California at Berkeley in 1919, it was declared a national society in 1925, when it had three regional chapters. Today it has as many as 184 chapters at various universities and colleges in the United States. The membership consists of those professors and university students of distinction who have shown particular enthusiasm for Hispanic subjects and the Spanish language. Its motto is "El amor por todo lo noble y bello que haya salido de la venerable España" (Love for all things noble and beautiful emerging from noble Spain), and its coat of arms consists of the four quarterings with castles and lions, a central circle containing the three Greek letters and a royal crown as a crest.

The candlelight ceremony at which members are received into the *sociedad* is only attended by initiates and is full of symbols of Hispanic culture, from the red candle with a yellow bow held by the new member to that typically Spanish flower, the carnation, which the candidate wears. Speeches on arms and letters from *Don Quixote* and a paragraph from Azorín are read aloud, and the members with doctorates take an oath, in keeping with the motto of the society. Some very eminent professors have been members of Sigma Delta Pi, and its honorary presidents have included Tomás Navarro Tomás, G. Griswold Morley and Leavitt O. Wright. Much has been done for the growth of the society by Professor James O. Swain (a specialist on Vicente Blasco Ibáñez), who was secretary of the society for 14 years. He was succeeded by F. Dewey Amner and Stuart M. Gross. A bulletin called *Entre Nosotros* has been issued periodically, informing the members of the chapters' activities, which include plays, lectures and film festivals, and noting new articles or books dealing with Hispanic subjects. For students at the secondary education level there is a society called the Sociedad Honoraria Hispánica. It publishes a quarterly bulletin called *Albricias*.

Other institutions that have done much to make Spanish language and culture more widespread include the Hispanic Society of America in New York and the

Hispanic Foundation of the Library of Congress, in Washington, D.C., both founded by the great Hispanic scholar Archer M. Huntington. The Instituto de las Españas (Institute of the Spains) of Columbia University has published the *Revista Hispánica Moderna* since 1934 and later launched the *Revista de Estudios Hispánicos.*

Many United States universities and colleges have institutes specializing in the study of Spanish America and houses where the students can immerse themselves in Hispanic culture, thereby helping them to master the language. To name only a few of the most outstanding journals, the University of Florida at Gainesville publishes the *Handbook of Latin American Studies* in cooperation with the Library of Congress; the University of Pennsylvania has a quarterly publication, *The Hispanic Review,* founded in 1933; and Duke University brings out *The Hispanic American Historical Review* four times a year, reporting on the most outstanding developments in the field of Hispanic history. Also covering Hispanic history is *The Americas* of the Academy of American Franciscan History. The *Revista de Estudios Hispánicos* of the University of Alabama is issued three times a year.

Studies of Catalan have been promoted by the North American Catalan Society, which has organized discussions at various universities. In some cases, Catalan is taught as well. The Basque language is encouraged by the Basque American Foundation, with a *Journal of Basque Studies.* The University of California at Santa Barbara, Indiana University, Cornell and the Universities of Wisconsin and Nevada offer Basque studies. Nevada also has a Center of Basque Studies and an extensive library of books in Spanish and Basque. The Asociación de Estudios Gallegos (The Association of Galician Studies) was the promoter of the Segundo Congreso de Estudios Gallegos (Second Congress of Galician Studies) at Brown University in November 1988.

Hispanic Scholars

Many Hispanic scholars are less well known than they should be. However, for the sake of brevity, the list given here only includes those not mentioned elsewhere in this volume: Alfred Coester, Harry C. Heaton, E. K. Mapes, George Tyler Northup, Charles E. Chapman, Donald Walsh, and James Brown Scott; and more recently, Paul Horgan, Gilbert Chase, Curtis Wilgus, Michael Kenny, James F. King, Joseph Schraibman, Roberto Lado, Nicholson Adams, Sterling A. Stoudemire, John J. Keller, W. H. Shoemaker, Edmund S. Urbanski, Elias Rivers, Inman Fox, James O. Swain, D.

W. McPheeters, Theodore Andersson, Jaime Casteñeda, Everett Hesse, Aurelio Espinosa, Rudolph and Isabel M. Schevill, Edgar Knowlton, Jack D. L. Holmes, Geoffrey Ribbans, etc.

Similarly, many scholars from Hispanic countries have cooperated with their American colleagues: Felipe Fernández, Felix Merino, León de la Costa, Miguel Cabrera de Nevares, Julio Soler, Luis F. Mantilla, Angel Herreros de la Mora and Javier Vingut in the past; and, more recently, Juan Marichal, Juan López Morillas, Jorge Guillén, Jaime Ferrán Homero Serís, Sofía Novoa, María Madariaga, Joaquín Casalduero, Angel del Río, Francisco Ayala, Tomás Navarro Tomás, Eugenio Florit, Vicente Llorens, Américo Castro, Rafael Supervía, Juan Rodríguez Castellano, Carlos Rojas, Joan Corominas, Antonio Sánchez Romeralo, Juan Luis Alborg, German Bleiberg, Ricardo Gullón, Max Insfrán, Ramón Sender, Enrique Ruiz Fornells, Jose Onís, José F. Montesinos, Antonio Rodríguez Moñino, Odón Betanzos, Graciela Nemes, Joaquín Segura and Gerardo Piña.

The presence of the Spanish in parts of the thirteen colonies and, after independence, the immigration to the United States of Spanish-speaking peoples from Mexico, Cuba, Puerto Rico, Spain and other countries have resulted in Spanish being spoken as the mother tongue of a very considerable number of U.S. citizens and residents today. In fact the figure is more than 28.26 million people. After English, Spanish is undoubtedly the most commonly used language, followed at a great distance by French, which is still used as a native language along the border with the Canadian province of Quebec and in some areas of Louisiana. To that figure must be added those citizens of Hispanic descent who, although born in the United States and using English as their first language, still retain the use of Spanish.

It is surprising to travel through the United States and, in distinct areas of the country, to hear the language of Cervantes used with different variations in each place. It is amazing to see how the Spanish introduced at the time of the Spanish colonization has survived. This is true in the states of New Mexico, Arizona, Colorado, Louisiana, Texas and California, and in smaller areas in Florida, Nevada and Alabama. There are some differences, for instance, between the Spanish spoken in New Mexico and in Arizona, and even within each of these regions some slight divergencies can be seen. At Tucson, in addition to the normal Spanish spoken in southern Arizona, there is that used by the Yaqui Indians and by Pachucos. Pachuco is a type of slang invented at El Paso, Texas, in the 1930s, and spread later—particularly after World War II—to California (Los Angeles) and Arizona. Though it is based on Spanish, it includes a mixture of anglicisms; local Mexican expressions and regional terms; Spanish words whose meanings or form or both have been changed; and invented terms. Often used by youths belonging to gangs, its main purpose is to be different and not to be understood by outsiders. Pachuco is such a curious phenomenon that songs have even been recorded in this jargon, some of them by Lalo Guerrero, such as the song called "La Pachuquilla," which sold 60,000 records in only a few months.

In Louisiana, Spanish has survived, among other places, in the parish of St. Bernard and the so-called brulis (Ascension and Assumption parishes), but there are even differences of speech between them, for the inhabitants of the former originally came from the Canary Islands, while the latter experienced a greater degree of French influence. It is a pleasure to hear the truer Spanish spoken in San Antonio, Texas, and throughout southwestern Texas; the same can be said of most of Colorado, particularly in the southern areas bordering New Mexico.

However, it is in New Mexico and southern Colorado that the original Spanish imported by the settlers in the 16th and 17th centuries has survived best. It contains a number of archaic expressions that have disappeared in Spain, and even in many South and Central America countries. This is due to its isolation from Mexican and Anglo-Saxon influence until relatively recently and contrasts with what has happened in Texas and California. It is not unusual to hear a New Mexican use such old-fashioned words as *asina, agora, morar* or *mesmo*. In those cases where idiomatic influences from Mexico can be found, these are attributable to Nahuatl, the language of the Aztecs, rather than to Mexican Spanish. Professor Aurelio M. Espinosa has described the Spanish of New Mexico as the most isolated remnant of the Spanish spoken during the Golden Age. A very useful scholarly contribution to the knowledge of areas in which Spanish-language use survives is professor Manuel Alvar's *El atlas del español en Estados Unidos.*

One perhaps inevitable aspect of the widespread use of the Spanish language is the emergence of Spanglish, with wrongly modified English words being added to the original Spanish.

Proof of the vitality of Spanish in the United States lies in the fact that during the past 10 years, the Spanish-speaking media has doubled. The 100 radio stations completely broadcasting in Spanish in 1978 became 211

in 1988. A good number of English radio stations include in their programs a few hours of Spanish. In California, for example, more than 65 of them broadcast between one and 20 hours in Spanish. The number of television channels in Spanish has gone from 16 to 22, without taking into consideration the six Mexican channels that can be picked up with the "Morelos" satellite. The SIN and Latinet TV stations had a wide coverage years ago. The newscast is served nowadays by Univisión backed by Hallmark Cards, and by Telemundo backed by Reliance Capital Group (this one started in January 1987, under the name of American Broadcasting Corporation). A new competitor is Univisa with Galavisión Spanish Cable service as its most easily recognized product.

There are also more than 200 Spanish-language newspapers in the country, intended for local readers (there are others whose market is primarily in Hispanic countries). They include daily papers: *Diario las Américas* (Miami), *El Diario–La Prensa* (New York), *El Tiempo* (New York), *Exito Chicago* (Chicago), *El Nuevo Tiempo* (Santa Barbara), *La Opinión* (Los Angeles), *El Continental* (El Paso) and *Laredo Times* (Laredo). The *Miami Herald* has been publishing a newspaper in Spanish called *El Nuevo Herald* since 1987. The Chicano community publishes *El Malcriado*.

As far as journalism is concerned, it is curious to note that in Louisiana, whereas only one newspaper, called *Moniteur de la Luisiane* (in French), was published in Spanish times, in the years after Louisiana became part of the United States several Spanish-language periodicals came into being, namely, *El Misisipi; El Mensagero Luisianés; El Telégrafo; El Español; El Correo Atlántico; Avispa de Nueva Orleáns; El Iris de Paz; La Patria, periódico mercantil, político y literario, único órgano de la población española de los Estados Unidos; La unión; El Indicador* (all at New Orleans) and *El Mexicano* (at Natchitoches). These publications lasted for different lengths of time, and some even until 1869. In total, according to the Asociación Nacional de Editores Hispanos (National Association of Hispanic Editors), the number of Spanish periodical publications, broken down by type of periodical, are as follows: "sheet" newspapers, 80; "tabloid" newspapers, 278; weeklies, 711; professional magazines, 93; and informative papers, 225.

A more detailed list of the Spanish-language media can be found in the appendix, at the back of this volume.

While of course Spanish was spoken in colonial times in different areas under Spanish rule, it persisted even when the old Spanish territories joined the Anglo-Saxon world. In New Mexico, Spanish became an official language in 1846, when General Stephen Watts Kearny ordered the preparation of the Organic Laws and Constitution, on August 18, two days after the peaceful taking of Santa Fe by the forces of the United States. From that time onward, Spanish could be used on a par with English in parliament and in the law courts; moreover, in 1910, a clause was included in the state constitution ordering that laws be published in English and in Spanish. Even today, modern acts of the state legislature are translated into Spanish; in the courts of justice and magistrates courts, the defense can, if necessary, use Spanish with the efficient assistance of translators; in newspa-

pers, edicts and legal announcements can still be seen in English and in Spanish, and the rights and privileges of citizens can be protected and promoted in both languages. In Colorado, Spanish was an official language until 1921 and could be used with English in congress and in the law courts.

The situation was somewhat similar with the states given by Mexico under the Treaty of Guadalupe Hidalgo of 1848, which, in fact, turned the United States into a bilingual nation. The California Constitution, passed in that same year, declared that all laws, decrees, regulations and provision whose nature requires their publication should be drafted in English and in Spanish.

Hispanic families like the Lugos of Bell, California, owned ranches in the Southwest long before the arrival of North European colonists. Smithsonian Institution.

Under a decision of the state of New York, Spanish-speaking United States citizens can take the oath on the Constitution in Spanish and, therefore, vote; this decision gave rise to a number of complaints on the part of other minorities, such as the Poles and Russians, but they were rejected on the grounds that there is a state—New Mexico—of the Union where Spanish is also an official language, and therefore its citizens can vote without knowing English. The federal government likewise passed a law enabling Spanish-speaking citizens to vote in their language, provided they had attended school through all grades under the United States flag, namely, Puerto Ricans, citizens born in the Panama Canal zone and Filipinos prior to independence.

On the occasion of the Hemisfair 1968, held at San Antonio, Texas, Spanish was considered an official language together with English in that state throughout the year.

The 1964 Civil Rights Act opposed any discrimination concerning race, color, religion, sex or nation of origin. The Cabinet Committee on Opportunities for Spanish Speaking People was set up in 1969 to promote the access of Spanish speakers to public office. The Voting Rights Acts of 1965 and 1975 eliminated requisites relating to language. The Bilingual Ballot has been promoted by the Fondo Puertorriqueño de Defensa Legal. Some states have even allowed driving examinations in Spanish.

Under a decision taken by the city council in 1967, Miami (Florida) had two official languages due to the large Hispanic population, mainly exiled Cubans. The same was the case in Dade County since 1973. Years later, a referendum overruled this official bilingualism. Likewise, in California in 1986, another referendum established English as the sole official language. Six other states, such as Florida and Colorado in 1988, have ruled the same.

A number of scholars have studied the influence of Spanish on the English language as spoken and written in America. Useful volumns on this subject include *A Dictionary of Spanish Terms in English,* by Professor Harold W. Bentrey, and *A History of Foreign Words in English,* by Mary S. Serjeantson. This influence is greater than would appear at first sight, quite apart from the countless names of towns, rivers, mountains, capes and other features scattered all over the geography of the country. Many Spanish words have been included in the present-day American vocabulary, and not only in the southwestern states, although those terms are most widespread there. Some words are obviously of Spanish origin, while others have been anglified and altered either in their spelling or pronunciation. Some curious examples of the latter include the word *alligator* (which comes from the Spanish word *lagarto,* for "lizard"), *cigar, huelga, grandee, negro, rodeo, tornado, hurricane* and *tobacco.* Likewise in frequent and widespread use throughout the country are words such as *siesta, guerrilla, plaza, mañana, adios, ranch* and many others. The same is the case with cowboy vocabulary, with such words as *sombrero, lasso, corral, caballo, vaca, vaquero, illano, matanza, manteca, stampede, adobe, cañon, piñon, bonanza, fandango* and *hacienda.* There are over 900 such words.

Geographical Names

America takes its name from the Florentine-born Americo Vespucio (Amerigo Vespucci), who undertook a number of voyages of discovery to the New World in the service of the kings of Spain. After he had obtained his naturalization in the Kingdoms of Castile and Leon in 1505, his account of the four voyages led Martin Waldseemüller to propose in 1507 that the great continent recently discovered by Christopher Columbus should be given the name by which it is known today. In maps of the area, the name was used by Pedro Margallo in his *Fiscae compendium* in 1520, in 1514 by Ludovicus Boulanger and in 1515 by Leonardo da Vinci.

The use of this name was not universal; the adjective *americano* is not to be found in the Spanish *Diccionario de Autoridades* of 1734 and was only included in the 1770 edition without reference to any authority. In the course of the 16th century, North America bore several names far removed from the present one, including Nueva España (New Spain), which contained Florida and all of the land north of the Rio Grande. Later, the northernmost areas were called New France. The name America as applying to the northern areas of the New World began to appear on the maps of Ortelius in 1570 and Cornelius de Judaeis in 1593. The planisphere accompanying the chronicle of Nicolás de Cardona in 1614 calls the north, "América Mexicana" and the south, "América Peruana."

Prior to the American Revolution, there was no name covering the provinces as a whole, but when they rebelled, they began to adopt the name United Colonies, United Colonies of America or United Colonies of

North America. The name United States of America was used in the Declaration of Independence, yet when Benjamin Franklin, Silas Deane and Arthur Lee asked for an interview with the Spanish ambassador in Paris, the count of Aranda, toward the end of 1776, they did so as "Plenipotentiaries of the Congress of the United Provinces of North America," and Franklin signed a consular treaty with France whereby the "Thirteen United States of North America" permitted French consuls to present their letters of credence to the governors of the states and not to Congress.

After their victorious rebellion against Britain, when the founding fathers wanted to give their land a meaningful name, many advocated Columbia in honor of Christopher Columbus. It was Philip Frenau who started this movement in Boston in 1775, in the publication *American Liberty;* for a while, he looked very likely to succeed. An opportunity for the change of name arose at the Constitutional Convention of 1787, but the many problems that had to be solved during that convention resulted in no decision being made.

Instead, the country became known as the United States of America. When the Spanish American colonies attained independence, it became clear how confusing the name chosen was; these states too were part of the Americas, but their origins did not share the same revolutionary past as the original 13 provinces. Nonetheless, "America" came to be used for the sake of brevity, and "Americans," to distinguish its citizens (though others on the North American continent consider themselves Americans as well). The name Columbia continued to be used as a poetic term for the nation. The 19th-century song "Columbia, the Gem of the Ocean" was widely popular, and when the federal capital was built, Thomas Crawford drew the statue "Columbia" for the dome (since then, all federal buildings have a statue of "Columbia"). The name Columbia was given to one of the U.S. space shuttles.

The origins of several state names are related in one way or another to their Spanish background. Florida was given its name by Juan Ponce de León on April 2, 1513. As he had not yet disembarked, he did not know the name by which it was known to the inhabitants. Since there was no priest on that expedition, perhaps he could not recall which saint's feast was celebrated on that day and so honor him according to the widespread Spanish custom. One may wonder whether it ever occurred to him to call it New León. His chronicler, He-

rrera, explains that he chose the name Florida because it was six days after Easter Sunday (Pascua Florida) and the countryside was a mass of spring flowers. In time, the intonation was to change from the Spanish, where the stress is on the letter *i*, to its present pronunciation. For a long time, the area known as Florida was to include a vast amount of territory stretching at least as far as the Chesapeake Bay. The term remained in use during the British occupation of the peninsula state and was retained when it joined the Union.

Spain also gave Texas its name. In 1683, seven Indians from the East visited the Spanish governor at El Paso to ask him for missionaries and assistance in war. They spoke of certain tribes, and particularly of what the Spaniards understood to be "the Kingdom of Texas." An expedition was sent out, but found no such kingdom. Years later, in 1689, when news was heard of La Salle's travels in those parts, another expedition was organized under the command of Alonso de León, and the Spaniards were greeted by the Hasinai Indians with cries of "Techas, Techas!" meaning "Friends, Friends!" Although the Spaniards realized that the word did not have any geographical connotations, they continued to use the name for the new territories explored by the expedition of Domingo de Terán and Friar Damián Massanet in 1691. (Previously they had been called Panuco and new Philippines [Nuevas Filipinas].)

Nuevo México (New Mexico) appears for the first time in the reports made by Francisco de Ibarra, a gold prospector, who set off northward in 1563, and, guided by an Indian woman, came to a large settlement. There, he saw people dressed like the Aztecs and playing drums in the same way. When he returned, he claimed to have discovered a new Mexico. Friar Marcos de Niza had visited the region many years earlier, in 1539, and had named it Nuevo Reino de San Francisco (New Kingdom of St. Francis). Coronado called the region Tiguex. The Group of Nine, led by Sánchez Chamuscado and Brother Rodríguez, called it San Felipe (St. Philip). The following year, Antonio Espejo reported that he had been north "to the provinces and settlements of New Mexico, which I called New Andalusia, in honor of the land of my birth." In 1598, Juan Oñate took possession of what he called the "kingdoms and provinces of New Mexico."

When Colorado was claimed by Spain in 1706, it was called Santo Domingo. When it was oganized into a territory as such, many other names were proposed, including San Juan (St. John). But in 1859 when the matter came before the legislature, the name suggested was Colona, derived from *Colón,* the Spanish version of the name Columbus. However, this proposal did not prosper. It was Senator Green of Missouri who successfully proposed the present name, from the river, which the Spaniards claimed ran red with earth.

Several explanations have been given for the name California. The most likely one is that it derives from "Las Sergas de Esplandián," the fifth part of the book of chivalry *Amadís de Gaula,* by Garci Ordoñez de Montalvo. The novel mentions an island governed by Queen Calafia and populated by women, where only those few men needed to maintain the reproduction of the species were admitted. The Spaniards of New Spain undoubtedly were acquainted with the novel, and when they heard about the discovery of a large island (for Lower, or Baja, California was originally thought to be an island) they easily accepted the name. Herrera also mentions this in his chronicles.

The name Montana, which was eventually given to the territory and later to the state, was hotly disputed. The debates in the House of Representatives and in the Senate are curious. In the House, James M. Ashley vigorously defended the name Montana and explained the meaning of the original Spanish word, appropriate for such a mountainous territory. He thus prevented its being given the name Jefferson, which a group of Democrats, and even some inhabitants, were demanding; in the Senate, mention was also made of its Spanish etymology. Naturally, the tilde on the Spanish ñ was omitted because it is unknown in English.

The choice of the name Nevada for the adjacent territory was due to the Committee for Territories, which noting the existence of Sierra Nevada nearby, decided to shorten the name of Nevada. The inhabitants of the future territory were not too pleased with the choice; the mountain range only covered a very small part of the region and seemed to suggest a climate and scenery far removed from reality. Other names were proposed: Washoe, from the native Indian tribe, and Sierra Plata and Oro Plata, (in Spanish) owing to the mines all over the territory. But, ultimately, the first choice prevailed.

The name Arizona (meaning arid land) was used in the 18th century by Father Ortega, referring to an old mining district, and in the mid-19th century, the Arizona Mining and Trade Company was formed. In 1854, when Congress proposed dividing the territory of New Mexico, various names were considered for the western sector: Gadsonia (for Gadsden, the name of the man who negotiated with Mexico for the purchase of the belt of land included in the territory), Pimeria (for Land of the Pima, the name used by the Spaniards) and Arizona. At the convention, which met at Tucson two years later, a Mr. N. P. Cook, who had interests in the mining company, forcefully urged that the name Arizona be adopted. It was under this name that the region was made into a territory by the Confederates in 1861, and when it passed into the hands of the Union in 1863, Congress maintained that name.

Among the possible etymologies of Oregon are the Spanish words *orégano* (marjoram), *orejón* (big ear), *origen* (origin) and even *Aragón* (Aragon). The most likely explanation seems to be that Spanish navigators encountered some Indians with large ears (in Spanish, *orejas*) and called them *orejones.* Seemingly, when transcribed into English in the singular, the *j* was changed to a *g* in accordance with the English pronunciation. In 1853, the inhabitants of the northern area of the territory asked Congress to arrange for the creation of another separate territory called Columbia, thereby honoring the memory of the discoveror. The bill reached the House of Representatives but was defeated because the District of Columbia already existed, and therefore, confusion might arise. (It is curious to note that the city is usually called Washington, which can equally easily be confused with the state.)

The original federal capital was, of course, Philadelphia. However, it was felt that the capital should be established at a strategic point between the then-existing 13 states, in order to free it from the particular influence of any one of them. Consequently Virginia and Maryland ceded land in Washington and Alexandria Counties, respectively, to form a block 10 miles square. The fact that George Washington's Mount Vernon residence was nearby had some bearing on the choice; indeed, Washington had interests in the area. The name District of Columbia—which was mentioned for the first time in a letter from the Board of Architects to Architect L'Enfant dated September 9, 1791, and was included in the minutes of Congress on May 6, 1796—is a remnant of the determined efforts made to call the new country Columbia in homage to Columbus.

CONTRIBUTIONS TO THE ECONOMY AND THE LAW

Agriculture and Livestock

The Spaniards made many early contributions to American culture. They introduced the wheel in North America and also brought with them iron, the plow, various types of cereals, fruits and vegetables, horses, cows, pigs and other animals.

It was on his second voyage to America, specifically to the island of Santo Domingo, that Columbus introduced these species of animals. Gregorio de Villa Lobos brought the first heifers to New Spain in 1521, two years after its conquest by Hernán Cortés. The imported livestock soon multiplied so that by 1540 Vázquez de Coronado could easily gather no less than 500 horses, 500 head of cattle and 5,000 sheep, goats and pigs. During the same period, when Hernando de Soto disembarked in Florida, a considerable number of cows, sheep and pigs accompanied him on his long travels overland. In 1521, on his second visit to the Florida peninsula, Ponce de León had also brought young cows with him. They were the first of their species to enter the present territory of the United States. No planned breeding took place on those occasions, although a number of animals strayed into the wilds where they reproduced abundantly. The razorback hogs that the pioneers found on arriving in Alabama and Arkansas were in fact descended from the pigs that accompanied Hernando de Soto. The horses that escaped from captivity later became known by the name *cimarrones* (strays).

Sheep and cows were introduced into New Mexico with Juan Oñate's expedition in 1598. As a result of the colonization that followed the expedition, livestock raising prospered; sheep were particularly well suited to the conditions prevailing in those parts. The Indians soon became adept breeders and learned to spin the wool with which they then manufactured blankets, shawls and other articles and came to be masters of such handicrafts. Cattle raising spread later to New Mexico from Texas, where the first known breeding took place in eastern Texas in 1690, around the missions at Nacogdoches. By 1790, there were herds at Santa Cruz, San Pedro and Sorona, in what is now southern Arizona. Tristán de Luna—like Pánfilo de Narváez and Hernando de Soto before him—provided his settlers with a considerable number of head of cattle. But, Menéndez de Avilés can claim to have been the first successful cattle raiser in United States territory.

Although breeding got off to a difficult start between 1655 and 1702, and particularly in the last 20 years of that period, cattle breeding subsequently experienced a period of prosperity in Florida, with ranches in Palatka, Gainesville and Tallahassee; as many as 25 ranches are known to have existed in the first two areas, and nine in the third. The cattle bred by Horruytiner, Arcipreste de Hita and Salazar became deservedly famous. The ship *San Carlos* is known as the "Mayflower of the West," because cattle, chickens and other domestic livestock were disembarked in 1769 on the first expedition by Gaspar de Portola and Junípero Serra. Cattle breeding quickly progressed on the missions so that by the end of the century, there were more than a million head of cattle in the province of California.

The famous Texas longhorn dates back to Spanish colonial times, the beginnings of the rugged tradition of cattle breeding. By 1770, 40,000 head of branded and unbranded cattle were counted on the Espíritu Santo (Holy Spirit) Mission, near Goliad, while the neighboring mission of Rosario could boast 10,000 branded and 20,000 unbranded head of cattle. The unbranded animals came to be known by the Spanish name *mesteños*, which gave rise eventually to the English word *mustang*, later applied to wild horses as well. In fact, Spanish cattle breeding resulted in many Castilian words becoming a part of the language of the Texas cowboys, and ultimately throughout the country. Texas cattle spread to other areas of the country, both westward to the far west and northward to the great prairie states, endowing the United States with one of its major sources of wealth.

The Spanish *vaquero* lies at the origin of the popular figure of the cowboy: The first horsemen to ride through the western lands were Spaniards. As can be seen by comparing them with Andalusian country attire, cowboy clothes are essentially Spanish in style and type. It was Spanish horses that frightened the Indians when they saw them for the first time and wondered whether they were animals or beings physically joined to their riders. The Pueblo Indians first saw horses in 1540, when Coronado and his followers arrived, while in the Southeast, it was the horses brought by Narváez and de Soto that struck terror into the natives.

The presence of horses caused a tremendous revolution in the art of warfare. The Indians soon got over their fright, realized the advantages of such animals and became splendid horsemen; from sedentary farmers they turned into nomads. Once they owned horses and learned to make the most of them, the lifestyle of the Indians changed completely; they traveled much faster and more freely, acquiring the ability to flee after making an attack. As a result, the possession of horses became a major objective in Indian warfare and was often the cause of bloody attacks. Stealing horses became an end in itself, and once achieved, a real scourge for the Spaniards, because the Indians often attained superiority over the Spaniards in battle by having a larger proportion of mounted forces. Thanks to horses the Indians were also able to follow the migratory routes of the huge herds of bison over the prairies and have been compared favorably with the mounted hordes of the Mongol Genghis Khan. As Patrick Patterson, director of the Woolaroc Museum in Oklahoma, says, every painting with a horse in the United States is an acknowledgment of the Spanish influence. Many horses turned wild and came to be called *cimarrones,* a name borne by towns in various states, and even by a Cadillac car.

The contributions made to farming were no less important than those in livestock raising. All Spanish expeditions arriving on the continent for the purpose of setting up permanent settlements brought seeds and farm implements with them, including those settlements organized by Ayllón at San Miguel de Gualdape, by Tristán de Luna at Pensacola and by Coronado in New Mexico.

Juan Oñate and his men brought many new seeds, planted them in properly prepared fields and showed the Indians how to cultivate them. These crops included wheat, oats, rye, onions, chile, peas, melons, watermelons, apricots, peaches, apples and certain varieties of beans, plums, figs, dates, almonds, walnuts, hazelnuts, olives and other things hitherto unknown in North America. These crops gradually prospered, and no small part was played in this by the friars at the different missions that gradually sprang up. The Spaniards likewise were instrumental in acclimatizing grapevines, orange and lemon trees, and other citrus fruits on the new continent. The methods of irrigation that the Spaniards had inherited from the Arabs played an important part in the progress of all these crops. The grapevine and horticultural produce that are so important for the economy of California arrived at San Diego about the Spanish ship *San Carlos* in 1769.

Roads

Alvar Núñez Cabeza de Vaca rightly bears the title of first pedestrian in the United States, for he was the first man to cross North America from east to west centuries ago. His hike is difficult to understand even today, for he passed through the states of Florida, Alabama, Mississippi and Louisiana as a member of the expedition led by Narváez; and afterward, on his own, took eight years to travel through Texas, New Mexico and Arizona, before reaching New Spain, through which he also traveled on foot to the capital of Mexico. This first transcontinental journey was duly commemorated in 1935 by a 50-cent coin minted in the United States showing a map of those states and the name of this legendary Spaniard. This feat was not to be repeated until 1805, by the Lewis and Clark expedition. The merit of Cabeza de Vaca's trek is even greater when it is remembered that when he set out on his tremendous journey, Queen Elizabeth of England had not yet been born, and she only acceded to the throne 20 years after he had completed his long walk. Cabeza de Vaca walked more than 11,000 miles (15,000 kilometers) and his companion, Andrés Dorantes, walked even farther. Historian Charles Lummis notes, however, that their names are practically unknown to the vast majority of Americans, although they are persons "who should be considered with profound interest and admiration."

The Spanish expeditions that later explored the country gradually opened up routes, more often than not along barely marked tracks, and always through regions inhabited by hostile tribes. Those routes eventually became consolidated and have served as the basis for several modern highways. That is the case with the so-called Atlantic, Gulf and Pacific Safeway, which links St. Augustine on the east coast with Los Angeles on the west coast. It follows the route of former highways 90, 80, 70 and 86, which coincided with the Old Spanish Trail. At St. Augustine, Florida, there is a stone marking point zero on that route. Old Spanish Trail is the evocative name that the safeway was given during the ceremonies held at St. Augustine in 1929. Though it was later absorbed by other routes, in its publicity leaflets and brochures the old name has been retained. The

2,743 miles (4,115 kilometers) comprising this route cost the Spaniards 200 years of endeavor, from the foundation of St. Augustine in 1565 to that of San Diego in 1769. In Florida, the trail established by the Spaniards linked St. Augustine with San Luis (in the vicinity of Tallahassee) via a number of missions or staging posts, which include present-day Gainesville.

During 40 years of rule in Louisiana, after she took over the territory in 1763, Spain succeeded in establishing the physical link between her possessions in Florida and those in the Southwest. In Texas, the trail linked up Atascosito, which passed through Beaumont, Houston, Victoria, La Bahía and San Antonio, and extended as far as El Paso. Another route in Texas was the Camino Real (King's Highway) stretching from Los Adaes—capital of the eastern sector—to Saltillo, in New Spain, via San Antonio and Guerrero (although later it was extended as far as Natchitoches). This is Highway 21, along which are signs recalling its age and history. San Antonio was soon linked permanently with Santa Fe, and later with Albuquerque. New Mexico was to be linked with California via Arizona by the Gila Trail, which had first been used by Melchor Díaz in 1539 but was not to become fully established until Juan Bautista de Anza, accompanied by Father Francisco Hermenegildo Garcés and Father Juan Díaz, opened the route from Sonora to the Pacific via Yuma in 1774.

Santa Fe became an important center of communications as the Spanish explorations gradually progressed. In 1776, they advanced westward thanks to the efforts of Father Silvestre Vélez de Escalante and Father José Juan Domínguez, who when seeking a way to California via Utah blazed the Crossing of the Fathers; these efforts were to be completed in 1829 by the Mexican, Antonio Armijo (this route, called the Spanish Trail, was much used between 1830 and 1850). The roads to the east were opened up by Pedro Vial, who in 1792 crossed the territories of Missouri, Kansas and Colorado and linked the capital of New Mexico to St. Louis, Missouri. The reports given in his diary marked the precedent for what was to become an important route for civilization and trade in the 19th century, the Santa Fe Trail. St. Louis was linked to New Orleans by a permanent route, partly by river and partly overland, which coincides in Missouri with today's Highway 61 from New Madrid. Signposts marking this old Camino Real, or King's Highway, can still be found in St. Louis, among other places. Similar signposts can be seen along Californian Route 101 from San Diego to San Francisco, opened up by Father Junípero Serra. Reproductions of the mission bells have been placed every 10 miles along the Camino Real, and in Florida, signposts mark every five miles of the De Soto Trail.

The Spanish Dollar

Spanish contributions to the United States also include the dollar, which was instrumental in attaining independence. In the early stages of their history, the economy of the colonies had been based on barter, but the need was soon felt to use a commodity of intrinsic uniform value. The prevailing scarcity of coinage led New England to set up a mint in 1651, followed by Maryland's 10 years later. The scarcity of metals in the colonies and the ban on the importation of metals and British coins decreed by Britain forced the different legislatures to issue "legal tender" or paper money. In 1690, when soldiers returned home from the attack on Canada, they had to be paid in notes, which were used for paying taxes; as a result, these notes were kept in circulation. In 1712, South Carolina organized a public bank and issued $148,000 in credit notes; 20 years later, Maryland ordained that tobacco should be used as legal tender at a penny the pound, and Indian corn at 20 pence the bushel (other provinces resorted to analogous measures).

Spanish currency, the Spanish silver dollar, or peso, helped to remedy this situation. Known in Spanish territories as the *peso*, this Spanish dollar was found in use among the natives when La Salle reached Texas in 1686. The remote origin of the name "dollar" can be traced to a valley in Bohemia, called the Joachimsthal, or Valley of Joachim. In 1486, the feudal lord of the valley went into the lucrative business of minting sterling silver coins of a given weight and size. The Joachimsthaler therefore became a currency in great demand and was soon known as the "thaler." When it reached the Nether-

Centennial coins honoring our Spanish heritage. Carlos M. Fernández-Shaw.

lands the name became "daler," and later, both in Spain and in London, it was quoted as the "dolar." Since Spanish currency had a very high gold content as a result of the abundance of gold mined in Peru and Mexico, it became known as the Spanish dollar.

Sometimes known as a "piece of eight" (*pieza de ocho* or *real de a 8*) because it was equivalent to eight *reales*, it was worth four shillings and six pence in relation to the pound sterling, although the rate of exchange quoted in each province differed: in Georgia and South Carolina, four shillings and eight pence; in Virginia and New England, six shillings; in New York, eight shillings; and in the other colonies, seven shillings and six pence. The piece of eight became the predominant coin in circulation, although other foreign currencies were also used on a smaller scale. The Spanish gold *pistola,* or pistole, was equivalent to four dollars; the doubloon was worth 16 dollars. As a result of this overvaluation of the Spanish dollar, the colonies thought they would retain the coins in their domains, but the result was that they had to be sent to England to pay for goods. In 1740, the British Parliament forbade the use of paper currency issued by the colonies using the Spanish dollar as a standard and years later banned the notes issued by the provincial treasuries as legal tender, thereby giving rise to the discontent that eventually exploded when the laws on taxation were enacted.

At the time of the uprising against Britain, one of the points raised was the organization of an independent monetary system. It was then that the Spanish dollar was taken as standard instead of sterling. In 1775, the Continental Congress declared that the 2 million credit notes whose issue it authorized should be redeemed in Spanish dollars. Thus, in 1775 and 1776, notes were printed in Philadelphia bearing the name United Colonies, while from 1777, they appeared with the name United States of North America. The text in English reads as follows: "Three Dollars. This bill entitles the bearer to receive three Spanish Milled dollars, according to a Resolution of Congress passed at Philadelphia February 17, 1776." They were also issued in the same way in Virginia and Rhode Island.

The choice of the Spanish milled dollar displaced the British monetary units and meant the introduction of a decimal coinage system. Thomas Jefferson proposed the Spanish dollar as the monetary unit, and recommended that the new dollar be defined in terms of silver and gold. Along those guidelines, in 1785 Congress passed a resolution describing the dollar as the monetary unit of the United States and subdividing it according to the decimal system. In order to set a value for the unit chosen, Secretary of the Treasury Alexander Hamilton had a number of Spanish dollars, chosen at random, weighed: Their average weight was 371.25 grams of pure silver, and as a result, that was the figure taken as the basis for the new dollar. This was also a step toward the separation of the American dollar from the Spanish dollar. In the Act Establishing a Mint and Regulating the Coins of the United States of April 2, 1792, references were made indistinctly to the dollar and to the "unit," undoubtedly with the idea of suggesting an alternative denomination for the currency. However, the second term never gained acceptance, and people preferred using the Spanish term.

Foreign currency continued to circulate in the United States, and Spanish dollars in particular were declared legal tender by Congress in 1793 and again in 1806. Only in 1857 did Congress repeal this privilege in favor of the Spanish dollar and other foreign currencies. When it ceased to be the monetary standard of the United States, the term *Spanish* was dropped, but the term *dollar,* which had been used on the first banknotes, was retained.

The dollars mentioned on the Continental Congress notes were coins with milled edges, minted in this way primarily to avoid counterfeiting (another common practice to avoid counterfeits was to cut the familiar Spanish coins in half). The Spanish dollar was also known as the pillar dollar, owing to the Pillars of Hercules shown on it as part of the Spanish coat of arms. The dollar sign by which the United States dollar is commonly known is also of Spanish origin. According to the most authoritative sources, the origin lies in those same Pillars of Hercules (two of which could be seen on the Spanish coat of arms), which have a ribbon spiraling down them on which can be read the words "Plus Ultra" (Further on!). This was the Spanish motto, adopted because by discovering America she had destroyed the ancient legend of the dreaded sea beyond the Straits of Gibraltar, which were known in ancient times as the Pillars of Hercules. According to other sources, the dollar sign stands for the Pillars of Hercules and the figure eight, which encompasses them like a pennant on pieces of eight. In *A History of the Dollar,* Arthur Nussbaum writes that the two parallel lines are one of the many abbreviations of the letter *p* standing for the Spanish peso coin, whereas the *s* indicates the plural. In any case, it is curious to note that this abbreviation has been used for the national currency of Argentina, the Argentine peso.

Spanish subjects can be found on coins, bank notes and postage stamps, and are sometimes exceptionally important features. The first commemorative coin struck in the United States appeared in 1892 on the occasion of the Columbus Exhibition at Chicago. It was the half-dollar, bearing the effigy of Christopher Columbus on one side and the caravel *Santa María* on the other. Almost at the same time, the quarter appeared with the effigy of Queen Isabella of Castile, the only one to bear the likeness of a foreign monarch.

In 1934, the 50-cent coin commemorating the centennial of the state of Texas showed the Spanish mission at El Alamo on the reverse side. The following year, the subject of the Old Spanish Trail received minting honors in a 50-cent coin bearing the name of Alvar Núñez Cabeza de Vaca on the obverse side accompanied by the head of a cow (*cabeza de vaca*), since it had not been possible to find even an approximate portrait of the Spanish *conquistador*. On the reverse side was a yucca tree in flower, on a map of the states of Florida, Alabama, Mississippi, Louisiana and Texas, with the dates 1535–1935. Across the states runs a line marking the route of the Old Trail with points representing St. Augustine, Jacksonville, Tallahasee, Mobile, New Orleans, Galveston, San Antonio and El Paso. It was minted for the purpose of erecting a monument to human endurance.

The first commemorative stamps in the United States were also issued on the occasion of the Columbus Exhibition in Chicago in January 1893. The set consisted of 16 stamps covering various subjects and stages of the Discovery, with Spain featured prominently. Other commemorative stamps issued in the United States have been related to Spanish subjects: the Arkansas Post; the Palace of the Governors at Santa Fe; the old Spanish gate at St. Augustine and the figure of a *conquistador* bearing the banner with castle and lion quarterings (in 1965, to celebrate the fourth centennial of the foundation of St. Augustine a Spanish postage stamp bore the same design printed in red and yellow); San Francisco Bay, discovered by Sergeant Ortega and his exploring party in 1769; the El Capitan Rock in Yosemite Park, California; the Grand Canyon in Arizona; Mesa Verde Park; the likenesses of Núñez de Balboa, Vázquez de Coronado, Bernardo de Gálvez, Ponce de León and Fray Junípero Serra; and a number of other stamps issued to commemorate various anniversaries showing states connected with Spain. One stamp is inscribed "Hispanic-Americans, A Proud Heritage."

Land Grants

While there were Spaniards who settled in the present territory of the United States, there were also Anglo-Saxon settlers from the East who sought permission from the Spanish authorities to live within their dominions. Many immigrants were unable to settle down in their new country for reasons of hardship, disappointments, a love of adventure and the search for wealth in new areas. As a result they preferred to continue their migration. The natural place for them to move to was Spanish territory on the same continent.

For a long time, the Spanish authorities were not inclined to allow foreigners to settle in their territory, largely for religious reasons. However, a time came when the Spanish population proved incapable of colonizing such huge possessions; settlers were needed to defend them from the attacks of foreigners and Indians and to make the land productive by their work. Therefore, Spanish policy changed, and a number of permits were granted, particularly in the territories of Louisiana (before Louisiana passed into the hands of the United States) and later in Texas. New settlers, who invariably had to take an oath of fealty to the king of Spain as future loyal subjects, were mainly ordinary people, but some achieved great importance in the annals of the United States. There can be no doubt whatsoever that they were staunch American patriots, for their record in the Revolution is more than sufficient proof. The fact that they had taken an oath of loyalty to the king of Spain was not extraordinary as they did not see Spain as an enemy to the cause of their country.

One such famous settler is Daniel Boone, the Kentucky pioneer who settled in Spanish territory in Missouri. He obtained a grant of 1,000 arpents of land and became a Spanish civil servant, acting as receiver in the Femme Osage section of St. Charles district between 1800 and 1804. When Moses Austin sought to settle in Texas in the fall of 1820, he promised to give up his United States nationality and become a Spanish subject (as he had been in Upper Louisiana in 1798). His request was granted on January 17, 1821. Earlier, in 1797, he had lived in Spanish Missouri, helped to found the locality of Potosi and improved lead ore smelting processes and built furnaces at Herculaneum. On March 15, 1788, George Rogers Clark wrote to the Spanish ambassador Diego de Gardoqui seeking permission to found a colony in Spanish territory (though his petition was refused). Andrew Jackson was attorney general in the district of Miró (named after the Spanish governor of Louisiana) in the region of Cumberland (Tennessee). When he reached Kentucky in July 1788, he took part in the so-called Spanish Conspiracy, which sought the independence of Cumberland from United States rule and its inclusion within the Spanish sphere of influence. In 1789 Jackson swore his allegiance to King Carlos IV.

In view of the imminence of a war with Britain, the governor of Louisiana, Baron de Carondelet, adopted a policy of encouraging foreigners to settle in the territories under his authority. Some 2,000 families took advantage of that decision. In 1795, he authorized the lieutenant governor at St. Louis, Zenón Trudeau, to proceed in this respect, and the following year, the latter reported: "American families are arriving here every day." In June 1795, Philippe Enrique Neri, Baron de Bastrop, was authorized to settle 500 families at Bayou de Lair, on the present boundary between Arkansas and Louisiana (a group of French families had already settled in the neighborhood of Lauratown in 1766) and on June 20, 1797, the marquis de la Maison Rouge obtained permission to bring 30 families to settle in the present county of Camden, Arkansas.

The granting of residence permits often likewise entailed grants of land. The latter were sometimes made for reasons of military strategy or political convenience; sometimes they were a mark of gratitude on the part of the Crown to those who had served loyally in war or peace; some were simply due to the need to repopulate an area, for which attractive conditions had to be offered. In the latter two cases, namely gratitude and repopulation, they were called *composiciones* in Spanish, literally meaning "settlements" or "agreements"; or, sometimes, they took the form of bills of sale. There were even cases where land was granted by royal grace and favor. Such gifts of land were common practice throughout Spanish colonial history, and in territories that had not formerly belonged to Spain, such as Louisiana, it was Spain that introduced this practice, an example subsequently followed by Mexico and the United States. No grant was made by sale in Upper Louisiana.

The grants at Vigil and St. Vrain, Sangre de Cristo, etc., in Colorado also date from that period. The origin of the town of Dubuque (Iowa) lies in a grant made in November 1796 to Julien Dubuque, who called the township Les Mines d'Espagne. Several other grants were made in Upper Louisiana, such as one to Jorge Morgan, who founded New Madrid with a group of pioneers from Pennsylvania.

Soldiers and civilians accompanying Friar Junípero Serra in the colonization of California likewise received rustic properties that soon became known as *ranchos*, such as Rancho de Nuestra Señora de Refugio, owned by José Francisco Ortega; Rancho San Antonio owned by Antonio María Lugo; Rancho San Pedro belonging to José Juan Domínguez; Rancho Santiago de Santa Ana owned by Juan Pablo Grijalva; and Rancho de las Pulgas, belonging to the Argüello family. Inland from San Diego, there are areas that, due to their aridness and inhospitable conditions, have not changed since they were granted in Spanish times. During the Spanish period, 40 real estate title deeds were granted in California; 800 were granted under Mexican rule. At Mobile (Alabama) some real estate is still based on grants made by the Spanish governors.

When sovereignty over the territories changed, the new authorities undertook to respect the royal grace and favor grants. According to the reports of the American commissioner, Spain had distributed 1,463,333 acres, only half of which had been confirmed by the governor at New Orleans, but either because the title deeds did not appear to be sufficiently clear or because the new occupants simply seized what belonged to the previous occupiers, a number of lawsuits ensued, many of which have not yet been concluded. So it is that United States courts are still obliged to study those grants and the whole legal system on which they were based.

Consequently, a substantial number of United States real estate owners find their proprietorship rooted in Spanish legal provisions. According to the historian Hubert Bancroft, 205 grants still existed in New Mexico in 1886. Many suits are still pending in New Mexico, lodged by Hispanics who claim that their rights have been infringed by Anglos; a group called Alianza Federal de Mercedes (Federal Alliance of Graces and Favors) was formed to defend them at Albuquerque. Reyes Lopez Tijerina and other promoters of the alliance grew impatient when they found that their petitions were not receiving attention, and in 1967 proclaimed the Republic of San Joaquín del Río de Chama and sent delegates to Sante Fe and Washington, D.C. The conquest of Tierra Amarilla and the freeing of 12 colleagues from jail only lasted two hours. The ringleaders were captured. In December 1964, the court at Albuquerque heard the case of the Atrisco Grant, involving an area of 50,000 acres and 17,000 heirs. Well-known lawsuits concerning grants include the Peralta Reavis case in Arizona and the Maxwell Grant case in New Mexico, both dating from the time of Mexican governor Armijo. Generally speaking, most of those validly made under Spanish law can be said to have been accepted by the courts of the Union, even in the present century.

Spanish Law

Lawsuits concerning ownership of land distributed by the king of Spain or his representatives are not the only reason for the continued presence of Spanish law in U.S. courts.

In 1806, the territorial legislature of Louisiana passed a Code of Civil Law based on Spanish medieval and colonial law. In addition, a mercantile law was enacted deriving from a Spanish mercantile code. Jurist H. P. Dart states that it is easy to find in the Digest of 1808 and the Civil Code of 1825 the principles contained in the famous *Quinta Partida*, or Fifth Book of Laws, of King Alphonso X. He points out the influence of Spanish sources on the Procedural Code of 1825. Curiously enough, however, the promoters of this legislation were citizens of French origin; this confirms the great influence left by Spain in the territory purchased by Thomas Jefferson, for its inhabitants might well have sought inspiration in Napoleonic Codes, recently promulgated and made known in New Orleans. But, in the name of the democratic principles introduced by the new nation, the people of Louisiana proclaimed their cultural autonomy and political self-determination by including the right to choose their own language and legal system. In this they were guided by their theoretician Edward Livingston (whose name was certainly neither Spanish nor French). For that reason, in addition to Spanish law, they tried to give the Spanish language official status. According to the act of that legislature, apart from Roman law, the Spanish legislation involved included none other than the *Recopilaciones de Castilla* (compilations of Castile) and *Autos Acordados* (judicial decrees), the *Siete Partidas*, the *Leyes de Toro* (Toro Laws), the *Recopilación de Indias* (Compilations of the Indies), the *Ordenanza Comercial de Bilbao* (Commercial Ordinance of Bilbao), and the Royal Orders and Decrees formerly applied in Louisiana.

When General Stephen Watts Kearny took the city of Santa Fe in 1846, New Mexico passed into the hands of the United States. On August 18 of that year, acting as governor, he commissioned Colonel Doniphan and lawyer Willard P. Hall to compile the Organic Laws and Constitution of the country by studying the old laws and the way in which they could be made compatible with the institutions and laws of the United States. This work was drafted in English and Donaciano Vigil translated it into Spanish; in this way the Kearny Code became the territorial law in New Mexico and a *modus vivendi* between two civilizations. The result was faultless and, thanks to the new law, New Mexicans were permitted to apply those Spanish or Mexican laws not contrary to the principles of the United States Constitution. The best of Spain and Mexico was thus included in New Mexican law, and this legal code is still in force today. Any laws enacted since then, although drafted in English, have always been translated into Spanish. In the law courts and Congress of the state of Colorado, Spanish or English could be used until 1921.

Another area in which Spanish law is still in force, not only in New Mexico, as Oliver La Farge recalls, but in Arizona, Texas and Colorado, is water and mining rights. On these subjects British common law did not provide regulations capable of ousting the old Spanish ordinances. In the discussions held at El Escorial in 1978, Professor Donald Cutter recalled that the 1873 Code of Benefits of Mines of the United States, originated by the California gold rushes, is based on Spanish mining methods, and that the treatment of Indians as citizens was based on the Spanish Laws of the Indies.

Spanish law is likewise still applied in another very important area, the economic regulation of family partnership. Matrimonial financial relations governed by the Spanish system of *gananciales* involved common property held by husband and wife or acquired or increased during marriage by onerous title. In the case of many citizens of Texas, this system at one time proved so advantageous that it constituted a tax privilege with respect of U.S. citizens governed by other family systems. A general tax reduction to the Texan level was successfully advocated in the federal Congress.

Texas inherited other laws of Spain as well. Following its independence from Spain, the state maintained Spanish civil law under the Constitution of 1836, passed once national life had got under way. The constitution declared that all previous laws not incompatible with the constitution should remain in force until they were declared void, rejected, amended or lapsed owing to their own statute of limitations. However, on January 20, 1840, British Common Law was considered as decisive insofar as it was not contrary to the constitution or the acts of Congress of the Texan Republic, and all previous laws in force were excluded unless expressly accepted.

When joining the Union, a constitution along the lines of those of other states with a British tradition was superimposed on the traditional Spanish backdrop. Nonetheless, some components of Spanish law have endured due to the fact that English common law was construed as meaning the common law of the states that gained their independence from Britain (which was different from English common law as such, owing to the long time during which the respective bodies of law had led separate lives). It was also only applicable where no statutes existed on the subject, or the statutory provisions were silent as on some aspects of marriage law, property rights, adoption laws, river rights, domicile and other subjects.

Texas jurisprudence particularly contains references to those cases where courts should accept Spanish law in relevant cases, as a body of law which was once enforced in the territory; it likewise states that Spanish law is applicable to obligations incurred during Spanish times, arguing that it is the law when and where the contract was executed that applies. (The works of Professor Joseph W. McKnight on the law in the Anglo-Hispanic frontier and the effect of the Hispanic legal doctrine in the Republic of Texas are worth reading. He emphasizes the incorporation of the principles of traditional Spanish law to the new American legal system.)

PART II:
THE ATLANTIC COAST STATES

◆   *NEW ENGLAND*   ◆

Let us begin with the states along the northern Atlantic seaboard, since they led the way in the historical development of Anglo-Saxon civilization in the United States.

In the far north lies New England, full of names reminiscent of Europe, names that add the adjective *new* to the region of origin of the founders. The name New England is preserved with affection; a household word, even though it is not an official administrative entity as such. Before the immigrants from England arrived however, Diego de Ribeiro drew a map of the eastern coast in 1529 from the information given to him by the navigator Esteban Gómez, who had explored the area, and named it Tierras de Gómez.

Vermont and New Hampshire

These two states have the least Spanish connections in the Union. A prominent feature of Vermont is Lake Champlain, the impressive scene of many battles in the course of the struggles in the colonial period between Britain and France, and between Britain and the United States. It stretches along the boundary between Vermont and New York. The Spanish summer courses run by Middlebury College are particu-

larly famous and have been attended by many of the best students and teachers now teaching Spanish in the United States.

Wolfeboro, New Hampshire is the home of the Brewster Academy, a well-known, old educational institution. Surprisingly in such an unlikely place, the Brewster Academy Spanish Club has awakened great interest in Spain and Hispanic affairs. It was in Putney that the philanthropic Experiment on International Living was founded, and is still run, organizing exchanges of high school students, allowing Spanish and American students the opportunity of living with foreign families during a school year while attending classes at the level corresponding to their knowledge.

Maine

In 1525, long before the name *Maine* was given to the ship whose sinking led the United States to declare war against Spain in 1898, Esteban Gómez, pilot to the Emperor Charles V (King Charles I of Spain), visited the coast of Maine and left records of his voyage. A local historian has described his visit as memorable and more thorough than those of any of his European predecessors, including the Vikings.

In order to identify places with a view to subsequent expeditions, Gómez named a number of major features. Some of those names still survive: Campo Bello, an attractive island on which he landed; Bahía del Casco, or Casco Bay, so named because it is shaped like a helmet (*casco* in Spanish); Bahí del Saco, or Saco Bay, a sacklike bay; Bahía Profunda, now the Bay of Fundy, with dark waters and high waves breaking against the rocks. He sailed up a river that he mistakenly took to be a strait and called it Estrecho de los Gamos, now Penobscot Bay. Cape Elizabeth was to appear on the map drawn up by Gutiérrez in 1562 as Cabo de las Muchas Islas, or Cape of Many Islands.

Massachusetts

Esteban Gómez also reached Cape Cod in 1525, long before the Pilgrims arrived, and called it Cabo de Santa Maróa, as it is shown on the map made by Diego Gutiérrez in 1562.

Part of the Spanish aid sent during the Revolution reached the rebels through the port of Boston. There is a letter from Benjamin Franklin thanking the count of Aranda for the 12,000 rifles and other assistance provided at the command of King Charles of Spain.

Boston is unquestionably the capital not only of Massachusetts but of all New England. Since its foundation in 1630 it has maintained a leadership that has been spread to the whole nation. The area as a whole, and Boston in particular, can claim to be the home of the oldest society life in the United States; in 1898, that society fled inland with its belongings to take refuge at Worcester for fear of a Spanish invasion, as Theodore Roosevelt recounted afterward. The well-known saying that "the Lowells only speak to the Cabots and the Cabots only speak to God" evoked from Juan Ramón Jiménez, the Spanish poet and Nobel prize winner, the remark: "How boring for the Lowells. . . and for God."

From an architectural standpoint, impressive buildings in Boston include the Beacon Hill area and Marlborough, Commonwealth and Newberry Streets, described by the author of *Platero and I,* Juan Ramón Jiménez, as three parallel scissors of chocolate houses, which day lengthens and night shrinks. Among the fine buildings and noteworthy historic sites are the Capitol; the Fanueil Hall, the original scene of the Revolution and present home of the Ancient and Honorable Artillery Company; Trinity Church, which shows the influence of the old Cathedral at Salamanca; and Boston Public Library, whose dome was built by Spanish archi-

Archer M. Huntington, Hispanist, poet and president of the Hispanic Society of America. Library of Congress.

tect Guastavino. John Singer Sargent, who painted its mural, *Dogma of the Redemption,* traveled to Spain to absorb some of the spirit of medieval Christendom.

Another noteworthy work by Sargent connected with Spain can be seen in the collection of Mrs. Isabella Stewart Gardner, housed in the building known as Fenway Court: this is his popular painting *El Jaleo,* displayed in a setting consisting of a Spanish cloister with Moorish arches. Other Spanish works of art in the collection include *Santa Engracia* by Bartolomé Bermejo and *Doctor of Law* by Francisco de Zurbarán.

There is also a good selection of Spanish works in the Museum of Fine Arts, which houses such paintings as *Fray Félix Hortensio Paravicino* and *St. Dominic Kneeling in Prayer* both by El Greco; the portraits of *Infanta Maróa Teresa* and poet *Luis de Góngora y Argote* by Diego de Velázquez; *Don Baltasar Carlos and his Dwarf,* also by Velázquez; and *St. Cyril and St. Thomas,* by Zurbarán. In addition the museum houses the 13th-century Romanesque apse from the Church of Santa María del Mar, in Catalonia, and the romantic portico of the Church of San Miguel from Uncastillo, in the Spanish province of Zaragoza.

It was also in Boston that Madrilenian poet Pedro Salinas spent the last days of his life in 1951.

At the nearby locality of Lincoln, the De Cordova Museum can be visited. It is housed in the Norman-style castle left to the city in his will by Julian de Cordova (1851–1954), owner of the Union Glass Co. of Somerville, Massachusetts, who used to style himself count of Cabra and marquis of Almodóvar, as a descendant of the Gran Capitán, or Great Captain, the Spaniard Gonzalo Fernández de Córdoba. The museum carries on active work in the artistic field and maintains a fine arts school attended by 500 students, special exhibition programs, seminars and lectures on artistic subjects, film shows, and dance and poetry recitals.

Boston was the American home of the philosopher George Santayana. Born in Madrid, he lived in Boston from the age of nine onward, and studied and taught philosophy at Harvard University until he decided to end his university career in 1912 and devote himself entirely to intellectual pursuits in Europe, where he made Rome his home city. While he wrote all his works in English, Santayana never abandoned his original nationality and left an indelible Hispanic hallmark on his writings.

Discussion of Santayana leads us to Harvard University, in the suburb of Cambridge on the opposite bank of the Charles River, without which no perspective of this region would be complete. The interest at Harvard in Spanish subjects goes back at least as far as 1750, when ships plied to and from Barcelona, Cádiz, Málaga, the Caribbean ports and South America. Professor Stanley T. Williams has studied Spanish influence in the United States and early Spanish-American contacts through sailors and merchants during the wars waged by Britain against Spain when Massachusetts was a colony, or by European settlers who possibly absorbed Spanish culture before crossing the Atlantic. The aesthetic limitations of the New England Puritans were to prevent initial influence from the Continent, in contrast to that in Dutch New York, German Pennsylvania or Swedish Delaware. The presence of Spain throughout most of the North American continent at that time must inevitably have been a decisive factor. In 1650, there are known to have been colonists in New England who spoke Spanish, and Spanish dictionaries from that time have been found in libraries. Cotton Mather could write Spanish correctly, and Samuel Sewall used to send to London for Spanish books. Mather was the author of the first book written in Spanish in the northern colonies. By learning Spanish both men intended to extend Protestantism throughout the continent.

There were Spanish teachers in New England in the 17th century, although not so many as in the 18th century, when they began to advertise in the newspapers. The name of Miguel de Cervantes was, by that time, included in the catalogs of several libraries, and, for instance, George Alcock, a student of medicine at Harvard who died in 1676, had an English version of *Don Quixote* and another of the *Labors of Persiles and Sigismunda.* It is also curious to note the existence in Boston in 1683 of a translation of *Sueños de Quevedo (The Visions of Quevedo)*, while the library of Harvard College boasted another of *La Celestina.* In the 18th century, *Don Quixote* won a resounding victory in America, and the Smollet version in four volumes could be found at any bookseller's. (In 1986, it was re-edited with a prologue by Carlos Fuentes.) The works of Garcilaso de la Vega, Fernando Herrera, Juan de Mariana, Antonio de Solís, José de Acosta, Jerónimo de Zurita or Pedro Mártir de Angleria were available. The London translation of the *History of the Conquest of New Spain* by Bernal Díaz del Castillo was reprinted at Salem in 1803.

The 19th century was the golden age of Spanish scholarship in New England. When he died in 1815, Abiel Smith, who had graduated from Harvard in 1764, left a legacy of $20,000 at 3% interest for the purpose of founding the chair that bears his name for a professor of French or Spanish at Harvard. The creation of this chair (behind which can perhaps be seen his passion for Spanish theater and novels) was instrumental in introducing Spanish in the syllabus at Harvard.

By 1817 the duties of the holder of the new chair had been defined, and in 1819 George Ticknor received the appointment. His duties consisted of giving lectures on Spanish and French literature. To prepare them he had to carry out thorough research and obtain suitable books. In consequence, he wrote his famous *History of Spanish Literature*, published in 1849, a masterpiece that is unrivaled even in Spain. The result of those acquisitions was the gathering of an enormous Spanish bibliographical collection that is still kept intact by Harvard University. In 1876, Ticknor was also the author of a remarkable account of his travels in Europe, in which he devoted 80 pages to Spain, possibly the best written by an American traveler in the 19th century.

In 1836, Henry Wadsworth Longfellow succeeded Ticknor in the Smith chair. He, too, lectured on literature and wrote about the Spanish language in his "Castles in Spain." Longfellow was attracted to the Golden Century in the works of Lope de Vega, Cervantes, and Pedro Calderón de la Barca, and his knowledge of Spanish literature was complete, as was his command of spoken and written Spanish. He published a number of poetic descriptions of Spain in his book *Outre-Mer,* as well as impeccable translations of the *coplas,* or stanzas, of Jorge Manrique.

In 1855, James Russell Lowell took charge of the chair, which he held until 1891. He devoted himself fully to teaching Spanish and made his advanced studies on Cervantes available to his students. From 1877 to 1880, he was the United States minister in Madrid, and his beautiful little book *Impressions of Spain,* based on his correspondence, dates from that period; in it he relates, among other things, the visit of General Ulysses Grant to the Spanish court. Since he was also the author of *The Biglow Papers,* in which the presence of the hero invented by Cervantes can be seen, the Spaniards took to calling the popular American diplomat "José Biglow."

J. D. M. Ford was the fourth holder of the Smith chair and was the first in the 20th century. The holding of the chair at Harvard by Ticknor, Longfellow and Lowell in succession had a tremendous impact, and a large number of Spanish scholars trained under their guidance were to become the basis for the great revival of Spanish studies in the United States today. Among their pupils was Henry David Thoreau, who in his later years, learned Spanish at Harvard.

Francis Sales, who was a native of Perpignan and resided in Spain for a long time, became a professor at Harvard in 1817 and spent 35 years teaching Spanish to the university students. In addition, he wrote and edited several didactic texts: *Colmena Española,* a selection of drama master works, an edition of Josse's *Grammar of the Spanish Language* and others.

Journalist and poet William C. Bryant, from Massachusetts, was a diplomat and lived in Madrid; he later wrote *Letters from Spain and Other Countries.*

Between 1830 and 1850, a major group of historians flourished in New England. Prescott, Motley, Merriman and Bancroft, who were interested in Spain. Spain was a real hobby for William Prescott, who was a friend of Professor Ticknor. The first edition of his *History of the Reign of Ferdinand and Isabella* (a typical Christmas gift in Boston in 1837) was sold out in five months, and on the day his *History of the Conquest of Peru* was published, 7,500 copies were sold. He spent six years preparing his important *History of the Conquest of Mexico* (1843) and left his *History of the Reign of Phillip II* unfinished when he died.

John Lothrop Motley was more partisan in his approach to Spanish history, and Phillip II is not seen in a favorable light in his work of that name any more than the Spaniards are in his *This Rise of the Dutch Republic* (1856). Roger B. Merriman, author of the four-volume study *The Rise of the Spanish Empire,* spent 43 years teaching in the Department of History at Harvard. Thanks to this work, Merriman occupies a leading position among Hispanist historians. Add to this brief list of New England historians Katherine Lee Bates, a professor at Wellesley College, who wrote her first book at the turn of the century, *Spanish Highways and Byways,* a witty, anecdotal and analytic work, followed by a dozen other books and articles on Spanish subjects. (Hubert Howe Bancroft's work will be discussed in the chapter on California.)

Admiral Samuel Eliot Morison, the leading U.S. specialist on Columbus, published the important study *Admiral of the Ocean Sea.* To write it, Morison sailed from New England to Palos on the brig *Capitana* (in 1939–1940) and returned on her from Gomera using Columbus's log book in order to follow the route taken by the discoverer on his third voyage. (Morison's book is still available, in a paperback edition.)

At the end of 1891, the Instituto Cultural Español organized a commemoration of Enrique Granados, the Spanish composer who died in the sinking of the *Sussex,* in 1916; soprano María Coronada took part in the event. José María Sert and Rafael Moneo have been deans of the Harvard Faculty of Architecture.

In 1899, Spanish Nobel Prize winner Santiago Ramón y Cajal was invited to give three lectures at Clark University in Worcester. He recounted his impressions of his trip in his memor *Recuerdos de mi vida.* In 1984, King Juan Carlos I received an honorary doctorate from Harvard. The John Kennedy Library of Harvard was visited by the monarch of Spain in 1997.

Rhode Island

Esteben Gómez, pilot to Charles V, visited Narragansett Bay in 1525, which resulted in its inclusion in Gutiérrez's map of 1562. The capital, Providence, was founded in 1636 by Roger Williams, and the surroundings inspired Spanish writer Miguel Delibes to write his novel *La sombra del ciprés es alargada* (The Long Shadow of the Cypress).

The second most important city in Rhode Island, with its major textile industry, is Newport, which still has vestiges of the splendor it enjoyed at the turn of the century and fabulous residences, which impress local people and visitors alike. Newport also has the Touro Synagogue, which celebrated its second centenary in 1963, making it the oldest synagogue in the United States. This synagogue is of particular significance for Spaniards because it was built by a group of Sephardim. They probably reached Rhode Island around 1658 but were unable to pay the cost for a building for worship at the time. However, they did manage to buy some land for the cemetery in 1677.

When Newport became an important trade center at the beginning of the 18th century, more Jews arrived, and it clearly became necessary to build a synagogue. The foundation stone was laid in 1759, and it took four years to complete the building. The head of the community was Rabbi Isaac Touro, while a prominent member of the local Sephardim was merchant Aaron Lopez, known as the "Merchant Prince of New England" because his ships and agents were well known on both sides of the Atlantic. It was in this synagogue that President George Washington made his famous declaration on religious freedom in the course of his visit to Newport in 1790.

Connecticut

In 1525, Esteban Gómez arrived with his caravel at the mouth of the Connecticut River, which he called Río de la Buena Madre (River of the Good Mother). It was at Derby (Connecticut) that the U.S. ambassador in Madrid, David Humphreys, imported the first Spanish merino sheep, which were to become so famous and so important for the later development of Australia.

New Haven is, of course, famous for Yale University. The interest of Yale University in teaching Spanish dates back to the 1826–1827 academic year, when Spanish was made an optional subject for students in their junior year. Charles Roux headed the program, and two years later, these responsibilities were taken on by José Antonio Pizarro. The teaching of Spanish was given new impetus from 1879 onward, thanks to Professor William Ireland Knapp, who had studied in Spain. He wrote a *Grammar of the Modern Spanish Language (Gramática del Idioma Español Moderno)* for his students and published the works of Juan Boscán and Diego Hurtado de Mendoza for their benefit. The Department of History has also produced some leading Hispanic scholars, including Edward Gaylord Bourne, the author of the magnificent *Spain in America*, published in 1904 and reprinted in recent years. In 1869 *The Romance of Spanish History (El Romance de la Historia Espaáola)* by a Congregationalist pastor, John S. C. Abbot was published in New Haven. It is a skillfully knitted series of "well-authenticated" incidents, "from the many centuries which have passed away" and "which prove most interesting and instructive to American readers." Today, the Department of Spanish at Yale is one of the best in the United States. The Beinecke Library has some magnificent Spanish incunabula and manuscripts. Yale's professor Manuel Durán was a president of the North American Catalan Society.

Spanish Place-Names

In New England can be found the following localities bearing Spanish names: Carmel, Columbia Falls, East Peru, Madrid, Mexico, Saco and West Peru, all in Maine; and Ayer in Massachusetts.

NEW YORK

At Niagara Falls, one of the thrills for visitors is to cross from one bank to the other in a suspended cable car. In fact, this car was invented by a Spanish engineer, Leonardo Torres Quevedo (who also invented a system of remote control and the Astra-Torres dirigible). In nearby Buffalo is a campus of State University of New York, which hosted Spanish writer Guillermo Díaz Plaja during the 1964–1965 academic year. To the south in Syracuse University, where in June 1964 Spanish author Camilo José Cela was awarded an honorary degree; he received the Nobel Prize in 1989. Not far away, in Hamilton, is Colgate University, with an Institute of Spanish Studies that publishes the review *Symposium*. Close by is Lake George where in July 1758 French general Montcalm defeated Abercromby at the Battle of Ticonderoga; a number of cannons housed at the museum at Fort Ticonderoga bear the Spanish coat of arms. The writer Washington Irving, keenly interested in Spanish culture, is buried at Tarrytown.

New York City

So we come to New York City. The sight of the Statue of Liberty and the view of the downtown skyscrapers make an unforgettable impression and are both a suitable premonition and a splendid symbol of what is to be found on the mainland. Fine essays on New York City have been published in all languages. Anybody wishing to learn the opinion of some Spaniards on the city should read *La Ciudad Automática* by Julio Camba; *El País del Futuro* by Ramón Pérez de Ayala; Joaquín Belda in *En el país del bluff, veinte días en Nueva York; Diario de un Poeta Recién Casado* by Juan Ramón Jiménez; *Poeta en Nueva York* by Federico García Lorca; and more recently, *Los Estados Unidos en Escorzo* by Julián Marías; *U.S.A., el Paraíso del Proletariado* by Rodrigo Royo; *Irbe de casa* by Carmen Martín Gaite; and *Cuadernos de Nueva York* by José Hierro, to mention but a few.

"Had Columbus not changed his course, New York would now be Spanish," writes the Spanish playwright Fernando Arrabal. In fact, the Hispanic community was chiefly formed by small groups who arrived before the 1924 immigration laws or after 1939. With the relatively recent influx of Puerto Ricans, and the even more recent arrival of Cubans and people of other Hispanic nationalities, the overall Spanish and Hispanic population has grown enormously, and many contributions are being made by the Spanish-speaking people. In fact, they are here in such large numbers (over 1 million Puerto Ricans) that people speaking in Spanish can be found constantly in the streets and in many public places. It was estimated in 1989 that in New York City, one out of five inhabitants over the age of 16 was Hispanic. In Suffolk County, the Hispanic population reached 100,000. This is made all the more noticeable by the number of Spanish radio stations and television channels; Spanish language newspapers with a considerable circulation, such as *La Prensa–El Diario de Nueva York,* and, in their day, *El Tiempo, El Mirador de Nueva York* (which later became *El Mirador del Tiempo), El ABC de las Américas,* and the review *Temas;* dozens of cinemas showing Hispanic films; frequent performances of plays in Spanish; large numbers of clubs or associations of all kinds like Casa de España, Círculo Isabel la Católica, and Club Taurino; and restaurants specializing in food from Spain, Portugal, the Caribbean and Latin American countries. The Spanish bookstore of Eliseo Torres and his successors is a landmark in the city.

It is quite possible to live in New York City for months and even years speaking Spanish only and without the need to use English. There are districts, around 14th Street, up Broadway and in East Harlem, where the shop signs are written in Spanish and give the pedestrian the impression of being south of the Rio Grande or abroad. In several parts of the city, including parts of the Bronx, Brooklyn and Queens, traffic signs have been installed in Spanish. It is not unusual to come across signs saying "Cruce en las esquinas" or "Obedezca las luces del tráfico." Advertisements and directions appear in Spanish on the subways, and even the telephone directory has a Spanish Yellow Pages. Under the laws of the state of New York, Spanish-speaking United States citizens can vote and can take the oath on the Constitution in Spanish. At present, the Hispanic population of the city of Brooklyn has reached 16% to 18%.

Adapting to this metropolis has not always been easy for Spanish speakers. They face discrimination in educational opportunities and at work and unjust assertions of juvenile delinquency. However, better prospects are in store for them, if only because of the influence of the Hispanic vote at election time. The Asociación de Voluntarios Bilingües (Association of Bilingual Volunteers) was founded recently to provide free education for the needy. An outstanding personality from New York at the end of the 19th century was José Francisco Navarro, builder of the New York Metropolitan Elevated Railway, founder of Ingersoll-Rand and cofounder with Thomas Alva Edison of the Edison Electric Light Company.

Another branch of the Spanish colony, although there are many years of time between them and recent immigrants, are the Sephardim, descendants of the Jews expelled from Spain in 1492, of whom there are about 40,000 in New York City. They were the first Jews to arrive when New York was still New Amsterdam, for they took advantage of the permission granted them by Holland to settle in her territory. During this period, in 1654, the first synagogue, which still exists today, was founded. They opened typical Mediterranean cafés in East Manhattan, where they spent their leisure time. In recent years, the Sephardim have spread to the Bronx, Brooklyn and other districts. They have preserved their original language, Ladino, and use synagogues specially for Spanish-speaking Jews. Their main synagogue is located at 8 West 70th Street. The Bronx Sephardi Center has a synagogue and religious school, and a Sephardi home for old people is planned. In St. James' Place, near Chinatown, there is still a triangle of the cemetery of the Spanish and Portuguese synagogue, which occupied what is now Chatham Square and dates back to 1656. This makes it the second oldest cemetery in the city and the oldest Jewish cemetery in the country. A commemorative plaque has been placed at the entrance. It was of this cemetery that García Lorca wrote:

La hierba celeste y sola de la que huye con miedo el rocío y las blancas entradas de mármol que conducen al aire duro, mostraban su silencio roto por las huellas dormidas de los zapatos . . .

A second Hispano-Portuguese cemetery, which opened in 1805 and closed in 1829, is at West 11th Street, near the southwest corner of the Avenue of the Americas.

Finally, there is a Jewish University in New York, the Yeshiva, that bestowed on King Juan Carlos an honorary doctorate in 1997.

The Spanish association Club de la Hispanidad was founded to recognize the Spanish role in the discovery of America, and other groups have followed suit. In 1964, Mayor Wagner proclaimed Spain Week, which has taken place annually, usually including a ceremony in honor of Columbus, a parade down Fifth Avenue, a Mass, a gala dinner and other events. On one such occasion, in 1970, the former Instituto de Cultura Hispánica (Institute of Hispanic Culture) of Madrid, exhibited Spanish documents of great geographical, historical and cartographical value, mostly concerning the explorations of Ponce de León, Vózquez de Ayllón, Esteban Gómez, Hernando de Soto and other *conquistadores* in North America. In 1971, the festivities were attended by the late duke of Veragua, the direct descendant of Columbus. In 1986, Governor Mario Cuomo and Mayor Ed Koch declared Hispanic Community Week from September 14–20, and in 1987, Mayor Koch announced that New York would be the official city for the Fifth Centennial of the Discovery of America. In 1992, Prince Felipe de Borbón presided over the largest sailing ship parade in the bay of New York, which celebrated the fifth centennial of Columbus's arrival in America.

Historically, similar activities have greeted the occasion of the discovery. On April 18, 1893, Her Royal Highness Infanta Doña Eulalia and her husband arrived aboard the steamship *Reina Cristina* as delegates of the regent queen of Spain. They were received by a representative of President Grover Cleveland and by the consul general of Spain, Arturo Baldasano. The dignitaries were greeted by a port jammed with steamships, whose occupants, like the Spanish colony waiting at the quayside, cheered the royal visitors as they arrived. The duke of Veragua was also present.

On April 24, the reproductions of the caravels of the Discovery arrived, with other ships of the Spanish fleet, to take part in the big naval review at which President Cleveland presided on April 27, 1893. After a very bad voyage owing to storms in which the caravels almost sank, the Spanish fleet anchored initially at Delaware Bay and later at Hampton. The warships were the *Infanta Isabel* towing the caravel *Pinta*; the *Nueva Espana* towing the *Niña;* and the *Reina Regente,* with the *Santa María* in tow. The American warships *Philadelphia, Newark, Atlanta, San Francisco, Bancroft, Bennington, Baltimore, Chicago, Yorktown* and *Concord* took part in the naval review, together with Argentinian, Dutch, German, British, Russian, French, Italian and Brazilian ships. Ironically, a few years later, some of these American warships would fight against Spain, and the Spanish ship *Reina Regente* would be captured by the American fleet.

In Lower Manhattan, the oldest part of the city, where the first group of skyscrapers were built, set among other proud buildings such as the City Hall, the New York Stock Exchange and the headquarters of major banks and financial corporations, there stands a parish church that was built primarily with Spanish help, the Church of Saint Peter, the first Catholic church in New York State.

In his residence on Broadway, Spain's first minister plenipotentiary to the United States, Diego de Gardoqui, had a chapel in which Mass was celebrated and attended by Catholics who had no other place of worship. As their numbers increased, Gardoqui opened a collection to which he was the first subscriber, and the proceeds made it possible to buy a piece of land on Barclay Street, close to Broadway and City Hall. Gardoqui presided at the laying of the foundation stone on October 5, 1785, and deposited beside it a metal container with several gold coins sent by King Charles III as a symbol of Spanish financial assistance for this project. Gardoqui obtained a further $1,000 from the count of Floridablanca, then prime minister, and obtained permission for an Irish priest, Father O'Brien, to travel to Cuba and Mexico to collect funds, where he obtained $6,000 and an oil painting of *The Crucifixion* by José María Vallejo, from Mexico, which is still hung above the High Altar. Thanks to these efforts, the Church of Saint Peter was opened in the presence of the Spanish representative with a solemn High Mass, on November 4, 1786, the feast of the patron saint of King Charles III of Spain. At the ensuing banquet, George Washington sat on Gardoqui's right. As a mark of gratitude to Gardoqui, the church trustees decided to reserve "forever, a bench situated in a preferential position for the use of the representatives of His Catholic Majesty the King of Spain." In 1956, General Francisco Franco presented the church with a valuable chalice, thereby continuing the sponsorship started by the Bourbon monarchs. In 1965, Hispanidad Day was marked by the holding of a religious ceremony for the first time at the Church of Saint Peter.

Spaniards also played a decisive role in founding an orphanage for 160 children in the care of the Sisters of Charity. A famous Spanish artist, María Felicidad García, known as La Malibran, sang in the cathedral to raise funds for this project, and her example so moved Catholics to contribute that building began in 1826. Another Catholic church, the Cathedral-Basilica of St. James (the patron saint of Spain), established some years ago the Compostela Award, to honor men and women "whose lives represent the noblest ideals of the Cathedral tradition of fidelity to justice, truth, beauty and peace."

Universities and Other Institutions

The large-scale presence of people of Hispanic origin was not necessary for New York to take an interest in Spanish as a language. As early as 1735, teachers of Spanish advertised in the *New York Gazette*. On October 26, 1747, Augustus Vaughan opened "a school on New Street near the corner of Beaver Street, where English, Latin, Spanish and Italian are correctly and expeditiously taught." There is also evidence to show that, during the 17th century, copies of the works of Baltasar Gracián, *Diana* by Jorge de Montemayor, and *Guzmán de Alfarache* by Mateo Alemán were to be found in New York, and the New York Society Library had volumes such as *La Celestina* or *La Historáa de Méjico* by Francisco Clavijero. By the end of the century the bibliography on Spain and Spanish America had become considerable. In 1815, the *North American Review* began publication and became a vital artery for knowledge of the Hispanic peoples, thanks to the excellent writers who contributed, particularly after Jared Sparks became editor in 1824.

The facilities for studying Spanish in New York today are undoubtedly excellent. Leaders in this trend are the important universities such as New York, Columbia, Fordham (Jesuits), Yeshiva and the College of the City of New York. New York University and Columbia University have dozens of teachers in their Spanish departments, for both post-graduate and graduate courses, including those organized by the well-known Barnard College for women at Columbia, where teachers and students put on performances of plays and have also organized functions to honor Spanish authors, such as the celebration of the centenary of Lope de Vega. Mariano Velázquez de la Cadena, author of the best Spanish-English/English-Spanish dictionary of the day, which is still in use, taught at Columbia in the 1830s. An outstanding member of Columbia's history department was Professor Lewis Hanke, who, together with historian William Thomas Walsh and writer Waldo Frank, formed a group of major American Hispanic scholars in recent years. In 1934, Columbia University brought out the *Revista Hispánica Moderna* (formerly *Revista de Estudios Hispánicos*), one of the best publications of its kind.

New York University is centered around Washington Square, where the Spanish poet Juan Ramón Jiménez sat, one spring afternoon, in the shade of a tree that he claimed was thicker with birds than with leaves. NYU is one of the largest universities in the United States, with over 40,000 students on several campuses. For a long time, NYU has run a junior year in Madrid program, always attended by a large number of students, and more recently, expanded its program to make it possible to obtain a master's degree in Spain.

Other institutions in the field of United States–Spanish cultural relations are the Institute of International Education (a key organization for the exchange of students) and the American Field Service (active in secondary education), both of which have their headquarters in New York. The Hispanic Institute, originally founded in 1920 under the name Instituto de las Españas, did beneficial work as a result of the joint efforts of several Spanish universities and various federal agencies. Its first director was Federico de Onís. Today, the leading Hispanic cultural center in New York is the Spanish Institute, founded in 1954 and supported since then by a number of prominent figures such as E. Laroque Tinker, George S. Moore, Beatriz Bermejillo, Teodoro Rousseau, Rosita Noyes, Dr. Ramón Castroviejo, Angier Biddle Duke, Barleton Sprague Smith and William H. Hickey. The work of this institute became full of promise for the future upon acquiring a building on Park Avenue, thanks to the generosity of the marquesa de Cuevas; called Spanish House, it spreads Spanish culture through its library, lecture halls, theatrical groups and the Academia Norteamericana de Altos Estudios (North American Academy of Higher Studies). This center was opened officially in April 1970.

Hispanic Art

An event of outstanding importance for Spanish culture was the foundation of the Hispanic Society of America by Archer M. Huntington and the opening in 1908 of the building constructed on Broadway, between 155th and 156th Streets, as a museum to house the works of art and books selected by this great Hispanist. The library contains many manuscripts and books published in the 17th and successive centuries and totals approximately 100,000 volumes. A new building was needed by 1930. In the central patio visitors are greeted by a statue of the El Cid, bas-reliefs of Boabdil and Don Quixote, and a frieze with the names of the leading figures of Hispanic culture, all of which is the work of sculptress Anna Vaughn Hyatt, the wife of the founder. Hyatt also sculpted the group called *Los Portadores de la Antorcha (The Torchbearers)* in the University City of Madrid, and various reproductions of her statue of El Cid can be found in Spain.

The Hispanic Society houses Spanish paintings by Luis de Morales, El Greco *(St. Luke)*, Zurbarán, Juan Carreño de Mirando, Velázquez *(The Count-Duke of Olivares)* and Goya *(The Duchess of Alba)*, among the great masters. Among the modern artists are Mariano Fortuny, Martín Rico, José María López Mezquita, Miguel Viladrich, Ignacio Zuloaga and Joaquín Sorolla. The 14 enormous Sorolla canvases on the Spanish provinces give exceptional light, color and atmosphere to the hall that bears his name, specially built in 1926. Two exhibitions held there in 1909 made a great impact; one was of paintings by Sorolla, when the artist traveled to New York for the first time, and the other, of works by Zuloaga. The Hispanic Society also houses splendid collections of sculptures; furniture; wrought iron, gold and silver work; ceramics; and fabrics. The program of publications of the society, once presided by A. Hyatt Mayor and directed by Theodore S. Beardsley Jr. for many years, has been on a large scale, covering the collections of the society or various aspects relating to it. The number of full members appointed by its directors is limited to 100, while there are 300 corresponding members.

The Hispanic Society is not the only place where Spanish art can be seen. The Metropolitan Museum of Art houses several impressive exhibits. (A Spaniard, Carmen Gómez Moreno, has been assistant curator of medieval art.) The collection of paintings in the Metropolitan is exceptional. Works by El Greco *(View of Toledo)*, Velázquez and Goya abound and served as the core for an exhibition in 1928, which included 13 Grecos, seven Murillos, six Riberas, seven Velázquez's, four Zurbarán's and 22 Goyas, brought from all parts of the country.

On the ground floor, beyond the monumental staircase, is the imposing screen from the Cathedral of Valladolid in a specially adapted room. As an antechamber to the Thomas J. Watson Library of art books, there is the beautiful Spanish Renaissance patio from the Palace at Velez Blanco. Built by Pedro Fajardo between 1506 and 1515, it was bought by a French antiques dealer, who then sold it to George Blumenthal, who installed it at his mansion on Park Avenue. When the building was razed in 1945, the owner presented the patio to the Metropolitan Museum, which after several years of study, reassembled

Detail of the exterior of the Apse from Fuentidueña, a Spanish national monument from the ruins of the 12th century church of St. Martin, as installed at The Cloisters in Fort Tryon Park, New York. On loan from Spain to the Metropolitan Museum of Art.

it stone by stone. The solemn opening to the public in November 1964 was a major artistic and social event.

No less important was the inauguration of the apse from San Martín de Fuentidueña in the Cloisters in Upper Manhattan. This museum of medieval art, which is part of the Metropolitan, has a collection of cloisters, chambers, archways, sculptures and every kind of work of art in Romanesque and Gothic styles. They are all original works brought from different European countries, including Spain, and are well grouped together.

The Museum of Modern Art, renovated a few years ago, also has many exceptional works by Spanish artists: Juan Gris, Joan Miró, Pablo Picasso (*Fishing by Night in Antibes* and *Les Desmoiselles d'Avignon*), Salvador Dalí (*The Persistence of Memory*), Antoni Tapies and Eduardo Chillida.

The Huntington Hartford Museum was opened a few years ago opposite Central Park, its star exhibits being the great paintings by Dalí *The Taking of Tetuan* and *Columbus Discovers America*. The museum recently closed, and its paintings were auctioned (the second one mentioned is now in the St. Petersburg's Dalí Museum).

More examples of Spanish art can be seen in the Frick Collection: *Purification of the Temple, St. Jerome* and *Vincentio Anastagi* by El Greco; *Philip IV* by Velázquez; *Doña María Martínez de Puga, The Count of Teba, The Duke of Osuna* and *La Forja* by Goya.

Historically a strong impact was made by the Spanish Pavilion at the New York Fair (1964–1965), where works by the latest masters and outstanding painters of the new generation were shown side by side in the pavilion with Goya's *Majas* or El Greco's *Knight with his Hand on his Breast*, sent from the Prado Museum in Madrid. The exhibition was completed by the murals of Joaquín Vaquero Turcios, the stained glass of Ramón Vázquez de Molezun, the statues of Fray Junípero by Pablo Serrano and of Queen Isabella by José Luis Sánchez, a ceramic mural by Antonio Cumella, the surfaces by José María de Labra and the grille by Amadeo Gabino. The building itself was designed by architect Javier Carvajal. In order to make the most of the impact of the fair, the Spanish Pavilion Awards for the Arts were created. Also present at the fair was an exact replica of the caravel *Santa María*.

Another event that made an artistic impact was the exhibition of Spanish photography between 1920 and 1945 housed at the International Center of Photography at the beginning of 1986. In the last few years, the city has been the scene of large exhibitions of Joaquín Sorolla (simultaneously at the IBM Gallery and in the His-

panic Society, 1989), Ignacio Zuloaga (Spanish Institute, 1989), Francisco de Goya (Metropolitan Museum, 1989) and others.

Spanish artistic flair can also be admired in the murals of the buildings forming part of the Rockefeller Center. Opposite is Saint Patrick's Cathedral, whose Altar of the Americas is the work of Spanish sculptor Enrique Monjó. In the large vestibule of the International Building, there are two impressive frescos by Spanish painter José María Sert, with his characteristic combination of shades of sepia: one is a mural on the theme of the achievements of man, featuring Lincoln and Emerson, while the other, a truly amazing piece of work, shows figures representing the past, present and future surrounded by spiraling airplanes. Monjó sculpted the huge high-relief called the *United States-Twentieth Century* set in the forecourt of the First National City Bank skyscraper on Park Avenue; it was inaugurated in June 1968. On the panel dedicated to the discovery of America, Christopher Columbus is seen holding the *Santa María* in his hands.

Another contribution of Spanish art to New York architecture is not very well known. These are the works of Rafael Guastavino, a Valencian who immigrated to the United States bringing with him his experience of the system commonly known as the Catalonian vault, which he patented as the Guastavino system. Assisted and succeeded by his son, Rafael, he used his method on many buildings, including the chapel of Columbia University (the experimental building using the system), the domes over the old Pennsylvania railroad station and the Cathedral of St. John the Divine, subway stations, the approaches to the Queensborough Bridge and the basement of Taunton Court House. Several artists are residents of New York, including Esteban Vicente and Luis Sanguino.

Theater and Music

Spanish themes have been used on the New York stage throughout the 19th and 20th centuries. William Dunlap had three comedies produced in a single year, 1800: *La Virgen del Sol (The Virgin of the Sun)* on March 12; *Pizarro in Peru* on March 26; and *El Caballero del Guadalquivir (The Knight of the Guadalquivir)* on December 5. Ernest Hemingway used counterespionage in Madrid during the Spanish Civil War as his theme in *La Quinta Columna,* or *The Fifth Column,* which had its premiere at the Alvin Theater, on March 6, 1940.

The literature of Cervantes has been a frequently used source of inspiration (for example, the *Slaves of Algeria,* by Susan Haswell Rowson at the end of the 17th century, and the musical *Man of La Mancha*) as has the story of Don Juan (for instance, the versions by Langner in 1921 and by Rostand in 1925), as well as historical tales on the subjects of the succession to the Spanish throne on the death of Alfonso XI (*Leonor de Guzmán* by George Henry Boker), the wars of the Comuneros, or Communities, (*Ladies of Castile*) and Catalonia in 1500 (*The Three Dukes* by Robert Montgomery Bird and the stage version of a novel by Francis Marion Crawford, *In the Palace of the King*).

Spanish plays have also been seen in New York, either in the original, or else suitably adapted. In 1832, *La Estrella de Sevilla* by Lope de Vega and directed by Fanny Kemble Butler was a great success. Two versions of *Un Drama Nuevo* by Manuel Tamayo y Baus have been performed, one by Agustín Daly and another by William Dean Howells, the latter version being particularly well received. José de Echegaray has been one of the most popular Spanish authors in New York. In 1908, *El Gran Galeoto* was rewarded with 100 curtain calls, and *Marianna* was included in the repertoire of Mrs. Patrick Campbell from 1902 onward. In 1903, *Terra Baixa* by Angel Guimerá played at the Manhattan Theater for three weeks. Between 1910 and 1930, another favorite was Jacinto Benavente; the same can be said of the Alvarez Quintero brothers (Serafín and Joaquín) and Gregorio Martínez Sierra, whose *Canción de Cuna (Cradle Song)* of 1927 and *El Reino de Dios (The Kingdom of God)* of 1929 enjoyed long runs. A big hit in April 1932, at the New York Theater, was the company of María Guerrero and Fernando Díaz de Mendoza, which performed plays by classical and contemporary Spanish authors, together with other works by European playwrights. In 1927, another hit was made by Argentinian actress Camila Quiroga, in her performances of Spanish plays.

The Spanish Civil War and the ensuing world war brought a gap in Spanish theatricals on the American stage, with the exception of the works of García Lorca, translated into English, which were performed and made popular on television, and Spanish theater was confined almost exclusively to universities. The classical plays *El Caballero de Olmedo* by Lope de Vega, in 1962, and *La Drama Duende* by Pedro Calderón de la Barca in the spring of 1965, were produced by the Institute of Advanced Studies in Theater Arts (IASTA) under the guidance of Spaniards José Tamayo and José Luis Alonso, respectively. A praiseworthy effort was made by Spanish veteran actor José Crespo and his company in 1964 when they performed *La Vida es Sueño* by Calderón, in Spanish and in an English translation (*Life Is a Dream*).

In recent years there has been a considerable growth of Spanish-speaking theatrical groups, such as Laboratorio de Teatro Español, Teatro Rodante Puertorriqueño (with Miriam Colón), Dumé Spanish Theatre (whose founder was Heriberto Dumé), Intar (directed by Max Ferré) and Compañía de Teatro Repertorio Español (promoted by Gilberto Zaldívar). Among other plays, performances have been given of *Anillos para una dama* by Antonio Gala. There have also been tours by Spanish companies, mostly subsidized by the Joint Spanish American Committee, such as Pequeño Teatro de Madrid and the Zascandil group, which have also performed in other cities.

Spanish theater and cinema has also become popular due to the plays of Jaime Salom, Fernando Arrabal, and Fermín Cabal as well as the films of Pedro Almodóvar and Oscar winners Garci and Trueba.

In the world of music, author Stanley T. Williams has called Manuel García a "musical Columbus." Born in Seville in 1775, he sailed from Liverpool to New York in 1825, with his son Manuel and his daughter María (who has been mentioned before as the well-known singer La Malibran). With them they brought an opera company. The season opened on November 29, 1825, at the New York Theater with *The Barber of Seville* (part of whose music is attributed to García), the first full-length opera sung in New York in a language other than English. At the New York Theater, and later at the Park Theater, the company gave a total of 79 performances, including 11 new operas, such as Mozart's *Don Juan*, until September 30, 1826, when the company departed. The season was a resounding success. Another excellent company, from Havana and directed by Francisco Martínez y Torrens, performed in New York in 1847. Zarzuela companies have also always been popular, and New York is the headquarters of an Association of Friends of the Zarzuela. In 1985, an *Anthology of Zarzuela,* directed by José Tamayo, with performances by Plácido Domingo, was staged at Madison Square Garden.

From her first performance for the New York public on April 14, 1926, the singer Raquel Meller scored a great success. Also extremely popular was La Argentinita with her Spanish dancing. Spanish composer Enrique Granados attended the premiere performance of his opera *Goyescas;* he lost his life on his return voyage to Spain in 1916, when the Germans sank the steamship *Sussex*. The Valencian singer, Lucrecia Bori, was for a long time prima donna at the Metropolitan until her retirement in 1936; she lived in New York and, until her death a few years ago, keenly promoted Spanish artistic activities in New York. Among the newer generations of Spanish opera or concert singers who have performed in New York, mention should be made of Victoria de los Angeles, as well as Consuelo Rubio, Teresa Berganza, Pilar Lorengar, Montserrat Cabellé, Alfredo Kraus, Plácido Domingo and José Carreras.

The New York dock workers had an unusual companion in Spanish composer Isaac Albéniz; they had the benefit of his talents when he earned his fare back to Spain by performing in dockside taverns, sometimes putting on a circus act by playing the piano with his back to the instrument and his hands crossed on the keyboard behind him. Earlier, between 1870 and 1890, the great violinist Pablo Sarasate (who was painted by James Abbott McNeill Whistler) had been a popular figure, as was the case with cellist Pablo Casals.

It is to Andrés Segovia that world recognition of the guitar as a noble instrument is due. Other guitarists whose names frequently appear on programs include the Madrilenian veteran Carlos Montoya, Sabicas, the Romeros, Serranito and Juan Serrano. Outstanding performers with the harp include Nicanor Zabaleta and María Rosa Calvo Manzano, while Alicia de Larrocha has often played the piano here, and Genoveva Gálvez the harpsichord. A well-known composer, Leonardo

Balada, lives in New York. The actress Rosita Díaz also lived in the metropolis until her death in 1986. It must be admitted that Spanish folklore has contributed considerably to keeping the name of Spain in the public eye. The Spanish ballet companies of José Greco, Jiménez and Vargas, José Molina, Antonio, Antonio Gades and Ana Lorca, together with musical groups such as Los Chavales de España or choirs such as the Orfeón of Pamplona, or Coros y Danzas de España can be included among them.

Leaving New York by crossing the Hudson River is a reminder that its original name was the San Antonio River. It received this name when Esteban Gómez sailed up it in 1525. Francisco López de Gómara, when speaking of the navigator's voyage, inserts the heading "Río de San Antón," and Oviedo places it at 41° north latitude. Going on the information provided by Esteban Gómez, Diego de Ribeiro calls all the land between what is now Chesapeake Bay and the north of Cape Cod Tierras de Gómez on his famous map.

Spanish Place-Names

In New York State, towns with Spanish names include: Alma, Aurora, Bolivar, Cadiz, Carmel, Cuba, Lima, Madrid, Medina, Mexico, Panama, Peru and Salamanca; there is also a country, Columbia, with a name that recalls Spain's presence.

◆ THE MID-ATLANTIC STATES ◆

New Jersey

The small locality of Morristown, in the west of New Jersey, is especially meaningful for Spain. While headquartered here General George Washington, met with the representative of the French government, M. La Luzerne, and the unofficial Spanish representative, Juan Miralles, who came to the camp to persuade him to reinforce his armies in the Carolinas as a means of thwarting British plans to attack the Spanish possessions in the South. During his stay there (Miralles wrote to Governor Gálvez for the last time on April 12, 1780) the Span-

ish envoy fell ill and died a few days later on April 28. Miralles's remains were borne to the cemetery on the shoulders of army captains, and he was buried with military honors. Washington presided at the funeral. The marquis de Lafayette broke the news to the Spanish ambassador in Paris, the count of Aranda, who reported it to the Spanish count of Floridablanca in a dispatch dated June 30, 1780.

Two universities are particularly well known in this part of New Jersey: Princeton and Rutgers. The Princeton campus has long shown interest in the Spanish language: John Witherspoon, president from 1768 to 1794, considered Cervantes superior to Homer and Boileau for irony and wit. The Spanish department today is an important one; Spanish historian Américo Castro was a member of the department for a long time before retiring to La Jolla, California.

In the bustling city of Newark, a Club of Spain sponsors the local Spain's Day proclaimed annually by the City Hall.

When traveling the 125 miles from Sandy Hook to Cape May, it can be remembered that Esteban Gómez also sailed along this stretch of coast and called Sandy Hook "Cabo de Arenas," as it is shown on the Ribeiro map, of which the present name is a translation.

On entering Delaware Bay one approaches Point Breeze, which was chosen by Joseph Bonaparte as a retreat during his exile in the United States after he was ousted from the throne of Spain, on which he had been placed by his brother Napoleon Bonaparte. The Spanish populace had nicknamed him "Pepe Botella," (Joe Bottle). There would be no reason to mention Point Breeze if Joseph Bonaparte had simply spent his time reflecting on the past. But, he spent his retirement conspiring against the Spanish Empire and trying to find a throne of his own.

In 1816, he contacted a certain Francisco Javier Mina, who organized an expedition of an assortment of volunteers from various places, with the idea of disembarking at the mouth of the Nuevo Santander River in the Gulf of Mexico and capturing the capital of New Spain. For this purpose Joseph Bonaparte provided Mina with a letter of credit for $100,000 against at London bank, which enabled the expedition to set sail.

In April 1817, it reached the Rio Grande. There, seeing that Mina was flying the Spanish flag, a Spanish lookout post at the mouth of the river supplied him with drinking water, meat and other provisions. Meanwhile, having brought a printing press with him, Mina proceeded to publish a bulletin; dated April 12, 1817, this can be considered as the first publication in Texas. The squadron weighed anchor shortly afterward and a few weeks later disappeared in a complete fiasco, its leaders dead and the other expeditionaries scattered.

That was not the last of the plots hatched by Joseph Bonaparte from Point Breeze. He made funds available to French general Charles Lallemand to finance his plans to establish a colony in Texas, a Spanish dominion, providing a refuge for Napoléon if his planned escape from St. Helena was successful. Lallemand and his men disembarked on the coast of Texas in 1818 and founded the colony of Champ d'Asile. However, in view of the pressure of the Indians and rumors of the approach of a Spanish expedition, they razed camp six months after their arrival.

Nowadays, a large Cuban population has taken residence in Union City.

Spanish Place-Names

The localities with Spanish names in New Jersey include Belmar, Buena, Carmel, Columbus, Malaga and Rio Grande.

Pennsylvania

According to the duke de la Rochefoucauld, the Spaniards also explored parts of Pennsylvania. They built forts on the river Tioga, as outputs of their penetration up the Susquehanna from Chesapeake Bay (which they called Bahía de Santa María). In the Oneida District (in the center of the triangle formed by Harrisburg, Allentown and Scranton) the so-called Pompeya stone was discovered bearing the inscription "Leo de Lon. VI 1520," the origin of which is attributed to the expeditions of Esteban Gómez or Lucas Vasquez de Ayllón, or later parties of explorers.

At the time of the uprising of the colonies, and after the Declaration of Independence, Spain considered it advisable to appoint an unofficial agent to act as observer and provide information at first hand concerning the course of the war and the standpoints of the new nation. Consequently, the count of Floridablanca, then secretary of state, appointed Juan de Miralles to hold that post when his name was proposed by the commander-in-chief of the Spanish forces at Havana, Diego Navarro. Miralles reached Charleston on January 9, 1778, and stayed there until the spring, when he moved to Philadelphia.

In spite of his position as a mere agent, he succeeded in maintaining close contact with members of Congress and other authorities. According to inquiries made by Victor Pradera, former Spanish consul in Philadelphia (1966), Miralles lived in a house at number 110 South Third Street; the house, which no longer exists, stood next to Powell House, one of the best preserved on Society Hill, and was the home of John Penn, the last colonial governor of Pennsylvania, and of Benjamin Chew, the last president of the High Court of the colony. Everything seems to indicate that the Spanish "ambassador" was held in high repute; he certainly entertained lavishly in the building and adjacent gardens, which were profusely illuminated.

Until the arrival of Diego de Gardoqui in 1785, Francisco Rendón, secretary to Miralles, acted as unofficial Spanish agent and initially occupied the same house as his predecessor. There, Rendón had the honor of being host to General George Washington, his wife and children. At the end of 1781, when Washington and his army arrived to take up winter quarters at Charleston, it became necessary to accommodate the visitors in private homes, and the leading townspeople came forward to offer their hospitality. Rendón was no exception and offered his home accordingly. Washington accepted it gladly but would not accept the hospitality of his table, since he considered that the food for his family and officers should be paid for out of the public coffers. A plaque was recently placed on the house in question bearing the following inscription: "On this site stood the home, 1778–1780, of Juan de Miralles (1715–1780), first Spanish Diplomatic Representative to the United States of America. He died April 28, 1780, while visiting General Washington at his Morristown Headquarters. The same home became the residence of his successor, Francisco Rondon (Rendón), who lent it to General Washington for the Winter of 1781–1782. Through these officials Spanish military and financial assistance was channeled to the American Patriots. Tribute from the Government of Spain, 1967."

Rendó subsequently moved to a house owned by the Shippen family, at the corner of Fourth Street and Locust Street, likewise on Society Hill, and one of the oldest and best preserved buildings in the town. Not far away is St. Mary's Church, the first Catholic church in Philadelphia, with a plaque on the facade recalling the presence of the Spanish and French diplomatic envoys, together with the president, members of his government, members of Congress and representatives of the armed forces at the first public religious commemoration of the Declaration of Independence on July 4, 1779.

While Miralles was the first de facto Spanish agent in the United States, Diego de Gardoqui was the first official Spanish representative. He received from King Charles III letters of credence dated September 27, 1784, addressed to "Our great and well-beloved friends the United States of North America," appointing him chargé d'affaires before the Continental Congress.

From May 20, 1785, when he reached Philadelphia, until October 12, 1789, when he returned to Spain, Gardoqui worked incessantly, but he resided mostly in New York.

Gardoqui was not a newcomer to relations with the rebellious colonies. A member of the powerful Bilbao firm Gardoqui e hijos, he knew Britain and her possessions well. For that very reason he had been chosen to hold discussions with Arthur Lee, when this American emissary was sent by Franklin from Paris to act as the official envoy of Congress in Spain. He first acted as interpreter at the talks held between Lee and Grimaldi, at Burgos, but was later appointed intermediary in order to channel Spanish aid to the revolutionaries, a mission in which he often had to advance sums that the King had undertaken to furnish. In this respect he acted in the same way as Pierre Caron de Beaumarchains in France (author of *The Barber of Seville*), who handled such affairs through the Spanish firm of Rodríguez, Hortales y Compañía.

As a Spanish diplomatic representative, Gardoqui had to cope with the difficult postrevolutionary period, in which the interests of the United States did not always coincide with those of Spain. The clauses of the Anglo-American peace treaty did not respect the rights claimed by Spain with respect to the territories west of the Mississippi. Moreover, the inevitable difficulties experienced by a new country gave rise to attempts at separatism.

By his actions Gardoqui certainly showed his affection for the United States, and his letters corroborate this. In one of his letters to George Washington, dated November 18, 1785, he said: "I have been, am & will be a true friend to your United States." The general in his turn, wrote to him as follows on January 20, 1786: "The sentiments which you have been pleased to entertain of my conduct are very flattering; and the friendly manner in which they are expressed is highly pleasing. To meet the approbation of a gentleman whose good wishes were early engaged in the American cause, & who has attended to its progress thro' the various stages of the revolution, must be considered as a happy circumstance for me; & I shall seek occasionally to testify my sense of it." In a letter dated August 30 of that same year, Washington wrote: "I can omit no occasion of assuring your Excellency of the high gauge I entertain of the many marks of polite attention I have received from you; nor of the pleasure I should feel in the honor of expressing it at this seat of my retirement from public life if you should ever feel an inclination to make an excursion into the middle States."

When Gardoqui departed from the country, the Spanish representatives whom he left behind in Philadelphia were José de Jóudenes and José de Viar, who had accompanied him from Spain as secretaries. Holding the appointment of commissioners, in 1791 they are recorded as living at 127 Mulberry Street, now Arch Street; in 1794, the chancellery was at 37 South Fourth Street; and in 1796, at 297 Arch Street. They succeeded in intervening at decisive moments, for, on orders from baron de Carondelet, governor of Louisiana, they warned Jefferson that any United States violation of Spanish territory or of that of the allies of Spain would mean war.

In May 1796, the Spanish diplomatic mission was headed by a minister plenipotentiary, Carlos Martínez de Yrujo. He is known to have lived at number 315 High Street, which stood between numbers 800 and 1300 of what is now Market Street. Yrujo married Sara McKean, the daughter of one of the signatories of the Declaration of Independence and president of the Continental Congress. Well-known painter Gilbert Stuart painted the McKean and Yrujo families, and the four portraits were exhibited at the Metropolitan Museum of Art in New York in 1976. When the government moved to the federal capital in 1800, only a consulate was left open in Philadelphia.

The most outstanding personality in revolutionary Philadelphia was undoubtedly Benjamin Franklin. Endowed with great curiosity and a very broad range of interests, he not only has to his credit some fine scientific achievements, but played an enormous part in the shaping of the new nation and, from his post as official envoy in Paris, was extraordinarily influential in obtaining effective aid from France for the rebels. In addition to the part he played in obtaining Spanish cooperation during the war against Britain, Franklin was important because of his interest in spreading knowledge of the Spanish language in the United States.

Franklin began to study Spanish in 1733 as part of his program for the study of modern languages and instructed that Spanish be included in the syllabus of the Academy of Philadelphia, founded in 1749. The circles in which Franklin moved were frequented by the Franciscan encyclopedist Antonio José Ruiz de Padrón from 1784 onward. In 1784, the Royal Academy of His-

tory, in Madrid, appointed Franklin their correspondent academician; the American Philosophical Society was to grant a similar honor to an eminent Spanish botanist, Alejandro Ramírez.

In 1776, the first Spanish university course was given in Philadelphia, which thus became the first of the higher educational institutions to take an active interest in Spanish. But, it was not until 1830 that students at the University of Pennsylvania were free to study Spanish (or another language), provided that it was requested by their parents. These studies did not achieve a high standard until the presence of that dynamic personality, Hugh Rennert, at the end of the 19th century. Outstanding professors have been part of the Department of Spanish during the present century, including Romera-Navarro, author of an important work, *El hispanismo en Norteamérica.*

A familiarity with the works of Cervantes was evident in Philadelphia in the middle of the 18th century. Inspired by the Spanish work, a play called *Don Quixote in England,* by Henry Fielding, was performed on May 21, 1766, and a comic opera by Isaac Bickerstaffe, called *The Padlock,* based on *El celoso extremeño,* became popular from 1769 on. His influence was also seen in the comedy by H. H. Brackenridge, *Modern Chivalry* (Philadelphia, 1792–1797). The latter years of the century also saw one of the first performances in the United States of a work by Calderón de la Barca: *El escondido y la tapada.* Georgina King was the author of *El Camino de Santiago (The Road to Santiago).*

The International Exhibition of 1876 was of fundamental importance for the dissemination of art, and particularly, Spanish art in this area. Spain took part on a large scale in various fields, such as agriculture and industry, under the guidance of the royal commissioner, Francisco López Fabra; he was assisted by a party of military engineers. During the exhibition, on April 23, a resounding homage was paid to Cervantes. At the closing banquet, on November 10, with President Ulysses Grant presiding, in the official toast, General Hawley saluted Spain, "our sister country, our friend, whose flag was the first to fly on American soil."

Stephen Ferris, a professor at the Academy of Fine Arts of Pennsylvania, was instrumental in making Spanish sketching more widely known; thanks to his guidance, Robert F. Blum became a devotee of Daniel Urrabieta Vierge and a disciple of Mariano Fortuny. The Fine Arts Museum, houses the finest collection of Pablo

Picasso's work in North America (among others his *Self Portrait*, the *Bread Girl*, *Violin and Guitar* and *Three Musicians*); the *Plate with Fruits* by Juan Gris; the famous *Dog Barking at the Moon* and *Personage in the Presence of Nature* by Joan Miró; and *Presage of the Civil War* by Salvador Dalí, to mention only a few. A medieval patio with its cloister has been rebuilt in the middle of the museum, mostly consisting of Spanish work. The select picture gallery at the exclusive Barnes Foundation houses works by Picasso and other Spanish masters. In the course of the 1960s, exhibitions held in Philadelphia included the works of Benjamín Palencia, Vaquero Turcios and Spanish engravings, while Spanish singers at the magnificent opera house included the baritone Manuel Ausensi.

Duquesne University, in Pittsburgh, published for many years the *Hispanic Review.*

Spanish Place-Names

The list of Spanish names in Pennsylvania includes Carbon and Columbia Counties and the towns of Adrian, Almedia, Andalusia, Anita, Antes Fort, Bolivar, Columbia, Columbus, Gibraltar, Jacobus, Lopez, Madera, Matamoras, Molino, Sacramento, Valencia and Villanova.

Delaware

A Spanish galleon is thought to have sunk in the area off the coast of Rehoboth Beach, as some years ago coins bearing the arms of the king of Spain were found in the sand in this area.

Wilmington is the headquarters of the E.I. Du Pont de Nemours Corporation, founded in 1892 when the firm's founder built its first gunpower plant; a Spaniard would make his fortune with the company as well. Born in Cádiz in 1880, Elías Ahuja emigrated to the United States at the age of 17. After various vicissitudes, he studied at the Massachusetts Institute of Technology, started work with Du Pont and rose to a high position in the corporation. He traveled to Spain and in 1937 returned to Wilmington, where he founded a charitable society, Good Samaritan, Inc., to provide aid for noteworthy Spanish students wanting to study in the United States. The physicist Francisco Balta Calleja won the Dupont '96 prize for research.

Spanish Place-Names

The only towns in Delaware with Spanish names are Columbia, Delmar, Laurel and Magnolia.

Maryland

The annals of Maryland include visits to this coast by Spanish ships only a few years after the discovery by Christopher Columbus. In 1525, a Spanish ship (probably that of Esteban Gómez) was severely damaged by storms and thick ice, and had to be towed from the shore by its crew and repaired at the mouth of the river Wilcomico, near the present locality of White Haven, in Chesapeake Bay. The ship set sail shortly afterward and as a record of its passing, left a flag and an inscription on wood recounting the event.

Close to Washington lies Annapolis, the state capital. Its greatest fame is owed to the U.S. Naval Academy, where are exhibited artifacts from the not always amicable relationship between the United States and Spain. Many souvenirs remain from the Spanish-American War of 1898, including one of the masts of the *Maine*. The cruiser *Reina Mercedes* was once moored at a nearby quay, where it served as a calaboose for cadets! One can also find an old Spanish bronze cannon, captured from the Mexicans in California in 1847.

The museum houses many souvenirs from Cuba and the Philippines: the red and gold insignia, with the coat of arms, belonging to the Spanish warship *Jorge Juan,* sunk by the U.S.S. *Annapolis* at Nipe Bay, on July 21, 1898; the colors of Rear Admiral Patricio Montojo, commander of the Spanish squadron at Manila, taken from the warship *Reina Cristina*; the first red and gold Spanish flag captured from the sailing ship *Matilde* by the U.S.S. *New York* near Havana; the Spanish flag from the cruiser *María Teresa*, commanded by Admiral Pascual Cervera at the Battle of Santiago; a commemorative plaque of the *Maine* made from metal recovered from the ship; a tray from the cruiser *Cristóbal Colón*; a statuette of Abraham Lincoln made by a Spanish artist and found screwed down in the office of the Spanish commander of the Olangapo naval station in the Philippines; a set of Spanish silver coins melted by the explosion of an American shell, in August 1898, and found in the possession of a member of the crew of the *Almirante Oquendo*, to judge by the pieces of bone mingled with the coins; and many other such exhibits. In the library can be seen five large display cabinets full of Spanish flags: a complete list and description of these flags would be wearisome for the reader.

Also at the naval academy is the figure of the first admiral of the United States, David Glasgow Farragut, the son of a Minorcan, Jorge Ferragut. The academy, library and museum are all full of his memory and souvenirs. In the museum can be seen his signature under his oath as a cadet, signed on December 19, 1810; a reproduction of the plaque summarizing his life placed on the destroyer U.S.S. *Farrugut* and the original plaque commissioned by the city council of Ciudadela (Minorca) honoring his memory, presented in Ciudadela to the American ambassador J. C. Dunn, on June 27, 1953.

In 1792, Baltimore held important celebrations to commemorate the discovery of America. In 1825, it was here that the popular Spanish grammar text by Mariano Cubó was first published and in the space of a few years ran to six editions. Cubí taught at St. Mary's College, where the first teacher of Spanish had been Father Peter Babad. Another teacher at this college was a Spanish vice-consul in Baltimore, José Antonio Pizarro, to whom Severn Teackle Wallis dedicated his *Glimpses of Spain* (1849), in which the author set out, on the grounds of his own personal knowledge of Spain, to correct many widespread errors about the country. In 1984, President Reagan unveiled a monument to Columbus here.

Today, the standard-bearer of Spanish culture in Baltimore is the Department of Spanish at the renowned Johns Hopkins University. The great Spanish poet Pedro Salinas spent a long time here, prior to his death in Boston, in 1951. One of the distinguished professors at the Peabody Institute, a magnificent institution in the musical world, was the Spanish pianist Julio Esteban, president of the Association of Pianists of the United States in 1966. The Walters Art Gallery, opposite the conservatory on the other side of Charles Street, houses some fine works of art, some of which are Spanish. Also worth mentioning is the Museum of Art, which, among other Spanish paintings, has the well-known *Family of Acrobats* by Pablo Picasso, as well as his words *Leo Stein* and *Monkey.*

For many years, the writer John dos Passos wintered in Baltimore and spent the summer at Westmoreland, Virginia. The author of *Midcentury* was acquainted with the works of the Spanish novelist Camilo José Cela and had a good command of Spanish. He made numerous visits to Spain, which crystalized in *Rosinante to the Road Again* (1922) and *Adventures of a Young Man,* with scenes from the Spanish Civil War.

A few miles outside Washington, D.C., in Bethesda is the Academy of American Franciscan History, which has an artistically interesting chapel built by the Franciscan fathers. It was built in 1961 to the design of Peruvian architect Harth Terré, who likewise directed the construction of the altars and the statues, made in the workshop of Spanish sculptor José Ramón Zaragoza, at Lima. The chapel is inspired by a missionary church of colonial times in Peru, and high altar, in American Baroque style, has a central statue of the Virgin of Guadalupe, flanked by statues of St. Toribio de Mogrovejo, St. Rose of Lima, St. Francisco Solano and St. Felipe de Jesús, all of the 16th century. The side altar on the right, in Neoclassical style, analogous to the one used by the Franciscans in Peru, has statues of St. Anthony of Padua and a copy of the statue of St. Francis by Spanish sculptor Pedro de Mena. The left-hand side altar is in 17th-century Spanish-American style; here, in addition to a Christ in Chains, there is a high relief of St. James the Elder at the Battle of Clavijo. The tabernacle is a modern Spanish work, while the altar lamps are inspired by those at the Basilica of St. Francis of Assisi; the Crucifix on the high altar is an old one in the style common at Quito, while the windows are made of onyx from Puebla de los Angeles, Mexico. The Stations of the Cross, in 18th-century Sevillian ceramic, were a gift from the Escuela de Estudios Hispanoamericanos (School of Hispano-American Studies) at Seville. In the little courtyard outside the chapel entrance is a *picota,* a column crowned by a cross of the type so frequently found in Spain, to welcome those attending the Sunday Mass in Spanish. This academy publishes important historical works and a quarterly review, *The Americas,* and grants an annual award, the Sierra Award of the Americas. Spanish historian Father Lino Gómez Canedo and his colleagues Kieman and MacCarthy, among others, have resided here.

Spanish Place-Names

The only towns in the state bearing Spanish names are Cordova, La Plata, Mayo and Villa Heights.

WASHINGTON, D.C.

The Potomac River flows through a long wide estuary into the Chesapeake Bay. This bay was visited quite frequently by the Spaniards during the 16th and early 17th centuries, and some of the earliest, most detailed and precise descriptions of it were provided by them. Apart from the expeditions of Angel Villafañe, Father Juan Bautista Segura and Menéndez de Avilés, the martyrs of Axacán, which will be covered in the next chapter on Virginia, other Spaniards visited the bay, known to them indistinctly as Santa María or Madre de Dios.

Bahía de la Madre de Dios (Bay of the Mother of God) was named by Pedro de Quexós when he was sent in 1525 by Vázquez de Ayllón with two caravels to explore the unknown northern lands and sailed along 500 miles of coast. This voyage was marked on the world map drawn by Juan Vespucio, Américo's nephew, in 1526. Treasurer of Florida Juan Menéndez Marqués, Juan Lara and Vicente González in 1588 accompanied Governor Pedro Menéndez Marqués of Florida to investigate reports of an English settlement in the area (Roanoke Island). The first two give a vivid description of the great bay they had seen in the course of a search for better harbors than St. Augustine, which had been established by the Crown in Florida in 1602.

Juan Menéndez's report stated that the bay, situated at 37° latitude, was particularly good and very big. The entrance to the bay ran in a northwest–southeast direction, he reported, and was not too shallow, lacked reefs either inside or outside it, and measured about two nautical leagues across. The bay was so spacious that one shore was not visible from the other and at the narrowest part, was as wide as at the entrance. Sailing northward up the bay, there were a multitude of smaller bays, each of considerable size. Particularly abundant in inlets, rivers and valleys was the sector comprised between the 38th and 40th parallels; on reaching that point the bay ended in beautiful scenery with gently rolling hills and valleys (Menéndez undoubtedly was referring to the area of Annapolis, Baltimore and Havre de Grace). The soil was rich for farming and livestock and the rivers flowing into the bay were so numerous and deep that in some places the water in the bay itself was sweet. In the region of the 38th parallel (the boundary between the states of Maryland and Virginia),

Menéndez found an Indian wearing a gold necklace, who told him of the existence of gold not far from Madre de Dios, which the Indians called Tapisco, at the foot of a mountain chain that lay half a day's journey away (perhaps the Appalachians). The Indian was baptized and given the name Vicente, or Vincent, and was taken aboard by Menéndez so that he could report personally in Spain; but he died on the voyage and was buried at a monastery in Santo Domingo.

The statement given by a soldier, Juan López Avilés, in the course of the inquiries, confirmed the previous reports and the excellent condition and width of the bay, based on details that he received from an expeditionary, Vincent González. A detailed description of the Chesapeake area is given in a letter that a later governor of St. Augustine, Gonzalo Méndez Canzo, wrote to the king on February 28, 1600, and likewise confirmed that the coast between the 37th and 40th parallels had many good havens. The Bay of Santa María received a further Spanish visit in 1609, when Francisco Fernández Ecija, who held the post of sargento mayor at St. Augustine (commander of the infantry and substitute for the governor in the event of his absence or illness), was commissioned by the Crown to sail up the coast and bring news about the British colony at Jamestown.

The District of Columbia naturally takes its name from Christopher Columbus, the discoverer of the New World, and has been symbolized as a statuesque woman with flowing white robes, wearing a helmet crowned with stars. Since the revolutionary leaders had considered calling their new country Columbia in honor of Columbus, it is fitting that its capital should be called the District of Columbia. Subsequently, Columbia came to mean freedom.

A statue of Columbus stands in front of Union Station, serving as a modest annual rallying point on October 12. Since its erection in 1966, the commemoration of the discovery has also been celebrated before the statue of Queen Isabella on the steps of the Pan-American Union. In 1967, Hispanidad Day was organized by the Inter-American Defense Board. Some streets of the capital bear the Spanish navigator's name, and the Capitol hosts some artistic works with him as a protagonist.

The original grid of Washington's streets has lasted to this day and has elicited praise from foreigners. The capital looks more like a garden than a city, and horizontal lines predominate in public buildings and private mansions in residential areas. Spanish novelist Miguel Delibes, visiting professor at the University of Maryland, described Washington as "The anti-New York, a builder of groundscrapers or recumbent skyscrapers."

The main entrance to the White House is in the center of Lafayette Square, where number 14, at that time the Spanish legation, was occupied by Juan Valera for part of his diplomatic mission in Washington (1883–1886). North from the very entrance to the White House is 16th Street; halfway along it stands the present Spanish Embassy building. Near Lafayette Square is Farragut Square, in the center of which stands the statue of the first admiral of the United States; here, in October 1964, the then minister of information and tourism of Spain, Manuel Fraga Iribarne, rendered homage to this descendant of Spain.

Going up Massachusetts Avenue where the largest number of foreign embassies stand, near the progressive Brookings Institution, is number 1447, another spot once occupied by the Spanish legate, who apparently was something of a heartbreaker: the daughter of the secretary of state, Thomas Francis Bayard, committed suicide when she heard of the departure from the United States of the Spanish minister, Don Juan Valera, who was not exactly young, but seemingly lived up to his first name. Nearby, the National Geographic Society building houses many records of Spanish contributions to world geography; the popular magazine has published dozens of articles about Hispanic history and culture. In December 1964, a major exhibition was held here of treasures rescued from a Spanish galleon sun in Florida waters in 1715: the exhibits included not only a beautiful artistic chain and gold coins of various sizes (some the size of saucers), but cutlery of modern appearance and fine china brought to America on the Manila galleon, all in perfect condition. In 1976, Queen Sofía of Spain opened an exhibition of the articles raised from the *Atocha*, which sank in 1622.

In the foyer of the diplomatic entrance to the huge State Department building can be seen the flags of those many countries with which the United States has diplomatic relations, including, therefore, the red and yellow flag of Spain; the permanent exhibition on the ground floor includes a number of items referring to the common history of Spain and North America. Before this building stands a statue of the Spanish governor Bernardo de Gálvez on horseback. This work of Juan de Avalos, was unveiled by King Juan Carlos in 1976. In the following years, the Spanish Heritage Weeks proclaimed in September every year by the different presidents, often started in front of this statue.

Not far away, on Pennsylvania Avenue, is the massive building of the World Bank for Reconstruction and Development. Its neighboring institution, the International Monetary Fund, has had, like the bank, an enormous influence on the economic progress of Hispanic nations in the past 40 years. In the central courtyard can be seen a sculpture by Spanish artist Eduardo Chillida.

The Capitol houses many fine works of art, some of which highlight the Hispanic contribution to the history of America and mankind. The frieze around the rotunda includes 18 scenes from American history, the first seven by Constantino Brumidi, eight by Filippo Costaggini and the last three by David Cox. Number one shows *The Landing of Columbus*; number two, *Cortés Entering the Palace of Montezuma*; number three, *The Conquest of Peru by Pizarro*; number four, *The Burial of De Soto, at Midnight, in the Mississippi*; and number 17, *The War between Spain and the United States*. Eight giant oil paintings hang on the walls of the rotunda (in the center of which is placed the catafalque for those accorded this honor, such as President John F. Kennedy, General Douglas MacArthur and President Herbert Hoover). Two of these paintings are of interest here: the *Landing of Columbus on San Salvador* by John Vanderlyn and the *Discovery of the Mississippi River by De Soto*, by W. H. Powell. Other works of art on the subject of Columbus can be seen at the Capitol. On the bronze door leading into the rotunda, Randolph Rogers sculpted eight scenes from the life of Columbus in 1857, in which Bartholomew Columbus also appears; In the President's Hall (near the Senate) is full-length portrait of Columbus by Constantino Brumidi accompanied by other personages and allegories that adorn the ceiling, and, in the western corridor on the first floor is another work by Brumidi illustrating *Columbus and the Indian Maidens*.

In the Capitol's Statuary Hall can be seen the statues of Father Junípero Serra, who was a missionary in California, and Father Eusebio Kino, who was an evangelizer of the Indians in Arizona. On the high walls of the House can be seen a collection of marble medallions with effigies of the most famous legislators in the history of world law, those born in Spain include the Rabbi Maimonides (1135–1204) from Córdoba, who codified Jewish oral law, and King Alphonso X the Wise (1221–1284), author of the Siete Partidas, a recomplication of Roman and Canon law. Important buildings around the Capitol include the Supreme Court, the Library of Congress and the Folger Library.

The Library of Congress houses a collection of particular interest to students of Hispanic culture. The building houses the Hispanic Foundation, which was established in 1939 by Archer Huntington, the founder of the Hispanic Society of America. Realizing that the society could not keep abreast of all noteworthy publications of interest on Spain in Spanish America, and acquire them for its library, in 1927 he made a substantial donation for that purpose; in 1930 he made a further donation, which provided enough funds to set up the present foundation.

The Hispanic Room was inaugurated on Columbus Day, October 12, 1939, and the stainless steel Columbus Coat of Arms was dedicated in 1940. The coat of arms has in the first and second quarters the royal arms of Castilla and León, the castle and the lion, granted to him by the monarchs Isabella and Ferdinand. The third quarter represents "a few islands and sea-waves" and the last one five anchors. Above the shield, the words in Spanish "Por Castilla y por León" appear, and below it, the words "Nuevo Mundo halló Colón" (For Castile and for León, Columbus found a New World). It possesses some valuable Spanish books and first editions and in recent years, organized an exhibition on Cervantes and Lope de Vega.

In the main hall, decorated with a colorful canvas by Cándido Portinari, a fine group of Hispanists draft (in cooperation with the University of Florida) the useful *Handbook of Latin American Studies*. The Word Archive (Archivo de la Palabra) contains recordings of the voices of outstanding writers in the Spanish language. In 1962 and 1965, the IASTA gave performances in English at the Coolidge Auditorium of *El Caballero de Olmedo* by

Statue of Queen Isabella of Spain in the Pan-American building in Washington, D.C. Carlos Fernández-Shaw.

Lope de Vega and of *La Dama Duende* by Calderón de la Barca. In 1970, the Hispanic Foundation received a valuable collection of documents on the Spanish colonization of America, donated the New York bookdealer Hans Kraus. It also houses the Lowry Collection, with matchless treasures of the Spanish past.

The National Gallery of Art was a gift to the nation from Andrew W. Mellon. It is one of the finest art galleries in the country and includes some important Spanish works: *The Adoration of the Magi*, by a Hispano-Flemish master of the 15th century; *The Nativity*, by Juan de Flandes; *The Marriage at Cana* and *Christ Among the Doctors* by the Master of the Retable of the Catholic Kings; *The Virgin with St. Agnes and St. Tecla, St. Ildephonsus, The Laoconte, St. Martin and the Beggar, St. Jerome, The Holy Family* and *Christ Clearing the Temple* by El Greco; *Still Life* by Juan Van der Hamen; *St. Lucy* by Zurbarán; *Pope Innocent X, The Needle-Woman*, and *Portrait of a Youth* by Velázquez; *The Return of the Prodigal Son* and *A Girl with her Duenna* by Bartolomé Esteban Murillo; *The Assumption of the Virgin* by Juan de Valdés Leal; and *The Marquesa de Pontejos, Don Bartolomé Sure-*

The Portinari murals: Cultural Beginnings and Mining. Library of Congress.

Letter from George Washington to Don Diego de Gardoqui of Spain, dated January 20, 1786. Spain was an effective ally in the Revolution.

da, *La Señora Sabasa, The Condesa de Chinchón* (or *Countess of Chinchón*), *The Duke of Wellington, Charles IV, Queen María Luisa,* and *The Book-Seller* by Goya.

Exhibits of modern Spanish painters include several outstandings Picassos, such as *The Family of Mountebanks* and other paintings of his Blue period, several paintings by Joan Miró, Juan Gris and the large, popular *The Last Supper* by Salvador Dalí, one of the main attractions of the museum, which share a room with the following paintings by Ignacio Zuloaga: *La Rubia del Abanico, Merceditas, Mrs. Philip Lydig* and *Achieta.*

Other art museums include the Corcoran Gallery, dedicated to American painting, which houses a curious coat of arms of Castile in ceramics, and the excellent private museum housing the Phillips Collection, which displays two versions of *Peter Repentant* by Greco and Goya, Goya's etching *Beware of Advice* (*Cuidado con los Consejos*), three works by Juan Gris (*Abstraction, Cup and Pack of Cigarettes* and *Still Life of Newspapers*); *The Minstrel Bullfight* and *The Blue Room* by Pablo Picasso; *Orange Grove* by Sorolla; *A Girl of Montmartre* by Zuloaga and *Red Sun* by Miró.

The modern National Museum of American History has an exhibit devoted to Spanish homes, and a replica of the caravel *Santa María,* the gem of the collection of scale models of ships made by the Maritime Museum in Barcelona. In the Naval Historical Exhibition Center, installed in another building, can be seen an artistic Spanish coat of arms from the cruiser *Reina Mercedes,* as well as wooden reliefs from several Spanish ships that took part in the Cuban War.

The Plaza of the Americas with statues of Simón Bolívar and José Gervasio Artigas, lies between the two buildings of the Pan-American Union. Although these buildings are in the unmistakable style of the Spanish Renaissance, the first to be built and the most important one, designed by architects Albert Kelsey and Paul Cret, is of greater interest from the architectural standpoint. It is the headquarters of the Organization of American States (OAS); in the gardens in front of the building stands the statue of Queen Isabella by José Luis Sánchez, donated to the OAS on April 14, 1996—Americas Day—by the Spanish government, represented by then-Minister of Foreign Affairs Fernando María Castiella. Two years earlier, Castiella had also been instrumental in securing the installation of a bust of Father Francisco de Vitoria, the father of international law. Sculpted by Victorio Macho, the bust is in one of the spacious galleries in the building, which houses statues of eminent Americans. The center of the building is a typical colonial patio, adorned with Maya, Aztec and Zapotec motifs. An outstanding collection of books on America and its history can be consulted in the Christopher Columbus Library on the ground floor.

In the fall of 1964, then Undersecretary for Cultural Affairs of the OAS Jaime Posada signed an agreement with the director of the Instituto de Cultura Hispánica (Institute of Hispanic Culture, ICH) Gregorio Marañón. A major part was played in this agreement by the director of culture, Rafael Squirru, and the assistant director, Guillermo de Zéndegui, who was at the same time editor of the prestigious cultural monthly *Americas.* This agreement was the first of its kind that the office of the secretary general of the OAS signed with a government of a nonmember country and bore fruit in the Festival of Music of America and Spain, held in Spain in October 1964 and, again, in 1967, with the Colombian conductor

Guillermo Espinosa as the chief promoter. The capital of Spain was also the venue of the seminar on Latin America and Spain in January 1969 under the sponsorship of the OAS, the Inter-American Development Bank (IDB), the Inter-American Committee of the Alliance for Progress (CIAP) and the Instituto de Cultura Hispánica (ICH). In May 1970, the secretary general Galo Plaza visited Spain, and letters were exchanged between him and the Spanish minister of foreign affairs laying down the general guidelines for cooperation between Spain and the OAS for the development of certain projects affecting several Latin American countries.

Another building houses the Pan-American Health Organization. Designed by Uruguayan architect Román Fresnedo, it was opened in the fall of 1965; in the foyer is a bust of Francisco Hernández, physician to King Philip II, sculpted by César Montaña, which was presented by Enrique Suárez de Puga on behalf of the Instituto de Cultura Hispánica and the Spanish Professional Medical Associations. Other agencies in Washington, D.C., and the surrounding area in which the Hispanic countries participate include the Inter-American Defense Board (with its college) and the Inter-American Development Bank (IDB). Other institutions in the area concerned with Hispanic affairs include the Hispanic American Heritage Committee, the Centro Anglo-Español, the Club de las Américas, the Club de Puerto Rico and the Foundation for the Advancement of Hispanic-Americans.

The present Spanish Embassy building is by no means Spanish in style. It was built for use by the vice president of the United States. It is situated on 16th Street and Meridian Hill, so named because a stone was placed there to mark the zero meridian of the nation. A covered patio was built later—with Spanish tiling and a fountain, presided over by a ceramic picture of the Virgin of the Kings—and a vestibule with Spanish chairs and other pieces of Spanish furniture; portraits of King Alphonso X and Queen Victoria Eugenia, painted by Fernando Alvarez de Sotomayor; an alabaster bust of Charles V, possibly by Pompeyo Leoni; and a Spanish coat of arms that belonged to the first Spanish legation in Philadelphia. On the walls of one of the chambers in the embassy is a fine collection of small paintings by Eugenio Lucas and in another, a collection of princesses painted by Jacobo Van Loo. The ballroom is presided over by a portrait of Charles II by Antonio Rafael Mengs, flanked by two colossal Gobelin tapestries on the side walls. A screen depicting the departure of Columbus from the port of Palos and other paintings, such as the portrait of the baron of Carondelet, governor of Louisiana, complete the collection of works of art owned by the Spanish state in the ambassador's residence.

The chancellery, for many years on the other side of the patio, was adorned with a tapestry by David Teniers, and an oil painting of Pedro de Luján, Silva, Góngora y Menéndez de Avilés, duke of Almodóvar del Río, and *adelantado* of Florida. On the walls of the different offices hung various portraits of former heads of the Spanish mission and other diplomats who had served here. Today, it has been moved to an independent building.

There are many more buildings in Washington showing Spanish influence. Many have been constructed with the Guastavino vault invented by the Spanish-American architect Rafael Guastavino: the parish of the Sacred Heart (near the Spanish Embassy); the church of St. Anne; Washington Cathedral (Episcopalian), which has in its south door eight sculptures by Spanish artist Enrique Monjó; the Supreme Court building; the Army War College; the Trinity College chapel; the buildings of the National Archives (holding much material of interest for the history of Spain in America); the Departments of Commerce and of the Interior; the buildings housing the offices of senators and representatives; the National Academy of Science; the Scottish Rite Masonic Temple (opposite the Spanish Embassy); some buildings at Georgetown University; and the Basilica of the Immaculate Conception.

The Basilica of the Immaculate Conception is impressive chiefly on account of its immensity. Above one of the altars is venerated a reproduction in mosaic of the Immaculate Conception by Bartolomé Esteban Murillo. The basilica forms part of the campus of the Catholic University of America, which has an important department of Spanish, the Oliveira Lima Library and the Ibero-American Institute. The university grants annual scholarships endowed by the Association of Daughters of Isabella.

Georgetown University, run by the Jesuits, is the oldest in the area. In December 1964 various events were held to commemorate the 175th anniversary of its foundation and the most important universities of the world were invited. The Spanish Universities of Zaragoza and Madrid represented all Spanish universities. The Institute of Languages and Linguistics of Georgetown University, directed for many years by Professor Roberto Lado, is famous. Apart from Spanish, 20 other modern languages can be studied here. The prince of Asturias, heir to the Spanish Crown, graduated here with a master's degree in international relations. The university awards the Axacan Prize in memory of the Spanish Jesuits who suffered martyrdom there in nearby Virginia (see below). Also important are the Departments of Spanish of American University, George Washington University, Howard University and Maryland University where distinguished visiting professors have included for many years Juan Ramón Jiménez, Gregorio Salvador in 1963, Miguel Delibes in 1964 and others.

Spanish Place-Names
There are not many streets in greater Washington, D.C., bearing Spanish names. However, several streets include the name Farragut, four use Columbia (Columbia Road, Columbus, Columbia Pike and Columbia Avenue), and there are as well streets named Alamo, Galvez, Hayas, Magellan Avenue, Portal, Quintana, Toledo Road, Toledo Terrace and others.

◆ THE TWO VIRGINIAS ◆

This area was called Tierras de Ayllón by the Spaniards, due to the landing in 1526 of Vázquez de Ayllón and his colonists in the Carolinas, and was used on maps drawn of the surrounding coasts thereafter.

The English colony of Jamestown was founded on May 24, 1607. A museum, which housed a copy of Tordesillas's treaty, donated by the Archive of the Indies, Seville, was built when it celebrated its 350th anniversary. Not faraway, in Yorktown, the British Cornwallis surrendered to Washington's and Rochambeau's armies on October 18, 1781, after fundamental Spanish cooperation. In the neighboring city, Newport News, stands the Mariners' Museum, built by Archer Huntington, who was the donor of many items, such as a painting by Joaquín Sorolla of Columbus leaving Palos on his first voyage and José María López Mezquita's portraits of the trustees and officers. Richmond, the capital of Virginia, keeps many Spanish art pieces in its museum.

Despite its predominantly Anglo-Saxon history, the state of Virginia was introduced to Western civilization by Spaniards. (A French map of the 17th century includes in Virginia ["Americae Pars Septentrionalis"] a region called "Medano Hispanis.") The first European language spoken on Virginian soil was the Spanish of Garcilaso de la Vega or the marquis de Santillana and of the missions that were established by the Jesuits at Chesapeake Bay between 1570 and 1571, 37 years before the first Englishman set foot in this area—although there has been much debate among scholars about this point.

At one time the site of the first mission was believed to coincide with a spot called Triangle not far from the Marine Corps base at Quantico, a few miles from Washington. (It is reached by traveling south on highway 1 and a large crucifix on the left-hand side of the road indicates its direction.) Nearby, at Aquia Creek, a plaque unveiled in 1933 commemorates the foundation of the Spanish missions in the area. However, while an organized Catholic settlement in Virginia certainly dates back to around 1650—confirmed in 1924 by the discovery of the remains of the cemetery wall and the headstones of several Catholic families, such as the Brents (Mary, the wife of George Brent, was the daughter of Lord Baltimore)—a more probable location is in the surroundings of what was eventually to be Jamestown.

This district, where the Indian township of Axacán stood, was visited in September 1570 by a seven-man Spanish expedition including Fathers Juan Bautista Segura and Luis de Quirós, Brothers Sancho de Cevallos and Gabriel Gómez, and Don Luis, the brother of the Indian chief of this area. In 1561, he had been taken prisoner by the expedition led by Angel Villafañe, had been sent to Mexico and, there, had been protected by Viceroy Luis de Velasco, who had him baptized, gave him the name Luis and took him to Spain, where he even presented him to Philip II. In 1566 he had accompanied some Dominicans to Axacán in an unsuccessful missionary venture. Back in Mexico, Don Luis appeared to be thoroughly certain of the Catholic faith and was chosen to take part in the missionary expedition of Father Segura.

The Spaniards were surprised at the conditions in the area, which conflicted with the description given by the convert. Six years of poor crops had brought famine and

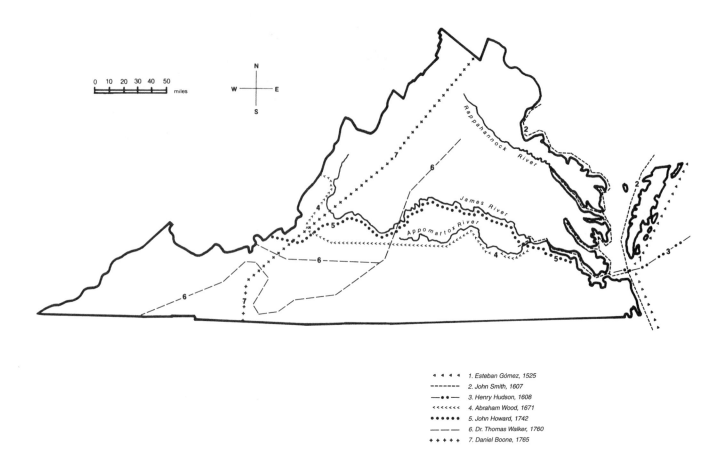

Explorers in Virginia, 1525–1765. Facts On File.

Legend:
◄ ◄ ◄ ◄ 1. Esteban Gómez, 1525
- - - - - - 2. John Smith, 1607
—•—•— 3. Henry Hudson, 1608
<<<<<< 4. Abraham Wood, 1671
••••• 5. John Howard, 1742
— — — 6. Dr. Thomas Walker, 1760
+ + + + 7. Daniel Boone, 1765

a marked decrease in the local population. Such were the impressions that Father Segura and Father Quirós conveyed in a letter to Juan de Henestrosa, governor of Cuba, asking for aid and for seed to be sent by March or April. They spent the winter awaiting these provisions and, in the meanwhile, built some huts as accommodation and to serve as a chapel. Don Luis stayed with them as their interpreter and as teacher of the native language, until, in February, he disappeared. Father Quirós and two brothers set out for the Indian village in search of Don Luis. Although they were received warmly by him and his companions, on the way home they were ambushed and shot to death with arrows. Don Luis donned the habit of Father Quirós and appeared in this disguise before Father Segura and his remaining companions, who were martyred on their knees. Only one youth, Alonso, escaped with the help of the brother of Don Luis by whose account the history of the tragic deaths of these missionaries is known.

The aid requested from Governor Henestrosa arrived in the spring on a small boat, accompanied by Vicente González and Brother Juan Salcedo. Seeing no sign of the missionaries, they grew suspicious and even more so when they saw some Indians wearing the Jesuit habits. Not wishing to fall into a trap that the Indians were endeavoring to lay for them by making every sign of friendship, they succeeded in capturing two Indians and weighing anchor. When Admiral Menéndez de Avilés heard this story, he decided to punish the culprits and set sail from St. Augustine bound for Axacán, stopping on the way at Santa Elena to pick up Juan Rogel and Francisco de Villarreal.

At Axacán, he disembarked with 30 soldiers and captured a considerable number of Indians, who accused Don Luis of being the culprit. He promised to spare the lives of the prisoners if they brought Don Luis to him; when they were unsuccessful, he hanged eight of them from the mainmast of the vessel. Rogel wanted to continue the search inland with the help of Alonso, who had returned to the scene, but the admiral decided to withdraw and set sail for Santa Elena. The martyrdom of the Jesuits at Axacán was the reason why the general of the order, the Spaniard Francis Borgia, decided to recall his missionaries from United States territory, and they abandoned their evangelizing efforts in North America for a time.

Due homage was paid to the martyrs of Axacán in the course of ceremonies held to commemorate the 350th anniversary of Virginia. The celebrations were held on November 10, 1957, at the Jamestown Festival Park, organized by the Axacán Memorial Society, and attended by the Spanish ambassador and his wife the countess of Motrico.

From the earliest days, Virginia shared the interest shown by the other colonies in Spanish and Hispanic civilization. Spaniards also visited Virginia (one Francisco Miguel is recorded as having spent eight months in Jamestown around 1610), and Spanish books could be found in the colonists libraries. Thomas Jefferson spoke excellent Spanish and maintained contact with booksellers in Madrid. Although his knowledge of Spanish is thought to have been advanced by 1775, his visits to Europe and, specifically, to France, contributed to his perfecting it. Jefferson's interest in Spanish stemmed from obvious reasons: the existence of the language in America together with English, its usefulness for the future relations of the new country with Spain and Spanish America, and Spanish participation in events on the North American continent.

Jefferson's interest is reflected in his insistence that Spanish be taught at William and Mary College at Williamsburg and in the institution of a chair of modern languages, Spanish among others, at the University of Virginia, which he founded. The personal influence of Jefferson in the direction of this institution should not be overlooked. Even the plans of the harmonious main buildings, which are still standing today, were drawn by him, as were those of his home at Monticello, near Charlottesville, where the university stands.

Jefferson wished George Ticknor, a prominent Hispanicist at Harvard, to oversee the teaching of Spanish, but when the latter declined the invitation, he recommended George Blaetterman, who held the chair from 1825 to 1840. He was succeeded by Maximilian Schele de Vere, of Swedish origin, who had a decisive influence on hundreds of students of Spanish between 1844 and 1895. The University of Virginia has continued to keep its interest in the Spanish language very much alive, as have other schools in the region.

Across the Potomac from Washington, D.C., in Virginia stands Mount Vernon, George Washington's home, where he and his wife are buried. While he was in retirement here, in 1786, he received a gift of a vicuna blanket from the Spanish representative Gardoqui, and a donkey sent by the count of Florida-blanca on behalf of Charles IV; to judge from Washington's letter to the Spanish diplomat dated January 20, 1786, these gifts were greatly appreciated.

Spanish Place-Names

Localities with Spanish names in Virginia include Altavista, Buena Vista, Callao, Columbia, Columbia Pines and Saluda; in West Virginia, Adrian, Alma, Arista, Aurora, Bolivar, Buena, Julia, Leon and Mingo.

NORTH CAROLINA

Spanish ships appeared off the coasts of North Carolina one day at the beginning of the 16th century. Licenciado Lucas Vázquez de Ayllón, a native of Toledo, reached the New World in 1504 and held the post of alcalde mayor (senior mayor) on the island of Hispaniola, where he married Ana Becerra, a wealthy landowner. Having financial means, in 1520 he sent a caravel under the command of Francisco Gordillo to explore the Atlantic coast to the north. At the Lucayas Islands, Gordillo found another caravel commanded by Pedro Quexós, to whom Juan Ortiz de Matienzo had entrusted a similar mission, and they decided to join forces. On June 24, 1521, Gordillo and Quexós landed at a point, which the local inhabitants called Chicora, near the present Cape Fear River; they called it Jordan and set up a wooden cross as a symbol of Spanish sovereignty over the land.

Various contacts with the local Indians were pursued, but ultimately a group of them were kidnapped by the Spaniards to take with them on their return south. Some Indians died on the voyage during a storm in which one of the caravels sank, while others refused to eat and died of hunger. When Gordillo reached Santo Domingo with his cargo, he was imprisoned for disobeying the superior's orders not to disturb the natives; Diego Colón (Columbus) ordered the surviving Indians to be set free and placed in the care of Ayllón and de Matienzo until they could be returned to their homes.

One of the Indians entered the service of Ayllón as a servant, was baptized and given the name cf Francisco Chicora; he learned Spanish and was therefore able to describe his country to his master in detail. Armed with this information, Ayllón traveled to Spain, where, on June 12, 1523, he obtained from Emperor Charles V a charter authorizing him to colonize the new territory, under which he undertook to take missionaries with him, to build churches, not to enslave the Indians, to furnish a report on what he discovered and to provide the expeditionaries with supplies, medicines, a doctor and a surgeon. The expedition sailed in mid-July 1526. It was composed of five ships (among them the *Bretona*, the *Santa Catalina* and the *Churruca*) under the command of Ayllón himself, with the navigator Pedro de Quexós, the Dominican fathers Pedro Estrada, Antonio Montesinos and Antonio de Cervantes, 500 men, and a considerable party of Negroes, Indians and women.

The expedition landed in the vicinity of Cape Fear and the river previously called Jordan, Ayllón immediately set his men to work building a vessel to replace one which had been lost when entering the river. He himself designed it with a mast so that it was usable with sails or oars. But, the place chosen was not suitable, being marshy and unhealthy.

Moreover, Chicora and other native guides disappeared, thus depriving the expedition of their assistance to gain the friendship of the Indians, their relatives and friends. A second site was chosen, in the neighborhood of the present locality of Georgetown, in South Carolina. As a result of these explorations and establishments, the name Ayllón appeared on many maps of the New World thereafter, and the area more or less between Florida and the Chesapeake Bay was called Tierras de Ayllón (Ayllón's Land).

The first English attempt to establish a colony on the continent was that of Walter Raleigh, on Roanoke Island, North Carolina, in 1584, part of the chain of sandbanks parallel to the mainland, which protect it and provide its splendid beaches. However, these four arcs along the coasts of Carolina had also been explored by the Spanish: the first of them is marked "Barra de S. Tjago" on a French map of the early 17th century, which vertices at Capes Hatteras (called Cape Fernando on the map), Look-out (Cape Engaño) and Fear (Cape Trafalgar on that map, which had been called Cape Terra Falgar on the map drawn by Gutiérrez in 1562 and Traffalgar in a previous one by Ribeiro, dating from 1529).

De Soto, Pardo and Boyano

Driving south from Virginia along the Blue Ridge Parkway, one comes to the village of Cherokee, on the southern slopes of the Great Smokies, a reserve of the Cherokee Indians found by the Spanish Hernando de Soto and a group of his soldiers, in 1540. The conquistador passed through this region in what are now Highlands, Franklin, Hayesville and Murphy, skirting Lake Hiwassee. Some stones with inscriptions recall this Spanish pioneer trek.

In the winter of 1566–1567, Spaniards taking part in the Pardo and Boyano expedition appeared in this region at the township of Xualla, in the present Polk County. After negotiating with the natives and in view of the snow that had fallen on the nearby mountains, Captain Juan Pardo decided to halt their westward march and construct a fort, which they called San Juan de Xualla, near the source of the Wateree River. In two weeks the building was completed and left in charge of Sergeant Hernando Boyano and 13 soldiers.

Pardo continued his explorations eastward across fertile countryside until he reached Guatari, the residence of two noble chiefs and a veritable court, where the expeditionaries stayed for two weeks enjoying the generous hospitality of the natives, who expressed a desire to become Christians. Pardo left the chaplain Father Sebastián Montero, accompanied by four soldiers, in this locality to found a mission, and Guatari became the first successful mission in the United States. In view of some alarming news that he received from Santa Elena, Pardo decided to return to that post.

In the meanwhile, Sergeant Hernando Boyano fought two bloody battles in which he defeated two bellicose chieftains; the second of these battles cost the defeated chieftain the lives of 1,500 Indians. These results made it possible for Boyano to head west and reach the Little Tennessee River, in Jackson County, through which de Soto had passed a few years earlier.

Heading into Georgia, into the rich Chiaha area, he rejoined Pardo's party at a point near present-day Rome. After exploring that region and Alabama, Pardo turned back toward North Carolina. Near Cauchi (in the westernmost area), he erected a fortified outpost to which he assigned a garrison of a corporal and 12 soldiers, together with the interpreter Olmedo. He visited Xualla once more and reinforced the garrison with 30 men under the command of Alberto Escudero; at Guatari, he decided to provide military defenses for the mission and left a garrison consisting of a corporal and 17 soldiers. He then returned to his base on March 2, 1568.

Historian Herbert Ketchan found a 900-page narrative of Pardo's second expedition, written in April 1569, by the notary Juan de la Bandera at Santa Elena. According to the tale, Pardo reached Charlotte, North Carolina, and a town de Soto had called Xuala on September 24, which Charles Hudson places near Marion. They then pushed on to the present Ashville and crossed the Great Smoky Mountains.

The results of de Soto's efforts, however, were short lived. In view of the impossibility of receiving assistance from Santa Elena, the garrisons grew impatient and there were Indians uprisings. Subsequently, some destroyed and others abandoned, the outposts set up by Pardo during his expedition gradually disappeared so that not the slightest trace of them remains. Nonetheless, the Spaniards had established settlements in North Carolina many years before the British attempted to found a colony in Virginia.

The State of Franklin

Less well known than the early explorations are the ties established between Spain and part of the territory of North Carolina only a few years after independence, in the attempt to create the new State of Franklin.

The inhabitants of the countries of Virginia and North Carolina lying to the west of the Appalachians were united in their displeasure at the isolation that independence had brought them and the few advantages achieved. The rural policy of North Carolina only increased their discontent. When the state legislature declared the West open, this encouraged speculation rather than new settlements so that dealers in the East grew rich without setting foot in the West, at the expense of the pioneers by whose personal effort the land was being brought under cultivation. The disgust of the inhabitants in the region of the Holston River reached a peak in the spring of 1784, following the vote of the state legislature to grant the western areas to the federal state and the appearance of the ordinance passed by Congress in Washington, D.C., from which could be deduced an invitation to form new states. Meeting in August at Jonesboro (today in the state of Tennessee), they voted unanimously in favor of forming a new state, which in principle would be called Frankland (a land of free men).

At a later meeting in December, the name Franklin was chosen, John Sevier was appointed governor and petitions were sent to North Carolina, Virginia and the federal Congress for recognition of the new state. It was to be formed from territories belonging to those states and also to Georgia and the present states of Alabama and Tennessee. In spite of the authorization given by the new legislature to take those territories by force if necessary, Sevier encountered difficulties of all kinds. Georgia and South Carolina claimed problems with the Indians along the frontier; the Virginian countries ultimately gave way to pressure from the prestigious governor, Patrick Henry; and the federal Congress did not approve the petition. Sevier, who enjoyed great prestige following his military actions in the War of Independence and his expeditions west of the Appalachians, felt that the only solution to the situation was to commission James White, the former superintendent of Indian affairs in the South, to open negotiations with Diego de Gardoqui, the Spanish diplomatic representative to the United States in New York, and with the Spanish governors at Havana and New Orleans, suggesting a plan whereby the independent State of Franklin would unite with Spain.

Gardoqui gave White his blessing to return to Sevier and encourage him to enter into correspondence with him. As a result, Sevier offered to transfer the State of Franklin from the United States to Spain. On September 17, 1788, Sevier wrote Gardoqui a letter, which was delivered personally by his son James, stating, "The people of this region have come to truly realize upon what part of the world and upon which nation their future happiness and security depend and they immediately infer that their interest and prosperity entirely depend upon the protection and liberality of your Government." Equipped with a passport provided by Gardoqui, White sailed to Havana for talks with the Spanish captain general, Bernardo de Gálvez (who had

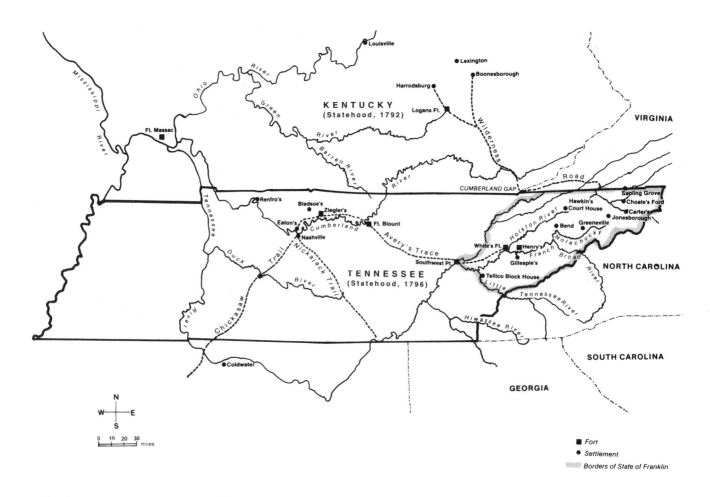

The State of Franklin, 1779–1796. Facts On File.

fought against the British during the War of Independence) and with Manuel Gayoso, commander of the Spanish stronghold on the Mississippi, Natchez.

On April 15, 1789, White reached New Orleans, where he informed Governor Miró of his requests of Spain: recognition of the independence of the State of Franklin, extension of the boundaries of Franklin farther south (into Tennessee) and permission to establish trade on the Alabama and Mississippi Rivers. Miró gave him assurances regarding the trade privileges sought and the sympathy of Spain toward the new state, but he confessed that he did not have authority to ensure the assistance of Spain for sedition from a country with which Spain was at peace.

Armed conflict broke out on February 27, 1788, between Sevier's followers and North Carolinians, commanded by John Tipton, and the continued refusal of the federal Congress and that of North Carolina to recognize independence, thus further strengthening the determi-

nation of the governor of Franklin to seek the cooperation of Spain. On April 18, 1788, Gardoqui informed Sevier that "His Majesty is very favorably inclined to give the inhabitants of that region all the protection that they asked for," together with permission to use the Mississippi in the event of association with Spain.

On June 21, 1788, the Constitution of the United States came into force when it was ratified by the ninth state, New Hampshire, thereby consolidating the power of the central government. Moreover, Spanish assistance was inadequate. The frontier territory constantly came under attack from Indians, who in the summer of 1788, destroyed four supply caravans. The State of Franklin required the protection of a superior power; if aid were not forthcoming from Spain or Britain, all dreams of independence would have to be abandoned. In frustration John Sevier took to drink, making it possible for his enemy, Tipton, to arrest him on October 10 and put him in chains. All plans for the State of Franklin were dashed.

◆ ◆ ◆

James B. Duke was a responsible for the foundation, in 1925, of the university that bears his name at Durham. The library is remarkable for its large collection of works about Latin America, particularly Peru, Colombia, Bolivia, Brazil and Ecuador. The Spanish department publishes an important quarterly review, *The Hispanic American Historical Review*.

Founded in 1792, the University of North Carolina has a Spanish department and university press that have been known for their quality for many years, and for their attention to past and present Spanish affairs. The library, which contains many Spanish and Spanish-American books, has a noteworthy collection of Spanish plays, numbering over 20,000. The university publishes the journal *Hispanófilo* three times a year.

The North Carolina Museum of Art, at Raleigh, has a fine collection of still lifes by Gerardo Meléndez and Jesús Romero Gorriá; a portable altar of the Bermejo school; *Christ Before Pilate* by Luis Borrassá; *St. John the Baptist* by José Ribera; and *Blessed Giles Before Pope Gregory IX* by Bartolomé Esteban Murillo.

Spanish Place-Names

Although the name Ayllón was to disappear from local geography in time, other Spanish names have survived in this state. They include Cabarrus and Columbus Counties, and the towns Aurora, Barco, Celo, Cerro Gordo, Columbia, Columbus, Lola, Manteo, Oliva, Peru, Ronda and Saluda.

◆   # SOUTH CAROLINA   ◆

Vázquez de Ayllón and the First Settlement: San Miguel de Gualdape

The first words that the English heard the Indians utter when they arrived on the shores of South Carolina were words of welcome in broken Spanish. This was due to the fact that Licenciado Lucas Vázquez de Ayllón had established the colony of San Miguel de Gualdape in 1526 in the neighborhood of present-day Georgetown, at the mouth of the Maccamaw or Black River in Winyah Bay; this was the first European attempt to establish a permanent settlement on the North American continent. It has not been possible to determine its position exactly, because the land used to be owned by the daughter of the famous financier Bernard Baruch, who refused to allow any archaeological work there. Following her death a few years ago, little more precise information concerning the whereabouts of the colony has been unearthed.

In 1520, as we have seen, Ayllón dispatched a ship from North Carolina under the command of Francisco Gordillo to explore the Atlantic coast to the north. In the light of the information provided on their return by Francisco Gordillo and Pedro Quexós, Ayllón obtained a charter from the emperor and organized the expedi-

tion of 1526, which did not succeed in establishing a settlement at the first site chosen, near Cape Fear, but moved farther south to a point not far from Pee Dee River. This second site was named San Miguel de Gualdape. The men traveled to the spot overland on foot, while the supplies, women and children came by sea.

The abundant vegetation, trees and plants, and a large variety of animals, not all wild, seemed to augur well for the future of the new colonists. They might have succeeded had they not been decimated by diseases and epidemics (smallpox, typhus, dysentery and malaria), and if the cold climate had not proved so hard to endure for those accustomed to tropical temperatures. As a result, Ayllón himself died on October 18, 1526, after appointing his nephew, Juan Ramírez, as his successor. Ramírez was away at the time, and Francisco Gómez, as lieutenant to Ayllón, therefore took command. Taking advantage of the prevailing discontent, Ginés Doncel and Pedro de Bazán imprisoned Gómez and committed all kinds of outrages, until the Negro slaves rebelled and freed the prisoners. Bazán was executed. Disheartened and discontented, the colonists decided to return to Hispaniola, where 150 of them arrived after tragic vicissitudes and burying Lucas Vázquez de Ayllón at sea. Ayllón's rights were subsequently claimed by his son Luis but were refused by the Spanish Crown. (Some scholars believed that San Miguel was located on the coast of Georgia.)

Santa Elena and the Hazards of Survival

As Tristán de Luna had been unsuccessful in colonizing Pensacola, the viceroy of New Spain, Luis de Velasco, sent Angel de Villafañe to Florida to transport his settlers to the eastern Atlantic coast. (King Philip II considered that a site there would be more practical for the purposes of his American policy.) Villafañe reached Pensacola on March 14, 1561, with two ships and after leaving victuals for the garrison, set course for the future settlement. Although some expeditionaries deserted at Havana, in May he sailed for the coast of Carolina, which he explored as far as the Chesapeake Bay, including the colony in Axacán (Virginia). On May 27, he reached Santa Elena (present-day Port Royal, South Carolina) and entered the mouth of the river. Although it was hard to make headway upstream he succeeded in penetrating some five or six leagues inland. There, Villafañe took possession of the territory in the name of the king, carved crosses on the trees and erected a large cross on the beach. Since there were no inhabitants and the land was marshy, he weighed anchor and sailed round Cape Román (marked on the map by Ribeiro), now called Cape Romain. On June 8, he took possession of the Pee Dee River and called it the Jordan River, at a spot not far from Ayllán's unsuccessful colony. Not finding anywhere that he considered suitable for a settlement, he abandoned the project and returned to Hispaniola in July 1561.

In May 1562, French ships commanded by Jean Ribaut appeared on the Atlantic coast. After exploring the coast of Florida, they came to a large river, which they took to be Ayllón's Jordan River. Encouraged by the enthusiasm of his men at the conditions of the place, Ribaut decided to found a settlement, which he called Port Royal (the name which it still bears to this day) and built a fort, named Charles Fort in honor of French king Charles IX.

But the presence of the French at Port Royal was short lived. Famine and other problems gave rise to a revolt among the settlers until, making use of what few tools they had at their disposal, and with the help of the Indians (who were eager for them to leave), they succeeded in building a vessel. Not all of them reached France; the survivors of shipwreck and cannibalism among themselves were imprisoned in England after being seized by an English ship.

No traces of the French were left in the region when Admiral Menéndez de Avilés carried out a tour of inspection in 1566. He intervened in a local feud between the chieftain of Orista and the chieftain of the neighboring region of Guale to the south and Orista Indians who had been taken as prisoners by their rivals were set free. Great celebrations ensued in honor of Menéndez. At the end of the feast, the admiral, seated on a high dais, received an oath of fealty from all the chiefs who had gathered, amid the whoops and cries of their subjects who were present. This visit by Menéndez de Avilés marked the beginning of the construction of a mission and fort, San Felipe, at the mouth of the Coosawatchie River (on a later French map, it is shown with the name Cruz Hispanis).

As a result of expeditions into the interior by Captain Juan Pardo, two caravels from Spain brought 193 farmers and their families. By October 1569, the settlement, which was called Santa Elena, numbered 237, under the command of Esteban de las Alas. A Jesuit, Father Rogel, was put in charge of the mission; he had recently arrived in America with the first batch of missionaries sent by Francis Borgia (later made a saint) at the request of Menéndez and became the first resident priest in South Carolina. His work at Orista, which lay 12 leagues from the fort, was helped by his quick mastery of the native tongue (in six months). He built a chapel and a house with the Indians' assistance, but failed in his attempts to turn them into a sedentary people. Gradually a rift began to grow between Father Juan Rogel and his new parishioners because of the Jesuit missionary's attacks on Satan, whom the Indians liked because they felt him to be the dispenser of ferocity and courage, and the inevitable requisitioning of food (owing to the lack of supplies) on orders from the commander of the *presidio*, Juan de Vandera. Discouraged, Father Rogel returned to Santa Elena on July 13, 1570. In the course of the summer, beset by the heat, mosquitoes and other insects that made life unbearable, Esteban de las Alas decided to abandon the fort and sail home to Spain with 120 of his men, arguing that the sharp reduction in the garrison would give those staying behind a better chance of survival.

The ensuing years did not bring peace to Santa Elena. While the commander of the *presidio*, Captain Alonso de Solís, was away, his second-in-command, Hernando de Miranda, adopted a provocative attitude that gave rise to the first serious Indian rising with which the Spaniards had to contend. As before, the scarcity of food made it necessary to requisition supplies, which met with the opposition of the Indians. Boyano, with 20 men, had been entrusted with the task, but deceived by the apparently well-disposed Indians, they perished in a surprise attack on July 22, 1576. The only survivor was a soldier named Andrés Calderón, who succeeded in making his way back to the fort to report what had happened. Two Indians were executed, including Hemalo, who had traveled to Spain, where he had been widely feted. When Solís returned, he sallied from the fort to take reprisals, but he and his men were ambushed. Two thousand Indians then assaulted the fort and killed more than 20 Spaniards. Considering it impossible to hold out any longer Hernando de Miranda made his escape to St. Augustine with the other survivors aboard a pinnace and was promptly dismissed for doing so.

Burned to the ground by the Indians, the fort was rebuilt in 1577 at another spot and called San Marcos by Governor Pedro Menéndez Marqués. (It was discovered in 1949.) Nevertheless, calm did not return. In 1578, Captain Diego de Ordoño, Miguel Moreno and 17 other officers on their way to Santa Elena called at Sapelo Island. Although the Indians received them hospitably at first, the visitors were later murdered. A similar fate was met at Tolomato by the squadron sent from Santa Elena under the command of Gaspar Arias: the captain and the soldiers Nicolás de Aguirre, Sancho de Arango and Pedro Menéndez, nicknamed "El Bizco" (squint-eye), died in the trap laid for them. This unstable situation forced Governor Pedro Menéndez Marqués, a nephew of the admiral, to organize a punitive expedition, but it was not until they reached the township of Cocapoy, in the vicinity of Santa Elena, that they managed to catch up with the main body of fleeing Indians on whom they inflicted a resounding defeat and heavy casualties. The French settlers who had encouraged the Indian rising were exchanged for the Indian prisoners and executed.

A fresh Indian revolt took place in 1580, when they again succeeded in taking the *presidio*. By 1582 it had been reestablished once more, but in 1587, acting on orders from his superiors, the commander, Hernando de Miranda, withdrew the Spanish garrison for good. That same year, the English pirate Francis Drake passed near Santa Elena with the intention of setting fire to the place but was prevented from landing by contrary winds and heavy seas. The withdrawal of the Spaniards marked the end of their permanent presence in South Carolina. Consequently, Santa Elena was abandoned by Spain 100 years before the British arrived.

In 1612, the name Santa Elena was given to the recently created ecclesiastical province that comprised the present states of South Carolina, Georgia and Florida. From 1670 onward, Port Royal—which resumed the French name—became a major center of Anglo-Saxon expansion. On the grounds that it lay in Spanish territory (as even the British recognized) in September 1686, the governor of St. Augustine, Juan Cabrera, dispatched three ships under the command of Tomás de León, who destroyed the colony of Lord Cardross. In 1715, the proximity of the Yamasee, who were on friendly terms with the Spaniards, made it necessary to evacuate the inhabitants of Port Royal. The war placed all the British colonies in the Carolinas in jeopardy, for all the Indian tribes except the Cherokee joined the Yamasee. Thomas Nairne, the official leader of the British traffickers, was surprised at his home at Pocotaligo, 11 miles from Port Royal, tortured and burned to death. Ultimately defeated in war and decimated, the Yamasee sought refuge at St. Augustine and placed themselves under Spanish protection. (The ruins of Santa Elena and Fort San Felipe were discovered in 1979, on Parris Island, by a team of archaeologists and historians.)

Pardo, Boyano and de Soto

In 1566, Menéndez de Avilés's deputy, Captain Juan Pardo, departed from Fort San Felipe, at Santa Elena, and headed into the interior with reinforcements sent from Spain in the Arciniegas expedition. He had with him Sergeant Hernando Boyano, Ensign Alberto Escudero and 125 volunteer soldiers. On November 10 they set out in a northwesterly direction, passing through the friendly districts of Escamacu and Cazao and on the seventh day, reached the locality of Guiamae, in present-day Orangeburg County. They were received cordially by the local chieftains, who took an oath of loyalty to Spain and the Gospel was preached.

The expedition continued on its way, until two days later they came to fertile fields of corn and wild grapes, an ideal spot to found a large town: they were at the confluence of the Congaree and Wateree Rivers, near present-day Columbia, capital of South Carolina. They then came to the fertile area of Tagaya, with abundant springs and brooks, and the Issa district. On the return journey, Boyano found "three mines of very good crystal," and all the expeditionaries took a number of diamonds. According to Juan Ribas (a member of the party who married an Indian woman during the course of the expedition, thereafter known as Luisa Menéndez), Boyano sold one of these stones to a Seville jeweler, who praised its value greatly. They at last reached areas farther north, in what is now North Carolina, and followed the same route back. Pardo repeated the same itinerary on a second expedition in the following September. According to Joseph Judge, "From Santa Elena and Port Royal Sound, Pardo traveled west and north to the village named Guiamae at the juncture of the Congaree and Wateree Rivers. Here he picked up Soto's route, a well-trod trail leading up the Wateree to the town of Cofitachequi. What remains of the town today is an assemblage of mounds on the riverbank outside Camden, South Carolina . . . From here the trails follow the River to Charlotte, North Carolina." On March 2, 1568, Pardo reached Santa Elena and described the visited lands as "good for bread and wine and any kind of livestock." On their travels throughout 1566 and 1567, Pardo and Boyano set up five strategic outposts to serve as a link for the Spanish colonization of the interior and traveled through parts of North Carolina, Georgia and Alabama.

When Hernando de Soto was passing through the northwestern area of South Carolina with his troops, one of the strangest events of his whole trek took place. On May 1, 1540, they reached Cofitachequi, which some historians place in the neighborhood of the state capital, Columbia, while most consider it to have been on the left bank of the Savannah River, by present-day Silver Bluff, near Augusta. They soon saw a young woman approaching; she introduced herself as the niece of the princess governing that province and offered to send a canoe to take the Spanish leader to the presence of her mistress. When the emissary returned to the princess and informed her of the Spaniard's friendly disposition, she decided to meet the visitor herself. The encounter must have been memorable, to judge by the attire of the princess, the members of her retinue, the gifts that were exchanged and the flirtation that ensued between the "red-skinned Cleopatra" and the "Spanish Mark Antony." The whole party was regaled with blankets and skins, wild duck, corn and other food, and half the houses in the township were placed at their disposal as accommodations. The huge pearls given to de Soto were seen as a taste of the many that they could obtain in the future; taken from tombs on the advice of the princess, they weighed as much as 350 pounds. Not satisfied with what he had found so far, Hernando de Soto wished to

head westward for the rich province of Chiaha, which the princess praised so highly. In order to be sure of the truth of her assertions, de Soto invited her to follow him, which she did with ill grace. The romance soon ended. Making their way up the Savannah River, the expeditionaries passed through the present localities of Greenwood and Anderson, and through Oconee County. Here, the princess succeeded in escaping, although de Soto does not appear to have made much effort to retain her, perhaps feeling some remorse. According to the chronicler Hidalgo de Elvas, the princess sought consolation afterward by joining a fugitive negro.

Charleston

Charleston was the spearhead of the British colonial advance southward. Heavy storms scattered two Spanish expeditions sent from St. Augustine to destroy the new settlement, one in 1670, under the command of Juan Menéndez Marqués, and the other in 1686. The commander of the second of these expeditions, Tomás de León, went down with his ship *Rosario*. Charleston was also the starting point for the Woodward expeditions, which proved so troublesome for the Spanish settlements in the Appalachians, and the Moore expeditions, which destroyed the missions around San Luis, Florida. Charleston was attacked in 1706 by a combined French and Spanish fleet; its colonists disapproved of the treaty between Spain and Great Britain, signed in 1739.

It was to Charleston that the enterprising Minorcan Jorge Ferragut came with his ship to help the cause of independence and, in addition to his personal efforts, gave his new country a famous son, Admiral David Farragut. When Charleston was besieged by the British, Jorge Ferragut fought them at sea and later on land with the cannons from his ship when she was disabled in combat. On May 12, 1780, he was taken prisoner when the town fell to the assailing forces but was exchanged later.

On January 9, 1778, Juan Miralles, a businessman in Havana, came to Charleston commissioned by Spain to act as an unofficial observer in the struggle of the revolutionaries against Britain. He remained there until the spring, holding a great deal of correspondence with the governor of Cuba, Diego José Navarro, and with the minister for the Indies. He even dispatched a schooner, which Navarro returned laden with the provisions requested.

The nearby Brookgreen Gardens was established by the outstanding Hispanists Anna H. and Archer M.

Huntington. In 1930, Archer Huntington purchased several plantations in order to turn them into a garden where his wife's sculptures could be exhibited adequately. The philanthropist also commissioned works from various famous artists during the difficult Depression years. In this way an exceptional open-air museum was created with 288 works by 156 artists, in addition to a small zoo for native animals and birds. Mrs. Huntington designed a butterfly-shaped ensemble of walks, and water was pumped from the river to feed an irrigation system along the lines of the Arab irrigation systems in Spain in order to water about 600 different species of trees and plants. Decorative Spanish bricks were used to a wall separating the forest from the gardens. The Huntingtons built a mansion to preside over the gardens and called it Atalaya (Watchtower), like the towers in Andalusia built as lookout points to warn of the approach of Barbary pirates. It was in this retreat that Anna Huntington sculpted her *Don Quixote* for the Hispanic Society in New York.

Spanish Place-Names

Spanish-sounding names in South Carolina include the localities of Columbia, Lamar, Saluda, Seneca, Una and West Columbia, as well as Saluda County.

GEORGIA

The presence of the Spaniards in Georgia is little known, but it lasted from 1566 to 1702, a period marked by the beginning and end of the missions (not counting the unsuccessful Spanish invasion of St. Simons Island in 1742). It also covered a considerable area that stretched up the coast as far as the boundary of South Carolina and west as far as present-day Columbus. The Spaniards can be said to have explored practically the whole territory south of a line drawn from Columbus to Savannah. In his speech at a luncheon given in his honor by King Juan Carlos at the Royal Palace in Madrid in June 1980, President Jimmy Carter pointed out that his home state, Georgia, had been a Spanish colony for much longer than it had been a British one.

Conquistadores and Explorers: De Soto, Pardo, Boyano and Others

There is a possibility, still unverified, that the colony of San Miguel de Gualdape was founded in 1526, in the lands of what today is the state of Georgia. If this were true, it would be 207 years before Oglethorpe sailed up the Savannah River to begin the English colony of Georgia.

Hernando de Soto was the first European to set foot on Georgia soil. He and his expeditionaries passed through this region between March 3 (the date on which they abandoned Apalachee) and May 1, 1540, when they arrived at Cofitachequi. They followed an itinerary that today more or less passes through Bainbridge, Cordele (after passing close to Albany), Hawkinsville (going up the Ocmulgee River), Louisville (not far from Dublin) and Augusta. They visited a number of native townships of better appearance than those seen in Florida. The chronicler Hidalgo de Elvas describes the houses, built like ovens to protect their inmates from the cold, and the barbecues to be found in the homes of the leading inhabitants, where the tributes offered by members of the tribe were deposited. The Indian women reminded him of Spanish Gypsies in their brief attire. Although it seems somewhat unlikely, some authors maintain that, in the course of their westward march, they followed the Savannah River upstream, rested in Habersham and Murray Counties, and passed through Chiaha, now Rome.

In 1567, Captain Juan Pardo and Sergeant Hernando Boyano, on their way from North Carolina, reached the area in which Rome stands today, the famous old region of Chiaha, fertile and set amid plentiful rivers. They spent 10 days here, and the chronicler of the expedition, Juan de Vandera, speaks of it with glowing praise. Farther west, the expeditionaries found gold and silver mines at Chalaume, but their plans to proceed were foiled by the growing hostility of the local Indians, who

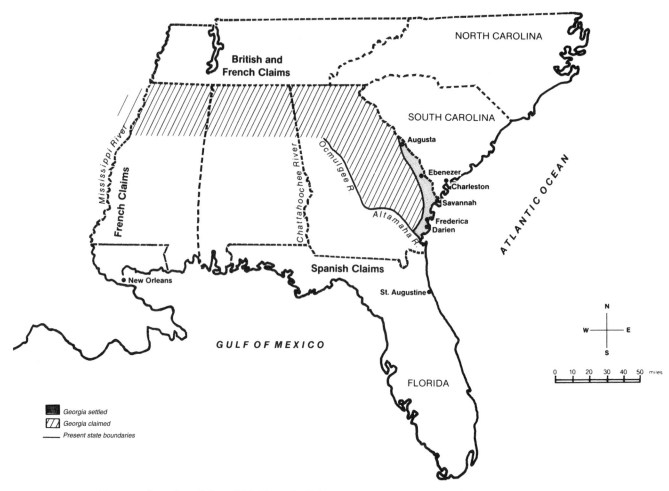

European boundary claims, 1750. Facts On File.

were about 7,000 strong and gave every sign of becoming more and more bellicose. Pardo considered it wiser to retrace their steps but allowed a soldier, Juan de Ribas, to set off for what is now the territory of Alabama. When they reached Chiaha again, Pardo proceeded to build a fort as an outpost to mark the westernmost point under the rule of the Spanish Crown. It took two weeks to build, after which the expedition departed, leaving a corporal and 15 soldiers in charge of the fort. However, he was unable to keep his promise to the chief that he would return within three or four moons. The Indian grew impatient, problems arose among the garrison and the fort had to be abandoned shortly afterward.

On the banks of the Talaje River, now the Altamaha, not far from its confluence with the Ocmulgee, lay the Tama region, the colonization of which caused the governor of Florida, Gonzalo Méndez Canzo, much worry. Favorable reports about the area had been given by the Pardo and Boyano expedition, and an expeditionary, the soldier Juan de Ribas, had married one of the two Indian women brought back. Canzo commissioned a soldier, Gaspar de Salas, and the Franciscans Chozas and Velascola to visit Tama. After an eight-day journey, they were able to report that the area was fertile (in contrast to the poverty of the land known until then), and had abundant vegetation, fruit and game, silver mines, and a marvelous medicinal herb, the *guitamo real*. At the westernmost point, at Ocute (now Hawkinsville), they were given a friendly welcome and departed again amid tears (so the chronicler said). The visitors found traces of a previous Spanish visit: years earlier, Hernando de Soto and his men had come this way and had abandoned a useless artillery piece.

In order to confirm these repeated accounts, Canzo again sent an old soldier and good scout, Juan de Lara, to this area. After nine days' march westward, Juan de Lara came to a mountain chain and a large township,

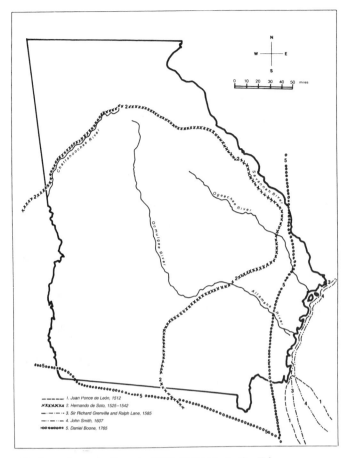

Early explorers in Georgia, 1512–1765. Facts On File.

Olatama. He then turned north and found fertile land stretching as far as a broad river (the Altamaha). From that point he returned home. From this account given it can be deduced that Lara visited the center of Georgia and approached its western boundaries.

Canzo concluded that St. Augustine was situated in an inhospitable and unproductive area, and must depend on the Guale region and its hinterland, the Tama area. This would also extend the Spanish sphere of influence northward and, with it, the area under Spanish rule. King Philip III considered the governor's proposal and ordered the governor of Cuba to inquire as to the advisability of the site chosen for St. Augustine. Pardo de Valdés chose his own son, Fernando, for the task; sailing in the *San Roque*, he landed at St. Augustine on August 30, 1602, and on his return, supported Canzo's proposal. St. Augustine should be maintained on account of its strategic situation affording protection to the fleets bound for Spain, while developing the riches of the Tama area. Consequently, Canzo set to work to consolidate the area for Spain and to repair the damage

done by the uprising of Juanillo. A number of circumstances, including the transfer of Canzo himself, were to prevent the fulfillment of those enterprising projects.

Missionaries

A fundamental book on the subject of Spanish colonization by Professor John Tate Lanning, *The Spanish Missions of Georgia*, and the archaeological work carried out by Professor Lewis H. Larson of Georgia State College have helped make this history better known. Recently the initiatives of Jack Spalding, editor of the *Atlanta Journal*, concerning the development of the Spanish historic sites, and the proposals made by some members of the Georgia Historical Commission as to building a museum at Darien to tell the story of the Spanish missions have sought to revive this history. The ruins that Lanning mentioned in 1934 have now disappeared so that the task of reviving the Spanish past is likely to be even more arduous.

National Geographic magazine published an important article in March 1988, and Dr. David Hurst Thomas carried out excavations with his team and published a book on the island of Santa Catalina where he states the following: "The Spanish mission system in Georgia and Florida was founded earlier, involved more people and lasted longer than the Southwestern system which is so familiar to Americans . . . Few people realize that Georgia and Florida once boasted a string of missions fully comparable to their better-known western counterparts." An initial difficulty in researching this history lies in the differences between the Spanish and the present-day place-names. Ossabaw Island used to be called Asopo; St. Catherines Island, Santa Catalina de Guale; Sapelo Island, Zapala; St. Simons Island, Asao; Jekyll, Ospo; and Cumberland Island, San Pedro. On the mainland, hardly any Hispano-Indian place-names coincide with the present ones. Three Indian groups inhabited the area and therefore maintained relations (peaceful or otherwise) with the Spaniards: the Cusabo Indians, near North Carolina; the Guale Indians, in the center; and the Timucua, in the southern area near Florida.

The history of Spain's presence in Georgia can be characterized as an initial period of imperial eagerness to expand for the purpose of winning new souls for Christendom; a period endeavoring to maintain what had already been achieved; and a final period in which it was impossible to keep a foothold, during which the British appeared and the Spaniards fell back toward the vicinity of St. Augustine, Florida. The first period can be placed between 1566 and 1615; the second, until 1656, the time of the Indian rebellion against Governor Diego de Rebolledo; and the third period, from that year until 1704. The Spanish withdrawal was slow, faced with the scarcity of the material goods needed in such a vast territory, which were increased by the pressure of the British to the north and of the Indians, encouraged and financed by the British. The early years of the 17th century can be considered as the moment of greatest splendor, when the territories received the successive visits of Governors Canzo and Pedro de Ibarra, and of Bishop Altamirano of Santiago, in Cuba, under whose episcopal jurisdiction those territories lay. The missions in the east were the first to be established and the longest lasting; those in the west were less successful, since they were founded at a time when the Spanish imperial impetus was beginning to weaken and British expansionism was awakening.

St. Catherines Island

The first contact of the Spaniards with St. Catherines Island was due to Admiral Pedro Menéndez de Avilés. In the course of his quick tour of the area, he landed on the island on April 4, 1566, and stayed there for four days. He took advantage of his stay to teach the natives about Catholicism, and impressed by their willingness to learn and the need for missionaries there, he decided to ask for them during his next visit to Spain (in fact, he approached the Council of the Indies and his good friend, the general of the Society of Jesus, the former duke of Gandia and future saint Francis Borgia). For fun, two Spanish youths in his party promised the Indian chief to pray to their god for rain, and as a result the chieftain presented them with a number of gifts, such as fish and deerskins, for they were in the midst of a severe drought.

When Menéndez heard about the conduct of his subordinates he was very angry; he decided to punish them for their frivolous and dangerous behavior in matters that could be of great importance for the evangelization of the area. Since he had forbidden them to carry the matter further, the chieftain complained that Menéndez did not wish to pray to his god for help, which proved that his attitude was not as friendly as he claimed. To extricate himself from this situation, Menéndez replied that it would rain if he became a Christian, and the chief in turn declared that he was prepared to do so. He then assembled the Spaniards and the Indians, and kneeling

before an improvised cross, they all sang the litanies and adored and kissed the cross. An hour and a half later a storm burst; it rained abundantly for 24 hours in a radius of five leagues. The amazement of the Indians at the miracle worked by the God of the white men was indescribable.

Despite this fortunate start, the Jesuit priests assigned to St. Catherines Island did not find it easy to preach the gospel among the Guale Indians: after 14 months' work by Father Antonio Sedeño, six by Father Juan B. Segura, four by Father Alamo Gonzalo and six by Father Francisco, only seven people had been baptized, three of them on their deathbeds, and this in spite of the crops distributed among the Indians in a time of need, which had been sent all the way from Cuba by Bishop Juan del Castillo. In 1569, Brother Domingo Agustín Báez also worked there, although only for a year, for he died while doing his missionary work; nevertheless, he had time to draw up a grammar of the Guale language, the first book written within the present borders of the United States. The lack of converts led to the withdrawal of the Jesuits. When the Franciscans arrived in Florida, two were assigned to St. Catherines Island in 1593; they were Father Miguel de Auñón and lay-brother Antonio de Badajoz, who increased the Spanish contingent on the island, where a small garrison had been posted at the *presidio* since the times of Menéndez.

The work of Father Miguel de Auñón and Brother Antonio de Badajoz was flourishing when the rebellion of the Indian Juanillo caused a general upheaval. As an account of the rebellion follows, suffice it to say that the chief on the island was required by the rebels, under threat of death, to kill the missionaries. Since he wished to save their lives, three times he sent messengers to the Franciscans stationed at Asopo urging them to flee and take refuge in the *presidio* so that they could not be found when the attempt was made to assassinate them. Since his pleas were disregarded, the chief himself came to the missionaries and advised them to run away; the missionaries gratefully replied that they were prepared for martyrdom and only wished to say Mass beforehand; the chief promised to give their bodies a Christian burial. The rebels arrived on September 17. First they killed the lay-brother and then Father Auñón, in spite of the quarrel which broke out among the murderers themselves owing to the popularity of their victim among the Indians. The two dead men were buried at the foot of the large cross that Father Auñón had erected.

When Sergeant Alonzo Díaz de Badajoz arrived at the island, sent by Governor Canzo to put down the revolt, he found the mission church and adjoining building gutted and the two tombs open; the bodies had been quartered and tied by the ankles. As a punishment, Governor Canzo issued an order authorizing the enslavement of the Indians in the rebellious areas, but a royal decree, made known on January 31, 1600, at the seat of government at St. Augustine countermanded the order, and Canzo therefore ordered Sergeant Alonso Díaz to return the captives to their homes. The following May, once the rebel leader had been killed, the chiefs in the area took an oath of loyalty to Spain at St. Augustine, with the chiefs from St. Catherines Island among them. The result was that Governor Canzo visited the missionary territories and on February 15, 1603, reached St. Catherines Island, where he was received by the chieftain, Don Alonso, and another six elders, with whom he discussed past and future relations. After abjuring their errors, they received absolution from Father Pedro Ruiz, who had accompanied the governor.

Once the groundwork had been laid, the new governor, Pedro de Ibarra, went on a triumphal tour of the territories at the end of 1604. He landed at St. Catherines Island on November 24 and was received by the new chief of the island, Bartolomé, and other chiefs. The troops accompanying the governor marched in formation for half a league before they reached the township; this made a deep impression on the islanders, who greeted the governor and Father Ruiz, who had accompanied him, by kissing their hands. The visitor responded by embracing them and distributing gifts of all kinds, and by inviting the principal chiefs to his table (an unusual gesture). On November 24, once the church had been rebuilt, Mass was celebrated before a large crowd of people; afterward, speaking through his interpreters Juan de Junco and Santiago, the governor addressed those present and expressed his joy at the visit and the paternal care of the king of Spain for his subjects, proof of which lay in the journey that he was making from distant lands.

In reply the chiefs expressed the joy of their people at seeing and hearing him. As a result of Ibarra's promise to send missionaries, Father Ruiz was posted at St. Catherines Island permanently. He arranged the transfer of the remains of Father Auñón and Brother Antonio to St. Augustine, and prepared the way for the visit that Bishop Altamirano paid on April 30, 1606. The occasion was celebrated with all kinds of festivities, and the Indians showed overwhelming enthusiasm at seeing the bishop, who was most gratified; 286 Indians received confirmation, and a large number of chiefs, led by the chief of the island, Don Diego, took part in the warm welcome. The future of the mission was assured, and the effects of the revolt led by Juanillo had been overcome.

The mission progressed until 1656. However, against the better judgment of the Franciscans, Governor Rebolledo took certain steps to offset the danger of a British attack, and an Indian rebellion broke out. Years of famine and epidemics ensued. In 1670, a British ship appeared and sent a small party ashore; they were attacked immediately, and all were either killed or taken prisoner. In 1673, a Spanish garrison sent to St. Catherines began to build a stone fort, which was completed by the time Governor Diego de Quiroga arrived in 1677. In 1680, there was an outbreak of fighting with various Indian tribes as a result of their alliance with the British. A party of 300 Indians, equipped with British firearms, attacked the fort defended by Captain Francisco Fuentes. The defenders were victorious, but the episode had disastrous consequences: all the natives fled from the island, which therefore had to be abandoned. Plans to repopulate it by bringing 100 families from the Canary Islands could not be implemented owing to the speed with which subsequent events took place.

The anthropologist Dr. David Hurst Thomas, of the American Museum of Natural History in New York, states that the mission of Santa Catalina is the only one in Georgia whose location is exactly known thanks to new radar and magnetometric devices. Owing to this, his team was able to recover 430 human remains, household dishes, musket shots, rosary beads, wheat, crucifixes and glass trading beads numbering in the tens of thousands. "Santa Catalina" says Dr. Thomas "was the northernmost Spanish outpost of the Eastern Seaboard and this historical fact implied considerable size and permanence."

The Neighboring Coastline and the Domain of Juanillo

The inhabitants of St. Catherines Island belonged to the Guale tribe, who also inhabited the nearby coastline and other important population centers during the Spanish period. In present-day McIntosh County, with its center at the town of Darien, the missions of Tolomato and Espogache have been located (the latter in fact being the successor of the former), together with that of Tupique. A little farther south, in neighboring Glynn County, lay the mission of Santo Domingo de Talexe.

Following the fruitless attempts of the Jesuits to evangelize the area and their withdrawal in 1572, 10 years went by without any Spanish missionaries residing there. In 1573, a Spanish officer and 14 soldiers were slaughtered, and in July 1576, a company of 22 white men, with Sergeant Hernando Boyano at their head, perished in an ambush while requisitioning food among the Indians for the *presidio* at Santa Elena. The reprisals applied by Governor Pedro Menéndez Marquéz were not effective, for in 1580 the Indians rose and took the *presidio*. A fresh uprising took place in 1582.

In view of this state of affairs, a Franciscan, Alonso de Reynoso, succeeded in convincing the Council of the Indies in Spain of the need to send missionaries to Florida in considerable numbers. The first group of missionaries arrived in 1584, although it was not until 1593 that a missionary, Father Pedro Corpa, could be stationed permanently at Tolomato. The mission was set up there because it was the place of residence of the *mico*, or principal chief, but the missionary frequently went on visits to subordinate townships with sub-missions. The success of Father Corpa and his fellows in the Guale province was remarkable. They quickly won the Indians over with preaching, gifts and the example of their own good works. The submission that the king's soldiers had not achieved was won by these Spanish sons of St. Francis, who adapted themselves admirably to the hard local conditions and the poverty of the area, but were rewarded by hearing the Ave Maria and Pater Noster intoned with Indian accents.

They attempted to curb the practice of polygamy but were not successful. Indeed, this was one of the reasons that led to the revolt by Juanillo, together with their interference in the government of the tribes. The appointment, through the influence of Father Corpa, of a big chief, or *mico*, other than Juanillo, who would normally have inherited the post, resulted in Juanillo's boundless hatred to which he gave vent by leading a group of disgruntled Indians in a rebellion. Hiding in the church at Tolomato on the morning of September 13, 1597, they dealt Father Corpa a mortal blow on the head as he was entering the church. But Juanillo was not satisfied by the disappearance of his enemy; he wanted to wipe out all the missionaries in the area. The following day he called a number of neighboring chieftains to a conference and encouraged them to uproot the Spanish throughout their territory. His words were undoubtedly convincing, for they resulted in the ensuing murders of the different missionaries in the area.

Impressed by these atrocities, Governor Canzo sent Captain Vicente González with 22 men to Tolomato. As they approached, they found that the natives had fled to the mountains for fear of reprisals, and only one, wounded from a distance by a harquebus shot, could be interrogated. When the governor himself arrived shortly afterward, he found the church and mission buildings in the township burnt down, and only in a few instances was it possible to recover some ornaments, an altar and a statue of St. Anthony of Padua. At the township of Tupique where Father Blas Rodríquez had been posted, his tomb was found open with the head severed from the body; he had been killed on September 16 after singing Mass. It was only in the following spring that Canzo learned of the survival of the only missionary to escape Juanillo's uprising: Father Francisco Dávila had been enslaved at Tulufina, not far from Tolomato, on the banks of the Talaje River, now the Altamaha. Canzo dispatched Lieutenant Francisco Fernández Ecija to look for him; after negotiations with his captors he succeeded in obtaining Dávila's freedom in exchange for some Indians who were being held prisoners at St. Augustine. At first Father Dávila was unrecognizable, such had been his sufferings during captivity. Not only had he been forced to work without respite and subjected to barbarous games by the young Indians, but he had begun to be burned alive: told he would be set free if only he adored the native gods and denied Christ, he staunchly refused and would have suffered martyrdom if an Indian woman had not interceded. As the mother of some Indians who were prisoners of the Spaniards, she urged her people to accept the proposed exchange. Not far from Talaje itself, up the Talaje River, lay the town of Yfusinique. Here Juanillo took refuge and died with 24 of his fellow rebels when an Indian war party, led by the chief of Asao and including many of Juanillo's former allies, launched an attack. His death restored peace to the area for a time.

In May 1600, at St. Augustine, Canzo received a delegation of Indian chiefs led by the *mico* of Espogache, who declared their willingness to swear obedience to the king of Spain, represented by the governor of Florida. Their proposal was accepted on the following conditions: a commitment to cease fighting with the Spaniards and to cooperate loyally with them; an undertaking to submit any complaints to the governor, and not to take the law into their own hands as they had in 1597; and a willingness to receive the governor or his representatives with due honor and respect when he visited their towns. Once the Indians had taken the oath, the governor sent his visitors home aboard Spanish ships. The example set by these chiefs spread, and many others followed suit, with the exception of the chief of Tolomato, who had been a great friend of Juanillo. He was duly punished by the same war party, which put an end to the rebel chief, led by the chief of Asao (St. Simons Island), called Don Domingo, who was duly appointed big chief of the region, a post previously held by the chief of Tolomato. The central mission was moved to Talaxe, and those at Tolomato and Tupique were not reopened.

As big chief, it fell to Don Domingo to receive Governor Canzo at the mouth of the Altamaha River when he visited the region in 1603. In his address to the Indians Canzo discussed trade with them, the rebuilding of the missions and renewed unity between the Spaniards and the Guale people. In his sermon, Father Ruiz stressed similar points and the following day gave absolution at the end of a mass attended by the entire population. After receiving the oaths of loyalty of the chiefs, the governor left Talaxe, where the Indians built the mission of Santo Domingo de Talaxe shortly afterward. On February 10, Canzo arrived at Tupique, where he was received by the local chief and the chief of Espogache, whom he already knew following his visit to St. Augustine. In view of the marks of friendship and submission that he received, the punishments imposed earlier were lifted. The Indians promised to give up their nomadic way of life and settle in the township to be built at Tupique. The visit of a new governor, Pedro de Ibarra, aboard the *San José,* on November 21, 1604, was equally successful: the Spaniards expounded the same viewpoints, and the Indians, the same adherence. Ibarra promised to build a church at Espogache.

As promised, a Franciscan friar was sent to the region. Father Diego Delgado set to work at the Santo Domingo de Talaxe Mission, where he welcomed Bishop Altamirano on his visit on April 22, 1606, and proudly presented 262 Indians to be confirmed, with their chief Don Diego and his brother Don Mateo at their head. The sedentary lifestyle had begun to bear fruit, and consequently, the fruit was literally harvested: the visitor was offered an abundant banquet of local produce. Two days later, the bishop was welcomed at Espogache, where he administered baptism and confirmation on the same day since there were no resident missionaries. Among those to receive the sacraments was Tuguepi, chief of the fierce Salchiches tribe, and one of the followers of Juanillo during his revolt. This visit was followed by a long period of great prosperity.

The revolt against Governor Diego de Rebolledo in 1656 contributed to a gradual deterioration of the situation. The raids by the British and their Indian allies caused a state of great confusion in Guale country, so Governor Juan Marqués Cabrera decided, in 1683, that the Indians should withdraw from the area to greater safety in the vicinity of St. Augustine. Many opposed this move and sought the protection of the British instead, in spite of the advice of the friars. In 1685, a party of Indians led by Altamaha attacked the Timucua town of Afuyca, where they set fire to Santa Catalina Mission and killed or kidnapped the inhabitants. They stopped at Tama on their way home and celebrated their victory. In view of the continual attacks from the north and the fact that many Indians had abandoned the region, those who remained loyal to Spain obeyed the governor's orders. Since they could not hold out any longer, the garrison of the *presidio* at Espogache and the missions in the Tolomato area were abandoned definitively in 1686.

On nearby Sapelo Island (Zápala) there were also a military garrison and a mission station, although the latter was only considered as an occasional "visiting" mission until 1655, when it became possible to post a friar there permanently. It was called San José de Zápala. The *presidio* was built in 1680, on orders from Governor Cabrera, by Captain Francisco Fuentes, when he and his men withdrew from St. Catherines Island. The garrison was so small (at that time there were no more than 290 soldiers in all Florida) that the Spaniards had a hard time when the island was attacked by the British pirate Kinckley.

St. Simons Island and Jekyll Island

Traces of a Spanish past can be found at what is now called St. Simons Island, where a plaque recounts the history of the Spaniards, together with a flag bearing the castles and lions of Castile. The island was known as Asao in Spanish times, and two missions were built here: Santo Domingo de Asao and Ocotonico in the south of the island. Father Francisco de Velascola, a missionary of Herculean stature from Cantabria in the north of Spain was posted to Santo Domingo de Asao and greatly impressed the Indians. He was at St. Augustine when Juanillo rose in revolt; the rebels therefore awaited his return and struck him down as he landed. His habit, worn by one of the Indians, alerted the missions near St. Augustine that a bloody rising was taking place. Don Domingo, the local chief, submitted to Spain again and led the expedition that put an end to Juanillo, and the new mission of San Buenaventura was built on St. Simons Island. This mission encountered the same hardships as others in the region, and they were all abandoned in 1702.

The Spaniards would return to St. Simons Island during the War of the Austrian Succession (1740–1748), known as the War of Jenkins' Ear, during which Britain declared war against Spain on the trumped up pretext that the loss of the pirate's ear was proof of Spanish brutality. In response to the unsuccessful attempts of the British commander James Oglethorpe to take St. Augustine, King Philip V of Spain ordered the Spanish governor, Manuel de Montiano, to lead an expedition to destroy the British settlements in Georgia and the Carolinas. Thirty ships, with 1,300 men aboard, set sail from St. Augustine on June 20, 1742. On July 5, the fleet eluded the fire from the batteries on Fort St. Simon and entered the southern bay. After fierce fighting, Oglethorpe abandoned the fort and withdrew with his men to Fort Frederica, situated in the north of the island. On the morning of July 7, after occupying Fort St. Simon, Montiano sent Captain Sebastián Sánchez to reconnoitre along the way to Fort Frederica. In a battle with Oglethorpe and his men, he was defeated and taken prisoner. When Montiano heard the news, he dispatched Captain Antonio Barba, with 300 men, to set their companions free, and they succeeded in forcing the British to withdraw. The Spaniards halted to rest and prepare a meal and, not foreseeing an ambush, stacked their arms. A British attack took them by surprise, panic ensued, and they beat a hasty retreat. Another strategem led Montiano to believe that powerful reinforcements had arrived, and on the advice of his officers, he was induced to weigh anchor and abandon the venture. The British now found the road to Florida open, and Georgia remained in their hands for good.

This thwarted invasion is depicted in an information center built near the ruins of Fort Frederica, at whose entrance visitors are greeted by the flag of Castile, side by side with the British and United States flags. A commemorative plaque was unveiled in 1913, on the site of Spanish defeat, known as the Battle of Bloody Marsh.

It was to Jekyll Island that Father Francisco Dávila was posted in 1593. Surprised at home by Juanillo and his fellow rebels, he succeeded in escaping by hiding in a palm grove but was discovered in the moonlight, and received several arrow wounds. However, he was not killed thanks to the local chief, who wanted Dávila for himself. He later sold Father Dávila as a slave. He was eventually set free at Tulufina. The island fell upon difficult times afterward, until the mission was reestablished as Santiago de Ocone; it was still among those existing in 1655. Indians allied to the British attacked in 1680; the assault was repulsed thanks to the courage of the Spanish commander and his Indian friends. The order issued by the governor to withdraw southward in 1683, met with resistance among the Indians. The situation worsened as a result of the terror spread through the island by a British pirate attack in 1684. The Spaniards finally abandoned the place at the turn of the century.

One of the historical plaques to be seen on Jekyll Island reads: "In 1736, Spanish Commissioners Don Pedro Lamberto and Don Manuel d'Arcy, sent by Governor Sanchez of St. Augustine, to discuss rival claims to the Georgia coast, were feted on Jekyll . . . Agreeing to leave all questions to the courts of Spain and England, the emissaries returned to St. Augustine pleased with their mission . . ."

Cumberland Island and the Mainland

On the East Coast, missions and *presidios* were established in the territory of the Timucua. The Spanish missionaries continued to live on Cumberland Island (known at that time as San Pedro) and on the mainland (at the mouth of the St. Mary River, formerly the San Mateo River), until their withdrawal to the area around St. Augustine. Cumberland Island would receive the first blood of the martyrs. The Jesuits, urged by Governor Menéndez de Avilés to go as missionaries, sailed on July 28, 1566, from Spain on a ship that was struck by a hurricane near the coast of Florida. After various incidents, the captain sent Father Pedro Martínez ashore in a boat. Several Indians who initially appeared to be friendly set upon the visitors, all of whom managed to escape except the priest, who did not flee. He was killed when a single blow from a club crushed his skull. When Menéndez toured the coast of Georgia in the course of that year, he left a garrison on the island.

When a new batch of Franciscans arrived in 1593, Cumberland was assigned to Father Pedro Fernández de Chozas (who went to the mission later called San Pedro y San Pablo, at Poturibato, with a chapel), Father Baltasar López (who replaced the former at the time of his trip to the Tama region) and Father Francisco Pareja (who worked both on the island, at the village of Chief Don Juan, and on the mainland, at Nombre de Dios Mission). North of the St. Mary River, in what is now Camden County, Father Pedro Ruiz was placed in charge of the villages of San Sebastián and Tocoy, while Father Pedro de Vermejo was in charge of seven villages. These missions, which were the most fruitful in the area, went well from the start and remained loyal to the Spanish. A fundamental factor in their development was the chief of Cumberland, Don Juan, who was an early convert to Christianity and piously attended Mass and the Holy Week celebrations. At that time, different confraternities used to carry statues through the streets of San Pedro in processions inevitably reminiscent of distant Seville.

In the course of their revolt, Juanillo and his followers ventured to land on the island with the intention of murdering the missionaries, the chief and the soldiers at the *presidio*. On October 4, 1597, 400 Indians disembarked silently some distance away, but the barking of a dog alerted several loyal Indians, who managed to warn their chief. Father Chozas and Father Pareja prepared for any eventuality and wrote an urgent note to Governor Canzo asking for reinforcements. The presence of a Spanish brigantine nearby bewildered the intruders as they cautiously approached, and Don Juan took advantage of this to spread further confusion among them so that many took flight in their boats, while others hid in the forests until they were taken prisoner one by one. The reinforcements sent by the governor arrived on October 10, commanded by Sergeant Juan de Santiago; Governor Canzo himself, at the head of 150 Spanish infantry, reached the island a week later. The governor rewarded the loyalty of the islanders by reducing their tributes to symbolic sums. When Don Juan died in 1600, his authority passed into the hands of his niece, Doña Ana.

In the years following the revolt, Fathers López, Pareja and Ruiz left their missions and moved into the northern areas, which were now devoid of missionaries. It was at Cumberland that Governor Canzo began his tour of inspection in January 1603, where he built a model mission. On his return from his visit, he attended a conference of chiefs on February 28 and confirmed the senior authority of Doña Ana. The inauguration on March 10, of the Church of San Pedro de Mocamo, which was fairly large and had a high altar and choir, was a major event; the awed Indians finally overcame their restraint and received assurances that even those on the mainland would be protected thanks to the garrison at the *presidio*. The young chieftainess was appointed the custodian—together with Father López—of the fine building. When Governor Ibarra reached Cumberland Island on November 14, 1604, he was received not by Doña Ana, who had died, but by Doña María Meléndez. Friendly greetings were exchanged, and the loyalty of the natives to Spain became firmly established. When Bishop Juan de las Cabezas Altamirano arrived with his retinue on April 11, 1606, his hosts in Doña María's absence were a newcomer, Father Capilla, and Doña María's son. More than 300 Indians, including several local chiefs, received confirmation.

Santa María Mission, on the banks of the St. Mary River, became the focal point of evangelization on the mainland. Governor Pedro Menéndez de Avilés had built a chapel in the area in 1566, and it became the center of missionary work when the Indians and missionaries were withdrawn provisionally from Cumberland Island, as a precaution following the revolt of Juanillo. When Canzo built a church on Cumberland Island, it again became the centerpiece of the missions, and those on the mainland became "visiting" missions in the charge of Father Juan Bautista Capilla. In 1615, however, a permanent missionary was assigned to the area, and Santa María de Sena became the link between St. Augustine and Talaxe. Near the present locality of St. Mary, the historian John Tate Lanning found the best-preserved ruins in all Georgia, with columns in perfect condition and 34 small windows in the large wall of a two-storied building shaped like a fortress and crowned with battlements of sorts. Jonathan Dickinson visited this mission in 1697, while making his way back to South Carolina after being shipwrecked on the coast of Florida; he was accommodated in a spacious circular room 10 meters in diameter and saw the high standard of learning to which the missionaries had raised the alert Indian boys.

The Southwest

The Apalache missions in Southwest Georgia came into being at the beginning of the 17th century. Established in an area peopled by Muskogi Indians, originally between the Aucilla and Ochleckonee Rivers, and around the present town of Tallahassee (Florida), they belonged to the Franciscan province of Potano, in which there were 1,000 Christians by 1607, according to the reports of Father Francisco Pareja and Father Alonso de Peñaranda. The apostolic harvest must have seemed promising, in contrast with the scant personal and material means available. The constant requests made by missionaries and governors alike in this respect show the growing number of converts and the need for more missionaries to work in the region. By 1655 there were nine missions dependent on the *presidio* and mission of San Luis, in Florida, namely: San Lorenzo de Apalache, San Francisco de Apalache, Concepción de Apalache, San José de Apalache, San Juan de Apalache, San Pedro de Apalache, San Cosme y San Damián, San Luis de Apalache and San Martín de Apalache. Of the 38 mission stations that the Franciscans were running by that time throughout the area (which comprised present-day Georgia and Florida) there were 70 friars and 26,000 Indian inhabitants. The San Francisco de Apalache Mission, for instance, was established among the Oconee Indians, whose main center lay in the neighborhood of what is now Milledgeville; there was another mission for the same Indians, as we have seen, on Jekyll Island. The mission of Nuestra Señora de la Candelaria de Tama was founded in 1680 in the Tamali Indian region (not far from Hawkinsville) and was followed later by that of San Luis de Tamalí.

Several missions were built to care for the Chacato Indians. In 1681, Father Francisco Gutiérrez de Vera is recorded as looking after a mission on the banks of the Ocmulgee River, at Coweta, near the present town of Macon, in Butts County. The Coweta area was a cause of friction between the British and the Spaniards, and became a pawn played alternately by one side or the other. It was the scene of the doings of trader and explorer Dr. Henry Woodward, in 1682, and the attempts to capture him by the Spanish commander of the Apalache garrison, Antonio Mateos, who failed due to the agile flight of the Englishman and the complicity of the local Indians. (He succeeded in destroying the fort built by Woodward and his allies. This chapter ended in Woodward's death.)

The repeated British raids led Governor Quiroga y Losada to erect a fort at Coweta by Captain Primo de Rivera in 1687. The presence of Captain Fabián Angulo with 20 Spanish infantry and 20 loyal Apalachee brought results; at a meeting convened there by regional chiefs, the following May, they voted unanimously to keep faith with Spain. The need for troops to defend St. Augustine forced the governor to withdraw the Coweta garrison after destroying the fort in order to prevent its use by the British. A son of the emperor of Coweta, Chipacasi, was a great friend of Spain, who after being feted by the Spanish governor at St. Augustine, advocated an alliance of the Creek Indians with Spain, thus opposing his father, who favored the British. His personal intervention saved the life of a Spanish cavalry officer, Lieutenant Diego de Peña. A council of war was also held at Coweta, where an Englishman, known to the Spaniards as "Antonio," drew a number of tribes into an alliance against Spain. In a campaign during the early months of 1702, the Apalache missions in Georgia lying between the Flint River and the Chattahoochee River were destroyed, and those of their inhabitants who did not flee southward were killed or taken prisoner. The final blow to the missions in the area was struck by another Englishman, James Moore, in his attacks during January 1704, which had further consequences in the north of Florida.

Also among the first group of settlers to reach Georgia was a group of Sephardim, or Jews of Spanish descent, who had come from England. Three prominent members of their community in London collected the funds needed for the journey: Francis Salvador, director of the Dutch East India Company; Anthony da Costa, the first Jewish director of the Bank of England; and Baron Suasso. Having settled in Savannah, they were not integrated into the community at first, but the services of Dr. Samuel Núñez during an epidemic earned them the grateful acknowledgement of the colonists.

Spanish Place-Names

In light of its colorful past, Georgia certainly deserves an important place in Hispanic-American history. A short list of places that have Spanish names include Adrian, Alamo, Alma, Alto, Aragon, Arco, Buena Vista, Camilla, Celeste, Chula, Colon, De Soto, Engima, Juniper, Martin, Martinez, Mora, Nunez, Pavo, Portal, Resaca, Rincon, Vidalia and Villa Rica, in addition to Columbia County.

FLORIDA

◆   ◆

Florida, the first U.S. territory to come within the European sphere of influence after its discovery by Juan Ponce de León, did not play an active part in the national affairs of the Anglo-Saxon population until the middle of the 19th century. Its history under the Spanish flag, the Stars and Stripes, the Confederate flag and those flags of France and Britain support Florida's claim to be the State of the Five Flags. For 300 years, Florida was a Spanish possession and its Hispanic community is today numerous and influential.

Florida was named by Ponce de León when he landed on Easter—Pascua Florida—in 1513, its name prompted by the exuberant vegetation and the variety of species found there. While still situated in the temperate zone, the shores of Florida are bathed by the warm Gulf stream and have some of the most varied flora in the country. With 3,000 kinds of native flowers and those introduced from Europe, today Florida is a huge multicolored garden set amid lakes, of which there are 30,000. It seems all garden and forest, for dense masses of trees stretch north and south forming forests, some small, but others covering many square miles. The nature reserve of the Everglades, in the southwest, is possibly the best preserved of all the forest beauty spots

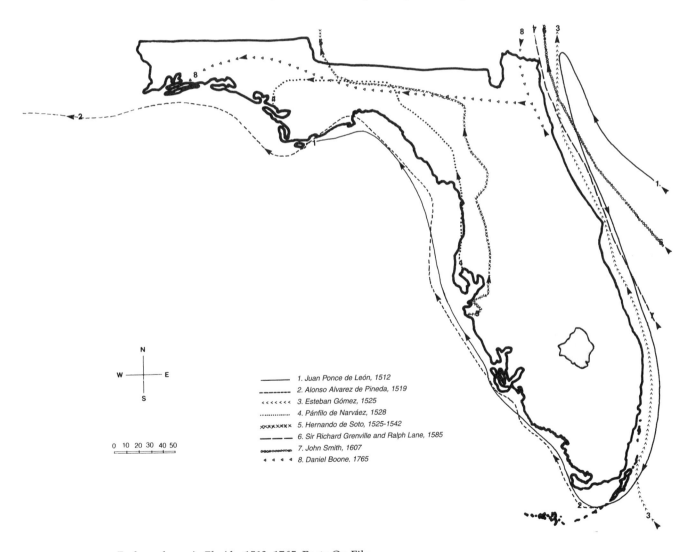

N
W ——+—— E
S

0 10 20 30 40 50

————— 1. Juan Ponce de León, 1512
- - - - - - 2. Alonso Alvarez de Pineda, 1519
< < < < < < 3. Esteban Gómez, 1525
.... 4. Pánfilo de Narváez, 1528
xxxxxxxx 5. Hernando de Soto, 1525-1542
— — — 6. Sir Richard Grenville and Ralph Lane, 1585
ooooooooo 7. John Smith, 1607
◄ ◄ ◄ ◄ 8. Daniel Boone, 1765

Early explorers in Florida, 1512–1765. Facts On File.

and animal reserves in the country. At Palatka visitors can see a vast collection of plants and flowers including 100,000 azaleas, 25,000 chrysanthemums, 2,000 magnolias, 100,000 pines, and thousands of dogwoods, roses and bougainvilleas. There, next to the thick palmettos or slender cypresses, precious mahogany or beautiful mangroves, sight and senses can take in the giant orchid, citrine verbena, colorful azaleas, or orange blossoms. Like the other members of the citrus family, the orange tree is a lasting contribution made by Spain to the scenery in Florida and to its economic development as a predominantly agricultural state. The orange and lemon trees in the Orlando area, in the center of the peninsula or on the west coasts, inevitably remind any Spanish visitor of the banks of the Guadalquivir or the Spanish coast around Valencia.

Concerned at his advancing age and enamored of his young protégée, Ponce de León did not hesitate to hazard his considerable fortune in his search for the Fountain of Youth, and embarking for the miraculous island of Bimini, he sighted and trod the soil of Florida for the first time. He did not achieve his purpose of rejuvenation, but his informants were not far wrong regarding the existence of marvelous medicinal springs, for there are over 27 important springs of that type in Florida (including Silver Springs, Junipero Springs and Rainbow Springs). The name Florida was soon applied to the territories to the north, even as far as Canada, on the first maps proclaiming news of the discovery of North American territory.

East Coast: Independent Republics on Amelia Island

Amelia Island and the town of Fernandina Beach were named after King Ferdinand (Fernando) VII of Spain. Fort San Carlos was built in the vicinity by the Spaniards in 1686 and completed in 1816. All that is left today are two signs, in the surroundings of Bosque Bello Cemetery, indicating its site, as follows:

PLAZA SAN CARLOS

This land high above the Amelia River was a campsite for Indians in pre-historic times, as early as 2,000–1,000 B.C. In the early history of the state, it assumed military importance because of the fine protected harbor on the northern boundary of Spanish Florida. In the first Spanish period, a village of Franciscans and Indians was established here by 1675, and a Spanish sentinel's house

Spanish Florida and the Yazoo Territory, 1783. Facts On File.

was documented in 1696. From 1736 to 1742, James Oglethorpe stationed Highlanders on this site. After the withdrawal of Oglethorpe's troops in 1742, the area served as a buffer zone between the English and the Spanish until 1763, when Florida became a British possession. When Spain regained possession of Florida in 1783, this harbor was an embarkation point for British Loyalists leaving Florida. The U.S. Embargo Act of 1807, which closed all U.S. ports to European trade, made the border town of Fernandina a center for smuggling. On March 17, 1812, a group of Americans known as the Patriots overthrew the Spanish battery, but the U.S. flag replaced the Patriots' standard after one day. Spain regained control in May, 1813, and completed Fort San Carlos in 1816. As the fort's parade ground, this site was named Plaza San Carlos.

FORT SAN CARLOS

On this bluff overlooking the Amelia River, Fort San Carlos was completed by the Spanish in 1816. The fort was made of wood and earthworks and was armed with eight or ten guns. As the Spanish Empire disintegrated, Fort San Carlos became increasingly vulnerable to foreign intervention. Commissioned by representatives of revolting South American countries to liberate Florida from Spanish control, Sir Gregor MacGregor seized the fort in June 1817. After his withdrawal in September, the Spanish attempt to re-assert their

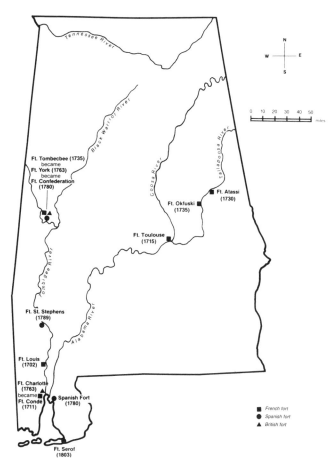

Colonial forts in Alabama (West Florida), 1670–1813. Facts On File.

British. The fort built in 1690 by Governor Quiroga y Losada nearby was also destroyed then.

In 1817, this eastern sector of the peninsula witnessed a series of events that seem closer to fiction than to fact. A Scotsman, Gregor McGregor, who had fought with Francisco de Miranda and Simón Bolívar for the independence of Venezuela (where he married Josefa Lovera), was envious of the glory achieved by the Libertador. Wishing to obtain the wealth and power that had hitherto eluded him, he decided to try his luck in the United States. He obtained support in New York and set sail from Savannah with 150 men aboard two ships bound for Amelia Island. When some of his party disembarked, the Spanish commander, Francisco Morales, thought that the contingent was much larger and surrendered without firing a shot. McGregor then hoisted his flag, which he called the Green Cross of Florida. He sent his prisoners to St. Augustine, where the governor, José Coppinger, suspecting Morales of cowardice, threw him into prison and brought him to trial, at which he was found guilty and condemned to death (although he was not actually executed).

From Fernandina, McGregor sent out enthusiastic proclamations of independence to the countries to the south. Moreover, he invited all the pirates and smugglers infesting the West Indies to use the island as a deposit for their prizes and a market for their cargoes, while his soldiers gave themselves over to pillaging, much to the alarm of the settlers on the island. On one occasion, Coppinger heard that a group of these armed men were near St. Augustine and sent out a detachment that killed 10 of them while the rest were sacking and robbing in the neighborhood. As a result of this setback and the fact that his men began to disband, McGregor decided to abandon the island and leave its government in the hands of two of his followers, James Irwin and David Hubbard, who repulsed the attack launched against the island by Coppinger's reinforced troops shortly afterward.

A few days later, the French pirate Louis Aury appeared off Fernandina and proclaimed himself master of Amelia Island. With the consent of Manuel Herrera, who called himself minister plenipotentiary of the "Republic of Mexico" (Mexico had not yet attained its independence) Aury set up his government, in which he himself held civilian and military powers. When he came ashore, he ordered Irwin and Hubbard to hand the island over to him, to which they agreed for financial reasons, provided that Aury allowed Hubbard to wield civilian power and appointed Irwin his second-in-command of

authority was repelled by forces led by MacGregor's lieutenants, Jared Irwin and Ruggles Hubbard. Somewhat later, the pirate Luis Aury gained control of the fort. Because Aury's privateering threatened negotiations concerning the cession of Florida, United States troops occupied Fort San Carlos in December, 1817. Although upset by U.S. interference at Fort San Carlos, Spain did cede Florida in 1821, and the U.S. abandoned the fort shortly after the transferral. Archaeologists estimate that two-thirds of the area has disappeared through erosion.

It is hard to find the spot, since it is not shown on maps and is little known among the local populace. The same is not the case with Fort Clinch nearby. Built after the Spanish period, it houses mementos of the different stages of local history.

Along the course of Harrison Creek, a group of archaeologists together with Kenneth Hardin and Dr. Clark Larsen began excavating in 1986 what they attributed to the missions of Santa María and the later Santa Catalina built in 1686 and destroyed in 1702 by the

the military forces. On September 21, 1817, to the accompaniment of a salute fired by cannon, he solemnly proclaimed the annexation of Amelia Island to the "Republic of Mexico." Disputes soon arose between the two factions but ended when Hubbard died of yellow fever. Furthermore, President James Monroe ordered the naval forces of the United States to expel Aury from the island. Instead, Aury proclaimed Amelia Island an independent republic, appointed Irwin its president, and sent Monroe a message reminding him of the rights of the island as a sovereign nation. When the United States troops landed, he offered little resistance and left for Nicaragua at the beginning of 1818.

Amelia Island had been the scene of another international incident some years earlier. In January 1811, President James Madison requested and obtained from Congress authorization to take temporary possession of any part of the Floridas, in compliance with an agreement to be reached, in the event, with the Spanish authorities, or if any part of Florida fell into the hands of a foreign power. Colonel John McKee and George Mathews, former governor of Georgia, were appointed to study the potential offered by the license thus obtained. Although they did not find the atmosphere in western Florida to be favorable, they saw chances of success in eastern Florida, mainly thanks to the cooperation of a settler on the St. John River, John H. McIntosh.

In mid-March, with the help of a group that they had formed and called "patriots," McKee and Mathews decided to embark upon a military venture and wrote to Monroe requesting assistance. Considering Monroe's silence as tacit approval of their plans, they went a step further and decided to conquer Amelia Island. The commander of Fernandina, Justo López, only had a garrison of 10 men but did not allow himself to be intimidated by superior forces, since he had news that the United States authorities across the St. Mary River were not cooperating with the rebels. However, he decided to surrender when he discovered that there were eight armed vessels in the vicinity.

Mathews then failed in an attempt to attack St. Augustine and received a letter from Monroe dated April 4, 1812, expressing his mortification at the harm that the two men's activities could do to his secret negotiations with Spain to relinquish her control of Florida. In his letter, he dismissed Mathews and appointed David B. Mitchell as governor of Georgia in his stead. Monroe ordered Mitchell to withdraw the United States forces gradually from Florida and to make arrangements with the Spanish authorities for the grant of an

amnesty for the insurgents. The new Spanish governor, Sebastian Kindelan, insisted on the immediate withdrawal of the troops before opening negotiations. In March 1813, Kindelan and a new representative appointed by Monroe, General Thomas Pinckney, negotiated the withdrawal of the troops, while Luis de Onís, the Spanish minister in Washington, D.C., sent Monroe a momorandum of amnesty in favor of the rebels.

Jacksonville

From Amelia Island to St. Augustine, along the coast road, there are some places with names reminiscent of Spain, such as Ponte Vedra Beach and South Ponte Vedra; not far away is Palm Valley, where once stood Fort Diego, which played a major part in Oglethorpe's attack on St. Augustine in 1740. But, before proceeding, let's look at Jacksonville, where the Liga Hispánica de Florida was founded at Jacksonville University some years ago. Here, on the right bank of the St. John River, near its mouth into the Atlantic, Fort Caroline was founded by a French Huguenot, René de Laudonnière, who landed with three ships (one the *Isabella*) and 300 settlers on June 22, 1564. Standing on the banks of the river not far from the coast, the triangular fort experienced hard times, starvation and mutinies, relieved by the visit of the English pirate John Hawkins. The arrival of Jean Ribaut (who had explored the area earlier with Laudonnière) with seven vessels on August 28, 1564, did not improve the situation. On September 4, six Spanish ships appeared in those waters. King Philip II wished to expel the Huguenots from Florida and had entrusted the task to Admiral Pedro Menéndez de Avilés.

On the feast of St. Augustine in 1565, the Spanish force sighted the Dolphins River, but, not finding the French there, sailed on northward to the mouth of the St. John River. After a cannonade with the French vessels, the ships passed so close that the combatants shouted threats and curses at one another. The Spanish attempts to grapple failed, and Menéndez returned to the point from which he had set out, where three vessels were unloading provisions, and proceeded to found St. Augustine on September 8.

Meanwhile, Ribaut prepared to attack his enemy, and, on September 10, sailed in search of Menéndez with 400 soldiers and 200 sailors. Several attempts to surprise the Spaniards and land were thwarted by a heavy gale, which forced the expeditionaries to withdraw and take refuge in a distant haven. This delay gave Menéndez time to hatch a daring plan: an overland attack on Fort Caroline with 500 men. The plan was not well received among his subordinates, but after three days of difficult progress through swamps and bogs, they went into action. At daybreak on the fourth day, to the traditional Spanish war cry of "Santiago y cierra España!" (For St. James, and close Spain!) the expeditionaries leaped upon the still sleeping garrison. With the exception of the women and children, all those who did not flee were killed, without any loss of life on the part of the assailants. René de Laudonnière and some fellow fugitives succeeded in escaping to France. Once taken, the fort was renamed San Mateo, as it had been captured on the feast of St. Matthew. After a short respite, Menéndez left a garrison there and returned to St. Augustine on September 24, where he was joyously welcomed by the surprised inhabitants, who had feared the worst on account of his prolonged absence.

In this area, between the frontier and St. Augustine, a number of Spanish missions sprang up and became the most prosperous and longest lasting of all those on the East Coast. They originated with the tour of inspection carried out by Menéndez de Avilés in 1566, on his return from the Guale Indian territory to the north. Sailing up the San Juan (later St. John) River as far as the Timucua township of Utina, he was received with much ceremony by the Indians, who begged him to pray to his God for rain (the news of his intercession at St. Catherines Island, described in the section on Georgia, had spread). Fortunately for the visitor, a heavy cloudburst relieved the drought shortly afterward. It is hardly surprising that first the Jesuit missionaries and then the Franciscans were given a warm welcome.

At the beginning of the 17th century, the Indians in this part of Florida were divided up into three districts (the fourth, San Pedro, was in Georgia): Nombre de Dios, Río Dulce and San Sebastián, all close to St. Augustine. Together with Santa María Mission on what is now Amelia Island, they were tended by Fathers Blas de Montes, Francisco Pareja, Pedro Viniegra and Pedro Bermejo. In time, the missions of Santa Cruz and San Juan del Puerto (on Fort George Island, near Jacksonville) were founded, like that of Nuestra Señora de Guadalupe at Tolomato, for the Guale people who retreated southward as a result of the invasions of the Chichuneco Indians. Protected by Fort San Marcos nearby, they remained in Spanish hands until Florida was handed over to the British. With the exception of Nombre de Dios Mission, as will be seen, no traces of these missions remain, though archaeological work has begun on the site of the San Juan del Puerto Mission.

St. Augustine: The First City and the "Fountain of Youth"

St. Augustine is the place where Juan Ponce de León thought he would find the "Fountain of Youth." Although the exact point where the discoverer landed is not certain, there is much evidence to believe that it was in St. Augustine. By a spring that still flows before a Spanish-style building, with a fresco depicting the arrival of the Spanish *conquistador*, a statue of Ponce de León, an obelisk and an explorer's globe mark the spot where he set foot ashore, in the spring of 1513, when Florida was discovered by the Europeans at *Pascua florida*, Eastertide, when the flowers were in bloom.

Ponce de León was a soldier whose courage had been renowned during the wars to evict the Moors from Granada, and who had sailed to America with Columbus on his second voyage. Victorious in various pacification campaigns in the Antilles, where he was accompanied loyally by his famous dog Becerillo, Ponce de León was appointed governor of Puerto Rico in 1509. On February 23, 1512, King Ferdinand signed the charter authorizing him to explore and colonize the island of Bimini, appointed him *adelantado* and governor, and entrusted the Christianization of the Indians to him. The governor, rich and powerful, but not exactly young, had fallen in love with the orphaned daughter of his own first, yet unrequited, love. Owing to the difference in their ages, he realized that it was useless to expect anything other than a submissive and reverent love. Hearing through some Indians that in a land to the north there was a wonderful spring of water that returned youth to those who drank it, he decided to stake everything, even his life if need be, on this single chance, for he thought the prize was well worth it.

With a brigantine, a caravel and a galleon, and Antón de Alaminos as his navigator, he weighed anchor on March 3, 1513, bound from San Germán to Aguadillo, in Puerto Rico, and from there set a northerly course. After calling at the island of San Salvador, discovered by Columbus on his first voyage, he sighted the continent on March 27, Easter Sunday, but did not land near St. Augustine until April 2. He spent six days there, duly taking possession of the territory in the name of his king, and fruitlessly testing the rejuvenating qualities of the local springs. He then continued his exploratory voyage northward until he encountered the cold sea currents and decided to turn south. (He believed that Florida was an island.) Nevertheless, he discovered the warm current of the Gulf Stream, also known as that of Ponce de León.

The 450th anniversary of that discovery was duly celebrated at St. Augustine on March 11, 1963. The Hispanic Institute of Florida honored the Spanish ambassador, Don Antonio Garrigues, with a luncheon; the house that once belonged to the Avero family was opened to the public after careful restoration in a ceremony at which Vice President Lyndon B. Johnson presided. The foundation stone of a building that Spain undertook to rebuild for the centennial festivities was then laid.

Johnson's speech recalled his youthful contacts as a Texan with the Hispanic world and praised the Spanish participation in American history.

On the occasion of the Bicentennial of the United States Independence, the consulate general of Spain in Miami opened a contest for the Ponce de León Prize. It was granted to José A. Cubeñas, author of the work *The Spanish and Hispanic Presence in Florida since the Discovery until the Bicentennial.*

In 1976 and 1985, excavations were carried out under the supervision of Dr. Kathleen Deagan. Remains from the constructions of Pedro Menéndez's colony were found.

Approaching Old St. Augustine, the Spanish Gate, flanked by two towers, greets visitors with its United States and Spanish flags fluttering. The presence of the Spanish flag here is a well-deserved homage to the blood that so many Spaniards gave in this area. The red and gold of Spain is found time and time again in St. Augustine: at the entrance to important buildings, over San Marcos Castle (in this case, the flag with the Cross of Burgundy), and the length and breadth of the streets in the form of pennants and bunting. The local coat of arms is that of Spain with the Golden Fleece and is borne by the municipal police as a shoulder badge showing their authority. St. Augustine was capital of Florida for two and one-half centuries, in days when the territory governed from this point was not confined to the present boundaries of the state of Florida. Once a key point in Spanish policy in the area, through the ups and downs of history it became the earliest town in the United States; some of its buildings can claim to be the oldest in the country, and it can boast the most imposing and best preserved military fortification anywhere

on the North American continent: San Marcos Castle. The fourth centenary of the foundation of St. Augustine was fittingly celebrated in 1965.

The city gate can be seen to form part of the walls that the Spaniards built at the beginning of the 18th century, crowned, like a barbed wire fence, with the glorious yucca plant, or Spanish bayonet. The present towers, which date from 1804, stand beside a deep moat which was spanned by the only entrance to the town on the landward side, a drawbridge. The main street, St. George (now known once more as Calle Real), has a number of interesting buildings: the old schoolhouse (the only wooden building dating from the mid-18th century that was saved from a fire); the Arrivas and Avero Houses (duly restored), seat of the St. Augustine Historical Restoration and Preservation Commission; the mansion of Governor Don Pablo de Hita y Salazar (rebuilt, with many features brought from Spain by the owner, Senator Walter P. Frazer), which was used as a chapel during the British occupation; the Old Spanish Treasury, originally a wooden building, but built of masonry in the 18th century by its owner Esteban de Peán; the Oliveros House and Benet House; and, finally, the Casa de Hidalgo, the replica of a Spanish house built by the Spanish government in 1955 based on the plans by architect Javier Barroso, to house an information and tourist bureau.

The Plaza de la Constitución is certainly reminiscent of Spain in its layout, its restful atmosphere, the vegetation, the buildings around it and the cathedral on the north side of the square. Building of the cathedral began in 1793, for only ruins remained of the church after the British occupation, however, the old records of the former church are still preserved and date back to 1594. Planned by Spanish engineer Mariano de la Rocque and built with funds provided by the Spanish Royal Treasury and its congregation, it caught fire in 1887 (it had been consecrated as a cathedral in 1870) and was repaired in the following year, when some additions, such as the tower, were made. Today, it has recovered its Hispanic character. On the frontal wall, a fresco stands out which depicts scenes of the history of the city. Next to the main entrance to the church, a marker explains in detail its history and emphasizes that the Parish Church, built in 1565, is the oldest in the United States.

On the west side of the square, Governor Canzo built his private house at the beginning of the 17th century; this house was to become the official residence of the Spanish governors, and later of the British governors. Used in recent years as a post office, it has now recovered its original features and has been turned into an exhibition center. Governor Canzo established a public market on the opposite side of the square, where weights and measures were checked; the 19th-century building is still standing and is known as the slave market.

The plaza was laid out in 1598 in accordance with royal instructions on urban planning enacted in 1573. An obelisk in the center is a memorial to the first Spanish constitution of 1812, from which the plaza gets its name, erected under the guidance of Fernando de la Maza Arredondo, who was jokingly nicknamed Don Fernando de la Plaza. Although, in 1814, King Ferdinand VII ordered the destruction of all monuments to the constitution drawn up by the Spanish Cortes, or parliament, which met at Cadiz, this obelisk remains.

In St. Francis Street stands the convent or friary of San Francisco, whose superiors included, among others, Fray Alonso de Reinosa, Fray Blas Montes, Fray Luis Jerónimo Oré—the great chronicler of Florida—and Fray Alonso Gregorio Escobedo—the author of the poem "La Florida." During the 17th and 18th centuries this was the hub of the missions in Florida and the eastern United States. During the British occupation, they were converted into barracks and remain as such today in the service of the Florida National Guard. Currently, there are a series of excavations under way. Also on St. Francis Street are the Llambias House, built before 1763, and the Oldest House, which dates back to 1703, where a Canary Islander, Tomás González, lived until he left Florida in 1763. Now owned by the St. Augustine Historical Society, the masonry walls of this building house a well-recreated Hispanic atmosphere, as do the adjacent gardens, which lead into the library of the Historical Society, which specializes in local history. Various flags, with the Spanish flag at their head, are at the entrance.

Nearby is Avilés Street, named in honor of the birthplace of the founder of St. Augustine, Pedro Menéndez de Avilés. This link has served as an incentive for Avilés and St. Augustine to establish a program as twin cities. On October 18, 1962, Spanish ambassador Garrigues presented a bilingual parchment in which the city of Avilés declared St. Augustine to be its twin. The ceremony took place at the traditional Ponce de León Hotel, a large Spanish Renaissance–style building (constructed in 1885 by Henry M. Flagler, one of the cofounders of the Standard Oil Company), which houses many Spanish mementos, including the escutcheons of the Spanish provinces. The building is the seat of the Flagler College.

Houses on Avilés Street include the Fatio House, the Casa O'Reilly (so-called after the Irish chaplain who toiled at St. Augustine during the second Spanish period) and the Don Toledo House, all of which are of Spanish origin. In parallel Córdova Street was the Hotel Córdova (formerly Casa Mónica), now the St. John's County Courthouse. The Museum Theatre can also be found there. In it, two informative films are screened: *Dream of Empire* and *Struggle to Survive* relating to the first years of the city.

Other streets bearing Spanish names are those of Cadiz, Granada, Sevilla, Malaga, Saragossa, Valencia, Riberia, Cuna and Carrera. St. Augustine is bounded on the western side by the San Sebastian River, which is crossed by King Street, a remnant of the Camino Real, or King's Highway, which led to the interior and the west of the peninsula. The Pan American Building in Charlotte Street has been the venue for all kinds of exhibitions concerning the Hispanic countries.

Nombre de Dios Mission

On the outskirts of the town, close to the spot first sighted by Ponce de León, stands the Nombre de Dios Mission, on land owned by the Catholic Church. It was here that Pedro Menéndez de Avilés landed on September 8, 1565. He had been honored by King Philip II with the title of *adelantado* and commissioned to set up three fortified posts on the costs of Florida to prevent French expansion along the American seaboard and to destroy any existing settlements organized by the Huguenots. Moreover, Menéndez had lost his son, Juan, who disappeared in a gale off the Florida coast, and he was, therefore, prepared to carry out the royal commission at his own expense in order to have an opportunity of perhaps finding his heir still alive. The expedition commanded by the Asturian admiral had sighted the coast of Florida on August 28, the feast day of St. Augustine, hence the name of the town that was later built. Although some of the expeditionaries had disembarked, he had not done so, for, having heard that the French had a settlement nearby, he wished to seek them out. His encounter with the French took place, as we have seen, at the mouth of the St. John River.

Consequently, the foundation of the oldest community in the United States took place on the feast of the Nativity of the Virgin Mary, when Don Pedro came ashore amid great pomp, accompanied by Father Solís de Merás and other members of the expedition. They were received by Father Francisco López de Mendoza Grajales, who had landed the previous evening with another party.

The *adelantado* then solemnly took possession of the territory in the name of King Philip. Father López de Mendoza Grajales then said the first Mass on the continent. A simple altar erected in the gardens at the mission recalls this event, while the diorama in the nearby museum shows the Spanish leaders kneeling before the surprised Indians. A large bronze monument to Father López, sculpted by Ivan Mestrovic, was unveiled in 1958; the Spanish missionary is shown with his arms outstretched in his first encounter with the natives of America. A steel cross, more than 200 feet tall, was consecrated nearby in 1966.

On the same piece of land as Nombre de Dios Mission, there now stands the Shrine of Our Lady of La Leche, an advocation that is greatly venerated and encouraged among United States Catholics. According to the brochure available, which includes prayers to the Virgin Mary for expectant and new mothers, this devotion originated from a miracle that took place in Madrid in 1598 when a statue of the Blessed Virgin had been rescued from sacrilegious hands; a mother and her unborn child were saved by the prayers of a distressed father. As a result, King Philip III built a shrine in the capital of Spain at his own expense under this advocation. The original statue was burned when mobs set fire to the Church of San Luis in Madrid on March 13, 1936, but a replica can still be seen at St. Augustine, in the chapel built as a small, quiet refuge of faith in 1915.

Nombre de Dios Mission was the first of a chain of mission stations that spread out from St. Augustine, Florida, to Georgia and even South Carolina. It started to function as a mission in 1566 or 1567, although there is not thought to have been a stone chapel until 1597, the foundations of which were discovered a few years ago. A distinguishing feature of this mission, where Father Francisco Pareja worked so fruitfully, was that the chiefs and other members of the tribe remained faithful following their conversion to Christianity: Doña María, a chieftainess who lived in the early 17th century, was married to a Spanish soldier, Clemente Vernal, and they had several children. Governors Canzo and Ibarra consolidated the authority of the chieftainess, and Bishop Altamirano administered the Sacrament of Confirmation to her and her children, 200 Indians and 20 Spaniards, on April 2, 1606. This mission served as a refuge for Indians fleeing from the north, and as an oasis of hospitality for visitors, whether they were governors or ecclesiastical dignitaries (like Bishop Altamirano), Spaniards or foreigners. Also near St. Augustine were the missionary districts of Río Dulce and San Sebastián. Chief Gaspar, at San Sebastián Mission, was an unwavering friend of Spain.

Menéndez de Avilés, the Founder

Once he had taken possession of the land, Menéndez de Avilés proceeded to unload his ships. Two of them, *Capitana* and *San Pelayo*, had too much draft for Matanzas Bay and had to cast anchor some way out; their cargoes were transferred to boats and brought ashore, after which the two vessels were dispatched to Cuba in search of further support. This work was proceeding when, at dawn on September 11, 1565, the ships commanded by Jean Ribaut appeared silhouetted against the horizon. The barely established Spaniards could hardly have endured the attack of the numerous French forces if a storm had not arisen, as if by a miracle; not only did it prevent the enemy from entering the bay or returning to their starting point, but in the midst of driving rain and hurricane winds, it also dispersed their fleet, sank some ships, threw others onto the coast and drove another group southward. It was then that the Spanish admiral decided to carry out the risky overland assault on Fort Caroline, which as has been seen, proved to be victorious. On their return, four priests came forth to welcome him bearing a cross and accompanied by all the soldiers, sailors, women and children, singing the "Te Deum Laudamus."

Four days later, some Indians brought the admiral news to the effect that a substantial party of Frenchmen had been shipwrecked on an islet lying about 12 miles from St. Augustine, where, unarmed and without food, they were trying to fend off the attacks of the natives. The admiral at once sent out a patrol to reconnoiter, and some 200 survivors of the wreck were located. Told of the disaster at Fort Caroline, and faced with the prospect of dying of starvation, they surrendered unconditionally on September 29, but only those who abjured their Protestant religion were saved. On October 12, another 150 (including Ribaut himself) died in similar circumstances, after arriving at the island from the south two days later. From that time onward, the place was known as Matanzas, meaning "slaughters" in Spanish.

Owing to its strategic position protecting St. Augustine, a small fort for a garrison of 50 soldiers was built at Matanzas in 1569. From a wooden lookout tower, six soldiers kept a permanent watch for the possible enemy ships in order to warn San Marcos. This fort fulfilled its mission at the time of the pirate attack in March 1683 and during the blockade by James Oglethorpe in June and

July 1740. The need for a stone fort was eventually seen, and it was completed by 1742; 50 men with six cannons forced Oglethorpe to give up his fresh attempt in 1743.

In judging the conduct of Menéndez, which has been the subject of much controversy, allowance should be made for the overwhelming superiority of the French forces compared to those of the Spaniards. Moreover, he achieved his objective, for he put a permanent end to French attempts to establish themselves on the East Coast (the successful attack by pirate Dominique de Gourges in the spring of 1568 only resulted in the death of those Spaniards taken prisoner). In view of the refusal of the governor of Cuba to send him aid, Don Pedro went to Cuba personally to fetch it. Subsequently, he sailed along the southern coasts of Florida. His absence resulted in disquiet at St. Augustine and San Mateo; the situation was alleviated by the arrival of a fleet of 14 ships from Spain under the command of Sancho de Arciniega, with 1,500 people and abundant provisions.

The admiral undertook a fruitful voyage northward up the coast and founded a fort at Santa Elena. After this, in 1567, he considered it advisable to return to Spain to report to the Crown on the situation in Florida. Contrary to his expectations and hopes, he was never to return to Florida, firstly owing to the time taken by his work on behalf of his new beloved land, and secondly because in 1574, King Philip II appointed him captain general of the Spanish Armada, which was then preparing to attack the Netherlands and the British Isles. On September 17, 1574, he died at Santander, at the age of 55. The remains of Pedro Menéndez de Avilés lie in the Church of San Francisco at Avilés, to which they were transferred in 1956 from the Church of San Nicolás, in compliance with the wishes expressed in his will. A red and yellow Spanish flag was presented for delivery to the city hall of St. Augustine. At the Shrine of Our Lady of La Leche can be seen the funerary casket in which the admiral's coffin was deposited. At St. Augustine, where there are so many statues of Ponce de León, this was the only reminder of its founder in sight, with the exception of the painting of Don Pedro by Spanish artist Alberto Duce (presented by the Spanish embassy through the local historical society, at the end of the "pilgrimage to St. Augustine" on January 24 and 26, 1958, organized by the Hispanic Institute and the Casa Ibérica at Rollins College), until the city council of Avilés presented a statue of the *adelantado*—a replica of which stands in the park at Avilés—that now stands in Menendez Park.

The commemoration of the foundation of St. Augustine by Pedro Menéndez de Avilés was celebrated with particular enthusiasm in 1965, on the occasion of the city's fourth centennial. The postal services in both the United States and Spain simultaneously launched a nationwide issue of the same stamp showing a *conquistador* bearing a flag of red and gold with the castle and lion quarterings and a caravel in the background. The commemoration ended in a 12-day celebration between August 28 and September 8. In the preceding months various events had taken place, like the meeting of monument and park curators sponsored by the Pan-American Union in Washington, D.C. The premiere performance of a historical play, *The Cross and the Sword* by Paul Green (which is still performed), took place in the new amphitheater, exhalting the figure of Menéndez de Avilés and recounting the early days of the colony.

The inauguration of the Casa de Hidalgo was a principal event, the speakers being the Spanish minister of the interior and the United States secretary of the interior, Stewart Udall, who said:

> We owe much to the bravery, the faith, the dreams of our predecessors from Spain. Thus always we shall recall with equal appreciation and respect, as we do today, those Iberian deeds and qualities that helped to build the Americas. . . . the rich heritage they left us is evident today in every one of our American States: faith in a destiny, determination to achieve the high goals we have set, a pride in the brotherhood of free and active men.

A most symbolic ceremony was held earlier, when work was started on the Hispanic Garden, and the statue of Isabella, sculpted by Anna H. Huntington, was unveiled.

History of St. Augustine After Its Foundation

In a short history of St. Augustine in the years following its foundation, the outstanding figure must be Pedro Menéndez Marqués, the nephew of the admiral, to whom St. Augustine owes its survival. In 1570, when the lack of supplies led to a mutiny of the garrisons of Santa Elena, San Mateo and St. Augustine he saved the situation. His period of government from 1577 to 1589 was crucial and coincide with, among other events, the famous attack by Francis Drake in 1586, with a fleet of 20 ships with 2,000 men abroad. Although the small garrison of 150 men endeavored to prevent it, the town and fort were burned down. Menéndez Marqués had no alternative but to abandon Fort Santa Elena in order to support the decimated forces at St. Augustine.

Each year in June, the "Night Watch" commemorates this mournful event. Men and women in period dress go out into the streets and appear at the governor's house and then at the castle, where they camp overnight.

Menéndez Marqués was succeeded by Governors Domingo Martínez de Avendaño and Gonzalo Méndez Canzo, a distinguished admiral. During the term of office of the latter, St. Augustine caught fire in 1599 and was ravaged by a storm a few months later. The Indian Juanillo and his friends rose in revolt (the fatal results for the Georgia missions have already been discussed). Claims that there were better harbors closer to fertile land led the Council of the Indies to carry out an inquiry concerning the conversion of the Indians in Florida, the agricultural potential of the region and its mineral resources, and the advisability of moving the site of the *presidio*. Governor Canzo urged that no changes be made, his ambition being to explore the regions of Tama (Georgia) and Apalachee (West Florida), which would spread Spanish expansion from the Florida Keys to Chesapeake Bay and ensure provisions for the *presidios* while developing a prosperous economy in Florida.

On August 30, 1602, Don Fernando Valdés, the son of the governor of Cuba, disembarked at St. Augustine armed with a royal order to investigate all these matters. At that time, St. Augustine had 225 soldiers and 400 other inhabitants, including 57 wives and 107 children. From August 31 to September 23, the first court hearing held in the territory of the United States took place: the Florida proceedings. It began with a simple ceremony as Valdés handed the royal order to the governor, in the presence of Pedro Redondo Villegas, the royal investigator into financial matters, and Juan Oñate, a military adviser. Méndez Canzo kissed the document and proclaimed in a loud voice his desire to obey and to cooperate, together with his subordinates, in fulfilling the orders of the king, after which he returned the order to Valdés. A record of the proceedings was drawn up by the royal notary, Alonso García La Vera, Valdés then called upon Canzo to summon the royal treasurer, Juan Menéndez Marqués; the royal comptroller, Bartolomé Argüelles; and the auditor, Alonso de las Alas so that they could proceed to select between 12 and 18 inhabitants to give evidence in the proceedings. The three men chose 18 people from among the soldiers and missionaries. The hearings were presided over by a royal investigator and the governor, with the royal notary and the commission in attendance. Twenty-one witnesses were heard, and their testimonials are an invaluable source of information about Florida at the beginning of the 17th

century. (Their evidence is now available for anybody to read thanks to the historian Charles Arnade.) The court of inquiry ruled in favor of those who wished to maintain the settlement in St. Augustine, and the town survived once again.

The danger from the British increased throughout the 17th century, as pirates increasingly preyed upon Spanish shipping. In the spring of 1668, a Spanish ship fell into the hands of an English pirate, Robert Searles (alias Davis). When it was seen at St. Augustine, the captain answered with the correct identifying countersign and was assumed to be a Spaniard; the unwary citizens did not realize that the ship held a much feared pirate crew. While the town slept calmly, the pirates invaded the streets and killed some 60 Spaniards, sacked homes and burned everything in their path, with the sole exception of the fort, where the governor had succeeded in taking refuge accompanied by other inhabitants who had not fled to the surrounding woods.

This attack persuaded the Spanish authorities of the pressing need to build a solid masonry fort capable of protecting the population in a fresh assault, and not prone to the fires, which had hitherto damaged or destroyed their wooden forts. In the fall of 1669, the queen regent, Doña Mariana of Austria, issued a royal order to the viceroy of Mexico to provide adequate funds for an impregnable fortress to be built of the stone formed by seashells, which abounded on the nearby Anastasia Island.

San Marcos Castle

Close to San Marcos Castle can be seen the Zero Stone, which marks the starting point of the route that during and after the Spanish period, linked the eastern coast of Florida with the coast of California. With four bastions at its corners and in a magnificent state of repair, the massive castle stands out against the horizon, a testimony to the excellence of Spanish military engineering, thanks to which it has withstood the ravages of time, of humans and of 19th-century indifference.

Smaller than some other Spanish castles, such as El Morro at Havana or San Felipe at Cartagena de Indias, it was nevertheless big enough for its purpose: that neither the castle itself nor the town or region should fall into enemy hands. The building was commenced in 1672 and was finished by August of 1696. Ignacio Daza was the military engineer who planned and directed the building work in the early stages. Others who contributed

The San Marcos Castle in St. Augustine, Florida, was built by Spaniards between the years 1672 and 1756. USIS Photo Lab, Madrid, Spain.

decisively through their effort and determination in the endeavor included Governors Manuel de Cendoya (who began it), Nicolás Ponce de León, Pablo de Hita y Salazar, Juan Marquéz Cabrera, Diego de Quiroga y Losada and Laureano de Torres y Ayala. The cost was originally estimated by Cendoya at 70,000 pesos, but eventually amounted to 138,375 pesos (about $220,000).

Surrounded by a shallow but wide moat, entry is gained by a footbridge leading to a wide passageway, which in turn leads into the large central courtyard. A flight of steps (once a ramp) leads from the courtyard to the upper story, on which are situated the artillery pieces that defended the fort on four sides. One of the cannons still to be seen, called "La Sibila," bears the date 1737 and the name of the artificer, Juan Solano.

In the fall of 1702 the new fort received its baptism of fire, while José de Zúñiga y Cerda was governor. Eight ships commanded by James Moore, the British governor of Carolina, and supported by detachments led overland by Colonel Daniel, laid siege to the town. Realizing his inferiority, Zúñiga had time to order the 1,500 inhabitants to take refuge within the castle. The fruitless siege lasted for two months, until the appearance of two Spanish ships sent to aid the defenders forced the British to withdraw overland after burning their transports, materials and provisions, together with the town itself. All burned, with the exception of the shrine of Our Lady of Soledad and about 20 other buildings. This fire showed the need for defense works; two lines of fortifications were built little by little

*(From left to right, top to bottom) The governor's house, Fort Matanzas and the Flagler Building, in
St. Augustine, Florida, and the Teatro San Carlos in Key West, Florida.* Carlos M. Fernández-Shaw.

around the fort between Matanzas Bay and the San
Sebastián River, and another defense work was built to
the south, all with the necessary sentry posts. In addition, a new redoubt, Fort Mosa, was built two miles
north of the town, to protect the growing number of

blacks who were deserting from the British colonies
and seeking refuge in Spanish territory.

In May 1740, the fort was put to the test once again
when it was attacked by the British general James
Oglethorpe from Georgia. Fortunately, the castle

defenses had been reinforced by military engineer Antonio Arredondo, and six ships succeeded in bringing supplies from Cuba. After occupying the small neighboring forts, Picolata (on the banks of the St. Johns River), Diego and Mosa, the British found they were unable to command the bay on account of the presence of Spanish ships and the greater draft the British ships required. Oglethorpe put some cannon ashore on Anastasia Island and began a regular siege, bombarding the town and fort incessantly for 27 days. On June 26, patrols formed by Spaniards and blacks took Fort Mosa by surprise, killing Colonel Palmer and 50 of his men. On July 7, the besieged governor, Manuel de Montiano, received two new supply ships. The summer heat, shortage of drinking water and the increasing ravages of disease forced the assailants to raise the siege. Oglethorpe withdrew, to the joy of the defenders, whose homes had scarcely suffered as a result of the siege.

The ensuing years, until 1763, can be considered the golden age of St. Augustine; its 3,000 inhabitants enjoyed peace, social life saw a period of splendor and the population experienced relative financial well-being.

Today, members of the St. Augustine Garrison and the Men of Menéndez relive the military days dressed in the uniforms and carrying the arms of that period.

St. Augustine, British and Spanish

On March 16, 1763, a lieutenant from the British schooner *Bonetta* brought Governor Melchor Feliú and the inhabitants of St. Augustine news of the cession of Florida by Spain to Great Britain. This was the price exacted for the return of Cuba, which the British had taken in the course of the Seven Years' War, in which Spain had been involved as an ally of France, who had herself lost Canada. All the Spanish residents prepared to depart, with the exception of some civil servants appointed to handle the sale of the properties of those who were leaving. On June 21, 1764, the governor and the last few families abandoned the town; very few of them were to return.

Manuel de Céspedes was the governor who received Florida back again on July 12, 1784. In the 20 years that had elapsed, the thirteen colonies had fought for independence, and Florida had been a rallying point for loyalists to the British Crown and a haven for fugitives. In 1768, some Minorcans had been brought to New Smyrna by Dr. Andrew Turnbull. (The Minorcans specialized in fishing shrimps and turtles. Some of their descen-

dants maintain the tradition.) In 1777, the survivors moved to St. Augustine, where they formed the nucleus for the Spanish population during the second period of Spanish rule in Florida (and who were ancestors of the oldest local families today). A leading member of the group was Father Pedro Camps, who died in 1790. A memorial statue was erected in the square of the Catholic cathedral in St. Augustine in 1975.

In the course of the War of 1812, General George Matthews was encouraged by President James Madison to act in Florida, with the result that Fernandina and Fort Mosa fell into the hands of the patriots; the president, however, was forced to order their withdrawal following sharp Spanish and British protests. On the pretext of restoring order, frequent raids were made into Spanish territory during the second decade of the 19th century. These conflicts ended when the treaty ceding Florida was signed. On June 10, 1821, Spanish governor José Coppinger handed eastern Florida and San Marcos Castle over to Colonel Robert Butler.

The moving text of the edict with which the Spanish authority said goodbye to the Spanish subjects under her jurisdiction on July 7, 1821, follows.

Inhabitants of Eastern Florida: this coming tenth day, the Commissioner of the United States, Colonel Mr. Roberto Butler, legitimately authorized to receive it, will take over this Province. The Spanish Officials and Troops will evacuate the territory which the American Officials and Troops are to occupy in accordance with the Treaty celebrated in Washington on February 22nd, 1819, the Royal Charter from October 24th of the previous years, and other warrants which I have as Commissioner for the hand over. Once this is accomplished, the Spanish authorities cease to perform their functions and the American ones begin to carry out theirs. It is my obligation to inform you of this important political change. I have previously let you know what has been stipulated by our government in order to safeguard your free practice of the Catholic Religion, your properties and possessions which the same treaty guarantees. I have also revealed to you the exemptions, grace and protection that our government offers to those who wish to move to some places of the Spanish Monarchy and especially to the Island of Cuba. I cease to be in command, but I shall remain among you the time necessary to conclude some points of the Commission, whose decision I await from the Superior Government. Meanwhile, I am ready to give all the assistance within my reach to all those who seek the transfer to Havana, and wherever I am I shall willingly give testimony of how highly I think of you and of the appreciation you all deserve.

Floridians, you are about to give the last proof of your virtues by obeying the orders of His Majesty. I hope that with this change all the vicissitudes which the circumstances have made you suffer with heroic resignation shall cease! As witness of this and of all the sacrifices you have done for your country, I shall reveal whatever I have evidence of each one of you as I usually did for all, if you so wish. I am pleased with the idea that you will all be happy, which is all that one wishes for you your

Friend and Citizen,
Colonel Jose Coppinger
St. Augustine of Florida, July 7th, 1821.

South of St. Augustine

As St. Augustine and Matanzas are left behind, one approaches Daytona Beach. Inland are localities with such Spanish names as San Mateo, Andalusia and Seville. A popular spa, De Leon Springs, is nearby. Highway 17 passes near the sites of various Franciscan missions: San Diego de Salamototo, San Diego de Laca, San Antonio de Ecanape, San Luis de Acuera, San Salvador de Macaya and Santa Lucía.

Highway 1 leads to New Smyrna, founded in 1768 by Dr. Andrew Turnbull, where Minorcans played an important part in its early history. When Smyrna was established, Minorca, in the Mediterranean near Spain, had fallen into British hands. Dr. Turnbull thought that the islanders (of Spanish origin, yet now subjects of Britain), would be of great assistance in the British colonies. But the colony of Les Mesquites, as it was called, came to an end in 1777; trouble with the Indian natives, disease, heat and other adversities resulted in the survivors deciding to relocate to St. Augustine while Turnbull was away in England. In St. Augustine they were sympathetically received by the British governor Patrick Tonyn. Stephen Vincent Benét, a descendant of those colonists, wrote "Spanish Bayonet" in 1926, the story of Sebastián Zafortezas and the Minorcans in Florida.

Some time ago, the remains of Spanish shipwrecks were discovered near Sebastian. But more recently the Fort Pierce area was the site of the successful salvaging of treasures that sank on July 31, 1715, along this coast, aboard 10 Spanish galleons. The ships had sailed from Havana bound for Spain three days earlier, but ran into one of the terrible hurricanes so common in the area. They were transporting, among other things, gold and silver ingots and coins from Mexico, Peru and New Granada. The Spaniards succeeded in saving part of the treasure, valued at $14 million, with the help of native divers, but most of it was buried in the sands along the coast, where optimistic treasure seekers often explored but, more often than not, gave up without success.

However, Kip Wagner and his team, the Real 8 Corporation, succeeded in recovering a number of valuable objects from the ocean bed from May 1, 1964, onward. The state of Florida granted them exclusive rights along part of the coast. Those who attended the "Pieces of Eight" exhibition organized in the National Geographic Society exhibition rooms, in Washington, D.C., at the end of December 1964, appreciated just how interesting these finds were: many gold and silver coins, some the size of the bottom of a tumbler; a silver service in such good condition that it could be used on the most refined table; marvelous porcelain brought from China on the Acapulco galleon; an anchor covered in a mass of rust, plants and mollusks; an amazing gold necklace, very finely worked and of great length, which looked as if it had been fashioned only yesterday; and many other exhibits worth seeing. A Catalonian expert, Francisco Xavier Calico, handled the sale of the coins to collectors all over the world: ironically, that was to be Spain's only part in the matter. The auction of over 1,000 pieces at the Waldorf-Astoria Hotel in New York, in May 1973, caused a great sensation. The same group of treasure seekers attained in 1965 similar findings in Sebastian Inlet, with an estimated value of $60,000, which belonged to another ship that was part of the same fleet sunk in 1715.

Southward, we pass by Cape Canaveral Kennedy Space Center and Walt Disney World. Fort Pierce lies about 92 miles from Miami. Today the A1A highway crosses the St. Lucie River near the spot where Ponce de León saw some uninhabited Indian huts on April 21, 1513, and then Jupiter Inlet with a creek nearby, which Ponce called Río de la Cruz, or Cross River. Here the Spanish *conquistador* saw Indians of both sexes almost entirely naked. They attacked him, and he succeeded in capturing one to serve him as an interpreter from that time onward. In 1696, an expedition of Quakers bound for Philadephia was shipwrecked in Hobe Sound not far from this point. After two months of captivity in the hands of the local savages, they were rescued by a Spanish patrol commanded by Captain López, who accompanied them safe and sound to British territory. Among those set free was Jonathan Dickinson, who later recounted all he had seen and heard.

Highway A1A runs for many miles parallel to the beach-studded islands protecting the coast along Palm Beach, Boca Raton, Pompano Beach, Fort Lauderdale and Hollywood. The origin of Palm Beach dates from 1878, when a Spanish merchant ship, *Providencia*, shipwrecked on its coast. Its cargo of 20,000 coconuts was sold and a good number planted, allowing palm trees to grow, as was characteristic of the island, which gave this beach its name. In 1893, Flagler built the Spanish Renaissance–style hotel, the Royal Poinciana, and in 1900, the Breakers, which was reconstructed in 1926 after two fires. The boom at Palm Beach began in the 1920s, with the result that many of its mansions are markedly Spanish in style due to the influence of architect Addison Mizner: among others, the Everglades Club, the buildings of El Mirasol farm (with its Stotesbury Arch of mauresque style), St. Edward's Catholic Church and the Tennis Club (with mission touches). In that boom period, Mrs. Horace Elgin Dodge, millionaire Dodge's widow, built Playa Riente at Palm Beach in a Spanish Renaissance style, decorated with furnishings from Spain, among them—according to Areilza's testimony–the benches from the old Casa de Juntas of Guernica. After the death of Mrs. Dodge, the house was sold and torn down. The millionairess Mrs. Marjorie Merriweather built in 1923 her magnificent mansion (with 120 rooms) named Mara-Lago. Its style is Hispanic and Moorish, with many Hispanic objects and artistic details. Many of the Palm Beach streets bear Spanish names, such as Del Rio and del Mar.

The place where Boca Raton stands today was visited for the first time by Menéndez de Avilés in 1565; there are grounds for believing that it was in the vicinity that his son, Juan, died. Today, Boca Raton is a progressive locality with the thriving new Florida Atlantic University. Moreover, the inhabitants take pride in their Spanish ancestry, and the annual festivities in February are called Fiestas de Boca de Raton, during which shows, attire, decorations, food and drink are centered around Spanish themes, in a modern urban setting that also boasts Spanish-style building designed by Mizner. The annual festival that recalls the jazz age is named after this architect. In 1984, the architect William Fox planned the central Seaborn Square, essentially Spanish in style.

In 1567, shortly after their arrival in Florida, the Jesuits founded a mission among the Tequesta Indians situated near Miami river's mouth. This mission, run by Brother Francisco de Villarreal was shortlived. Earlier, Menéndez de Avilés had built a fort here with the cooperation of Doña Antonia, the Indian wife offered to him by her brother Carlos, the Calusa Indian chief. She is considered to have led the first Miami settlement.

The garrison met a violent end. In a nearby cemetery, located near where today's Hyatt Hotel stands, reads a marker: "Tequesta Indians lived at the mouth of the Miami river (200 yards southwest of this spot) for more than 15 centuries before white men came. The principal town of the Tequesta Indians, including six mounds used for dwelling, burial and religious rites, was discovered here by the Spaniards. They built in it the earliest white settlement in S.E. Florida, a fort and Jesuit mission, in 1567. When the British obtained Florida in 1763, most of the Tequestas departed with the Spaniards to Havana and thereafter vanished as a tribe."

Miami

Miami is today a crucial point in intercontinental communications, keystone in the relations among the Americas themselves and with Europe, especially Spain. Her modern international airport attends to some 20 million travelers a year, second largest after New York's Kennedy airport in passenger traffic and international cargo tonnage. Its port, on the other hand, is first in the world in cruise traffic: some 2.5 million passengers passed through in 1985. In the last 25 years the presence of Hispanics has grown, with more than 800,000 residing in Dade County (three-fourths of whom are in exile from Fidel Castro's Cuba). However, the percentage has slightly decreased in the last few years due to an increased arrival of immigrants from Central America and from other areas.

Miami is often confused with Dade County, which consists of 27 independent municipalities, among them Miami, Miami Beach, North Miami, Hialeah, South Miami and Coral Gables, reaching together a population of some 950,000 inhabitants (to which can be added those of the nearby areas amounting to 850,000 people more).

The Hispanic minority almost constitutes a majority that has caused moments of friction with the native Anglo Saxons. The fact is that the language of Cervantes is heard today, with a Caribbean air, more than English and is used in all kinds of publications, posters and announcements. In 1973 the county was declared officially bilingual (a later referendum revoked that condition by a few votes). The Yellow Pages of the telephone book are also published in Spanish, and the driver's license exam can be taken in Spanish. Spanish may be used for court appearances. The Spanish-speaking population is more or less concentrated in certain neighborhoods, resulting in Hispanic mayors in Miami, North Miami and Hialeah. The area around Southwest Eighth Street, or Calle Ocho, nicknamed Little Havana, is especially attractive, full of life and activity. It's not surprising then, that among the 20 most common last names in Greater Miami, the first six are Rodriguez, Gonzalez, Garcia, Lopez, Hernandez and Fernandez.

There are Spanish restaurants, and some stores display the sign "English Spoken"; it's possible to read in Spanish *El Diario Las Americas* and *El Nuevo Herald,* a special edition of the *Miami Herald* (as well as other numerous publications). Spanish is heard on radio stations such as Radio Mambi, "la Cubanísima," Cadena Azul and Radio Suave. TV channels 23 and 51, and periodically others, offer Spanish programs. Spanish booksellers and editors were, at one time, grouped together in LESA, a company that has since closed, but one can acquire Spanish works in several bookstores in the area of Calle Ocho. On nearby Flagler Street the public is served by the Hispanic Branch Library, well stocked in the humanist sector, as well as the Central Library and other municipal branches. Several *pelotaris* play in this area's jai alai frontons, and several Iberian artists work here fruitfully, some permanently. Singers and musicians Julio Iglesias, Raphael and Rocío Jurado are residents, and visitors such as Lola Flores, María Dolores Pradera and José Luis Perales, appear frequently. In theater, in which the universities are quite active, the works of Federico García Lorca, Ramón María del Valle-Inclán and others are performed. In flamenco, within Dade County, it's possible to see five different shows in one month. The *Anthology of the Zarzuela* was a tremendous success not long ago, and this operetta form has a great following here. There are representative offices of 11 banks of Spain, peninsular companies like Iberian Airline and a Spain-U.S. chamber of commerce.

Official representation includes the consulate general, a commercial office and a tourist office. The Spaniards get together socially in different Spanish clubs, as well as through other associations, such as AGUE (Society of Graduates from Spanish Universities), which has several hundred members.

On October 12, 1968, the ambassador of Spain inaugurated a monument by the vanguard sculptor M. Martí, on the *Discovery of America,* donated to Dade County by the government of Spain. On that occasion, the mayor proclaimed the first Spanish Week, which after 1973 took the name of Hispanic Heritage Week. One October 12, 1977, the statue of *Ponce de León,* a work by Enrique Monjó, was unveiled in a city park. An exhibit relating to that *conquistador* was opened in April 1985, by H.R.H. the count of Barcelona. Miami also boasts a statue of Columbus.

Around the date of the anniversary of the discovery of America, a series of Hispanic commemorations within the frame of the Hispanic Heritage Festival, directed by Eloy Vazquez, have been celebrated for some 16 years, gaining more importance each year. Groups and artists from all the Hispanic countries participate; a Miss Hispanidad is elected; a giant *paella* is prepared in the open air for some thousands of people; and several kinds of cultural exhibits are held with the assistance of local authorities, radio stations, television stations and reporters. Miami has also been the scene of the first Ferias de Andalucía, which aims to become an annual event.

In July 1987, the Plaza de la Evangelización was opened, in the downtown area, close to the water. Promoted by F. Amando Llorente, this is a tribute to the Spanish missionary effort. It is centered by an obelisk and backed by a typical mission facade, with two bronze bells brought from Saldana, Spain.

Besides the University of Miami, Florida International University and St. Thomas University are located here. In 1998, José M. Aznar, head of the Spanish government, was honored by FIU with the doctorate *honoris causa* in law. Miami-Dade Community College also enjoys a very high prestige.

Miami Beach, first visited by Ponce de León in July 1513, is the area of Dade County that traditionally has been more famous (with downtown Miami now close behind) for its hotel row, expensive shops and luxurious villas, with areas of recreation like the Convention Center and the Miami Beach Center of the Performing Arts for the "snowbirds" (tourists from the North who come south for the winter). A plaque on Ocean Drive commemorates Columbus and his Discovery. An art deco district surrounding Española Way in Miami Beach contains buildings in Spanish style, which aspire to evoke old world romance. The nearby Bass Museum has held exhibitions of Spanish artists, such as the Primitivos Modernos (Modern Primitives) in 1986.

Due to the populous Jewish community, a tribute was paid to Maimonides on August 18, 1985, on the 850th anniversary of his birth, in a plaza beside Temple

Moses. A plaque dedicated to the Cordovan philosopher was unveiled in the presence of authorities and Sephardic representatives of nine Spanish-American countries, members of the Latin American Sephardic Federation (FESELA). Congressman Alberto Gutman, a Sephardic of Cuban origin also participated. In the synagogue, the National Congress of American Sephardics was celebrated in 1988. The president of the World Sephardic Federation, Nessim Gaon, also visited this community that same year.

At North Miami Beach is the Monastery of San Bernardo de Sacramenia. This is a 12th-century Cistercian cloister, in which stand statues of Kings Alphonso VII and Alphonso VIII of León amid the greenery of a well-kept garden around a convent wall. The monastery was founded in the province of Segovia and was inhabited by the monks until Spanish Church properties were sold and religious orders disbanded by Mendizábal in 1835.

Since 1464, Sacramenia has been the ancestral home of the Casa de Alburquerque, which explains why among the coat of arms that adorn its walls is the one from Don Beltrán de la Cueva, the first *duque* to hold that title. In 1925, William Randolph Hearst purchased what was left of the monastery (many houses in the village had been built with stones taken from its ruined walls). After being numbered, the stones were packed into 10,751 crates; for this purpose it was necessary to send to Sacramenia the equipment for two sawmills, buy a local wood for the necessary timber and build a road to the nearest railroad station. The cargo was placed in quarantine on its arrival at New York because the stones were packed in hay, which had to be replaced by excelsior, which meant every single crate had to be opened and then closed again. This work was halted during the Depression, and the crates were left in storage in New York. After 1951, two Cincinnati industrialists, E. Raymond Moss and William S. Edgemon, purchased the stones; when the boxes were opened, it was discovered that the numbers had been changed, and the task of rearranging them took several years and $1.5 million. The Catholic monastery was bought in 1964 by an Episcopalian congregation for its religious services. The former refectory is used as a chapel, and the monastery is now known as St. Bernard of Clairvaux, with the result that all mention of Sacramenia, its place of origin and *raison d'être* is lost.

South of Miami, the Vizcaya House and Garden can be visited. In spite of its Spanish name, the style is Italian Renaissance, in accordance with the wishes of the builder and owner, James Deering, founder of International Harvester Corporation, the agricultural machinery manufacturer. Begun in 1914, it was not completed until 1925, shortly before Deering's death. The whole place is sumptuous, inside and out, with gardens stretching down to the luxurious pier on the coast. In addition to a wrought iron replica of the old Spanish caraval *Vizcaya* at the entrance, there are some valuable Spanish exhibits on the first floor: magnificent carpets in several chambers, outstanding among which is one dating from the 15th century, which belonged to Don Faurique Enríquez, admiral of Castile; the great lamps from a Spanish cathedral; the portrait of Francisco de Altamira, attributed to Juan Carreño de Miranda; and the portrait of Queen Barbara de Braganza.

The University of Miami is located in Coral Gables. The university has the important Department of Inter-American Affairs, a language department that includes Spanish and the Institute of Iberian Studies located in the Graduate School of International Studies. Its dean, Ambassador Ambler Moss, founder of the Casal Catala, was the promoter along with American Express of the literary competition Letras de Oro (Letters of Gold) in five categories, constituting the first national competition in Spanish.

The city of Coral Gables was planned by a romantic dreamer, George Merrick, who was ruined in his endeavor by a hurricane. He gave Spanish names to most of the streets and plazas and constructed entrances to the city with a Spanish flavor and fomented the construction of colonial-style homes. Thus in the street directory there are up to 20 names of historic persons (Ponce de León, Coronado, Columbus, Fonseca, Pizarro, etc.) and seven place-names from Biscay (Viscay, Alava, Deva, etc.), 12 from Andalusia (Andalusia, Granada, Sevilla, Almeria, etc.), seven from Catalonia (Catalonia, Gerona, Sarria, Monserrate, etc.), 12 from Castile (Castile, Segovia, Avila, etc.), five from the Kingdom of León (Salamanca, Palencia, etc.), two from Aragon (Aragon and Saragossa), three from Murcia (Murcia, Lorca and Cartagena), two from Cantabria (Santander and Santillana), others from Galicia (Coruna and Lugo), several names of monuments (Alhambra, Alcazar, Giralda) and saints' names (San Ignacio, San Domingo), among other Spanish names. King Alfonso XIII of Spain decorated Merrick with the Encomienda de Isabel la Católica in 1926, as a result of the consul of Spain in Tampa's proposal.

Coral Gables inspired the great Spanish poets, Juan Ramón Jiménez and Agustín de Foxá: "Spanish tiles," wrote the latter, "cause the roofs of Coral Gables to blush." Jiménez, the poet of Moguer, lived a few years of his exile in "a white house on Alhambra Circle." Another Spaniard, the poet from Asturias Alfonso Camín devoted verses to the tallest building of the city: the Biltmore Hotel, with the Giralda Tower, "The Giralda Girl." Coral Gables, whose foundation was so influenced by the works of Washington Irving, especially *Tales of the Alhambra,* signed in 1989 a sisterhood pact with Granada.

The Keys and Fort Santa Lucía

The famous Florida Keys, or *cayos,* are a collection of coral islands and reefs extending in a wide arc in a southwesterly direction for some 95 miles, with their tip, Key West, only a few miles from Cuba. On his voyage of discovery in 1513, Ponce de León called them "martyrs," because "seen from afar, the emerging rocks resembled suffering men." They must have been unhospitable places in Spanish times. Menéndez de Avilés founded Fort Santa Lucía on one of them, but the garrison died of starvation because they could find nothing but fish to eat and the provisions sent to relieve them never arrived owing to the dangers of navigation in the area.

At the tip of this chain of islands is Key West, called Cayo Hueso by the Spaniards, lying beyond Key Largo, Islamorada, Vaca, Paloma, Bahía Honda and the others. Farther out to sea lie the Tortugas, named by Ponce de León in June 1513, and the Marquesas, named in honor of the marquis of Cadereita, admiral of the Spanish fleet of the Indies in 1622. The first inhabitants of the Keys, the Matecumbes Indians, commercialized fishing and began its exportation to Cuba. Basque fishermen related the news of such wealth in Europe.

Key West is an attractive mixture of Spanish, Cuban and North American elements; two miles wide by three miles long, it has a romantic atmosphere of adventure. A community founded by castaways shipwrecked during hurricanes, it grew as it became an important port of call due to its location and frequent visits by regular ships and corsairs or buccaneer ships. The Old Pirate House still stands on Elizabeth Street, once a refuge for José Gaspar and Juan Gómez, notorious villains of the sea. Not long ago a calaboose was discovered in the house, with a sword that belonged to Gómez. Many other buildings still show a marked Spanish influence, and Spanish woodwork can be seen on balconies, windows, terraces and balustrades. As a result of a hurricane in 1622, the Spanish ships *Santa María de Atocha*

and *Santa Margarita* were wrecked; the former displaced 550 tons and was the flagship of a fleet of 23 vessels. In 1973, the first finds of the wreck were made, and since then Mel Fisher and his company Treasure Salvors have continued efforts to locate more of the wrecks. The *Santa Margarita* was discovered in 1980, and an exhibition was mounted that year of the objects salvaged, said to be worth $20 million. In 1985, they discovered the *Atocha* about 40 miles from Key West, with a treasure estimated to be worth about $400 million in gold bars, silver pieces of eight (about 47 tons), jewels, cannon, etc. In May 1989, the Seahawk Company found what it hoped to be the remains of the vessel *Nuestra Señora de la Merced.* The newly discovered galleon lies about 75 miles southwest of Key West, or about 25 miles directly south of the Dry Tortugas. It sank together with the above mentioned ships and appears to be practically intact. A maritime museum in Key West houses artifacts from this and other sites.

Key West also played a strategic role during the Cuban Revolution. The newly restored San Carlos building was the site of many revolutionary meetings. In that building, on January 3, 1892, José Martí spoke for an hour. The next day, Martí visited the buildings of the tobacco factory, among them that of the Spaniard Domingo Villamil, "La Rosa Española," and other minor workshops. This factory strike produced the second exodus from Key West in 1893 (the first one was in 1886) and the beginning of the end of the tobacco industry. Key West was also of great importance in the course of the Spanish-American War of 1898.

The huge Everglades park nearby is the last sanctuary of the Miccosukee, a group of Seminole Indians descended from those who refused to move to follow the paths of forced migration to Oklahoma in the 19th century. Four delegates, headed by Buffalo-Tiger, visited the Spanish embassy in Washington, D.C., in 1958, to present treaties signed between the Seminole Nation and Spain at the end of the 18th century, whereby the Kingdom of Spain undertook to help the Indians and, in the event, make them subjects of the Crown. The Seminole conveyed a message written on buckskin for the Spanish chief of state.

On one of the key islands, probably Estero Island, the first Jesuit mission in the New World was established: San Carlos. In the spring of 1567, Governor Menéndez de Avilés escorted the Jesuit missionaries, Father Juan Rogel and Father Francisco de Villareal, to San Carlos, where a *presidio* commanded by Francisco de Reinosa had been established the preceding year. The governor had ordered that a house be built for the converted chieftainess, Doña Antonia, together with a chapel. He was also hopeful of finding his vanished son (lost in a shipwreck) among the Indians. Father Rogel worked there until 1568, converting the Indians and attending to the spiritual welfare of the garrison, but the mission was shortlived.

The island had first been visited by Ponce de Léon in May 1513, after calling at Charlotte Harbor and Captiva and Sanibel Islands. He cast anchor at Estero, took water and firewood aboard, and was informed that a chief called Carlos lived a short distance to the north, or so he understood, and hence the name of the mission. The Indians in the area were known as "Calos," which may have been what Ponce de Léon heard. Following several attempts to land, and bloody clashes with the Indians, Ponce weighed anchor and sailed south on June 14.

Ponce de Léon visited Charlotte Harbor again in February 1521, in the course of his second expedition to Florida in search of the Fountain of Youth. It is a wide bay with its mouth protected by the islands called Gasparilla (including Boca Grande and South Boca Grande), Costa, Captiva and Sanibel, among others. During Ponce de Léon's absence, Francisco Hernández de Córdoba and some other adventurers had appeared there and, by their conduct, had earned the natives' hostility. When the 200 expeditionaries accompanying Ponce began to build houses, after disembarking with 50 horses, other animals and a number of implements for cultivating the soil, they were repeatedly attacked by the Indians, who succeeded in wounding the Spanish commander. Feeling near death, he chose to return to his own people, and the rest of the expedition followed him. He died a few days after his arrival in Havana. Ponce's venture, the miraculous fountain and his tragic end are poetically depicted by Eugene O'Neill in his play *The Fountain*. (The story of Ponce de Léon has also been the subject of the novel *Boyuca* [1832] by Robert C. Sands and of the work *Donna Florida* [1843] and the poem "Ponce de Léon" by Edwin Arlington Robinson.) In Punta Gorda, in the vicinity of Charlotte Harbor, a Ponce de Léon Historical Park stands. A marker reminds that on those shores "the first European settlement in what is now the United States was established . . . by explorer Juan Ponce de Léon and a band of more than 200 soldiers, priests, farmers, artisans and monks. The colony lasted for about six months, finally collapsing after a battle with hostile Caloosa Indians in which Juan Ponce de Léon was mortally wounded. The exact location of the colony is still unknown . . ."

The Royal Order of the Ponce de Léon Conquistadors was founded in 1980 and sponsors every February many activities with Spanish flavor, among others the re-creation of the landing of Ponce and his group. Punta Gorda has also signed a sisterhood pact with Palencia, Spain, the province in which Ponce was born, and with San Juan, Puerto Rico.

At Warm Mineral Springs, north of Punta Gorda at Charlotte Harbor, those suffering from arthritis find relief in the hot springs. At the entrance a map of considerable size highlights the exploits of the Spaniards in Florida.

Sarasota is reached after passing near to Siesta Key. It is the perhaps unlikely home of the Ringling Museum of Art, established by John and Mable Ringling (of the Ringling and Barnum and Bailey Circus), and their residence, called Ca D'Azan. Included in the museum are four monumental cartoons for tapestries painted by Rubens for the king of Spain, two paintings by El Greco, including a *Christ on the Cross;* two paintings by Velázquez, such as the portrait of Philip IV; three Murillos (one, an Immaculate Conception); *Doña Mariana de Austria,* by Juan Carreño de Miranda; and a Zurbarán. The residence of the founders, with its gardens and pools, is beautifully kept and likewise houses some valuable works of art (including a fine Goya).

Bradenton and Hernando de Soto

Bradenton is the headquarters of the Hernando de Soto Historical Society, more commonly known as the Conquistadors. This society is well known in Spain, as are its members; since 1962, they have visited Spain every two or three years and toured different Spanish cities on the way to the village of Barcarrota (Badajoz), the birthplace of *conquistador* Hernando de Soto and the twin town of Bradenton. In 1967, they were received at the White House by President Lyndon Johnson and conferred on Johnson the title of honorary conquistador.

After making a fortune in Peru and marrying the aristocratic Doña Isabel de Bobadilla in Spain, Hernando de Soto wished to continue his exploits in North America, much impressed by the tales told by Cabeza de Vaca; in 1537, he therefore obtained from the emperor his appointment as *adelantado* of Florida. They sailed from Havana on May 18, after spending almost a year in Cuba, at Santiago, gathering livestock and supplies of all kinds. De Soto left behind his wife and his friend Juan de Rojas as governor. The departure had been a solemn yet dazzling occasion with seven large and three small vessels, all bedecked with bunting and flags. They were unable to go ashore quickly in Florida, and their presence off the coast was relayed with smoke signals sent up by the coastal Indians to warn other more distant tribes of the approach of strangers.

For many years there were doubts as to the exact spot where de Soto landed. A commission appointed by Congress in 1935 to commemorate the 400th anniversary of the event reached the conclusion that they had disembarked at a spot now known as Shaw's Point, part of Bradenton, at the entrance to Tampa Bay. At the point can be seen the first stone of the De Soto Trail, a carved stone with Spanish coat of arms and two bronzes under the headings Knight of Santiago and The Spanish Crown.

The township of Ucita was the first to receive the expeditionaries. At Ucita, one of the patrols found Juan Ortíz, who would have been killed by the expeditionaries themselves in the course of a counterattack if he had not shouted at the top of his voice in Spanish "For the love of God and the Blessed Virgin, do not kill me!" A member of the expedition organized by Pánfilo de Narváez, Juan Ortíz had been taken prisoner by the Indians at Ucita. He would have been burned at the stake but for the pleadings of the daughter of the chief. This encounter with Ortíz was to be of great importance for de Soto, because after almost 10 years in the country, Ortíz knew the local dialect well and became invaluable as an interpreter for his new leader. The vanguard of the army remained in the area until August 1, when the 550 men, 200 horses and numerous livestock accompanying the expedition set out on a long journey, fraught with vicissitudes. Though few were to return, de Soto's expedition embarked on one of the most exciting campaigns of discovery in the modern world.

In spring every year, Bradenton commemorates the arrival of de Soto and his companions. The Friday called De Soto Day is a legal holiday in Manatee County. Thanks to the initiative of Dr. W. D. Sugg and other local personalities, De Soto Week has been celebrated since 1939. Various events take place, to which state officials and representatives of the Spanish embassy are invited. The commemoration ceremonies are organized by the Conquistadors, made up of 133 members, the same number as the horsemen who accompanied Don Hernando. Every year, the members hold a secret ballot to elect the one who is to play the part of the Spanish *conquistador* and the 25 men who are to accompany him in the mock landing. An enormous personal and financial effort is called for on the part of those elected, who must spend a lot of time throughout the year traveling and representing both the town and the association. "Don Hernando" is accompanied by the "queen," also elected yearly by the Conquistadors, who must give generously of her time as well.

The first day of De Soto Week for many years began with the commemoration of the landing of de Soto and his men on the beach in the De Soto National Park, which occupies land donated by Dr. Sugg at Shaw's Point. Preceded by a ritual dance performed by "Indians," the presence of the Spaniards is announced by the roar of cannons and harquebus salvos (a matchlock gun) fired by the invaders. Two boats anchored off the beach suddenly explode, while their occupants (realistic mannequins) fall before the Spanish soldiers. De Soto and his men disembark, spreading out in arrow formation. With their leader, a Franciscan friar, the royal standard and a cross at their head, they advance up the beach and kneel as they take possession of the place in the name of the kings of Spain. The *conquistadores* wear splendid 16th-century costumes and thick beards.

The neighboring city of St. Petersburg houses the Salvador Dalí Museum, the world's most complete collection of works by the painter of Port Lligat. It was made possible thanks to the foundation created by Reynolds and Leonor Morse.

More modern tributes to de Soto can also be found in Bradenton. The great bridge linking town with neighboring Palmetto is called De Soto Bridge; on land near the national park, the Catholic Church has erected a statue of the *conquistador* accompanied by two bas-reliefs by Pérez Comendador; and downtown, in the Plaza de Hernando de Soto, a reproduction of the *conquistador's* birthplace and a typical Extremadura church have been built. A Spanish-style building to house a museum and the headquarters of the Conquistadors have also been constructed. The South Florida Museum exhibits two large paintings: one devoted to the landing of de Soto and the other to the first Mass. In the center of the square, there is a bronze statue of Don Hernando on horseback, sword in hand, sculpted by that same artist and unveiled in March 1972.

Tampa Bay

The Tampa Bay area was the site of numerous episodes in early Spanish-American history. Having obtained a royal grant, the explorer Pánfilo de Narváez took possession of the Tampa Bay area in the name of the emperor Charles V and his mother, Queen Juana La Loca (Joanna the Mad), on April 16, 1528. This event took place at the entrance to the bay, or perhaps on one of the islets at its mouth. He was accompanied by 600 settlers and soldiers, some with their wives, and several friars, among others Friar Juan Suárez; 42 horses and a variety of other livestock; Alonso Enrique; and the explorer who was to become the most famous of all, Alvar Núñez Cabeza de Vaca. On the shores of the bay, Narváez came into contact with the Indians for the first time and was told of the existence of rich land to the north of the province of Apalachee; consequently, he convened a council a few days later and decided to send part of the expedition to skirt the coast aboard the ships, while the vanguard of his army proceeded overland.

A ship sent by Mendoza, viceroy of New Spain, also arrived at Tampa Bay on the feast of the Ascension, 1549, bringing the Dominicans Fray Luis Cáncer, Fray Gregorio de Beteta, Fray Diego de Tolosa, Fray Juan García, Brother Fuentes, a converted Indian woman called Magdalena and a party of expeditionaries. In spite of the cold welcome they received from the Indians while reconnoitering, Fray Luis, Fray Juan and Brother Fuentes spent the night on one of the islands at the entrance to the bay. Returning aboard, they sailed into the bay, where they sighted a village. Fray Luis, Fray Diego, Brother Fuentes and Magdalena came ashore and held a friendly parley with the inhabitants. Told that there was a magnificent haven a day and a half away, Fray Luis agreed to the request of the natives that his companions should make the journey by land while he and the rest of the expeditionaries would proceed by sea.

It took the inexperienced pilot a week to locate the haven, and another week to enter it. On the feast of Corpus Christi, Fray Luis and Fray Juan went ashore, celebrated Mass and looked for their companions; the following day they continued their inquiries, and a few Indians eventually appeared and promised to come back with them the following morning. The Indians kept the rendezvous; among them was Magdalena, who having been reunited with her people, was as naked as the other women of the tribe. The missionary fathers were not with them, although Magdalena assured them that they were alive. Returning aboard encouraged by this news, they soon discovered that it was untrue. Juan Muñoz, a member of the de Soto expedition, who had been captured by the Indians but had now succeeded in escaping in a canoe, reported the martyrdom of Fray Diego and Brother Fuentes. Those on board decided to leave, but

Fray Luis considered it his duty to stay behind. He spent June 24 writing notes that would serve as a testimonial of what had happened and despite the pleas of his companions, ordered that he should be taken ashore in a boat to where a group of Indians had gathered. Kneeling on the sand, he was immediately bludgeoned to death. Being unable to assist him, those aboard the ship weighed anchor and set course for Veracruz.

Menéndez de Avilés founded a fort in the vicinity of Tampa Bay or Tocabaga, where he left Captain García de Cos in command of 30 soldiers. After being visited by Pedro Menéndez Marqués and Father Rogel, the Jesuits set up a mission there. The artifacts recovered in Safety Harbor and at Siete Robles, in the same area, has provided fundamental information about their vicissitudes.

After the United States acquired Florida from Spain in 1821, the first American soldiers began arriving in Tampa in 1824 to establish Fort Brooke and to rid the area of pirates, fugitive slaves, slave smugglers, Indians, contrabandists and adventurers. There they found Spanish "fish ranchos" along Spanishtown Creek, and descendants of those who had been established since the beginning of the second Spanish period in Florida in 1783, according to Professor Tony Pizzo. To this group belonged Juan Montes de Oca who, because of his knowledge of the Seminole language, became a guide and interpreter for Colonel Brooke.

Tampa itself came into being when Henry Bradley Plant built the Jacksonville railroad in 1884. In 1891, he opened the Tampa Bay Hotel. Thirteen hundred feet long, with five stories and 500 rooms, it became the main tourist attraction on the west coast of Florida until, for various reasons, it was ceded to the town, and later to the University of Tampa in 1933 under a 99-year contract. This peculiar building in Arab style, with 13 minarets (one for each month in the Muslim calendar) is said to have been "inspired" by the Alhambra at Granada; in fact, it in no way resembled the Palace of the Abencerrajes. During the Spanish-American War, the hotel was the headquarters of Theodore Roosevelt's Rough Riders. There are new additions to the old building, which include a fine boardroom in true Spanish style containing a walnut table with 12 chairs and two armchairs with 17th-century carvings, an 18th-century Catalonian cabinet, two inlaid chests of drawers, carpets, wrought iron work and two copies by José Sanz of the paintings *Prince Baltasar Carlos* and the *Infanta Margarita de Austria* by Velázquez. One wing of the building houses the Tampa Municipal Museum containing all the furniture and objects of value from the old hotel, including among other pieces, a cabinet that is claimed to have belonged to the Catholic monarchs.

In the garden stands a venerable oak tree, in the shade of which Hernando de Soto held parleys with the Timucua Indians of the area. When he set off toward Ocala, de Soto left a small force at Tampa under the command of Pedro de Calderón, with supplies for two years. Today two civic centers and youth clubs bear the names of the *conquistadores* de Soto and Ponce de Léon. The thriving University of South Florida is also situated in the vicinity.

Also nearby is the municipality of Temple Terrace on the banks of the Hillsborough River (Río de San Julián y Arriaga). On April 25, 1757, Francisco María Celi, together with 19 armed men, appeared in this area. Their objective was to explore the pine trees in order to use them as masts on the ships of the Royal Spanish Navy. They camped on the surroundings until April 26. They named the forest El Piñal de la Cruz de Santa Teresa and drew a map of the Great Bay of Tampa, which can be found today in the Naval Museum in Madrid, containing such names as Ensenada de Aguirre, Punta de Montalvo and Canal de San Juan y Navarro. A memorial marker was inaugurated in October 1988 through the initiative of historian Dr. Tony Pizzo.

Another point of Hispanic interest in Tampa is Ybor City, a quarter predominantly populated by Spaniards (or their descendants) and Italians. It owes its name and existence to Vicente Martínez Ybor, who first came from Cuba in 1869 and settled at Key West. In 1886, accompanied by his brother Eduardo, he settled in that sector of the bay and started the business that was to make Tampa the center of the United States cigar industry. Most of the residents are from Asturias and Cuba (there are about 40,000, making this one of the largest Spanish communities in the United States), however, not all the Spanish-speaking population are Hispanics, for the many Italians living here speak perfect Spanish with hardly a trace of an accent. Before radios existed, it was the custom in the cigar factory to read novels aloud for the entertainment of the workers. Consequently, Benito Pérez Galdós, Armando Palacio Valdés, Leopoldo Alas (Clarín) and other Spanish novelists became household names to the cigar makers at Tampa, and their style and their language became familiar. It was in this way that the Italians in Tampa came to master the language of Cervantes.

José Martí arrived in Ybor City in November 1891. He stayed at the Cherokee Hotel and pronounced a rousing

A 1755 map of Tampa Bay, Florida. Carlos M. Fernández-Shaw.

speech at the Cuban Lyceum. There can be found a Park of Marti's Friends with a statue of him. At the end of the 19th century, there were over 50 tobacco factories and 40,000 tobacconists who twisted about 10 million Havana cigars per year. With the depression and automation of the tobacco industry, Ybor City entered a decline. How-

A map drawn by the expedition of Francisco María de Celi to Tampa Bay, Florida, 1755. Carlos M. Fernández-Shaw.

ever, a group of university students began reconstructing the city and giving it new life at the end of the 1970s. As such, the old factory, Martínez Ybor, has been turned into a thriving shopping center, Ybor Square.

Walking through the streets of Ybor City, visiting its stores or frequenting its restaurants or casinos is like being in a Hispanic country. Everybody speaks Spanish as their first language, although they can use English if required. There are local Spanish radio and television stations.

Prominent members of the community have been Bob Martinez, former governor of the state of Florida; and Emiliano Salcines, ex-state attorney general and honorary viceconsul of Spain.

The writer and journalist José Iglesias has written a series of three comedies entitled *Cuban Immigration in Ybor City*. These works take place in 1912 with the arrival of an immigrant family, in 1920 with the new generation, and in 1978 with the encounter with the exiled Cubans.

The Hispanic festivities in Tampa reach a climax in February when a mass of little boats go out on the bay to escort the ship of the famous pirate José Gaspar, better known as "Gasparilla," who becomes the protagonist of a colorful week-long carnival. Tampa organizes a dazzling parade of floats, while Ybor City sponsors the parade at night. The Latin American fiesta in March is presided over by a queen elected from among the Hispanic community. Spacious buildings house the Spanish Center, Asturian Center and the Cuban Civic Center. The Spanish-Iberian Club is also active. Local newspapers include the weekly *La Gaceta*.

Central Florida: Narváez and de Soto

The route to Gainesville is approximately the same as those taken by Pánfilo de Narváez or Hernando de Soto. When crossing the Withlacoochee River, the expedition of Narváez had to work to cross the river on mere logs; a little farther north, the expedition was met by a troop of Indians playing flutes and carrying their chief, Dulchanchellin, who gave the Spaniards a friendly welcome. In this area they also saw an opossum for the first time; Cabeza de Vaca gave a very graphic description of the animal, quite different from the one given years later by Hidalgo de Elvas. In the Ocala area (where Osceola became involved in the Seminole War of 1835–1842), de Soto and his men spent some time, and his leadership and courage were put to the test by two Indian attacks,

in the course of which he and his horse (Aceituno) were felled. (In recent years, a state commission has placed milestones along the de Soto route at five-mile intervals. Roadside exhibits have been located along the trail to interpret de Soto's exploration and the Indians he contacted [Inverness, Williston, Gainesville]. Near Withlacoochee River [Inverness], Spanish armor and beads, iron spikes and bones have recently been discovered.)

On this route, Ocala can be found. In its westerly sector, Marti City was founded in 1894, which is said to be the first municipality of independent Cuba. Martí had visited Ocala on two occasions. The municipal experiment lasted only a short time.

North Florida: Gainesville and Tallahassee

The University of Florida at Gainesville is of great importance in Spanish-American studies. It is the headquarters for the Center of Latin American Studies and the P. K. Yonge Library containing copies and photocopies of more than 100,000 pages of documents concerning Spanish Florida (from 1519 to 1819) taken from Archive of the Indies at Seville by historian Irene A. Wright (with funds provided by John B. Stetson Jr.). The Florida Historical Society owns hundreds of documents and business papers of the firm Panton, Leslie and Co., which was active in western Florida under Spanish rule, and publishes the well-known review *Florida Historical Quarterly*. The university sponsored, together with the Instituto de Cooperación Iberoamericana, in December 1983, a symposium on the topic of the relations between Spain and the United States. Its Institute for Early Contact Period Studies, directed by Professor Michael V. Gannon, also organized in April 1988 a conference on the subject: "Rethinking the Encounter." Other projects it has been in charge of are the translation and editing of the *Libro de Armadas (Book of the Navies)*, found in the Archives of the Indies by Professor Eugene Lyon (it describes in detail *La Niña*, the caravel used on Columbus's voyages); the excavation of Navidad, first settlement by Columbus in the New World, and Puerto Real, the fourth settlement; the microfiling of the Archives of Count Revillagigedo, descendant of Menéndez de Avilés; and the De Soto Trail in Florida.

Professor Charles Fairbanks has begun excavation of a Spanish mission near Gainesville called San Felasco. In the hall of the state capitol flies the flag of castles and lions among the five historical flags of Florida. Close by, a fresco geographically describes the history of the

United States with an old Spanish colonial map and a prominent portrait of Pedro Menéndez de Avilés. There is a Museum of History of Florida, which contains a few Spanish mementos: a glass case with objects from a sunken galleon and a reference to the Minorcans of St. Augustine. At the center of Tallahassee, close to the capitol building, the Hernando de Soto camp was discovered in March 1987, where among other things, a 16th-century Spanish coin, a crossbow arrow and an iron piece of a considerable diameter have been unearthed.

The discovery, made by B. Clavin Jones, took place when a builder about to start work on two buildings, alerted authorities of his findings. He agreed to put off construction until all the excavations were completed. When an archaeologist confirmed the importance of that location, the Trust for Public Land purchased the nearby lands until the state could contribute the necessary funds. The excavations were carried out over an extensive area, with the permission of the respective owners.

The route to Tallahassee follows fairly closely those taken by Pánfilo de Narváez and Hernando de Soto, crossing the Suwannee River (called San Juan de Guácara by the Spaniards) and its tributary, the Santa Fe River. The expeditionaries under Narváez succeeded in crossing the river with the help of Indians who were enemies of the Apalachee. Modern travelers fortunately do not suffer the same disappointment experienced by Pánfilo and his men when they reached the town of Apalachee: they had been told of a town comparable to those in Mexico, with gold dazzling on the rooftops and splendid stone buildings. Instead, the advance party sent out to explore under Cabeza de Vaca found a village of 40 huts built with palm fronds, clustered together in disorder and separated by narrow muddy lanes. They found only women and children, and the only booty was corn and deerskins. Their inquiries confirmed that Apalachee was the main settlement in the area, and all that the visitors found here was privation and death caused by the constant attacks of the natives, who wanted their unwelcome guests to depart. Among their victims was the Aztec prince Pedro de Tezcuco, a loyal follower of Fray Suárez; his death caused great dismay among the Spaniards.

After 25 arduous days, Narváez decided to go to Aute, an Indian village on the site of present-day St. Marks. However, renewed Indians attacks, a shortage of food (the oysters on the coast provided some sustenance) and malaria sapped the morale of the soldiers, whose officers, convened in council by Narváez, decided to abandon the area. The lack of boats seemed an impossible obstacle; nobody knew how to build them, and they were without even the most elementary tools. Nevertheless, one of the expeditionaries offered to direct the building of some rudimentary vessels, and his proposal was accepted in view of their eagerness to depart and their desperate plight. Seven weeks later, they launched five boats about 10 meters long, the result of heroic ingenuity and effort. Finally, on September 22, the 243 survivors set out, their boats only two hand-breadths out of the water once laden, using their shirts as sails. They called the bay Bahía de los Caballos (Bay of the Horses), in grateful tribute to their own animals whose meat had sustained them throughout their ordeal.

A patrol commanded by Francisco Maldonado, sent out by Hernando de Soto shortly after their arrival in the Apalachee area on October 6, 1539, found the remains of those dead horses. De Soto had sent Juan de Añasco with orders for Bishop Calderón and his men to abandon Tampa and rejoin the expedition; when the uncertain fate of the Narváez expedition was known, de Soto decided to send Maldonado to Havana in the pinnace remaining at Tampa to bring provisions and rejoin the expedition during the summer at Ochussee Bay. On March 3, 1540, de Soto left the Apalachee area (Florida) after following an itinerary that more or less coincides with the present localities of Gainesville, Lake City, Live Oak and Tallahassee, where he observed the first Christmas on the North American continent.

Missions Along El Camino Real

From 1633 onward, intensified efforts were made to civilize the area between the Aucilla and Apalachicola Rivers (known to the Spaniards as the Asile and Apalachicolo Rivers) and straddling the Ochlockonee River (Lanas or Amarillo River). By their efforts the missionaries succeeded in establishing many mission stations that with the exception of one or two revolts, were peaceful and reached their peak when Bishop Calderón came on a pastoral visit in 1675. As we have seen in Georgia, the growing pressure and presence of the British from the north served to increase Spanish interest in making a claim in the area, had sufficient material means been available. But the growing disaffection of the Apalachicolo, encouraged by the British, and the presence of the French on the western flank, where they founded Biloxi in 1699, further weakened the position of the Spaniards, who were eventually unable to withstand the pressure.

A king's highway, or *camino real,* was established to link the mission with St. Augustine, where the governor had his residence; in fact, a whole string of such missions could be found along the highway. According to the historian Mark F. Boyd, after leaving St. Augustine, the highway crossed the St. Johns River (Salamototo or San Juan) via the township of Picolata, then turned south along the boundary between Clay and Putnam Counties, entered Alachua County, where the Santo Tomás de Santa Fe Mission or Santa Fe de Toluco Mission stood, and proceeded a little farther south to that of San Francisco de Potano, near Gainesville. From there the route continued northwest, fording the Santa Fe River, to reach the Santa Catalina de Afuyca Mission, not far from Hildred, on the boundary between Columbia and Suwannee Counties (in 1987 the mission cemetery and the remains of some of its buildings were found). The road continued in a fairly straight line as far as Dell, on the left bank of the Suwannee River, where the San Juan de Guácara Mission stood, after passing the Missions of Afuyca and Santa Cruz de Tarihica, at equal distances along the present O'Brien line. The route crossed the river and followed the right bank upstream through Lafayette County until, once in Madison County, it turned almost 90 degrees west not far from and parallel to the boundary with Taylor County, with the missions of San Pedro de Potohiriba, Santa Elena de Machava and San Mateo de Tolapatafi, before reaching San Miguel de Asile, on the banks of the Aucilla River, in the locality of Lamont. The route then followed the same itinerary as Highway 27 as far as Tallahassee, with another string of missions: San Lorenzo de Ivitachuco, Nuestra Señora de la Purísma Concepción de Ayubale, San Francisco de Ocone, San Juan de Aspalaga and San José de Ocuia, where the highway forked, leading to Santa Cruz de Capola, San Martín de Tomole and Purificación de Tama on one branch, and to San Pedro y San Pablo de Patale, San Antonio de Pacuqua and San Cosme y San Damián de Escambe on the other, after which the branches converged again at San Luis de Tamalí. Not all these missions were among the Apalachee Indians: Purificación de Tama was established among the Yamassee; San Carlos de Chacatos and San Pedro de los Chines, among the Chatots Indians; and San Francisco de Ocone among the Oconee Indians (Professor John H. Hann's synoptic list of missions contains up to 52). In March 1989, the mission of San Martín de Ayacuto (in the state park at Ichetucknee Spring) was discovered along with spearheads and other artifacts.

All the cereals that the fertile land in West Florida produced and that the inhabitants of barren East Florida needed were transported along the King's Highway or by the sea route from St. Marks to St. Augustine. Little else is known about the sea traffic except, through Governor Damián de Vega Castro y Pardo, that a frigate was dispatched in 1639 from the capital to Apalachee, that Captain Juan de Florencia transported provisions for the *presidio* aboard the *San Martín* in 1646 and that a ship owned by one Ignacio de Losa arrived at St. Augustine years later, from Apalachee, with a cargo of corn.

San Luis is the most important of all the missions along the Camino Real and was probably founded in 1655; its fort is mentioned in documents as early as 1675. It lay two miles west of Tallahassee and has been located thanks to the meritorious excavations of Dr. John W. Griffin (as Dr. Hale G. Smith must take the credit for finding San Francisco de Ocone, 23 miles southeast of Tallahassee, near the township of Waukeenah). When strategic requirements made it advisable to abandon the missions in Georgia, Spanish efforts concentrated on St. Augustine, in the east, and San Luis, in the west. St. Augustine, however, withstood the ravages of history, whereas San Luis succumbed. It met its end when the British commander, Colonel James Moore, attacked the area in 1704.

A five-year excavation project started in 1983. The archaeologists have found the fort, the council house and the Indian village, and excavations of the church, cemetery and convent are under way.

With a considerable number of Indian allies and British soldiers under his command, Moore took Ayubale by surprise on January 25, 1704. Father Angel de Miranda and a group of Spaniards and Apalachee Indians held out heroically all day long, after taking up positions in the church and convent, but their resistance ended when their ammunition was exhausted and when the assailants set fire to the buildings. When he heard the news, Captain Juan Ruiz Mexía set out from the *presidio* at San Luis with 30 Spaniards and 400 Indians. They spent the night at Patale, and, at dawn the next day, after being exhorted by Father Juan de Parga, they met the British at Ayubale. The ensuing battle ended in the defeat of the Spaniards; Father Parga was killed and beheaded, and Mexía was taken prisoner and forced to watch the martyrdom of the missionary. The forces accompanying Moore committed atrocities of all kinds, torturing and murdering the prisoners. Thirteen missions were destroyed, and that of San Lorenzo de Ivitachuco (with it exemplary leader) Don Patricio, was saved only by handing over everything of value that they possessed.

"The demential way in which this systematic destructive task was accomplished," Guillermo de Zéndegui writes, "could not be explained as tactical motivations, since the Missions were not, in fact, military objectives. Its true reasons have to be found in the innermost feelings where disavowed prejudices, rivalries and hatred nest."

Further attacks against the rest of the missions continued throughout June and July, and Father Manuel de Mendoza was killed at Patale. Only San Luis de Tamalí and San Lorenzo de Ivitachuco can be said to have survived. Consequently, in view of the possibility of further attacks, which the Spaniards would have been too weak to repulse, Manuel Solana, the lieutenant governor who had succeeded Mexía at San Luis, recommended to Governor Zúñiga, at St. Augustine, that the Apalachee region be abandoned. This was done, and most of the settlers and friendly Indians left for Pensacola, while another group relocated in St. Augustine. San Luis was evacuated and destroyed by the Spaniards in July 1704 and was never revived.

Fort St. Marks

St. Marks, or San Marcos, was mentioned earlier as a camp used by Narváez and a harbor handling export trade. The first Fort San Marcos de Apalache was begun, under the supervision of Artillery Captain Enrique Primo de Rivera, on December 3, 1678, and was completed on April 7 the following year. San Marcos de Apalache retained its influence throughout the period of Spanish rule and the subsequent British period. As a result of the agricultural characteristics of the area and the growing shipping trade, by 1683 it had become a settlement of considerable size, described as a town on a map of that period, but a violent attack on the wooden fort by a numerous combined force of French and British pirates took the Spanish and Indian garrison by surprise during the first half of 1682.

By royal command, Governor Juan Márquez de Cabrera immediately commissioned engineer Juan de Siscara to build a second wooden fort with bastions at the corners, situated at the confluence of the Warcol and St. Marks Rivers. Command of the fort was given to Captain Francisco Fuentes. The fort fell into complete ruin following the dismemberment of the Spanish settlements after the raid by British general Sir John Moore

in 1704. When rivalries sprang up among the Creek Indians, due to their alliance with either British or Spanish settlers, the faction friendly to Spain sought protection, and the Spanish authorities brought the old fort back into use again.

The square wooden fort was rebuilt with four bastions and a harbor for vessels with a shallow draft. Within it were a church, some stores and quarters for the troops. As the low-lying fort was in constant risk of flooding, it soon became clearly necessary to build a stone fort. After several delays, the acting governor, Fulgencio García de Solís, engaged the services of an expert engineer in 1754. For five years, as "engineer extraordinary of Florida," Juan de la Cotilla designed and directed the construction of the fort, for the sum of 800 pesos; the work had not been entirely finished when Florida was ceded to Great Britain in 1763. The fort itself changed hands in 1764.

British rule was short lived. When the British capitulated to the army of Bernardo de Gálvez, the governor of Louisiana, at Pensacola, on March 9, 1781, West Florida passed into the hands of Spain once again, ceded under the Treaty of Versailles of 1783. Taking advantage of the special authorization to negotiate with the Creek Indians, which the Spanish government granted as a monopoly to the firm Panton, Leslie and Co. (established by the Scottish traders William Panton and John Leslie), a member of the company, Charles McLatchey, set up a trading post near St. Marks. The Spaniards did not recover the fort until 1787, and it underwent considerable repairs in 1790, as shown in the plan drawn by Luis de Bertucat. The fort stands today not far from Tallahassee. The ruins are worth seeing and some plaques explain to the visitor the features of the fort. Inside the area a comprehensive museum has been built.

In 1792, the English adventurer William A. Bowles, who was married to an Apalachicola or Creek woman, sacked the Panton Co. warehouses. As a result of this and a number of other misdeeds, he was kept in prison for five years and saw the inside of jails at Havana, Madrid, and Manila, until he succeeded in escaping to the British colony of Sierra Leone while being taken back to Spain. With the enthusiastic support of the British, he then organized a small expedition and returned to the region. On October 26, 1799, he proclaimed the Independent State of Muscogee. The Creek Indians supported him, and on April 5, 1800, he declared war on Spain and captured Fort St. Marks on May 19. Spanish troops from Pensacola soon ousted the upstart, and he went into hiding in the hinterland; the

Spanish governor Vicente Folch offered a $4,500 reward to anyone who delivered him dead or alive. He was arrested in 1803, so the State of Muscogee had a de facto existence of a little more than three years. This time, Bowles was unable to escape, and he died in El Morro Castle at Havana on December 23, 1805. Following Bowles's disappearance, St. Marks experienced a period of peace, so much so that, in 1808, the Spanish authorities considered evacuating the fort.

However, a garrison remained there, and in 1814 was commanded by Francisco Caso y Luengo. In the course of the Anglo-U.S. war, British agents agitated the Indians against the territories entrusted to Andrew Jackson; claiming that the Spanish authorities were incapable of preventing such raids, Jackson ordered his troops to proceed to St. Marks, where they arrived on April 6, 1818. When Major Caso y Luengo refused to surrender, Captain Twiggs took the fort the following morning. This event caused a major commotion in Congress, and in the respective parliaments in Spain and Britain. The government of the United States changed its mind and ordered the withdrawal of its forces from there and from Pensacola in the summer of 1819. The Spanish troops reoccupied St. Marks until their final withdrawal, following the Treaty of Cession of Florida to the United States in 1821.

Pensacola

It remains for us to look at events in the western sector of Florida. Highway 90 from Tallahassee leads to Pensacola (former capital of Spanish West Florida), crosses the Apalachicola River and passes the towns of Marianna, Ponce de Léon (from which the highest peak of Florida can be seen) and Crestview, where in April the annual Old Spanish Trail Festival is held. Highway 98, along the coast, passes through such Spanish-sounding places as Mexico Beach, not far from Cape San Blas, fair-sized towns such as Panama City and smaller centers such as San Blas, Santa Rosa and Valparaiso.

When landing at Pensacola municipal airport, travelers are greeted by a large plaque reading "Pensacola. Fiesta of the Five Flags" and visitors are soon acquainted with the history of the city revealed by the five flags that have flown over the town through the centuries: Spain possessed Pensacola from 1559 to 1719, from 1722 to 1763, and from 1781 until 1821; France held it between 1719 and 1722; Great Britain, from 1763 to 1781; the United States, from 1821 until 1861, and again from 1862 onward; and the Confederate states held Pensacola in the period between 1861 and 1862.

These sandy beaches were probably first visited by white men on the arrival of the Spanish navigators Miruelos and Pineda around 1519. In 1528, they were visited by the Narváez expedition, for whom they were anything but welcoming. The overladen boats only avoided sinking thanks to the canoes placed alongside them, taken from some Indians who fled when they saw the Spaniards. When they reached Santa Rosa Island, a storm broke out and forced them to disembark. Literally dying of thirst because the water supply on board had become undrinkable, several men perished after drinking salt water. Faced with the prospect of inevitable dehydration, the rest decided to risk setting sail again. So they ventured into Pensacola Bay, where they were welcomed by the Indians in a friendly fashion initially but were later ambushed and forced to withdraw (with Cabeza de Vaca covering the retreat) and to put to sea again; all of them had been wounded.

Francisco Maldonado came to this same bay at the end of 1539, when, on orders from Hernando de Soto, he explored the area in search of a navigable river and a well-protected harbor. Either here or at Mobile Bay (the latter would appear to be more likely), Maldonado waited fruitlessly for his leader throughout the following summer at the rendezvous that they had arranged to supply the *conquistador* with the necessary reinforcements of men and supplies brought from Havana.

The Early Spanish Settlements

In 1557, urged by his viceroy in New Spain, Luis de Velasco, to settle and evangelize Florida, King Philip II of Spain ordered him to appoint a governor to organize an expedition bound for two points, one unspecified, and the other, Santa Elena or St. Helena on the coast of South Carolina, to offset the presence of the French. Velasco chose for the task Don Tristán de Luna, a rich nobleman and deputy to the explorer Francisco Vázquez de Coronado during his discoveries. In June 1559, he set sail for Veracruz with 500 soldiers, 1,000 settlers, numerous Indians, 240 horses and abundant provisions, aboard 13 ships. After a hazardous voyage, in which a fair number of animals and supplies were lost, Luna considered it more advisable to settle in Pensacola Bay. They landed on Santa Rosa Island, where the first Mass was said. (In commemoration, a cross stands today on Highway 399, which traverses the island to

Fort Pickens, a massive fortress dating from 1834, situated at the mouth of the bay; it was used as a prison for the Indian rebel Geronimo and was fortified specially in 1898, at the time of the war with Spain.)

When Luna realized that he only had provisions for 80 days, he dispatched a galleon to Mexico and ordered to patrols to scout through the region in search of food. While one, in which Fray Pedro de Feria took part, followed the Escambia River upstream, the other, with Father Domingo de la Anunciación, explored the easternmost sector of the mainland. Neither party achieved its purpose. Moreover, on August 19, a terrible hurricane sank the anchored ships, with the exception of one driven inland by the wind, which everybody considered to be the work of the Devil. A solution had to be found to relieve the situation, and Luna himself therefore took command of an expedition that set out inland as far as what is now Talladega County, in Alabama. After much hardship, he was forced to return to his starting point, where he ordered his lieutenant, Mateo del Saúz, to abandon the endeavor after seven months, owing to the discouragement and even insubordination that was spreading among the settlers, led by Jorge Cerón.

On Palm Sunday 1561, Fray Domingo de la Anunciación celebrated Mass, and before the Communion, turned to the congregation; with the consecrated Host in his hand, he asked Luna to approach. He then asked him solemnly whether he confessed to being a good Catholic and, when Luna replied that he was, whether he did not declare himself guilty of injustices and misgovernment. Overcome, Luna asked all those present for forgiveness of his sins and errors, which brought a similar response from the dissidents, who proclaimed their renewed loyalty to their leader. But starvation still threatened, with no remedy in sight.

Fortunately, the aid requested from Mexico arrived on March 14, 1561, aboard two ships commanded by Angel de Villafañe, who brought with him the order to move the colony to the east coast of Florida, at Santa Elena, and to replace Luna, who was ill. In compliance with these orders, Luna sailed via Havana in April. Accompanied by the settlers (although many stayed behind at Havana), Villafaña set course for their new destination, while a garrison of about 70 men was left at Pensacola with orders to return to New Spain unless orders to the contrary were received within six months. That was the end of the first Spanish attempt to settle in the area, which, at that time, according to the so-called Luna Papers published by well-known experts on the subject, was called Bahía Filipina del Puerto de Santa María, or "Philippine Bay of St. Mary's Port."

The second Spanish settlement at Pensacola was the result of disquiet caused among the Spanish authorities by the presence of the French explorer René-Robert Cavelier, sieur de La Salle in the Gulf of Mexico, and the interest taken by France in the area. Under the command of Admiral Andrés Matías de Paz and Doctor Carlos de Sigüenza y Góngora, an expedition reconnoitered the coastline of the Gulf of Mexico in 1639, from Pensacola to the mouth of the Mississippi, and recommended the occupation of Pensacola Bay. Therefore, the viceroy of New Spain, Count of Montezuma, ordered the senior *alcalde* (mayor) of Santa Fe de Guanajuato, Don Andrés de Arriola, to prepare the expedition. With the rank of *maestre de campo*, he weighed anchor at Veracruz with 200 men aboard three ships, on October 15, 1698, but did not reach his destination until November 21. There he found Captain Juan Jordán de Reina, who had arrived from Spain via Havana two days earlier. As soon as they disembarked, the expeditionaries set to work to mount the 18 cannon, which they had brought, and to erect the living quarters. Fort San Carlos de Austria began to be built as soon as the necessary timber became available; designed by Jayme Franck, who was present to direct the work, it was about 280 feet square and had four bastions.

Their occupation of the area could not have been more timely, for three months after they began to settle in, a large French fleet commanded by Pierre Le Moyne, seigneur of Iberville, appeared and requested permission to enter the bay. When permission was refused, the French sailed west and proceeded to settle on Dauphin Island (later Mobile) and at Biloxi. Once he considered that the fortification works had reached a stage at which they could be defended, Arriola departed and left the command to Sargento Mayor Francisco Martínez, and in his absence, to Captain Jordán. Being built of timber, in such a particularly humid area with strong winds, the fort soon began to suffer the effects of the weather. Moreover, the unhealthiness of the area and the difficulty in obtaining provisions directly raised the cost of maintaining the *presidio* to the considerable figure of 100,000 pesos a year. Several fires broke out, one in 1704, which caused the destruction of buildings attached to the fort. For all these reasons, Governor Salinas Verona proposed that it should be transferred to Santa Rosa Island in 1712.

The War of the Spanish Succession resulted in Spain becoming allied with France, with the result that their respective establishments on the Gulf of Mexico gave each other mutual aid against the Indians and British. Once the war was over, however, their relations gradually deteriorated so that, when Governor Salinas left his post in 1718, he warned of an imminent French attack on Fort San Carlos and advised that the garrison be reinforced. On May 14, 1719, Monsieur de Bienville ordered a combined sea and land attack, which took the Spaniards by surprise and forced the new governor, Juan Pedro Matamoros, to surrender. The prisoners were sent to Havana. A fleet that the governor of Cuba, Gregorio Guazo, was preparing to attack Fort George, in the Carolinas, was sent to Pensacola under Admiral de la Torre and took the fort on August 6, together with 350 prisoners. In response, a large French expedition commanded by Count de Champmeslin, attacked the Spanish settlement on September 18 and after 10 hours of fighting, won the day. The fort was destroyed, the buildings set on fire, and the Spanish cannons were thrown into the bay. In four months, Pensacola had changed hands four times! However, under the peace treaty that ended the War of the Quadruple Alliance, France returned Pensacola to Spain in 1722.

The remains of Fort San Carlos de Austria (yet another place in the United States under the Spanish advocation of St. Charles) can still be seen on some heights commanding the entrance to the bay. At the site of present-day Fort Barrancas (built by the United States in 1839), the height of the definitive structure of San Carlos, measuring 33 by 33 meters, was raised between 1781 and 1790 and turned into a semicircular shape, built in brick and surrounded by a deep moat. It was in the hands of the British in 1814, and was taken by their American ene- mies, who returned it to Spain at the end of the British-American war. Following the Indian uprising of 1818, the United States took possession of the fort again but returned it to Spain the following year. It ultimately came into the hands of the United States at the time of the cession of Florida by Spain in 1821.

To recover Pensacola and carry out what was to be the third Spanish settlement, the viceroy of New Spain chose Alexander Wauchope, a Scottish Catholic and second-in-command of the Armada de Barlovento, or Windward Fleet. He again chose Santa Rosa Island on account of its strategic situation, its good defensive position against Indian attacks and the plentiful supply of drinking water. A village soon sprang up, and the records show that by February 1723, there was a storehouse 13 meters long, a powder magazine, two large barracks, the house of the captain-governor and 32 dwellings. On a map dated 1739 are included gardens and fields that the Spaniards cultivated on the other shore of the bay, at the spot previously occupied by the second Spanish settlement. The sketches drawn by a trader, Serres, who visited Pensacola in 1743 on behalf of a company at Havana, show no less than 50 buildings.

In 1752 a hurricane destroyed the town, so the Spaniards built an outpost called San Miguel where today stands Seville Square. In 1763, when Florida was ceded to Great Britain, the third Spanish period came to an end. In the years that followed, the British built two forts, Fort Barrancas, on a site near old Fort San Carlos (1771), and Fort George, situated on the left-hand hill commanding the town. Archaeologist Norman Simons discovered it in 1961. This archaeological find, the result of several years' work, has been researched during the summers by teams

Two views of Fort Barrancas in Pensacola, Florida. Carlos M. Fernández-Shaw.

of students from Florida State University at Tallahassee, under the guidance of Professor Hale Smith.

Conquest of the City by Gálvez

When Spain declared war on Britain to assist the American revolutionaries seeking their independence, the governor of Louisiana and Mobile, Bernardo de Gálvez (who had been appointed commander of all Spanish operations in America by King Charles III after the taking of Mobile) convened the Council of War, or Junta, which decided on a plan of action to take Pensacola. After a first attempt to organize an expedition of 2,065 men, and a second that likewise failed to materialize, in August 1781, at Havana, Gálvez gathered a force of 3,800 men belonging to the army corps that had recently arrived from Spain. This force was joined by another 2,000 men from Mexico, Puerto Rico and Santo Domingo. But the fleet was dispersed in mid-October by a hurricane.

Gálvez soon recovered from his disappointment and convinced the Junta that the expedition should be recognized and that it was time to deal a final blow to British power at Pensacola. On March 8, Gálvez and his convoy sighted their first objective, Santa Rosa Island. The fire from the 140 British cannons on Barrancas Coloradas gave rise to a difference of opinion between the general and the commander of his fleet, Calbó, which was settled when the marshal decided personally to force the entrance to the bay with the felucca *Valenzuela* and the brigantine *Galveztown*. The operation succeeded, amid the applause of the fleet, and little damage was sustained. As a result, on the following night the whole fleet forced the passage without a single ship being hit (Calbó decided to retire to Havana). On March 22, the expeditionary force was joined by Ezpeleta and 500 men from Mobile, and the following day, the fleet from New Orleans arrived. To this force was added 1,600 veterans who arrived on April 19 under the command of Field Marshal Juan Manuel de Cagigal, in 20 ships commanded by José Solano. In this way, the forces at Gálvez's disposal now numbered over 7,000 men.

Gálvez was determined to carry out a decisive assault. After a month studying the situation, he ordered his men to dig a trench for three nights running, by which a 24-centimeter battery could be brought up close to the British fortifications. Several artillery duels and assaults took place with casualties on both sides, until at dawn on May 8, a Spanish projectile hit the magazine in the fort and resulted in an awesome explosion that killed between 80 and 100 defenders. Gálvez immediately ordered an assault, and at 3:00 P.M., General Archibald Campbell raised the white flag in surrender. Under the terms of capitulation, the British general handed over to the Spanish general the whole of West Florida in exchange for a commitment to grant his adversaries the honors of war, protect noncombatants, return slaves and send the prisoners to any port of their choice with the exception of Jamaica and St. Augustine. The formal surrender of the fort took place on May 10, 1781.

The news was received amid great rejoicing by those in Havana, and in Spain itself, where the *Gaceta de Madrid* printed the report from the victor to his uncle, Don José de Gálvez, president of the Council of the Indies. The fall of Pensacola was a serious setback for the British cause in North America and brought great satisfaction and relief to the weary armies of General George Washington. By his victory, the young Spanish general had, according to the historian Buchanan Parker Thompson, given the most vital aid contributed by any other man to the struggling American colonies. In winning this triumphant victory over the last great British outpost, he had not only served his king to the limit of his strength, but had made to the United States the most important gift any ally could ever offer: the security of their southeastern and western frontiers.

Acknowledging the importance of the event, King Charles III ordered that Pensacola be renamed Santa María de Gálvez; likewise, Fort George was renamed San Miguel (St. Michael); Fort Barrancas was given the name San Carlos; Queen's Redoubt was renamed Fort San Bernardo; and Prince of Wales Battery became Fort Sombrero. Gálvez was promoted to lieutenant general and West Florida was added to his governorship and made independent of New Spain; his personal pay was raised by 10,000 pesos during the war; he was given the title of count; and the royal order of November 12, 1781, read as follows: ". . . to perpetuate for posterity the memory of the heroic action in which you alone forced the passage into the bay, you may place as a crest over your coat of arms the brigantine *Galveztown*, with the motto: 'Yo Solo' ['I Alone']."

The Fourth Spanish Settlement

It was in this way that the fourth and last Spanish period at Pensacola began. After Florida was ceded to Spain by Britain under the Treaty of Versailles of September 3, 1783, the British division of the two Floridas was maintained; Pensacola became the Spanish capital in West Florida and had as many as nine governors.

Lying on the mainland, on the shores of Escambia Bay (the same name is still borne by the corresponding county) not far from Perdido River, present-day Pensacola can be said to have been born in 1750, when the Spaniards considered it advisable to build the San Miguel Palisade to defend the Christian Indians in the area. This really marked the start of the fourth Spanish settlement at Pensacola, although the new foundation work did not commence on a large scale until 1756, when the site of the third settlement was abandoned completely after a destructive hurricane.

As was deduced at the beginning of this visit to Pensacola, the street names have three origins: Aragon, Catalonia and the Spanish War of Independence against Napoleon. An important connection with events on the peninsula can be seen in the names of two squares that, in addition to that of Extremadura, are still the most important ones in the town: Ferdinand VII Plaza and Seville Square. (Seville Square was formerly called Plaza de la Constitución, while Ferdinand VII Square used to be called Sevilla. The change in name reflects how the absolutism of the son of King Charles IV had repercussions in distant Pensacola; the original name was in the honor of the constitution passed by the Cortes, or Parliament, at Cadiz.) The part of the town including these streets is identified with the old Spanish town. Period houses are still standing, such as Quina House (dating from 1815, owned by Desiderio Quina, an apothecary), Julee House (built in 1790 and reputed to be the oldest surviving house) and the Home of Illustrious Ladies (built by Gabriel Hernández in 1810); the sites occupied by the house of the governor, the jail and others are known.

It was in Ferdinand VII Plaza that the transfer of Florida from Spain to the United States took place and where Spanish troops drilled and public ceremonies took place. The City Hall and law courts still stand on this square. On July 17, 1821, General Andrew Jackson, with the fourth Regiment, appeared from the north side, while from the south came the Spanish governor José Callava, followed by his assistants and the Dragoons of Tarragona. With the two commanders situated in the center of the square, the Spanish flag was lowered to half-mast, while on another flagstaff, the American flag with 24 stars was raised. For a few moments the two flags remained at the same height, until the Spanish flag was lowered completely and the red, white and blue rose to the top of the flagstaff. Shouts of jubilation came from the throats of the Americans, while the Spaniards wept silently: seeing this painful contrast, Jackson ordered that all shows of jubilation cease. Just a few days earlier, however, his relations with Callava had not been friendly, for the Spaniard (who was unaware of the sale) had refused to hand over command to Jackson. Jackson decided to throw the governor into jail, but, as he was at home celebrating a family party, he preferred not to put up any resistance and took his friends and relations to prison with him and continued the party there.

These scenes have been graphically recorded by artists Rudeen and Manuel Runyan in the Pensacola Historical Museum (housed in an old Episcopalian church on Zaragossa Street), where many other Spanish mementos can also be seen: flags, plans of the town at different stages, the history of the different settlements and period costumes, all of which were arranged by the late director, Leila Abercrombie, together with a collection of photographs of Peñíscola, Spain, and its castle, sent to the museum by the wife of actor Charlton Heston, who starred in the film El Cid, which was filmed at Peñíscola. The name of Pensacola is thought by some to be derived, through successive changes in pronunciation, from Peñíscola. Near the museum lies the eight-acre St. Michael Cemetery, which was donated to the Catholics of Pensacola by the king of Spain in 1781. Administered by the Church for many years, today it depends on City Hall, which keeps it in perfect order. In it lie the remains of some prominent citizens, 257 born abroad and 215 on the American continent including Moreno, González, the wife of one of the signatories of the Declaration of Independence, two federal senators and the secretary of the navy of the Confederacy. To restore the burial ground, a foundation has been established, to which the Spanish government has contributed.

Governor Zéspedes considered the services of the Scottish traders William Panton and John Leslie to be indispensible in maintaining trade with the Creek Indians led by Alexander McGillivray against competition from the United States and Great Britain. Consequently, in 1785, he authorized Panton and Leslie to settle at Pensacola and set up business in cooperation with the Indian chief. So began a trading firm, Panton, Leslie and Co., which played an important part in Spanish policy. When McGillivray died in 1793, he was buried in the garden of the house.

Even side streets in Pensacola, such as Gonzalez and Moreno, have ties to a rich history. Jaime González, a wealthy Spanish landowner, was very influential in the affairs of the colony and retained that influence even after Florida became part of the United States, when he defended the rights of the Spaniards against the new occupiers. Francisco Moreno was the son of the doctor who accompanied Governor Gálvez when he conquered Pensacola in 1781; he married three times and had 27 children. The first banker in Pensacola (the chest that he used as a safe for his money can still be seen), his name on his own account and on that of his descendants has been linked with the history of the city ever since.

But these are not the only streets of the town bearing Spanish names. The truly surprising thing is that streets bearing Anglo-Saxon names are the exception, while Spanish names abound. Apart from the fact that the two main streets are called Cervantes and Palafox, they are followed in quick succession by names such as Alcañiz, Zaragossa, Barcelona, Tarragona, Manresa, Reus, Intendencia, Commendancia and Baylen. Palafox is by far the most important street in the town: broad, well laid out, with a fine garden in the center. At the point where the street begins there is a plaque explaining the Aragonese origin of the name. It is on this street that the Fiesta of the Five Flags has been held every spring since 1949 with a big parade of floats.

Various ceremonies took place at Pensacola in 1959 for the commemoration of the arrival here of Tristán de Luna and his companions 400 years earlier, with various festivities attended by a host of American and Spanish dignitaries. Parades, pageants, dances and a reenactment of the landing of Tristán de Luna with his spectac-

ular court were the climax of two major cultural events: the organization of an exhibition and the construction of a replica of the Spanish township as drawn by Serres. The exhibition installed on two floors of a new building had been opened the previous May; it consisted of exhibits largely from Spain (loans from the Naval and Army Museums and other centers, installed and tended by Matilde Medina), conveying a sense of Spanish culture of the time of Philip II and Spanish influence in North America since. The Spanish *aldea*, or village, whose buildings are still standing, contained a replica of the chapel, the fort, the house of the governor and a number of houses existing in 1743, all built of wood; in them could be seen a select group of Spanish craftsmen (potters, blacksmiths, silversmiths and embroiderers) dressed in their regional costumes and brought expressly from Spain to demonstrate their trades.

Pensacola quite often receives the visit of the Spanish training ship *Juan Sebastián Elcano*. For her visit in 1998, José M. Aznar, head of the Spanish government, was present.

Spanish Place-Names

Apart from the towns in Florida already mentioned that bear Spanish names, others include Alturas, Andalusia, Arredonda, Columbia, Cortez, El Portal, Hernando, Mayo, Naranja, Pedro, Ponce de Leon, Punta Gorda, San Blas, San Mateo, Seville and Valparaiso, in addition to Leon, De Soto and Santa Rosa counties.

PART III:
STATES ON THE EAST BANK OF THE MISSISSIPPI RIVER

Two criteria, geographic and historical, have prevailed in grouping these states together. Any river basin is always a homogeneous geographical complex, but this is all the more true in the case of the "Father of Rivers," one of the greatest water courses on Earth owing to its length, sheer size and the area that it irrigates and for which it serves as a fundamental means of transport. From the historical angle, it would have been possible to deal at the same time with those states situated on both banks, but historically speaking, the two banks have led separate lives, particularly with regard to their Spanish history.

When the war between France, Spain and Britain was ended by the Treaty of Paris of 1763, whereby France relinquished Canada and the rest of her colonies in North America to Britain, Spain gained possession of the lands lying to the west of the Mississippi and the island of New Orleans situated to the east, which comprised most of former French Louisiana, whereas Britain received the land on the left or eastern bank of the river. In the course of the preliminary peace negotiations, France had offered Britain Louisiana, but as Britain then held Cuba, she preferred to demand Florida in exchange for the recovery of Cuba by Spain. In order to overcome Spanish reluctance to lose such a strategic territory, which had been defended staunchly in earlier times, France offered her southern neighbor the territories of Louisiana situated on the west bank of the Mississippi. Strange though it may seem, this gift was not received enthusiastically at court in Madrid, for it only entailed greater expenditure, renewed efforts, increasing sources of concern for a declining state that was facing the many problems which her far-flung kingdoms already caused her. Nevertheless, the prevailing idea was that the large possessions that thus came into the hands of the Spanish Crown would serve as a buffer for New Spain and the dependent governorships, such as Texas and New Mexico, and would help to contain possible attempts at expansion by neighbors, whether they were British or colonists (who, in time, would acquire independence), or the French (whose presence had already proved to be a headache for the Spanish authorities in Texas). Therefore it was considered that France's disappearance, by transfer of its territories to Spain, would provide a period of tranquility. This, unfortunately, was not to last for many years.

It will be helpful to give a general outline of the Spanish presence in the states in question and the way in which her close links with them were forged. The primary reasons lay in the rebellion of the colonists against Great Britain, the proclamation of independence, the ensuing war and the Treaty of Paris of 1783 between Great Britain and the new nation. Had the revolution not broken out, the Spanish presence in the area would perhaps have been confined to frontier relations and to solving the problems caused for the French residents by the cession of Louisiana by France. Most of those French residents chose to submit to rule by Spain rather than by Britain, rightly assuming that, as Catholics, they would find greater protection and understanding among the representatives of the Spanish Bourbon monarchy than on the part of the Anglo-Saxon Protestant rulers. Consequently, many French people crossed the Mississippi and abandoned their places of residence on the east bank.

In Spain, the outbreak of war between Britain and her colonies aroused sympathy for the rebels from the outset, and that sympathy was to acquire concrete form in a number of steps that were of great importance for their cause, and would later become one of the essential reasons for Spain to declare war against her traditional enemy, as France had done earlier, on June 21, 1779, and for the participation of Spanish armies in the war.

It was in the region in question (together with that lying on the right bank of the Mississippi) that Spanish intervention in the war took place (with the exception of Pensacola, which was also taken from the British by troops under Bernardo de Gálvez in a timely fashion). The part played by the Spanish armies, as will be seen, became considerable and entailed military aid of a very specific nature for the colonists; it was the only assistance given to the new nation by another nation as such, with its regular army under the command of its own generals, acting as a friend and cobelligerent on orders emanating from the government itself. The direct French collaboration in the form of men and material means undoubtedly attained higher figures than that provided by Spain. But initially, the French only took part as volunteers, and later, by forming part of the revolutionary army under the supreme command of General George Washington. Thanks to the Spanish decision to go to war, many natives of Spanish territory (future citizens of the Union) were in a position to help achieve independence against Britain. Hence, their descendants can pride themselves (on a par with people in the East) on belonging to the prestigious Associations of Sons and Daughters of the American Revolution.

Furthermore, the Spanish military operations were successful. There were resounding victories at Fort Manchac, Baton Rouge, Natchez, Mobile, Pensacola, St. Louis and St. Joseph and no defeats; the only British forts left in the Mississippi valley were Detroit and Mackinac. The British had not made allowances for such results when they planned their campaigns (with the assistance of their Indian allies) to achieve freedom of navigation up the Mississippi River by taking such strategic points as New Orleans. As a result of their victories, and with a view to protecting the territories west of the Mississippi, the Spaniards began to consider their rights over the land east of the river, part of which had literally fallen into their hands, and where, at some

points, the forts erected clearly proclaimed the presence of Spain; Spanish activities in the area during the War of Independence included other steps aimed at laying the foundations for subsequent claims to sovereignty.

The Spanish claims to the territories to the east of the Mississippi received the support of France, and when Congress met in Philadelphia, the French diplomatic representative, Monsieur Chevalier de la Luzerne, insistently demanded that such Spanish claims be acknowledged, and even made this a condition for essential aid from France. The state of Virginia was an exception and took steps to contradict the Spanish arguments when the explorer George Rogers Clark built Fort Jefferson on the east bank of the Mississippi, with the approval of Thomas Jefferson in 1780; but the attacks of the Chickasaw Indians and difficulties over supplies forced him to abandon the fort the following year. The only American garrison remaining was that at Fort Nelson, in Louisville, named after King Louis XVI of France out of gratitude for French cooperation. By taking such steps, Virginia and the southern states, such as North Carolina, even angered those in the North, which lacked any territorial interests in the West and feared that such conduct might alienate French support and friendship. When the attempted mediation of Russia and Austria, offered to the United States on May 20, 1781, failed owing to the refusal of Britain, Minister La Luzerne felt able to report to his government that the Americans, realizing the true nature of their situation, were prepared to accept the Ohio River and even the Appalachians as the future frontier between the United States and Spain. Supreme responsibility in the ensuing peace negotiations lay with Benjamin Franklin, and in the summer of 1781, a difficult period for the American cause, he took a realistic view and declared himself ready to make concessions in order to achieve victory.

In August 1782, John Jay, who had served as delegate of the faithful Indian allies, was cast aside almost without discussion, and, instead, the British territories west of the Appalachians and south of the Great Lakes were recognized as belonging to the United States; thus, the dominions of several Indian nations were placed within the sphere of the new country. The boundary with Canada was traced along lines that coincide with the present ones, and the Spanish claims were made to recede to the west bank of the Mississippi and the territories south of the 31st parallel.

As a result of the new situation, both the United States and Spain wished to solve the problem of boundaries between their respective territories. It fell to the count of

Aranda to negotiate with Jay, who was residing in Paris again, in the course of talks that began in the middle of 1782. The Spanish ambassador began by drawing the frontier that Spain claimed in red pencil on one of the maps in the Mitchell Atlas: the line began at Lake Superior, descended to cross Lake Erie, continued via the confluence of the Conhaway River with the Ohio River, proceeded to the innermost tip of South Carolina and then continued in a straight line to a lake in Apalachee territory, formed by a river whose name was unknown and flowed into the Altamaha or George River, but without actually reaching it, thus leaving an undecided point.

Realizing his scant cartographical knowledge, Aranda resorted to the expertise of Rayneval, undersecretary to French foreign minister, the count of Vergonnes, and laid down as a cardinal point in the negotiations with Jay the existence of two categories of British territory in North America: the colonies themselves, with an established population and established boundaries, and the crowns territories that had been conquered from other empires, for example, Canada, Louisiana and Florida. Jay proposed a compromise boundary line that would run from Kanawha to the frontier of Georgia, thus retaining Pennsylvania and most of the settlements in the Holston area for the emerging states, but leaving Kentucky and Tennessee in Spanish territory. The British, on the other hand, were clearly unwilling to cede to the rebels anything beyond the Proclamation Line of 1763, those being territories which had been denied to the subjects loyal to the Spanish Crown.

Count Floridablanca, the Spanish chief minister, rejected the Russian and Austrian offers of mediation. He made the loyalty of Spain quite plain by not agreeing to leave the way open for future outrages against the rebels, and by his unwillingness to sign the peace unless they were granted their desired independence.

However, the attitude of Britain's government suddenly changed when Lord Shelburne was appointed to lead the cabinet. The British negotiators realized that their position should be precisely the opposite to that of the French. If France was in favor of a western frontier for the new nation, which would limit its expansion in that direction, Britain should argue in favor of the contrary. So it was that the astonished American delegates received peace proposals that would have been out of the question years or even months earlier; they were included in the provisional peace treaty signed on November 30, 1782. The memorandum drafted by Rayneval suited the Spaniards, since it made them successors of the rights acquired by France in Louisiana, although it placed the boundary line somewhat differently to that proposed by Aranda. Internal difficulties in the United States and the appointment of Diego Gardoqui as Spanish representative to the United States Congress deferred the reaching of an agreement.

Meanwhile, the active but not always peaceful expansionism of the colonists and the growing weakness of Spain, in spite of the patriotism and ability of her representatives in America, led to American domination over the upper part of the east banks to the Mississippi being de facto uncontested. The same was not the case at the southern end of the area under dispute, where dangerous tension arose. The absence of any legal basis for the American claims to this sector has been recognized by historians such as Flagg Bemis. Both sides resorted to invaluable alliances with the Indians, who on this occasion, openly sided with the Spaniards. Continued American pressure and the steady Spanish decline ended in the signing of the Treaty of San Lorenzo in 1795, under which Spain practically abandoned her previous stand and gave way to her neighbor. This coincided in practice with the policy that Aranda had advised Floridablanca to pursue in a letter dated March 2, 1783, where he said, among other things, that "since that new dominion . . . looks as if it will be tranquil in its settlement, which is everything that we could desire, for the same reason it would seem to be in our interests for it to begin to live with such a disposition, without any immediate cause remaining that it may look upon with resentment, so that neither in those living today nor in the tradition of their successors, any ill-will shall be engendered among neighbors . . ."

But the presence of Spain gave rise to another most important aspect: while accepting the fact of the material occupation of the regions of Kentucky and Tennessee by the colonists in the East, Spain looked with sympathy upon their desires to become independent from the thirteen provinces and to associate with Spain on certain conditions. There was a time in 1787 when everybody believed that the West would become Spanish, and the Spanish authorities in the area were of that opinion themselves. Of their own free will, the Anglo-Saxon inhabitants of the territories now comprising Kentucky and Tennessee were on the point of becoming dependent on the Crown of Spain in the last quarter of the 18th century, just five years after independence. What had proved impossible to retain by force was almost achieved by peaceful means. Little imagination is needed to realize what would have become of the new nation if the cessionist wishes of a fraction of its inhabitants had come true.

◆ ILLINOIS, WISCONSIN, INDIANA, MICHIGAN AND OHIO ◆

Illinois

Illinois is a familiar name in Spanish documents kept at the Archive of the Indies in Seville and in history books dealing with Spain's past. Illinois became a part of the Spanish world and events at the period when Spain took over possession of Louisiana as a result of the Treaty of Paris, whereby France ceded these vast territories, in 1763. From that time onward, the name Illinois, taken from some of the Indians in the region, began to appear, albeit with peculiar Hispanified spelling as in many other cases. Thus, references are made to *Ylinoa* and *Ylinois* and to the district of the *Ylinenses*. In his report to Governor Alexander O'Reilly on October 29, 1769, Francisco Rui states that the leading township of the Ylinenses is one called Santa Genoveva, otherwise known as Misera. His report dated two days later to Lieutenant Governor Pedro Piernas includes a description that begins as follows: "The land of the 'Ylinoeses' is, on the whole, healthy and fertile, with a delightful climate and suitable for all kinds of plants."

These Spanish reports obviously mention Ylinois as covering a larger area than that occupied by the state of Illinois today; the Spaniards undoubtedly meant Upper Louisiana, which comprised the land north of what is now half of the state of Arkansas.

Chicago

Hispanics—from Puerto Rico, Mexico and Colombia, as well as natives—are becoming a major force in Chicago (in 1976, they provided the mayoral candidate John Howlett with 200,000 votes), and it is the most populous Catholic archdiocese in the United States. While it was once the setting for the anti-Spanish editorials of William Randolph Hearst's newspapers, which urged war against Spain in 1898, today it is home for several important Hispanic organizations, including the Spanish Association of the Midwest. Every other year it is the site of the convention of the Modern Language Association and the American Association of Teachers of Spanish and Portuguese.

In spring 1988, the Cultural Center of the Public Library of Chicago showed an exhibition called "Nueva Epoca" (New Epoch) dedicated to the paintings and sculptures of young Spanish artists. Among them were José Manuel Broto, Chema Cobo, Ferrán García Sevilla, Miguel Navarro, José María Sicilia, Juan Uslé and Susana Solano.

Chicago has an exceptional art institute containing a number of Spanish works of art: a splendid medieval retable of Chancellor López de Ayala; two works by Bernat Martorell and Bartolomé Bermejo; *St. Francis and the Skull, The Feast in the House of Simon, The Assumption of the Blessed Virgin* and *St. Francis* by El Greco; *St. John, Job* and *The Servant Girl* by Diego Rodríguez de Silva Velázquez; *Two Monks in the Country* by Bartolomé Murillo; *Crucifixion, Still Life* and *St. Romain* by Francisco Zurbarán; *Isidoro Máiquez* and *Six Episodes from the Capture of the Bandit Morgato by the Monk Pedro de Zaldívar* by Francisco Goya; together with such works by Pablo Picasso as *Sylvette, The Old Guitarist* and *Mother and Child*; Salvador Dalí's *Mae West* and *Inventions of the Monsters*; Joan Miró's *People with Stars, Chessboard* and *A Woman and Birds in Front of the Sun*; and others.

In the Civic Center Square, the imposing steel sculpture depicting a fanciful bird with its head bent down, donated to the city by Picasso, lends a Hispanic note to the colossal urban setting, as does the sculpture in front by Miró. Its inauguration, in the summer of 1967, was attended by 50,000 people.

The Museum of Science and Industry is all that remains of the Columbian World Exposition of October 1892, organized to celebrate the third centenary of the discovery of America. Spain was represented on that occasion by Infanta Eulalia. The ceremonies were presided over by Vice President Levy P. Morton, together with several members of the government, in the absence of President Benjamin Harrison. A parade of

80,000 men, with Indians and cowboys, 150 bands playing (John Philip Sousa conducted the navy band) and a concert in which a choir 1,000 strong took part, were some of the events during the exposition. At a time when the suffragist campaign to obtain voting rights for women was at its peak, a board of women was asked to help organize the commemorative ceremonies with the slogan that, but for Queen Isabella, "Columbus would never have discovered America."

In the field of higher studies, the city has, among others, the University of Chicago, founded in 1890 with funds provided by John D. Rockefeller. Here, the library contains the Durret Collection, documents relating to the attempt of Kentucky to achieve independence, and the Gardoqui Collection, containing copies from the Spanish archives concerning his diplomatic mission in the United States. Loyola University, run by the Jesuits, houses an Institute of History of the Society of Jesus, which has studied the Spanish missions in North America; publishes the quarterly review *Mid-America*; and awards every year the Sword of Loyola to "persons exemplifying Ignatius of Loyola's courage, dedication and service."

Western Illinois

Sixty-odd years before the Mormons arrived, the Spaniards overran the western sector of Illinois. The inhabitants of Cahokia, near present-day East St. Louis, made common cause with the Spaniards (who were stationed on the opposite bank of the Mississippi) in 1780, to defend themselves from Indian attacks. A company totaling 300 took reprisals (under the command of Colonel John Montgomery) near Bear River and Prairie du Chien, in the vicinity of Keokuk, on the border of Iowa, Illinois and Missouri.

Down the Mississippi, some 60 miles from St. Louis, was Kaskasia, opposite St. Geneviève. This settlement, together with that of Cahokia, played a particularly important role in the days of the Revolution, and it is worth noting the Spanish participation in events there. General George Rogers Clark arrived at Kaskasia on July 4, 1778, in compliance with instructions from the governor of Virginia, Patrick Henry, who had approved the plan submitted to him by Clark the previous December. The lack of munitions, supplies and money to pay his troops jeopardized his situation, which was saved thanks to the drafts and bills of exchange that Clark sent to New Orleans to the agent for Virginia, Oliver Pollock.

They were accepted by the Spanish governor, who advanced Pollock as much as $74,087 for the purchase of gunpowder and other provisions, and helped him to obtain them. Bernardo de Gálvez likewise allowed the men of James Willing, who had arrived from Pittsburgh in an armed boat, to join forces with Clark by crossing Spanish territory. Subsequently, Pollock was to undertake a personal commitment for the sum of $136,466, which caused his ruin when the state of Virginia did not honor its debts; 10 years later he was duly reimbursed by the Virginian and federal governments.

Clark also received a sympathetic hearing from Fernando de Leyba, the Spanish lieutenant governor at St. Louis, who anticipated his arrival due to confidential information that he had received (like other Spanish commanders on the Mississippi) from the Spanish agent in Philadelphia, Juan Miralles, who had been informed of the venture planned. Clark was welcomed very cordially by Leyba; in a letter to Patrick Henry, he stated that the Spaniard had offered him all the forces that he could raise in the event of an attack by the Indians from Detroit. (Leyba and Clark became close friends.) All the resources of the settlements at St. Louis were open to those of Kentucky and later included even the hospitality of the home of the lieutenant governor himself and the warm affection of the ladies of his family (the love between Clark and the lieutenant governor's sister, Teresa de Leyba, is a matter of record).

The campaign undertaken by Clark was to end with the definitive capture of Vincennes, today in the state of Indiana, whose victory was aided by the assistance provided by Gálvez and Pollock. Clark had not only relied on them for supplies for his troops but, thanks to the credit they had extended to him, had been able to continue the conquest of the region and hold it. Without their assistance, Vincennes would have fallen into British hands, and the British plan to conquer the Mississippi basin would have resulted in the loss of the West and dire consequences for the course of the war.

The ties of Kaskasia and Cahokia with the Spaniards increased as more and more French Catholic inhabitants of those townships fled to the right bank of the Mississippi; Father Pierre Gibault was appointed parish priest of St. Geneviève in 1778; Gabriel Cerré, one of the wealthy citizens of Kaskasia, immigrated to the Spanish side in 1779; Charles Gratiot, from Cahokia, followed him shortly afterward. Years later, miners working under Julien Dubuque, a Spanish subject, worked lead mines on the Aple River, near the present town of Elizabeth, in the west.

Spanish Place-Names

In the state of Illinois there are the following localities bearing Spanish names: Aledo, Alma, Alto Pass, Andalusia, Arena, Argenta, Aurora, Cerro Gordo, Cisne, Columbia, Cordova, Cuba, De Soto, Eldorado, El Paso, Galena, Havana, Hidalgo, Lima, Manito, New Columbia, Nevada, Noble, Palos Heights, Palos Park, Peru, Plano, Polo, Sacramento, San Jose, Seneca, Serena, Toledo and Trilla. Toledo belongs to the world association of towns that take pride in the same name.

Wisconsin

Wisconsin is one of the states with few historical connections with Spain. Nevertheless, western Wisconsin was the scene of a feat of arms in which Julien Dubuque, mentioned above, proved victorious. During the Spanish-British war in 1797, he led an expedition from his home in Iowa (Mines d'Espagne) to Prairie du Chien, 50 miles north, in Wisconsin, succeeded in ousting the British and their Indian allies, and returned to his base with considerable booty.

Spanish Place-Names

Spanish names are borne by Columbia and Vigas Counties, and the following towns: Alma, Almena, Barron, Casco, Centuria, Columbia, Cornucopia, Cuba, Deronda, De Soto, Lima Center, Polar, Potosi, Rio and West Lima.

Indiana

In the southwest of Indiana on the banks of the Wabash River, stands Vincennes, named for the French captain killed in 1736. During the Revolution, the citizens of Wabash were independent; since most of them were French, they opposed British domination and therefore helped General Clark to take the town on February 24, 1779. Spanish assistance was invaluable in achieving this objective, not only through the materials provided for the revolutionary leader, but through the personal cooperation of a Spanish subject, Colonel Juan María Vigo, a trader who acted on orders from the Spanish

governor of St. Louis. Having a considerable fortune, Vigo used it in the fight against Britain (one of the counties in Indiana was later to be called after him). While Clark was at Kaskasia, he commissioned Vigo to reconnoiter after Vincennes was taken by British general George Hamilton on December 15, 1778. Five miles before reaching his destination, he was taken prisoner by the British and, although considered a rebel spy, no steps were taken against him owing to his popularity among the citizens of Vincennes and his being a subject of the king of Spain. Hamilton released him on condition that he should take no further part in the Revolution. Although he remained neutral, he did report his impressions to Clark, and these were of great assistance in the taking of Vincennes.

Years later, in 1786, Clark fell back to Vincennes in the course of his unsuccessful expedition against the Indians, and there he confiscated the merchandise of three Spanish traders, thus making the final mistake that led to the appointment of a committee of inquiry into his conduct; the findings of the commission were unfavorable and led to his dismissal and the decline of the good luck that had accompanied him until then.

The Spanish expedition under Eugenio Purré that conquered Fort St. Joseph (San José) in Michigan in 1781 passed through the northern region of Indiana twice while going there and back.

In the state capital, Indianapolis, is the John Herron Institute of Art, which among other notable works, has the paintings of *The Philosopher* by Ignacio Zuloaga; *A Boy Blowing Bubbles,* attributed to Bartolomé Murillo; an anonymous Spanish painting of the 16th century; five sketches by Joaquín Sorolla; and two engravings by Francisco de Goya and Pablo Picasso. In February 1963, the institute hung the outstanding exhibit "From Greco to Goya," consisting of Spanish paintings from American collections. The Universities of Purdue, Notre Dame and Indiana have important Departments of Spanish. In 1781, John Hay, an Indiana politician, wrote the perceptive book on Spanish customs *Castilian Days.*

Spanish Place-Names

Spanish names in Indiana include Vigo County, and the towns of Amo, Aurora, Avila, Buena Vista, Cadiz, Carmel, Francisco, Galveztown (in honor of Gálvez), Honduras, Largo, Lopez, Navarra, Plato, Point Isabel, San Jacinto, Santa Fe, Valparaiso, Veracruz, and Vigo.

Michigan

Strange as it may seem at first sight, the Spanish flag flew in Michigan in 1781 with full sovereign rights, deriving from conquest. The fact that Spanish arms had been victorious in this area provided a basis for the court at Madrid to defend its claims to the land east of the Mississippi River. What happened was as follows: the new lieutenant governor of St. Louis, Francisco Cruzat, heard that the British were renewing preparations to attempt to conquer the town for the second time, and they were building up their forces at Fort St. Joseph. He therefore decided to resort to the strategic maxim of attacking to avoid being attacked, and to make the best possible use of surprise. He was helped in his project by the Indians Heturno and Naguiquen, and by the French population of Cahokia, who wished to make good the losses suffered in an earlier assault on the fort (as was the case with the successful conquest of Vincennes by Clark, in 1779).

The expedition departed from St. Louis on January 2, 1781, under the command of a Spanish subject, Eugenio Purré (or Pourée), with Carlos Tayon as second-in-command and Louis Chevalier acting as guide and interpreter; the latter was the son of the French commander of the fort in question, who had been ill-treated by the British when they took it. The expedition was completed by 65 soldiers and about 200 Indian allies. With the addition of 12 Spanish soldiers stationed along the Illinois River, the force marched almost 400 miles across snow-bound country and through the territories of Indian tribes (who did not hinder the travelers), with a plentiful supply of provisions to survive and buy the neutrality of the natives, but with little clothing to protect them from the low temperatures. The days that followed until February 12 were therefore difficult. Fortunately the tiny army was able to cross the frozen St. Joseph River on foot and attacked the fort and adjacent fortifications by surprise. No lives were lost among the attackers, and the provisions found in the fort were distributed among those who had taken part, including the Indians. The Spanish flag was raised ceremoniously (while the British flag was captured and later taken to St. Louis as a trophy), and they took possession of the country in the name of King Charles III.

Since the purpose of the expedition was defensive, intended to destroy British provisions and their support base for a future attack on Spanish positions, and since the forces available to Cruzat were not sufficiently large for him to leave a suitable garrison at St. Joseph, so far from St. Louis, Purré gave the order to withdraw, after a short rest and burning the fort and adjacent buildings, except for the chapel. The contingent experienced similar hardship on the way home, but arrived safely in early March.

The lieutenant governor gave his superiors in New Orleans and Madrid a colorful report on the successful venture, and the *Gaceta de Madrid* published the news in its issue of March 12, 1782. John Jay, the representative of those seeking independence, read the issue and wrote a somewhat anxious letter to his secretary of foreign relations in Philadelphia, on April 28, 1782; his disquiet was shared by the American negotiators in Paris, whose prospects had not yet been improved by the eventual British decision to cede to the new nation all territories on the east bank of the Mississippi. José de Gálvez, at that time prime minister to the king of Spain, in letter number 62, dated at El Pardo on January 15, 1782, congratulated his nephew Bernardo Gálvez, governor of Louisiana, and conferred upon Eugenio Purré the rank of lieutenant of the army on half-pay; on Carlos Tayon, the rank of sublieutenant on half-pay; and on Louis Chevalier, whatever reward the governor saw fit.

Fort St. Joseph stood at a spot that now belongs to the town of Niles (which, for that reason, calls itself "The Town of the Four Flags": France, Britain, Spain and the United States), very near South Bend. There, a 70-ton stone bears the inscription "Fort St. Joseph. 1691–1781," and a placard nearby gives a short description of its history. This monument was inaugurated on July 5, 1913. There have been plans to rebuild the fort and make a large park around it for the organization of an annual festival; the main obstacle encountered has been the lack of reliable information on the characteristics of the original fortification. There is a museum in which, unfortunately, there is little detail concerning its Spanish history.

Detroit is known as the home of the auto industry; Spaniard José Ignacio López Arriortua was for a period of time the world vice president of General Motors.

Spanish Place-Names

In the state of Michigan, Spanish names are borne by Isabella County and the towns of Adrian, Alamo, Alba, Alpena, Amasa, Armada, California, Caro, Coloma, Colon, Columbus, Coronna, Disco, Eldorado, Luna, Manton, Moran, Palo and Santiago, in addition to St. Ignace, in honor of the Basque Jesuit saint.

Ohio

While the state capital, Columbus, is named after the discoverer, other localities bear names such as Columbiana (the seat of the county of the same name), Columbia, Columbia Station, Columbia Hills and Columbus Grove.

In the art museum at Cleveland can be seen such Spanish paintings as *A Portrait of Don Luis de Borbón* by Goya and *The Death of Adonis* by José de Ribera. Spanish departments can be found at the Universities of Bowling Green, Ohio State and Ohio Wesleyan (which also has an outstanding library and newspaper collection concerning the Spanish Civil War), as well as the College of Wooster, among others.

The Ohio River forms the southern and most of the eastern boundary of the state territory. In the course of the peace negotiations that led to independence, the possibility arose, opposed by some representatives of the United Provinces in Paris, of the Ohio River forming the frontier with the territories of the king of Spain. Had that idea prospered, today Spanish might be spoken on the shores of Lake Erie or in the surroundings of Chillicothe!

The prettiest route to Toledo, Ohio, is the road skirting the lake, which passes through an area where Sandusky lies, a town that seems practically German. While imperial Toledo, in Spain, stands on the river Tagus, Toledo, Ohio, lies on the Maumee River (Ferdinand La Salle claimed the region in the name of Louis XIV in 1689). Needless to say, Toledo, Ohio, is named after the Spanish Toledo, seemingly based on descriptions from Washington Irving's accounts from Spain. Once the name Toledo had been chosen, the city was consolidated officially under that name in 1837. When it celebrated its first centenary there was a growing civic movement in favor of establishing relations with the imperial city, and thanks to the enthusiasm of a Spaniard, Germán

Erausquin, and other distinguished citizens, an agreement was reached to make the two municipalities twin cities. The relationship is maintained by respective commissions; every year, on the same day, both cities celebrate the Day of the Two Toledos, which consists of various ceremonies and events that end with a banquet and speeches. The university contains the swords, damascene work, ceramics and photographs donated by the commission from Spanish Toledo.

Toledo takes pride in its museum of art. The Spanish paintings include two El Grecos, *The Annunciation* and *Christ at Gethsemane*; a Velázquez, *Man with a Goblet of Wine*; a Zurbarán, the very famous *The Flight into Egypt*; a José de Ribera, *A Musician*; and a Goya, *Children with a Barrow*. Its university takes the Spanish imperial arms for its coat of arms: an eagle and quarterings of castles, lions, bars, etc., surrounded by the motto in Spanish: *Coadyuvando el presente, formando el porvenir,* meaning "Helping the present, forming the future."

Spanish Place-Names

Apart from the names based on Columbus, many towns in Ohio bear the names of Spanish provinces, such as Cadiz, Malaga, Navarre, Seville and Toledo, and also of Hispanic cities such as Lima (a city of considerable size), Medina, Limaville, North Lima and Santa Fe. Other place-names connected with the Hispanic world include Alma, Aurora, Bolivar, Buena Vista, Carmel, Delta, Era, Fresno, Morral, Nevada, New Matamoras, Point Isabel, Rio Grande, Saltillo, Seneca, Toboso and Vega.

◆ *KENTUCKY AND TENNESSEE* ◆

Kentucky

The European colonization of Kentucky can be said to have started in 1774, following the battle between the British settlers and the Shawnee at Point Pleasant. None of the 350 settlers inhabiting Kentucky in 1775 had brought a family with him, until Daniel Boone, an agent of the Henderson Company, fetched his wife and daughters. They therefore became the first women to live in Kentucky, just as Daniel Boone himself had been the first European to explore and settle in the area.

Another of the pioneers was George Rogers Clark, who was soon entrusted by his fellow pioneers with defending them from Indian attacks. Realizing the abuses which the Transylvania Land Company was committing by raising land prices, thus making it useless for immigrants to make the effort to venture westward only to find no recompense, Clark called a meeting of the inhabitants of the villages of the area at Harrodsburg on June 6, 1776. There they decided to appoint him their representative and that he should travel to the capital of Williamsburg, Virginia, in order to arrange for the territory to become part of Virginia, with a seat in the provincial assembly for its delegate. After many obstacles were overcome, Kentucky was admitted as a Virginian county on December 7. Clark's able leadership and the loyalty of his troops were to be proved shortly afterward in the fight for independence, when they invaded British territory and took Vincennes. This victory and those of other patriots, such as John Sullivan, Daniel Brohead and Isaac Shelby, took immediate effect and gave a feeling of security to people who had heard fabulous tales about Kentucky. Hundreds of families rushed to the area, and about 20,000 people settled there in the space of six months.

In December 1783, James Wilkinson arrived; he was to become the master of political affairs in Kentucky for a quarter of a century. Wilkinson was a physically striking and intelligent man. He had soldiered under Benedict Arnold in Quebec and under Horatio Gates at Saratoga, but it was as a politician that he was to make his mark. Ever ambitious for more money, he accepted considerable sums as payment for spying on France, Spain and Great Britain. He had not the slightest scruple about betraying friends or benefactors, as long as he could turn that betrayal to his own advantage. In spite of the risks he ran and the money he accepted, he was clever enough to weather public outcries, inquiries by Congress, courts martial and trials for treason, without ever being found guilty, and yet he died an expatriate in Mexico on December 25, 1825.

Part of the Wilkinson story is linked with Spanish policy, which he served for purely personal reasons, rather than ideological ones. Although at one time he had espoused the Spanish cause, he had no scruples about commanding the occupation troops at New Orleans or Mobile, or ordering the taking of Spanish forts, such as San Fernando. His influence in Kentucky eclipsed the preeminent position of Clark in the region.

For the first year after peace was restored, Kentucky remained in a state of turmoil. The arrival of new colonists added to the uncertainty already existing concerning the title deeds of earlier settlers; the Indians continued their persistent, isolated and devastating attacks, which made life in the area uneasy; and local laws were passed and administered by legislatures in Virginia, whose governor and council alone were entitled to recruit militia to repulse the Indian attacks. In the summer of 1784, the Indian peril worsened, and in the fall a Cherokee invasion seemed imminent. The pioneer Benjamin Logan then called an informal meeting of the militia at Danville for November 7, to discuss the defense of the frontier. At the meeting its was decided to apply for the admission of Kentucky as a separate state, and for this purpose preliminary elections of delegates were called in every district.

Three conventions took place at Danville (December 27, 1784; May 23, 1785; and August 8, 1785), all of which raised the question of the need for Kentucky to be recognized as a free, sovereign independent state and for it to join the recently established Confederation. On July 10, 1786, the Virginia Assembly voted its separation as a state, provided that a convention elected by the people approved the proposal. Meanwhile, the repeated Indian skirmishes, perpetrated here and there by small patrols, confirmed the urgency of making a decision from the military standpoint to compensate for the ineffectiveness of the 300 men of General Josiah Harmar's national army, distributed between Fort Harmar and Fort Finney. The solution would be proposed by Clark, who suggested an offensive against the Indians as the best means of defense.

In spite of the difficulties that he encountered in recruiting his men and the onset of winter, Clark set out in September 1786. He had to overcome adversities of every kind: gradual desertions; indiscipline on the part of Logan, who carried out a separate attack instead of reinforcing the vanguard of the expedition; the decision to withdraw from Vincennes in view of the lack of supplies; and the general abandonment of the strategy planned. Wilkinson had begun to spread rumors about Clark being a drunkard, questioning his ability for effective command; now, he took advantage of the failure of the expedition to redouble his attacks on his rival, who eventually gave Wilkinson the pretext to discredit him.

In order to feed his garrison at Vincennes, Clark had confiscated merchandise from three Spanish traders, claiming that they were operating on national soil without a license and had been supplying the Indians, and that, in any case, this move was merely a reprisal for the Spaniards impounding American goods in transit on the Mississippi. Moreover, there was a widespread rumor—which Clark himself did his best to propagate—that Clark was organizing an expedition of volunteers against Natchez, in order to open up trade for the United States via the Big River; this rumor was confirmed by a letter from adventurer Thomas Green, dated December 4, 1786.

These circumstances were used by Wilkinson to persuade his fellow citizens at the Fourth Convention, which met at Danville in September 1786, just how dangerous Clark's activities were since it might easily entail war with Spain, for which neither Kentucky, Virginia nor the United States was prepared; on this point everyone agreed, and there was open concern. A specially appointed committee officially reproved Clark for his conduct and dismissed him from his military command. The Virginian delegation in Congress was entrusted with an apology to the Spanish representative in Philadelphia, Diego Gardoqui. Wilkinson and two of his associates were appointed Indian commissioners instead of Clark and two of his men.

Gardoqui had arrived in Philadelphia in July 1785, entrusted by the Spanish government to explore the possibilities of establishing full diplomatic relations with the United States, provided the latter accepted full Spanish control over both banks of the Mississippi south of the Ohio River. In exchange, Spain offered to grant trade privileges; these were particularly attractive in view of the size of the Spanish Empire and the Spanish custom of paying in gold and silver, which were scarce in the United States, whose paper money had become depreciated as a result of years of war.

The secretary for foreign affairs, John Jay, held several talks on the matter with Gardoqui, and at a secret session on August 29, 1786, Congress passed by seven votes to five their acceptance of the Spanish proposal, provided Spanish control over the Mississippi should last for 25 years. With the idea of obtaining trade advantages that would benefit the eastern states, Congress was prepared to sacrifice the western states—if only for 25 years—as regards their hopes of expansion and of obtaining a direct outlet via the Mississippi.

Through the parallel acceptance by Congress of Britain's continued possession of her positions on the Great Lakes, Spain and Great Britain now flanked the United States, supporting the Indians, whose constant raids made life impossible in Kentucky and neighboring territories. Although the policy of Congress was justified by the desire to strengthen the régime in the new country before undertaking ventures beyond its means (which rather than consolidating the country, would have seriously jeopardized its stability), serious unrest spread among the inhabitants of the West, who realized that they had been abandoned and saw the lack of interest in their problems in federal circles. This disquiet was encouraged by those interested in secession and by the recently founded newspaper *The Kentucky Gazette*. At the Fifth Convention, held in September 1787, there were renewed demands for separation from Virginia and admission as a new state.

Meanwhile, Wilkinson had begun to put into practice a scheme whereby he planned to obtain financial gains

and the consolidation of his political position in Kentucky. On December 20, 1786, he had written to Francisco Cruzat, the Spanish commander at St. Louis, warning him about Clark's military preparations, and had asked Gardoqui for a passport to visit New Orleans. Despite Gardoqui's refusal Wilkinson did not hesitate to go ahead with his plan. In June 1787, he embarked for New Orleans with a cargo of cereals and tobacco. He was right in his forecasts, for he was given a warm welcome by the governor of Louisiana, Esteban Miró, and succeeded in selling his merchandise tax-free at the substantial profit of $35,000. The Spanish authorities were eager to establish friendly relations with prominent people on the frontier who might be in favor of maintaining the peaceful status quo and could help to avoid the growing pressure of the colonists from the East on Spanish territories. Moreover, the Spanish posts, far apart and short of men and material, had to rely on the river for their communications (a hard slow voyage upstream), whereas the trip downstream (the direction from which an enemy attack would come) appeared simple and fast.

Wilkinson spent three months as a guest of the Spaniards, in daily contact with Miró. Wilkinson offered to lead a secessionist movement in Kentucky, which would influence the other territories west of the mountains in favor of closer ties with Spain. To confirm his intentions, he swore an oath of loyalty to the king of Spain on August 22, 1787. On September 5, he drafted a memorandum addressed to the king in which he suggested, in the first place, that he be granted exclusive trading rights via the Mississippi, claiming that the profits from this privilege would encourage his fellow citizens of Kentucky to separate from the United States and draw closer to Spain; in the second place, he offered his services as sole agent to organize the settlement of colonists in Spanish territory, thus promoting new links between Spain and the frontier. Miro received these proposals most enthusiastically and forwarded them with his support to Madrid.

In February 1788, Wilkinson returned in triumph to Kentucky, after traveling by sea and visiting Richmond, Pittsburg and Ohio. His impressive trading profits swayed public opinion in favor of Spain. Prices rose overnight, and what was bought for two dollars sold for nine. Wilkinson, who began to consider himself the "Washington of the West" made a further move in his plans as future leader of the new, expanding independent republic east of the Mississippi. Hearing at Richmond that the federal Constitution was being drafted, Wilkinson hastened back to Kentucky to prepare the ground to combat ratification and favor his plans for secession; simultaneously, he sent a number of barges downstream to New Orleans laden with tobacco, butter, ham and other merchandise in order to prove the advantages of good relations with Spain to his fellow citizens.

The entry into force of the federal Constitution upon its ratification by the ninth state, New Hampshire, on June 21, 1788, struck the westerners as a new source of profits for the eastern states and of scant benefit to the territories on the western side of the mountains. The continual depredations and numerous murders committed by the Indians in 1788, and the inability of the federal government to protect the colonists in such mortal peril, strengthened their belief that their future did not lie in the United States, but rather in their independence and association with Great Britain and Spain, their powerful neighbors to the north and south, respectively. In the course of a parley with a view to signing a peace agreement, together with other chiefs, the Cherokee chief Old Tassel was treacherously murdered; this resulted in a general Indian uprising with disastrous results for practically all the settlements.

The Sixth Kentucky Convention met on July 28, 1788. Gardoqui had held talks in advance with John Brown, the new Kentuckian member of the Virginia delegation in Congress, who wrote a confidential letter (dated July 10, 1788) to inform his friends in Kentucky of the assurances given by Gardoqui to the effect that, if Kentucky declared its independence and authorized somebody suitable to negotiate with him, he (Gardoqui) was authorized to grant permission for navigation on the Mississippi, a privilege that could never be granted if Kentucky continued to form part of the United States. Miró, for his part, had sent Wilkinson as much as $18,700 for distribution among 21 leading Kentucky citizens of his choice. Among Wilkinson's "confidential friends" were Secretary of Justice Harry Innes, John Brown, Caleb Wallace and Benjamin Sebastian; among those "favoring separation from Virginia and a friendly agreement with Spain" were pioneer Benjamin Logan and Isaac Shelby, later governor of Kentucky.

The Sixth Convention did not reach a definitive conclusion but did decide to call a fresh assembly for November 3. Meanwhile, the letter written by Brown became widely known, as did Britain's plans to support secession for her own benefit. When taking their decisions, citizens became more and more inclined to give priority to local interests and their own region rather than to the distant interests of the Union, of whose benefits they had not yet partaken.

Wilkinson was gathering support for his project at private meetings and conversations. At the Seventh Convention, therefore, he was able to read the contents of his memorandum to the king of Spain and persuade the delegates of the disadvantages of the present situation compared to the benefits of future connection with Spain. The time had come to take the final step: he asked Brown to list the offers made by Gardoqui, but Brown, surprised and annoyed, did not react as Wilkinson had expected. Wilkinson wisely preferred not to take the situation any further for the time being, and the convention broke up after approving the memorandum to the king asking for navigation rights on the Mississippi and after convening another meeting for the following August. In that interlude the people of Kentucky hoped to see a change in the attitude of the new government, under the Constitution, with greater understanding for the problems in the West than the previous government under the confederacy.

At the end of 1789, Wilkinson traveled for the second time to New Orleans, where he submitted a second memorandum to the king of Spain, and returned to Kentucky with two mules laden with silver. These, however, could not really compensate him for the hesitant Spanish policy, which showed little inclination to make a definite move in support of the secessionists. Wilkinson was inevitably disenchanted by the attitude of the Spaniards. In March that year, Miró had received a new definition of Spanish foreign policy formulated by the Council of Ministers: he was ordered to avoid at all costs any open action encouraging insurrection in the West of the new republic; furthermore, to reduce the ill will of the frontiersmen, the tariff on their exports of merchandise was cut to 15%, and, in some cases, to 6%, while facilities were given for the immigration of American colonists to Spanish territory. The result of that policy was to strip Wilkinson of his trade monopoly and, consequently, of the huge profits that he had been making until then and still intended to make. On the other hand, hostilities were on the point of breaking out between Britain and Spain, and Thomas Jefferson, who was then secretary of state, declared himself willing to help Spain and even reach an alliance with her, on condition that the British did not occupy her Louisiana territories, an eventuality that the United States had to oppose by every possible means.

Nevertheless, Wilkinson continued to act as a secret agent for Spain and, when promoted to higher rank in the army in 1791, considered that he should make the most of it, and asked Miró to raise his salary as a spy. When promoted to brigadier general at the beginning of

1792, his earnings rose accordingly to the sum of $2,000 a year. His services were useful to prevent the attempts of the French revolutionaries (who had just beheaded Louis XVI) to restore French rule in Louisiana. Those involved in the affair were the French representative Edmond Genet, who arrived on May 16, 1793; naturalist André Michaux; and the omnipresent Clark. When the governor of Louisiana sent an emphatic protest to George Washington, the response of his government was to disapprove these plots, which were also reproved by Genet's successor, Joseph Fauchet. Clark, however, did not halt his preparations for war and on February 25, 1794, made an appeal in Kentucky for volunteers, offering 2,000 acres of Spanish territory as a reward. Washington ordered Clark and his followers to drop their plans, arranged for the reconstruction of Fort Massac in lower Ohio so that its garrison could prevent any attempt by Clark to go down river and persuaded Congress to consider it a crime for any citizen to take hostile action against a country with which the United States was at peace.

In spite of this, John Montgomery, second-in-command to Clark, built a small fort on the Ohio and began to interrupt river-borne traffic bound for Spanish territory. In addition, Elijah Clarke, a Georgian pioneer, crossed the Oconee River with a party of volunteers and defying the federal government and the state of Georgia, took possession of a belt of land belonging to the Creek Indians where they set up an independent republic. Governor Baron de Carondelet, for his part, took the pertinent countermeasures: he sent messages to the allied Indians asking for their assistance, requested permission from the captain-general at Havana to counterattack Clarke, reinforced the Spanish garrisons on the Mississippi, armed a fleet of barges which were sufficiently mobile to bring relief to any place where their assistance was needed most, built a new fort on the Tombigbee River and increased the sums of money furnished to Wilkinson and other agents. The mere fact of his taking these steps was sufficient for Montgomery to stop obstructing river traffic, but the possibility of an incident arising might undoubtedly entail the outbreak of hostilities between Spain and the United States, which neither of the two countries desired at this time.

The movement of British forces, who remained allies of the Spaniards, seemed to forebode an inevitable clash; all the more so when the American colonists gradually increased their pressure and impatience to expand westward. In 1794, WiLkinson asked for more money as a reward for his success (according to him) in betraying the Clark expedition, and as the only means of keeping his group of friends in Kentucky inclined in favor of Spain; a boat with $6,000 hidden aboard was later captured, and Wilkinson barely escaped being implicated. However, the victory at Fallen Timbers in 1794, when the federal army under General Anthony Wayne defeated the Indian allies of the British, dispelled for good the danger of their raids in the area occupied by the colonists, and calm reigned once more. The central government gained prestige, and the territories in the West began to perceive that they, too, mattered in the Union. Inevitably, the idea of secession started to wane. The settlers in Kentucky were to number 200,000 by 1795, and their influx made ambitions for an alliance with Spain untenable.

Under the Treaty of San Lorenzo, signed by Thomas Pinckney on October 27, 1795, the Spanish government acknowledged the unfavorable situation (not without some bitterness) and waived in favor of the United States all claims to the territories east of the Mississippi as far as a point in the South, and granted freedom of navigation on the Mississippi, together with the right of deposit at New Orleans. As chance would have it, in his capacity as commander of the United States army of occupation, it was Wilkinson who presided over the transfer by Spain of the territories ceded under the treaty.

Spanish Place-Names

Today, the only Spanish mementos remaining in Kentucky are pictures in such museums as the one at Louisville and a few scattered names: Alonzo, Aurora, Buena Vista, Cadiz, Columbia, Columbus, Cordova, Delta, Lola, Meador, Mexico, Palma, Sacramento, Sonora and Varilla, as well as the Columbus Belmont State Park.

Tennessee

Hernando de Soto Passes Through

East Tennessee is crossed by the southern ranges of the Appalachians, known in this area as the Great Smokies. In 1540, this mountainous area was visited by the first European to set foot on the territory of the state, Hernando de Soto and his expeditionaries. In the pages on North Carolina, we ceased to follow their itinerary after leaving present-day Murphy and preparing to cross the present boundary line. They may well have passed through Angelico Gap and followed an itinerary coinciding with Highway 64; in any case, they camped near the city of Chattanooga. Some claim that de Soto continued on his way west and reached the vicinity of Manchester (where he built a fort) or Franklin. What is certain is that he soon changed direction and headed south, until he entered the present state of Alabama. Months later, de Soto and his expeditionaries reentered the state in west Tennessee.

On May 8, 1541, they saw the Mississippi for the first time. The description penned by one of those present, the *hidalgo* de Elvas, reads as follows: "The river is at least half a league in width. If a man stood still on the opposite bank, it could not be seen if he was a man or not. The river was of great depth and had strong currents; the water was always muddy and carried many trees and branches." The river was the broadest of those seen so far by the overawed Spaniards, accustomed to the small rivers in Spain, and de Soto therefore called it El Río Grande de la Florida (the Great River of Florida); the Indians called it "Father of Rivers," or Mississippi. In De Soto Park, in the heart of Memphis, a block of granite recalls the fact that it was near this spot that de Soto discovered the Mississippi in May 1541. From Memphis, the Spaniards proceeded on their dangerous journey westward after crossing the broad waters with great difficulty. It seems that after their presence, a mestizo group, called "Melungeon," was formed in the eastern side of the state.

Memphis is near the site of the old Chickasaw Bluffs, where in 1739, Jean-Baptiste Bienville built the short-lived Fort Assumption. The governor of Natchez, Manuel Gayoso de Lemos, in pursuing the policy of containing the expansion of colonists from the East, obtained permission from the Chickasaw Indians to establish a fort at the "Ecores à Margot." With support from the Mississippi Naval Squadron, Gayoso arrived there on May 30, 1795, and began work on the fortified outpost, which he called San Fernando de las Barrancas. He personally chose the site and gave specific orders concerning its construction. By the summer of that year, the fort was ready to repulse a possible attack. As a consequence of the signature of the Treaty of San Lorenzo on March 16, 1797, San Fernando was evacuated by its garrison, and the arms and ammunition were transferred to the opposite bank of the river, to Fort Esperanza, while the building itself was destroyed before they left. The commanders of the fort had been Elias Beauregard, Vicente Folch and Josef Deville Degoutin Bellechase.

At the time of the Revolution, the bluffs had seen the passage of the boats of patriots carrying arms and provisions supplied by the Spaniards of Louisiana upstream to Fort Pitt (Pittsburgh).

The Independence of Cumberland

Like Daniel Boone in Kentucky, James Robertson is the epitome of the early pioneer in Tennessee, when the name most commonly used was Cumberland. He

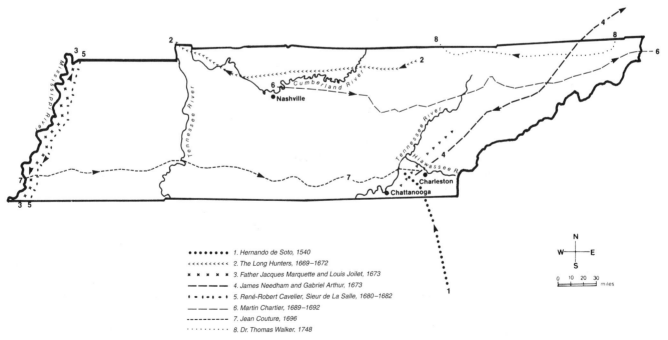

European exploration in Tennessee, 1540–1748. Facts On File.

1. Hernando de Soto, 1540
2. The Long Hunters, 1669–1672
3. Father Jacques Marquette and Louis Joilet, 1673
4. James Needham and Gabriel Arthur, 1673
5. René-Robert Cavelier, Sieur de La Salle, 1680–1682
6. Martin Chartier, 1689–1692
7. Jean Couture, 1696
8. Dr. Thomas Walker, 1748

played a major part in the events of its first 20 years, including his contacts with Spain, with a view to its independence and possible annexation. When the Transylvania Company lost its rights in Kentucky, when it became a county of Virginia, Robertson decided to compensate for these losses by organizing a similar settlement in the region of Cumberland, which he reckoned would fall within the area of North Carolina.

At the end of 1778, accompanied by eight comrades, Robertson went on an exploratory trip covering almost 250 miles, to a point where the capital stands today. The site was chosen as the most convenient spot for the future settlement, which would be called Nashboro after Francis Nash, a Carolinian who had died at Germantown. Later, a French suffix was added to the name, following the fashion introduced as a result of alliance with France: Nashville. The new colonists arrived in the winter of 1780 in two expeditions: one, led by John Donelson, on boats transporting the women and children along the Tennessee and Cumberland Rivers, and the other, overland, through Kentucky. Both expeditions endured serious hardship.

The government of North Carolina (once the spheres of influence had been defined) lay at a great distance, some 470 miles, with a high, intervening mountain chain. On May 13, 1780, this led the colonists to sign the Cumberland Compact, whereby they undertook to be ruled by their own laws. Indian attacks and the difficulties of the early days threatened the colony with extinction; so much so that Donelson withdrew to Kentucky with his family. The settlement was saved by Robertson's determination and by the grants of land by North Carolina to his soldiers; individually or by companies they took this opportunity and immigrated en masse to the West so that, by 1785, there were already as many as 40 villages. Their geographical distribution in the river valley, however, made them very hard to defend against Indian raids. To put an end to such incursions Robertson decided to attack, and, leading a force of 130 volunteers on horseback, crossed the Tennessee River during the night and took the Creek Indian camp by surprise at Coldwater, where they killed 20 and put the rest to flight.

In reprisal, the Indian leader Alexander McGillivray (of Scotch-Indian descent) unleashed a whole series of attacks on Cumberland, seriously jeopardizing its survival. (See section on Alabama for more on McGillivray.) Robertson had no alternative but to seek the urgent effective support of the governor of North Carolina, Samuel Johnson, who received him coldly; in general,

there was neither the desire nor the means available to come to the assistance of the distant colonists.

The inhabitants of Cumberland then discussed the possibility of seeking the necessary help and protection from Britain and Spain. Aware of his primary responsibility for these settlements, which he had sponsored, Robertson considered it advisable to contact McGillivray and suggest a combined Cumberland-Creek attack against Spanish possessions on the Gulf of Mexico in order to open up an independent outlet. When his proposal met with McGillivray's indifference, Robertson decided, at the end of 1788, to inform Esteban Rodríguez Miró of his willingness for Cumberland to establish a community of interests with Spain, to which proposal Miró reacted most favorably.

As has been seen, Robertson was not the only westerner to turn to Spain when faced with the neglect of the federal government. Another leading figure in these contacts with Spain was James White, who maintained personal relations with Gardoqui, Miró, Sevier and Wilkinson, all of whom were working to annex their territories to Spain. The Spanish governor at Pensacola, Arturo O'Neill, received a letter from McGillivray dated April 25, 1788, in which he was informed that McGillivray had received a delegation from Cumberland who had told him of the desire of the inhabitants to become subjects of the king of Spain and that the region was determined to seek independence from Congress, since the latter could not safeguard their persons or property nor promote their trade. The news brought back to Cumberland by Andrew Jackson concerning the ratification of the federal Constitution did not change the separatist intentions of the inhabitants, who considered the new Constitution to be favorable to the easterners and of scant interest to the inhabitants west of the mountains. White brought a message to Robertson from Gardoqui, in which Gardoqui stated that the king was well disposed toward providing the inhabitants of Cumberland with the safeguards they needed.

The plan received a temporary setback when none of the settlements in Cumberland escaped the disastrous Cherokee attack of 1788. (Among the dead were Colonel Anthony Bledsoe, Robertson's deputy.) But in August that year, North Carolina agreed to Robertson's request that Cumberland should henceforth be called Miró District, as a mark of admiration of its settlers toward the Spanish governor. On September 2, Robertson wrote another letter in favor of linking his fortunes with the nation that controlled the Mississippi. In September 1789, Robertson again wrote to Miró:

We have just held a Convention which has agreed that our members shall insist on being separated from North Carolina. Unprotected, we are to be obedient to the new Congress of the United States; but we cannot but wish for a more interesting connection. The United States affords us no protection. The District of Miró is daily plundered and the inhabitants murdered by the Creeks and Cherokees, unprovoked. For my own part, I conceive highly of the advantages of your Government.

We have seen the instructions of the Council of Ministers to Miró to avoid any action likely to encourage insurrection in the West; it follows that Robertson must also have been disappointed. On the other hand, the building of a new road to Nashville had resulted in the arrival of a new wave of immigrants, unaffected as yet by the troubles that had beset the earlier settlers. In a clever move, George Washington appointed Robertson brigadier general of the militia of the new territory of the Northwest. Nashville became the target for a planned invasion of Creek, Chickamauga and Chickasaw Indians in 1792, encouraged by Carondelet, as a first step to bring about the evacuation of Cumberland, but the resistance of the nearby fort at Buchanan's Station demoralized the disunited Indian attackers. The Treaty of San Lorenzo of October 27, 1795, marked the end of Spanish ambitions in the region. Cumberland and the south of Holston joined together in 1796 and obtained admission to the Union as a state called Tennessee, on June 1, 1795.

The Minorcan Admiral

Ten miles from Knoxville on the road to Nashville, at a place called Stony Point, Campbell Station, David Glasgow Farragut was born on July 5, 1801; he was to become the first admiral of the United States. This is of particular interest to Spaniards because it was here that his mother and father, Jorge Ferragut, a Spaniard from Minorca, lived. As he told his son, Jorge was born at Ciudadela, on the island of Minorca, on September 29, 1755, and had left the island on April 2, 1772. Some claim that he reached North America with the expedition of Minorcans organized by Dr. Andrew Turnbull, who founded New Smyrna in Florida.

According to Admiral Farragut's biographer, Charles Lee Lewis, Jorge Ferragut undoubtedly reached New Orleans at the time of the outbreak of the Revolution at Lexington, on April 19, 1775: he formed part of a crew of small merchant ship trading between Havana and Vera-cruz. When he heard of the uprising of the colonies he decided to enlist against the British (whose domination he had experienced in his native island) "in order to participate with his life and fortune in the struggle for American independence." He set sail for Puerto Príncipe where he exchanged his cargo for a cannon, side arms and ammunition, with which he disembarked at Charleston, South Carolina, in March 1776. In 1778, he supervised the construction of warships at Charleston, and entrusted with the command of one of them, he fought bravely in the defense of Savannah. When Savannah fell into the hands of the British, he withdrew to Charleston, which likewise was soon besieged by the enemy. There he fought until he was taken prisoner on May 12, 1780. He was later exchanged. He then fought with the army and is even said to have saved George Washington's life at the battle of Cowpens.

At the end of the war, Jorge retired with the rank of cavalry major. He then settled down as a colonist in Tennessee. For 15 hard years he alternated the work of farmer and woodsman (living in a log cabin) with the more dangerous task of fighting the Indians. When he was 40 he married Elizabeth Shine, and later their son, David, was born. With a family to look after, Jorge did not feel safe in Tennessee, which was constantly prone to Indian attacks. He moved to New Orleans, where there were many Spanish inhabitants since Louisiana had only recently been a Spanish dependency, and the prevalent religion (among the French inhabitants as well) was Catholicism.

David Glasgow Farragut (the original spelling of Ferragut was adapted to the English pronunciation) spoke elegant Spanish and proudly bore on his coat of arms the horseshoe, or *ferradura*, taken from the escutcheons of his ancestors. During the Civil War he fought on the side of the Union and led the fleet to victory on the Mississippi, in New Orleans and in Mobile. He died on August 14, 1870, at Portsmouth, New Hampshire. Today, two streets in his birthplace, Stony Point, bear his name.

Spanish Place-Names

Many names in Tennessee, reveal its Spanish past, such as Alamo, Alto, Bogota, Bolivar, Cerro Gordo, Columbia, Cordova, Cuba, Medina, Nobles, Quito, Saltillo and Santa Fe.

Vanderbilt University, in Nashville, maintains a chair of Spanish history.

◆ *ALABAMA* ◆

The presence of the Spaniards in Alabama can be divided into several stages. As state historian Albert James Pickett recalls, Alabama was discovered by Hernando de Soto and his expedition. They were the first European men to see its scenery, cross its rivers and encounter the natives, who defended their land to the limit of their endurance. While other Spaniards had previously set foot on territory along the coast, de Soto was the pioneer explorer who penetrated miles and miles of the interior and as a traveler became thoroughly acquainted with its people and geography. We will look at Alabama from the north first and end our tour on the Gulf of Mexico.

Hernando de Soto and Other Explorers

In 1540, Hernando de Soto and his expedition entered what is today the state of Alabama from the north and followed an itinerary that more or less traces today's Highway 72, alongside the Tennessee River from Bridgeport to Scottsboro, in Jackson County.

Undoubtedly wishing to head south, Hernando de Soto left the Tennessee River, and later, after reconnoitering in the area of the present towns of Guntersville and Albertville, found himself on the banks of the Coosa River. He followed the Coosa downstream to its confluence with the Tallapoosa River at a point near the present state capital, Montgomery, through what are today Attalla, Gadsden, Talladega, Childersburg, Lay Lake, Lay Dam, Mitchell Lake, Jordan Lake and Wetumpka. This route had taken him through the Coosa region, whose capital was the largest Indian town they had yet seen. The *conquistador* continued his march downstream, in October 1540, toward Talisin, in Dallas County, Camden, in Wilcox County, and Piache (present-day Claiborne), in Monroe County; he followed the Alabama River through country inhabited by the Mobile Indians. In the latter area, de Soto found that the tribal chief was a giant called Tuscaloosa, whom he took prisoner when he refused to provide the assistance of Indian bearers as requested by de Soto. Although Tuscaloosa then appeared to relent and provided him with the services of 400 of his subjects, he hatched a plot

that was to prove the most dangerous episode in de Soto's march on the mainland. Endeavoring to win the trust of the Spaniards, Tuscaloosa led them to the fortified village of Mabila, which probably lay in Clarke County, between the Alabama and Tombigbee Rivers. They arrived there on October 18, and de Soto entered the place with a group of his followers, in spite of the warnings of his second-in-command, Luis de Moscoso, who scouted ahead of the main party.

The Spaniards barely succeeded in escaping from the trap and regrouped outside the walls. A terrible battle ensued between the numerous Indians and hardened Spaniards, who, clad in armor, felt the heat from the flames of the burning township. The outcome of the battle was that the Spaniards lost 20 dead and 148 were

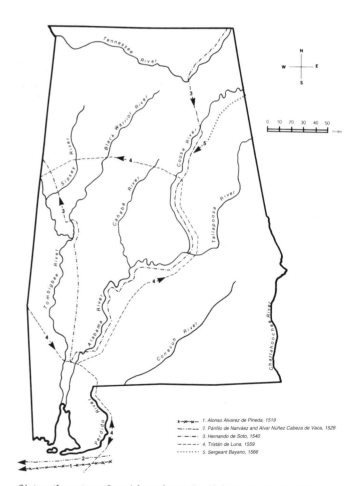

Sixteenth-century Spanish explorers in Alabama. Facts On File.

wounded; nearly 2,000 Indians were killed (including Tuscaloosa himself and his son) and hundreds more, wounded.

De Soto and his men camped at Mabila for a month to recover from this fray. While there, he received news of the arrival of Maldonado with ships and provisions at nearby Achusi Bay. Instead of being overjoyed at this news in the midst of so many hardships, de Soto feared that his troops might mutiny and decide to embark for Mexico. He preferred possible death to acknowledging failure and decided to forgo any assistance. On December 9, 1540, the expedition set out once more in a northerly direction. (In February 1987 news spread that the site of Mabila had been found at Cahawba, due to the unearthing of an Indian moat. But more digs have to be made to verify the findings.)

Highway 43 traces the last part of de Soto's itinerary through Alabama, passing through Grove Hill, Thomasville, Dixons Mills, Linden and Old Spring Hill. Some miles east of Demopolis, he discovered the Black Warrior River, which he crossed near Erie, and proceeded to Eutaw, crossed the Sipsey River (which he likewise discovered), passed near Carrollton, in Pickens County, and crossed the boundary into the state of Mississippi.

At the end of 1559, Tristán de Luna, head of the Spanish colony in Pensacola, reached a locality called Nanipacana de la Santa Cruz, in the vicinity of Claiborne, accompanied by about 1,000 Spanish settlers; he had left a lieutenant and 50 men and black slaves to look after the harbor in Florida. The expedition made its way upriver after receiving the reports of four companies of cavalry, who under the command of Mateo del Saúz, had returned announcing that they had found corn, beans and vegetables, of which the starving Spaniards were so greatly in need. The Indians told them that de Soto and his party had been there 19 years earlier, and recounted the destruction of Mabila and the death of its inhabitants. When their food supplies had run out, de Luna sent Saúz to Coosa with 150 soldiers in search of provisions. Saúz arrived in the Coosa region in the spring of 1560 and spent seven months there. The journey to Coosa was one long trail of adversity; many died on the way after eating poisonous grass and herbs to try to overcome their hunger. After 43 days, a forest of chestnut and walnut trees helped to restore their failing strength and enabled them to reach their destination, where they enjoyed the hospitality of the Indians for three months.

Father de la Anunciación and Domingo de Salazar, who had accompanied Saúz, unsuccessfully tried to convert their hosts to Christianity. The Coosa Indians were not in the mood for sermons at that time, for they were preparing to attack their hated enemies, the Natchez Indians. They asked the Spaniards to assist them in this venture, and unable to refuse, Saúz provided them with two captains, 50 infantrymen and some horsemen, in addition to Father de la Anunciación who wished to accompany them. The outcome of this punitive raid (into what is now the state of Mississippi) was satisfactory; apart from providing them with considerable quantities of foodstuffs, it resulted in the Spaniards using their good offices to settle the rivalries between the two Indian factions with little bloodshed.

Meanwhile, in Saúz's absence, the settlers at Nanipacana experienced all manner of hardships, disease and starvation. To maintain discipline, de Luna imposed severe measures, which did not improve morale; several months passed, and after convening a council of war, de Luna acknowledged his dire circumstances. Jorge Cerón, one of the settlers, argued that the best solution was to abandon the venture and return to Pensacola. His view prevailed and de Luna ordered the return of the settlers to Florida and sent Fray Pedro de la Feria with two small vessels (with some soldiers with wives in Cuba aboard) to seek aid at Havana or in Mexico. Saúz and his men learned of the end of the settlement when Captain Cristóbal Ramírez y Arellano (de Luna's nephew), dispatched by Saúz with news of his arrival at Coosa and an advance guard of 17 men, found the Nanipacana deserted. A note buried at the foot of a tree recounted the colony's abandonment, and Saúz decided to return with his group to Pensacola as well.

Some years later, in 1567, another Spanish expeditionary group appeared in the Chiaha frontier region, sent by Menéndez de Avilés. This was the expedition led by Juan Pardo and Sergeant Boyano, who built a fort on the spot, near modern-day Rome, Georgia. A soldier and interpreter with the party, Juan de Ribas, succeeded in reaching Coosa. Here he found a village large enough to accommodate 150 families and vestiges of de Soto's expedition: lances, coats of mail, weapons and European clothing in the natives' possession. However, this scouting by Ribas did not achieve one of the objectives sought by his superiors, namely to establish a link via the interior between the Atlantic coast and the Gulf of Mexico.

Fort Esteban and the Ellicott Line

We have followed de Soto through the region flanking the Tombigbee and Black Warrior Rivers and have seen the experiences of the expeditionaries accompanying de Luna at Nanipacana, now Monroe County, between the Tombigbee and Alabama Rivers. Over two centuries later, Spaniards returned to this area following the taking of Natchez and Mobile by the governor of Louisiana, Bernardo de Gálvez, in 1779 and 1780. The Spaniards had two forts protecting these settlements: Fort Confederación (built by the French before 1763 and called Tombecbé), situated in Sumter County, between the Tombigbee River and the state boundary with Mississippi; and Fort Esteban, built on orders from Governor Esteban Miró in 1789, in Clarke County, near Jackson. Known by the name St. Stephens (the town of that name still exists), it was to play an important part as the capital of the Alabama Territory, created in 1817, before becoming a state on December 14, 1819. In addition to the small fort there was a church and a house for the garrison commander, and other buildings. The mission at Fort Esteban played a defensive role, but also served primarily as a trading post: vessels sailing up the Tombigbee could not go any farther because of the rapids upstream, and American traders therefore came downriver to Fort Esteban to collect merchandise.

Fort Esteban remained in Spanish hands until it was ceded to the United States on May 5, 1799, as a result of the Treaty of San Lorenzo, signed on October 27, 1795, by Thomas Pinckney as George Washington's representative. (As we have seen, this treaty stipulated that Spain would abandon all territorial claims east of the Mississippi as far as a point south of Natchez, between parallels 32°28" and 31° north latitude, and granted freedom of navigation on the Mississippi, with the right to deposit merchandise at New Orleans.) By accepting the treaty, Spain acknowledged the pressure on those regions by the neighboring Americans and the impossibility of resisting it by force, while at the same time laying the foundations for future progressive friendship with her neighbor.

The new boundary line was not clearly marked out in the treaty. Various conflicts arose when the northeners laid claims to areas, which those in the south were reluctant to hand over. These problems grew more acute as a result of rumors of Spanish plans to return the territories of Louisiana to the French, who had repeatedly shown interest in them since the Directoire had reached power in 1795 and, in March 1796, had sent general Victor Collot as a spy. In view of this news, the American colonists were not prepared to allow France to give rein to further imperialist schemes (more would come shortly afterward under the absolute power of Napoleonic

government). In 1797, Andrew Ellicott, the American commissioner sent to settle the new boundary line, reported to his government the existence of three conspiracies: the revival of the pro-Spanish conspiracy by James Wilkinson and his cohorts, that of the western settlers to organize a revolution by Americans and French living in Louisiana and Florida, and the planned invasion of Spanish territories by frontiersmen acting on behalf of Great Britain or the United States.

Spain ultimately accepted the boundary line that had been defined, after great difficulties, by Ellicott and Sir William Dunbar, acting on behalf of Spain. The Ellicott Line entailed a surprise: Fort Esteban lay to the north of the line and was therefore included in the cession. On the banks of the Mobile River, a boundary stone was set up bearing an inscription; on the northern side it read "U.S. lat. 31°, 1799"; on the other side, another inscription read "Dominion de S. M. Carlos IV, Lat. 31°, 1799" (Dominions of His Majesty Charles IV, Latitude 31°, 1799). In the vicinity, the Americans built Fort Stoddert, which had a customs post as well as a garrison.

Mobile

The Spaniards' presence along the coastal belt of Alabama dated from the early days, centered around Mobile Bay. The first appearance of westerners along the Alabama coastline was through Alonso Alvarez de Pineda. Sent out by Francisco de Garay, governor of Jamaica, to explore the lands to the north, Pineda entered Mobile Bay in 1519 four ships and called it Bahía del Espíritu Santo, or Bay of the Holy Spirit. Pineda included Mobile on the map of his voyage in the Gulf of Mexico and made a report on his 40-day stay there.

The next Spaniard to arrive was Pánfilo de Narváez and his party, in the fall of 1528, in three makeshift boats after three scorching days sailing from Pensacola. When Cabeza de Vaca made signs that they were thirsty to the Indians on the shore, they were offered drinking water. The Greek Doroteo Teodoro, who had caulked the vessels, could not wait to slake his thirst. Accompanied by a black man, he decided to go ashore with the Indians, in spite of the warnings of his companions. On the following morning, the Indians came back demanding the two hostages whom they had left in exchange for the vanished expeditionaries and invited the Spaniards to come ashore if they wished to eat and drink.

Teodoro and his companion never returned. In view of an imminent attack by growing numbers of Indians, the travelers decided to depart and set a westward course.

Maldonado was in charge of the next exploratory, expedition, sent out at the end of 1539 by Hernando de Soto to reconnoiter and seek information; this was followed by a second expedition in the summer of 1540 to rendezvous with de Soto as arranged after traveling to Cuba to fetch more men and provisions. Historians disagree as to whether Achusi, or Ochuse, Bay, where they had arranged to meet, is present-day Pensacola Bay or Mobile Bay, although Mobile is the more likely spot.

Nor do historians agree as to the presence, during the later visit, of Doña Isabel, Hernando de Soto's wife. The legend of her stay at the mouth of the bay on Dauphin Island persists, however, and the fig trees that still grow there are said to have been planted by her. According to this story, on the morning of the departure of the ships from Havana, Maldonado, Juan de Añasco (de Soto's treasurer) and Gómez Arias found Doña Isabel on board, together with Doña Leonor, her companion and first cousin, and several maidservants; shortly after reaching the island, Doña Isabel had an orchard and garden planted with the seeds she had brought, and while digging discovered some pagan idols. She spent the summer excavating, after which the party moved to the mainland to the place where Mobile now stands, until news arrived about other white men in the vicinity and a bloody battle that had taken place (the Battle of Mabila).

Eventually the messengers dispatched returned with Rodrigo Rangel, de Soto's secretary, who brought news of the scarcely favorable outcome of the enterprise and de Soto's decision to continue the expedition and not to inform his men of the arrival of the relief ships. He told Maldonado of their leader's orders to return to Cuba and meet him once again, a year later, at the mouth of the Big River (the Mississippi). He also conveyed de Soto's disapproval of his wife's disobedience in embarking and reported the death of Nuño de Tobar, Leonor's husband. Isabel is also said to have decided that the party should not return to Cuba, but wait on the island until the following summer and the second rendezvous; apparently, she only consented to reembark when they received news of the disastrous end of de Soto, and she buried her jewels in a pit dug out of the sand.

Almost 20 years went by before the next Spanish visit. When King Philip II decided to establish colonies on the north coast of the Gulf of Mexico, he sent Guido de los Bazares on an exploratory mission with three ships and 60 men, who set sail from Veracruz on September 3, 1558. On reaching Mobile Bay, they called it Filipina (after King Philip). Bazares's men reached the Tensaw River and Montrose, in Baldwin County (on the opposite shore of the bay). There they remained until December 3, when they weighed anchor and set course for Mexico, reaching the port of Veracruz 11 days later. The enthusiastic report submitted concerning the conditions at Mobile recommended that a colony should be established there.

The result of that exploration was the organization of the expedition of Tristán de Luna the following year. Filipina Bay was visited by the expedition, but Pensacola Bay was the preferred site for a settlement.

The coast of Alabama was untouched for a long time afterward, until the French eventually set eyes on it. Pierre Le Moyne, sieur d'Iberville visited the bay and island in 1699, landing at Biloxi. After disembarking his men and materials, he soon realized that the spot he had chosen was not ideal for a settlement, and he therefore obtained from the minister of the marine in France, Pontchartrain, permission to move 25 miles up the Mobile River. His brother, Jean-Baptiste Le Moyne, sieur de Bienville, was put in charge of the venture, and the colonists were sent out at the beginning of 1702. They immediately began building Fort Louis de la Louisiane—in honor of King Louis the XIV—or Louis de la Mobile, as it was to be known subsequently. Mobile was to become the main center of French colonial activities in Louisiana until 1720 and was visited by the leading colonial personalities of the time.

In the course of the Pensacola War between Spain and France, Mobile was unsuccessfully attacked by a Spanish squadron, as a reprisal for French attacks on Pensacola. Under the 1720 peace treaty, the Spanish and French governments accepted the respective proposals of their establishments at Pensacola and Mobile to consider the Perdido River as a frontier between them. Following the signing of the Treaty of Paris in 1763, Mobile came into the hands of the British, who repaired former Fort Condé and renamed it Fort Charlotte. Mobile remained in British hands until it was captured by Bernardo de Gálvez in March 1780.

Spanish Rule in Mobile

Spain had declared war on Great Britain, and the Spanish governor cooperated with George Washington in the struggle for independence. Following his victories at Fort Manchac, Baton Rouge and Fort Panmure, the young commander had been appointed by King Charles III to achieve the main purpose of his troops in America: the expulsion of the British from the Gulf of Mexico and the banks of the Mississippi, "where their establishments do so much harm to our trade, as also to the security of our most valuable possessions." After overcoming the reluctance of his superiors at Havana, Governor Bernardo de Gálvez in Louisiana obtained 567 men; this brought his contingent up to 754 and 12 vessels of different sizes. On January 11, 1780, the expedition sailed from New Orleans, but was becalmed and then fell foul of a hurricane. The losses suffered when his vessels were wrecked were compensated for by the arrival of 20 ships from Cuba.

On February 29, Gálvez opened fire on the enemy for the first time, and a long chivalrous correspondence began between him and the British commander, Elias Durnford. On March 9, the Spanish general harangued his troops, and they began to build a series of trenches in order to bring their batteries up into a suitable position. Several artillery duels ensued, and a number of engagements took place until the white flag of surrender was raised over the fortifications at Mobile. At 10:00 A.M. on March 14, the Spanish forces claimed possession of Mobile, taking 300 prisoners and suffering very few casualties. Fortunately for the besiegers, the relief expedition of 1,100 men from Pensacola under the command of Archibald Campbell did not take part in the fighting, although their vanguard was within view; they raised camp and withdrew from Pensacola. To offset any further attack by the enemy, Gálvez ordered a fort to be built, the site of which is still known as Spanish Fort, on the banks of the first arm of the river encountered on the way from Pensacola. As a mark of the king's appreciation of his victory, Gálvez was given command of all Spanish operations in America with the traditional title of governor of Louisiana and Mobile. Gálvez was a native of Málaga in Spain, and it is said that Málaga cathedral has one tower missing due to the fact that the money available to build it was spent on aid for American independence.

Throughout its 33 years of Spanish rule, Mobile was dependent on West Florida, with Pensacola as its capital, and the region was divided into two districts: Baton Rouge, between the Pearl and Mississippi Rivers, and Mobile, between the Pearl and Perdido Rivers. A commander resided in the town and lived in a house near the fort. Twelve officers held that post over the years, the most distinguished ones being Vicente Folch, Manuel Lanzos, Joaquín Osorno and Cayetano Pérez. The commander held both civil and military authority and acted as judge and notary. Other authorities included the mayor, or *alcalde,* and the royal treasurer, a post in which Miguel Eslava acquired considerable fame; his

descendants continued to live in the town throughout the 19th century and were prominent in politics and business. Thirteen priests ministered here, under the jurisdiction of the bishop of Louisiana and Florida, who, for many years, was Bishop Peñalver. The main church in Mobile during French times was Notre Dame, but the Spaniards changed its name to Immaculada Concepción, or Immaculate Conception, the name given to the cathedral built years later. Many French and British traders and merchants remained in the town and continued to use their respective languages, although Spanish was the official language. That period saw marked progress in livestock breeding, and there were a fair number of mills and several cotton gins, which brought their owners quick profits. The Spanish authorities made numerous land grants and confirmed some of those made under British rule so that today, most of the real estate in Mobile and its surroundings is based on Spanish documents.

At the time of the sale of Louisiana by France to the United States, Thomas Jefferson claimed that Mobile was included in the sale according to its status in French colonial times, whereas Spain argued that Mobile had been separated from Louisiana since the Treaty of Paris of 1763, and that, when Spain recovered Florida in 1783, Mobile had been absorbed into the western sector of Florida, just as it had been under British rule. Although Mobile remained in Spanish hands, it came under constant internal and external pressure from the surrounding United States territories. The colonists in the Tombigbee area—who did not have the benefit of the now free port of New Orleans but had to use the Spanish port of Mobile, where there were customs—sent a petition to Congress in 1809 asking permission to create the Territory of Mobile of the United States. This request brought no response whatsoever. However, the American citizens in the Baton Rouge District rebelled and captured the fort, and proclaimed the State of West Florida in 1810, hoisting a blue flag with a silver star; their independence was shortlived, and the district was incorporated with Louisiana. As the district of Mobile was still in Spanish hands, Reuben Kemper organized an expedition to take the capital. While in camp nearby, an excessive intake of whisky prior to the attack prevented their assault on the town and led to the besiegers being captured by the Spaniards; their leaders were sent to El Morro castle at Havana.

The Spanish-British alliance against Napoleon led to nonbelligerence on the part of Spain in favor of Britain during her war against the United States in 1812, with the result that the Spanish ports, including Mobile, were used by British ships. This resulted in Congress annexing the district of Mobile to the United States on May 11, 1812. President James Madison ordered its occupation; although the United States was not at war with Spain, General James Wilkinson—formerly a spy for Spain—set sail from New Orleans and occupied Mobile in March 1813. The Spanish commander, Cayetano Pérez, evacuated Fort Carlota on April 13, the date on which the United States flag was raised.

In the course of the War of Secession, Mobile, which was in the hands of the Confederates, was the scene of one of the major victories of Vice-Admiral Farragut, on August 5, 1864. The solid construction of the Spanish fort played a key role in the stout resistance that the Confederates showed to the attackers until the last minute.

More than 175 years have passed since Spain abandoned Mobile, and yet, the town and its inhabitants keep reminders of that era alive. There are still descendants of Spaniards who are proud of their heritage, and as a result of the city's Franco-Spanish past, the Catholic population is predominant. The Spanish castle and lion quarterings are featured on the coat of arms of the town and near the classic-style cathedral an inscription recalls that the land on which it stands was granted by Spain for a cemetery.

Touring the town, visitors can find the old city limits and buildings in the Spanish style, such as the home of the Confederate admiral Semmes, the site of the Spanish Fort and the Spanish parts of Fort Carlota, or the magnificent Plaza de España, before the modern auditorium in the center of the rebuilt old town. There are many streets still bearing Spanish names.

McGillivray

Between 1763 and 1799, the territories east of the Mississippi were of special concern to Spain. From the American War of Independence onward, when British authority over the territories was disputed and Spain took some parts by military action, they became the subject of conflicting claims. As we have already seen, in the peace treaty negotiations the new United States were at one time prepared to give way to Spanish claims, but Great Britain ultimately deliberately endeavored to cause a conflict between the former Spanish and American allies by granting rights to all her possessions between the Appalachians and the Missis-

sippi River as far as the 31st parallel, in the south, near Mobile. Spain, refusing to acknowledge those limits, insisted on ownership of the east bank of the Mississippi as far as the Ohio River, and of the district south of the Tennessee River and west of the Flint River, in what is now the center of Georgia.

This difference of opinion was to cause tension between the two countries for several years and resulted in Spain's delay in acknowledging the independence of the United States. In order to defend her rights in the area described, Spain reinforced her military defenses, closed the Mississippi to shipping other than Spanish vessels on June 14, 1784, and pursued a policy of friendship with the Indian nations, who greatly assisted her. Faced with this Spanish opposition, and similar British opposition in the north, for three years Congress did not take any action in the West other than forbidding immigrants to settle there. The federal army, under General Josiah Harmar, even went so far as to burn down the cabins built by those who had already settled and prevented their returning. Historians agree that Spain maintained her policy throughout the 1780s, when she formed close links with the settlements in Kentucky, Franklin and Cumberland, which sought to secede and allied themselves with Spain. However, the growing pressure of the settlers, the consolidation of federal power and the gradual weakening of Spain led to a less fortunate period in the 1790s, which ended with her eventual waiving of all claims.

Under the territorial distribution made in 1763, Britain received possession of the land east of the Mississippi, from which the French and the Spaniards emigrated. By means of the Proclamation Line, which forbade the settlement of colonists on the western side of the line, Spain gained the gratitude and unconditional alliance of the Creek Indians in the subsequent difficult days of the struggle for independence. When independence was won and the British retreated, Spain supported Indian claims against the new enemy, the young confederation of North America. In those difficult days, in 1783, the Creek Nation turned for leadership to a youth of 24, Alexander McGillivray.

The son of a Scotsman and an Indian woman (who was in turn the daughter of a Frenchman named Marchand, the commander of Fort Toulouse), McGillivray had been born at Little Tallasie not far from the present-day capital, Montgomery. When 14 years old, he had been taken to Charleston to receive a Western education and acquired a good command of the English language during the three years he spent there. With the outbreak of the Revolution, the family, who was loyal to the British Crown, lost all its property, and this resulted in Alexander's decision to fight for the British, who appointed him colonel and commissioner of the Creek Indians. So it was that his acceptance by his brother Indians seemed only natural, and his leadership became unquestionable not only as a result of force of arms, but due to his ability to communicate with his allies in English. At that time, the Creek Nation occupied areas comprising most of the state of Georgia, the state of Alabama and part of Mississippi, and had been in contact (not always peacefully) with westerners since the times of Ponce de León, Narváez and de Soto.

McGillivray opposed the Treaty of Augusta, signed on November 1, 1783, by a group of Creek chiefs, who relinquished a large area lying between the Ogeechee and Oconee Rivers to the state of Georgia. On January 1, 1784, he wrote to the Spanish governor of Pensacola, Arturo O'Neill, asking for the protection of the king of Spain for the Creek Nation inasmuch as, being an independent people, it could not be handed over by Britain to the United States against its will and interests. Having received a favorable reply from O'Neill, on March 28 he turned to the governor of Louisiana, Esteban Miró, asking for Spanish aid and permission to carry on trade with the British firm of Panton, Leslie and Co., based in New Orleans, on which the Indians depended for a livelihood that the Spanish organization of affairs could not provide. Faced with the danger that, otherwise, this trade might be channeled through the North Americans, Miró eventually accepted.

On June 1, 1784, the Treaty of Pensacola was signed, under which Spain appointed McGillivray commissioner to the Creeks and undertook to defend them and their territory west of the Flint River and south of the Tennessee. On July 10, 1785, McGillivray sent a memorandum to the king of Spain on behalf of the Creek, Chickasaw and Cherokee Indian chiefs, in which he rejected the treaty between the United States and Great Britain under which the territories inhabited by those nations had been transferred; his memorandum likewise insisted that force would be used to prevent colonists settling there and on the need to obtain more aid from Spain. In letters dated March 28, 1786, and May 1, 1786, he reported to O'Neill and to Miró, respectively, on the course of the war that the Creek Indians had declared against the United States in order to eradicate the new settlements. He failed to obtain the approval of the Spanish authorities for that decision and therefore found that the military aid provided him was reduced considerably (a situation that Miró later changed in view of McGillivray's threat to reach an agreement with the British or Americans).

In February 1787, McGillivray was visited by James White, acting as superintendent for Indian affairs appointed by Congress. White endeavored unsuccessfully to get the Indian chief to change his violent approach to the settlements. The efforts made by Richard Winn, who succeeded White, were no more successful in the spring of 1788; the murder of the Indian chief Old Tassel had enraged his Cherokee Indians, who had previously been disposed toward peace. A proclamation by Congress on September 1, ordering the withdrawal of immigrants from Indian territory, did not produce results, owing to the difficulty of putting it into practice with scant coercive forces and the continued Indian attacks on the white townships. On September 2, James Robertson, who was at the same time proposing annexation of Cumberland (Tennessee) with Spain, wrote to McGillivray saying that the West should adjoin the nation that controlled the Mississippi. The delegates sent out by George Washington in 1789 were no better received by the Indian chief than their predecessors.

The situation changed the following year, however, when Spain insisted on a more peaceful policy to avoid further frontier incidents. McGillivray decided to accept an invitation to visit New York, trusting that this would spur the Spaniards to furnish more aid in view of their disquiet at a possible rapprochement with the United States. To judge by the report sent in by Spanish agent José de Viar, the visitors, McGillivray and 30 other Creek chiefs, were received in New York as if they were royalty and signed, first with Henry Knox and later with Washington himself, the Treaty of New York, dated August 13, 1790. Under the treaty, McGillivray waived the claim to the belt of territory in Georgia between the Oconee and Ogeechee Rivers, and received assurances from Washington that the federal government would oppose new settlements under the so-called Yazoo Project. McGillivray was also appointed a general and obtained an annual pension of $1,500; but he did not renounce his connections with Spain or the trade monopoly that he enjoyed with Panton.

As McGillivray had expected, the Spanish reaction to the treaty took the form of more substantial promise of aid and the annual payment of $2,000, which Miró was authorized to increase if circumstances so advised, and peace between the Cherokee and the United States was shortlived. The governor of Louisiana, Carondelet, summoned the Indian chief to New Orleans, where he signed the Treaty of New Orleans on July 6, 1792. Under this treaty McGillivray undertook to declare war on the United States until he had recovered the territory belonging to the Creeks under British rule, and Spain promised an adequate supply of arms, border guarantees and an annual pension of $3,500.

The foreseen invasion by the Creek, Cherokee and Chickamauga took place in September. The ultimate objective was Nashville, on which the three columns converged, the first commanded by Doublehead, the second under the command of Middlestriker and the third commanded by Watts. Stricken by a mortal illness and bedridden, McGillivray was unable to take part in the invasion. His absence was felt, owing to the disputes that broke out among the chiefs when they were nearing Nashville, and resulted in the expedition coming to a disastrous end. The death of McGillivray on February

17, 1793, was a heavy blow to the survival of his political plans and the Creek Nation. The business of Panton, Leslie and Co., was to continue, however, and the mortal remains of the warrior were laid to rest in the garden of Leslie's home at Pensacola.

Spanish Place-Names

There are various Spanish place-names in Alabama, including De Soto State Park, in DeKalb County, Monte Sano State Park, in Madison County, and the towns called Alma, Almeria, Alta, Andalusia, Angel, Ardilla, Bexar, Columbia, Columbiana, Cordova, Cuba, Delta, Docena, Fleta, Francisco, Galera, Gordo, Lavaca, Madrid, Magnolia, Manila, Triana, Valhermoso Springs and Vida.

MISSISSIPPI

In Mississippi, as in the other southern states, Spanish moss festoons the trees and lends the scenery the appearance of a theatrical set. This is the scene of the adventures of Tom Sawyer and Huckleberry Finn, Mark Twain's characters whose paths mirror the wanderings of Don Quixote and Sancho Panza. The state of Mississippi boasts major towns such as Natchez and Vicksburg on the banks of the Mississippi, both of which are linked with Spanish history (Fort Nogales was situated at Vicksburg). Columbus, in the northwestern sector of the state, holds an Annual Pilgrimage in April, with the discoverer accompanied by Spanish soldiers bearing the banner of Isabella and Ferdinand.

The district of Mobile, along the coastal belt, was not included in the republic of West Florida, which was transferred to the United States and therefore remained in Spanish hands. Although the Mississippi region was first explored by Spain, it was populated by French settlements (both along the coast and inland), until it fell into British hands in 1763, when France handed over all the possessions along the eastern bank of the Mississippi. In the years following the outbreak of the Revolution, it was claimed by Spain as a result of her military occupation, claims that United States rejected. Under

the Treaty of San Lorenzo of 1795, Spain waived her rights to the district north of parallel 31, and consequently, in 1798, the territory of Mississippi was created, to which were added parts of Georgia and South Carolina. It covered the states of Alabama and Mississippi, with the exception of the coastal belt south of the 31st parallel, and eventually came into the possession of the United States when Spanish troops abandoned Mobile on April 13, 1813, following the occupation of the town by 600 men under General James Wilkinson, on orders from President James Madison to seize lands adjacent to West Florida as far as the Perdido River.

Along that coastal belt the modern towns of Biloxi and Gulfport have fine beaches and resort facilities. Near the boundary of the state of Alabama, in Pascagoula, stands an old Spanish fort where visitors can see the reenactment of events that took place within its walls and in the surrounding area. It was founded in 1721 by Joseph de la Pointe, whose granddaughter married a Spanish army captain, Enrique de Grimarest. The fort is the oldest building in the area and is built of wood, oyster shells, adobe and moss. It was held by Spain from 1780 to 1810.

Pascagoula was also the home of Jorge Ferragut, the Minorcan father of Admiral Farragut, who moved here in 1809, following the death of his wife in New Orleans, to live with his children at a spot called Point Plaquet, which had been known since then as Farragut's Point. He died at Pascagoula on June 4, 1817, and is buried in the local cemetery.

The Spanish History

This state bears the Indian name that means "Father of the Waters." The first Spaniard to claim to have sighted the river was Alonzo Alvarez de Pineda in 1519, who discovered that the water was drinkable at the wide estuary. He named in Espíritu Santo, or Holy Spirit. He was followed by Pánfilo de Narváez and his unfortunate companions in the fall of 1528, when they sailed first through Lake Borgne, on their way from Mobile, and later changed course for Chandeleur Sound, where they sighted the islands of that name and set foot on dry land on one of the riverbanks. Farther upstream, Hernando de Soto crossed the Mississippi in May 1513, and called it Rio Grande de la Florida, or the Big River of Florida.

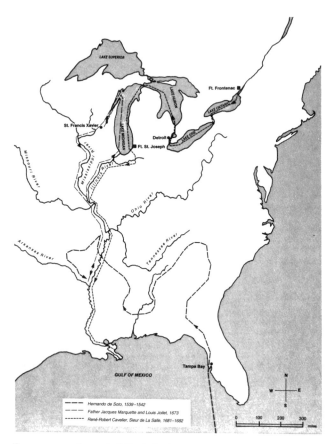

European explorers in Mississippi, 1539–1682. Facts On File.

Toward the middle of December 1540, Hernando de Soto and his men entered the territory of Mississippi, where they found fruit and other foodstuffs plentiful and decided to spend the winter. During their stay there, an unusual incident took place. Some Indians stole several pigs; two Indians were killed in the attempt, while another was sentenced to having his hands cut off. Shortly afterward, four Spaniards were found thieving in Indian tents: displaying equal justice, Hernando de Soto condemned two of them to death and confiscated the properties of the other two.

Before departing westward in March 1541, finding that he needed bearers, de Soto asked the Chickasaw chiefs to provide them. His request was refused and the Spaniards' camp was burned down during the night. In spite of the confusion this caused among the sleeping Spaniards, order was restored but not before soldiers and 50 horses had been killed (de Soto himself was unhorsed); many others were without clothing and supplies. They left the camp and in May, reached the great Mississippi River at a spot that many historians claim is present-day Sunflower Landing, while others say that it was in the neighborhood of Memphis. Could this be the spot where the writer William Gilmore Simms found a crude cross marking the tomb of one of de Soto's soldiers? It was this find that led the writer to embark on his long novel *Pelayo* (1835) and its sequel, *Count Julian* (1845).

Another party of Spaniards crossed the territory from east to west and back in 1560. The group included two captains, 50 infantrymen and a number of men on horseback, in addition to Father Domingo de la Anunciación. This contingent was pressed into service by Mateo del Saúz, deputy to Tristán de Luna at Coosa, to assist the Coosa Indians in their expedition against their enemies, the Natchez Indians. After a spectacular farewell, the expeditionaries set out accompanied by 300 Indian warriors. On reaching the Big River (perhaps the Pearl River) in the vicinity of a large township, the Indian chief asked the Spaniards not to sound their customary reveille so that the attack would be a compete surprise. To his disappointment, however, they found the town abandoned except for a single ailing enemy. Although the Spaniards tried to save him and Father Anunciación attempted in vain to convert him, he was killed by the Coosa. They set fire to the huts and took some of the corn they found, which was to be sent to Saúz. The Indians and the Spanish soldiers continued their advance without finding any trace of their antagonists until, as they reached the Mississippi, they were greeted with the submission of the Natchez Indians, who had crossed to the other bank out of fear; the Natchez Indians paid them a tribute three times a year, consisting of chestnuts, walnuts and other fruits and, with the daunting presence of the Spaniards, the former enemies entered into a truce.

Natchez

The Spaniards were instrumental again when the colonists on the East Coast rose against Britain in 1776. Bernardo de Gálvez, at that time governor of Louisiana, favored the patriots, in spite of Spain's neutrality. He provided them with considerable aid, as we have seen, through Oliver Pollock, an Irish merchant in New Orleans, who had placed himself and his fortune at the disposal of the Revolution, and James Willing, to whom he supplied arms, ammunition and other provisions. On January 10, 1778, Willing departed from Pittsburgh aboard an armed vessel and sailed down the Ohio and the Mississippi to New Orleans, burning British-owned settlements and plantations as he passed through. Gálvez allowed them to sell the booty obtained on their voyage and ignored the capture of two British vessels by Willing. However, in view of Willing's unpredictable conduct, Gálvez did not allow him to return through Spanish territory, but authorized Robert George to lead his men through it to Illinois territory, on condition that they refrain from any action against British settlements.

Spain declared war on Britain on the side of the rebels on June 21, 1779, which Gálvez knew in advance of his British neighbors. On September 6, he attacked Fort Manchac, and the garrison had no alternative but to surrender. He was equally successful with the fort at Baton Rouge, whose commander, Alexander Dickson, raised the white flag on September 21. Fort Panmure, at Natchez, with its garrison of 80 men, was included in the terms of capitulation. Captain Juan de la Villebeuvre had the duty of relieving the town and fort of Natchez of Captain Anthony Forster on October 5. Accompanied by 50 soldiers, the Spanish captain was the bearer of the order to surrender and a letter from Oliver Pollock praising the spirit of liberty and generous behavior of Gálvez; the letter also extolled the advantages in trade that would derive from their permanent alignment with New Orleans. On November 22, 1780, Spanish captain Baltasar de Villiers led a detachment of troops from Arkansas Post to the opposite east bank of the Mississippi and took formal possession of the Territory of Mississippi in the name of the king of Spain.

Almost two years after these victories, while Gálvez continued his efforts against the British, some British royalists near Natchez, including Anthony Hutchins, planned to retake Fort Panmure and sought help from General Campbell, governor of Pensacola, who encouraged them in their venture. Alexander MacIntosh, a colonist who was prospering under Spanish rule, reported the conspiracy to the commander of the fort, Captain Juan de la Villebeuvre. The captain succeeded in repulsing an attack by the rebels, but confronted with a forged letter from MacIntosh in which the fort's destruction seemed imminent, he surrendered on condition that it play no part in the war from that time onward. The British flag was raised, but not for long; the bloody defeat of a group of their followers and the news that Pensacola had fallen into Gálvez's hands discouraged the ringleaders, who fled. The Spaniards recovered the fort and the inhabitants of Natchez renewed their oath of loyalty to Spain. The rebels were treated benevolently.

Natchez soon became a key point in Spanish–North American relations, and the commander of the fort, Manuel Gayoso de Lemos, played an active role, aided, according to all accounts, by his intelligence, his excellent English, his marriage to an American and his popularity among the settlers in the region. Historian Jack Holmes comments that he brought to the final period of Spanish administration on the Mississippi a reputation for liberality, honesty and progress. The Natchez District at that time covered the area from Punta Cortada (Point Coupée) in the south as far as the mouth of the Yazoo River, in the north; from the Mississippi in the west to an unclear frontier in the east. (Prior to Gayoso, its commanders included Carlos de Grand Pré, Esteban Miró, Pedro José Piernas, Francisco Collele, Felipe Treviño and Francisco Bouligny and, again, Carlos de Grand Pré.)

From the day when he took possession of his post on May 19, 1789, until his transfer to New Orleans on July 29, 1797, Gayoso was a strong and capable administrator. He was effective in managing Indian affairs. The Treaties of Natchez and Nogales that he executed with the Indians consolidated Spain's position.

Gayoso was responsible for the construction, on orders from Baron de Carondelet, governor of Louisiana, of Forts San Fernando de las Barrancas, Esteban and Confederación, and played an essential part in the creation of the Mississippi naval squadron and a citizen's militia.

O'Fallon and Clark

The state of Georgia, which had recently ratified the federal Constitution, claimed part of Mississippi and other western territories, which she was anxious to sell before the federal Congress should deny those alleged rights and decide to turn the lands into federal territory. Under the Act of December 21, 1789, Georgia sold 25 million acres at five-sixths of a cent per acre to the Tennessee, Virginia and South Carolina Yazoo Companies. The land in question was inhabited by Indians and was also subject to claims by Spain. Among the participants in that huge deal were Patrick Henry, William Blount, John Sevier, James Wilkinson, George Morgan, George Rogers Clark and Baron von Steuben. Of the three projects, the most ambitious was that of the South Carolina company, which was to develop an enormous belt of land along the east bank of the Mississippi, and between the Mississippi and the Yazoo River, north of the town of Vicksburg. William Davenport had failed in earlier attempts to organize the County of Bourbon in the Natchez area in 1785, and a colony at Chickasaw Bluffs in 1787.

In an attempt to overcome the foreseeable Spanish objections to the sale, the South Carolina company appointed James O'Fallon, an Irishman and former Catholic priest, as their general agent. In order to obtain Spanish approval, O'Fallon maintained correspondence with Diego de Gardoqui, Miró and McGillivray; he contended that Spain should allow the establishment of the settlement, which would become an independent free state, a center of trade, a major deposit for merchandise going up and down the Mississippi and a considerable slave market. In view of the strategic importance of New Orleans to this state, it was important for it to maintain close ties with Spain, and it could be of great use to Spain as a buffer between the United States and New Spain, which would thus be protected from the possible ambitions of aggressive American settlers.

Although Miró continued the correspondence with O'Fallon for the purpose of finding out his true intentions, it does not seem likely that the project was viewed favorably by Spain. In view of Miró's ambivalence, O'Fallon grew impatient and joined his brother-in-law, George Rogers Clark, in the recruitment of settlers from Kentucky for the conquest of Natchez and New Orleans. George Washington, who had been appointed president only a year earlier, was alarmed at the prospect of his country becoming involved in an international war, and therefore, on August 26, 1790, he issued a proclamation denouncing the Clark-O'Fallon expedition. The scheme was further discredited by the well-founded accusations made by Wilkinson to the company concerning numerous irregularities.

The outbreak of the French Revolution and the execution of Louis XVI on January 21, 1793, led to war between France, on the one hand, and Britain, Spain, Holland, Austria and Prussia on the other. After much debate, on April 22, Washington signed the Neutrality Proclamation outlining a "friendly and impartial" posture toward all parties in the conflict. On April 8, Edmond Genet, the diplomatic representative of the French revolutionaries, disembarked at Charleston after being diverted from Philadelphia by unfavorable winds. Among the business that had brought him was the revival of French interests in the Mississippi basin and the possible recovery of Louisiana. To this end he sought Clark's cooperation, knowing of his plans to attack Spanish settlements with forces recruited in Kentucky, with the help of certain French elements in Spanish territory. To act as an intermediate agent Genet sent André Michaux, an outstanding naturalist, who visited Clark on September 17 in Louisville. Michaux had authorization to promote the insurrection in Spanish territory and the negotiation of treaties with the Indians. At the same time, democratic societies encouraged the enlistment of volunteers and the collection of funds; Clark himself contributed $4,680.

In view of indignant protests by Spain, conveyed to Washington by Governor Carondelet, the federal government ordered the arrest of Genet's agents and asked the French government to withdraw their representative. The new French minister, Joseph Fauchet, who arrived on February 21, 1794, reluctantly withdrew French support for Clark, who, nevertheless, went ahead with his preparations. His main objectives were to take Natchez and New Orleans. On March 24, Washington published a decree ordering Clark and his friends to desist from their venture, and on March 31, the secretary of defense, Henry Knox, began fortification of Fort Massac, on the Ohio, to prevent the rebel expedition from descending the river. In June, Congress classified as a criminal offense the participation of citizens in hostile acts against any foreign power with which the United States maintained peaceful relations.

The federal troops, however, were not strong enough to compel George Rogers Clark to stop. John Montgomery made his way down the Cumberland as far as the Ohio, at the head of a contingent of frontier settlers and French volunteers, where he built a fortified palisade to interrupt traffic bound for Spanish territory. Elijah Clarke, who had given up a plan to invade Florida owing to lack of French support, crossed the Oconee River with a group of followers, thus defying the United States, Georgia, Spain and the Creek Indians. Taking possession of a large area of land occupied by the Indians, he proclaimed an independent republic. Carondelet asked the friendly Indians for assistance and the captain general at Havana for permission to counterattack Clarke. To forestall an attack along the Mississippi, the Spanish garrisons were reinforced, and a fleet of warships was equipped and armed. Fort Confederación was built to withstand possible invasion by land and Luis Lorimier, the Spanish commander at Nuevo Madrid, raised a war party of 600 Indians. Montgomery was forced to desist, no blood was shed and the danger of a war between Spain and the United States was averted. Clarke remained among the Indians, while Clark bitterly withdrew forever from public affairs.

As the Napoleonic wars raged in Europe, Britain wanted to avoid the United States entering the war on the side of their former ally, France, or to at least ensure its neutrality. It therefore agreed to hand over posts that it had retained by force since the end of the War of Independence in the Northwestern Territory. So it was that the Jay Treaty was signed on November 19, 1794. Abandoned by the British (as they had already been in 1783, and by the French in 1763) and defeated at Fallen Timbers, the Indian nations ceased their warlike activities and were prepared to start a period of peaceful relations with their powerful new neighbors: on February 22, hostilities ceased, and on August 3, 1795, they signed the Treaty of Greenville under which they accepted certain areas of territory in the state of Ohio, so that the Proclamation Line became a part of history.

The collapse of British and Indian opposition in 1795 did not meet with a parallel Spanish approach. On the contrary, Baron de Carondelet, the governor of Louisiana, went ahead with his plans to support a new conspiracy in Kentucky led by Wilkinson, Benjamin Sebastian, Harry Innes and others. At the same time, he lent military support to Spanish claims to districts south and west of the Tennessee River, when Governor Gayoso of Natchez erected Fort San Fernando on May 30, 1795, at the spot called Chickasaw Bluffs, near present-day Memphis. On June 13, 1795, Carondelet reported to his superiors that Gayoso had started building work on the establishment called Las Barracas de Marot, situated 420 leagues from New Orleans, on the east bank of the Mississippi, to ensure communications with the outposts in the Ylinoa (Illinois) region.

But the authorities in Spain did not follow the same policy as Carondelet, who strove to maintain her power on the North American continent. The wars waged in Europe made the threat of conflict in the faraway Mississippi valley a dangerous prospect, while maintaining the borders of a frontier pressed by the growing numbers of American settlers seemed near impossible. Consequently, on October 27, 1795, Prime Minister Manuel Godoy signed the Treaty of San Lorenzo with the American emissary, Thomas Pinckney, committing what the historian Holmes has called "the most serious blunder of her [Spanish] American colonial policy." Under the treaty, Spain renounced the positions that she had maintained for so many years south of the 31st parallel, east of the Mississippi River, and granted free navigation up the Mississippi and rights of deposit at New Orleans for a period of three years. This Treaty of Friendship, Limits, Trade and Navigation was the first of those signed between Spain and the new country. (In the Academy of Fine Arts of San Fernando in Madrid today, a portrait of Washington given to Manuel Godoy commemorates this event. Painted in Philadelphia in 1796 by Joseph Perovani, who was influenced by the artist Gilbert Stuart, the portrait depicts Washington pointing at this treaty, with another document, "Plan of the City of Washington, State of Maryland," at his fingertips.)

As a loyal subject of the king, Carondelet had no alternative but to prepare to obey successive orders from his superior Godoy, who wished to rid himself of the problems and expenses that the possession of Louisiana caused Spain, the direction of which changed according to the favorable or unfavorable progress of the negotiations. Natchez, which was to be included in the deal, became the key point in the formalities conducive to transferring possession of the territories covered by the treaty.

In order to carry out the transfer of territory, President Washington appointed Andrew Ellicott, who arrived at Natchez on February 14, 1797. En route, he received word that Carondelet had given orders to prevent him from proceeding downstream until the new posts could be evacuated when the river waters rose; at Chickasaw Bluffs he received a letter from the governor of Natchez, Gayoso, notifying him that evacuation could not be undertaken for lack of boats and requesting him to leave his escort of 25 men at Bayou Pierre in order to avoid a possible incident. Ellicott was received at Natchez with great courtesy, and when Gayoso began preparations for the withdrawal, he received counterorders from Carondelet. When a few months later, new orders were given, the American delegate been to lose patience.

A dispute that arose on June 1 between Catholics and Protestants led to a group of inhabitants at Natchez forming a Committee of Public Safety (to which Ellicott belonged), which drew up a set of four articles declaring themselves American citizens, but respecting temporary Spanish rule; Gayoso accepted these articles, and they were later accepted by Carondelet. When Carondelet left the territory, Gayoso succeeded him as governor of Louisiana, appointed his former secretary, Captain Stephen Minor, as temporary commander of the fort and civil and military governor of the district of Natchez. Minor received irrevocable orders from Godoy to evacuate the fort, and in January 1798, Gayoso reported the king's decision to Ellicott. On March 30, the Spanish troops abandoned the different forts. With the assistance of Sir William Dunbar, appointed by Spain to represent her in defining the frontiers, Ellicott proceeded to mark out the new boundary, a task in which he had to contend with mosquitos, malaria, torrential rain, the enmity of the Indians and the incompetence of his assistants.

After the transfer of land, Spain still retained the Baton Rouge and Manchac sectors, between Orleans Island and Natchez, and land along the coastal belt as far as Mobile. There were many residents in Baton Rouge who favored separation from Spain, complaining against the exclusion of their territory from the Louisiana Purchase; among them were the brothers Reuben and Samuel Kemper, living on American soil, who one day suddenly took Bayou Sara by surprise while it was under Spanish control. The commander at Baton Rouge, Captain Carlos de Grand Pré, requested help from the marquis de Casa Calvo, the Spanish governor of Louisiana in New Orleans. The dispatch of an armed vessel with a few militiamen sufficed to expel the rebels. Similar incidents occurred in 1804 and 1805, including the proclamation by the Kempers, in August 1804, of the independence of the district and the unfurling of a flag consisting of seven white and blue stripes with two stars on a blue field; subsequently they sought a pardon for this conduct from the military authority, Grand Pré.

In 1807, Grand Pré was succeeded as commander by Carlos Dehault de Lassus, who was less successful in putting down disturbances, while the inhabitants of Baton Rouge grew more discontent. Rumors began that Napoléon intended to take possession of the province. On July 20, 1810, the settlers gathered at St. John's Plains, which John Rhea presiding, and, after declaring their opposition to occupation by the French, swore loyalty to Spain; at a second meeting held on August 25, a new government was formed. A letter was composed by de Lassus to the governor at Pensacola requesting military aid, but it was intercepted and revealed that de Lassus disagreed with the plotters. The rebels convened and raised the flag of a new independent sovereign state: a blue background with a silver star in the center. On September 23 they advanced against the fort and surprised de Lassus and fatally wounded his second-in-command, Louis de Grand Pré, the son of Carlos. Three days later, the rebels formed a provisional government, issued a declaration of independence and elected Fulwar Skipwith president of the Republic of West Florida.

The government of the United States, not surprisingly, was not prepared to tolerate this dissension. On October 27, the governor of the Territory of Orleans, William Claiborne, received orders to take the secessionist district. Fort Baton Rouge surrendered easily, and the stars and stripes were immediately hoisted. The Republic of West Florida had lasted for less than three months.

Spanish Place-Names

Together with the mortal remains of those Spaniards who lost their lives here, Mississippi still preserves some names that recall its Spanish history: Bolivar, De Soto, Grenada and Tunica Counties; and the towns of Anguila, Clara, Columbia, Columbus, Cuevas, Delta, Doloroso, Flora, Grenada, Hernando, Quito, Rio, Saltillo, Santa Rosa and Tunica.

PART IV:
STATES ON THE WEST BANK OF THE MISSISSIPPI RIVER

While Part III covered those states in the Mississippi basin on the left bank of the river, which fell to Britain in 1763 when France gave up her American dominions, we'll look here at another group of states along the "Big River" and its tributaries, lying on the right bank and stretching westward, that were handed over to Spain by her French neighbor also in 1763. This territory, the so-called French Louisiana, which increased the dominions of King Charles III of Spain, had more or less clear limits in the south, and its eastern boundary was defined by the Mississippi River. Its frontiers were not clear in the west and north, and this lack of precision had to be clarified during the years of Spanish rule, although the task was never completed owing to the huge area involved.

The Spanish presence in these states diminishes with the distance from St. Louis and New Orleans in a northerly and westerly direction, simply because of that distance itself and the short time available under Spanish rule for exploration and settlement. Those ventures might have been consummated had the course of Spain's internal and European policy been different, and if it had not been for the problems that American independence caused for the Spanish governors of Louisiana. From the outset, the settlers west of the Appalachians exerted pressure on the Spanish territories to include them within their area of influence and bring them under their own rule.

How did all these states come into the hands of Spain? The assignment of these lands by France to Spain occurred under King Louis XV. He relinquished the lands on the right bank of the Mississippi River, together with

Orleans Island, in favor of the kings of Spain under the Treaty of Fontainebleau of November 3, 1762, confirmed (with the exception of the so-called parishes of Florida) by the Treaty of Paris of February 10, 1763. Louisiana remained in Spanish hands until the secret Treaty of San Ildefonso of October 1, 1800 and the subsequent treaty of the same name of March 21, 1801, by which Louisiana was once again transferred to France, who hastened to sell it to the United States by the Treaty of Paris of April 30, 1803. Spain considered that sale as illegal, since, according to Article Seven of the Treaty of San Ildefonso, France had undertaken not to assign Louisiana to any power other than Spain. Again, Napoléon had treated Spain disgracefully; Spain was left without her territory, and without the money that the United States had paid Napoléon. It had taken little effort for Napoléon to obtain it, and he had no compunction about selling it at a ludicrously low price.

The acquisition of such vast domains in 1763 was not accompanied by popular rejoicing in Spain, firstly owing to ignorance of the exact size and enormous potential of the territories involved, and, secondly, due to the growing problems that such a territorial acquisition implied for the faltering power of Spain, who was already overwhelmed by the problems entailed in her enormous dominions in America, Asia and Africa, and her key position in the European revolt of the 18th century. Louisiana was accepted, however, as an enormous buffer to protect Spain's interests in the viceroyship of New Spain from French expansion attempts, which disappeared entirely, and from British expansion.

Given its name by French explorer René-Robert Cavelier, sieur de La Salle in honor of Louis XIV, Louisiana has been considered generally as a French territory and venture inherited by the United States, with an insignificant interlude under Spanish rule. But, it should be remembered that the first permanent settlement in the present-day state of Louisiana was founded in 1714 at Natchitoches by St. Denis (Fort de La Boulaye, founded in 1699, was of scant importance and, being so isolated, was abandoned shortly afterward) and the French port of New Orleans was not founded until 1719. Moreover, the Treaty of Fontainebleau in 1762 included the transfer of the territory to Spain, with the result that in fact Louisiana was nominally under French rule for about 50 years (or at the most 60). Therefore, counting the years between 1762 and November 30, 1803, when the French recovered possession of their old territories, it can be seen that Spain ruled Louisiana for over 40 years, which is not much shorter than the period of French rule.

Furthermore, historically speaking, the French period was marked by attempts to explore and settle that were not fully successful and only covered small areas of the territory, which lacked governmental organization. The years of Spanish rule, on the other hand, set the colony on its feet and laid the foundations for its subsequent progress. This was a period of organization, prudent measures, increase in population, and the conversion of New Orleans into the most important city on the North American continent. The Spanish rulers applied a sensible policy and upright conduct so that when the last of them departed, the French inhabitants viewed the French governors with uncertainty, having come to accept the progressive Spanish rule.

In addition, Louisiana contributed to American independence with the help of Spain, who rendered services of the cause of the Revolution, including the expulsion of Britain from the Mississippi basin and the South of the United States, thereby preventing her strategic plan, which could have had a decisive influence on the final outcome of the uprising. Britain strove to surround the revolutionaries by means of an arc stretching between Canada and Florida, which would use the Mississippi basin, with New Orleans as a supply point, to build pressure eastward and corner the revolutionaries on the eastern side of the Appalachians. (These were the same tactics used by Louis XIV against the British colonies when he set up a number of forts in the Mississippi valley to obtain the alliance of the Indians and cut off the expansion of the British colonies westward, as well as the maneuver attempted subsequently by the British at the time of their invasion of Louisiana in 1814–1815, which, had it succeeded, would have cancelled the effects of the Louisiana Purchase and changed the course of the history of the United States.)

The Louisiana Purchase has been described as the biggest real estate deal in history. President Thomas Jefferson, hearing rumors in 1801 of the purchase of Louisiana from Spain by Napoléon, commissioned his minister in Paris, Robert R. Livingston, in 1802, to negotiate with France for the purchase of Orleans Island and West Florida, namely, along the coast of the Gulf of Mexico. Napoléon had planned the revival of French military power in the gulf. Various events would thwart his plans: on the island of Santo Domingo, the black ruler Toussaint Louverture, had gained control in the uprising of 1791 and an army bound for Louisiana had to be diverted to the island. The attempted uprising of the French in Louisiana ended in failure, yellow fever decimating the ranks of the soldiers and the imminence of a war with Britain giving rise to fears as to the conquest of New Orleans—and of Louisiana—by British forces. All these factors led Napoléon to put an end to his American dreams and hand over Louisiana to the United States, for a sum of money that he needed badly. The American negotiators, Livingston and James Monroe, were understandably amazed when offered the purchase of this great tract of territory. Although they lacked authorization from the president, they signed the Treaty of Transfer on April 30, 1803, with the French plenipotentiary, Charles-Maurice de Talleyrand.

Strange as it may seem today, the acquisition was not received with unanimous praise by the beneficiaries, and Jefferson, when ratifying the actions of his envoys, was criticized for having spent a considerable sum of money on useless land. The treaty was not made known immediately. The last Spanish governor of Louisiana, Juan Manuel de Salcedo, actually handed over the southern sector at a ceremony at the municipal hall in New Orleans on November 30, 1803. The French representative, Pierre Clement de Laussat, had arrived in March, and it was he who acted also on behalf of France at the transfer of power to the American commissioners, W. C. C. Claiborne and General James Wilkinson, which took place at New Orleans on December 20, 1803. Upper Louisiana was handed over by the lieutenant governor, Carlos Dehault de Lassus, at St. Louis, on March 9, 1804.

LOUISIANA

The *Conquistadores:* Pineda, Narváez and de Soto

The Spaniards were the first Europeans to discover Louisiana. In 1519, Alonso Alvarez de Pineda sighted the Mississippi delta, and nine years later, the expeditionaries accompanying Pánfilo de Narváez, including Cabeza de Vaca, explored Lake Borgne, Chandeleur Sound and one of the arms of the great Mississippi.

Hernando de Soto and his men set foot on the soil of this state in March 1542, when they entered from the north following the course of the Ouachita River down to its confluence with the Mississippi, passing through the present localities of Monroe and Columbia, in the hope of sighting the sea once more. The conquistador, with only 300 men and 40 horses left, all lacking the most elementary supplies, recognized the need to build two brigantines on the coast to send one to Mexico and the other to Cuba to seek assistance and report on his vicissitudes and survival.

The vanguard of the expedition arrived at a township called Guachoya, near present-day Ferriday, on the banks of the Mississippi opposite Natchez. De Soto then selected a small exploratory party under the command of Juan de Añasco, to go downstream and find the sea. A week later, they returned without having sighted the sea or any trace of it (the local Indians did not even know of its existence). In a desperate attempt to extricate himself from this situation, since he felt that his strength was failing him, he asked a neighboring Indian chief for assistance. When aid was refused, a dispute broke out, and the Spaniards inflicted heavy casualties on the Indians.

De Soto, however, became ill, and fever was gradually consuming him. On May 20, feeling that his end war near, he gathered his officers and, with their consent, elected Luis de Moscoso to be his successor. He then made his will, confessed and expired. Lest the news of de Soto's death should cause an Indian uprising, the Indians were told that he had ascended to the sun (for he had appeared to them to be the Son of the Sun). His body was placed aboard a canoe during the night; it sank little by little in midstream. The Mississippi is therefore the tomb of Hernando de Soto, one of the greatest of Spanish *conquistadores.*

After the burial, Moscoso immediately gathered his men and gave orders to return to Mexico overland. The expeditionaries set out westward and entered the region of the Naguatex Indians, in Texas, until they reached the Trinity River; however, with winter approaching, they chose to turn back to the spot where their leader had died. They then decided to build seven brigantines on the banks of the Mississippi and set off downstream bound for the sea on July 3. It took them 17 days to reach the Gulf of Mexico, across which they sailed to New Spain and disembarked at the Panuco River about 150 miles north of Veracruz. Viceroy Antonio de Mendoza gave the defeated expeditionaries a splendid welcome in Mexico City, where they went to church to make their thanksgiving.

Early explorers in Louisiana, 1527–1682. Facts On File.

The Spanish Governors: Ulloa, O'Reilly and Unzaga

In the summer of 1765, Antonio de Ulloa, who had been appointed Spanish governor, wrote from Havana announcing his plans to take possession of the territory.

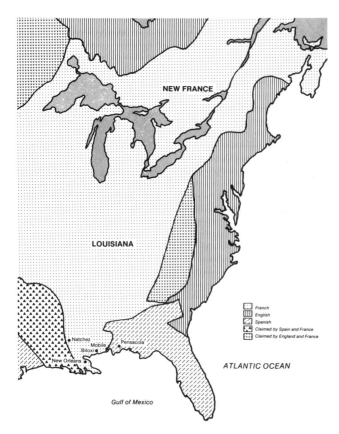

European claims in North America, 1689–1763. Facts On File.

This plan was delayed until the following spring, when he disembarked with 90 soldiers at New Orleans. There he met with stubborn resistance on the part of an influential minority who were reluctant to accept rule by Spain. He had to confine himself to dealing with Philippe Aubry and issuing a number of intelligent measures concerning trade and public order. His policies were beneficial to the settlers but were not well received among the community leaders, whose attitude worsened, as did even that of the clergy, when Ulloa left for Balize, at the mouth of the Mississippi, and returned married to a Peruvian. Realizing that little could be done with the force at his disposal, he had to bow to the pressure of the New Orleans Superior Council and departed in November 1768 aboard a French ship bound for Havana, where he reported the revolt. With Ulloa had arrived the grandfather of the well-known historian of Louisiana, Charles Etienne Gayarré, of Aragonese birth and the author of such important works as *History of Louisiana* and *Philip II*.

In August 1769 the new governor, the Irishman Alexander O'Reilly, took up his post, accompanied by 24 ships and 3,000 soldiers. This time the rebellious colonists could do nothing and had no alternative but to resign themselves to Spanish rule. As a preemptive step, O'Reilly arrested 11 of the ringleaders of the rebellion, five of whom were later shot, including Nicolas Chauvin de Lafranière. His second step was to begin to reorganize the colony. He proclaimed Spanish to be the official language and enforced the laws of Spain. The superior council was replaced by the institution known as the *cabildo* (chapter), composed of 10 members, presided over by the governor. He fixed the prices of foodstuffs and other commodities, promoted trade with the outside world, established a system of land grants and encouraged good relations with the Indians. When he left Louisiana in March 1770, leaving Luis de Unzaga y Amézaga as governor, O'Reilly had served his office well.

Luis de Unzaga, the next governor, concentrated his efforts on pacifying all the inhabitants and pursued the policy introduced by his predecessor of entrusting key positions in the administration to Creoles, and encouraged the Spaniards to marry Creoles (as he himself had done). Unzaga promoted education, immigration, agriculture and good government; tobacco planting was introduced, and trade with all countries was encouraged. By the time he was appointed captain general in Caracas in 1777, he had contributed greatly toward the prosperity of Louisiana.

It was Unzaga who initiated Spanish cooperation with the rebellious thirteen colonies. In favoring their cause, he followed the example set by his predecessor, O'Reilly. An Irishman, O'Reilly had become friendly with a New Orleans trade, Oliver Pollock, introduced to him by another Irishman, Father Butler, rector of the Jesuit College at Havana. This triumvirate of Irish Catholics, as enemies of Britain for religious and historical reasons, were to have a decisive influence on the action taken by Spain during the American Revolution.

Bernardo de Gálvez and the War of Independence

At the outbreak of the American Revolution, Bernardo de Gálvez was left temporarily in charge of the government in New Orleans. He was then a young colonel who received royal confirmation as governor in 1779, when notified of the declaration of war on Great Britain. American ambassador Joseph Jova described him as a dapper and chivalrous military officer. In the period until 1785, when he was appointed viceroy of New Spain, he boosted trade, cut taxes on exports and improved agriculture. His generous grants of land encouraged immigrants to settle, and he encouraged a hospitable policy toward the Indians. However, the matter in which he achieved most distinction was with respect to the rebellion of the colonies, by assisting them during the early stages, and subsequently by playing an active military part. The descendants of the people of Louisiana who fought against Britain under Gálvez, members of the highly esteemed and patriotic Society of Sons of the American Revolution, are still proud of their feats, as Professor Alcée Fortier, of Tulane University, chairman of the Commission for the Louisiana State-hood Centennial, acknowledged on the occasion of the centenary.

The new governor was the son of Matías de Gálvez, former viceroy of Mexico, and a nephew of José de Gálvez, then president of the Consejo de Indias, or Council of the Indies. He had served in Nueva Vizcaya and Sonora while his uncle was inspector-general and therefore had acquired considerable experience of America by the time he disembarked at New Orleans in 1776. He soon became friendly with Oliver Pollock and showed his sympathy for the new American cause. He opened the port to free trade on the part of the colonists and allowed the sale of prizes that they had taken, according to the provisions of the Royal Ordinance of October 23, 1776. But he went even further; the following April, he used his own means to capture 11 British ships engaged in smuggling and ordered British subjects to abandon Louisiana within two weeks.

Louisiana became a refuge for Americans fleeing from the British across the river and a source of supplies of all kinds needed by the colonists. Pollock acted as an official agent of Congress, given financial assistance by the coffers of the local government. By the end of 1777, Gálvez had lent Pollock $74,087, and cargo worth 25,000 gold doubloons had been dispatched directly from government depots. At the beginning of 1778, Pollock, acting on his own account, purchased goods worth 10,900 gold doubloons, which were shipped upstream to Philadelphia. These and other sums advanced placed the Irishman in a difficult financial situation. He was assisted by Gálvez, while Pollock was obliged to apply to Congress for reimbursement. According to some sources, in his first year in office Gálvez sent provisions worth $100,000, together with other shipments sent by Pollock.

When supplies sent by the government in Madrid, in response to a request from General Charles Lee through former governor Unzaga, were brought to New Orleans by Eduardo Miguel, Gálvez took every precaution to prevent the British from becoming aware of the cargo. Captain James Willing arrived to collect the cargo on behalf of Congress, but his disorderly conduct proved to be a headache for the governor and Pollock and certainly did not benefit the cause that he claimed to serve. Willing sailed down the Mississippi in command of the ship *Rattletrap,* capturing other vessels, burning plantations, plundering and robbing all in his path, and allowing his men to indulge in all kinds of unruliness and cruelty. His notorious and rowdy presence posed difficulties for the governor, who was still neutral and had to oblige Willing to return the stolen property. The sojourn of his unwanted guests forced the governor to provide Pollock with an additional sum of 24,023 pesos, and later, a further 15,948 pesos, in order to fit out the frigate *Rebeca* for the party to return to their starting point. Gálvez had misgivings about Willing's conduct, and authorized his party to return overland through Spanish territory on condition that they were commanded by Robert George. This was effected, and they reached their destination safe and sound with the cargo sent by the Spanish government. Willing returned to Philadelphia by sea aboard the *Rebeca,* laden by Pollock with munitions, muskets, food, blankets and medicine, all forming part of the large quantity of supplies from Spain. But, the frigate was captured by the British, and Willing was sent to jail in New York (he was subsequently exchanged). The American general George Rogers Clark wrote to the commander of St. Louis, Leyba, concerning the Willing incident as follows: "I am now convinced of what I have long suspected: the bad conduct of an American Officer in that Quarter. When plunder is the prevailing passion of any Body of troops whether great or small, their Country can expect but little service from them."

Mention should also be made here of the assistance given by Gálvez and Pollock to Clark's troops in their operations in the northwest. Gálvez and Pollock's teamwork proved most effective in providing supplies for the conquest of the town of Vincennes by the American leader, and in pegging down the British general, George Hamilton, before he was taken prisoner. Supplies were provided not only for Clark, but also for John Montgomery and Fort Jefferson. Had it not been for timely assistance from Pollock, the fort would have fallen. Such were the financial demands placed on the generous Irishman that he was forced to mortgage his home and plantations, sell his slaves and undertake loans. It should not be forgotten that the merchants in the Illinois district refused to accept from Clark payment in paper money issued by the Continental Congress and only accepted orders to pay drawn on Pollock at New Orleans. While Robert Morris, the Philadelphia banker, is usually considered the great financer of the Revolution, Professor James Alton argues that Oliver Pollock made the largest individual contribution of money to the cause.

The royal order outlining Spain's declaration of war on Britain, on June 21, 1779, reached Gálvez at the beginning of August. He then convened the inhabitants of New Orleans, informed them that Spain and Britain were at war as "a consequence of the recognition of American independence," and appealed to them for assistance. He immediately drew up his plans for war, being well aware that the advantage in war lies with whomever takes the initiative, and that only by doing so could he make the most of the scant forces at his disposal. A hurricane that caused serious damage to his preparations did not alter his determination to attack Fort Manchac by surprise. On the morning of August 27, the small army departed; its ranks swelled on the way until they numbered 1,472 men. After an arduous march, they sighted the fort on September 6 and on the next day, launched their assault and took it. The following month, Fort Baton Rouge surrendered, followed by Fort Panmure, at Natchez. On March 14, 1780, the forces under Gálvez took Mobile after a difficult siege, and on May 10, 1781, the formal surrender of Pensacola took place. This marked the end of the British threat in the West and South, and the independence fighters could concentrate on dealing the final blow against British power.

Bernardo de Gálvez left a lasting impression on Louisiana. His unquestionable political talent, his marriage to the young Creole Felicia de St. Maxen d'Estrehan and his attractive personality won him a popularity among the inhabitants of the territory, which grew in line with his success as an administrator and his victories as a general. He played an important role in the revolution of the colonists, not only from the military standpoint, but also from that of provisions supplied to the armies of Washington and Clark. He used all the funds available in his coffers, which were officially assigned for the province under his rule, but were in fact employed to further the cause of independence. "The daring triumvirate, Gálvez, Pollock and Clark, all men of imagination and courage," writes Thomson, "was now complete. The story of their collaboration would remain forever a glorious affirmation of the friendship between Spain, the forgotten ally, and the struggling new nation of the United States." As a result, Pollock drew the attention of Congress to the important services rendered by Gálvez to the common cause and expressed to his friend his desire that Gálvez's portrait hang in the Capitol "in order to perpetuate to your memory in the United States of America, as ranking in your Exalted Nation, as a Soldier and a Gentleman with those that have been of Singular Service in the Glorious Contest of Liberty."

Those singular services were duly acknowledged by President Gerald Ford during the bicentennial of America's independence when he recalled that "Don Bernardo de Gálvez, Spanish Captain General and Governor of Spanish Louisiana, conducted these victorious campaigns [to protect the southern front of the colonies and keep the Mississippi River open to navigation] and in 1781 captured the heavily fortified city of Pensacola from the British. The assistance given to the Revolution by Gálvez and the Spanish troops under his command has not always been given the recognition it deserves by our history books." Thanks to the Spanish government, however, in 1976 New Orleans erected a statute of Bernardo de Gálvez on horseback by sculptor Juan de Avalos. September 21 of each year has been proclaimed by the governor of Louisiana as Bernardo de Gálvez Day. On that date in 1779, Gálvez conquered Baton Rouge "helping to further the cause of the American Revolution." In 1987, the Count of Gálvez Historical Society was founded in Miami to promote a better understanding of the Hispanic past.

The Later Governors

Esteban Rodríguez Miró succeeded Gálvez as governor in 1785, although he had already been acting in that capacity while the latter was absent on campaign. He pursued the same policy as his predecessors in all fields, and the liberal trade policy recommended by Gálvez was approved by the king, so business and prosperity in Louisiana increased. It was while Miró was governor that the fire of 1788 broke out in New Orleans, causing the destruction of the buildings in the center of the town. Miró immediately set in hand plans for rebuilding and resorted to the wealthier citizens for assistance. One of them, a Spaniard, Andrés Almonester, a native of Mairena, in Andalusia, paid out of his own pocket for the town hall, cathedral, presbytery, hospital, public school and church of the Ursuline convent; this explains why the buildings of the so-called Vieux Carré in the French quarter are all Spanish, not French, as is widely believed. The French Market of New Orleans also dates from the Spanish period.

Miró was returned to Spain in 1791, and Don Francisco Luis Héctor, baron de Carondelet, was appointed governor. His term of office was one of administrative reform and of efforts to maintain and expand the area under his rule. He organized the city of New Orleans, built the New Orleans Canal and oversaw the recovery from a fire that once again broke out in the city in 1794. His timely steps thwarted the outbreak of rebellion led by a number of citizens of French origin, following the receipt of news about the revolution in France in 1789. During the mandate of Carondelet, the first theater was opened in New Orleans on October 4, 1792. In 1794, Etienne de Boré succeeded in granulating the sugar planted the previous year; this signaled the beginning of the sugar industry in Louisiana. With the transfer of Carondelet to Ecuador in 1797, his fruitful rule came to an end. One of the main streets in New Orleans bears his name, as did a warship, the U.S.S. *Carondelet,* which played an active part in the War of Secession, and whose flag is now at the Naval Museum at Annapolis, Maryland.

During the period from 1797 to 1803, three officers held the post of governor: Manuel Gayoso de Lemos held the post until his death in 1799; he was followed for two years by the marquis de Casa Calvo; and then by Don Juan Manuel de Salcedo. At the end of 1802, Salcedo suspended the privilege of tax-free deposit of American goods in New Orleans, a decision that caused unrest among those affected. Salcedo was charged with handling over the Spanish territory to France on November 30, 1803.

New Orleans

The colorful character of Louisiana is the result of the mix of people of different origins: Anglo Saxons, blacks, French and Spanish. The mixture of the latter two gave rise to the Creoles, derived from the Spanish *criollos,* particular to this region. Because of their ancestry, they form one of the largest Catholic populations in the country.

If Louisiana certainly provides unique opportunities for the palate, its effect on the ear is also extraordinary. The mixture of origins among the population has led to accents found in no other part of the country, providing an exceptional opportunity for linguists, sociologists and musicians. These sounds can be heard especially during the popular Mardi Gras carnival along Canal Street, which has become a hallmark since a group of bored students decided to enjoy themselves before the arrival of Lent in 1830.

A visit to New Orleans uncovers numerous vestiges of its Spanish past. Canal Street links the Mississippi River with Pontchartrain Lake, on the banks of which stands a beautiful residential area, while the farther shore can be reached by crossing a bridge 25 miles long. In the sector is Spanish Fort Street together with the ruins of Fort St. John. A sign calls it "Spanish Fort" and explains that, although of French origin, it was rebuilt by the Spaniards in 1779. In Canal Street the lampposts bear plaques on all four sides recalling the "four rules" to which the town was subject in the past: French, Spanish, Confederate and American. Two streets leading into Canal Street bear the names of Spanish governors: Carondelet and Gálvez. At the point where Canal Street gives onto the river winding through the city lies the large Plaza de España, centered around an old monumental fountain, surrounded by benches adorned with the coats of arms of the provinces of Spain. The mayors of Madrid and Barcelona, Carlos Arias and José María de Porcioles, attended the ceremony at which the first stone was laid in December 1968.

The Spanish Vieux Carré

The most attractive item on a visit to New Orleans is the Spanish Vieux Carré. With the help of a guidebook, it is possible to locate the houses and other spots in the city dating from colonial times; almost without exception, the major historical buildings and monuments date from the Spanish period, following the two fires that devastated New Orleans. To win the goodwill and cooperation of the residents of French origin, who were more numerous than the Spaniards, the Spanish governors maintained the French style; in this policy they proved successful. So it is that most buildings are not in a style similar to those found in Spain or to the colonial architecture found elsewhere in America.

In the largest square in this quarter, Jackson Square (known as Plaza de Armas in Spanish times), stand some buildings that bear a distinctly Spanish air dating from the 18th century, similar to the palace of the captain general at Havana or the ministry of finance in

Madrid. One of these buildings is the Cabildo, built in 1795 thanks to the generosity of Andrés Almonester y Rojas (his portrait, painted in 1796, hangs in one of the chambers) to replace the previous building, which had been burned down. It was the seat of the "Muy Ilustre Cabildo" and was the setting for major events in the governing of Louisiana during the Spanish period, for the executive, legislative and judicial powers were centered here, and it was from here that the whole territory was ruled. The coat of arms of Spain once presided over the main doorway but has been replaced by the eagle supporting the American colors. In the chapter hall of this building, which was erected under the guidance of Almonester himself with the assistance of Gilberto Guilleman, the successive transfers of rule in Louisiana took place. Today it houses the historical and artistic sections of the Louisiana State Museum. A stroll through the building or beneath its arcades is like being on the other side of the Atlantic.

The municipal building in New Orleans, one of the oldest structures in the United States, the seat of the governor when Louisiana belonged to the Spanish Crown. USIS Photo Lab, Madrid.

Matching the Cabildo and flanking the cathedral on the same side of Jackson Square is the presbytery, or Presbytere. Planned by Almonester with the same dimensions and features as the Cabildo, in order to give the square a certain balance, the building was begun before the Cabildo but had not been completed by the time Louisiana was transferred. It was finished in 1813 in the original style planned and is a beautiful building. The church was handed over to the city in 1853, and today it also houses other sections of the Louisiana State Museum. There can be seen the flags bearing the castle and lion quarterings and the flag of the Spanish monarch Charles III. Exhibits include the plan of the city drawn up by a Spaniard, Carlos Trudeau, and the edict issued by Governor Carondelet severely punishing the owners of slaves.

St. Louis Cathedral, standing between the Cabildo and the Presbytere, dates from 1794 and replaced the earlier building, erected in 1722 but destroyed by fire. The cost of building the cathedral was defrayed by Andrés Almonester, for which he was granted civic honors and a weekly mass was to be offered for the repose of his soul perpetually. The interior lacks any Spanish atmosphere other than the stained glass windows presented by Spain in recent years, in which various episodes of the Spanish period are portrayed. In the cathedral lie the remains of Andrés Almonester, whose tomb is at the foot of the altar of Our Lady of the Rosary, with an epitaph in Spanish. Governor Manuel Gayoso is also buried here.

Until 1793 Louisiana belonged to the diocese of Cuba. In that year the first bishopric was set up and Bishop Luis de Peñalver y Cárdenas took charge of his see in July 1795. St. Louis (San Luis) became a cathedral and is thus the oldest surviving cathedral in the present territory of the United States. The bishop was accompanied by a Capuchin father, Francisco Antonio Moreno y Arze, a native of Sedella (Granada), who was appointed parish priest at the cathedral and remained in that post until his death in 1829. His burial was attended by thousands of people, a mark of the popularity of this controversial figure, known for his intelligence and virtue, and popularly known as Fray Antonio de Sedella. He and the pirate Jean Lafitte share the honors of being the most romantic figures of the Vieux Carré, and have not been forgotten in New Orleans.

While the Cabildo, cathedral and presbytery flank the north side of Jackson Square, the twin buildings of the baronesa de Pontalba occupy the right and left sides, with the south side opening onto the river. The baroness of Pontalba, known by that title owing to her unfortu-

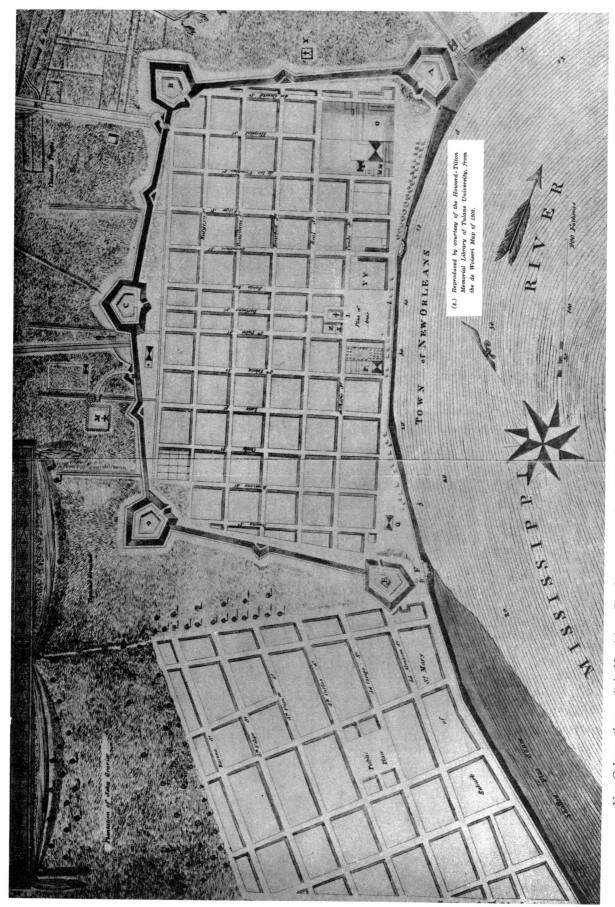

New Orleans, then capital of Louisiana. Based on a map made in 1762, the year the king of France ceded Louisiana and New Orleans to the king of Spain. Consulado de España, New Orleans.

nate marriage to Joseph Xavier Celestin Delfau de Pontalba, was named Micaela, the daughter of Andrés Almonester and the heiress to his considerable fortune, which she succeeded in increasing.

After the death of her parents, the baroness spent a long time in France, where, in 1834, she was almost murdered by her father-in-law, who then promptly committed suicide. Subsequently she traveled to New Orleans, accompanied by her two children. Impetuous yet remarkably intelligent, she succeeded in completing her project of building the first apartment buildings in the United States and even helped with the actual drawings of the different parts of the buildings. Their noble proportions and spacious balconies stretching along the three-story facades, with beautifully worked wrought iron railings bearing the interlaced letters A (Almonester) and P (Pontalba), with their arcades, the harmony of the color scheme of red brick with the black balconies and gray roofs, make this an impressive ensemble and a tribute to the talent of their creator.

In the fall of 1850 she moved into the new buildings, which contained 16 apartments and were publicly advertised for rent. Shortly afterward she returned to Paris, where she died in 1874. Her heirs owned the Pontalba buildings until 1920; today, they are the property of the city of New Orleans. The furniture on view there came from Fernando Puig's home, which was known to be more than a century old.

It was in New Orleans that the poet Antonio Crespo y Neva died on September 9, 1783; a cavalry lieutenant, he had been taken prisoner by corsairs and had endured countless hardships until he succeeded in reaching the city a month earlier. He left a manuscript collection of poems dedicated in 1782 to Governor Bernardo de Gálvez, whose portrait on the front page of the work had been drawn by Crespo himself.

Spanish Streets and Houses

The Spanish origin of the old mansions of the Vieux Carré can easily be seen. Fine plaques composed of Talavera tiles adorn the main street corners, indicating the Spanish names formerly borne by the streets. Those responsible for the initiative include the former Instituto de Cultura Hispánica, directed at the time by Blas Piñar, and the man behind the idea, José Luis Aparicio, Spanish consul general at New Orleans for several years. The plaques recall the existence of streets called

Calle Real, Tolosa, San Pedro, Del Arsenal, San Felipe and Del Muelle, among others.

On Royal Street (Calle Real) stand a number of old houses; taken at random, a few examples include the Old Gaz Bank (number 339), built in 1880 by Pablo Lanuesse; the Patio Royal (number 417), erected by Spanish merchant José Faurie, before the end of the 18th century; the Spanish Comandancia (number 519), where the horses of Governor Miró were originally stabled; in 1792, the Casa Merieult (number 529) was built by Pedro Aragón y Villegas, from whose heirs it was purchased by merchant Merieult; the Court of Two Lions (number 641) was built in 1798 by Merieult, and is used as a *casa de comercio*, or trade building; the Royal Castilian Arms building was erected in 1795 thanks to Charles Lonbies; and Patti's Court—so-called because it housed the famous singer Adelina Patti in 1860—is known to have escaped the fire of 1794.

New Orleans was the home of the well-known novelist Frances Parkinson Keyes, who wrote about such Spanish personalities as St. Theresa, St. Rose and Sister María de Agreda. She was a dame of the Order of Isabella the Catholic. She lived at 1113 Chartres Street, in a large mansion called Beauregard House, and her home, furnished in the style of its day (the early 19th century), was full of Spanish mementos.

One of the most outstanding museums is named after Delgado, the Creole who donated the funds for its creation. In 1989, the Cabot-Delgado Foundation was created to oversee a museum to be established on the aircraft carrier U.S.S. *Cabot* (later sold to Spain and called *Dedalo* and given back to the United States by Spain) housing exhibits relating to Hispanic-American history, particularly naval history.

Loyola and Tulane Universities have Spanish departments, and Tulane has hosted three conventions on "Louisiana Hispanic Languages and Literatures"; another three have been organized by the State University at Baton Rouge. The organization Hispanidad 88 has sought to bring together different Hispanic institutes in the city to emphasize Louisiana's Hispanic roots and to commemorate the discovery of America. The monthly magazine *Que Pasa* is also published in New Orleans.

South Louisiana

The surrounding areas of Louisiana fall into two different categories: one, north of the Red River, is Anglo

Saxon, English-speaking, Protestant and largely industrial; the other, to the south, is French-speaking (and in some areas Spanish-speaking), inhabited predominantly by people of French and Spanish origin, Catholic and largely agricultural—farming and fishing (though the boundary line between these two worlds is becoming more and more blurred).

It was in the south that the immigrants arriving during the 18th century settled; with some exceptions, the north was preferred by American colonists arriving in Louisiana from the east or north. The south is the land of the bayous, or arms into which the Mississippi becomes dispersed, marshland where reptiles and alligators have their habitat amid cypress trees festooned with Spanish moss. It was to the south that the Acadians, or French colonists, expelled by the British from their Canadian Acadia (later known as Nova Scotia) settled. Their troubles began in 1713, when France transferred them to Britain under the Treaty of Utrecht. In spite of the stipulations as to their freedom of settlement and religion, the British rulers strove to assimilate them. In view of the failure of these attempts, they were expelled from Canada in 1755, and their properties were confiscated; New Haven, Boston, New York, Philadelphia, Charleston and Savannah became the destinations for this scattered community. Feeling out of place on British soil, by different routes they managed to become reunited in the hospitable, Catholic and French territory of Louisiana. The first Acadians—"Cajuns," as they were called—arrived in 1756 and went to St. James Parish. A census drawn up by the Spaniards in 1787 reveals the existence of 1,587 Cajuns in Louisiana, the population rising to 4,000 in 1790, while their descendants numbered 50,000 in 1900.

It is worth visiting some localities in this southern area. Lake Charles takes its name from Carlos Salía, a Spaniard who settled here toward 1781 and built the first house within the limits of the town. New Iberia derives from the Colonia de Iberia founded by a group of Canary Islanders who were brought here after 1778 at the expense of the king, during Governor Gálvez's administration. The colony was included in the census carried out by the Spanish authorities between 1785 and 1788, and in the latter year, the population stood at about 200 inhabitants. The colony's numbers multiplied, and the descendants still live today on the land settled by their forbears. In the neighborhood of Opelousas there is a plantation, with a magnificent brick building, which was granted to Hipólito Chretien by the Spanish governor in 1776.

South of New Orleans is the parish of St. Bernard, on the shores of Lake Borgne, with a sector called Terre aux Boeufs where in 1778 a group of Canary Islanders, or *isleños*, settled during the governorship of Bernardo de Gálvez. From that time until World War II, the group remained isolated from outside influences, so the descendants of the first colonists managed to preserve their Spanish tongue and customs, unlike other Spanish groups in Louisiana. This is a unique case, due largely, not only to intermarriage within the same community rather than with strangers, but to the predominant livelihoods—shrimp and prawn fishing, trapping, sugar cane farming—which set them apart from their neighbors and in constant contact within their own community, thus encouraging the maintenance of a national folklore. This group has kept Spanish as its own language, but owing to their isolation, the powerful influences of English and French, and exposure to Spanish idioms as spoken in the Caribbean, their language has acquired certain characteristics of phonetics and vocabulary which make it a highly interesting case for those studying the Spanish language, its survival and evolution. These aspects have been thoroughly studied by Professor Raymond R. MacCurdy. De la Croix is the largest town in the parish, with 1,000 inhabitants; the localities of Regio, Shell Beach and Yscloskey together total a similar figure. Not far from St. Bernard Parish, likewise south of New Orleans, lies a town called Barataria.

In 1814, Gato, or Cat, Island in the Mississippi delta was given by the state to the Spanish envoy Juan de las Cuevas for having helped save New Orleans from the British assault in 1812. (His great-great-grandson was a Democratic congressman for Louisiana, Hale Boggs.)

Baton Rouge

Earlier references to the part played by Baton Rouge in the fight for national independence call for a complementary, but short account here. Following the taking of Fort Manchac by the troops under the Spanish governor of Louisiana, Bernardo de Gálvez, after the declaration of war against Britain on June 21, 1779, the need arose to follow up this success by taking Baton Rouge. The Spanish commander allowed his weary troops a few days to recover and meanwhile took advantage of the respite to obtain information about the defenses. He reached the conclusion that Baton Rouge must have 13 cannon, as opposed to his 10 pieces of artillery, and that there were about 500 men. Only by making a breach in the walls of the fortress with his artillery could his infantry have a chance of piercing the defenses. He resorted to the stratagem of distracting the attention of the defenders in order to bring a battery up to within a short distance; this ploy was successful, and when he opened fire in the early hours of September 21, he was able to wreak such destruction on the fort that the commander, Alexander Dickson, had no alternative but to seek a truce just after midday. Dickson surrendered the fort at Baton Rouge and Fort Panmure.

In the meanwhile, the captain in command at Pointe Coupé, Carlos de Grand Pré, and his volunteers had occupied the British outposts at Thompson's Creek and Amite. Galvez rewarded him by appointing him commander of the district. The governor of New Orleans completed his military successes by gaining command over Lake Pontchartrain, and by capturing eight enemy vessels on the Mississippi.

Today, the capital of Louisiana boasts a number of points of interest in Spanish-American history. In the hall of the Capitol fly 10 flags, including the Spanish flag with the castle and lion quarterings and that of King Charles III. The antechamber of the state's House of Representatives is decorated with Spanish pink marble. On the facade of the building are eight medallions with silhouettes of the most representative figures in the history of the state: the first is that of Hernando de Soto.

In the park adjoining the Capitol is the Old Arsenal Museum, housed in the former Spanish arsenal. Ten showcases in the spacious main hall, accompanied by 10 flags, refer to the different powers that were involved in the history of the city: first there is a model of de Soto, shown with a musket of the day; in fourth place is Bernardo de Gálvez with a Spanish chair. Surrounding the arsenal are gardens with a promontory overlooking the river: here two old cannons flank a plaque recounting the Battle of Baton Rouge in 1779 and recalling the fact that it was the only one during the Revolution won outside the thirteen colonies. A plague nearby explains that Gálvez's troops and his native allies defeated the British on that spot. Not far away, the old Capitol shows a mixture of Gothic and Arab influence, while, beyond, stands the house of Prince Napoléon-Lucien-Charles, nephew of the emperor Napoléon and son of Joachim Murat, who invaded Spain, and lived here in 1821.

In recent years, Baton Rouge has maintained particularly close contact with the city of Vigo, Spain, and the mayor of Vigo, Rafael J. Portanet, was made honorary mayor of Baton Rouge.

Galveztown

Baton Rouge can be taken as a starting point for several day trips to discover traces and recollections of the Spanish period. Highway 168 leads downstream to Donaldsonville, center of the former parish of Ascensión, called after a mission so named by Father Revillagodos prior to 1772. In this parish and the neighboring one of Assumption, groups of isleños, or settlers from the Canary Islands, settled in 1778, with the assistance of Governor Bernardo de Gálvez. It was in his honor that Galveztown was founded in Ascensión Parish between 1775 and 1789. The commander of the local fort was Francisco Collel, from whom Colyell Bay, not far from Lake Maurepas, received its name. The main locality in Assumption Parish was Valenzuela, with 1,057 inhabitants. During the 19th century, Spanish remained the predominant language in both areas, and although it has fought for survival in the course of the 20th century, it has declined very considerably in recent times.

There are also still Spanish-speaking people—not more than 300—at the following places: in Barton, Brusly Sacramento, Brusly Capite, Brusly Vives and Brusly McCall, all in Ascensión Parish; and Brusly St. Martin, St. Maurin and Belle Rose, in Assumption Parish. "Brusly" is the Anglicized version of the French word brulé and refers to land covered in trees and bushes burned in order to grow horticultural produce. In the local Spanish tongue, those fields are called brulis.

Comprised within the area is the town of Gonzales, and a little farther east is Hammond, the strawberry growing center. Across the river, near Burnside is the Bocage Plantation, built by Marius Pons and given to his daughter Françoise as a wedding present in 1801, when she married Cristophe Colomb, who claimed to be a descendant of the admiral.

Northward on Highway 63 from Baton Rouge can be found tombs with Spanish names in the Church of St. Gabriel. On Highway 61–65 heading north, along the Old Spanish Trail, you pass El Cipresal del Diablo before reaching St. Francisville, founded by the Capuchins at the end of the 18th century, thanks to a grant by the king of Spain; it stands in the parish of West Feliciana, which, like its neighbor East Feliciana, bears a name of Spanish origin and, in its day, was inhabited by Spaniards. Turning onto Highway 124, you come to the Greenwood Plantation, whose first owner was Oliver Pollock, who had very close ties with his good friend Governor Gálvez.

Central Louisiana

Following the Red River upstream, one comes to the city of Natchitoches, the oldest French settlement in Louisiana, founded in 1714. There was no better guide to become acquainted with the area than Charles Cunningham, editor of the two local newspapers and chairman of the organizing committee for the events held on May 8 and 9, 1964, to celebrate the 250th anniversary of its foundation. The Instituto de Cultura Hispánica at Madrid participated by presenting a stone plaque for the facade of the parish church, which had been recently restored, with an inscription recalling the first mass said on this spot by Father Margil, from the neighboring *presidio* of Los Adaes.

French explorer St. Denis (who married a Spaniard, Manuela Ramón) founded Fort St. Jean Baptiste; St. Denis, who lived in the locality for many years, died here and was buried—according to the records—on a plot of land where a drugstore now stands. Religious services, during that period, were administered by the Spanish friars from Los Adaes, and surviving parish records are in Spanish. The town has considerable atmosphere, and several buildings retain their old appearance. In the outlying area there are still traditional plantations, some having an area of 10,000 acres. It is municipal policy that new buildings should have a certain Old World appearance.

When Louisiana came into the hands of Spain in 1763, Natchitoches naturally fell within the new sphere of influence, but its French commander, M. Athanase de Mezières et Clugny, a leading Parisian (whose sister had married the duke of Orleans), remained in his post in spite of the change of sovereignty. Realizing the friendly relations existing between Mezières and the Indians in the area, governor Alexander O'Reilly summoned him to New Orleans and, after holding conference with him, confirmed him in his post. So Mezières was one of the many Frenchmen who became subjects of the king of Spain during the years of Spanish rule in Louisiana. Some called his loyalty into question, but his deeds, his good relationship with the Spanish commander at Los Adaes, Lieutenant González, and his success in getting the friendly tribes to be equally friendly to Spain all confirmed the farsightedness of O'Reilly. Mezières was appointed temporary governor of Texas during the absence of Domingo Cabello, and on September 30, 1779, he was appointed governor for life.

Although the Crown rewarded Mezières for his services, he was unable to take up the post because he died at San Antonio on November 2 that same year, but not before he had recommended to the king his four sons—two of whom were already army officers—and his two daughters.

When the French founded Natchitoches, the Spanish authorities were fearful of French encroachment on Texas territory. The missions set up in 1690 by Domingo de Terán, which had been abandoned a few years later, appeared to be necessary to contain expansion by their neighbors; consequently in 1716 another expedition commanded by Domingo Ramón, with Father Antonio Margil taking part, laid the foundations for several missions around the present-day locality of Nacogdoches, in eastern Texas. Crossing the Sabine River (which now serves as a boundary between Texas and Louisiana), they built the Los Adaes Mission some eight miles from Natchitoches. Having survived a few difficult years of French raids, the marquis of San Miguel de Aguayo, governor of Coahuila, consolidated the missions with the *presidio* of Nuestra Señora del Pilar de los Adaes in 1721.

In the town of Robeline, a narrow road leads to a fork, where a stone announces the proximity of Los Adaes. It is to be found in a grove of trees spread over two hills: on one stood the *presidio*, and on the other, the mission. Two plaques make a brief reference to the site's history, but no traces can be seen, only a few dips and hillocks, which hint at the existence of passages, trenches or walls, which might perhaps be revealed in an archaeological exploration.

Despite the fact that so little of the Spanish capital of east Texas remains, it held that status for 50 years, until the government was moved to San Antonio in 1772. This step was taken as a result of the publication of the Nuevas Regulaciones, based on the report made by the representative of the king, Cayetano María Pignatelli Rubí, following a tour of some 5,600 miles that he made in 1766 visiting the *presidios* north of New Spain. Efforts were being made to cut expenditure for the Spanish exchequer while strengthening military establishments—by suppressing those which were ill equipped and, therefore, open to attack by the Indians—a policy that would enable them to make an effective contribution to defense and protection; this meant that there was no further reason to maintain Los Adaes once Spanish sovereignty was enforced in Louisiana and there were no further fears of French infiltration. Consequently, Governor Juan María de Riperdá ordered the commander, soldiers, missionaries and colonists at Los Adaes to be transferred to San Antonio. Not all of them accepted these orders willingly; obeying the order caused the travelers many difficulties and some even met their death in the process.

Owing to the special system of government in Louisiana, the frontier was maintained between Louisiana and neighboring Texas, which was included among the so-called Inner Provinces, and a special passport was required to cross the frontier: in this system can be seen the origins of the boundaries of Texas and Louisiana. In the period from the Louisiana Purchase by the United States in 1803 until 1822—the year in which Spain lost her sovereignty in Texas—a number of Spanish-American disputes arose concerning the sector lying between the Sabine and Red Rivers; eventually it was declared to be neutral, although open to colonization. Several land grants made during the Spanish period are on record in this region; for example, in 1795, Don Jacinto Mora received 207,360 acres east of Sabine, which were given the name Las Ormegas. In 1797, 12 square miles, including the locality of Many, were attributed to Ed Murphy.

The Protestant pastor Timothy Flint visited Los Adaes, in the early 19th century, and his well-known account is one of the few that have survived concerning that period. The wooden church had four bells and several paintings of saints, which were severely criticized by the traveler on aesthetic grounds. The local people, who differed in appearance from the French, spoke Spanish slowly and adopted the passive attitude of listeners rather than of speakers; they showed him great hospitality and were simple and friendly in manner. By that time they were living in considerable poverty, as was shown by their mud-walled homes, corn bread (the making of which Flint describes) and their clothing, among other things. The descendants of the people who received Flint are now more progressive and are centered around Robeline; the district is known as Spanish Lake, and some of the inhabitants still speak Spanish. Their appearance is decidedly Spanish, and the family names, such as Mora, Orcón, Hernández and Hidalgo, are unquestionably Spanish.

North Louisiana

North of the Red River lies the Anglo-Saxon sector of Louisiana. Concordia Parish lies some distance up the Mississippi from its confluence with the Red River; the parish includes the locality of Vidalia, near Ferriday, in the vicinity of which Hernando de Soto is thought to have died. Many place-names are Spanish. In central Louisiana the capital is Alexandria, farther north is Columbia, and following Highway 165, progressive Monroe stands on the banks of the Ouachita River; de Soto is claimed to have passed through this area. In February 1783, Juan Bautista Filhiol was appointed commander of the output of the Washita. Departing from New Orleans with a party of soldiers and settlers, he followed the Mississippi, Red River and the Ouachita River upstream as far as the future site of Monroe, where they disembarked in 1785. To defend themselves from Indian attacks, they built Fort Miró, named in honor of Spanish governor Esteban Miró; it changed its name in 1819 after the first steamboat on the river, *James Monroe,* brought prosperity to the area.

Monroe is linked by Highway 80 to Shreveport, where the King's Highway, or Camino Real of Spanish times, can still be seen. Shreveport is mentioned frequently in letters written by Juan Valera from Washington. Santos Ollo, a member of a Spanish trading firm from Larache, had bought cotton from the Confederate government during the American Civil War and had then exported it to Mexico. Shortly after the end of the Civil War, the federal government seized 1,369 bales of cotton at Shreveport, valued at $700,000, sold them at New Orleans and pocketed the money. Ollo claimed the sum in question, and Juan Valera hoped to extricate himself from his financial difficulties through diplomatic channels, thanks to the percentage that he would receive according to the customs tariff. However, Valera eventually left without payment, and it was his successor, Emilio Muruaga, who had to press the Spanish claims before Secretary of State Thomas Bayard.

Spanish Place-Names

Spanish place-names in Louisiana include the parishes of Ascension, Concordia, De Soto, East Feliciana, Iberia and West Feliciana, and the towns of Alto, Ama, Barataria, Bolivar, Bonita, Castor, Columbia, Columbus, Gonzales, Lake Charles, Lamar, Lunita, Magnolia, Marrero, New Iberia, Toro and Vidalia.

MISSOURI

Historically speaking, Missouri was developed by a number of successive influxes, first in a north to south direction, and then from south to north; these trends decided its Franco-Spanish background. The French from Canada and afterward from New Orleans, were followed by the Spaniards, setting out from New Orleans. Although under Spanish rule there were contacts between Missouri, Texas and New Mexico, these influences lacked the importance of those coming up the Camino Real from the south or down the exceptional waterways of the Mississippi and its tributaries. The Eastern part of the state bears the strongest Franco-Spanish imprint.

Early Spanish History

St. Louis was founded in 1764 by two Frenchmen, Pierre Laclede and his young protégé, Auguste Chouteau. With permission from the French commander at New Orleans, M. d'Abbadie, they departed upstream with a group of settlers in August 1763 and after some preliminary explorations, began to prepare the land for their settlement on February 14, 1764. It was not until April that lots of land were distributed and the township given the name of the patron saint of the reigning French monarch, Louis XV.

The French flag only flew until Spain took possession of the town. But while the actual French command did not last longer than the difficult early days of its foundation and the progress of the town was due largely to the work of the Spanish government, the population was almost entirely French.

St. Louis was the capital of the Spanish territories of Upper Louisiana, and the system of government was organized as follows: the captain general, with his headquarters at Havana, was the supreme authority, and on him depended the governor of New Orleans, with direct command throughout the territory. In order to deal more directly with Upper Louisiana, powers were delegated to a lieutenant or deputy governor, who resided at St. Louis and had, in turn, several commanders under him posted in different places; only three of them received payment for their services, namely, those at St. Geneviève (Santa Genoveva), New Bourbon (Nuevo Borbón) and Cape

Girardeau (Cabo Girardeau). The successive lieutenant governors of St. Louis were in 1770, Pedro Piernas; 1775, Francisco Cruzat; 1778, Fernando de Leyba; 1780, Francisco Cruzat; 1787, Manuel Pérez; 1792, Zenón Trudeau; and 1799, Carlos Dehault de Lassus. Some of them were of French origin, and a number of Spanish lieutenant governors were married to French women.

When France withdrew from Louisiana and was replaced by Britain on the left bank of the Mississippi, considerable numbers of French settlers who wished to settle in the new Spanish dominions began to arrive. The reason was that the Spanish territory was governed by Latins and Catholics, as opposed to the Protestant Anglo-Saxon government on the other bank. This signaled the start of a fruitful cooperation between the Spanish governors and their French subjects, which resulted in the progress of the region and the laying of the foundations of the prosperity eventually attained by Missouri and other neighboring states. An example of this Franco-Spanish harmony is as follows: when the British appeared, in the fall of 1765, to take possession of Fort Chartres—on the opposite bank of the river from St. Louis—its commander, Monsieur Saint-Ange de Bellerive, sought refuge at St. Louis and was appointed to command the outpost until he was succeeded by the lieutenant governor, Pedro Piernas, in 1770.

On July 11, 1778, Fernando de Leyba wrote a letter to Governor Bernardo de Gálvez reporting that he had taken up his post as commander after a journey lasting 93 days. Throughout his mandate, until his death at St. Louis on June 28, 1780 (he was buried in the church), he played a key role in crucial years for the American Revolution. General George Rogers Clark, on the other bank, often turned to Leyba for money, weapons and clothing for his needy troops, and had to seek his protection on more than one difficult occasion. The war was not the only reason for these contacts, for, in addition, Clark fell in love with the governor's sister, Teresa de Leyba. Hearing that the Leyba family had been ruined owing to the depreciation of the bonds of the state of Virginia subscribed by the governor, Clark sought Teresa's hand in marriage (he had saved her from a fire at the convent); she declined because she had taken religious vows and eventually entered a convent of Ursuline nuns at New Orleans following Fernando de Leyba's premature death.

Few people realize that one of the battles during the Revolution was fought in Spanish Missouri. Wanting to recover Fort Cahokia and Vincennes, conquered by Clark, the British prepared a force 300 strong to capture them and St. Louis, with the help of 1,000 Indian allies. Leyba had a small garrison under his command and managed to reinforce it with the help of some Indian allies, but only had two months in which to prepare to confront the invasion from the north, announced by reliable sources. On April 17, 1780, Father Bernard de Limpach blessed the laying of the foundation stone of the fort that Leyba built on the hilltop near the church commanding the river; the fort was called San Carlos in honor of King Charles III of Spain. Leyba likewise placed five cannon at key points around the perimeter of the town. When the enemy forces under Emmanuel Hesse appeared, they surprised several unfortunates in nearby fields, who were killed. At 1:00 P.M. on May 26, 650 Indians launched the attack but were repulsed by the Spanish garrison, consisting of 25 soldiers and 289 civilians. Two hours of fighting sufficed to make them abandon their plans and withdraw, after killing 32 prisoners. A bronze inscription installed in the Spanish International Pavilion nearby reads "To the memory of Fort San Carlos, which was built here by Commander Leyba and his Spanish soldiers, who defeated the British army and thus defended the endurance of the American Revolution."

As a result of their defeat, the British proved unable to gain command of the Mississippi valley and carry out their enveloping operation from the west around the rebellious colonies, as their strategists had planned. This defeat and the previous one at Vincennes signaled the loss of the war in the west on the part of the British long before the Peace of Paris brought the fighting to a formal close. (This important victory was noted by St. Louisan, Jean Baptiste Trudeau [the owner of a school from 1774, where he taught for 50 years] who composed the poem "Ballad of the Year of the Surprise.") Leyba was promoted to lieutenant colonel. The fine map of the town of St. Louis drawn up by Francisco Cruzat is dated 1780. In 1788, Lieutenant Governor Manuel Pérez put forward a proposal to Esteban Miró, the Spanish governor in Louisiana, concerning repairs to the fortifications of St. Louis and obtained permis-

sion to proceed. Governor Baron de Carondelet issued instructions to Carlos Howard on November 26, 1795, to organize an expedition to defend Upper Louisiana against raids from across the Mississippi and, if necessary, to gather the Spanish forces at St. Louis and other subordinate outposts.

The years following the independence of the United States brought unrest, uncertainty and uneasiness west of the Appalachians. This resulted in an upsurge of emigration to the lands west of the Mississippi, and this influx would have been even greater if the Spanish authorities had not at first made it a requisite that immigrants should be Catholics. In 1790, a wave of French settlers arrived for two reasons: the failure of the Barlow-Playfair colonization in the Ohio region, and the flight from the terror spreading through France as a result of the revolution, which guillotined Louis XVI. In 1795, Governor Carondelet gave permission for American colonists to settle in Spanish territory regardless of their religion. In 1796, Lieutenant Governor Trudeau reported the daily arrival of families from the United States. Between 1796 and 1804, 5,000 families can be estimated to have settled here. According to a report by Dehault de Lassus, the population of Spanish Missouri was about 8,000 in 1799.

In 1793, the governor of New Orleans granted the merchants of St. Louis permission to form a single company, the Company of Explorers of Upper Missouri, to handle trade the length of the Missouri River. The company sent three major trading and exploratory expeditions out from St. Louis: one in 1794, commanded by Jean Baptiste Trudeau, proved to be disastrous; one in 1795, was unsuccessful owing to the attacks by Ponca Indians; and the third, in 1796, commanded by James MacKay, was no more successful. Years later, John Evans, a Welshman in the service of the company, traveled up the Missouri to its source, carving the name of Charless III on rocks and trees to mark his discoveries. In 1808, a Spaniard, Manuel Lisa, established the Missouri Fur Co., which proved to be a highly successful venture until his death in 1820.

The first church in the township, a modest wooden building, was blessed by Father Pierre Gibault in June 1770, in the presence of the new lieutenant governor. Father Gibault played an invaluable part in the struggle for American independence in later years, and when Clark conquered Kaskasia and gave him assurances that Catholics would enjoy full religious freedom under the new regime, he gave Clark his enthusiastic cooperation and played a decisive role in the taking of Vincennes in 1779, thanks to his influence over the French population. His active role in the war earned him the hatred of the British, and he would have suffered dearly if he had not taken refuge in Spanish territory. A Capuchin priest, Father Valentine Neufchateau, spent three years at St. Louis, but it is Friar Bernard de Limpach who should be considered as the first pastor over the inhabitants of St. Louis, where he was formally instated on May 19, 1776, by Lieutenant Governor Francisco Cruzat, and where he remained until 1789, two years prior to his death.

It is interesting to read the report dated October 31, 1769, sent by Pedro Piernas to Governor O'Reilly about the land and post to which he had been sent: "The land of Ylinoeses is," it reads, "healthy and fertile on the whole; the climate, delightful and suitable for all kinds of plants, fruit and grain. Some parts are mountainous and others flat . . . the territory abounds in game . . ." (earlier, he had difficulty with the ice when traveling upstream); he considered the situation of St. Louis high and pleasant, built on rocks and therefore in no danger from floods. The Spaniards called this region Ylinois, and sometimes Ylinoa or the District of the Ylinenses.

The diary of another Spanish cleric, Pedro Vial begins in 1792; in it he relates his journey from Santa Fe to St. Louis on orders from the governor of New Mexico, Fernando de la Concha, accompanied by José Vincente Villanueva and Vicenta Espinosa. This diary was one of the highlights of the day, for it opened up a whole new, unexpected field of communications between such distant regions. At a later date, full advantage was taken of these reports by Zebulon Pike and all who followed him along the Santa Fe Trail.

The Transfer of Upper Louisiana

In February 1804, a company of American infantry commanded by Captain Amos Stoddard billeted at Cahokia and subsequently crossed the river to arrange with the Spanish authorities the details of the transfer of Upper Louisiana to its new owners. Stoddard was acting as the representative of France and the United States. Everything went well, except for the fact that Carlos Dehault de Lassus caught an unfortunate chill, which caused a delay of one day in the transfer. Finally, on March 9, the company of infantry formed up before the house of the governor in the Calle Real, where a large crowd gathered. The ceremony consisted in the signature of the deed of transfer of dominion, and a speech made by the Spaniard to his well-loved Franco-Spanish citizens and the Delaware, Shawnee and Sac Indians, somewhat along these lines: "Your former fathers, the Spaniards and the French, who now shake the hand of your new father, the United States, have renounced these lands as an act of goodwill and by virtue of the latest treaty. The new father will maintain and defend the land and protect all white men and redskins living here. You will live as happily as if the Spaniards were still here." At a signal, the cannons at the fort fired a salute. The Spanish flag was struck. The French flag was then raised, but, instead of being lowered in order to make way for the Stars and Stripes, it was left on the flagstaff throughout the rest of the day. The American flag was not raised until the following day. So it was that the presence of Spain in Missouri came to an end officially.

St. Louis

St. Louis today can be approached along Kingshighway, the former Camino Real. The only old building still standing in St. Louis is the Antigua Catedral, or Old Cathedral, consecrated to St. Louis; this was the fourth cathedral to be built in North America and was opened in 1834. Above the high altar is a very fine copy of the Christ by Velázquez, painted by Charles Quest. In the museum can be seen a finely tuned bell, presented in 1774 by the Spanish lieutenant governor Pedro J. Piernas and his wife to the first Catholic church built in St. Louis, whose first resident priest was one Father Valentine; the bell was given the name Pedro José Felicitas.

In 1899, Spanish engineer Ricardo Galbis built a pelota court at St. Louis, the first in the United States. It was a short-lived venture, because permission was not given for betting and the interest of the public waned as a result. It was used as an exhibition hall during the world's fair at the turn of the century.

In May 1969, the Spanish Pavilion from the New York World's Fair was reinaugurated at St. Louis, as a gift from Spain to the city. Its foundation stone is one from the tomb of Queen Isabella at Granada, and in the pavilion stands a statue of the Spanish queen, a replica of the one that stood in one of the courtyards in the pavilion, donated by the Foundation Patronato Doce de Octubre, as well as other works of art displayed there. The opening of the pavilion in 1969 was attended by Spanish minister Manuel Fraga Iribarne. The pavilion was for some years a cultural center and is now owned by the Marriot Corporation. A reproduction of the caravel *Santa María* was anchored for years beside the city's famous arch.

The City Art Museum has a fine collection of Spanish art, including an apostle by El Greco, two saints by Juan de Valdés Leal, a monk and a still life by Francisco de Zurbarán, a portrait by Bartolomé Murillo, a Juan Gris, a Tapies and several Picassos, among them *The Mother*, painted in 1900. The museum has a Hispano-Arab art room containing furniture and tapestries, brought from the Convent of Santa Isabel at Toledo, where outstanding exhibits, apart from several cabinets, include a high door consisting of two leaves and a splendid coffered ceiling.

Northern Missouri

Not far away, to the north of St. Louis, is the district of St. Charles. Its original raison d'être was the protection of St. Louis. As early as January 7, 1767, Governor Ulloa issued instructions to Captain Francisco Rui to set up two forts on the Missouri River at its confluence with the Mississippi. But the difficult conditions prevailing at that spot led Rui to call a council of his subordinates and on October 2, 1767, send a query on the matter to Ulloa. Nevertheless, as instructed, Rui fulfilled his mission and on March 10, 1769, handed over to the first lieutenant governor, Pedro Piernas, the fort Don Carlos, Señor Príncipe de Asturias (Don Carlos, the Lord Prince of Asturias) and the smaller fort Don Carlos Tercero, el Rey (Charles the Third, the King). The former stood on the southern bank of the mouth of the Missouri, while the second lay to the north. A description of the forts is given in the deed drawn up for them to be handed over, and in the report that Francisco Rui himself sent to Governor O'Reilly on October 29, 1769.

St. Charles was founded in 1769, upstream on the banks of the Missouri, in the Femme Osage sector, on Highway 94. Pioneer Daniel Boone, who held an official Spanish post as receiver between 1800 and 1804, received a grant of 1,000 "arpents" of land. The house he built there with his son, from 1803 to 1810, is still standing, and it is there that he was buried. St. Charles also boasts some other old buildings. The defenses were completed by the Portage de Sioux in 1779, La Charette in 1797 and Côte Sans Desseins in 1808, under United States rule.

Also to the north of St. Louis, San Fernando de Florissant came into being in 1786. That was the year in which the first commander came to reside in this fertile valley, where a number of colonists had settled earlier; François Dunegant was appointed to hold civil and military authority there. According to the Spanish archives at Havana, at the time of the census in 1787 there were 40 inhabitants and seven plantations. The township, as its name indicates, was placed under the patronage of St. Ferdinand III, king of Spain, who conquered Seville, and a church was built in his honor in 1789. The present church of the same name replaced the original one in 1821 and is the oldest Catholic church in Upper Louisiana. Within its walls, Father J. Didier was buried in 1790. Mother Phillippine Duchesne later lived in the convent next door between 1819 and 1827; a member of the Order of the Sacred Heart, she was beatified in 1940. Father Pierre-Jean De Smet, who had great influence in later years, was ordained priest in the church here. The high altar has a statue of St. Ferdinand. The strip of land near the main entrance was used by the Spanish troops for drill. Nearby, in St. Denis Street, the house of Eugenio Alvarez still stands; built in 1790, and formerly the residence of the military commander, it is the only surviving building of the Spanish period.

Carondelet, which now belongs to the southern outskirts of St. Louis, was given this name to honor the Spanish governor Baron de Carondelet. Originally in 1767, it was called Prairie à Catalan, and it still has some buildings dating back more than a century.

Crève Coeur and Point Labadie complete the outposts that, with Florissant, comprise the outer districts of St. Louis.

Southern Missouri

The districts to the south of St. Louis can be reached by traveling downstream or taking Highway 61, the Royal Highway that once linked St. Louis and New Madrid (or Nuevo Madrid; see below). The Ste. Geneviève district initially comprised this area down the Mississippi, the oldest permanent settlement in Missouri. Founded in 1737, it served as a meeting point for French lead prospectors; the Jesuits from Kaskasia, on the opposite bank of the river, paid periodical visits to the town. Ste. Geneviève was an essential halting place both at the time of the foundation of St. Louis and for the different Spanish expeditions bound for the latter. The report by Captain Francisco Rui to Governor O'Reilly dated October 29, 1769, describes Ste. Geneviève (under the name, Misera) as the main town of the Ylinenses. Also writing in 1769, Pedro Piernas described it as being inhabited by some 600 people, including blacks and Indians (only 10% were Europeans), and with scattered houses so that the town looked larger than it really was. He gave particulars of several of the wealthier inhabitants. In 1785 there were serious floods along the Mississippi, and according to the report from Governor Esteban Miró to Count Bernardo de Gálvez at Havana, on July 19, 1785, the inhabitants had to abandon their homes and lost all their belongings, while seeking refuge on a nearby mountain.

A number of old houses are still standing in the town, at least three dating from the Spanish period: J. B. Valle House, dating from 1782 (with prison cells in its cellars); Bolduc House, dating from 1770; and Janis-Ziegler House, dating from 1790. Ste. Geneviève has maintained the atmosphere of bygone times in its buildings, streets and squares: the bell in the parish church standing in Du Bourg Square still rings for the Angelus at six, 12 and 18 hours, processions pass through the streets on religious feastdays and, on New Year's Eve, people wear fancy dress, sing "La Guignolée" and knock on their neighbors' doors, demanding wine.

The town called Mine à Breton also used to be part of the Ste. Geneviève district. It was founded by Francisco Azor as a result of his discovery of a lead mine in 1773. In 1797 Moses Austin, from Virginia, settled here and improved the process of smelting the lead ore; he obtained the grant of a mine, built new furnaces and a tower at Herculaneum and helped establish the township of Potosi. New Bourbon, or Nuevo Borbón, was founded in 1793, and the inhabitants made a patriotic collection in November 1799 to help the Spanish commander defray the military expenses caused by conflict with the United States. Another town that began during the Spanish period was St. Michaels, later called Fredericktown. Not far away is the locality called De Soto.

The Cape Girardeau district is closely linked with the figure of Canadian Louis Lorimier, who founded the capital in 1793 while in the service of Spain. The Spanish government granted him exclusive trading rights with the Shawnee and Delaware Indians living between the Mississippi and the Arkansas. It was at this point that the Cherokee Indians crossed the great river on the Trail of Tears, when they were expelled from their land in the east and sent to settle in Oklahoma Territory.

Farther south on the banks of the Mississippi stands New Madrid, or Nuevo Madrid. Its foundations were laid when the Spanish representative in Philadelphia, Diego Gardoqui, made a grant of land to the group led by George Morgan on February 14, 1788; Morgan had considerable correspondence with Gardoqui and Governor Miró on the matter. In a letter to Miró, dated April 14, 1789, he reports the choice of the site for the new settlement to their friends at Fort Pitt (now Pittsburgh), saying that they were all in perfect health and most encouraged by the discovery of such a magnificent climate and territory. Pedro Foucher was appointed the first commander of the new town, whose inhabitants signed a number of oaths of loyalty to the king of Spain over the period between 1789 and 1796. The commander welcomed American general David Forman in 1790, and the latter reported: "He gave me a splendid dinner after the Spanish style, with plenty of good wine and coffee without cream."

In 1794, while commander of New Madrid, Louis Lorimier forced American general John Montgomery, with a force of 600 men, to abandon the blockade of the Mississippi and the fort built on orders from General Clark. Another of the commanders, Henri Peyroux de la Coudrenière, played an active part in 1803 in the capture of the famous bandits Harpe and Samuel Mason, whose misdeeds brought them to a disastrous end. New Madrid weathered the earthquakes of 1811 and 1812.

Spanish Place-Names

In addition to the towns already mentioned, originating from grants made by the governor of New Orleans during Spanish rule, there are a number of other towns in Missouri with names reminiscent of Spain: Alba, Amazonia, Aurora, Avilla, Bolivar, Brazito, Callao, Chula, Columbia, Concordia, Cuba, Delta, De Soto, El Dorado Springs, Florida, Galena, Hercules, Iberia, Isabella, Lamar, Lamonte, La Plata, Laredo, Meta, Mexico, Molino, Montserrat, Nevada, Polo, Potosi, Risco, Rollo, Saco, Salcedo, Santa Fe, Santa Rosa, Seneca, Spanish Lake, Terresita and Tunas.

◆ ARKANSAS, OKLAHOMA, KANSAS AND NEBRASKA ◆

Hernando de Soto in Arkansas

Hernando de Soto and his companions were the first Europeans to explore Arkansas, toward the end of 1541. He may have entered Arkansas at a point near the present site of West Memphis, or a short way below the confluence of the St. Francis River with the Mississippi, but in any event in the province of Pacaha, he found the local Indian chief at war with his neighbor, the chief of Casqui. He managed to reconcile them and invited them to dine; as a mark of gratitude the Casqui chief presented him with his daughter, while his erstwhile enemy made him a gift of two sisters with large breasts, so we are told by the chronicler Hidalgo de Elvas.

Hernando de Soto continued on his way following a route more or less coinciding with today's Highway 70 and passed through an area that fits the description of the state capital, until he reached Hot Springs, where 47 hot springs spill forth 1 million gallons of water a day, De Soto and his men set up their quarters for the winter in the Indian village of Autiamque, where they built a high palisade to protect them during their three-month stay from the natives, who had fled when they arrived and left the village deserted. Thanks to the abundant food abandoned by the Indians, and such rabbits and game as they could hunt and the fires that they built with firewood taken from the local woods, they man-

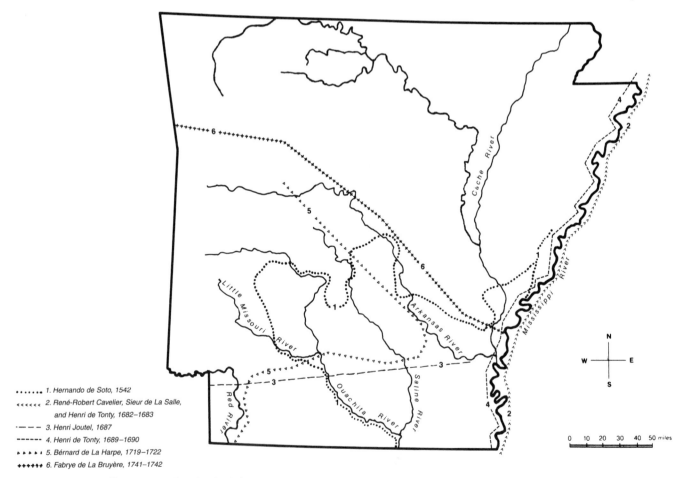

······· 1. Hernando de Soto, 1542
‹‹‹‹‹‹ 2. René-Robert Cavelier, Sieur de La Salle,
    and Henri de Tonty, 1682–1683
·— — — 3. Henri Joutel, 1687
------ 4. Henri de Tonty, 1689–1690
▸ ▸ ▸ ▸ ▸ 5. Bérnard de La Harpe, 1719–1722
✦✦✦✦✦ 6. Fabrye de La Bruyère, 1741–1742

European exploration in Arkansas, 1541–1742. Facts On File.

aged to endure the hard winter and heavy snowfalls. In March 1542, the expedition set out once more and, after passing near the present towns of Arkadelphia and Camden, followed the Ouachita River downstream until it joined the Mississippi.

A number of pigs brought along on the expedition were left behind and, in time, their descendants turned wild; razor-back hogs have now become a symbol of Arkansas. In spite of their great size, they are said to run as fast as a deer and can slip along mountain defiles on ledges three inches wide.

Arkansas Post and Esperanza

Spanish Arkansas was divided into two districts: Arkansas Post and Esperanza, both of which came under the lieutenant governor at St. Louis. The names of some of the Spanish commanders at Arkansas Post are known to us: Captain Chalmette, in 1780; Captain Joseph Vallière, from 1786 to 1790; Carlos Villemont, from 1790 to 1801; Francisco Luengo, from 1802 to 1803; and Ignacio Leno from 1803 to 1804.

The Protestant pastor Timothy Flint visited Arkansas Post in the 1820s and, besides describing the surrounding plain, left an account of the shortcomings of the government in the recently created territory and the violent character of the people. He described the town, which then had a population of 10,000 inhabitants, and mentioned the days of Spanish rule when the authorities consisted of a commander, a priest and a detachment of soldiers. He likewise met an aged Quawpaw Indian chief, who had done a great favor for the Spanish commander. It so happened that a group of Muskogee or Creek Indians arrived at Arkansas Post and, finding it ungarrisoned at the time, succeeded in kidnapping the son of the commander. Seeing the anxiety of the commander when he discovered what had happened, the Quawpaw offered to recover him; he tracked the kidnappers down and, when he overtook them, sent a warrior to them bearing a challenge, as was the custom among those tribes when declaring war. The Creeks, who believed that a large Hispano-Indian contingent was approaching, hurriedly fled and abandoned everything, including the child, who was thus returned safe and sound to his grateful parents.

Arkansas Post played an important role during the American Revolution. Dependent on the government in New Orleans, it was used from the outside in its policy of assisting the rebels. On orders from Governor Luis de Unzaga, Arkansas Post warmly welcomed the exhausted men under the command of William Linn, known as "Gibson's Lambs," who brought with them 900 pounds of gunpowder and other supplies with which they had departed from New Orleans in the early winter of 1777. At Arkansas Post they were able to recover until spring arrived, when they departed in good physical condition with the supplies and foodstuffs provided by the Spaniards; they then headed for Fort Pitt, protected by a military escort when passing through enemy country. Arkansas Fort was also a refuge for the expedition led by James Willing that sailed down the Mississippi aboard the *Rattletrap* in January 1778. Owing to the misdeeds committed by the party and the resultant uprising of the Indians, a group of American families applied to the commander for protection at the fort.

The National Park Service is now responsible for the Arkansas Post National Memorial. The site has changed greatly compared to Spanish times; in fact, the only structure still standing is an old well that has been bricked up and roofed over.

Nearby, where the White River joins the Mississippi, in 1776 François d'Armond obtained permission from the Spanish to found what was in time to be known as Montgomery's Landing, after it had been taken by General John Montgomery.

In the southern sector of the state, through which de Soto passed, some settlements were established 250 years later, authorized by the Spanish governor Baron de Carondelet. In this way, on June 20, 1797, the marquis de la Maison Rouge was given permission to bring 30 families to settle in a group of 133,165 acres forming the old locality of Ecore Fabre, now called Camden. In 1795, Baron Bastrop obtained permission from Carondelet to settle 500 families in present-day Ouachita County, namely 640,000 acres comprising Bayou de Lair and Bayou Bartholomew, in the vicinity of the Louisiana border.

The chief center in the Esperanza, or Hopefield, district is West Memphis, on the banks of the Mississippi. The settlements along the upper reaches of the White and Arkansas Rivers, around the town of Dardanelle, were dependent on Memphis. French immigrants bearing a royal grant settled as Lauratown in 1766 under the guidance of Antoine Vincents, Le Bass, Le Mieux and Peter Guignolett. There are still Le Mieux families in the county today, just as there are Guignoletts in Portia. A few years ago, 400 Spanish dollar coins were unearthed in a plowed field at Lauratown. Official records from these and other Spanish settlements in the state list family names (Winter, Stillwell, Phillips, Hew and Scull, among others) whose descendants can still be found here. In spite of the time that has elapsed, land grants made to such immigrants under valid Spanish law have been admitted in United States court rulings, some during the present century. Today, the red, white and blue Arkansas state flag bears three stars; one of them symbolizes Spain, which once ruled this territory.

Spanish Place-Names

Three counties in Arkansas bear Spanish names—Columbia, Nevada and Sebastian—as do the following towns: Alma, Alpena, Casa, Cerro Gordo, Columbus, El Dorado, Havana, Lamar, Lavaca, Lepanto, Magnolia, Manila, Marianna, Mena, Minorca, Moro, Ola and Saldo.

Coronado and Other Explorers in Oklahoma

Francisco Vázquez de Coronado was the first European to tread the soil of Oklahoma, in 1541, from the rolling plains to the panhandle lying between Texas and Kansas. (Historian Octavio Gil Munilla claims that Hernando de Soto arrived in 1542.) On his return journey he crossed a region of Oklahoma lying between Ponca City and Bartlesville. From that time onward, almost all Spanish expeditions to Kansas or Nebraska passed

through Oklahoma: Friar Juan de Padilla and his companions, Juan Oñate and his party, Governor Diego de Peñalosa, and Pedro de Villazur on his way to a tragic death, among others. It was in Oklahoma that the disastrous journey of Francisco Leyva de Bonilla and Antonio Gutiérrez de Humaña came to a tragic end when they perished at the hands of the Indians. The Spaniards controlled this part of the country until the transfer of Louisiana in 1803 and contributed to its progress with the introduction of horses and sheep, whose wool began to be used by the Navajo Indians for their much prized cloth and blankets.

Following the defeat of the Seminole chief Assunwha in 1854, the United States Congress ordered the mass deportation to what is now the state of Oklahoma of the so-called Five Civilized Tribes: the Choctaw, Chickasaw, Cherokee, Creek and Seminole. We have seen the dealings with the Seminole in the chapter on Florida. As for the Cherokee, in November 1966, the chief of the tribe named Spanish ambassador Merry del Val "Big Chief Bull-Killer" (Mata-Toro); the ambassador received all the attributes of his new rank in Washington, D.C. A few months later, in March 1967, the Creek Indians sent Francisco Franco, head of the Spanish state, a genuine pipe of peace through a delegate conveying a message of greetings inviting him to visit them in Oklahoma.

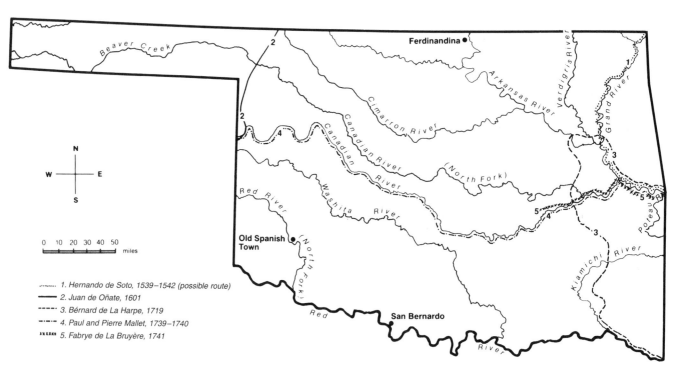

Spanish and French explorers in Oklahoma, 1539–1741. Facts On File.

Spanish Place-Names

Counties bearing Spanish names are Alfalfa and Cimarron, as do the towns of Alfalfa, Blanco, Calera, Camargo, Carmen, Castaneda, Cestos, Clarita, Concho, Eldorado, El Reno, Fonda, Isabella, Lamar, Loco, Optima, Panama, Ramona, Salinas, Sante Fe, Terral and Vinita. Local rivers with Spanish names include the Agua Frio Creek, Carrizozo Creek, Cieneguilla del Burro, Cimarron, Gallinas Creek, Palo Duro Creek and Verdigris.

Kansas

Making your way up from Oklahoma to Kansas you follow the same route as did Francisco Vázquez de Coronado, the first westerner to see its vast plains in 1541. (Due tribute is made to this fact in the mural painted by artist John Stewart Curry in the capitol building at Topeka, the state capital.) Here you enter the area known by some as the Great Plains and by others as the Great Desert. In his report to Emperor Charles V on October 20, 1541, the *conquistador* Coronado wrote: "I traveled for forty-two days from the time I left the forces (in New Mexico), living only on the meat of the oxen and cows that we killed . . . and marching for days without water, cooking the meat with the excrement of the cows, because there is no kind of wood in this country, except around the rivers or streams, which are few." This is the first description that the outside world received of these broad flat lands, subjected to extreme temperatures (short, hot summers, and long, bitterly cold winters), which have become the granary of the country. The rainfall in western Kansas, through which Coronado traveled, is extremely low. These lands did not appear to be extensively cultivated when the Spaniards set foot here. They were the home of buffalo, which roamed over the plains as undisputed masters. Moreover, the wind blew without any windbreak.

Vázquez de Coronado and Father Juan de Padilla

The expeditionaries continued on their way in a northeasterly direction until they reached present-day Lyons, in Rice County (where the armor of a *conquistador* was found recently). Later, they crossed the Smokey Hill River, first reaching Quivira, and afterward, an Indian township on the Republican River, near Belleville. (The monument erected at Junction City by the Quivira Historical Society therefore does not seem to be correctly sited as the northernmost and easternmost point reached on Coronado's travels.) A large hill southwest of Salina is called Coronado Heights and the *conquistador* is claimed to have climbed to that vantage point to scan the great valley and the Indian township of Quivira.

Coroando gave this description of the Kansas plains: "This province of Quivira . . . 950 leagues from Mexico . . . is the best that I have seen to produce all the produce of Spain, because, in addition to the soil being very black and rich, it is watered by brooks, springs and rivers, and I found in it plums like those found in Spain, and walnuts and very sweet grapes and blackberries." Moreover, there were rabbits, which ran alongside the horses and were therefore easily speared from the saddle. Here the Spaniards encountered Indians who ate raw meat—frequently wolf meat—and carried around their necks a fresh cow gut, from which, when thirsty, they drank blood and gastric juices; they were also in the habit of sharpening flint knives on their own teeth.

Historians do not agree as to the exact site of Quivira: some place it on the 40th parallel north latitude, others on parallel 39, between the Arkansas River at Great Bend and the confluence of the Republican and Kansas Rivers, or even between Salinas and Junction City. It was roughly at this point that the Indian "El Turco" perished, after being hung as a traitor. Coronado and his men had entered Kansas from Oklahoma and, on the feast of St. Peter and St. Paul, June 29, 1541 reached the broadest river seen on their expedition: the Arkansas, which they called after the saints in question. That point must have been roughly in the region of Spearville.

But despite the discovery of the Indian settlement, they would not find the gold that they sought, and the area seemed miserable compared to the description they had been given by El Turco in New Mexico. The Quivira that they had expected was very different, and Vázquez de Coronado—the "Don Quixote of America," according to Donald Culross Peattie—who had entered the plains of Kansas, his lance at the ready, in search of the gold of the Quivira of his dreams, found as he approached only the sun over the great flatlands, which in time was to be reflected on the fields of yellow wheat, and not the king of metals. There were no sources of wealth, no noble minerals as in Peru or Mexico, no abundance of pearls. The midsummer night's dream was shattered, and Coronado returned, dying, to New Spain, defeated in his enterprise.

The Spanish captain was accompanied on his expedition by a Franciscan friar, Juan de Padilla, who, during his sojourn at Quivira, planted a wooden cross in the main street of the township with the help of local Indians.

After the group returned to New Mexico in April 1542, Father Juan de Padilla gave a sermon during Mass in the open air, a few days prior to the departure of the army for New Spain. He commented on the Scriptures and on the fact that according to them he was under an obligation to stay behind to evangelize the Indians. He did so and saw his compatriots depart southward; with him were a lay brother, Father Luis de Escalona, and two oblates, Lucas and Sebastián, and they were joined by a soldier, Andrés do Campo, a free black man, and a Mexican Indian. The commander of the expedition left them a horse, mules and sheep. Father Luis stayed behind in New Mexico with his black servant Cristóbal (Christopher), while the others set off again northward.

Upon arriving at Quivira they were overjoyed to find a cross, the one that had been set up months earlier: this was a sign of the good disposition of the local Indians, the Pawnee, toward Christianity. Near them was camped another tribe of Guas Indians, who were the treacherous rivals of the Pawnee. Although he war warned of the danger, Padilla would not give up his attempt to convert them. There are several theories about the way in which he met his death, but the most likely one, taken from the statement made by do Campo, is that Father Juan entered the township after ordering his companions to wait for him outside. They watched as the missionary advanced toward the hostile Indians, and then, as he knelt down to pray for their conversion, he was shot down by a flurry of arrows.

Today, Council Grove and Herington, which lie some 28 miles apart, claim to be the site of this event, the first martyrdom in North America. The Quivira Historical Society has erected a monument at Herington, marking the spot on which he died, with the following inscription: "Quivira. Juan de Padilla. Martyr for the Faith yielded his life here in 1542. Coronado 1541—J.V. Brower 1896. Erected by Robert Henderson, C.R. Schillin and Rev. J.F. Leary for Quivira Historical Society, 1904. Kansas, U.S.A." Others claim that the monument to Coronado at Council Grove is more likely to have been the site of Padilla's martyrdom: it stands on a hilltop and can be seen for many miles around to the east and west of the town.

The Santa Fe Trail followed the same direction as Highway 56, which links the two towns; the trail played a very influential part in the days following Spanish rule, and, therefore, the monument to the "Madonna of the Trail" has been erected along this route as an act of homage to American women who accompanied their menfolk and contributed so greatly, through their self-sacrifice and courage, to opening up the broad territories of the West to colonization.

Do Campo, the oblates and the Indian were given permission to collect the body of Father Juan and buried it at a spot that they marked on a map, which they drew of the area. They then traveled to Mexico accompanied by two dogs that helped them to hunt rabbits during their journey. After several months, accompanied by a group of Franciscan fathers, they returned to the spot where Father Juan had been martyred and, thanks to the map, succeeded in finding his body. They placed it in a coffin and carried it to New Mexico, where it was buried in the chapel at Little Isleta Mission; there, according to tradition, a number of miracles later took place. The Franciscan fathers replaced the stones covering the tomb of Father Juan, which had helped them find the site.

This pile of stones remains to this day and used to be visited piously in the times of the Santa Fe Trail; today it is tended by the people of Council Grove, who prevent any depredation by souvenir hunters.

Juan de Oñate in the Kingdom of Quivira and Later Spanish Expeditions

In 1594, Francisco Leyva de Bonilla and Antonio Gutiérrez de Humaña ventured across the Arkansas River into Kansas territory; heading north for 12 days, they reached another river (possibly the Republican). On their way back they were killed by Indians. News of these events was obtained a few years later by Juan de Oñate and his fellow expeditionaries, who had left Mexico at the end of September 1601, and wandered through the Kingdom of Quivira for two months. On their return, all they had to report was that they had fought a pitched battle against some Indian tribes and heard the renewed claims of a prisoner whom they had taken, called Miguel, as to the fabulous riches to be found farther afield. They were afraid of being misled once again by the guile of the natives, and they headed southwest. Here, they confirmed the fact that the region was flat, and their wagons moved through this country easily: in time, this information was to prove most useful.

In 1706, in view of the encroachment of the French from Canada, Juan Ulibarri led an expedition from Santa Fe into Kansas. In 1709, Governor Antonio Valverde of New Mexico went to Quivira with a fairly large armed force but did not proceed beyond the Arkansas River. In 1720, Pedro de Villazur traveled through the area with another Spanish party likewise organized to prevent French encroachment; he met his death in the state of Nebraska.

When the American explorer Zebulon Pike departed from St. Louis in June 24, 1806, his expedition passed through the region of the Pawnee Indians in the neighborhood of the Republican River on September 25 of that same year. He found a Spanish flag flying there, having been presented to the Indians a few days earlier by an expedition of 300 horsemen from Santa Fe. Pike asked them to remove the Spanish colors so that the American colors could be raised in their stead; in view of the opposition on the part of the Indians, he agreed that the American colors should only fly during his stay there, and he returned the Spanish red and gold flag for them to raise after his departure. Pike later continued his trek along the Arkansas River westward as far as the town of Pueblo, Colorado, where he was captured by the Spaniards and taken to Santa Fe.

The real development of Kansas began during the period of Spanish rule. Pierre Laclède and Auguste Chouteau, who founded St. Louis in 1764, developed the fur trade in the years following the transfer of Louisiana to Spain and sent agents to the extensive territories in the West, including Kansas. Although not very numerous, these agents prepared the way for Kansas to become a territory. A Spaniard, Manuel Lisa, was the heart and soul of the Missouri Fur Co., founded at St. Louis in cooperation with the Chouteaus in 1808. A year earlier he had already set up a number of posts up the Missouri River and, until his death, was the most powerful fur trader in the United States.

Apart from the blood of the first martyr and the monuments described earlier, the Spaniards also left in their wake in Kansas a romantic memory: a two-edged sword was discovered in the late 1980s in Finney County and was handed over to the state historical society; it bears the name of one of the officers accompanying Coronado, Juan Gallego, and its blade has the following inscription: "No me desvaines sin razón; no me enfundes sin honor" (do not unsheathe me without reason; do

not sheathe me without honor). The discovery prompted a local writer to exclaim: "They came with color and glory, with hopes valorous as they were vain; they came on the sandaled feet of martyr priests; they came at the point of the invincible sword of the last Knight of Spain."

On April 18, 1989, the governor of Kansas, Mike Hayden, proclaimed April 22 Queen Isabella Day for various reasons, among which was his statement, "the history of America has direct linkages to the birth of Queen Isabella on April 22, 1451."

Spanish Place-Names

A number of towns in Kansas bear Spanish names: Alma, Agricola, Alta Vista, Arma, Bonita, Cimarron, Columbus, Concordia, De Soto, El Dorado, Galena, Havana, Isabel, Leon, Lucas, Moran, Navarre, Peru, Rolla, Salinas, Seneca and Victoria.

Nebraska: Coronado, Oñate and Other Explorers

Francisco Vázquez de Coronado was the first European to set foot in Nebraska, pursuing his dream: Quivira, a river nine kilometers wide, fishes as big as horses, huge canoes with golden eagles on their prows. (In fact, the *conquistador* was not far wrong: until the late 1980s, the Missouri used to overflow its banks and flood an area several miles wide; and its waters, and those of the Platte, are plied daily by vessels laden with great wealth, namely cattle descended from the Spanish longhorn from Texas, on their way to the markets in Omaha. While the *conquistadores* did not find gold themselves, the Black Hills eventually yielded the rich gold mine at Homestake.) Some historians argue that Coronado went beyond the 40th parallel, coinciding with the border with Kansas, and advanced as far as the site of Lincoln itself, in the area where the Indian El Turco is supposed to have been hanged as a traitor. According to historian Charles F. Lummis, the explorer Juan Oñate also set foot in Nebraska.

There are some doubts as to whether the expedition dispatched by Diego de Peñalosa from New Mexico in 1662 actually reached Nebraska. In any case, it establishes contact with the territory north of Quivira, and the chief of Quivira convened a council of 70 chiefs from the area. In 1720, the governor of Santa Fe proposed to destroy the French settlements in Illinois and replace their inhabitants with colonists from Mexico. Trappers and traders had discovered a route across the Great Plains from Santa Fe. The Spaniards met with cooperation on the part of the Osage Indians, who were enemies of the Missouri. The party consisted of 42 soldier-settlers, 60 Indians and a priest, in addition to a considerable number of animals and was under the command of Pedro de Villazur. They crossed three rivers: the Napestle (Arkansas), Jesús y María (the southern reaches of the Platte) and San Lorenzo (the northern reaches of the Platte). The guides made a mistake and led the expedition to the Missouri Indian camp. Since they spoke the same language as the Osages, at first the Spaniards did not realize the mistake and gave them 180 muskets. Before the travelers realized what was happening, the Indians fell upon them. In the fierce battle that ensued most of the Spanish party were killed. The priest saved his life by undertaking to show the Indians how to ride on horseback. Thanks to this, one day he succeeded in escaping and recounting what had happened. The battle must have taken place near what was later to be the town of North Platte or in the nieghborhood of Columbus, at the confluence of the Platte and Loup Rivers.

Several fur dealers under Spanish protection led explorations in the area inhabited by the Omaha and adjacent tribes. In 1789, a Juan Munico, from St. Louis, was the first to make contact with the Poncas Indians living on the Niobrara River, in the north of the state. The governor granted him a trading monopoly in that sector as a reward for his efforts. The following year Jacques d'Eglise obtained a license to hunt on the Missouri, and there were others who extended the influence of the Spanish authorities in Nebraska. To control and expand business on the Upper Missouri, a group of traders from St. Louis organized the Company of Explorers of the Upper Missouri in 1793. The royal delegate granted them exclusive rights to trade with the Indians to the north of the Poncas, and the company dispatched a number of trading expeditions.

Manuel Lisa

In 1812, Fort Lisa was built 10 miles north of Omaha, by the Spaniard Manuel Lisa, who arrived at St. Louis from New Orleans in 1799. When Meriwether Lewis and William Clark returned from their famous travels, Lisa planned to start trading with the Indians in the

Southwest and with the Spaniards at Santa Fe. Being unable to carry out these plans, in 1807 he started to open up trade with the Missouri. Between that year and his death in 1820, Lisa went on several expeditions upstream. In 1817, he transported to St. Louis a single consignment of furs worth $35,000, a very considerable sum in those days. Lisa won the friendship of most of the Indians with whom he dealt and provided them with seed to sow pumpkins, turnips, string beans and potatoes, and taught them how to farm. This friendship proved useful in the course of the War of 1812, in which, now a citizen of the United States, he took part against Great Britain. It was due to him that the Indians in the Missouri region were loyal to the United States.

Lisa eventually had more than 100 employees in his Missouri Fur Company, together with hundreds of horses and many head of cattle. In its heyday, the company is said to have handled furs and skins worth $600,000. Fort Lisa became the largest trading post in Nebraska. Between its walls Manuel Lisa himself lived for long periods, with his Indian wife and children (he had a white wife and children in St. Louis). His Indian wife was a princess of the Omaha tribe, a beautiful and courageous woman, who once saved the life of one of her children in an Indian attack. Their daughter, Rosalia, was educated at a convent school in St. Louis and married a farmer from Illinois. When Stephen H. Long camped near Fort Lisa in 1819, he gave a very elaborate dinner for the trader. Lisa and his company were particularly important for Nebraska, owing to the role they played in promoting the start of trade and permanent settlements in the region.

Nebraskans today are conscious of their Spanish past. In Omaha, the Joslyn Memorial for Music and Art displayed some exceptional Spanish art in the exhibition "Soldiers and Saints in Old and New Spain" in 1962. A painting in the west hall of the Capitol in Lincoln depicts the role of Spaniards and Frenchmen in state history and is a permanent tribute to Coronado's search for Quivira. In April 1989, the University of Nebraska sponsored a symposium, "The Hispanic Presence on the Great Plains."

Spanish Place-Names

The following Nebraska localities have Spanish names: Alma, Almeria, Anselmo, Aurora, Columbus, Cordova, El Dorado, Lamar, Loma, Lorenzo, Madrid, Panama, Peru, Rulo, Seneca and Valparaiso.

THE TWO DAKOTAS, MINNESOTA AND IOWA

South Dakota and North Dakota

Spain played a part in the early history of the Dakotas, between 1750 and 1850, when they were encompassed within the Louisiana territory. All the trading posts authorized by the governors of New Orleans to deal with the Indians on the prairies were more or less closely associated with the region. The first European settler to live here (in 1775) was Pierre Dorin, who married an Indian woman of the Sioux tribe and built a cabin on the site of Yankton.

The first permanent settlement was the work of the Northwest Fur Company at Pembina, near the Canadian frontier. The Compañia de Exploradores del Alto Missouri (The Company of Explorers of the Upper Missouri), known as the Spanish Missouri Company, began its operations in 1793, and in the course of the next few years several of its expeditions traveled for long distances and undoubtedly reached the Dakotas. At the end of the 18th century, the Welshman John Evans, in the service of the company, traveled up the Missouri River as far as its sources in Montana, and as he went he carved the name of the Spanish monarch Charles IV on rocks and trees to prove his discoveries.

As we have seen, Manuel Lisa played an active part in Kansas and Nebraska in opening up the Great Plains to the white man. His agents traveled long distances into the territories watered by the Missouri, and their friendship with the Sioux, Mandan, Poncas, Pawnee, Cheyenne, Crow and Arikara Indians—several of them predominant in the Dakotas—helped persuade the Indians to be loyal to the United States in the difficult days of the War of 1812 against Britain, who owned neighboring Canada. As the historian Herbert Bolton tells us, in an attempt to link St. Louis with the settlement at Nootka, Spain sent explorers up the Missouri River at least as far as Yellowstone.

Spanish Place-Names

Spanish names are borne by the following localities in North Dakota: Adrian, Alamo, Arena, Columbus, Fortuna, Grano, Havana, Juanita, Leal, Loma, Medina, Plaza, Portal, Raza, Ruso, and Silva. Those in South Dakota include Alpena, Aurora Center, Avance, Bonilla, Capa, Columbia, Conde, Corona, Hermosa, Isabel, Plana and Seneca, as well as Aurora County.

Minnesota

Part of the Louisiana territory, the land in Minnesota lying west of the Mississippi was transferred by France to Spain in 1763 and remained a Spanish possession until it was ceded to the United States in the Louisiana Purchase in 1803. Thus, the area was dependent on the Spanish Crown for 40 years.

Some towns in Minnesota today bear Spanish names like Adrian, Alma, Almora, Altura, Alvarado, Amor, Aurora, Carlos, Clara, Columbia Heights, Fernando, Granada, Isabella, Montevideo, Mora, Reno, St. Rosa, Santiago, Vergas and Victoria, in addition to Noble County.

Iowa

Although Iowa was discovered by Europeans in 1673, when Louis Joliet and Father Marquette traveled through the Upper Mississippi, the region was undeveloped until the period when Spain ruled over the Louisiana territory, to which Iowa belonged. In 1769 the first trader, Jean Marie Cardinal, set foot in this region; he died in a British assault on St. Louis on May 26, 1780, as a member of the Spanish garrison.

On April 9, 1780, on the bank of the Little Maquoketa River, north of Dubuque, British forces attacked Spanish, French and revolutionary traders and miners, and captured 17 of them. As a reprisal, a force was organized under the command of Colonel John Montgomery, with a total of 300 men (100 Spaniards were provided by Fernando de Leyba, lieutenant governor of St. Louis). This force proceeded up the Illinois River as far as Peoria, and from there to Rock River (in Illinois) and Prairie du Chien (on the present boundary between Iowa and Wisconsin). The Indians in the area fled, and their villages, arms and supplies were set on fire.

Years later, the Irishman Andrew Todd obtained from the Spanish governor at New Orleans, Baron de Carondelet, the grant of exclusive trading rights in the Upper Mississippi in exchange for a 6% tax. Governor Esteban Miró, for his part, planned the construction of two forts near the confluence of the Des Moines and Iowa rivers with the Mississippi. On the other side of the state, the east banks of the river may have been part of the area of which Welshman John Evans, working for the Compañía de Exploradores del Alto Missouri, took symbolic possession in the name of King Charles IV.

The most important Spanish contribution to Iowa history, however, was the fortified settlement called Les Mines d'Espagne, founded by Julien Dubuque near the town that bears his name. Born in Canada, Dubuque settled at that spot in 1785, to become the first permanent white settler in Iowa. In September 1788, he signed a contract with the Fox Indian chiefs whereby they recognized his possession of certain lands and his right to work his silver mines. Years later, he extended his operations to the other shore of the Mississippi, and opened up mines near present-day Elizabeth, Illinois, and in Wisconsin territory at the spot where Potosi stands today. The Spanish governor Baron de Carondelet formally acknowledged his rights in 1796, and Dubuque's petition for such recognition is on record. At the time, with war with Britain imminent, the Spanish authorities were encouraging pioneers to settle on the border of the Canadian frontier in order to help repulse a possible British attack. Dubuque proved to be a loyal subject and led an expedition against the British at Prairie du Chien, 45 miles to the north on the opposite side of the Mississippi; he forced them to withdraw and returned victoriously with considerable booty.

Business went well for Dubuque; in 1804, after taking charge of government in Upper Louisiana, the American commander Amos Stoddart reported that Dubuque's fur trade over the previous 15 years could be estimated at an annual figure of $203,000—quite a sum for that day! In Eagle Point Park, at Dubuque, can be seen one of the cabins in which the pioneer lived. He is buried beneath a high tower there.

Spanish Place-Names

Spanish names are borne by the following counties in Iowa: Buena Vista, Cerro Gordo and Palo Alto (in addition to Dubuque). The towns include Alta Anita, Buena Vista, California, Columbus Junction, De Soto, Durango, Eldorado, Farragut, Fonda, Ira, Leon, Lima, Madrid, Magnolia, Manila, Moran, Nevada, Palo, Panama, Peru, Plano, Rubio, Seneca, Toledo, Traer and Ventura.

PART V:
STATES OF THE SOUTHWEST

◆ *TEXAS* ◆

The characteristic warmth of Texas is not merely a question of climate, but also of temperament. Consequently, it is not hard to believe the story of the origins of the name of the state: the Spaniards understood that the Indians in the region, who greeted them saying "tejas" were informing them of the name of their nation, whereas, in fact, they were welcoming them and describing them as "friends"; hence the official motto, "Friendship."

When a native of Burgos, Martía de León, founded the town of Victoria in 1824, he named its main street (in which he himself lived with other fellow citizens) Calle de los Diez Amigos (Street of the Ten Friends); its original name was restored in 1962. At the intersection of that street and De Leon Plaza stands a monument of Six Flags, including the Spanish flag with castle and lion quarterings, and the Route of the Six Flags links Victoria with Cuero, Goliad, Refugio, Port Lavaca and Edna. These monuments reveal Texans' appreciation for the nations that contributed to its historical formation, and particularly Spain, who played an exceptional part.

The Spanish Past

"In 1519, only 27 years after the arrival of Christopher Columbus to America," King Juan Carlos I of Spain remarked in a speech when he visited Texas, "another navigator of the Spanish Crown, Captain Alonso Alvarez de Pineda, sighted the beautiful bay which he named Corpus Christi, in memory of that day's religious feast." Other voyages would not be blessed with such good fortune.

Galveston Island, bathed by the waters of the Gulf of Mexico, was probably discovered in 1518 by Juan de Grijalva. Shortly afterward it was visited by Alonso Alvarez de Pineda, who drew up the first map of the Texas coastline. Galveston is the point at which Alvar Núñez Cabeza de Vaca and his shipwrecked companions landed on November 6, 1528. Their forced disembarkation on this coast was the culmination of a disastrous voyage in crudely fashioned boats, their previous landfall having been at the mouth of the Mississippi. The 80 survivors—who did not include Pánfilo de Narváez, their leader—arrived naked, starving and exhausted. They were welcomed by the local Indians, but as time passed, scarcity of food and epidemics resulted in the Indians' hospitality changing to hostility so that the number of Spaniards had been reduced to 15 by the time spring came. The island was called Malhado, or "Ill Luck." To escape death, the men had to cure the wounded and sick with a certain amount of daring and plenty of prayer; Cabeza de Vaca even went so far as to perform a successful surgical operation.

After six years, in 1534, the future author of *Shipwrecks* succeeded in escaping; on the banks of the Guadalupe River he encountered three comrades in misfortune, Captains Andrés Dorantes and Alonso del

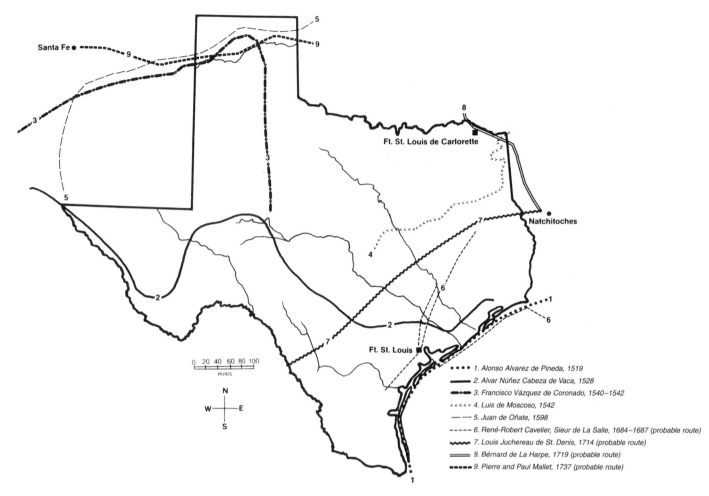

Spanish and French explorers in Texas, 1519–1737. Facts On File.

Castillo and the Moorish slave Estebanico. The four companions failed in an attempt to escape and postponed another attempt until the following year at the time of the prickly pear harvest in what are now Karnes and DeWitt Counties. They then set out for the west of Texas, making for the Big Spring region, and trekked as far as what they called Llano Estacado, before continuing westward and entering the territory of New Mexico. In the course of this venture, Cabeza de Vaca saw buffalo for the first time, and the scenery, inhabitants and characteristics of Texas were to become known in Europe thanks to his exciting accounts, which were published at Valladolid (Spain) in 1542.

Following the reports made by Cabeza de Vaca to the Spanish authorities, the expedition led by Vázquez de Coronado was organized and, on the way to Quivira (Kansas), passed through Texas; the first Thanksgiving in America was celebrated by Friar Juan de Padilla,

probably on May 29, 1541, in the Palo Duro Canyon in the northwest panhandle. (The Texas chapter of the Daughters of the American Colonists unveiled a commemorative plaque there, in 1959.)

A terrible hurricane hit the area in the spring of 1553; 20 ships had sailed from Veracruz bound for Cuba and Spain, but only three succeeded in reaching their destination, and one turned back to its starting point. The rest fell foul of the raging winds, and their crews, totaling some 300 men—including five Dominicans—were cast ashore on the south coast of Texas.

In *Great River, The Rio Grande in North American History,* the historian Paul Horgan relates the incidents that befell them. The only defense the 80 survivors had against the aggressive local Indians were two bows, which they lost shortly afterward when fording a river to try to return on foot to New Spain by skirting the coast. One day the Indians captured two Spaniards and,

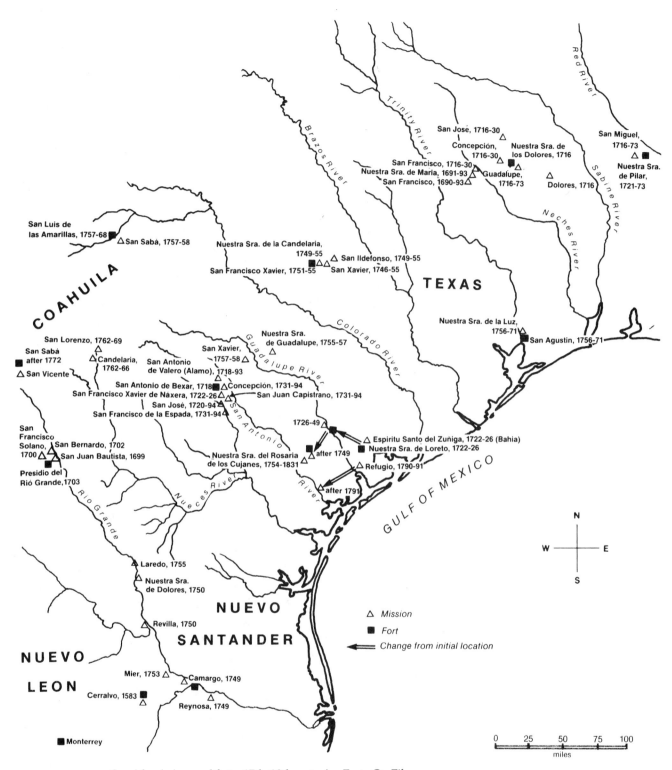

Spanish missions and forts, 17th–18th centuries. Facts On File.

stripping them of their clothing, returned them naked to the party. Led by confusion and despair at the hardships they were enduring, the survivors interpreted this as meaning that the natives resented the clothing of the intruders compared to their own nakedness; as a result all of them, men, women, children and friars, decided to strip in order to win the friendship and some peace from their belligerent hosts. However, their tragicomical decision was fruitless, for the Indians continued to attack them, and as many as 100 of the castaways were killed by arrows or died of sickness or starvation. When they reached the Rio Grande they succeeded in crossing it in small groups on a raft that they found, although they met with hostility on the part of the natives.

Among the wounded were Friar Diego de la Cruz and Friar Hernando Méndez, who nevertheless decided not to accompany the expedition southward, but to remain in the region and preach the Gospels to the natives. Having recrossed the river to the left bank, Friar Diego died there after receiving the last sacraments administered by his companion, who buried him on the river bank. Heading upstream, Friar Hernando encountered a Spaniard called Vázquez and a black woman, and they joined him in his efforts to survive. Their meeting must have been awkward, since all three were unclothed. But their struggle ended when the priest died, the black woman was murdered by the Indians and Vázquez fled in pursuit of the main party.

The absence of Friar Diego and Friar Hernando was felt by their three fellow priests, two of whom therefore turned back. Reaching the river, they traveled upstream on the raft that the expedition had used to cross the river. In midstream they found an island, where they decided to moor to gather their strength; to their horror the island suddenly sank, throwing them into the water, and then departed hurriedly downstream; it was an

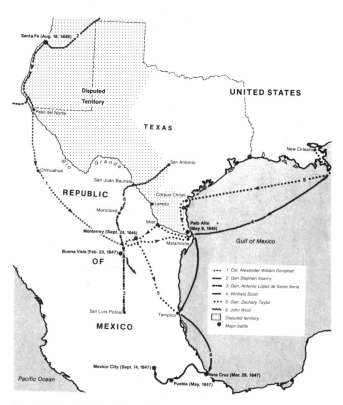

The Mexican War in Texas, 1846–1847. Facts On File.

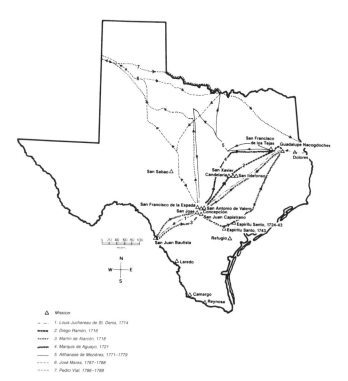

Eighteenth-century Spanish explorers in Texas. Facts On File.

enormous whale. Not finding their companions, they rejoined the main party, but of the three Dominicans only Friar Marcos de Mena was destined to reach Mexico City with a few other survivors, and there gave an account of their vicissitudes. They all considered it a dream to be safe and sound, but Friar Marcos must have been particularly grateful for he had already been buried. Set upon by the Indians when they came ashore, Friar Marcos seemingly received a fatal wound, and being unable to keep up with his companions in their flight, he was abandoned; they had buried him on a beach, just leaving a hole in his tomb so that he could breathe until he died; he did not die, however, but extricated himself from his grave and saw the bodies of a fair number of his gravediggers, killed by the Indians.

Juan de Oñate and his men followed a similar route in their search for the fabulous territories to the north in 1598. Some claim that Luis de Moscoso, accompanied by the troops entrusted to him by Hernando de Soto on his deathbed, came as far as eastern Texas. But none of those Spanish expeditions during the 16th century was organized with the intention of settling within Texas. Owing to the size of the territory, it would have been useless to make any such attempt in the early days of

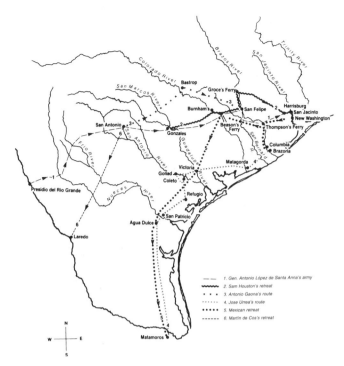

The Mexican invasion of Texas, 1836. Facts On File.

exploration. Only when the colonization of the north of Mexico began to become stabilized and the Spaniards heard news of the French intentions to settle there did Spanish activities in what is now Texas really begin. But, once begun, they withstood adversity. A dozen *presidios* were built, and as many as 39 Franciscan missions sprang up on all sides, with townships built around them. Surrounding Indians were taught the Christian religion, how to farm the land and how to breed cattle (now one of the sources of greatest wealth in the region). About 30 ranches are reckoned to have been founded at that time.

The visit of Frenchman René-Robert Cavalier, sieur de La Salle, to Texas signaled the start of the permanent presence of the Spaniards in the territory. He had disembarked at Pass Cavallo in February 1685, passing between Matagorda Island and the peninsula of the same name. After many vicissitudes, he decided to build Fort St. Louis, some five miles upstream from Garcitas. But things did not go well, and his attempt at colonization ended when he was murdered by his own men on March 20, 1686.

While the threat posed by French adventurer La Salle gave rise to the Spanish attempts at colonization at the end of the 17th century, at the beginning of the 18th century a French trader, Jean Jucherau de Saint Denis, led the Spanish authorities to organize a network of mis-

sions and *presidios* at strategic points in the territory. In 1716, in the course of the expedition commanded by Domingo Ramón (which was accompanied by Father Francisco Antonio Margil and Father Alonso Espinosa), the foundations were laid not far from the earlier mission stations for the missions of San Francisco de los Neches, San José de los Nazonis, Nuestra Señora de la Purísima Concepción de los Aynais and Nuestra Señora de los Dolores de los Ais (now Saint Augustine). Nuestra Señora de Guadalupe was founded at the site of present-day Nacogdoches, near which can be seen two springs called The Eyes of Father Margil (Los Ojos del Padre Margil) and a memorial plaque dedicated to the mission. About 1779, a fort was built at the town; now known as the Old Stone Fort, it can still be visited. To complete the plans, in 1717 Ramón founded the mission of San Miguel de los Adaes near Natchitoches, in what is now the state of Louisiana, and the *presidio* of Nuestra Señora de los Dolores, at present-day Douglas. These foundations were temporarily abandoned due to French raids, but the marquis de San Miguel de Aguayo, governor of Coahuila, reestablished them in 1721, and added the *presidio* of Nuestra Señora del Pilar de los Adaes, near the present-day town of Robeline (Louisiana), not far from the mission.

The leading role in the anti-French reaction over the easternmost sector of Texas was played by a Spanish officer, Alonso de León, governor of Coahuila, from 1688 onward, who came to be known as the "conqueror of Texas." He carried out five raids into Texas territory and in 1689 he ascertained the destruction of Fort St. Louis and the departure of the French, and heard about the tragic end met by its founder, La Salle. In 1690 he proceeded to lay foundations for settlements, accompanied by the Franciscan Father Damian Massanet in east Texas.

Alonso de León and one of Father Massanet's fellow priests, Father Miguel Fontcuberta, chose that area to set up two missions: San Francisco de los Texas, on May 24, 1690, close to where Weches stands today; and Santa María, near the Neches River, which was started by another colleague, Father Casañas. (Signposts along the highway indicate the site of the former mission, and a memorial stone reminds visitors of the exploits of a handful of Spaniards.) The recently rebuilt structure, though unoccupied, recalls those earlier hazardous times. One of the mission bells is now at Baylor University.

A province was founded in this area and Domingo de Terán de los Ríos was governor until 1693, when the area was abandoned as Spanish efforts centered in west

Florida. The Camino Real, or King's Highway, passed by San Francisco de los Texas on the way to Natchitoches, linking east Texas with San Antonio and Santa Fe. Today, along Highway 21, can be found signs recalling its history and foundation on orders from the king of Spain to his governor, Domingo de Terán. Texas was made a separate governorship, and Los Adaes became the capital for 50 years, until the provincial government was transferred to San Antonio in 1773. Antonio Gil y Barbo, a native of Burgos, did not accept the order to withdraw. He eventually used the abandoned walls of the Guadalupe Mission to set up a trading post. He and his colleagues were to be considered the founders of Nacogdoches. (One of his descendants, Henry Arechiga, lives at Waco and still preserves part of the family archives.) The will of Gil y Barbo was published recently and describes the interesting times in which he lived.

A Sovereign and Independent State

Texas is the only American state that can really claim to have been an independent state (apart from the incipient efforts in that direction in California, Louisiana and Florida) for almost 10 years. Anglo-Saxon settlement in Texas began with Moses Austin, with the permission of the viceroy of New Spain on January 17, 1821. When the region came under Mexican rule, following the end of Spanish rule, the number of immigrants increased, and there were continual incidents with the authorities until open war broke out, with two milestones: the Alamo, to which Mexican general Antonio López de Santa Anna laid siege, in the course of which William D. Travis, Davy Crockett and 187 men from Tennessee met their deaths on March 6, 1836; and the Battle of San Jacinto, won by Sam Houston on April 21, 1836, to the cry of "Remember the Alamo," when Santa Anna himself fell prisoner.

Subsequently, on October 22, the Independent Republic of Texas was proclaimed and Sam Houston was appointed its first president. Its flag had a lone star. Houston's successor was Mirabeau B. Lamar, who implemented an intensive policy to insure the independence of the new country and signed treaties with France, Holland, Belgium and Great Britain. Lamar was even tempted to expand, as is shown by his attempt to penetrate New Mexico. The Mexicans for their part invaded Texas in 1842 and conquered San Antonio and Corpus Christi. After a number of incidents, the arrangements made by parties interested in annexing Texas to the Union ended in the signing of a treaty on April 12, 1844, which received joint approval by Congress and the Senate on February 28, 1845.

Modern Cities

The state capital, Austin, honors the memory of Steven Fuller Austin, the son of Moses Austin, the father of Texan independence and its first minister of foreign affairs. Initially called Waterloo, the city is mainly Anglo Saxon, and yet in the central hall of the Capitol can be seen a large Spanish coat of arms forming a kind of artistic mosaic carpet in which it is combined harmoniously with five other coats of arms (those of France, Mexico, Texas, the Confederacy and the United States); set into the floor, a large number of place-names such as Gonzales, Bexar, Alamo, San Jacinto, Palo Alto and Palmito highlight milestones in local history. In a building next door housing the state archives, the Spanish flag with castle and lion quarterings flies beside the Spanish coat of arms.

Populous and progressive cities include Fort Worth and Dallas, not far away; between them lies the complex Six Flags Over Texas where visitors can see reproductions of other small towns with buildings, customs and outstanding events in the history of Texas under each of the flags.

Dallas has two museums with some fine representative collections of Spanish art: the Art Museum and the Meadows Museum at the Southern Methodist University. In addition to five etchings and a figure of Christ by Francisco José de Goya and a *Saint John* by El Greco, the Art Museum boasts a painting of *Saint Onofre the Hermit* by José Ribera, two Mirós, a Juan de Juanes and the *Aqueduct at Segovia* by Valentín de Zubiaurre. The Meadows Museum has *The Adoration of the Shepherds* by El Greco, *El Borracho (The Drunkard)* by Ribera, *El Pícaro (The Rascal)* by Bartolomé Esteban Murillo and *St. Catherine of Sienna* by Francisco de Zurbarán. This museum also holds two portraits by Juan Pantoja de la Cruz, *Capea* and *Picador* by Francisco de Goya and a number of works by Francisco Bayeu, Eduardo Maella, Vicente López, Leonardo Alenza and Joaquín Sorolla y Bastida.

Houston is another major city with a Spanish past. The Modern Museum houses a portrait by Juan Pantoja de la Cruz, a cartoon by Goya and a rendering of the Virgin Mary by Murillo, as well as paintings by Joan Miró, Antonio Tapíes, Luis Feito and Augustín Millares. Houston University has a granite sculpture by Eduardo Chillida. An Institute of Hispanic Culture was founded in 1966. In 1972, it became affiliated with the Instituto de

Cultura Hispánica in Madrid and annually celebrates the Americas' Night in which two prominent citizens perform the role of the Catholic monarchs. There is a similar institute at Corpus Christi.

On the occasion of the landing of the Apollo 11 astronauts on the moon, on July 21, 1969, Houston and Huelva, Spain, decided to sign a twin-city agreement. In 1970, the Spain and Texas Society received legal approval, and in 1975 a group of students from the University of Houston visited Madrigal de las Altas Torres, birthplace of Queen Isabella. The university's Spanish department commemorated the seventh centenary of the death of King Alphonso X the Wise. And in 1992, the university organized a symposium about "Spain and the American Frontier, 1763–1835."

On September 28, 1987, King Juan Carlos I of Spain inaugurated a bust of Cabeza de Vaca in Houston's Hermann Park. Here, he said: "It can be stated that the history of Texas begins with the chronicle of Alvar Núñez . . . *Naufragios [Shipwrecks]* . . . While honoring the memory of Cabeza Vaca, we would like to remember all those Spaniards who abandoned their native land for the adventure of the Discovery."

San Antonio

The true history of Texas begins with San Antonio. To finalize efforts at garrisoning east Texas, it was considered advisable to found a town in between so as not to leave the settlements so far apart. Thus San Antonio, which dates back to May 1, 1718, was established by Captain Martín de Alarcón (who had just been appointed governor of Texas) and Father Antonio de Buenaventura Olivares, of the Order of Saint Francis. Differences had arisen between them shortly after leaving Monclova, Mexico, and as a result they divided up their men and animals. Close to the banks of the San Pedro Creek, Captain Martín built a fort, which he called San Fernando de Béjar (San Fernando in honor of the then prince of Asturias, subsequently King Ferdinand VI; and Béjar, after the duke of Béjar, a brother of the viceroy, who had died in the defense of Budapest against the Turks). Half a mile away from the fort, Father Antonio built a mission, which he called San Antonio de Valero, in honor of the Franciscan saint and the marquis of Valero, who was currently viceroy of Mexico. A compromise was reached eventually, and the future town was called San Antonio de Béjar.

Sixteen families from the Canary Islands, sent out by King Philip V, reached San Antonio in 1731. They were the first colonists in the state of Texas; today, some of their descendants still live at San Antonio or in the surrounding area. The main square in San Antonio recently recovered its original name of Plaza Yslas, which can be seen on the plaque in front of the cathedral. The colonists received the rank of *hidalgos.*

Later, the mission was to be known and reverenced as the famous Alamo, and became one of the patriotic shrines of the United States following the staunch resistance in 1836 of a group of Anglo-Saxon citizens, led by the legendary Davy Crockett, against the Mexican troops of General Santa Anna. Between the *presidio* and the mission, a township of adobe houses gradually sprang up, and it was there that houses were built for the officers and soldiers with their Indian wives, as well as the workshops of craftsmen and the occasional saloon. The remnants of this past now, constitute the Hispanic corner known as La Villita. There, the four Nights of Old San Antonio are held yearly.

The success of the mission of San Antonio in attracting and converting the natives in the area led to the foundation of other missions. The first, in 1720, was the mission of San José y San Miguel de Aguayo, today known as San José Mission. In 1731 another three missions were built; Nuestra Señora de la Purísima Concepción de María de Acuña (in honor of the viceroy), San Francisco de la Espada and San Juan Capistrano. Built along the river not more then eight and a half miles apart, they were linked by a system of irrigation ditches and aqueducts. These missions have been very well preserved. Each is attractive in its own way, and all are notable for the size of their walls, the fine materials used and the importance that they attained, rightly

El Alamo Mission in San Antonio, Texas. Carlos Fernández-Shaw.

reflecting the considerable size attained by San Antonio from the earliest days.

It is not possible to give a detailed history of the Texas missions here, but their existence must certainly be noted in passing together with their influential role in history, and today in illuminating the Spanish cultural world.

Even those who are ignorant of its history must admire the splendid architecture of San José Mission now cared for by the National Park Service. The church (with its vaulted roof long since sunken inward by the rigors of time) has been rebuilt, as have the quarters where the Indians lived, where grain or farm implements were stored, or trades and industry were taught. Still in ruins are the dwellings of the friars. There can be seen the famous *ventana de la rosa* (rose window) attributed to the love of Creole sculptor Pedro de Huizar for a Spanish girl who was meant to come from Spain, but never arrived. Huizar was also the author of the fine facade of the church. The mission is a true gem of colonial art.

Its past has also been evoked in a work written by Ethel Wilson Harris, the *San Jose Story*, in collaboration with Frank Duane. This comedy is set in the year 1777 and is based on the visit of the inspector, Father Morphy, to this mission accompanied by Commander de Croix, while Pedro de Huizar was working there. Another work, *The Indians of San José*, was performed for the first time in July 1964, in the Historical Theatre of Texas (which opened in 1958), an open-air amphitheater situated on the grounds of the mission itself. Here, at Christmas, can also be seen the play *Los Pastores (The Shepherds)*, which has been performed at San Antonio almost without a break since missionary days.

Pope John Paul II visited San Antonio on September 13, 1987. During his stay there, he gave a complete speech in Spanish and said: "the Spanish Inheritance in San Antonio and the Southeast is very important to the Church. Spanish was the language of the first evangelists in this region. The Missions of San Antonio and across all of the southeast are visible signs of the many years of evangelization and services carried out by the first missionaries."

No less care has been lavished on the preservation of the Spanish Governor's Palace at San Antonio, built in 1722. It is still situated at the center of the city, and has been recognized as a National Historic Landmark. Although not outwardly outstanding in appearance, it has the sober dignity and appearance of Spanish architecture, and inside all the elegant simplicity of an 18th-century Spanish ancestral home; well cared for by its present owners, it is a magnificent symbol of epic Spanish days in Texas territory. The patio at the rear is quiet, full of musical sounds, with flowers and birds around a fountain flanked by a wide porch; the furniture exhibited is period furniture. Presiding over the whole is a portrait of the marquis de Valero. From this palace the affairs of Texas were ruled during the 18th century, and its chambers witnessed the dramatic years prior to independence from Spain. From here an appointment was dispatched in favor of Miguel Ramos Arizpe, empowering him to represent the province of Coahuila-Texas at the sessions of the renowned Cortes of Cadiz (1812), in Spain; indeed, he acquitted himself well in the course of those sessions.

When the occupant of the palace was Manuel Salcedo, it witnessed the rebellion of José Antonio Gutiérrez de Lara, who, like his brother, became enthusiastic over the hot-headed preachings of independence of Father Miguel Hidalgo; with a group of rebels, he succeeded in taking San Antonio and capturing the governor toward the end of 1810. He did not consolidate his victory; three months later Salcedo was set free and restored to his post at San Antonio. However, Lara was not discouraged and went to Washington, D.C., to obtain aid from President James Monroe in the form of men and arms, and in March 1813 laid siege to the capital once more, with the help of Augustus Magee. The town was assaulted on April 2. Salcedo and 16 Spanish officers were put to death and the first independent republic of Texas was proclaimed on April 17. It was to last four months; the royalist forces from Laredo proved victorious at the battle of Medina on August 18, 1813.

When entering San Antonio today, one finds its streets lined with Spanish balconies and flowers everywhere, and Spanish can be heard easily in the streets. The population is largely composed of Mexicans, relatively recent arrivals, and by the successors of the inhabitants of colonial times. These two communities comprise almost a third of the population. They have great influence in the life of the town at the present time, and throughout the state.

For years San Antonio had an Institute of Hispanic Culture. At the time of the American bicentennial, in 1976, the Order of Gálvez's Grenadiers and Ladies, composed of outstanding Texans was founded. Its purpose is to recover for American history not only the figure of Bernardo de Gálvez himself, but all those periods of history to which Spain contributed. The Spanish government donated to the new order uniforms of the type used by one of the regiments that fought for the independence of the United States under the Spanish governor, worn today on special occasions. There are also squads of grenadiers at San Antonio, El Paso Galveston and Houston. The Ladies of the order wear medals similar to that of the Spanish Order of Civil Merit, but in the Spanish colors, as a mark of distinction and rank. Under their statues, every three years the Grenadiers must pay a visit to the king of Spain, the first of which took place in 1978. They greeted the king and queen during their visit to San Antonio in 1987.

The main reason San Antonio became a capital was the abundance of water flowing nearby. A stroll along the well-paved banks beneath the streetlamps or along the Paseo del Alamo leads to the Arneson River Theater where from a packed amphitheater or from the riverboats themselves one can watch a performance of *Fiesta Noche del Río* reflected in the waters flowing between the stage and the audience. Spanish theater can also be enjoyed at the Teatro de la Esperanza (Theater of Hope), founded by Jorge A. Huertas, at the university, and each year in April the Fiesta San Antonio, which lasts 10 days, is celebrated, organized by the Paseo del Rio Association.

In 1968, under the slogan "Confluence of Civilizations in America," San Antonio was host of the Hemis-Fair, coinciding with the 250th anniversary of the founding of the city. The fair opened on April 6, presided over by Spanish and American dignitaries, and lasted six months. The Spanish Pavilion, built in characteristic Andalusian style, with tiles, wrought iron and horseshoe arches, included in its showrooms a historical and artistic itinerary through Spain, with special emphasis on the discovery of America, the exploration and colonization of the New World and Spanish assistance in the independence of the United States. Among the works of art exhibited were paintings by El Greco, Velázquez, Ribera, Murillo, Pereda, Zurbarán and Goya, in addition to the anonymous portrait of a Spanish *conquistador,* the Roman head of Agrippina, the armor of the "Gran Capitán," and the (18th-century) map of the viceroyship of New Spain drawn up by José Antonio de Alzate Ramírez. Spain Day was celebrated on April 7, and Laredo Day in June (the mayors of Laredo [Spain], Laredo [Texas] and Nuevo Laredo [Mexico] were present). At the end of the fair, the Spanish, consul general at New Orleans presented the keys of the pavilion to the city as a gift by the Spanish government. San Antonio is the twin of the Spanish cities of Las Palmas and Santa Cruz de Tenerife.

Central and Southern Texas: Missions and *Presidios*

The Texas Old Missions and Forts Restoration Association (TOMFRA) proposes to rebuild many of the old missions—once their original sites have been located—along a Texas Mission Trail. To this end, TOMFRA benefits from official and private aid, and above all the enthusiasm of its members. Since its foundation it has organized lectures and trips of historical interest, has promoted restoration work and has published the quarterly bulletin *El Campanario.* In one issue, Father Marion A. Habig claims that there were 36 missions and six sub-missions in Texas, as well as nine *presidios* and 18 settlements; another such article contains a select bibliography for the study of the missions and the Hispano-Texan forts. Thanks to the effort of TOMFRA, since October 1974, the home of Columbus at Valladolid, now a museum, has flown a United States flag and exhibits a coffer containing earth from the Spanish missions and *presidios* in Texas.

At Anahuac, at the mouth of the Trinity River in Galveston Bay, one can view the recent finds of Professor Curtis Tunnell from the mission of Nuestra Señora de la Luz del Orocoquisac and the *presidio* of San Augustín de Ahumada. A number of Spanish settlements were also situated in the area; the team led by Professor William C. Massey excavated the ruins of the San Francisco Xavier de los Horcasitas Mission, founded in 1746, and of the *presidio* of the same name. At the present time few traces are left of them, or of the missions of San Ildefonso and Nuestra Señora de la Candelaria, founded in 1748 and 1749, respectively; memorial stones raised in 1936 inform visitors of the major events in the history of each mission. Father Francisco Mariano de los Dolores y Viana founded the mission of San Ildefonso. The martyrdom of Father José Ganzábal there led to it being transferred, in 1755, to the more secure banks of the San Marcos River. All that can now be seen of the San Ildefonso Mission is a dike and various irrigation works, though the mission once housed as many as 349 Indians, according to the reports of Captain José Joaquín de Eca y Muzquiz. Nuestra Señora de la Candelaria Mission likewise suffered the consequences of the death of Father Ganzábal and was moved to a spot near the Nueces River, close to present-day Montell, on Highway 55. As experienced colonizers, the Spaniards were particularly mindful about the availability of water, and as this was a major problem in Texas, they endeavored to situate their missions on the banks of rivers and build aqueducts, irrigation channels and dikes to contain the liquid treasure and use it in irrigation.

Menard, a town with remnants of Spanish exploits, can be reached along Highways 81, 183 and 29, somewhat off the beaten track. The primary attraction is the Santa Cruz de San Saba Mission, which conjures up the tremendous scene of the fearful Comanche attack in 1758, which left the buildings in ruins and made martyrs of Fathers Alonso Giraldo de Terreros and José Santiesteban. The fort, built some distance away, could not prevent the attack and was abandoned following a visit to the area by the marqués de Rubí in 1766–1767, accompanied by a captain of engineers, Nicholas Lafora, who drew up a map and report on it.

Not far away can still be seen the ruins of the San Luis de las Amarillas *presidio*, built by Colonel Diego Ortíz y Parrilla. The San Saba River runs along one of the outer walls, and the remains give some idea of its considerable size. Here and there among the walls can be seen a ruined archway, and the many pieces viewed as a whole give an approximate idea of the size of the fort, one bastion of which still stands.

Camp Wood is the next stop on this tour of the missions. To reach it, visitors must travel through hilly country on a winding road, past dwarf oaks and twisted tree trunks, patches of evergreen oaks, sagebrush, walnut trees or pecans, from which the nearby Nueces River gets its name. The whitish soil in this area gives way to a richer gold, around Odessa and Lubbock, on the endless plain called the Ilano Estacado by the Spaniards. Camp Wood (reached by Highway 83) was the site of the San Lorenzo de la Santa Cruz Mission, founded by Felipe de Rábago y Terán and Father Diego Jiménez in 1762 to convert the Apache Indians and protect them against their rivals, the Comanche. With the information provided by a team of archaeologists from the University of Texas, some time ago some of the walls were rebuilt with the same types of adobe used in Spanish times, but this work was interrupted owing to a lack of accurate information. It is to be hoped that the Spanish or Mexican archives may soon yield the information required by members of the Camp Wood Historical Association to re-create the mission buildings and make the place one of the historical and tourist attractions not only of the region, but of the state.

Another mission and *presidio* were situated in the neighborhood of Goliad (this name being an anagram of the name Hidalgo, one of the heroes of the Mexican war of Independence); the town lies halfway between Houston and San Antonio, along the same road so often used by the Spaniards of the day. Both the mission and the *presidio* have been rebuilt with generous funding provided by Kathryn O'Connor, president of the Victoria Historical Association, who was decorated by King Juan Carlos I with the Order of Isabel la Católica (Queen Isabella). The Nuestra Señora del Espíritu Santo Mission was founded by José de Zúñiga on its present site in 1749 (the previous sites having been founded in 1722 at Fort St. Louis, and in 1726). This mission came to own some of the largest cattle ranches in Texas, numbering many thousands of head of cattle. After accurate reconstruction, the mission includes the church and the quarters of the friars and the Indians.

A few miles from the mission is the *presidio* of Nuestra Señora de Loreto de la Bahía, built by Captain Orobio y Basterra in 1749; it was first founded in 1722 by the Marquis de Aguayo close to the original mission. Under the guidance of his successors, Captain Manuel Ramírez de la Piscina and Francisco Tovar y Cazorla, the fortifications became more solid and proved useful in withstanding the frequent Indian attacks. They fell into the hands of the expedition led by José Gutiérrez de Lara and Augustus Magee in 1812, although the latter was unable to withstand the three-month siege laid to the place by Governor Juan Manuel Salcedo. Gutiérrez was tried and dismissed, and the expedition disbanded. A survivor, Henry Perry, returned in 1817 at the head of a considerable military force: his attempts to take the *presidio* by assault failed when royalist troops appeared on the scene, which led Perry to commit suicide. Another armed force, 50 or 60 strong, commanded by James Long, disembarked in the fall of 1821 at the mouth of the Guadalupe River and surrounded the fort; the attackers were defeated and taken prisoner within 24 hours.

To judge by the walls that are still standing and by the land marked out in line with the advanced stage of research here, La Bahía must have been important. Architect Railford Strippling and his technical assistants and diggers, mostly from Mexico, have done, much scientific and historical work excavating and building walls, and classifying finds: instruments, buttons, ironwork, nails and pieces of pottery, for example. In a side chapel in the church can be seen an admirable piece of artistic work, an old statue of the Virgin of Loreto. Sunday Mass is said by the parish priest of Goliad at the high altar before a modern fresco by a Mexican painter. Within the walls of La Bahía there is the same atmosphere as in a Spanish village, and one might well be on the high tableland of Castile rather than in America. However, the subsequent history of the *presidio* is very closely linked with that of the independence of Texas. In order to encourage interest and preserve the rich heritage associated with La Bahía in particular and the Spanish missions and forts in Texas in general, the Kathryn O'Connor Foundation has set up an annual prize, the La Bahía Award.

The Carbajal family of Goliad has donated their many artifacts to the *presidio*. Some locals are descendants of soldiers in the garrison dating back to the Spanish colonial era. Since 1986, each year in June the local citizens celebrate the role that the soldiers of the *presidio* played in helping the American colonists win their independence. The program begins with a flag-raising ceremony in the fortress quadrangle. Period clothing includes Spanish military uniforms from the 18th century. The event is cosponsored by the Crossroads of Texas Living History Association, a group of professional living-history interpreters, who portray notable events from the past. There is also a Spanish Nightwatch program, with a Grand Illumination and the old custom of the soldiers "locking up" the military outpost of La Bahía.

Near the previous mission stands the Mission of Nuestra Señora del Rosario, founded in 1754 by the Franciscans; it lasted for over 40 years and came to possess 30,000 head of cattle. Fortunately, from the point of view of preservation, it was chosen as a school for the families of soldiers and inhabitants in 1818, and the first teachers there were Juan Manuel Zambrano and José Galán. It later housed a girls' school.

Southwestern and Western Texas: Missions and *Presidios* on the Rio Grande

The southern sector of Texas and the territory near the Rio Grande have considerable connection with Spanish history, and today it is home to a large Spanish-speaking population from the other side of the border. In 31 counties of this region, and out of the state's 254 counties, more than 50% of the public school children have Spanish family names. Many of the smaller towns or villages have a large percentage of Hispanos.

One of the largest cities in the area is El Paso. Some historians believe that Juan de Oñate and his followers were the first Spanish settlers in the area in the year 1598. These historians argue that Oñate and his group celebrated the first "Thanksgiving Day" in North America on April 30, after they took possession of the land for the king of Spain. Traditionally, El Paso's origins have been believed to belong to a wattle and mud church and a monastery with a thatched roof, built among the area's peaceful Indians in 1659; in 1668 a larger church was completed and named Nuestra Señora de Guadalupe de El Paso. When the Spanish settlers at Santa Fe and other towns in New Mexico were forced to withdraw following the Pueblo Indian uprising in 1680, they sought refuge at El Paso del Norte. Then, in 1682 and 1683, Governor Antonio Otermín and Friar Francisco Ayeta founded the missions of San Antonio de la Isleta del Sur, San Francisco del Socorro del Sur, San Antonio de Senecu and San Lorenzo del Real, not far from the first of the group. In 1770 came a new addition, San Elizario, with the *presidio* of the same name. Throughout the period of Spanish rule El Paso played a major role owing to its location and size, for it was larger than other towns such as Santa Fe and Albuquerque. This area, called Chamizal, had been the subject of dispute by the United States and Mexico owing to the change of course of the Rio Grande; the matter was settled in 1965. In his volume *Memorias Exteriores*, José María de Areilza records his visit to the city in 1957 as the first one by a Spanish ambassador.

Presidio, in Presidio County, opposite the Mexican state of Chihuahua, was originally called Junta de los Ríos (Joining of the Rivers), but was given the name Presidio del Norte when Captain Alonso Rubín de Celis founded a military establishment here in 1759. In 1683–1684 the Franciscans had built the missions of San Antonio de los Puliques, San Francisco de los Julimes, Santa María la Redonda, San Pedro de Alcántara, Apóstol Santiago and San Cristóbal. This was due to the fact that the district was home to the Jumanos Indians, who proved very eager to receive Christian instruction because they had, reportedly, received mysterious visits from the "Lady in Blue," the Spanish nun, Sister María de Agreda (1602–1665), who had in fact never left Spain. As a consequence of their insistent demands that missionaries be sent to them, a party led by Captain Juan Domínguez de Mendoza and Father Nicolás López set out from El Paso on December 15, and following the course of the Rio Grande penetrated the vast territory spreading out from its left bank; their expedition lasted six months. As a result, on June 13 the following year, Mendoza took official legal possession of the land on the farther bank of the river, namely present-day Texas.

In the Mexican sector of Monterrey Spanish settlers came to work the mines discovered in 1579. They did not venture farther north for the time being. But, when rumors in New Spain were confirmed that the French had settled in Louisiana, and since the missions in east

Texas had been abandoned in 1693, it was decided to establish a defensive system in the region to serve as protection for Mexican territories. San Juan Bautista Mission, originally founded on the banks of the Sabinas River in Coahuila state, was transferred in 1700 to the plains flanking the Rio Grande. In the course of the next three years, two new missions were built, San Francisco Solano and San Bernardo, together with the necessary quarters to house the garrison of 30 men, the so-called compañía volante, or "flying company," commanded by Captain Diego Ramón. The whole complex became known as Presidio de San Juan Bautista del Río Grande, and in the ensuing decades was a key point in Spanish history of the region, playing a major role in revolutionary times. It became the nucleus of the Mexican city of Guerrero, south of Piedras Negras.

Across the river from Piedras Negras stands the U.S. city of Eagle Pass. The Indians in the area had alternately been at peace and war with the Spaniards during the first half of the 18th century. Following their repeated requests to be instructed in Christianity, Father Manuel de la Cruz crossed the river and made inquiries about the true good will of the local people. On orders from the governor of Coahuila, on April 30, 1675, Lieutenant Fernando del Bosque departed, accompanied by Father Juan Larios, Father Dionisio de San Buenaventura, 10 Spaniards and 20 Indian allies with their two chiefs. The party crossed what the Indians knew as the Northern, or North, River, at a point near Eagle Pass. Taking a northerly direction, the party explored the region and noted its features. On May 16, a small bell called worshipers to the first Mass sung in Texas, by Father Larios. There were 1,172 Indians present, many of whom asked to be baptized, but this was only granted to 55 children, until such time as the others had received instruction. The ceremony took place at a spot near present-day Del Rio, known then as San Ysidro (perhaps present-day San Felipe Springs?). South of Del Rio, Sacramento *presidio* was built in 1736.

On March 5, 1749, the township of Camargo—the first of the proposed townships in the Kingdom of New Santander, in the northeast at New Spain, alongside the Rio Grande—was formally founded at the end of a solemn mass attended by Lieutenant General José de Escandón. Earlier, in February 1747, Escandón had convened a meeting at the mouth of the river attended by seven armed detachments, 765 soldiers who had been stationed over an area of more than 120,000 square miles. As a result of their reports, he had carried out a thorough survey proposing the creation of 14 centers, six of them along the river, where colonists would be grouped together and missions should be built. His plan was different than those followed earlier: rather than establish missions supported by military detachments, they should form civilian settlements strong enough to fend off possible enemy attacks themselves, although naturally endowed with military forces and missionaries to preach the Gospel. In the execution of his plan he received enthusiastic cooperation from 500 families, who were to receive a certain area of free land, sums of up to 200 pesos and exemption from taxation for 10 years.

On March 14, 1747, the community of Reynosa was founded on the right bank, and a little farther upstream, Revilla, later known as Ciudad Guerrero, in the summer of 1750. In 1753, a township called Mier was built between them. On the left bank (present-day Texas) various other centers were developed: in the summer of 1750, Dolores, on the present site of San Ygnacio, established by José Vázquez Borrego (in the course of the same year, the Franciscans were to found Peñitas Mission, later Lomita, the beginnings of the township of Mission); in 1753, the townships that were to become the basis for Rio Grande City and Roma; and on May 15, 1755, Laredo, founded by Tomás Sánchez. (The names chosen for the sites were taken from Escandón's native province of Santander in the north of Spain.) In 1749 the king rewarded him with the title of count of Sierra Gorda, derived from one of the mountain chains in this region.

In the early years these establishments functioned collectively, and Escandón did not make individual grants of land until the colonists had become settled and the dangers of Indian attacks decreased, particularly on isolated farms. The only exception he made was that of Captain Blas María de la Garza Falcón, owing to the urgent need to set up a fortified stronghold halfway between Presidio de La Bahía and Rio Grande, on the banks of the Nueces River. Consequently, the captain, accompanied by his family, settlers and soldiers, set off in 1760 and settled on land which, in time, was to become the famous King Ranch, today the largest piece of real estate in the United States (over 975,000 acres), almost equivalent to the state of Connecticut, owned by the Kleberg family. The Rancho Real de Santa Petronila, so-called by the royal grant, fulfilled its role of promoting wealth in the area and providing defense against Indian raids. Garza gave names to many features within his domains and called part of his land and a brook after the patron saint of his daughter María Gertrudis; today, that river is the largest one on the King Ranch and has, in its turn, given its name to the famous Santa Gertrudis cattle.

In 1767, a royal commission arrived at Nuevo Santander (New Santander) in order to distribute land; the title deeds to many properties in this sector of Texas derive from the Actas de la visita General or Deeds of the General Visit of Inspection, and it is not unusual for the law courts even today to have to resort to them in cases of litigation. The commission distributed plots of land, the minimum size per family usually being 1,500 *varas* wide by 25,000 *varas* long, with the short end adjoining a watercourse. (One *vara* is approximately 2.8 feet; thus each plot would be roughly 6,750 acres.)

In 1772, Spaniard José Salvador de la Garza obtained a grant of 59 square leagues of El Potrero del Espíritu Santo at the southern limits of which Brownsville stands today. In 1781, a man from Reynosa, José Narciso Cavazos, obtained 500,000 acres, known as San Juan de Carricitos, comprising Willacy County and most of the neighborhood of Hidalgo and Kenedy. Between 1777 and 1798, Captain Juan José Hinojosa received the grant of Llano Grande, while José María Ballí received the adjoining estate of La Feria, both on the Rio Grande; Eugenio and Bartolomé Fernández acquired possession of Concepción de Carricitos, likewise on the big river.

In 1804, Juan José de la Garza obtained title to Casa Blanca on the Nueces River whereas Rincón de Corpus Cristi fell to Ramón de Hinojosa. In 1807, the Pérez Rey family, associated with Manuel García, settled legally on Rincón de los Laureles, which was a result of the Laureles, division of the King Ranch. The long narrow island on the farther side of the Madre Lagoon, San Carlos de los Malaguitos, was presented to Father Nicolás Ballí in the hopes of converting its inhabitants, the Karankawa; although he did not achieve his purpose, he gave his name, Padre Island, to that stretch of coastline, at the entrance to which can be seen a portrait of Isabella the Catholic.

Spanish Place-Names

It is worth giving a list, albeit shortened, of the places in Texas bearing Spanish names. Let us start with first names: Adrian, Anton, Candelaria, Celina, Cristobal, Clara, Concepcion, Elsa, Esperanza, Geronimo, Guadalupe, Inez, Joaquin, Lolita, Mercedes, Natalia, Perico, Petronilla, Ricardo, Sarita, Socorro and Sebastian. Family names are: Aguilares, Alba, Bolivar, Bustamante, Davila, De Leon, De Soto, Gomez, Gonzales, Guerra, Hidalgo, Los Saenz, Morales, Medina, Mendoza, Navarro, Palacios, Romero, Saltillo, Valera, Vera, Zapata and Zavalla. Colors: Amarillo, Blanco, Celeste, Colorado and Quemado. Features of nature are as follows: Agua Dulce, Agua Nueva, Alamo, Alamo Alto, Alta Loma, Alto, Boca Chica, Charco, Coyote, Cuevas, Del Rio, Del Valle, El Campo, El Lago, El Paso, El Sauz, Encinal, Encino, Era, Grulla, Hondo, Lagarto, La Paloma, Leona, Llano, Los Ebanos, Los Fresnos, Mico, Nevada, Palito Blanco, Palo Pinto, Plano, Rio Frio, Rio Grande, Rio Hondo, Riomedina, Rio Vista, Salado, Salmon, Sandia, Sierra Blanca, Veya and Viboras. Names of Spanish towns or foundations used in Texas are: Carmona, Corpus Christi, Galveston, Laredo, La Villa, Loyola, Los Angeles, Puerto Rico, Saragoza, Segovia and Vigo. Saints' names used are: San Antonio, San Benito, San Diego, San Elizario, San Felipe, San Gabriel, San Ignacio, San Isidro, San Juan, San Marcos, San Patricio, San Pedro, Santa Elena, Santa Maria and Santa Rosa. Names relating to cattle are used for some towns: Bovina, Bronco, Cornudas, Cuero, El Toro, Ganado, La Feria and Matador. Names having to do with buildings have also been used: Balcones, Camilla, Cason, Fronton, Lajitas, Presidio, Refugio, Spanish Fort and Tornillo. Others include Bandera, Bonanza, Bonita, Boquillas, Brazos, Canutillo Chico, Dinero, El Indio, La Joya, La Reforma, Loco, Nada, Orla, Progreso, Realitos and Talco.

NEW MEXICO

For students of Spanish history, the state of New Mexico is one of the most interesting. While Spain made its mark in many other states and buildings still stand as reminders of a Spanish past, no other state can rival New Mexico in the preservation of living monuments, namely the inhabitants, the descendants of the Spaniards who gradually settled in the "kingdom" in the course of four centuries.

The first European to set foot in New Mexico was Alvar Núñez Cabeza de Vaca, together with his companions, who had managed to survive the hardships of imprisonment by the native tribes after the shipwreck of the Narváez expedition near Galveston. However, his skill at curing sickness enabled him to survive until, in 1535, he and three other shipwrecked companions, Andrés Dorantes, Alonso del Castillo and Dorantes's Moorish slave Estebanico, succeeded in fleeing westward, crossing what was to become known as Llano Estacado, following the Pecos River upstream in a northerly direction for some way, then turning southwest not far from Artesia, and crossing the Rio Grande a little way upstream from El Paso, near Mesilla and Las Cruces. They eventually reached Mexico City, and their reports of the riches glimpsed during their long journey and the large buildings seen in some of the towns, led to the decision of the viceroy to organize an expedition to confirm the hopeful information supplied by the intrepid explorer.

In view of the refusal of Cabeza de Vaca to lead the expedition (because he planned to travel to Spain to obtain royal permission to carry out just such an enterprise for his own benefit), Viceroy Antonio de Mendoza chose Friar Marcos de Niza, who had accompanied Francisco Pizarro in the conquest of Peru, and appointed Esteban to act as a guide with an escort of soldiers. If reports are true, the governor of Nueva Galicia (New Galicia), Francisco Vázquez de Coronado, was to undertake the conquest of the areas to the north and organize the settlements of colonists.

Spaniards first inhabited this territory in 1539, and as recently as November 1820, the acting governor, Facundo Melgares, presided over a meeting of the *alcaldes* of New Mexico to discuss the journey to Spain of Don Pedro Bautista Pino, who represented the colony at the new sessions of parliament, or the Cortes, convened after the uprising led by Rafael del Riego at Cabezas de San Juan, Spain. Throughout its history, the Crown took unswerving interest in the distant kingdom, as did the viceroys and missionaries, who could expect little profit from such an arid region, inhabited by numerous native tribes, many of whom were hostile toward the Europeans and, often, to each other. Although it is true that exploration began owing to stories of the existence of the Seven Cities of Cibola or Gran Quivira, it is no less true that Spain's colonizing efforts persisted even after it had been concluded that these legends were groundless; in fact, those efforts can even be said to have intensified thereafter.

Early History

New Mexico is characteristically arid. Wherever water is found, crops can be grown and farms flourish; where no river is to be found, nature is barren and devoid of

the slightest basis for any economy. Hence the vital importance of the Rio Grande basin, realized from the outset by the Spaniards, who used it as a line of communication, a means of orientation in the vastness of the territory and a place for settlement for the colonists who gradually arrived and for the missions which were established. The Spaniards made the most of the waters of the Rio Grande and other rivers, developing irrigation systems based on their knowledge learned from the Moors. The Indians themselves lived for the most part on the land along the river banks. These were the sedentary Pueblo Indians, whom the Spaniards found grouped together in approximately 20 communities, inhabited by some 20,000 Indians. A community of Pueblos had been in the region for about five centuries. There were three main groups the Zuñi, the Tano and the Keresan, with the Zuñi living to the west, at some distance from the river.

These peoples were the builders of the famous four-story communal buildings, in which the ground floor had four rooms, the second floor three rooms, the third floor two rooms, and the fourth floor a single room, all with staggered terraces and small doorways or windows that had to be entered by a movable ladder. The

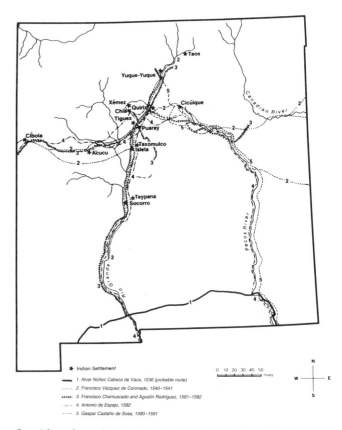

Spanish explorers in New Mexico, 1536–1591. Facts On File.

explanation for this unusual layout lies in the need for defense, protection from harsh climatic conditions, the natural resources available and a social organization based on matriarchy. These adobe buildings, which can still be seen at Taos and elsewhere, glittered in the sun and misled Father Marcos de Niza when he saw them from afar; his imagination led him to believe that he had seen the legendary cities of Cibola. The Spanish chronicles describe the existence at Pecos of two large groups of four-story communal buildings, one with 585 rooms and the other with 517, and boasting five squares and 16 *kivas,* or places of devotion. According to the historian Manuel Alvar, the *kivas* were indicative of a desire for permanence. (Later, Father Alonso de Benavides preached his own religion close to this site.)

The Pueblo Indians were in constant need of protection from their neighbors, the Comanche, the Apache and the Navajo, who were a continual nightmare for the Spanish governors as well. The evangelization of all these tribes, both sedentary and nomadic, was the primary reason for Spain's continued presence in New Mexico. (New Mexico would serve as an advanced protectorate of the viceroyalty of New Spain only during

The village of Galisteo, now in ruins, is one of a cluster of villages in this region of New Mexico, south of Santa Fe, that was home to Pueblo Indians of the Tano Nation during the 16th century. New Mexico State Tourist Bureau.

the 18th century, when other European countries began to show an interest in colonizing North America.)

The ventures in New Mexico were not good business: between 1609 and 1680, the conversion of the Indians cost Spain 1 million pesos, a considerable amount at that time. From a cultural point of view, however, it constituted a significant investment: today, in the very heart of North America there is a community with a population that is for the most part of Hispanic origin and Spanish-speaking; that still governs itself in many aspects by the laws promulgated by the kings of Spain; and that is loyal to the Catholic religion. According to the author Donald Cutter, the descendants of many of the native tribes, who speak Spanish, "live as Spaniards in spite of the fact that they do not have a drop of Spanish blood. They have the Spanish culture in their hearts, which is more important than blood."

A revolt in Texas, led by Bernardo Gutiérrez de Lara, carried over to New Mexico, linked, on the other hand, to the revolutionary events in New Spain. But the exchange of Spain's sovereignty to the new nation took place peacefully. News of the cession of the royal dominions, signed by the Viceroy Juan O'Donoju and Agustín de Iturbide on July 24, 1821, in Córdoba (which included territory in Central America, California, New Mexico and Texas), reached Sante Fe on December 26. On January 6, 1822, Governor Facundo Melgares presided over the celebrations of the birth of the new nation: artillery salutes thundered, a military

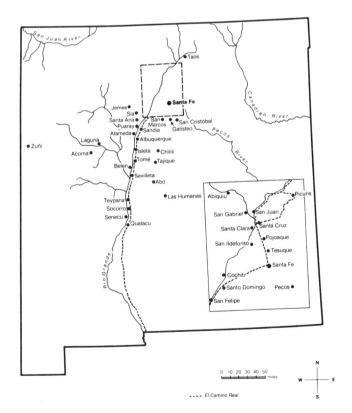

Spanish towns, 17th–18th centuries. Facts On File.

Many adobe houses like this one, said to be over 200 years old, can be found in the Espanola valley along the Rio Grande in New Mexico. New Mexico State Tourist Bureau.

parade enlivened the streets, a party was held in the palace by the *alcalde* Pedro Armendariz, and, that night, a play was performed recalling the Iguala Plan. The curtain was rising on a new act in the life of New Mexico.

New Mexico was not to remain long under the Mexican flag. By welcoming trade with the East, the new authorities lent support to the famous wagon train route between St. Louis and Sante Fe (the Sante Fe Trail); unwittingly, they aided in their own ruin by encouraging these contacts between New Mexicans and Americans, and even the settlement of many of the latter in their territory (some of whom, like Governor Charles Bent and Kit Carson, married local women). The fact that the United States was better organized, while Mexico was confronting the problems brought about by its

recent independence, as well as the increase in the number of Anglo-Saxon residents, friction between the residents and new arrivals, and a growing resentment over commercial exploitation and disregard of local traditions, led to increased animosity until hostilities finally broke out.

At the same time, there were signs of United States involvement in the 1837 rebellion of the Indians, who elected José González as governor at Taos but were defeated in January 1838 by the Mexican governor Antonio Armijo. Tensions were further heightened by the expedition to Santa Fe organized by the imperialistic president of the Independent State of Texas, Mirabeau B. Lamar, in 1842; his success led Governor Armijo to attempt an invasion of his neighbor, and in 1842 Mexican forces took San Antonio and Corpus Christi.

The mission of San Esteban Rey, built by Franciscan friars in the early 17th century, dominates the pueblo of Acoma. Carlos M. Fernández-Shaw.

A wooden cross stands out against the sky at the ruins of the Spanish mission at the pueblo of Pecos, near Santa Fe, New Mexico. The abandoned pueblo is now a state monument. New Mexico Department of Development.

The Santo Domingo Mission in New Mexico. Carlos M. Fernández-Shaw.

Conquest by the United States

The incorporation of Texas into the United States in 1845 brought with it the outbreak of war between the United States and Mexico. President James Polk included New Mexico in his plans for expansion toward California. However, no blood was spilled when the army of Stephen Watts Kearny occupied the territory and entered Sante Fe on August 18, 1845; another chapter in local history was about to begin.

Spanish civilization in New Mexico suffered following incorporation with the United States in 1848, under the Guadalupe Hidalgo treaty with Mexico. The inhabitants were isolated from their motherland (Mexico) and from their grandmotherland (Spain), and were subjected to pressure by the incoming Anglos, who were determined to impose their own language and customs. Their defense consisted in closing themselves in like a shell and isolating themselves as far as possible from outside influences; encouraging the survival of their religion, language and beloved traditions and the connections between the old families. Numerous incidents pitted the first Anglo-Saxon bishop of New Mexico, Jean-Baptiste Lamy, a man of French origin and not always a protector of the Spanish traditions and the clergy (of whom only 13 remained), against the mass of the faithful led by the famous Padre Antonio Martínez. The story of this clash of cultures has been

vividly told in the novels of Gertrude Atherton (including *The Splendid Idle Forties*), Willa Cather's *Death Comes for the Archbishop* and the play *Night Over Taos*, by Maxwell Anderson, which portrays the struggle of Pablo Montoya, a towering Hispanic figure, against the Anglos in the 1840s.

This tension ended in the Hispano-Indian uprising at Taos on January 19, 1847. On that occasion, the Indians made common cause with the Hispanics, their erstwhile enemies, and attempted to free themselves from the Anglo domination personified by Governor Charles Bent, who was killed at Taos. Colonel Sterling Price eventually overcame the rebels at the Battle of La Canada, on January 24.

In recent years, with migration to New Mexico from other areas, there has been a consequent decrease in the percentage of inhabitants of Spanish origin. The northern and western regions have preserved their traditions best, adjoining Colorado and Arizona, states that also have a marked Hispanic predominance. The east and south, influenced by their giant neighbor, Texas, have moved closer to the Anglo-Saxon world. The very names of the towns in the southern sector are predomi-

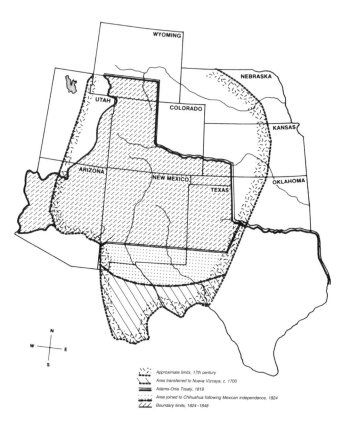

Southwest boundaries, 1600–1848. Facts On File.

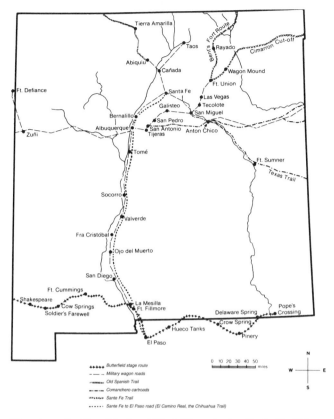

Historic trails, New Mexico, 17th–19th centuries. Facts On File.

comers embellished this type of construction with alterations of their own, and fortunately, this style has been preserved and is encouraged even in new buildings which, despite their skeleton of iron or reinforced concrete, outwardly show the same soft pink, sky blue, brown, yellow and turquoise hues used formerly. With so many contrasts of color it is hardly surprising that New Mexico is a paradise for artists, and whole streets in Santa Fe, such as Canyon Road, are lined with galleries.

The Spanish Heritage

In New Mexico, it is exciting to hear the language of Garcilaso in the streets of the United States spoken by people who have learned the language from their parents and grandparents, the language of descendants of the companions of Vázquez de Coronado, Juan de Oñate and so many other expeditions and settlements with which Spain peopled the land of New Mexico. Their Spanish is similar to that spoken in Spain.

There are radio stations that broadcast in Spanish, and Spanish readers find articles and news items in the weekly newspapers at Santa Fe, Bernalillo, Albuquerque, Santa Rosa and Española. New Mexico was inevitably far removed from peninsular Spain, for its contacts with the latter took place through New Spain (Nueva España) long before the airplane was invented, and this territory was even a long distance from Mexico considering the difficulty of communications in those days. On the other hand, this helped to preserve a greater purity of language so that the Spanish spoken here today largely bears the hallmark of the Renaissance and even of Medieval times. This is the Spanish that the Pueblo Indians learned, the Spanish heard even today under the porches of the old Spanish governor's palace at Santa Fe where the Indian vendors of pottery, jewelry and other crafts gather. Family names such as Lucero, Vigil, Apodaca, Aragón, Valencia and others still survive. Naturally, the Spanish language is not only spoken by the descendants of the Spaniards and by the Indians, but by Mexican immigrants, who number 300,000 (30% of the population) in this state. Spanish is considered an official language in New Mexico and can be used in the state legislature and law courts.

The ballads that the first Spanish settlers brought to America are still recited by the Hispanics and Indians of New Mexico. (Such songs as "Gerineldo," "Delgadina," "La Esposa Infiel" and others have been collected by Aurelio M. Espinosa in his volume *Romancero de Nuevo México*.) The same is true with popular folk songs, tales

nantly English and contrast with the numerous towns and cities in the rest of New Mexico, which preserve their Spanish names.

Nevertheless, New Mexico retains its Hispanic atmosphere, while at the same time contributing its own flavor to the great melting-pot of American culture. The racial discrimination endured by Hispanics has begun to wane and their political clout increased by their representation in Washington, D.C., by politicians like Senator Dennis Chávez and internationally by, for example, Ambassador Frank Ortíz (who has been stationed in Guatemala and Buenos Aires). The present moment is crucial for the future of Hispanic culture in New Mexico, as a matter of pride for all Spanish-speaking people and many others who are aware of the wealth of traditions in the United States and the harm done by their extinction. To assist in this effort, then Senator Pablo Montoya (from New Mexico) submitted a proposal to establish a special interdepartmental committee in Washington, D.C., on June 11, 1969.

When the Spaniards arrived, they found the Indians dwelling in modest buildings made of adobe. The new-

and sayings. Local fiestas resemble Spanish fiestas and are centered around religious ceremonies. Processions in the streets are common here. The strength of family ties can be seen in the importance given to christenings (newborn babies are given the name of the saint whose feast is celebrated on the day of birth) and weddings with a religious ceremony and a feast celebrated in true Spanish style; some are accompanied by the so-called *entrega,* recital of verses.

A number of plays have been preserved that were first performed here by Juan de Oñate's soldiers in 1598, when they were celebrating the foundation of the first capital before an audience of local Indians. The *Allegory of the Magi,* which was performed for example at Christmas 1964, dates from this period, as do the plays *Adam and Eve, The Shepherds* or *The Passion* during Holy Week. In addition to these Spanish plays, there are, of course, others in English for the English-speaking population, with Spanish subjects or the Hispanic history of New Mexico, namely *The Fiesta de Vargas Entrada (La Entrada a Santa Fe del reconquistador Don Diego de Vargas),* written by Pedro Ribera Ortega.

These traditions are kept alive with the help of two Hispanic organizations, La Sociedad Folklorística and Los Caballeros de Vargas. There is no sphere of activity in which the *sociedad* does not take part. One annual tradition is the *merienda,* or afternoon tea, at which the ladies wear dresses, shawls and mantillas (handed down from their ancestors and sometimes made many years ago, or in some cases acquired on a recent visit to Spain). The names of some leaders of the association—Alicia Romero, Josefina Ortega, Belina Ramírez—give evidence of their Spanish descent.

Los Caballeros de Vargas is an association for men, formed in 1956, whose members are descendants of the original *conquistadores.* Sixteen "Caballeros" and one man representing Diego de Zapata Luján Vargas commemorate the peaceful reconquest of Santa Fe by Vargas on September 14, 1692, following the Indian rebellion of 1680, which was on the verge of wiping out forever all trace of the Spanish world on the banks of the Rio Grande. The festivities began in 1712, on the initiative of Captain Juan Paez Hurtado and a group of leading citizens who sponsored publication of the "Proclamación y Ordenanza Cívico Religiosa" of that year; this is the oldest ongoing festival in the United States. At the present time, these festivities take place at the first weekend in September. The events include the burning, on the Friday, of Zozobra (a fat dummy), dancing in the streets, parades, the election of a queen, and other events, but the centerpiece of the festivities is a religious service and the *entrada,* or reenactment of the taking of the town by the Spaniards.

The *caballeros* use the coat of arms of the Vargas family, by courtesy of the descendants of Vargas, and wear 17th-century military dress at public ceremonies, whether they are civilian or religious events. One of the active members of the association, Pedro Ribera Ortega, described their purpose as keeping alive the fascinating history of Spanish America, maintaining good relations between the Spanish-speaking descendants of the *conquistadores* and their neighbors and taking part in the colorful historical festivities in Santa Fe (a delightful mixture of religious and civil celebrations) throughout the year. As Ortega expressed the feelings of his comrades: "With all our heart and soul we have not ceased to feel that we are the sons of our motherland Spain; we still preserve, although poorly, our faith, our speech (although it is spoken with a fair number of curious archaic expressions), our pride in the knowledge that we are true descendants of the Spanish conquistadors."

The knights, or *caballeros,* likewise take part (by escorting the processional float) in the other colorful festivities that take place in June, on the Sunday following Corpus Christi, to fulfill a vow made by Vargas in the event that the reconquest was carried out without loss of life; these festivities have been held ever since the year in which the town was retaken. They are predominantly religious and in honor of Our Lady of the Rosary, known in Spanish as La Conquistadora; a procession takes place from the cathedral at Santa Fe to the shrine of El Rosario, near the town, at the spot where the besieging army of Vargas camped and the Spanish leader built the original shrine. The statue of the Virgin is carried in a procession that retraces its steps nine days later, after a novena of masses offered by the grateful faithful.

An extraordinary statue of La Conquistadora can be seen to the left of the altar at the Cathedral of San Francisco, the only surviving altar from the mission of Nuestra Señora de la Asunción, built in 1627 by Friar Alonso de Benavides and rebuilt in 1713 after its destruction by the Indian rebellion in 1680. The beauty of this statue, the story of events surrounding it and the devotion that it inspires are remarkable. The statue was brought from Spain by a Franciscan friar in 1625 and is the oldest statue of the Virgin Mary in the United States. It escaped destruction during the revolt in 1680 because a devout woman, Josefa López Zambrano de Grijalba, clutched it to her and fled with her fellow citizens as they withdrew to El Paso, where the statue remained for 13 years. Once Santa Fe was retaken, the statue was returned in triumph to the town on December 16, 1693, and the tradition of the processions and thanksgiving masses began the following year; the annual celebration is the most important festival devoted to Mary in the United States. The confraternity of Nuestra Señora del Rosario, La Conquistadora, is a group of devotees who endeavor to maintain Marian piety.

The events described above were particularly meaningful in 1960, during the commemoration of the 350th anniversary of the foundation of Santa Fe by Governor Pedro de Peralta in 1610. The ceremonies were attended by the Misses Pérez Balsera, from Madrid, seventh generation descendants of Vargas himself, and the climax was the papal coronation of La Conquistadora statue by the legate of His Holiness Pope John XXIII, his apostolic delegate in the United States, Archbishop Egidio Vagnozzi.

In other towns, the festivities of the local patron saint are important and celebrated in great style, and Christmas is celebrated as a deeply religious event. The worshipers customarily attend midnight Mass, following the precedent set by Juan de Oñate and his men in 1598, and crèches are numerous. Children go caroling, called La Pedida de los Oremos, because they recite the verse:

Oremus, Oremus
angelitos somos;
a pedir aguinaldos
y rezando oremus.

Oremus, oremus
We are baby angels
Asking for Christmas gifts
And praying oremus.

The Mexican *posadas* are performed in the forecourt of a church and then go from door to door, recalling the search for a room by St. Joseph and the Virgin, until they reach the house chosen as a destination. Performances are staged of the medieval plays *Los Pastores, Adán y Eva, Las Apariciones de Nuestra Señora de Guadalupe* and *El Niño Perdido;* colorful *piñatas* are broken in a custom from Mexico, The festivities of the Reyes Magos, or the Three Magi, are particularly meaningful, and young and old alike await the arrival of the generous monarchs from the Far East bearing countless presents.

Santa Fe

Santa Fe was founded in 1610 by Governor Pedro de Peralta, the first representative of the king after the departure of Juan de Oñate, who called it La Villa Real de la Santa Fe de San Francisco de Asís. It is the second oldest city in the United States (after St. Augustine) and the oldest state capital in the Union. Governors in the colony spent their term of office (generally three years) in continual rivalry, as representatives of the state, with the missionaries, the militant arm of the Church. (For a list of governors, see the history Appendix.) As in all controversies neither one nor the other was entirely right or wrong, and just as there were magnificent governors and meddling friars, there were also arbitrary royal delegates and untiring missionaries defending the well-being of their flock. These disputes were a cause of increasing unrest among the Indians, who had not entirely adjusted to the presence of the Spaniards nor resigned themselves to abandoning their traditions; the Indians resented the lack of protection at times from attacks by their enemies, and rebelled, particularly at times of crisis, at supplying the Spaniards with provisions.

The 1680 Uprising and the Reconquest

This state of unrest gradually spread thanks to the strong personality of the Indian Popé, a well-known medicine man. For five years he prepared for the rebellion of his people. The uprising was planned for August 13, 1680, but took place four days earlier because the Spaniards had got wind of it that same day. By the time Governor Antonio de Otermín was in a position to react most of the harm had already been done. The uprising included almost all the Pueblo Indians and hit all the settlements founded thus far by the *conquistadores.* About 400 Spaniards, including women, children and missionaries, perished, and their properties were razed. The siege of Santa Fe began on August 15, after Otermín had rejected an ultimatum from the besiegers. On the morning of August 20, a sortie of 100 defenders won a victory in which 300 attackers were killed. But news of the general uprising and a conviction that it was impossible to hold out without any prospect of receiving relief led the governor to order the withdrawal of the 1,000 survivors from the town, which lay in ruins. The withdrawal took place on August 21, without confrontation by the Indians, who had been impressed by the carnage of the previous day.

Other Spaniards scattered nearby had rallied around Deputy Governor Alonso García at Isleta, farther south; García had not received Otermín's requests for assistence and did not even know about the struggle at Santa Fe. On September 13 the two parties were reunited, forming a total of 2,520 survivors. Together they made their way to El Paso, where the flag of New Mexico flew for 13 years. The work of almost a century had been destroyed in the space of a few days, and the economic effort made seemed fruitless; future events were to show that all had not been lost.

The unfortunate refugees, whose relatives and property had disappeared in the course of the uprising, followed a route parallel to the Rio Grande that had been used since the 16th century by the expeditions led by Francisco Sánchez Chamuscado, Antonio Espejo and Juan de Oñate, and, in the course of the 17th century, by the convoys that carried out the long task of supplying the missions and Spanish townships. Usually originating in Mexico City, these convoys would follow the route to Zacatecas, Durango, Parral and El Paso, and took six months to reach Santa Fe; it would take them about another six months to distribute their merchandise throughout the country and carry out repairs, and a further six months on the return journey that the round trip took about a year and a half. The convoys consisted of 32 wagons, drawn by eight mules, capable of transporting two tons of provisions each. On the

northward journey, the goods transported consisted of foodstuffs, building supplies, clothing and furniture, among other things; on the return trip, the wagons were loaded with pine nuts, sheep, leather, blankets and other goods crafted by the Indians.

It was on one of these convoys that Friar Francisco de Ayeta reached Santa Fe in 1647; he made the same journey several times in his efforts to prevent the gradual economic and military deterioration of the impoverished territory. His efforts were insufficient to prevent the outbreak of the rebellion. While Father Ayeta was at El Paso on August 25, 1680, he received two letters, one from Friar Diego de Mendoza, in charge of the Socorro Mission, and the other from a farmer, Juan Severiano Rodríguez de Suballe, informing him of the disaster. From El Paso he helped the commander, Pedro de Leiva, to organize relief expeditions of soldiers, as well as food for the retreating inhabitants of New Mexico. It was thanks to his perserverance that the Spanish presence in New Mexico did not disappear. Though he was aware of the natural desire of the settlers to flee forever from the area of their misfortunes, he realized that this would doom any attempt to recover what had been lost. The governor of Nueva Vizcaya (the Philippines), therefore, gave orders that refugees from New Mexico who departed without written permission from Governor Antonio Otermín should be arrested and returned to El Paso, on pain of death and treason against the king. The survivors set about building three camps, which grew into towns around the Guadalupe Mission.

Spanish efforts at reconquest would follow the same route used by the Oñate expedition, using the geographical landmarks that Oñate had named: Sierra de Robledo, called after the soldier buried on its slopes on March 21, 1598; Perrillo Spring, after the little dog that helped the thirsty expeditionaries to find a spring; Jornada del Muerto (Dead Man's March), a trek through 135 kilometers of waterless desert; and Fra Cristóbal, the name of the spot, and the nearby mountain range, where the Rio Grande turned back northward, in honor of the chaplain. On November 5, 1681, with trumpets blaring and flags unfurled, the troops commanded by Otermín set out. They found no sign of life until they reached Cochiti, where an advance party commanded by Juan Domínguez de Mendoza almost fell into a trap and decided to return. At Isleta they found waiting for them a group of loyal Indians 385 strong, who accompanied them on their return journey to El Paso the following February, and there settled and founded Isleta

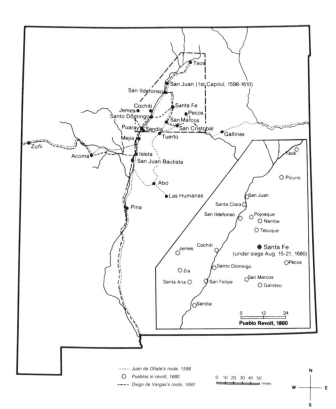

The Pueblo revolt and reconquest in New Mexico, 1598–1692. Facts On File.

del Sur. The expedition had failed. General Domingo de Cruzate, who succeeded Otermín, took up his post on August 30, 1683, and remained there until 1689 (for an interval between 1686 and 1688 Pedro Reneros Posada was left in charge). In 1689, Cruzate led a detachment that encountered the Sia Indians, 600 of whom were killed. His successor, Diego de Vargas Zapata Luján y Ponce de León, a man of noble family and considerable fortune, succeeded in reaching El Paso on February 22, 1691.

Vargas was outstanding for his courage, forcefulness, experience, diplomacy and noble mindedness, and these qualities were to stand him in good stead in his future campaign to recapture the territory. After six months of preparation, he departed at the head of a company of 60 Spaniards and 100 Indians, after carefully planning his strategy. When they approached a township, the Spaniards would lay siege to it so that no inhabitants could escape; no shot would be fired without orders from their leader. The soldiers would sing five times the praises of the Virgin Mary so that the besieged Indians could hear them, and the missionaries accompanying the party would then try to persuade the chiefs to return to the Church and submit to the Crown. If the Indians accepted, the priests would absolve them and christen the children born in the intervening period; should they refuse, the military siege would proceed and the township would be taken by force. This strategy seemed appropriate not only because the Indians would remember the Christian practices and the Spanish language, but also because major disputes had broken out among different factions, particularly owing to their disgust at the tyrannical government of Popé and the blood-thirsty attacks of the emboldened Apache. However, Vargas and his men found the townships deserted until they reached the capital.

At 4:00 A.M. on September 13, 1692, 200 voices broke the silence before the sleeping walls of Sante Fe entoning five times, "Alabado sea el Santísimo Sacramento del altar" (Praised be the Blessed Sacrament of the Altar). It was still dead of night, and the Indians rose shuddering with cold, fearing an Apache attack. Peering into the gloom cloaking the surrounding countryside, they heard the voice of Vargas proclaiming: "Do not be afraid, I am a Catholic, and when the sun rises you will be able to see my standard bearing the image of the Blessed Virgin." To reassure themselves the Indians asked the Spaniards to sound a trumpet, which they did. When day broke, several exhortations to peace

were made. The dike holding the water supply was broken and the Spaniards gave a show of force; the Indians eventually accepted their offer of peace toward the end of the day. Two unarmed Indians advanced, and Vargas dismounted and embraced them. The Spanish commander entered the town and the palace accompanied only by two Franciscans, while the army remained outside at the request of the Indians, who claimed that the women and children were frightened; in fact Vargas did so against the advice of his men. This mark of confidence won him a cordial welcome on the part of the populace, who enthusiastically replied to his cries of "Viva el rey" (Long live the king!) as he raised the royal pennant three times in the square and then knelt while the priests intoned the Te Deum Laudamos.

Vargas withdrew to spend the night with his troops nearby who remained on the alert; this further reinforced the first good impression he had made. His rest was undisturbed, for he had reconquered the capital of the kingdom without bloodshed. In the course of the days that followed, the chiefs of several townships came to Santa Fe to render obeisance, and their visit to the Pecos and Taos regions resulted in the submission of those tribes and of those at Sia and Jemez. Twenty-three towns had been pacified, and more than 2,000 Indians were baptized. All this had not cost the Crown a single *maravedi*, apart from the salaries of 50 men belonging to a relief force from Parral, in Mexico.

However, not everything would go well for Vargas. After his return to El Paso on December 20, he set about rebuilding the capital, returning the settlers to their homes and coaxing the farms into production once more. On October 4, 1693, an expedition set out, consisting of 100 Spanish soldiers, Indian allies, 70 families, 18 friars, 1,000 mules, 2,000 horses, 900 head of cattle, 18 wagons and three cannons. The expedition reached Santa Fe on December 16 surrounded by considerable tension, although there were no incidents en route. However, the Indians refused to leave the town, which had been returned to the Spanish councillors. In the days spent trying to get them to withdraw voluntarily, 21 Spaniards froze to death for lack of shelter. When the Indians were forced to withdraw, 70 of their leaders were executed.

Little by little the community flourished, the weather improved, the friars began to set their ruined missions in order, farms began to produce crops again and new families from Mexico were brought in. The first new settlements after Santa Fe and El Paso were founded at Santa Cruz, in the spring of 1695, and Bernalillo, in the fall, on the former site of the property of the Bernal family. A new uprising broke out on June 4, 1696, but did not spread like the previous conflict. Vargas took quick and severe action against the rebel tribes, who had killed five friars and 21 soldiers. By the end of the year the danger had passed, and the Pueblo Indians had submitted.

When Vargas asked to be appointed for a second term of office, however, his petition was refused, and January 1697 saw the arrival of his successor, Pedro Rodríguez Cubero, who, a few months later, imprisoned him and kept him behind bars for a year and a half. When King Philip II heard of this treatment, he ordered his immediate release. In Mexico City Vargas obtained a hearing and was appointed for another term of office as governor and captain-general of New Mexico; he also received the title of marquis de la Nava Brazinas. Royal justice had been served, and the governor-marquis returned to his beloved city of Santa Fe in November 1703.

Vargas had much to do to restore order after the disastrous administration of his enemy, Cubero; one of his first tasks was the reorganization of the army. A military campaign against the Apache seemed necessary, and the captain-general set out at the head of his troops. At the beginning of April they headed for Bemalillo, and later made for Taxique, where Vargas was overtaken by great pain and a high fever. Carried to the home of the *alcalde* of Bernalillo, Fernando Durán y Chávez, Vargas realized that his end was near and drew up his will on April 7. He died on April 8, 1704, and was buried under the high altar in the parish church of San Francisco. The name Vargas deserved to rank among those of the great *conquistadores*.

The Eighteenth and Nineteenth Centuries

The 18th century saw the missions flourish, with perfect harmony between the religious and civil authorities, and continual improvement in the quality of everyday life. However, the peaceful coexistence of settlers and Pueblo Indians was disturbed around 1763 by increasing French encroachment and the repeated attacks by the nomadic tribes, the Navajo, the Comanche and, in particular, the Apache. The reason for this increased hostility lay in the fact that the Comanche had moved southward from 1706 onward, forcing the Apache to shift westward, so that

both nations were on the warpath, gripping the kingdom of New Mexico in a pincer movement. The most irreconcilable enemies of the settlers were the Apache, for the powerful and dangerous Comanche kept periods of peace during which trading took place, and the *comancheros*, or traders, entered Indian territory freely. However, two campaigns dealt a heavy blow against the power of the Comanche: in 1717, the expedition led by Juan de Padellao, and, in 1779, another led by Governor Juan Bautista de Anza, during which the Indian chief perished. As for the Apache, the hesitant attitude of the Spaniards disappeared between 1775 and 1790, and successive attacks on the Indians' hideouts brought the destruction of their camps. Constant fighting took place, and many were killed. Clever military leaders such as Hugo O'Conor, Teodoro de Croix and Juan Bautista de Anza forced the Apache, faced with the prospect of annihilation, to sign peace treaties, which were to remain in force until 1810.

In 1746, José de Escandón was appointed lieutenant general. He proved influential in the regions around the Rio Grande and as reorganizer of the whole northwest of New Spain. In 1774, Eusebio Durán y Chávez set out from his estate near Albuquerque in order to visit King Charles III. In view of the deserving work done by his family on the Rio Grande, the king appointed him *alcalde* for life, with rights of succession, of the towns of Sandia, San Felipe, Santo Domingo and Cochiti. In 1776, Friar Silvestre de Escalante departed from Santa Fe to seek a pass in the West via which a link could be established with the California missions; and, in 1807, Zebulon Pike arrived at Santa Fe as a prisoner, the first American to have dared to enter the kingdom of New Mexico. With the publication of his diary upon return home he informed his fellow citizens for the first time of the existence of a vast land that might one day be theirs.

In 1805, Santa Fe was the starting point for a tour by Doctor Larrañaga to the different settlements and missions to administer preventive vaccinations, a great discovery of modern medicine; in spite of the reluctance he met, he was able to report mass vaccinations at El Paso, Cebolleta, Albuquerque, Santa Fe, Laguna and Zuñí. That same year, Governor Joaquín Real Alencaster accepted a proposal concerning trade with the Plains Indians that two natives and one James Pursley had brought to him in 1805. Alarmed at the infiltration of foreigners, this same governor warned his superiors of the need to reinforce the defenses of the province; but there was little relief, for Napoleon had invaded the Spanish peninsula and King Ferdinand VII had abdicated in his favor. In response to the convening of the

Spanish parliament, or Cortes, at Cadiz, in 1811, Pedro Bautista Pino, a rich landowner, was sent as a representative of New Mexico; he spent three years in Spain submitting an urgent program of recommendations for the benefit of his province.

Santa Fe Today

Santa Fe has preserved impressive harmony in its streets and squares and in its old and modern buildings, which are no more than two stories high. The old style is encouraged in new buildings; the modern post office, the Museum of Fine Arts, the Institute of Indian Arts and Crafts; even the gasoline stations and other shops fit in perfectly well with the Borrego, Rodríguez and Boyle houses, and with the later 19th-century buildings of Felipe B. Delgado, Juan José Prada or Padre Gallegos, as well as the San Miguel Mission and "The Oldest House."

Presiding over the central square in the town is the Governor's Palace, a simple building with a large portal piercing the main facade, reminiscent of so many buildings in Spain. In the entrance two plaques inform visitors of the history of the place, which was cleverly restored in 1909. The building houses an exhibition of archaeological and historical exhibits from the Southwest. The palace was begun in 1610, the year in which the city was founded, and suffered only slight damage at the time of the Indian rebellion in 1680.

The plaza is attractive, with its well-planned garden and peaceful Spanish atmosphere. At one corner stands the Museum of Fine Arts, and on the opposite side, a plaque states that Governor Antonio del Valle built the Church of Nuestra Señora de la Luz on that spot between 1754 and 1760; popularly known as La Castrense, this church was used by the garrison and remained standing until 1859, when it was torn down by Simón Delgado to build his own house. The church had been deserted since the American occupation and, in 1851, Judge Baker tried to install his court there, but had to desist, faced with the objections of Donaciano Vigil, the temporary governor. The reredos from La Castrense was first used in the Church of San Francisco, which once stood on the same site as the Cathedral of San Francisco; today, it can still be seen in the modern Church of Cristo Rey at one end of the town, with a painting of St. James (Santiago Matamoros) in the center, the Holy Family above, and St. Anthony and St. Ignatius on either side.

The cathedral is easily reached, for it is only one block along San Francisco Street. The foundation stone was laid on July 14, 1869, and the two towers are still unfinished. Building was urged by Archbishop Jean-Baptiste Lamy, who arrived in 1850, and the style is consequently markedly French and entirely alien to the local environment; in addition to the reredos with the statue of La Conquistadora, the cathedral contains the tombs of two Franciscans, Father Asensio Zárate (who died at San Lorenzo de los Pecuries on May 8, 1759) and Father Jerónimo de la Llana (who died at Quarai on April 1, 1759), as the Spanish inscriptions recount.

Standing not far from the center of Santa Fe, San Miguel Mission dates back to 1610 or, at the latest, 1620, according to Friar Alonso de Benavides, the Franciscan who became its custodian in 1625 and author of the well-known *Memorandum on the New Mexican Missions (Memorial sobre las misiones neo-mexicanas)*; thus it is the oldest church in use in the United States. Its age was confirmed by excavations carried out in 1955, evidence of which can be seen by the public through a sort of hatch near the high altar. Part of the roof was gutted by fire at the time of the 1680 uprising; the church was reopened after being renovated following the reconquest by Vargas, and in 1710, it was completely restored by the marquis de la Peñuela, as one of the beams in the church records. In 1630, Simón Delgado built a third roof, and further repairs were carried out in 1887 after a storm had caused the collapse of the tower in 1872.

The altar dates from 1798 and was a generous gift from José Antonio Ortíz. Replaced in the 19th century by another Victorian altar, it has now returned to its original place following restoration of the church, which was completed in 1955. Above the altar can be seen the "Santo," or statue of St. Michael, in a perfect state of repair, and six oil paintings depicting the archangel defeating Lucifer, St. Teresa of Avila, St. Gertrude, St. Louis and St. Francis, all dating from between 1710 and 1776 and in the possession of the church ever since. Two other oil paintings proved to be beyond repair, and their places have been taken by two paintings of St. Anthony and St. Francis. A great sonorous bell, now in the sacristy, bears an inscription that reads: "San José rogad por nosotros. 9 de agosto de 1356" (St. Joseph, pray for us. August 9th, 1356). This bell reached the New World in 1712 from Andalusia; the date of its arrival at Santa Fe is not known.

Opposite San Miguel Mission is the oldest house in the United States. The main walls were built of adobe in the 12th and 13th centuries by the Pueblo Indians inhab-

The town of Cimarron, New Mexico, was once a famous stop on the Santa Fe Trail. New Mexico Tourist Bureau.

iting the region, and the Spaniards made the most of them to erect the present building with adobe bricks. It was saved from the destruction of 1680 because the Indians respected it due to its indigenous origin. The mission has been used by a wide variety of people—Indians, witches, missionaries, slaves and adventurers—and all kinds of legends surround it. Restored in the manner of a home of two centuries ago, it is now a museum.

Not long ago the Colonial New Mexico Historical Foundation was established and has been installed in the capital's Old Cienaga Village Museum, the former Rancho de las Golondrinas, about eight miles southwest of Santa Fe.

Hotels such as La Fonda (where one wall is covered with a large mural of a map of New Mexico with the

Spanish coat of arms and figures of missionaries and *conquistadores*) retain a Spanish atmosphere. (Other hotels in Santa Fe bear Spanish names as well: El Rey, Hacienda El Gancho and others.) Picturesque streets greet the pedestrian, with such names as Don Gaspar, Don Diego, Coronado, De Vargas, García, Castillo, Delgado, Cerrillos and Agua Fria, among others.

Following the Alameda and the Camino del Monte, one comes to the Museums of Navajo Ceremonial Art and of International Folk Art. A section of the latter is devoted to local colonial art and houses many *santos* (paintings on wood) and *bultos* (sculptures) most of which are on religious subjects, showing a Spanish influence on the native artists of New Mexico, the *santeros*. Many *santos* by the Spaniard Rafael Aragón, who

The archbishop conducts High Mass at the opening of the Santa Fe Fiesta. The fiesta is held during Labor Day weekend each year in celebration of the reconquest of New Mexico by General de Vargas in 1693. New Mexico State Tourist Bureau.

The Museum of International Folk Art sponsors Spanish operettas, or *zarzuelas,* and the great flamenco dancer María Benitez lives in Santa Fe. Open-air performances of Spanish opera (such as *La Vida Breve,* by Carlos Fernández Shaw and Manuel de Falla) are held during the summer in a park nearby, with the Sangre de Cristo Mountains as a backdrop. In 1974, an Institute of Hispanic Culture was established in Santa Fe.

On September 29, 1987, Juan Carlos of Spain and his wife Sofía visited Sante Fe. The king remarked, "Santa Fe is a live relic of our past, and we still feel in her the palpitation of history . . . We feel that magnetism of New Mexico as the Spaniards who first took a chance in these lands must have felt."

Many well-known politicians come from Santa Fe. They include ambassadors, such as Frank Ortiz, Bill Richardson and Edward Romero (the current chief of the U.S. mission in Spain), Congressional Representative Manuel Lujan and Governor Tony Anaya.

arrived in New Mexico in 1820, show more modern Spanish influence. A niche with miniature figures depicts "the great power of God" and a reredos shows a red Holy Child of Atocha; a woolen bedspread or a piece of coarse cloth or carpet speaks of the skillful handicrafts of Hispanic women, while a chest, stool or seat, a cabinet or sideboard, a chair, table and bench for example, recreates the atmosphere of a home in 18th-century New Mexico.

This building, which houses the art gallery and auditorium of the state museum of New Mexico, is patterned after the American Indian pueblos. U.S. Department of State.

Western New Mexico

The state is divided down the center by the Rio Grande, and the western area is crossed in its turn by the imposing Rocky Mountains, which are subdivided at different heights into several mountain chains, almost all of which have Spanish names. The low winter temperatures, like the dry heat of summer on the plains, caused the *conquistadores* and settlers much hardship, and they suffered greatly from the cold when the provision convoys did not arrive or the Indian attacks or other circumstances destroyed their dwellings or heavy clothing.

In the spring of 1539 the exploratory party set out on foot led by Friar Marcos de Niza. Esteban went ahead with an advance guard and sent messages back to his leader, relaying the size of the townships encountered by means of crosses of varying sizes sent back with Indian runners. One day he sent a cross as large as a man. The joy of being close to their goal was marred by the death of Estebanico and his companions, who had advanced toward the town without waiting for the main party. The Indians with Friar Marcos refused to proceed any farther, fearing that they might meet the same end as their fellows. Only two consented to accompany the friar, who, at some distance from the town, had a vision—aided by his powerful imagination—of what he hoped to see: buildings with gold facades and terraces capable of holding a thousand people, forming a town larger than Mexico City. His enthusiasm knew no bounds when one of the Indians told him that this was the smallest of the now legendary cities of Cibola. Friar Marcos gave thanks to Divine Providence, called the lands he had discovered Reino de San Francisco (the Kingdom of San Francis), built an altar with stones topped by a cross and took possession of the whole region of Cibola in the name of the emperor. Returning in the summer, he reported to Coronado and the viceroy on the lands through which he had passed, the affability of the natives and the explorations carried out.

In view of this good news, the viceroy (who refused the enthusiastic offers of Hernán Cortés to command the venture) commissioned Francisco Vázquez de Coronado to undertake the expedition on June 6, 1540, and, thanks to the funds provided by Antonio Mendoza and Coronado's wife, the expedition set out with 336 fully equipped men, 100 Indians, 552 horses, 600 mules, 5,000 sheep and 500 head of cattle. Most of the members of the expedition were under 30 years of age (the general was just 30 himself) and were Spaniards, with the exception of the odd Portuguese, Scot, Sicilian or German. Only three of them were accompanied by their wives, one of whom acted as a nurse, and rode over 6,000 miles in the course of this venture. There were, of course, several religious men, led by Friar Marcos de Niza. Since Cibola was close to the Gulf of California—according to the reports submitted by the friar—a naval formation would accompany the party on land and would serve as a supply depot for their provisions. "It is perhaps the most elaborate single enterprise of exploration in North American history," wrote the historian Edward Gaylord Bourne.

The travelers soon realized that the Franciscan friar's accounts were exaggerated: the soil was not fertile, nor were the Indians so friendly, nor was the land they sought near the sea. (André Maurois describes the Indians as tricksters.) Coronado decided to turn in a northeasterly direction and lead an exploratory party of 50 men who, in view of the slowness of the main convoy, could announce the good news that undoubtedly awaited ahead. Entering Arizona, Coronado traveled through the southeast corner of the state (as far as what is now Highway 66) and then turned eastward. In mid-summer, the advance guard sighted the town glimpsed by Friar Marcos, and to their great chagrin it was not shining with gold, but only consisted of a few miserable adobe huts, for the Zuñi Indians who dwelt there lacked even sufficient food for subsistence. Friar Marcos was duly reprimanded.

The ruins of the city of Cibola, known as Hawikuh by the native people, still stand 14 miles southwest of the Zuñi pueblo, near Ojo Caliente. On July 7, 20 Indians met their death when they opposed the forces of the emperor. When the disappointed *conquistadores* entered the township, they found that the women and children had fled and that the uninteresting town was quite empty. Coronado at once set up his headquarters here and called the town Granada.

He wasted no time in sending out his lieutenants to explore the surrounding country: Pedro Tovar departed northwest on July 15, and in the space of a month crossed the land of the Hopi Indians and heard of the existence of that geological marvel, the Grand Canyon, which was to be seen for the first time by Europeans when García López de Cárdenas departed from Hawikuh with a patrol on August 25.

Four days later, Hernando de Alvarado marched eastward to try to confirm the optimistic reports obtained about that territory. It was not until the end of November that the vanguard of the expedition arrived under the command of Captain Tristán de Arrellano. Coronado allowed the expedition to rest for three weeks, before moving on to Alcanfor (near present-day Bernalillo), a site chosen by Cárdenas which pleased him when he arrived early in December. A garrison of 30 men was left at Granada until the expedition withdrew to New Spain in April 1542.

Francisco Sánchez Chamuscado and his party were the next Spaniards to visit the place 38 years later, followed by the merchant Antonio de Espejo in 1583. In 1598, Juan de Oñate assigned the area to Father Andrés Corchado, but missionary work did not begin in earnest until 1629, when Friars Roque de Figueredo, Agustín de Cuellar and Francisco de la Madre de Dios founded the first mission at Hawikuh. In 1632 Fathers Francisco de Letrado and Martín de Arvide suffered martyrdom, and as a result Governor Francisco de la Mora Ceballos sent a punitive expedition out commanded by Tomás de Albizu. An Apache attack caused the death of Father Pedro de Avila y Ayala on August 7, 1670; however, his successor is not thought to have died during the 1680 rebellion, for he had fled to the mountains with the Indians, who only returned when Diego de Vargas assured them that there would be peace.

Following the route taken by the Spanish expeditionaries on their journey eastward, and particularly the exploratory patrol led by Hernando de Alvarado (through country that seems to coincide with local Route 53) one comes to El Morro (47 miles southeast of Gallup). This famous rock, now a national monument, has 27 inscriptions carved on its various faces by as many *conquistadores* who camped in the surroundings and wished to leave a record of their passing. The oldest of these inscriptions was that made by Juan de Oñate on April 16, 1606, but the one by Coronado, if it ever existed, has not been preserved; others were made by Governor Francisco Manuel de Silva Nieto, Don Diego de Vargas, Governor Félix Martínez, José de Payba y Basconcelos, General Juan Pérez Hurtado, the bishop of Durango Don Martín de Eligacochea, in 1737 (the first bishop to visit New Mexico), and others. It is an imposing place, and a monument to the exploits of the Spaniards in United States territory.

Farther east is Acoma, now an Indian reservation, an impregnable rock sighted for the first time in 1540 by Alvarado and his men (by whom it was named Acuco), and subsequently by Antonio Espejo. On December 4, 1598, the nephew of the leader of the Oñate expedition, Captain Juan de Zaldívar, stopped at Acoma with 30 soldiers. At the invitation of the local people, not suspecting any treachery he climbed the narrow path leading up the steep rock accompanied by six of his men; a wave of Indians fell upon them, and only three escaped to tell the story.

When Juan de Oñate heard about the assault, after asking the friars for their counsel on a just war, he decided to attack Acoma and appointed Vicente de Zaldívar, the brother of the dead captain, to lead the

Bridge leading to Inscription Rock, part of El Morro National Monument of New Mexico, where 17th- and 18th-century Spanish explorers, such as Oñate and de Vargas, carved their names. New Mexico Department of Development.

punitive expedition. They arrived at their destination on January 21, 1599. As day broke on the following morning the first assault took place, and after only three days of raging battle, Acoma surrendered after the town had been burned down and 600 Indians had been killed. Severe justice was meted out to the prisoners and 60 Indian girls escorted by Captain Pérez de Villagrá—the future author of the poem "La Historia de la Nueva Mejico" (The History of New Mexico) recounting the assault on Acoma—were sent to the viceroy to be distributed among convents for their conversion and education. Oñate reported the events to his superior and asked him for reinforcements, which he obtained in the form of 73 soldiers, who reached the general's camp on Christmas Eve 1600. But the justice meted out after the assault had ended was to be one of the charges against Oñate during the customary court of inquiry conducted when he left New Mexico in the spring of 1605, having lost his only son in the course of the last skirmishes with the Indians. According to historian Charles Lummis, the assault on Acoma is one of the most extraordinary feats in American history. (In his novel *Los Tontos de la Concepción*, the Spanish writer Ramón J. Sender describes the difficult access to Acoma until a few years ago, via a secret route, on all fours and in single file.) In April 1998, a peace agreement was finally signed by Reginald Pasqual, chief of the Acoma Indians, and Manuel Gullón de Oñate, descendant of Juan de Oñate, and by witness Francisco Alvarez Cascos, the vice president of the Spanish government. Vice President Alvarez offered the New Mexico state governor a replica of the banner of the *conquistador* in the Plaza Mayor of Santa Fe. Later that year, to celebrate the fourth centennial of Oñate's arrival, the state government decorated some attending Spanish soldiers.

Corresponding to such a visit, the governor of New Mexico, Gary Johnson; the governor of San Juan Pueblo, Earl Salazar; and a group of Native American dancers paid a visit to Spain in November 1998. Johnson was decorated by Alvarez Cascos; the prince of Asturias opened an exhibition, "Reencounter of Three Cultures," in the Museo de América and a symposium took place in the Casa de América, commemorating the 400th anniversary of the Spanish arrival in New Mexico.

A few miles from Acoma lies Laguna, near Highway 66. Here, the San José Mission was built in 1699. Curiously enough, one of the most famous lawsuits in the history of New Mexico took place in 1852 between the towns of Acoma and Laguna over possession of a painting of St. Joseph, which was said to be miraculous and had been presented by King Charles II to Father Juan Ramírez. As long as it was at the mission at Acoma, the town enjoyed a prosperity that contrasted with the calamities of all kinds experienced by Laguna. Finally, a delegation of neighbors from Laguna, by dint of arduous negotiations, obtained the loan of the St. Joseph painting for a month; after that term—in light of the fortunate results of the presence of the painting—the people of Laguna refused to return it, and so months and years went by. The verdict of the court in 1852 ruled in favor of Acoma, and when a delegation was sent to fetch the miraculous picture, they found it beneath a tree halfway to their destination; they restored it to its original church, where it is still venerated.

Central New Mexico: Albuquerque

Albuquerque was rebuilt during the second period of Spanish rule in New Mexico, following reconquest of the kingdom by Diego de Vargas in 1692. A number of settlements had been planned, and on April 23, 1706, Governor Francisco Cuervo y Valdés decreed the foundation of this township under the name of La Villa de San Francisco de Alburquerque (in time, the first letter *r* in "Alburquerque" was to disappear), in honor of the duke of Alburquerque, then viceroy of New Spain. (The government in Madrid later ordered that the patron saint be changed from St. Francis Xavier to St. Philip Neri, patron of the first Bourbon king of Spain, who was on the throne at that time.) The new town was sited on the former estate of Luis Carbajal, which had been destroyed during the 1680 rebellion. Thirty families were brought from Santa Fe, and the governor donated a bell, the altar and the chasubles for worship. The official buildings and living quarters were built little by little according to plan, with the traditional *plaza mayor*, or *main square*, in the center, just as it can still be seen to this day.

Although it was the third city to be built here, Albuquerque is now the leading city in New Mexico in size and population. La Alianza Federal de Mercedes centers at Albuquerque the claims formulated before the pertinent authorities by the 75 heirs of those people benefiting by land grants made by Spain. For that reason, even today the law courts must study Spanish law.

The University of New Mexico, with adobe buildings, has its campus in Albuquerque. Its art museum and the collections kept in the Indian Pueblo Cultural Center highlight the state's early history. At the Spanish History Museum, maintained by Elmer Martinez and his family, the history of Spanish family names and of New Mexico in general can be traced.

Los Padillas Mission, founded in 1705, and Los Lunas, in 1716, both lie south of Albuquerque. In the same direction, along Highway 85, lies Isleta. Here, the local people did not take part in the general 1680 rebellion of the Indians, and Isleta served as a refuge for Governor Antonio de Otermín during his retreat from Santa Fe; the inhabitants settled near El Paso in the new township of Isleta del Sur. The Isleta Mission was known first as San Antonio and then San Agustín. Tradition has it that the remains of Father Juan de Padilla were buried there and that he walks through the streets of the town once a year.

Two other towns on the same route are Belen and Socorro, the latter named by Oñate to commemorate the friendly welcome given him by the natives. Like those from the mission at Sevilleta, they joined the Spaniards in their retreat toward El Paso in 1680. The founders of the Nuestra Señora del Socorro Mission were Fathers Antonio de Arteaga and García de Zúñiga, who planted the first vines in New Mexico within its walls. These missionaries were also the founders of San Antonio de Senecú, destroyed by the Apache in 1675.

Southeast of Albuquerque, not far from these missions, were others said to have "died of fear." They were attacked by the dreaded Apache and Comanche and had already been abandoned by the time of the 1680 rebellion. The Inmaculada Concepción Mission at Quarai was started up in 1629 by Father Francisco de Acevedo, as were the nearby missions of San Miguel de Tajique and San Gregorio de Abó; his successor, Father Gerónimo de la Llama, who died in 1659, was buried in Santa Fe's cathedral. In the vicinity of the ruins of Abó can be seen the two large churches and the Monastery of Gran Quivira. So long synonymous with the Promised Land or a place of fabulous wealth, as far as the Spaniards were concerned, the name Quivira was eventually given to this modest place. In spite of the size of the buildings erected, as evidenced by their walls, Quivira proved incapable of withstanding the ravages of the warlike Indians, for the inhabitants had no protection during the Indian raids. According to the Spanish scholar Manuel Alvar, the ruins of the Inmaculada Concepción Mission are as impressive as those of the classical world: "In few places will you feel such frightening insignificance as in front of the door of the ruins at Quarai."

Along the highway north from Albuquerque to Santa Fe, the road climbs little by little for over 50 miles, while the countryside changes color and vegetation becomes more sparse as the road emerges from the green basin of the Rio Grande. This route was first used by Hernando de Alvarado and his men in September 1540. After traveling through scenery that reminded him of Castile, he called the river Río de Nuestra Señora, or River of Our Lady this being one of the many names that the Rio Grande has received in the course of history. (A commemorative plaque along the way details its past.) The Indians whom he met on his journey greeted him most cordially. This encouraged him to press on north toward Taos, guided by Bigotes (Mustache) one of the chiefs from Pecos. Following the report that he sent to his general, Coronado, García López de Cárdenas with 14 knights and a group of Indians were entrusted with preparing a suitable place for the whole expedition to spend the winter. The district chosen was that of the Twelve Cities of Tiguex, on the west bank of the river, opposite present-day Bernalillo. Shortly afterward, in October, the first snows fell and the Spanish billeter saw no alternative but to beg the chief at Alcanfor, one of the nearby townships, to move his people to another township and leave his as accommodation for the Spaniards so that the main force would have somewhere to shelter when they arrived. The chief consented and departed with his subjects. The place chosen pleased Coronado when he arrived in December. The vanguard of the army joined them shortly after New Year's Day 1541.

Faced with resistance on the part of the town of Moho, some 10 miles farther north, Coronado launched a full-scale siege in February. After 77 days, the expeditionaries returned to their quarters, having achieved a victory intended to serve as an example for other neighboring Indians. Acting on information furnished by an Indian prisoner, El Turco, that the fabled Great Quivira lay to the north, the general departed with Father Juan de Padilla and a party of his men. The rest spent the winter at Alcanfor under the command of Captain Tristán de Arellano.

In the course of the following summer they went on expeditions into the surrounding regions but by the end of the summer began to question the fate of their leader. Leaving Francisco Barrionuevo in command, Arellano proceeded with 50 men to Pecos. There, he met Coronado, who returned discouraged, for neither Quivira nor the rich lands he had been promised by El Turco existed. (The traitor was executed.) On October 20, 1541, Coronado wrote to the emperor from Alcanfor expressing his disappointment; moreover, cold, hunger and insects seemed to hold dim prospects for the Spaniards camping comfortably there.

On December 27, Francisco de Coronado went out riding with Captain Rodrigo Maldonado, and they began to race. Owing to a faulty harness, Coronado fell and one of the hooves of his companion's horse struck his skull; he spent many days between life and death, but, once he recovered, was overcome by a desire to return home. He gave orders to return to New Spain. The expedition departed in April 1542. In view of the outcome, the Emperor Charles V ordered that no further funds be made available from the royal coffers for more ventures of this type.

Other missions were founded in this area as well. The mission of San Bartolomé was established in 1581 near Bernalillo by three friars, Agustín Rodríguez, Francisco López and Juan de Santa María, escorted by Francisco Sánchez Chamuscado with only eight soldiers and five Indians. The missionaries had obtained permission for their expedition on the grounds of the need to convert the Indians in the north, who were frequently victims of the slave hunters supplying workers for the newly established mines. They had crossed the Mexican frontier on June 5, 1581, near El Paso, and had headed up the Conchos River and later up the Rio Grande near Socorro. They got as far as Taos in the north and, as has been seen, as far as Acoma and Zuñí in the west. They must have shown great diplomatic ability to have been able to move about peacefully with such a small party over such a wide area. But, eventually, the friars suffered martyrdom, while Chamuscado met his death on his return journey, in April 1582. Hernando Gallegos, one of the survivors, reported the journey for posterity.

In Alameda, the ruins of the mission of San Francisco are still standing not far from the village of Santa Ana, which also has the remains of its old church. Also nearby in San Felipe (given this name by Castaño de Sosa), a mission built by Father Cristóbal de Quiñones in 1605. All of them were affected by the destruction wrought in 1680. That was not the case, however, with the mission of Santo Domingo, which was found intact by Governor Antonio de Otermín during his retreat southward, although its three friars (Francisco Antonio Lorenzana, Juan de Talabán and José Montes de Oca) were martyred on August 10. The mission was saved from fire but was not so fortunate when the river flooded. When rebuilt in 1885, it was moved a short distance away. Today, its annual festivities on August 4 attract people from the surrounding area.

Along Highway 44 one comes to the Sia pueblo, in the vicinity of which Friar Alonso de Lugo built the mission of Nuestra Señora de la Asunción in 1598. The local

Indians joined in the rebellion of 1680, and, when Governor Domingo de Cruzate attempted to reconquer New Mexico, it was at Sia, on August 1, 1689, that the bloodiest battle of the whole revolt took place: 600 Indians died and many were taken prisoner; they were never to forget this hard-learned lesson and gave Diego de Vargas Zapata Luján their cooperation when he appeared a few years later. Along the road, at Jemez, stand the ruins of three missions, San Diego, San José and San Juan. Captain Francisco Barrionuevo called the seven villages found in 1541 by the name Aguas Calientes, which coincides with modern Hot Springs. Not far from Highway 25 lies the township of Cochiti, a particularly attractive place with a well-known annual festival on July 14 called the Rain Dance. Discovered by Juan de Oñate in 1598, the township boasts old San Buenaventura Mission, built by Vargas to replace the earlier one which had been burned down, two kivas and a picturesque square in the center of the town.

Missions in Northern New Mexico

The first town along the road from Santa Fe to Taos is Tesuque, built after 1694 to the west of the original township, which was abandoned at the time of the 1680 rebellion. Two friendly Indians hastened to Santa Fe bringing news of the revolt. The leaders therefore decided to start the revolt earlier than planned, before the Spaniards could react, and it was at Tesuque that the first bloodshed took place on August 9, when the Spaniard Cristóbal de Herrera was murdered. Father Pío, who was absent at the time, was killed the following day.

The Nambé Mission, 13 miles away, was founded in 1598 by Father Cristóbal de Salazar; one of his successors, Father Tomás de Torres, was martyred in 1680, and his church was destroyed. The present one was built in 1729 at the expense of Governor Juan Domingo de Bustamante in order to accommodate the steadily growing number of converts. However, its appearance today is not entirely authentic; like other missions in New Mexico, its restoration has given it a modern appearance at the expense of its early character.

Set in a solitary region, the shrine Santuario de Chimayó is the goal for many who trust in its fame for miraculous cures; young and old alike, men and women, on horseback, in automobiles or on foot, lame or sick, all come to pray fervently and join the local residents in their worship. It is not known when this spot at Chimayó was found to be miraculous, but as early as 1816 the owner, Bernardo Abeyta, erected a large church. Tradition has it that a small quantity of earth from Chimayó diluted in water cures any ailment if whoever receives it has sincere faith. No money is charged for treatment, but devotees make offerings as a sign of gratitude. The Chimayó Shrine gave rise to a major incident in the middle of the last century: Mrs. Carmela Chávez inherited the shrine from her father and, with the money collected, carried out major repairs in the church and distributed large donations. Her relationship with the Franciscans was always excellent, even with the French Franciscans who replaced the Spaniards. However, a young priest came to the parish and wanted to force Mrs. Chávez to make a gift of the shrine to the Church on pain of excommunication. When she refused because it was her livelihood, he excommunicated her; however, when the bishop heard, he did not uphold the decision of his subordinate, and peace was restored. An image of the Santo Niño de Atocha (Holy Child of Atocha) is venerated in the shrine.

The mission of San Ildefonso is in this region along the road leading to Rito de los Frijoles. In the 1680 and 1696 revolts, Fathers Luis de Morales, Antonio Sánchez de Pro, Francisco Corvera and Antonio Moreno met their deaths, and two fierce battles took place in the surroundings between the rebel Indians and the troops led by Vargas, who won the day. The nearby mission of Santa Clara, although built in 1782, was kept in a good state of repair for a long time and was one of the finest examples of architecture of that type; however, when work began with a view to modernizing the structure, the roof fell in and the whole building collapsed.

Santa Cruz and San Juan

Santa Cruz lies some 28 miles north of the capital. Colonists who had accompanied Juan de Oñate settled here but were forced to flee or were killed at the time of the rebellion so that its definitive foundation did not take place until 1694, when 66 families were brought here by Vargas, making it the second town in the kingdom after Santa Fe. It was called La Villa Nueva de Santa Cruz de los Españoles Mexicanos del Rey Nuestro Señor Carlos Segundo (The New Town of Holy Cross of the Mexican Spaniards of Our Lord King Charles the Second), although the name given on documents was La Villa Nueva de Santa Cruz de la Cañada. The settlers were accompanied by Father Antonio Moreno, who died shortly afterward. The church erected by him was replaced by another in 1733, which stands to this day and is the largest and prettiest of the churches left by Spain in New Mexico; cruciform, it has two chapels, dedicated to the Virgin of Mount Carmel and to St. Francis. The statue of St. Francis is reputed to be one of the best made in the 17th century. Santa Cruz became the Spanish capital of the northern district of the province. In 1837 Mexican troops led by their governor fought in the area against rebel Indians, as did the army of Colonel Sterling Price in 1847, against the Taos Uprising.

About six miles from Santa Cruz lies San Juan. When Juan de Oñate reached New Mexico in July 1598, the Indians received the Spaniards with every show of friendship and vacated the early township in order to accommodate their unexpected guests. In view of such courtesy Oñate called the place San Juan de los Caballeros (Saint John of the Gentlemen). The relationship between the Indians and the Spaniards, however, would not remain so cordial.

San Juan was the home of Popé and therefore became the center of the anti-Spanish plot. It was from here that the order went out on August 10, 1680, for all the pueblos to rise against the white men, not less than 400 of whom were killed. Once the old system had been restored, the baptized Indians renounced Christianity and washed themselves with yucca juice to purify themselves; the use of the Spanish language was forbidden. Wearing ceremonial dress, Popé became the emperor of the Pueblo Indians and subjected them to his despotic rule for the next few years. Due to the resentment this unleashed and the renewed attacks of the traditional enemies of the Pueblo Indians, Popé was deposed, though restored to his post shortly afterward. His premature death prevented his witnessing the return of his enemies in the person of Vargas in 1692. Vargas built a fine church here, which would have survived if it had not been pulled down in 1913 to make room for a utility building. Today, San Juan is a progressive, industrious locality, where large crowds gather at the annual festivities on June 24.

Less than a mile to the west of San Juan is San Gabriel, the first Spanish settlement in the Southwest and the original capital of New Mexico. Founded by Juan de Oñate on September 8, 1598, on that day the mission chapel was consecrated, initially dedicated to St. Francis, and later to St. Michael. The existent ruins are the oldest remains of any European building erected in the United States. Several celebrations were organized for the event: a sung mass, attended by the chiefs from the area; a play; a tournament on horseback; a bullfight; and a simulated battle between Moors and Christians. On the morning of September 9, Oñate held a meeting with the Indian chiefs present and made a speech about the benevolent policy of Spain toward indigenous peoples and the duty of the latter to take an oath of fealty to the king of Spain.

San Gabriel became Oñate's capital and headquarters, and the starting point for expeditions to the outlying areas. It was from San Gabriel that the expedition against Acoma departed, and Oñate likewise left San Gabriel with a party of his men bound for the north. San Gabriel was to be the first experiment in farming with seeds and cuttings brought from Spain, including wheat, rye, oats, peas, onions, melons, peaches, apricots, figs, almonds, walnuts, chestnuts, vines and plums; it also saw the establishment of stock breeding with sheep (for their wool), cows and horses having been brought by the expeditionaries. Irrigation systems were set up and the Indians were given the necessary instruction for subsequent development. At the same time, the Spaniards became acquainted with native products like chocolate and tomatoes, and enjoyed the abundance of pine nuts.

The importance of the settlement was inevitable. It could not be otherwise, in view of the broad concessions obtained by Oñate (who was married to a granddaughter of Hernán Cortés) from the king, who not only had appointed him governor with a salary of 6,000 ducats a year, but sometimes exempted him from payment of up to one-tenth of the *quinto real,* or royal share of one-fifth of the fruits of conquest, and authorized him to distribute land and grant titles of *hidalgo.* The venture had developed well from the outset, and the group (composed of 129 soldiers, nine friars, 83 wagons and 7,000 head of cattle, in addition to 400 settlers—130 with their wives and children—and a considerable number of Indians) had reached El Paso without difficulty on April 26, 1598. On April 30, following a solemn mass, the governor had taken possession of the land of Rio Grande on behalf of his king and queen, and had knelt before the cross; the expeditionaries enjoyed a play, quickly written and rehearsed by Captain Marcos Farfán de los Godos, in which the *conquistadores,* friars and Indians appeared.

The University of New Mexico carried out archaeological research on this spot during the summers of 1959 and 1960, and some very outstanding finds were unearthed by Professor Florence Hawley Ellis, thanks to which the original site of San Gabriel has been clearly located.

Taos

A short way into the mountains near Taos is the mission of San Lorenzo de los Picuries, a well-preserved building in which a statue of St. Lawrence can be seen at the high altar, together with other statues of Our Lady of Mount Carmel and St. Joseph. Its out-of-the-way situation has been its salvation, for it preserves its original style with very little later influence. The township was first visited by Coronado, and building of the church was begun shortly after 1598 by Friar Francisco de Zamora; it was consumed by fire in 1680, as was the missionary, Friar Matías Rendón. The present building dates from the years after 1706, and one of its peculiarities is that the walls were built with mud poured into molds in the same way that reinforced concrete is made today.

Taos, 80 miles from Santa Fe, comprises the localities of Taos, Ranchos de Taos and Pueblo de Taos. The pueblo at Taos, with its five-story native communal buildings, were first seen by Hernando de Alvarado in 1540, and by Francisco de Barrionuevo the following year; they named it Valladolid. Nevertheless, Taos was the name that was to endure as the Spanish transcription of the native name Towih. Oñate visited the place in 1594 and assigned it to Friar Francisco de Zamora, who erected the mission of San Jerónimo. It would play an important role in Spanish-American history, not only owing to the martyrdom of the missionaries in 1680, but also because the pueblo at Taos played a leading part in the revolt of 1694 against Vargas, who had to lay siege to the townspeople in order to overcome them. The Indians would use it as a redoubt for their defense during the rebellion in 1847, when 150 died as the sound walls were shot to pieces by United States artillery; another uprising in 1910 was prevented by the arrival of the state militia.

The pueblo has preserved much of the language, religion and lands that Spain had bequeathed to it, and even the customs, dance and music such as "Los Matachines," of which recordings have been made.

The Millicent Rogers Museum houses a magnificent collection of native arts and crafts, including those by the well-known local artist María Martínez.

At Ranchos de Taos, the mission of San Francisco de Asís has been preserved in very good condition; built of adobe in 1755, it is 36 meters long and has two towers at the entrance. It is considered one of the most picturesque missions in New Mexico. The high altar has eight old paintings of great artistic merit. On the left-hand side of the transept crossing hangs a mysterious painting depicting Christ, which, when seen in the daytime, shows him full face and barefoot; but, if seen at night, he is bearing a cross with his shadow casting a silhouette illuminated by distant lights.

Taos, which is also known as Fernández de Taos or Don Fernando de Taos, is a locality equidistant between the previous two places, which are three miles away. It was hit by the destruction of the rebellion in 1680, when only two inhabitants survived: Fernando de Chávez and Sergeant Sebastián de Herrera. Reestablished after Vargas's reconquest, in December 1761, it experienced a terrible attack by the Apache, which forced Governor Manuel de Portillo y Urrizola to send out an expedition, during which more than 400 Indians met their deaths. Incidents from its post-Spanish history include the murder at his home of the first American governor, Charles Bent, in 1847, and also the sojourn of Kit Carson, who is buried in the local cemetery. The ministry here of the well-known Padre Martínez, from 1826 until 1856, is also noteworthy.

Taos celebrated the 350th anniversary of its second foundation in 1965, when an attractive medal was minted for the occasion. At the present time the locality is inhabited predominantly by artists, and art galleries abound. Although most of the buildings of Taos are modern, they all maintain a unified appearance in keeping with the original style of adobe building. In the Kit Carson State Park two Spanish flags fly permanently (together with those of the United States and New Mexico), and Spanish flags can be found on other buildings as well.

Pecos

Pecos, east of Santa Fe, has an exciting history. It was most important in the days of the Santa Fe Trail, but its last inhabitant, Agustín Pecos, disappeared in 1838; all the rest had moved little by little to Jemez, discouraged by their defenselessness against the constant attacks of enemy tribes and, particularly, owing to the terrible epidemics of measles, which had decimated the population twice. However, the church is still standing, and the caves of the Indian ancestors are still visited by their descendants.

Coronado visited the pueblo in 1540, at a time when the population was numerous and there were two large communal buildings. In 1582 Antonio de Espejo appeared, a wealthy merchant who, with a team of 13 soldiers and several Indians, in addition to Father Bernardino Beltrán, had decided to investigate the fate of Father Agustín Rodríguez and others who had accompanied Francisco Sánchez Chamuscado. They were welcomed by the Indian tribes encountered on the way in Alcanfor, Acoma and elsewhere and, to their consternation, were informed of the violent deaths of those whom they were seeking. Farther west, Espejo succeeded in collecting samples of minerals, which he took with him on his return journey.

Another expedition crossed the Rio Grande near Eagle Pass in December 1590. Comprised of a party of 170 people accompanied by a substantial baggage train, it was commanded by Gaspar Castaño de Sosa, lieutenant governor of the province of Nuevo León (New Leon). He had arrived at Pecos at the head of an exploratory patrol, after barely saving his skin; he had trusted too readily the cordial welcome of the natives. Showing an audacity worthy of the boldest *conquistadores*. Castaño with 19 soldiers and 17 Indian allies was not deterred by the substantial fortifications behind which the inhabitants had taken up their positions; with the help of two small cannons, he won the battle on the last day of the year and forced his opponents to accept peace. He later set up his headquarters at the spot that would in time be called Santo Domingo, and at all times observed a strict policy of protecting the Indians. However, he had carried out his expedition without a royal commission and was arrested; thinking that Captain Juan Morlete had come to bestow honors on him on behalf of the viceroy, he found that he was bearing an order for him to return to Mexico, where he was subsequently tried and found guilty. The chief of Pecos in 1680 was Juan Ye, who warned the missionary Father Fernando de Velasco of his imminent death; he did not save himself, however, but was killed when he went to Galisteo to warn his colleague there. Juan Ye cooperated with Vargas during his campaign against Taos.

Other missions in this area included San Cristóbal, San Lázaro, Santa Cruz de Galisteo, San Marcos and San Pedro del Cuchillo y Ciénaga.

Spanish Place-Names

In New Mexico, Spanish names by far exceed English names. The following will give an idea, when it is remembered that many more must go unmentioned: the counties include Bernalillo, Chaves, De Baca, Dona Ana, Guadalupe, Hidalgo, Los Alamos, Luna, Mora, Otero, Rio Arriba, Sandoval, San Juan, San Miguel, Santa Fe, Sierra, Socorro and Valencia; localities include Alameda, Alamogordo, Albuquerque, Alcalde, Archuleta, Belen, Bernalillo, Brazos, Capitan, Cardenas, Carne, Carrizozo, Cebolla,

Cienaga, Cimarron, Columbus, Cornudo Hills, Corona, Costilla, Cuba, Cuchillo, Del Macho, Dulce, El Huérfano, El Rito, El Vado, Encino, Española, Estancia, Flora Vista, Gallegos, Glorieta, Golondrinas, Guadalupita, Hachita, Hermanas, Isleta, Laguna, La Huerta, La Liendre, La Madera, La Mesa, Las Cruces, Las Vegas, Loco Hills, Los Almos, Los Chávez, Los Hueros, Los Lunas, Luis Lopez, Madrid, Magdalena, Mangas, Manuelito, Malaga, Mesilla Park, Mimbres, Mora, Mosquero, Ojo Feliz, Padilla, Penasco, Peralta, Pinos Altos, Portales, Ranchos of Taos, Raton, Rio Penasco, Rio Hondo, Romeroville, San Anto-nio, San Felipe, San Juan, San Rafael, Santa Cruz, Santa Fe, Santa Rita, Santa Rosa, Santo Domingo, Socorro, Solana, Tierra Amarilla, Trujillo, Villanueva and Yeso. As for the mountains, some are named after religious themes such as: Animas, Fra Cristobal, Guadalupe, Magdalena, Nacimiento, Sacramento, San Andres, Sangre de Cristo, San Juan, San Mateo and San Pedro; others are called after animals: Burro, Caballo Gallinas, Gallo and Portrillo or after features of nature: Alamo Huesco, Cebolleta, Dátil, Los Pinos, Manzano, Mimbres, Pedernal, Pinos Altos and Sandia.

◆ *ARIZONA* ◆

Arizona's very name, clearly of Spanish origin, gives some indication of the nature of the landscape. The intense heat is accompanied by a lack of water, which in the course of time has led to the formation of a tremendous desert covering two-thirds of the state. The scarcity of water and scanty vegetation in this part of the country are clearly visible from the air. The general appearance is pink, and although plains are predominant, there are a number of ridges crossing the center of the state in a north-south direction that give the surface a rolling appearance; they make the view less monotonous and give the impression of a huge sea of sand in which, for mysterious geological reasons, waves have been petrified before breaking: Santa Rita, Sierrita, Rincon, Santa Catalina, Santa Rosa, Quijotoa, Cimarron, Picacho and San Francisco are some of their names. The bold, enduring Spaniards, accustomed to hard climates, were equal to the arduous task of exploring and civilizing this part of the Southwest whose features are like those in the north of Mexico and, in particular, in the adjoining state of Sonora.

Several rivers cross the region and have gone down in history owing to their important role in colonizing enterprises: Santa Cruz, Gila, San Carlos, Verde. Their use for irrigation, prospecting artesian wells and the building of dams in the north have made it possible for flowers to brighten the desert landscape and large oases in valleys and elsewhere to provide delicious vegetables and fruit. These results, which were originally obtained long ago by the Spanish missionaries in the southern areas of the state, have increased enormously in recent times, particularly since the building of Boulder Dam; a third of the waters from the dam come to Arizona.

There is no record of the explorer Cabeza de Vaca and his three companions having set foot in the state of Arizona, but there is no doubt whatsoever that, as a result of his reports, the viceroy of New Spain sent Friar Marcos de Niza to reconnoiter accompanied by the former Moorish slave, Estebanico. In 1539 they were the first to set foot in Arizona territory, on their way to the now legendary Seven Cities of Cibola.

In 1540, Friar Marcos himself accompanied the expedition, which was organized as a result of his own report, under the command of Francisco Vázquez de Coronado and following the same route as before. Coronado and his men therefore entered Arizona territory from the southeast, and maintaining a northerly direction (along what is now Highway 66), they turned to the right and headed for New Mexico. Many geographical names in Arizona commemorate the venture—Coronado National Memorial Park, Coronado Mesa, Coronado Trail, Coronado Mountains, Padilla Mesa and Fray Marcos Mountains—as do streets in Tucson and Phoenix.

If missionary zeal is to be admired anywhere in the world, then certainly in this arid region it deserves special homage, in view of the climatic obstacles among others with which the sons of St. Ignatius and St. Francis had to contend. The land, which they named Pimería Alta after the Pima Indians, was relatively sparsely populated when the Spaniards appeared. Consequently, the

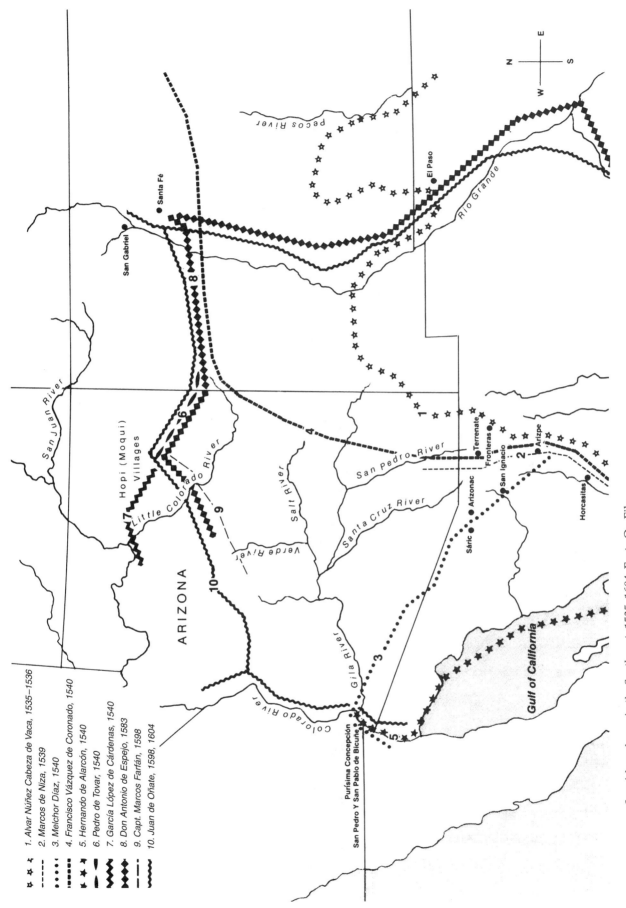

1. Alvar Núñez Cabeza de Vaca, 1535–1536
2. Marcos de Niza, 1539
3. Melchor Díaz, 1540
4. Francisco Vázquez de Coronado, 1540
5. Hernando de Alarcón, 1540
6. Pedro de Tovar, 1540
7. García López de Cárdenas, 1540
8. Don Antonio de Espejo, 1583
9. Capt. Marcos Farfán, 1598
10. Juan de Oñate, 1598, 1604

Spanish explorers in the Southwest, 1535–1604. Facts On File.

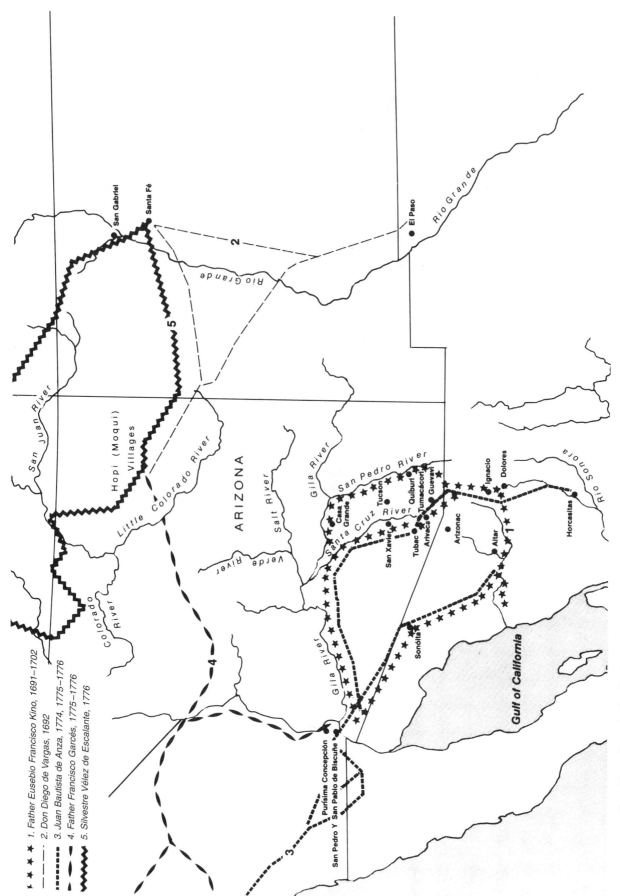

Spanish explorers in the Southwest, 1691–1776. Facts On File.

Legend

1. Father Eusebio Francisco Kino, 1691–1702
2. Don Diego de Vargas, 1692
3. Juan Bautista de Anza, 1774, 1775–1776
4. Father Francisco Garcés, 1775–1776
5. Silvestre Vélez de Escalante, 1776

Map labels

San Gabriel
Santa Fé
El Paso
Rio Grande
Rio Grande
San Juan River
Hopi (Moqui) Villages
Little Colorado River
ARIZONA
Colorado River
Colorado River
Salt River
Verde River
Gila River
Gila River
San Pedro River
Santa Cruz River
Casa Grande
Tucson
San Xavier
Tubac
Arivaca
Tumacácori
Quíburi
Guevavi
Ignacio
Dolores
Arizonac
Altar
Sonóita
Horcasitas
Río Sonora
Gulf of California
Purísima Concepción
San Pedro Y San Pablo de Biscuñe

enthusiasm of the Jesuits initially—from Father Eusebio Francisco Kino until the expulsion of the Jesuits in 1767—and of the Franciscans later—from the time when they replaced the former until, after the independence of Mexico, the missions disappeared—often had to overcome discouragement at the scant yield achieved with great effort and many leagues of territory covered. A burning spirit, like the burning climate, must have imbued these missionaries, bringing them to the northernmost territories of Spain's dominions to expose themselves to the trials that distance imposed upon them and to suffer the periodic devastation brought upon them by the fierce Apache, who in a single night would destroy the material and spiritual work of many years by death or the fear of death that they put into the converted Indians. It is true that the peaceful Sobaipuri or Papago Indians were ripe for evangelization, as is proved by the flourishing missions at Sonora and those set up in what is now the state of Arizona, but the rebellion of the Pimas in 1751 and the constant Apache attacks undid much that had already been achieved and gravely hampered the already arduous work of spreading Christianity.

Having once decided to build a fine mission, the Spanish Franciscans did so at San Xavier del Bac (not far from Tucson) in such a way that they could not be outdone, for it is the finest and, today, the best-preserved example of Spanish religious architecture in the United States. The handicrafts (pottery, fabrics and basketry, as examples) of the Navajo Indians inhabiting the reservations in the northwest of the state are renowned and much sought after all over the country thanks to their exceptional quality.

The Grand Canyon and the Lower Colorado

The first European to hear about the Grand Canyon was Spanish captain Pedro de Tovar, who as lieutenant to Francisco Vázquez de Coronado, received orders to explore for not more than one month in the region northwest of Hawikuh, where the vanguard of the Spanish forces lay. Having departed on July 15, 1540, he visited the villages of the Hopi Indians and from them heard reports about the existence of the canyon. However, since time was short, he returned to his starting point without seeing the canyon.

In view of the reports given by Tovar, Coronado dispatched a party on August 25, under García López de Cárdenas, who had the privilege of being the first European to sight this geological marvel. However, in spite of various attempts, he was unable to cross the canyon. The chronicler of the expedition, Pedro de Castañeda, informed the world of this discovery. Another Spaniard was later to be the first to cross the canyon, 236 years later: Father Francisco Garcés, who crossed the canyon from west to east on June 26, 1776, in the course of one of his exploratory expeditions. A few months later, on November 8, 1776, the Franciscans Silvestre Vélez de Escalante and Francisco Atanasio Domínguez would use the same crossing on their return journey from the expedition, which took them as far as Lake Utah. The spot became known as El Vado de los Padres, or Crossing of the Fathers. At the canyon information bureau there is a historical exhibition that traces the paths of Cárdenas and Father Garcés, and the translation of Castañeda's report is displayed. In the southeast of Arizona there are also heights or hills bearing the names Cárdenas, Coronado, Morán and Escalante, and at the end of the southwest tour, at Hermit's Point, a bell from one of the Spanish missions serves as a last reminder of their presence. A monument to Major John Wesley Powell, the first American to travel through the canyon in 1869, can be seen at one of the observation points looking out over the canyon, but there is no monument to the Spanish pioneers.

In order to bring provisions to the Coronado contingent mentioned above, some ships commanded by Hernando de Alarcón sailed up the Gulf of California and even up the Colorado River between California and

San Xavier del Bac Mission in Arizona was constructed of adobe brick more than 200 years ago. According to legend, the padres left one tower unfinished to avoid paying taxes to the Spanish Crown. Ansel Adams.

Arizona. However, in view of the lack of any news of Coronado's party (which arrived after they had departed), the captain decided to sail for home. Another Spaniard who set foot on Arizona soil in search of Alarcón, with whom he had arranged a rendezvous, was Melchor Díaz, a soldier and *alcalde* of Culiacán in command of a party of men.

Fifty years were to go by before the Spaniards explored these regions again, and so it was that Juan de Oñate crossed them from east to west in the fall of 1604, and retraced his steps in the following April. He had departed from San Juan, New Mexico, and came close to the mouth of the Colorado River (which he named), in the Gulf of California, in search of pearls and safe havens. That was to be the last expedition of this fine ruler.

A Spanish mission was established in Yuma by General Commander Teodoro de Croix in 1779 and directed by two Franciscan fathers, Francisco Garcés and Juan Díaz; there was also a *presidio* and a settlement of colonists. Relations between the settlers and the Indians were not very good, however, particularly due to the Spanish cattle encroaching on native crops. Things came to a head when an expeditionary party passed through Yuma and spent a few days resting here; commanded by Captain Fernando Rivera y Moncada, this party was traveling from Sonora to California. Irritated by the fact that the travelers' horses were using their pastures, the Yuma fell upon the white men on July 17, 1781, and killed Rivera, Garcés, Díaz and 100 other people. Pedro Fagés led three punitive expeditions on orders from Croix and succeeded in freeing 74 settlers who had been taken prisoner. The possibility of the Yuma repeating this bloodletting led the Spanish

The mission at the Southeast Tumacacori National Monument. Southwestern Monuments Association.

authorities to do without the overland communications route to California for a time, and communications were therefore conducted by sea alone.

In Winterhaven, California (near Yuma, Arizona), a memorial statue to Father Garcés in a town square is a reminder of the lives lost by the Spaniards in opening up the West.

Northern Arizona: Tusayan

During his expedition, Juan de Oñate visited an area that was to become the future province of Tusayan. There is a record of his passing in the inscription at El Morro Rock, a few miles away in the state of New Mexico, its walls acting as a record of the passing of a number of *conquistadores* and missionaries. Inhabited by the Hopi Indians (known as Moquis by the Spaniards), constant attempts were made to Christianize this area following the Oñate explorations. In fact it had been visited previously by Pedro de Tovar, accompanied by Father Juan de Padilla and 18 horsemen. They were not welcome. Arriving by night in the vicinity of the township of Awatobi, they waited in concealment until discovered by the Indians at dawn. Undeterred by the presence of the strange four-footed animals, the Indians put up a stout although useless resistance against the attempts of the Spaniards to pass through.

If Father Marcos de Niza—and consequently, Coronado—had not turned eastward, the much sought cities of Cibola would have been thought to be those in Hopi territory and not those of the Zuñi Indians. Some of the Hopi townships still exist and form part of a reservation that is included, in turn, in the much bigger reservations of the Navajo Indians, occupying the northern half of the state of Arizona and part of New Mexico. About 60,000 Indians live in these reservations, the two Apache reservations in the east, the Papago Indian reservation in the south and in the smaller ones of the Gila Indians not far from Phoenix, as well as in those near the Grand Canyon at Hualpai. In August, the Dance of the Snake and the Flute are still performed alternately some years at Hotevilla, Shipaulovi and Shongopovi, and other years at Walpi and Mishongnovi.

The San Bernardino Mission was constructed in Arizona in 1629. It was in the Hopi locality of Awatobi and was founded by Fathers Francisco Porras, Andrés Gutiérrez and Cristóbal de la Concepción, who reached the province of Tusayan on the feast of St. Bernardin. Other missions founded by these priests at the same period include San Francisco de Oraibi, San Buenaventura de Mishongnovi, San Bartolomé de Shongopovi and Kisakobi. The start of their missionary work was fruitful and was partly due to a miracle attributed to Father Porras when a son of the chief recovered his eyesight. However, this bonanza was short lived; on June 28, 1633, Father Porras was poisoned by the tribal witchdoctors and died; his companions are supposed to have met the same fate, although this is not certain. Subsequently, Fathers José de Espeleta, José de Trujillo, José Figueroa and Agustín de Santa María ran missions in the area until the Pueblo Indian rebellion of 1680, in New Mexico, when they perished at the hands of the Hopi Indians. According to a tradition that has come down to us, Espeleta and one of his companions were thrown off the cliffs at Oraibi. At the time of the reconquest of the territory by Vargas in 1692, the Spanish general marched to Tusayan and received the submission of almost all the Pueblo Indians. The chief of Awatobi even asked him to send a missionary, and as a result Father Garaycoechea visited Tusayan in the spring of 1700. Waiting for him at Awatobi was the church that had been burned down during the uprising and now rebuilt, and 73 Indians who wished to be baptized. But in the rest of the villages he was met with hostility, and when he departed, it was vented on their fellow Indians at Awatobi, who were taken by surprise one night and annihilated in revenge for their good will toward the Christians; their homes were completely destroyed.

In his diary, Father Vélez de Escalante recounts how he spent eight days at Tusayan in June 1775. He was the first missionary to venture into this territory after Father Garaycoechea, but when he realized the unswerving opposition of the Indians to evangelization, he recommended that a *presidio* be established. While there, he had the idea of linking Santa Fe with California by a route circumventing the canyon on the northern side. This he did the following year, when he departed from the capital of New Mexico on July 29, 1776. On his return journey to Santa Fe via the Crossing of the Fathers, he visited the Hopi Indian villages on November 16. Just previously, Father Francisco Garcés had spent the night of July 2, in the Hopi villages after crossing the canyon for the first time while on his way to the mission of San Xavier del Bac.

To the north of the Navajo reservation, about 120 miles from Flagstaff, stands Inscription House, so-called due to the barely legible "Carlos Arnaiz 1661," carved on one of the walls. It is not known who he was, although he may well have been one of the many Spaniards who ventured into the area on his own initiative and wished to leave some record of his passing.

Father Kino and Father Salvatierra in Southern Arizona

Apart from Spanish expeditions from New Mexico into northern Arizona, other more fruitful expeditions were undertaken in the south after 1680, following the Pueblo Indian rebellion. It was the Jesuit fathers who bore the brunt of this venture, among them, Father Eusebio Francisco Kino, a native of Segno, in the Tyrolean Alps. During his tenure as a professor at the University of Ingolstadt, he vowed to devote himself to the conversion of the Indians if he recovered from fever. From 1687 to 1711 he devoted his life to preaching to the Indians in the north of New Spain. He set up as many as 29 missions with 73 *visitas*, or missionary chapels (without a resident missionary), and he baptized more than 48,000 people. Eight of those missions were in the territory of modern Arizona.

Starting from the mission of Nuestra Señora de los Dolores, at Sonora, he visited tribe after tribe until he had made 13 expeditions into the state. In this way he became acquainted with practically all of south Arizona and drew up maps that are still admirable for their accuracy. His last visit to Arizona was in 1702. Subsequently, he remained at Dolores until March 1711, when, aged 70, he went to Magdalena to consecrate the chapel served by his fellow Jesuit Father Agustín de Campos. During the ceremony he was suddenly taken ill and died shortly afterward. Father Luis Valverde, who attended to him on his deathed, recounts that his bed consisted of two bullock skins used as a mattress, two blankets of the type used by the Indians and a pack saddle for a pillow. (The Mexican government announced the discovery of his remains in May 1966.)

In his apostolic work, from 1691 onward, Father Kino was assisted by another man, who accompanied him and was to complete his spiritual mission: Father Juan María Salvatierra. Appointed superior of the Society of Jesus at Sinaloa and Sonora in 1690, it fell to Father Salvatierra to set up the missions in Lower (Baja) California, with Loreto as a base. In 1701, Fathers Kino and Salvatierra set out together on their memorable journey westward to determine if California was a peninsula and if there was an outlet to the sea. Although they skirted the coasts of the gulf, they were unable to reach the northernmost tip because their mounts were exhausted, but they did see the opposite shore in the dusk and deduced that there was no passage for ships through it. Father Kino confirmed this on two further occasions and made maps of his findings. Another inseparable companion of the missionary was Captain Juan Mateo Manje, who shared his vicissitudes and did his utmost with his men to protect the "Sotana Negra" (black soutane), as the Indians called Father Kino. This missionary's wanderings have become known thanks to the discovery of his diary (in Spanish) by Hispanic scholar Dr. Herbert E. Bolton.

When a delegation of Sobaipuri Indians who had settled on the banks of the Santa Cruz River requested a missionary presence, Fathers Salvatierra and Kino proceeded to found San Gabriel de Guevavi at a spot near Nogales, on the present frontier with Mexico. Father Juan de San Martín took charge of the mission, with San Cayetano de Calabazas and San Luis de Bacuancos as chapels of ease. After the death of Father Kino, no missionaries remained at Guevavi until, in 1731, Father Bautista Grasshoffer was sent there. At the time of the Pima Indian rebellion in 1751, the priest at Guevavi was saved although not so for Fathers Francisco Xavier Saeta, Enrique Ruhen and Tomás Tello, who resided at Sonoita, Arizona, and Caborca, Sonora. They died together with about 100 other Spaniards, most of whom were miners working recently discovered mines. The rebellion was led by the Indian Luis Saric, who enjoyed the prestige of the title of captain general of the Pimas of the Mountains granted by Spanish governor Diego Ortíz Parrilla. The inspector of the Jesuits, Father Juan Antonio Balthasar, subsequently drew up a report criticizing the governor.

Although the missionaries returned to Arizona in 1752, there was no other permanent missionary at Guevavi until 1754. In 1763, Friar Ignacio Pfefferkorn took charge there and was succeeded by Friar Jimeno and Friar Pedro Rafael Díaz. When the Jesuits were expelled from Spanish dominions by decree of King Charles III in 1767, a Franciscan, Juan Crisóstomo Gil Bernabé took over Guevavi: the mission was then given the name Santos Angeles de Guevavi. Owing to the indifference of the Indians and the attacks by the Apache on several occasions, the mission declined quickly until it was abandoned in 1784. The walls crumbled, and time and treasure hunters finally destroyed it. The site now lies on private property. Some excavations have been carried out by archaeologists from Arizona State Museum; nevertheless, there is nothing standing today recalling the existence of the missionaries on this spot.

Tumacacori and Other Missions

In addition to Guevavi, the mission of Jamac was founded as a chapel of ease on a Sobaipuri ranch, like the Sonoita and Calabazas Missions. Little is known about the establishment and duration of the Jamac Mission, and as for its site, it is only known to have been in the Santa Cruz River valley, near the Mexican frontier. Not far away was San Marcelo de Sonoita, founded by Father Kino in the course of one of his journeys and later known as San Ignacio de Sonoita. It was here that Father Enrique Ruhen was murdered at the time of the Pima rebellion, on November 21, 1751. It was visited again years later but, like Guevavi, was abandoned in 1784. There are no ruins left of this mission.

There are traces, however, together with an explanatory plaque, of San Cayetano de Calabazas (close to Highway 19), a few miles from Nogales. It is said to have been founded by Father Kino, in 1694, for the service of the Papago Indians. When a church and a house were built for the missionary in 1791, it became an independent mission. When the Spanish missionaries disappeared after the independence of Mexico, the Calabazas region came into the possession of Manuel de la Gándara, governor of Sonora in the 1840s. The ranch, with its big adobe mansion surrounded by an army of peons and cowboys, became one of the most famous places of the day. Governor Manuel de la Gándara built a stone military fort on his property to protect it from Apache attacks. A change of political fortunes forced Gándara to flee to California, with the result that his ranch was lost and its buildings eventually collapsed.

Some other chapels of ease belonging to Guevavi included Arivaca, San Francisco de Ati and San Luis Bacuancos, which were probably abandoned following the death of Father Kino.

To the east of Nogales lies the Coronado National Memorial Park, a large park run by the National Park Service and so named because the Spanish *conquistador* is supposed to have entered Arizona in the vicinity. A little farther away, in Cochise County, the Rancho de San Bernardino once existed; it was very famous in the history of Arizona cattle breeding. The origins of this property covering 73,240 acres, part of which now belong to Mexico, lay in a grant of land by the Mexican government to Ignacio Pérez in 1822. It passed through several hands before coming into those of the famous sheriff John Slaughter, who lived there from 1890 until his death in 1922. The house, in Spanish style, became one of the meeting places of the Southwest. It took its name from the ruins of an old mission lying in the district about which nothing is known other than the mentions contained in the diary of Father Francisco Garcés.

Following the Santa Cruz River valley (along today's Highway 19) some 45 miles from Tucson, lies Tumacacori. Father Kino reached this area in 1691 and called the township San Cayetano; he said Mass there in a shed improvised by the Sobaipuri Indians themselves. In 1698, according to the missionary, there were already an adobe house, wheat fields and herds of cows, as well as flocks of sheep and goats. The mission, which acted as a chapel of ease for the Guevavi mission, became very prosperous, but the Pima rebellion was a setback. The following year, the Indian township moved to the present site of the mission, which had formerly been at some distance, and a *presidio* was founded for protection at Tubac, two and a half miles north; the mission was renamed San José de Tumacacori.

Following the expulsion of the Jesuits, San José was attacked in 1769 by the Apache, who took the inhabitants by surprise at midday, and burned their houses and church, of which only ruins were left standing. When Guevavi had to be abandoned, Tumacacori became a permanent mission and center for the other missions in the district. The present church is believed to have been begun in 1800 and was in use by 1822. The independence of Mexico brought with it the decadence of San José. The expulsion of Spanish missionaries, settlers and soldiers; the lack of defenses at Tumacacori to thwart the attacks of the Apache; and the lack of the annual aid given by the Spanish government, which the Mexican government did not continue to provide for upkeep, were some of the reasons for the mission's decline. It was sold to a private owner in 1840, and in 1848 the Indians abandoned the place, taking with them the statues and other objects of value to San Xavier del Bac, where they are today.

At Tumacacori the ruins of the church are in a relatively good state; with the exception of the mortuary chapel, of the buildings have collapsed. Archaeologists of the National Park Service are carrying out fruitful research work to locate the granaries, stables and accommodations. The floor of a recently built school has been pulled up to show the flooring of the old buildings beneath. The floor of a sort of cloister is in very fine condition. It is curious to note that most of the damage caused to the mission in general and to the church in particular has been caused by people hunting for Jesuit treasures. Here, as elsewhere, many believed the story of gold being buried by the Jesuit priests before departing; this supposition is of course mistaken, for church construction did not begin until 30 years after their departure. Reconstruction, which has not yet been completed, has been undertaken in various stages, one of the last in 1949, thanks to the procedures invented by Rutherford J. Gettens and Charlie R. Steen. Guided by the paintings that have been rescued, these experts came to the conclusion that the interior decor could be recreated fairly accurately.

The church is not large; apart from the walls and roof that are standing, there are traces of the side altars, the pulpit, the high altar and the characteristic colors of the reredos, which are still bright. There was once a choir, but the arch supporting it has collapsed. The dome over the high altar is in a perfect state of repair and rises to about 35 feet above ground level. It is topped by a lantern, which can be reached from the outside by climbing some steps sculpted out of its surface. The facade of the church rises in three sections: the first, the doorway flanked by two pilasters; the second, a window with similar adornments; and the third or upper section, consisting of a sort of pediment, the whole ending in a semicircle. Near the church is the old cemetery and a modern museum exhibiting a number of dioramas explaining the history of Tumacacori (the construction of the church, Apache attacks and the resistance of the defenders), a small equestrian bronze statue of Father Kino, some pistols and other firearms, sabers, a wooden bell, books used by the missionaries and other artifacts.

Tubac Presidio lies two and a half miles north of Tumacacori, the site of the former *presidio* of Tubac, established in 1752 by order of the governor of Sonara, Diego Ortíz Parrilla, on March 18 of that year, following the Pima rebellion. No trace whatsoever remains of it today, and a museum has been built on the spot in which are exhibited two Spanish flags—one, a white one, with the imperial coat of arms in the center; and the other, red and gold—as well as Spanish military jackets and items relating to the Indians of the area.

In 1745, Tubac had 400 inhabitants, while 10 years later the figure was higher than 500. Its commanders were Juan Bautista de Anza, both father and son (the son was born at the *presidio*). The younger Anza set out from Tubac on his expeditions to California, the first for the purpose of exploring a route from Sonora, and the second (on January 8, 1774), leading a party of carefully selected settlers, who founded San Francisco. Subsequently, the young Anza was to be appointed governor of New Mexico.

In 1754 a church was built at Tubac, dedicated to Saint Gertrude, for the use of the garrison and the Indians of the neighborhood. When Father Garcés founded the city of Tucson in 1772, the Tubac garrison was ordered to move to the new post but did not do so until 1776. Tubac would have been entirely destroyed by the Apache if a group of colonists had not stayed behind and a contingent of allied Pima Indians had not come to its defense. In the ensuing years it declined by stages, until in 1856 some mines were started in the nearby Santa Rita Mountains. Tubac then experienced a few years of plenty and even produced the state's first newspaper, *The Arizonian*. As a result of the order given by the Union government to withdraw all troops eastward when the Civil War broke out, the town was left undefended, and falling prey first to Apache and later to Mexican bandits, its walls crumbled and the rest of its residents migrated to Tucson.

San Xavier del Bac Mission

A path from Tubac to Tucson leads to the Papago Indian reservation and San Xavier del Bac, the prettiest of the Spanish missions in North America. It is unusual in that it continues to minister to the same Indians for whom it was founded.

Father Kino visited Bac for the first time at the request of the Sobaipuri Indians. (*Bac* means "place where underground water emerges.") It is interesting to note his reference to the Spaniards' own conversion; in one sermon, for example, he told the Indians how in ancient times the Spaniards were not Christians and recounted the coming of Saint James the Elder to Spain to teach them the faith, the difficulties encountered by the apostle for the first 14 years, in which he only baptized a few natives and the apparition (at Saragossa) of the Virgin Mary to console him and reveal that the Spaniards would themselves convert the other peoples of the world.

From 1692 onward, Father Kino often returned to Bac, where he was always welcomed cordially by the local Indians and received requests for a resident missionary. In November 1697 he stayed, accompanied by Captain Juan Mateo Manje, in an adobe house, with rafters and a flat roof, that the natives had built for the promised missionary. In April 1700 he ascertained from information provided by the Indians who had gathered at Bac that the blue shells seen in Pimería Alta were from the Pacific Ocean and not from the Gulf of Califor-

nia, thereby confirming his view that California was a peninsula, and the possibility of finding an overland route to the sea. On April 28, 1700, the foundations were laid for the first church, entrusted to the protection of the Spaniard St. Francis Xavier. Father Kino wrote to his superior, Father Leal, asking to be appointed the first resident there. In April 1701, Father Kino returned with Captain Manje to San Xavier and found the township half empty: half of the men had departed as volunteers on an expedition of the Compañía Volante de Sonora, or Sonora Flying Company; commanded by Ensign Juan Bautista de Escalante, the expedition had been organized to punish the Apache, who had rustled horses and murdered six Pima Indians.

The first permanent priest to be stationed here, in 1701, was not to be Father Kino, but Father Francisco Gonzalvo. Following the death of Father Gonzalvo, it was not possible to send new missionaries until 1731, when a Swiss Jesuit, Father Phillip Segesser von Brunegg, arrived and was installed by Captain Juan Bautista de Anza (the elder). However, his presence here was short lived, as was that of his successors, Fathers Stiger, Rapicani, José de Torres and Bauer. Father Alonso Espinosa was the most outstanding Jesuit after Father Kino and lived at Bac from 1756 until 1766. At the time of the expulsion of the Jesuits, Father José Neve was running the mission.

Father Francisco Hermenegildo Garcés, a Franciscan, arrived at San Xavier del Bac on June 29, 1768. Here, at the northernmost outpost of the dominions of Spain, he was awaited by 60 Indian families and an adobe church built by Espinosa. He remained in charge of San Xavier until 1799, although during that period he spent some time away on a number of journeys. In October 1768 he reached the Gila River, where he suffered from apoplexy and went on a second *entrada*, or expedition, the following March, in the course of which he suffered from sunstroke. Apart from some other travels, in between which he repaired the church, he accompanied the younger Anza on the first expedition to California, which lasted from January 8 until July 10, 1774, and also on the second expedition, from October 1775 until September 1776. During those periods the mission was tended by Fathers Juan Gorgoll and Félix de Gamarra, respectively. Friar Juan Antonio Valverde succeeded Father Garcés when he was transferred to Yuma in 1779.

Father Juan Bautista Velderrain, who was posted to Bac two years later, was responsible for the start of construction work on the present church of San Xavier, with funds loaned by Antonio Herreros secured by the prospect of future crops. When Father Velderain died in 1790, he was replaced by Friar Juan Bautista Llorenz, who finished the church in 1797. The names of the technical authors of this architectural marvel are unknown. Some suppose that it must have been Pedro Bojorquez (whose name can be seen on a door) while others claim that it was designed by Hermanes Gaona and his brother. Father Llorenz ran the mission until after 1814, and his successor, Father Juan Vaño, was there at the time of transfer of sovereignty from Spain to Mexico. Friar Rafael Díaz had to abandon the mission in 1828, and from then onward it was left without a spiritual father. Days of abandon ensued, and the building began to suffer from the ravages of time, treasure hunters and troops who sometimes took shelter there.

When the United States obtained the broad territories of the Southwest under the Treaty of Mexico, the land south of the Gila River, including San Xavier, remained in Mexican hands. Later, in 1854, under the Gadsden Purchase, the United States acquired the sector between the present frontier and the Gila River, including the territory discussed here. From 1866 onward priests from Tucson visited San Xavier. Throughout those periods and later, San Xavier and its works of art were saved thanks to the Indians, who cherished them and even took the statues to their homes only to return them later when permanent worship was reestablished. In 1873, nuns opened a school for Indians, and in 1895 the mission was commanded once again by the Franciscan Order. In 1913, Father Ferdinand Ortíz came to live here, and a few years later, Father Nicholas Perschl. The repair work carried out in 1906 saved the buildings and was due to Bishop Henry Granjon; he also devised the arch behind the mission, which is now known by his name.

The facade of the church has two white towers with terraces, the right tower still unfinished; in striking colorful contrast, they flank a reddish central section consisting of three parts: the big doorway, the balcony and the frontispiece, on which appear the lions of Castile. The church has a single aisle, and the transept is sufficiently wide to have, in addition to the high altar, two chapels on each side, rivaling each other in artistic ornamentation. Built of baked adobe (which has given it a marked degree of durability), it is 100 feet long by 20 feet wide. The walls are on average three feet thick. Above the transept crossing is a dome roughly 50 feet high. The high altar reredo in the style of Spanish master José Churruca has in its center a clothed statue of St. Francis Xavier, and above at one corner, the Immaculate Conception, with statues of St. Peter and St. Paul on either side. Crowning the reredos is a bust depicting God the Father, and medallions of Adam and Eve. In the left-hand side chapel of El Salvador (The Savior) is a reproduction of the tomb of St. Francis Xavier, topped with a statue of St. Francis of Assisi. The chapel opposite is under the advocation of Our Lady of Sorrows. One of the frescos in the church is dedicated to the Virgin of El Pilar, and the scallop shells of St. James abound as motifs above the doorways and at many other points in the aisles. Two Spanish lions guard the high altar.

There is a splendid view from the completed tower, whose bells can be heard over a long distance calling parishioners to Mass. From there can be seen the old cemetery and funerary chapel close to the church, the convent of the fathers, the hillock nearby where a grotto like that at Lourdes has been reproduced in recent times, the Indian township and the square in front of the church, which was formerly framed by other buildings. In a little chapel backing onto the church and leading out into the cloister are venerated two Spanish statues brought from Tumacacori; it is here that the resident priests say daily Mass.

San Xavier is the setting for a colorful festival organized by the Indians on the Friday after Easter, in the course of which they commemorate the arrival of the *conquistadores* and missionaries with a parade in period costumes. The white silhouette of its church outlined against the horizon entitles it to the name by which it is known, Paloma del Desierto, or Dove of the Desert.

Tucson

Tucson had its origins in a mission set up in an Indian village in the middle of the desert. Father Kino came here in 1694, when it was El Tusonino cattle ranch. A mission called San Cosme del Tucson was founded as a chapel of ease for the San Xavier del Bac Mission. Tucson is the Hispanicized version of the name of the place in Papago dialect, meaning "at the foot of the black mountain" (nearby Sentinel Peak), and the name was used for the first time by Father Kino on November 1, 1699. On the maps drawn up by the missionary in 1698 and 1701, mention is also made of an establishment called San Agustín del Oyaur, some four miles north of San Cosme, where the priest recommended the foundation of a mission in 1706. Following the death of Father Icino, there was no priest to take charge of the mission and in the ensuing years, the only mention is of San Agustín del Tucson. The efforts of another Jesuit, Father

Middendorff, to rebuild the mission in 1757, only lasted four months: his 10 soldiers were unable to withstand the attack of 500 Indians. In 1762, Captain Francisco Elías González escorted 250 Sobaipuri Indians to settle them at the village, which he called San José del Tucson because their arrival took place on the feast of St. Joseph. The following year, a church was built and given the same name.

The church had already collapsed by the time the Jesuits departed in 1767. When Father Francisco Garcés arrived from San Xavier in 1772, he proceeded to build accommodations, a church and a dwelling for the priest. It is not known exactly when the latter was completed, although in 1797, Father Iturralde visited an adobe church with a roof supported by beams. By the time Father Garcés died in 1781, the township of Tucson comprised the mission of San Agustín and the San José ranch land. As the Indian settlers from various places gradually increased in number, it became necessary to instruct and train them in various handicrafts.

After 1756, Spanish soldiers were posted intermittently in Tucson, but it was not until 1776 that a *presidio* was set up there, on the opposite side of the Santa Cruz River. As a result of the reorganization of frontier defenses recommended by the marquis de Rubí in 1767, the garrison was ordered to move from Tubac to Tucson, a site chosen personally by Hugo O'Conor, the chief inspector of the frontier on August 20, 1775. In the course of the construction of the royal *presidio* of San Agustín del Tucson, the soldiers camped in the pueblo. The first fortifications consisted of a wooden palisade raised by Pedro Allende y Saavedra, who took command on February 11, 1777. (The transfer of the garrison had been carried out under the command of Lieutenant Juan María Oliva.) Adobe walls were built together with the necessary buildings: the work was not finished until 1781, and the area on which it was built was considerable. Tucson therefore became the only walled city in United States history; this defensive nature was clearly necessary to fend off the continual attacks of the Apache. The years between 1780 and 1810 brought with them continued progress at the *presidio,* in which a major role was played by the commandant, José de Zúñiga, previously the commander of San Diego *presidio,* who held this command from 1795 to 1810.

There are no complete records about the formation of the *presidio;* the wall appears to have been about 13 feet high, and the corners of the fortified square had towers armed with two cannons. In the early days there was only one entrance (situated at the intersection of Main and Alameda Streets), although a second gate was added later. The stables were on the north side, with a military square in front of them; the soldiers' quarters lay on the south side giving onto a parade ground, while the granaries and stores were on the east side, together with the chapel. The wall remained standing until the area became a part of the United States, and lay approximately along the line coinciding with Pennington Street as far as the law courts, where it turned down Main Street (Camino Real) as far as Washington Street, along which it ran for some way before turning south to Pennington Street again. All that remains of the walls is a small stretch forming part of one of the buildings on these streets. A substantial town had grown up around the mission of San Augustín in Tucson, but the expulsion of Franciscans in 1828 led them to abandon the town to live at the *presidio.*

Spanish Tucson contributed the sum of 450 pesos to help the rebel colonies achieve their independence from England during the Revolutionary War. Today, Tucson is full of Spanish-style houses, either in the so-called colonial style or adobe houses after the style of those in New Mexico, with churches of all faiths inspired by San Xavier del Bac and a multitude of streets, most with Spanish names, rivaling the prettiest and most poetic names found in any Spanish city. The *conquistadores* and missionaries are honored by street names as well, and towns and regions of Spain are also represented in the nearly 800 Spanish place-names.

The Arizona State Museum in Tucson features the cultures of the Indians of the region. At the University of Arizona is the Museum of Art housing a large collection of works by Spanish painter Fernando Gallego, from the reredos of the cathedral at Ciudad Rodrigo. The collection consists of only half of the paintings in the reredos; even so there are 26, some of considerable size. They are late-15th-century works that suffered serious damage in the course of the two seiges of Ciudad Rodrigo during the Napoleonic invasion of Spain. Sold in 1877, they passed through several hands until they were bought by the Samuel H. Kress Foundation for the museum where they are exhibited. Forming part of the Gallagher Collection in the museum are paintings by the Spanish artists Pablo Picasso, Salvador Dalí, Joan Miró and Hipólito Hidalgo de Caviedes; a work by José Ribera can be seen in another room at the museum.

Not far from the university campus is the Arizona Pioneers' Historical Society, one corner of which is devoted to the Spanish past: two cabinets contain mementos of all kinds (pistols, swords, clothing, books, plans of the Kino missions, reproductions of documents, etc.). A Spanish flag hangs in this room, and a number of valuable documents are kept in a safe by historians. The library holds a collection of interesting artifacts as well. The modern Palace of Justice has a baroque air in keeping with the style of San Xavier; in the garden behind the Town Hall is a large bronze relief memorializing Eusebio Francisco Kino.

There are many Spanish speakers in Tucson; some are descendants of the Spanish colonists, but most have arrived with more recent Mexican immigration and the dialect known as "Pachuco" can also be heard. The novel *Cristo versus Arizona* is set here, and in 1987, the Nobel Prize–winning author Camilo José Cela spent several weeks here and was made an honorary citizen of Tucson.

Phoenix

North of Tucson stand the well-known Pueblo ruins of Casa Grande, now a national monument, visited by Father Kino in November 1694 after hearing reports by Captain Juan Mateo Manje. A little farther on lies Phoenix, the state capital.

There are buildings and churches in the Spanish style at Phoenix, and in the city and surrounding area there are as many as 170 streets bearing Spanish names. In the Capitol can be seen a number of mural paintings called *The Caravan of Arizona's Progress* that depict the state's history.

Some eight miles southeast of Phoenix is the Marcos Niza Rock on which is carved the friar's name and the date 1539, a witness to his search in the area for the Seven Cities of Cibola. Between Phoenix and Flagstaff lies Prescott; a Spaniard, Antonio de Espejo, visited this area, accompanied by nine men, during the winter of 1582–1583. There was one occasion during their journey on which they were confronted by 2,000 Indians.

It is interesting to note, albeit briefly, the history of the mines excavated by the Spaniards, who worked them for many years. Their history started with the expedition led by Espejo, who filed a silver and potassium salt claim at the sources of the Verde River. Juan de Oñate also found silver in 1604 on the banks of the Santa María and Bill Williams Rivers. But it was only after the prospecting carried out by Father Kino in 1705 that the mines were worked actively, and even acquired some importance in the course of the 18th century. Some mines lay in Mariposa County, near Phoenix; others, in the Santa Catalina Mountains, east of Tucson; a few were in the Painted Desert. While the famous "Bolas de Plata" claims were found in 1736 on the boundary with Sonora work began in the copper mines at Ajo in 1750; the Quijotoa district yielded gold in 1774, and in 1777 a mining community was working at Arivaca.

In any case, a golden legend persisted about the wealth of those deposits (the high altar at San Xavier del Bac is said to have contained silver worth $60,000), and they have drawn many prospectors in the 19th and 20th centuries, ever eager to find a seam. Some mines were in fact rediscovered and reopened; the location of many still remains a mystery. Among those reopened is the old Montezuma mine, near Vulture; those whose whereabouts are now unknown include the Iron Door mine, which is supposed to lie north of Tucson.

Among Phoenix's celebratory residents is opera theater director Theo Alcántara.

Spanish Place-Names

A short list of towns and cities in Arizona with Spanish names includes Ajo, Casa Grande, Eloy, Guadalupe, Mesa, Nogales, Patagonia, Picacho, Salome, San Carlos, San José, San Manuel, San Simón, Sierra Vista and Sonora as well as Aguila, Agua Caliente, Amado, Anita, Bonita, Bosque, Camp Verde, Cañon Diablo, Carrizo, Cazador, Concho, Dos Cabezas, Estrella, Ganado, La Palma, Pica, Piedra and Seneca.

PART VI:
THE ROCKY MOUNTAIN STATES

COLORADO

Spanish History

The rugged Rocky Mountains make Colorado one of the most scenic states in the country and the one with the highest average height above sea level. Six hundred peaks rise to a height of 12,000 feet; 300 rise to 12,600 feet; and 52 top approximately 14,000 feet. This topography has had considerable influence on Colorado history as it formed the western flank of the Spanish Louisiana Territory, at least in theory.

Southern Colorado shares a border with New Mexico and was the scene of a number of Spanish explorations. The Rocky Mountains in the center and the lower foothills at the eastern end offer wide valleys, providing a beautiful view, but sometimes hampering communications; this forced the Spaniards constantly to seek more suitable passes. There is no record that the early explorers, Coronado, Rodríguez and Espejo, Sosa or Oñate, set foot in this area, although some historians maintain that Juan de Zaldívar, one of Oñate's nephews, reached the vicinity of Denver and called the river Chato, due to its shallowness, more or less equivalent to the English name Platte.

However it is known that, with the colonizing ventures of Oñate to the south, the Spaniards gradually spread their sphere of influence and slowly secured a command over this area. In pursuing this policy, in 1644 the governor of New Mexico dispatched Juan de Archuleta and a party of soldiers with orders to bring back a number of Indians from Taos, who had taken refuge at a place which was later to be called El Cuartelejo. This expedition was definitely the first known exploration into Colorado territory by Europeans. One of the southern counties of Colorado bears the name Archuleta in honor of the *conquistador* (as does a locality in northern New Mexico). He is thought to have followed the Rio Grande upstream and to have gone as far as the San Luis Valley.

The diary of Governor Diego de Vargas was discovered recently by J. M. Espinosa, who reports that the pacifier of New Mexico set foot in Colorado in the year 1694 and stayed there with his men for several days. This document refers to geographical landmarks bearing Spanish names, which means that, prior to the Vargas expedition, there had undoubtedly already been other explorations that had given Spanish names to this unknown area.

The Vargas expedition left Taos on the night of July 6, 1694, in order to distract the Indian forces, who were alarmingly bellicose and were flocking to the area in increasing numbers following the Spanish reconquest of New Mexico in 1692 after the bloody uprising of 1680. The governor realized that if the Indians attacked he would not have sufficient forces to repulse them; he therefore considered it advisable to seek battle in the open, where the Spaniards would be able to make the most of their maneuverability and their advantage in horses and firearms. In any case, they should not return to Santa Fe by the short route. Preferring to take a roundabout route, they headed north up the Chama River basin, with the party commanded by Captain Lázaro de Misquía and with Mathias Luxán acting as interpreter.

On reaching Arroyo Hondo, Captain Juan de Olgín reported the presence of a large party of Indians whom they engaged in combat shortly afterward; the Spaniards won the day and forced the Indians to flee, leaving five dead and several wounded, together with two prisoners, who informed them that the Indians were aware of the movements of the Spaniards and that they had been following close on their heels since their departure the previous day. After crossing Colorado Creek, they followed Costilla Creek and entered present-day Colorado, where they reached the Culebra River before turning west. Shortly afterward they were faced with the problem of fording the Rio Grande (which Vargas called Río del Norte) but succeeded in doing so on July 10. They spent the rest of that day and the following hunting elk and buffalo to provide the Spanish party with badly needed meat. On July 12, the Ute Indians attacked unexpectedly, but were repulsed and, shortly afterward returned suing peace. As it happens, they had taken the Spaniards for Pueblo Indians—their enemies—in disguise, but realizing their mistake, they wished to resume the friendly relations that they had enjoyed with the Spaniards prior to the rebellion of the Pueblos in 1680.

Skirting the neighborhood of Antonito, they left Colorado territory to slip over the so-called San Antonio Range and reached the Ojo Caliente River and the confluence of the Chama with the Rio Grande. They recrossed the Rio Grande within view of San Juan pueblo and entered Santa Fe without further problems on July 16. Vargas was accompanied by Friar Juan de Alpuente, who was therefore the first priest to set foot in Colorado.

Years later, the Picuri Indians, like the Taos Indians before them, fled to El Cuartelejo; historians do not agree as to whether this occurred in 1696 or 1704 or both. The fact is that Juan Uribarri was dispatched in 1706 to bring them back; he was accompanied by 40 Spaniards and 100 Indian allies. Departing from Taos, they crossed Fernando Creek and headed for the mountains in an easterly direction as far as Urac Creek. There, advised by friendly Indians, they turned north until they reached the dividing line separating the Red River from the tributaries of the Purgatoire River. (The original name of the river was in fact El Río de las Animas Perdidas en el Purgatorio, or The River of the Souls Lost in Purgatory; it had received this name on account of the Spaniards who had died nearby after the priest who had accompanied them died, and were thus unable to receive absolution. This is the origin of the name of the town and the county of Las Animas.) Uribarri and his men crossed the Cuchara Pass, skirted the Spanish Peaks and approached the Green Horn Mountains by crossing the Arkansas River very close to the pueblo. From there they headed toward El Cuartelejo for five days.

There has been some dispute about the precise location of this point: while some claim that it lies in the present-day state of Kansas, historians Herbert Bolton and Alfred B. Thomas place it in Colorado (in the vicinity of Highway 50 today). On this leg of their journey, the Spaniards heard that the French were not far away. Once the group arrived at El Cuartelejo, Uribarri took possession of the country, accompanied by the customary ceremonies, on behalf of the king of Spain, Philip V. According to the report made by Uribarri himself, the royal ensign or standard-bearer, Francisco de Valdés, drew his sword and Uribarri cried: "Gentlemen, Comrades and Friends: let us pacify by our arms the great new province of San Luis and the great establishment of Santo Domingo de El Cuartelejo as vassals of our monarch, king and natural lord, King Philip V, may he live forever." The ensign inquired: "Is there anyone that contests this?" All answered together: "No." The leader of the party then cried: "Long live the King, long live the King, long live the King!" In response, the ensign then sliced the air in all four directions. They then fired their guns and threw their hats in the air.

The Spaniards did not reenter Colorado until 1719, when Governor Antonio Valverde of New Mexico wished to punish the Ute Indians and the Comanche. On September 15, 105 Spaniards and 500 allied Indians departed from Santa Fe following a route similar to that taken by Uribarri; they camped on the banks of Purgatoire, near the site of the future town of Trinidad. Proceeding to the Arkansas River in the vicinity, they had to fight off several groups of bears. They followed the Arkansas upstream for a distance where coincides with the town of Las Animas. Here, they received fairly accurate reports as to the proximity of the French and a few days later, returned to Santa Fe, apparently without difficulty.

Following the reports submitted by Valverde about the closeness of the French and other reports received by the viceroy of New Spain from other sources, a council of war was held in Mexico in January 1720; it was decided that Valverde should send out an expedition to pinpoint the French positions in the Northwest. So, on June 16, 1720, Pedro de Villazur left Santa Fe with 40 soldiers, a group of colonists and traders, 70 Indians and one priest. Taking a similar route to Uribarri, they turned northward from El Cuartelejo and traveled across almost the whole of the modern state of Colorado before reaching the South Platte River, which they followed as far as the state of Nebraska. As we have seen, they were met by the Missouri Indians and nearly all perished in a night attack, with the exception of the priest and some 10 or 12 of the expeditionaries, who succeeded in escaping and recounting what had happened.

The next Spanish visit to Colorado was in 1750, when Bustamante and Tagle led a punitive expedition against the Indians as far as the Arkansas River. A much more important venture was that led by Juan Bautista de Anza (Junior) shortly after taking up his position as governor of New Mexico. The purpose of the expedition was to punish the Comanche Indians, who, led by Chief Green Horn, had murdered a number of Spanish settlers. In August 1779, an army 645 strong left Santa Fe under the command of Anza. Their trail roughly followed the course of the Rio Grande, crossing brooks called Las Nutrias, San Antonio, Conejos, Las Jarras, Los Tumbres (Alamo River) and San Lorenzo (Piedra Pintada Creek). They crossed the river near the present-day locality of Del Norte and continued to skirt the Rocky Mountain massif until they reached the vicinity of what is now the township of Salida. After skirting the Arkansas River, they went down the Saint Charles River and then crossed it. On September 3, they encountered the forces of Green Horn, whom they defeated overwhelmingly near Rye; the Indian chief was killed in the course of the battle. The nearby mountains and a river were given his name. In 1932 a memorial was built by the Historical Society of Colorado nearby (along Highway 85), in Pueblo County, recounting the end of the "cruel scourge" of the Indians and the victory won by Anza, whose expedition is acknowledged as having been the first to cross certain parts of Colorado.

It is curious to note that shortly after defeating the Comanche, Anza tried to implement a policy of seeking peace with them. While the Comanche had originally settled in the south of Wyoming and north of Colorado, at the beginning of the 18th century their movements brought pressure to bear on the Apache. The resultant southward pressure of the Apache made it necessary for the Spaniards to abandon the missions in the San Gabriel and San Saba region in Texas. Then movements of the Apache also spread terror throughout the area and in the north of New Mexico. Hence the Spanish preoccupation between 1750 and 1786 with warding off Comanche and Apache attacks. Following the establishment of the interior provinces in 1776, the first general commander, Teodoro de Croix, made it a cardinal point of his policy to make peace with the Comanche. Governor Tomás Vélez Cachupín of New Mexico had already achieved a truce in 1762, and the commander of Natchitoches, Athanase de Mezières, who had made peace with several Indian nations, had directed his efforts to obtaining peace with the Comanche from 1769 to 1776. But the uprising of the thirteen colonies and the breaking of the peace by the Comanche, apart from other factors, led to a renewal of hostilities, the defense of New Mexico by Governor Pedro Fermín de Mendinueta and the organization of the Anza expedition mentioned above. Thanks to the ability of Anza, trade relations between the Spaniards and the Comanche gradually increased, and the principal Comanche chiefs visited Anza at Santa Fe in 1786 and, amid great ceremony, signed a treaty of peace and alliance.

The Spaniards bestowed the title of Comanche general in chief upon Chief Ecueracapa (Coat of Mail), who represented the four Comanche groups. The rivalry that this caused between the Comanche and the Ute Indians—former allies—was cleverly overcome by Anza. On July 14, 1787, Anza was in a position to report to General Commander Jacobo Ugarte y Loyola that the Indian Paruanarimuco had visited him and proposed that the Spaniards should help his people to become sedentary and to grow wheat and form villages along the banks of the Napestle River (the Arkansas). Since the Indian chief visited him again on July 25, in spite of the fact that Anza lacked authority to take action, he had no alternative but to approve the program of aid whereby he supplied him, on August 10, with 30 farmers equipped with implements and tools, under the guidance of a master-builder named Manuel Segura. The two leaders agreed to call the first settlement San Carlos de los Jupes (the Jupe formed one of the Comanche groups). The Spaniards supplied sheep, oxen, maize, corn and seed for the new village. By October, 19 houses had been completed, and many more were being built. The exact site of San Carlos is not certain; it is only known to have been on the banks of the Arkansas River.

The Ute Indians soon came to Anza asking for similar aid, and their request was granted with Ugarte's approval. However, Anza was transferred to another post at that crucial moment and was replaced by Fernando de la Concha; the Comanche saw this as a sign of the Spaniards withdrawing their support, and they therefore sent the farmers, the master-builder and the utensils back to New Mexico. Fortunately, Concha succeeded in regaining the trust of the Jupe; the work that had been interrupted was resumed and the houses were completed. The Comanche remained at San Carlos until January 1788, when they suddenly abandoned the site with the death of one of the wives whom Paruanarimuco esteemed most; the Comanche traditionally left a place associated with unfortunate circumstances and resettled a long distance away. This marked the end of Spanish-Indian cooperation and the attempt to settle nomadic tribes in Spanish outposts.

The Spaniards reached the Denver area as early as the 18th century. The existence of mines, reported by friendly Indians, attracted the Spaniards to the La Plata Mountains in La Plata and San Juan Counties. The governor of New Mexico, Tomás Vélez Cachupín, sent several exploratory expeditions in the 1760s. As the historians Hubert How Bancroft and Bernard De Voto tell us, one of them, commanded by Juan María de Rivera, departed from Santa Fe in 1761 (Alfred B. Thomas argues that the year was 1765). Rivera was accompanied by Joaquín Laín, Gregorio Sandoval and Pedro Mora, among others. Heading in a northwesterly direction, they crossed the foothills of the San Juan Mountains. In the La Plata canyons they obtained some samples of ore and continued on their way toward the Dolores River. From there they proceeded to the San Miguel River. Turning east, they crossed the Uncompahgre Plateau, before descending to the Uncompahgre River. They followed it downstream as far as Gannison River, where one of the men carved on the bark of a poplar tree a cross, his initials and the year of the expedition. This took place near the town of Sapinero. It was the first time the Europeans had crossed the Rocky Mountains. The party apparently returned home by the same route. In 1775, some of those who had accompanied Rivera returned to the Gannison River, along which they traveled for three days.

This western area of Colorado was also the setting for the ventures of Fathers Francisco Silvestre Vélez de Escalante and Atanasio Domínguez. Encouraged by Father Junípero Serra, they organized an expedition that departed from Santa Fe on July 29, 1776 (the same year as the revolutionary colonies were seeking independence). According to the historian Alfred B. Thomas, this was the most remarkable exploration in western Colorado in the 18th century. The priests were accompanied by 12 people, some of whom had been companions of Rivera, including Joaquín Laín, Pedro Cisneros and Bernardo Miera. Heading northwest toward the La Plata Mountains, they crossed a number of rivers flowing down from the San Juan chain. They drew some delightful pen sketches of these streams and the places, which they noted as excellent sites for future Spanish towns. Their itinerary was more or less as follows: Abiquiu, on the Chama River; San Juan River, which they reached on August 5 (they are thought to have crossed the boundary between Colorado and New Mexico in the neighborhood of the present town of Caracas). Turning northwest, they named a number of geographical points: Piedra Parada, Los Pinos, Florida and Las Animas. Escalante called the eastern part of La Plata, Sierra de la Grulla (crane), while the La Plata River was called San Joaquín. Descending to the Dolores River valley, their camps were called Asunción, Agua Tapada, Cañón Agua Escondida, Miera, Leberinto and Ancón San Bernardo.

In the second half of August they tried to locate a pass in the rocky defiles of the Dolores valley but, unable to find one, turned northwest in search of the Sapuagana Indians, who they knew lived in that direction. Finally they came to Cañon del Yeso (Gypsum Canyon) and from there climbed the mountains and descended to the San Miguel River, which they called the San Pedro River. This march was a trial of endurance, which left the horses' hooves bleeding. They spent two days in the valley, after which they climbed to the Uncompahgre Plateau, and once they reached the top, an Indian served them as a guide to lead them to the Uncompahgre River. They followed the river downstream to its confluence with the Gannison, near Robideau. There they rested for several days; afterward, the priests decided to continue their explorations—in spite of advice to the contrary from several friendly Indians—and to follow the Plateau Creek upstream to the Grand River in the vicinity of Battlement Creek. Heading northwest again through difficult country, they came to the White River, which they called San Clemente, and camped in the neighborhood of Rangely. About September 9, they crossed the boundary between Colorado and Utah following the Green River and, heading west, came to Lake Utah. This detailed account of their journey is provided by Father Escalante's diary.

Before that year, in Spanish days, colonists had naturally settled in the area on ranches or military outposts, or else in scattered groups, and Charles Lummis points out that the Spaniards began to populate Colorado half a century before the Anglo Saxons, just as they had discovered it several centuries earlier. A number of grants of land had been made by the king in that period, but the largest grants took place during the period of Mexican rule, namely Nolan, Sangre de Cristo, Vigil and St. Vrain, among others. The Sangre de Cristo grant was made in 1843 to Luis Lee, Narciso Beaubien and others, and included what was to become Costilla County and part of Taos County, New Mexico.

The preceding year, Antonio José Martínez, Juan Manuel Salazar, Julián Gallegos, Venancio Jácquez, and others had already tried to settle in the same territory but had not succeeded on account of the Indian attacks. When Narciso Beaubien died in the massacre at Taos, he was succeeded in his rights by his father Carlos Beaubien, who founded the town of San Luis de la Culebra, which was given this name because its first settlers— who included Faustino Medina, Mariano Pacheco, Ramón Rivera, Juan Manuel Salazar, Venancio Jácquez, Darío Gallegos, Antonio José Vallejos, Diego Gallegos, Juan Angel Vigil, Juan Ignacio Jácquez, José Gregorio Martínez and José Hilario Valdez—had arrived on the feast of St. Louis, June 21, 1851. All of them had come from Taos.

The foundation of San Luis was followed by that of San Pablo (then known as San Pedro), which took place in 1852, and San Acacio and Chama, in 1853, a short distance away on the banks of the Culebra River, settled entirely by Hispanics. The owner of the landgrant appointed a justice of the peace to exercise authority, who, together with the priest, ruled the fortunes of the new townships; protection against the Ute Indians, however, had to be entrusted to a federal garrison situated at Fort Massachusetts.

In the face of Indian attacks on Spanish settlers and the growing number of Americans, such as Zebulon Pike, who were entering Spanish territory, the viceroy of New Spain, Conde de Venadito, considered it advisable to construct a fort at a strategic spot lying about 21 miles east of Walsenburg, near Sangre de Cristo Pass. The governor of New Mexico, Facundo Melgares, is known to have performed the instructions received and built the fort on the eastern side of the pass between May and October 1819. On October 18, about 100 men dressed up as Indians attacked the fort but were repulsed by the small force commanded by José Antonio Valenzuela; they are thought to have been Americans in disguise, commanded by Benjamin O'Fallen. However, an expedition that explored the Rocky Mountain region in 1820, under the leadership of Major Stephen H. Long, obtained information from the Pawnee Indians concerning a battle that they had fought the previous year against the Spaniards, and from which they had returned with goods, money and horses. It is not known when the fort was abandoned. The Old Taos Trail passed close by, and Oak Creek flows at the foot of the hill on which the fort once stood.

Colorado Today

Denver was founded in 1858, at the time of the discovery of the silver mines. This area is said to have been visited for the first time by one of the Zaldívar brothers on the Oñate expedition, and the first trading post in the vicinity was founded in 1832 by Louis Vásquez. In spite of its late foundation, Denver has more than 70 streets bearing Spanish names, owing to a Hispanic population in excess of 25,000. These include Alameda Avenue, Alamo Drive, Barcelona, Cimarron Street, Columbia Place, Colorado Boulevard, Coronado Parkway, Cortez Street, Durango Street, El Camino Drive, Explorador Calle, Mariposa Street, Medina Way, Panorama Lane, Toledo Street, Tejon Street, De Soto Street, Verbena Street, Vista Lane and Linda Vista Drive.

Denver's Institute of Hispanic Culture has been presided over for many years by attorney Charles Vigil, a descendant of an old family of *conquistadores*. Colorado State Museum, dedicated to the history of the state, has a large number of very well executed dioramas showing various scenes from Indian life and the gold fever in the mid-19th century, although not much attention is paid its Spanish history: there is only one display cabinet with a historic map of the early days in Colorado, showing several Spanish expeditions, and another, called the Spanish Conquest, containing a hand-drawn map of the Vargas and Escalante expeditions, a cuirass, a coat of mail, a pair of silver stirrups (from Peru), a sword blade, and a drawing of the flag of Vargas, consisting of a cross of burgundy with a royal coat of arms in the center. On the upper floor of the museum, in the section dealing with weaponry, can be seen a number of items dating from the Spanish conquest.

The Art Museum houses a remarkable collection of *santos* and *bultos*, the work of the artists of New Mexico and from the south of Colorado, particularly during the period between 1750 and 1850, although the tradition continued later in some communities. Many of them were made for the *moradas* (floats) of the different confraternities of penitents whose origins are similar to those in Seville during Holy Week. (These confraternities are comprised of lay people who practice special religious ceremonies and, in particular, those commemorating the Passion.) Outstanding among the *santos*, or paintings on wood or leather, is a reredos formed by eight panels, attributed to a master of the early 19th century, Moreno Molleno; a painting in distemper depicting the three archangels, Michael, Raphael and Gabriel; and another showing the veil of Veronica. The *bultos*, or sculptures of wood covered in plaster and painted, include the *Carro de la Muerte* (Wagon of Death) a crudely realistic work by *santero* artist José Inez Herrera; several crucifixes of various sizes; a Saint Acacio crucified (dressed as a soldier with his men around him); and a Saint Librada on the Cross (the only woman depicted in this way).

The museum also has a Spanish baroque room, with a full-length portrait by Bartolomé Esteban Murillo of Diego Félix de Esquivel y Aldama, furnishings, and a splendid cabinet with candelabra and other objects. The walls are covered in cordovan leather and mirrors, while the ceiling consists of artistic coffer work. A *Saint George and the Dragon* by an anonymous Catalan artist of the 15th century, an "abbot with his crosier" by an anonymous Castillian painter of the same century, *The Adoration of the Magi* by the maestro of the retable of the Catholic kings, a 17th-century painting of St. Ferdinand the Third, and a still life by Pablo Picasso complete the Spanish art exhibits.

North of Denver, halfway to Platteville, stands Fort Vasquez now accurately rebuilt and well kept by the Historical Society of Colorado. It was founded in 1835 by traders Andrew Sublette and Louis Vasquez, who was the son of a Spaniard from the east and born a subject of King Charles IV at St. Louis, Missouri, on October 3, 1795. Having lost his father at an early age, Vasquez soon began to work in the skin and fur business for other traders, and had dealings with several Indian tribes. In this way he traveled through the basins of the Laramie, Green, Big Horn, Yellow Stone, North and South Platte Rivers, as well as Clear Creek. In pioneering days, Clear Creek was known as Vasquez Fork. Thanks to his long experience, he succeeded in setting up business on his own and founded, with his partner, a fort that became one of the trading centers for the area.

In 1838, he organized an expedition following the Santa Fe Trail and the Arkansas River before turning north and ending at South Platte. There is a description of the fort given in 1839 by E. Willard Smith as built of "daubies," or adobe sun-dried bricks. The fort was sold in 1842, and Vasquez began to work in the present states of Wyoming and Utah. Married in St. Louis in 1846, he died at Westport, Missouri, in 1868.

Also along Highway 85, following the Santa Fe Trail, is the Colorado town Trinidad. Well situated, it was founded in 1859 by Juan Ignacio Airiz and other Hispanics from the San Luis Valley and from Taos, who set up ranches there. Many names could be recalled by consulting the documents, photographs and other mementos to be seen at the Pioneer Museum in Old Baca House, the mansion occupied until 1920 by Felipe Baca, one of the pioneers of the region.

The Santa Fe Trail passed through Trinidad and turned northwest (coinciding with Highways 350 and 50), passing through the localities of La Junta, Las Animas (between them lies Fort Bent), Lamar, Granada and others, until the trail petered out in the state of Kansas, on the way to St. Louis, Missouri. From 1821 onward, the route was frequented by Kit Carson, Ceran St. Vrain and the Bent brothers, among others. Not far away, in the Purgatoire River valley are the foothills of the Sangre de Cristo Mountains; a village sprang up here when the nearby coal mines were worked, but they have now been abandoned; there is a chapel of San Saturnino, which is no longer open for worship.

Highway 85 continues in a northerly direction and passes through Aguilar (founded in 1867 by José Ramón Aguilar, a leading pioneer in South Colorado) before coming to Walsenburg. The latter was originally called Plaza de los Leones by its founder, Miguel Antonio León. The river was originally called San Juan River by Juan Uribarri, and later San Antonio by Antonio Valverde. It is not known exactly when they received the name, but they were known even to foreigners as early as 1808 and 1809, as can be deduced from documents of the day and an anonymous description of New Mexico given by a Frenchman, in 1818. The Huerfano River is crossed on the way toward Pueblo, and the solitary hill—which gave rise to its name, *huérfano* is Spanish for "orphan"—can be seen by travelers on that road.

Nearby, on the opposite side of the road, lies the locality of San Isabel, which, like San Isabel Forest, is called after Queen Isabella. West of Walsenburg lie the Spanish Peaks, Isabella and Ferdinand, also named after the Queen of Castile and her Aragonese husband. To the north lies the little village of La Veta, where there is the Francisco Plaza Museum. A few miles father west along Highway 160 is La Veta Pass, with a pink Colorado granite monument over six feet high to Félix Mestas, bearing the following inscription: "Mount Mestas Memorial. In honor of Felix B. Mestas Jr. Born Aug. 23, 1921, La Veta, Colo. Died Sept. 29, 1944 Mt. Battaglia, Italy. We pay tribute [a list of 62 Hispanic sons of Huerfano County dead in the World War II follows]."

Highway 160 leads to Fort Garland, now a museum run by the State Historical Society of Colorado, which houses a number of Spanish exhibits from the early days of the region, and also some dioramas and paintings depicting the arrival of various expeditions in Colorado. It was built in 1858 to house the garrison of Fort Massachusetts, which was closed down owing to the superior position occupied by the new fort and its ability to protect the isolated settlers in the area. Farther west lies Alamosa, another of the larger towns in the district.

The largest of all the municipal centers in southern Colorado, however, is Pueblo, on Highway 85. Together with the Arkansas River, which flows through it from west to east on the way to the state of Kansas, Pueblo forms the dividing line of the Hispanic region of Colorado. Thirty percent of its 125,000 inhabitants are Spanish speakers. One of the local stations only broadcasts in Spanish.

It was at Pueblo that the Spaniards took the American pioneer Zebulon Pike prisoner. He had started his exploratory travels on July 15, 1806, through the southwest area of the territories composed in the Louisiana Purchase and in the following February reached Sangre de Cristo, where he built a palisade at the confluence of the Conejos River with the Rio Grande. This area was certainly not included in the basin of the Mississippi and its tributaries, and Pike had therefore taken possession of foreign territory. Consequently he was led as a prisoner to Santa Fe and then to Chihuahua. In July 1807, he was released. On his return to the United States, he wrote an account of his travels and vicissitudes, which was a tremendous public success and opened the eyes of many people to the potential of future settlement in the West.

A few miles east of Pueblo, on the right bank of the Huerfano River at its confluence with the Arkansas River, there is a church, all that remains of Huerfano Abajo, a community founded in 1853 by Charles Autobees. On May 15 every year, the members of St. Isidore's Society come to venerate the statue of the saint from Madrid (Isadore being the translation of San Isidro). A

procession takes place, and the festivities end in a splendid banquet. In Pueblo, the Catholic religious organization called the Penitentes is also active. The streets at Pueblo include such Spanish names as Balboa, Coronado, De Soto, Cortez and many others.

Highway 550 leads down from Grand Junction to Delta, Montrose and Ouray, the latter so named in honor of Indian chief Ute, who was so influential in the signing of the peace treaty whereby his people agreed to withdraw westward. Ouray spoke Spanish, as did his assistants Ignacio and Severo. In the southwest corner of the state, lies the town of Durango and not far away, halfway to Utah, is the Mesa Verde National Park. It is worth noting that a point nearby is the only place in the United States common to four states: Arizona, New Mexico, Utah and Colorado. Mesa Verde is a high, isolated plateau; it was given that name by an unknown Spanish explorer, on account of the juniper and pine forests covering it. Owing to the topographical and climatic conditions of the area, the fertile soil and the possibility of digging out caves suitable for accommodation and storage in the steep walls of the plateau, this became a center of pre-Columbian civilization and settlement.

Basket Maker Indians inhabited Mesa Verde between the years A.D. 200 and 500, and with a modified form of culture, until the year 700; from that time onward they made progress in the building of houses and villages and in handicrafts. During the 11th century, most of the Indians took refuge in the rocky walls, building in their hollows such accommodation as could be adapted to the space available. The "cliff palace," with 200 dwellings forming terraces and 23 *kivas*, or chambers for ceremonies and meetings, was discovered by the Wetherill brothers in 1888. Father Escalante and his companions camped in the vicinity. The district had to be abandoned by its inhabitants in 1276, following 23 years of drought, which made it impossible for them to stay any longer, forcing them to emigrate and settle in the Rio Grande basin, where Coronado found them as the Pueblo Indians in 1540.

The leading museum at Colorado Springs is the Taylor Museum, which belongs to the Colorado Springs Art Center and houses the best collection of Hispanic colonial art in the Southwest. Apart from the *santos* and *bultos* exhibited in the rooms open to the public, this exceptional collection includes about 1,000 items. There are many exhibits depicting St. Francis, St. Joseph, St. Isidore, St. Michael, the Child Jesus of Atocha, several advocations of the Virgin Mary and curious interpretations of the Holy Trinity. The *santos* are usually made of wood, although there are some early ones made of leather. Many *bultos* are life-size sculptures, and a large number are clothed in the Spanish fashion. (The museum has a veritable wardrobe for the *bultos*). On show are some impressive *carros de la muerte* (wagons of death) together with a very large heavy cross belonging to a congregation of penitents. (Most of the works of art exhibited are from *moradas* [floats] belonging to such confraternities.) It is curious to note that many of the depictions of Christ on the cross show a goatee beard and highly varied clothing, some of them having a little angel in the wound in the side. This folk art executed by the *santeros* has continued down to the 20th century, as in the case of José Dolores López, a native of the town of Cordova, who died in 1938; the more recent style tends not to use colors, but only to fashion the wood and make the most of the raw material.

Spanish Place-Names

The counties with Spanish names in Colorado are as follows: Alamosa, Baca, Conejos, Costilla, Dolores, El Paso, La Plata, Las Animas, Mesa Mineral, Otero, Pueblo, Rio Blanco, Rio Grande, San Juan and San Miguel. The towns include Aguilar, Alamosa, Antonito, Arriba, Aurora, Blanca, Campo, Cortez, Del Norte, Dolores, Durango, El Dorado Springs, Granada, La Jarra, La Junta, Lamar, Las Animas, La Veta, Monte Vista, Pueblo, San Luis, Trinidad, Valdez and Vilas.

◆ *NEVADA AND UTAH* ◆

Nevada

The capital of Nevada is the small locality of Carson City, but the two largest cities are Reno and Las Vegas. Las Vegas was given its name by Antonio Armijo, a New Mexican, who, leading a group of traders, departed from Abiquiu in November 1829, following an itinerary similar to that chosen three years earlier by Jedediah Smith, and explored a route from Salt Lake City toward southern California. The 60-man convoy took 86 days to reach the San Gabriel Mission. The expedition succeeded in linking New Mexico with the Pacific via the Crossing of the Fathers, and established the route that was to be used so frequently, particularly during the years from 1830 to 1850, and became known as the Spanish Trail.

It is easy to see that the name Nevada is taken from the mountain chain skirting the western boundary, called the Sierra Nevada. It is said to have been given this name by a Spanish priest, Pedro Font, who saw the snow-covered peaks on April 3, 1776, near the confluence of the Sacramento and San Joaquín Rivers, while with an expeditionary group; the map that he drew in 1777 uses that name. The name was confirmed by Colonel John C. Frémont in his official report to the United States Senate on his journey to the West and his activities in California. He proposed that the new territory be called Sierra Nevada. (His suggestion, as we see, met with partial success.)

There is a story that Martín de Alarcón, Francisco de Ulloa, García López de Cárdenas and Father Francisco Garcés, among others, staked claims to a gold field at El Dorado, and hence the name they gave it. But the truth is that Alarcón and Ulloa only got as far as Yuma, some 280 miles from Nevada, and it is not thought likely that Cárdenas could have reached this territory.

The first European to set foot in Nevada was Father Francisco Garcés, who departed from Sonora in 1775 with an expedition commanded Juan Bautista de Anza (junior); he halted at the spot where the Colorado and Gila Rivers meet in order to seek a likely place for a mission. Father Pedro Font wrote about this expedition and drew up the map mentioned earlier. In January 1776, he set up a residence at the previous site of Fort Yuma and visited his religious brethren at San Gabriel. On April 9, he departed and returned along the San Fernando Valley to the Tulare valley, and crossed the Mojave River. (The inhabitants of Las Vegas have commemorated the first pioneering trip by giving the name Garcés to one of the central streets in the city and the Society of Daughters of the American Revolution have called their local group the Garcés Chapter.) Father Escalante's expeditions did not reach Nevada, but fell 20 miles short of it when he turned toward the Santa Clara valley at the southwestern tip of Utah.

There have been Basques in Nevada since the 1860s, when a group began to work as shepherds. Antonio Azcuénaga was already at McDemitt by 1877. From then onward, a large number of Basques came to the mountainous area of the state, and these Spaniards can be said to have focused particularly on Nevada and Idaho, and subsequently on Oregon. Some Basques have attained important positions in Nevada, such as Peter Echevarría, a senator for Nevada; Senator Bob Laxalt is also of French-Basque descent. In the south of Nevada, Pedro Altube founded his famous Spanish Ranch in 1873, with 1 million acres of land for sheep grazing. Pete Elia is said not to have known the real size of his properties, which were similar in size to that of Altube, and Smoke Creek, owned by Duc and Poco Iri-art boasted 40,000 sheep. Juan Calzagorta, a rancher in this area, was renowned for his strength: he could break even the strongest horse-shoes with his bare hands. Bob Laxalt has called the Basque shepherds the "lonely sentinels of the American West," thus doing justice to their solitude and permanent watch defending the interests entrusted to them.

Today at the end of May or early June the shepherds come down from the mountains for the sheep shearing. The Basque festivals at Elko have become a tradition and are usually attended by the governor and other authorities, together with Spanish representatives. The festivals consist of a colorful parade of regional costumes, an abundant meal of Basque cuisine and performances of folk songs and dances. On these occasions, the *Elko Daily Free Press* publishes articles in the Basque language. The University of Nevada has a center of Basque studies with a library well stocked with Spanish and Basque books. There is also a Euskaldunak Club. Finally, in Las Vegas and Reno there are jai alai courts.

Toward the end of 1988, the killing of 40 mustangs, who were drinking from an isolated gully, was reported in Nevada. These wild horses, which descend from those brought by the Spanish *conquistadores* in the 16th century, have been under the protection of federal law since 1971. In Nevada there are approximately 28,000 of them.

Spanish Place-Names

Spanish names can be found scattered all over the state: the cities of Las Vegas and Reno; Esmeralda County (which was given its name by J. M. Corey in 1860 because he liked the word); the localities of Mina, Caliente, Aguas Calientes and Golconda; and flag stations such as Hoya and Vista. Other place-names include Alamo, Amargosa Desert, Amargosa River, Aurora, Candelaria, Cortez Mountains, El Dorado, La Madre Mountains, Monte Cristo Range, Pinto Creek, Potosi Mountain, Rancho Romano, Sacramento Pass, San Antonio Mountains, San Jacinto, Santa Rosa Range and Virgin River (originally Río de la Virgen). In Las Vegas alone, there are dozens of Spanish street names, many bearing the names of saints.

Utah

Utah takes its name from the Ute Indians, who originally inhabited the territory. Flanked by Colorado and Nevada, it was once theoretically Spanish. Consequently, at the time of the independence of Mexico in 1822, the latter owned the territory and transferred it to the United States under the Treaty of Guadalupe Hidalgo.

The early Spaniards were the first Europeans to know about the area and the Indians inhabiting it, and the word Yutah can be found in their writings. Some historians claim that the García López de Cárdenas expedition set foot on land now forming part of San Juan County, in the southeast of the state, when wandering around the Grand Canyon in 1540.

However, the first confirmed Spanish expedition into Utah was that of two Franciscan friars, Francisco Silvestre Vélez de Escalante and Atanasio Domínguez, who were accompanied by Joaquín Laín, Pedro Cisneros, Bernardo Miera, and nine other colleagues. They left Santa Fe on July 29, 1776, on a mission intended to find a route for communications between New Mexico and California. The difficulties encountered, the harshness of the land through which they had to travel and the extreme climates endured make this one of the most remarkable feats in the annals of exploration, although it is one of the least known; indeed this venture led them along routes for a distance of some 1,560 miles, which took them little more than five months.

During the first part of their journey, they crossed the south and west of the state of Colorado and entered the state of Utah (near today's Highway 40) in the northeast sector. From the White valley they crossed to the Green River valley near the Dinosaur National Monument; they penetrated the Wasatch Mountains via the Duquesne River and reached Lake Utah on September 23. On climbing to a small height at the mouth of the canyon, they sighted the lake and the wide valley of Nuestra Señora de la Merced de los Timpanogotzis (Our

Lady of Mercy of the Timpanogotzis), as the friars called it. The Indians had fled at the sight of these strange visitors and had burned their fields, but the Spaniards considered the valley good and comfortable, and the lake had plenty of fish. Today Spanish Fork, on the shores of the lake, is a reminder of their presence.

On September 26, the Spanish expeditionaries set off for Monterey, having bought some dried fish from the Indians. On October 5, they arrived at Black Rock Springs near Milford. In addition to the difficulties posed by the terrain, the situation was further complicated when their guides deserted. With winter and the difficult mountain country ahead, they were faced with the dilemma of proceeding toward Monterey or returning to their starting point. They decided to settle the matter by drawing lots, trusting that with fervent prayer God would indirectly show the direction they should take; the answer was to return home, and they headed southeast.

Via Ash Creek they entered the Virgin River valley where, years later, the Mormon leader Brigham Young set up his "Dixie of the Desert." On October 14, they camped near present-day Toquerville. After climbing to a plateau and then descending to a plain, they spent three weeks trying to find their way through territory that now forms part of the frontier between Utah and Arizona, and seeking a way across the Colorado River. They underwent terrible hardships in this mountainous desert with scant water and sparse vegetation. On October 18, they recorded their presence at San Samuel, now called Cooper Pockets, and then at Santa Gertrudis, about nine miles south of Pipe Spring National Monument, in Arizona, in the vicinity of which they reached the northern tip of the Kaibab Mountains. On November 7, they at last found their way to the ford on the Colorado River and crossed without further trouble. The place would thereafter be known as El Vado de los Padres, or The Crossing of the Fathers. It so happened that it had likewise been discovered, only a few months earlier, by another Spaniard, Father Francisco Hermenegildo Garcés, who had crossed the river in the same direction. They reached the city of Santa Fe on January 2, 1777, after traveling nearly 1,600 miles.

On the grounds of the Palace of Justice at Provo today, there is a granite rock with a bronze plaque commemorating Fathers Escalante and Domínguez. While Father Domínguez was in fact the leader of the expedition, Father Escalante has become better known because he was the author of the famous diary, a very thorough report of their finds, including local plants and animals: his descriptions of birds and fish are remarkably scientific, and his opinions show an acute awareness of the local possibilities of irrigation. With his diary begins the written history of this part of the United States. A memorial stone situated on Highway 91 south of Scipio, recounts their travels, as do memorials in Spanish Fork and Cedar City. Near Monticello there is a bronze plaque placed above the Colorado River, at Lee's Ferry, and there is another monument at Jensen. In the southeast part of the state, a town and river bear the name Escalante, while the Escalante Desert can be found in the southwest. (Escalante's name is used for place-names in other states as well.)

A Spaniard called Mestas unsuccessfully followed the tracks of some stolen horses, following the Spanish-Ute Trail from New Mexico to the township of Timpanogos (near Lake Utah), in 1805. In 1813, traders Mauricio Arza and Lagos García spent some time in Utah trading in leather and slaves. Fort Buenaventura was built on the site of Ogden, west of the Wasatch Mountains by Miles Goodyear in 1844–1845. When James Ashley and his people visited Salt Lake in the 1820s, one member of the party was a Spaniard, Louis Vasquez, from Colorado; this expedition is considered to have been the first to circumnavigate the lake. Vasquez set up as a merchant at Salt Lake City in 1849, and in 1855 he sold his interest to the Mormons and returned to Missouri.

Other reminders of Utah's Spanish past include the local use of the word *cañón* for "canyon," for example Weber Cañon and Ogden Cañon. The floral emblem of Utah is the sego lily, also known as Spanish mariposa, because the Spaniards thought that it looked like a butterfly.

Finally, the very real presence of Spain in Utah continues today through the Basque shepherds. There is a large Basque colony in the state. Their influence is particularly noticeable in the capital, Salt Lake City. During the spring, summer and autumn, the shepherds spread out through the mountains, and in winter, descend to the ranches (sometimes very far apart) and to the capital.

Spanish Place-Names

Spanish names in Utah include the towns of Alta, Aurora, Bonanza, Callao, Columbia, Escalante, La Sal, Loa, Lola, Manila, Mona, Oasis, Pintura, Salina, San Rafael, Santa Clara, Spanish Fork and Vernal; there are also the Escalante, Paria and San Juan Rivers; while mountains bear the names Confusion, La Sal and San Rafael. Other geographic features with Spanish names are Alhambra Rock, Escalante Desert and Spanish Valley.

WYOMING, MONTANA AND IDAHO

Wyoming

Wyoming is crossed from northeast to southeast by the Continental Divide in the Rocky Mountains. The eastern sector (three-quarters) forms a part of the basin of the Mississippi River and its tributaries; part of the Louisiana territory, it was included in the transfer of the huge expanse of land from France to Spain in 1763. The western sector lies both above and below the 42nd parallel and was always considered by Spain as a port of Oregon; as a result it was divided between Spain and the United States along that line, following the Treaty of 1819 whereby the United States purchased Florida from Spain. Thus both the eastern and the western sectors of the state have existed under Spanish rule, albeit more in theory than in practice, for true sovereignty was not effectively exerted by the representatives of the Spanish Crown owing to the distance of Wyoming from the route followed by the Spanish *conquistadores* and missionaries.

In the eastern sector, this rule lasted for 40 years (the period of Spanish rule in Louisiana), and in the west, between dates that could in theory begin in 1542 (at the time of the discovery of Oregon by Bartolomé Ferrelo) and end between 1819 and 1822, those being the dates of the treaty and of the independence of Mexico, respectively. However there can be said to have been Spanish links with the territory throughout its history. Hubert Howe Brancroft mentions the possibility of the Spaniards having found gold here before 1650, opening channels for mines and building houses; a massacre in that year by the natives left no survivors and destroyed the town. Some maintain that the remains of that colonization were discovered in 1865. Near Laramie, a Spanish traveler, José Jordana y Morera, was surprised in 1876 to find the Spanish Trail opened up by Spanish explorers traveling from California to the interior and following the route that would one day be followed by the pioneers.

The Spanish trader Manuel Lisa, who settled in St. Louis, Missouri, founded a trade empire that spread throughout the lands west of the Missouri River between 1800 and 1820. He and his employees traveled all over this huge region and were on peaceful terms and did excellent business with the Indians, who provided them with furs and skins. They are also known to have traveled through Wyoming, and Lisa therefore had information about this region.

Another Spanish trader, Luis Vásquez, born in St. Louis in 1795, was a partner of Jim Bridger in the construction of Fort Bridger and in trading operations there from 1842 to 1855; moreover, in the winter of 1833–1834, Vásquez negotiated with the Crow Indians, with whom he was on good terms and the following spring, took 30 bales of buffalo hide and one bale of beaver pelts to Fort William (later renamed Fort Laramie). In 1855, he sold his interests to the Mormons. Situated at the southwest corner of the state of Wyoming, Fort Bridger was subsequently a strategic point for the Pony Express organized from St. Joseph, Missouri, to Sacramento, California; today the Pony Express building has been reconstructed and has an adjoining museum.

In the east of Wyoming and around Cheyenne, Basque shepherds can be found today. In the summer of 1988, Buffalo City hosted the 3,000 participants of the "XIV Convención Norteamericana-Vasca" (North American-Basque Convention.)

Spanish Place-Names

There are few Spanish names in Wyoming: Carbon County, and the towns of Alcova, Alta, Mona, Peru, Uva and Violan, in addition to Moran Mountain.

Montana

The eastern area of Montana formed part of Louisiana territory. It fell into the hands of Spain in 1763 and remained under Spain's control until its return to France in 1803. It was subsequently sold to the United States that same year. Spanish rights over the territory were transferred under the Treaty of 1819, whereby Spain sold Florida to the United States and settled a number of frontier conflicts. These territories were evangelized by French Jesuits, one of whom Father

Pierre-Jean De Smet, honored the founder of his order, the Spanish saint, Ignatius of Loyola, by writing the following words on a rock: "Sanctus Ignatius Patrones Montiun Die Julii 23, 1840" (St. Ignatius Montana's Patron July 23, 1840).

The state's name itself derives from the Spanish word *montaña* or mountain in view of its geographical features. The acceptance of the name was due to the efforts of an Ohio Congressman, James Ashley, when the creation of the new territory was proposed. On February 5, 1865, Governor Sidney Edgerton moved a joint resolution of the two state Houses, instituting the official state seal in which, beneath a scene consisting of mountains, waterfalls on the Missouri, a plow and a pickaxe, the official motto of Montana, "Oro y Plata" (gold and silver) appears.

When Manuel Lisa, the enterprising Spaniard born in New Orleans, heard at St. Louis, Missouri, of the results of the Meriwether Lewis and William Clark expedition, he fitted out an expedition of 42 men and led them up the Yellowstone River as far as its confluence with the Big Horn; there, in 1807, he built the first trading post in Montana. He named it Fort Ramón after his son, but the trappers and traders of the region knew it as Fort Lisa or Fort Manuel. His company, whose activity we have seen in other states, eventually employed a large number of people and prospered until Lisa's death in 1820. A Scotsman named David Mackay had ventured as far as Montana earlier, in 1796, in the service of Lisa's company and seeking furs for their trade, traveled up the Missouri River. The same is true of Welshman John Evans, who carved on the bark of many trees a record of his presence in the service of King Charles IV of Spain. The arrival of the Spaniards in these parts is described by that great historian Herbert Eugene Bolton.

Spanish Place-Names

One of the counties in Montana is called Carbon; towns bearing Spanish names include Alzada, Andes, Columbia Falls, Columbus, De Borgia, Laredo, Lima, Loma, Lustre, Ovando, Saco, Saint Ignatius and Santa Rita.

Idaho

In a novel by Carmen Laforet, *Paralelo 35*, Idaho is home to an American Basque community. "The land of America," she says, "has not melted them down or made them uniform in the course of generations."

In the state capital, Boise, an annual country festival has been held since 1929, originally organized by the American Basque Fraternity, later by the organization La Social Independencia and then, since 1962, by the Euskaldunak Organization. This institution runs the Basque Center at Boise, where there are more than 600 members, and sponsors the Basque dancing group, a choir and the "Baile de los Pastores," or "Shepherds Dance," which is held on December 27. (The telephone directory for Boise includes about 1,000 Basque names, representing at least 2,000 people of Basque origin; this city, with a population of 35,000 inhabitants, therefore, has the largest urban concentration of Basques outside Spain and France.)

The first Basque to reach Idaho is thought to have been Antonio Azcuénaga, who came via California, Oregon and Nevada. Many followed him, and although they started work as shepherds, they took up other professions as well. Today, there is a fourth generation of Basques here. Apart from the associations mentioned earlier, there are two mutual aid organizations, Sociedad de Socorros Mutuos and Fraternidad Vasco-Americana. Several Catholic churches are prominent among this community, for example, The Good Shepherd and the Cathedral of St. John the Evangelist, where Mass is said in the Basque tongue on Sundays at an altar donated by José Domingo Aldecoa in memory of his son, killed in World War II. Many Basques have attained important posts or leading social positions in Idaho, including Louis J. Bideganeta, secretary of the state supreme court, while others maintain ranches with more than 100,000 head of sheep. In Boise, KBAI radio broadcasts in the Basque language.

Spanish Place-Names

Towns with Spanish names in Idaho include Acequia, Alameda, Arco, Bonanza, Carmen, De Lamar, Lorenzo, Ola, Orofino, Salmon and Santa.

PART VII:
PACIFIC COAST STATES

◆ *CALIFORNIA* ◆

California became known to the Europeans largely through the efforts of Franciscans. The 21 missions formed the backbone of the early townships in this region, and the bells that ring along El Camino Real are reminders of the work of Father Junípero Serra and his religious brethren.

The origin of the name California has been the subject of much controversy. Was it an Indian word misunderstood by the Spaniards? Did it derive from the Latin words *callida fornax*, indicating the heat in California? As early as 1849, the historian George Ticknor ascribed it to the book of chivalry called *Las Sergas de Esplandián* (at San Clemente there is an Esplandian Avenue). Certainly this is the nicest and most acceptable theory. The author of that novel, Garci Ordóñez de Montalbo, presented it as the fifth book in his version of *Amadís de Gaula*, for the first edition produced at Saragossa, probably in 1508. In the book, Calafia, queen of the island of California, helps the pagan forces laying siege to Constantinople. "You should know," says the author, "that at the right-hand side of the Indies there was an island called California, very close to the paradise on earth, which was peopled by black women without any man being among them, for their way of life was almost like that of the Amazons. They had valiant bodies, vigorous ardent hearts, and great strength; the island itself being the strongest in the world with rocks and towering cliffs; their weapons were all of gold, as also were the harnesses of the wild beasts on which, after taming them, they rode; in all the island there was no other metal . . ." In this society, women were preeminent to the exclusion of men. (They killed most male children at birth, and only left those few needed for reproduction.)

The name California was already being used by Francisco Preciado, narrating the expedition of Francisco de Ulloa in 1539 and 1540, by Juan Rodríguez Cabrillo in the accounts of his voyage in 1542, by Bernal Díaz del Castillo when recounting the expeditions of Córtes in 1535 and elsewhere. But, in the early days, the word was limited to the bay (La Paz Bay), a cape (Punta Ballenas) or an island. The territory also received other names than that coined by Garci Ordóñez de Montalva; for instance, New Albion (given to it by the pirate Francis Drake), Carolina Island and New Russia. The first Spanish settlers were known as "Californios."

Discovery

The role of Spain in the history of California is undisputed. If the subject of the part played by Spain in the heritage of the United States is raised in this country, the California missions are immediately mentioned as a symbol of that presence. But, the extraordinarily interesting Spanish contribution to the history of California

237

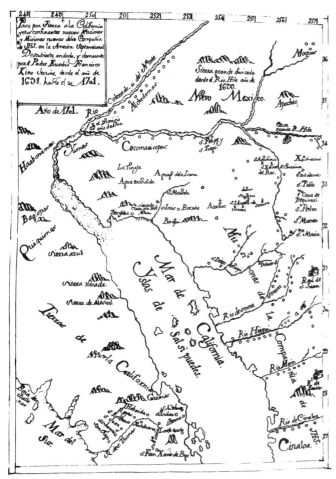

Spanish map detailing new missions in California and New Mexico, 1698–1701.

is not confined to a few chapels erected by some more or less elusive friars, as some would suggest.

The Spanish conquest and colonization of the westernmost lands of the present-day United States was not due to mere chance, nor was it an easy task that fell like a gift into the lap of the Spanish Empire. The result of a long chain of endeavors, it cost rivers of blood, consumed quantities of money and effort, and took many years. Moreover, it should not be forgotten that the overland route to California was fraught with difficulties while the sea route via the Pacific Ocean proved hazardous owing to the tremendous storms, interminable calms, treasure-seeking pirates and above all, the fact that it was unknown. The Spaniards were the first to chart the West Coast, and did so at the cost of a number of failures.

Looking at the fertile Central Valley, or the splendid highways running the length of the state, the large cities and flourishing industries found here and there, one forgets the different circumstances existing in the geography of this area in pre-Spanish times: untilled land,

scarcity of water and mountain chains that sometimes proved impossible to cross. Additionally, there existed a variety of Indian tribes, not always peaceful and friendly, who were the masters and overlords of this territory. André Maurois points out that the Spaniards brought orange, apricot, fig and olive trees to California, "much more precious than the gold and pearls which they took home from there."

After the discovery of the South Seas (now the Pacific) in 1513 by Vasco Núñez de Balboa, and the Magellan Strait—as a means of communication between this huge expanse of water and the Atlantic—by the great mariner, Ferdinand Magellan, after whom it is called, the need was felt not only to ascertain whether California was an island or a peninsula, but to seek a northern passage between the two oceans as a means of reaching the coasts of Asia and proving that the New World was not Cathay, as Columbus still believed when he died. Several centuries were spent on this tremendous enterprise, and various nations contributed their efforts in the hope of obtaining rewarding benefits. The Spaniards distinguished themselves by the quality and number of their expeditions.

Spanish ships sailed up the east and southern coasts of America in the early decades of the 16th century, and did the same along the western seaboards, where a venture was led by the tireless Hernán Cortés and navigators Cabrillo and Bartolmé Ferrelo. The viceroys Antonio de Mendoza, Antonio de Bucarelli y Ursua, Antonio Flores and Count Revillagigedo, among others, played a key role in the exploration saga. In the 17th century, and particularly throughout the 18th century, Spanish sailors persevered with the same enthusiasm as their Renaissance forbears. The names of navigators Sebastián Vizcaíno, Juan de Iturbe, Cestero, Nicolás de Cardona, Pedro Porter Cassanate, Juan Pérez, Bruno de Heceta, Esteban José Martínez, Juan Francisco de la Bodega y Quadra and Alejandro Malaspina will forever rank outstandingly amongst those who opened up the West of the United States.

Besides seeking the east-west passage, there were other reasons for organizing exploratory expeditions: in the first place, the desire to prevent any other foreign power from becoming established in the East Pacific area, a rivalry that soon began to take shape as far as England was concerned when the pirates Francis Drake and Thomas Cavendish appeared toward the end of the 16th century, and reached its climax in the Nootka controversy, which was settled in 1791 under an amicable agreement that avoided an imminent conflagration.

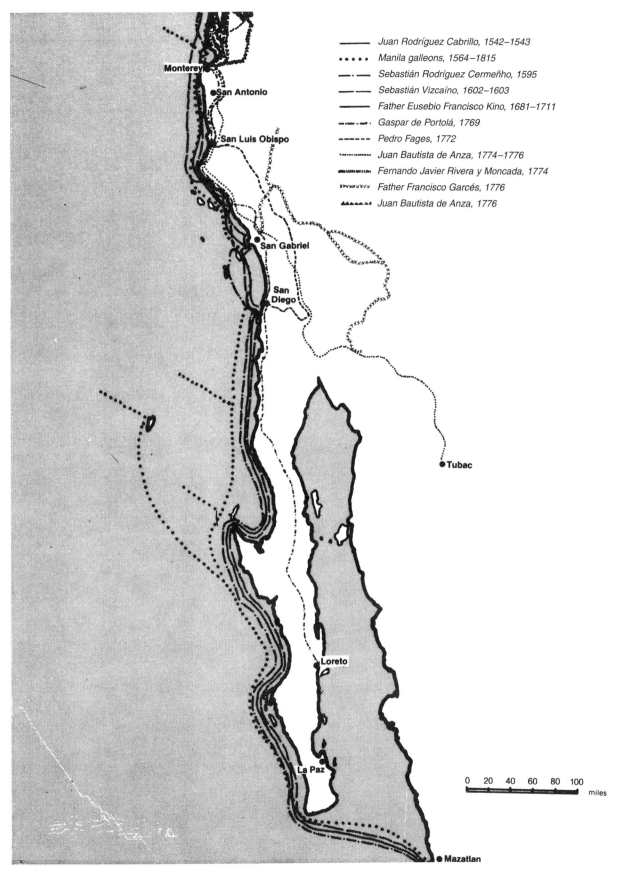

Legend:

——— Juan Rodríguez Cabrillo, 1542–1543
••••• Manila galleons, 1564–1815
—·—·— Sebastián Rodríguez Cermeño, 1595
— — — Sebastián Vizcaíno, 1602–1603
——— Father Eusebio Francisco Kino, 1681–1711
—··—··— Gaspar de Portolá, 1769
- - - - Pedro Fages, 1772
··—··—·· Juan Bautista de Anza, 1774–1776
▪▪▪▪▪ Fernando Javier Rivera y Moncada, 1774
xxxxxxx Father Francisco Garcés, 1776
▲▲▲▲▲ Juan Bautista de Anza, 1776

Monterey
●San Antonio
●San Luis Obispo
●San Gabriel
San Diego
●Tubac
Loreto
La Paz
0 20 40 60 80 100
miles
●Mazatlan

Spanish and Mexican explorers in California, 1542–1776. Facts On File.

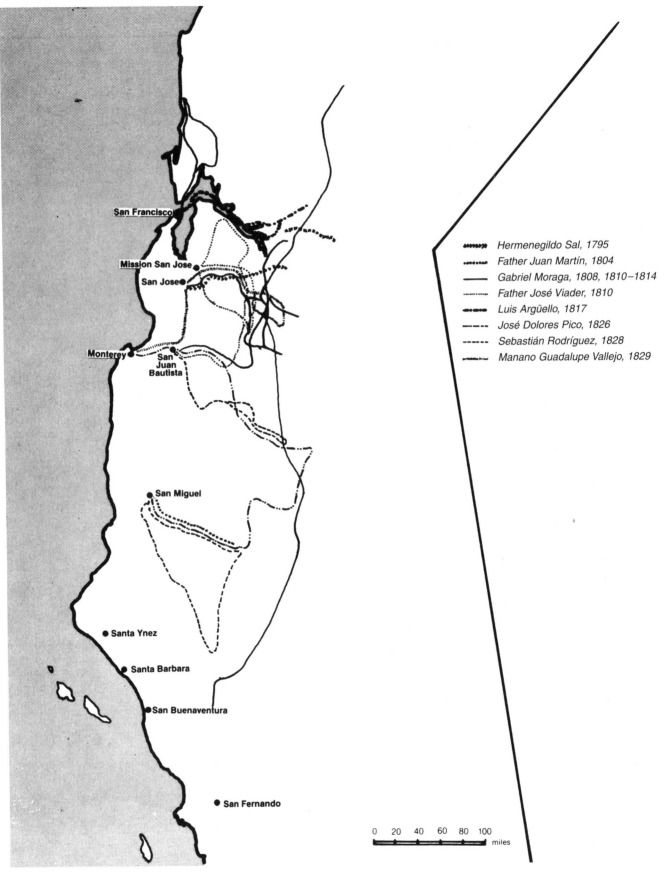

Legend:

- Hermenegildo Sal, 1795
- Father Juan Martín, 1804
- Gabriel Moraga, 1808, 1810–1814
- Father José Viader, 1810
- Luis Argüello, 1817
- José Dolores Pico, 1826
- Sebastián Rodríguez, 1828
- Manano Guadalupe Vallejo, 1829

San Francisco

Mission San Jose

San Jose

Monterey

San Juan Bautista

San Miguel

Santa Ynez

Santa Barbara

San Buenaventura

San Fernando

0 20 40 60 80 100 miles

Spanish and Mexican explorers in California, 1795–1829. Facts On File.

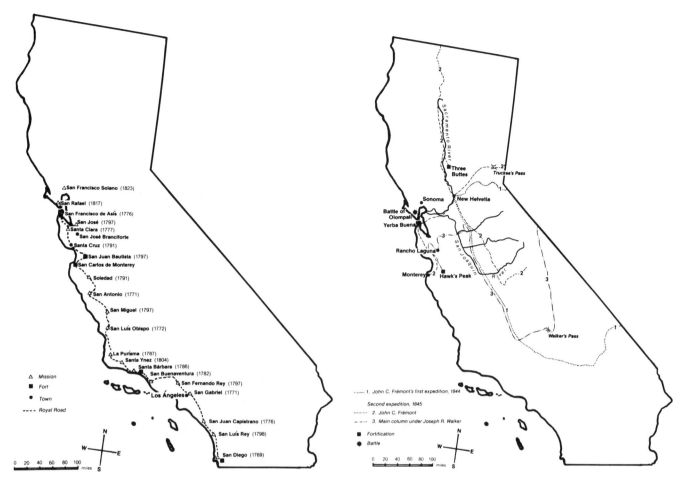

Spanish missions, forts and towns in California, 1769–1823. Facts On File.

John C. Frémont and the Bear Flag Revolt, 1844–1845. Facts On File.

With regard to the Russian presence in that area, which had begun with the discoveries of Vitus Bering and the subsequent colonization of Alaska, it is evident that had it not been for the quick effective action taken by men on orders from King Charles III (originating from a report submitted by his ambassador at St. Petersburg, Count Lacy, about Catherine the Great's plan to organize colonies), the coast of California would have been populated by subjects of the czar, and their settlements would have been harder to remove than those in the cold inhospitable territory of Alaska. It has been rightly claimed that Spain prevented California, and perhaps its neighboring territories, from becoming a Russian dominion, and thus did a great service to the achievement of the Manifest Destiny and the formation of the United States. The "Descripción de las costas de California (1513–1784)" by the bishop Iñigo Abbad y Lasierra describes this era.

There were three other reasons for the Spanish expeditions, although very different in nature. One was a material reason, the eagerness for riches expressed in the search for pearl oyster beds; another, a spiritual purpose in the unwavering desire of the kings of Spain to achieve the Christianization of the native Indian tribes in the territories lying north of New Spain; and a third reason, a systematic search for a haven at which the Manila galleon could take refuge safely from storms and pirates. More often than not, the initiative in these ventures was taken by the king, and they were organized at the expense of the royal exchequer; other ventures were undertaken as private enterprises, and some, such as those of Nicolás de Cardona or Pedro Porter Cassanate, invested huge sums that were not always recovered.

The report by a Jesuit, Father Gaspar Rodero, about the Spanish interest in colonizing California, written in 1737, claims that the California territories "possessed a healthy nature" and "the weather was regular according to the season of the year."

In Spain, a series of stamps commemorated in 1967 such figures as Esteban José Martínez, Francisco Antonio Mourelle, Cayetano Valdés and Juan Francisco de la

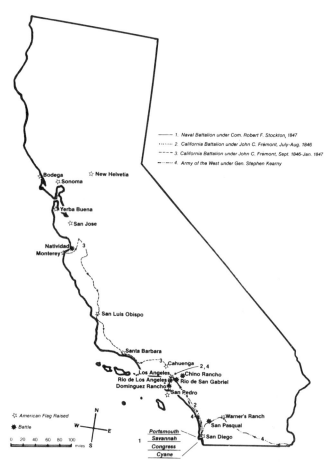

1. Naval Battalion under Com. Robert F. Stockton, 1847
2. California Battalion under John C. Fremont, July-Aug. 1846
3. California Battalion under John C. Fremont, Sept. 1846-Jan. 1847
4. Army of the West under Gen. Stephen Kearny

United States's conquest of California, 1846–1847. Facts On File.

Bodega y Quadra, as does a map of the northernmost American Pacific coastline and two landscapes, one of San Elías in Alaska, and a township at Nootka, based on drawings taken during the Malaspina expeditions. A stamp bearing a likeness of Fray Junípero Serra was issued to commemorate his bicentenary.

Missionaries

The fact that missionary zeal centered in this western area toward the second half of the 18th century can be said to be largely due to the personality of Franciscan friar Junípero Serra. On the other hand, it was not possible to preach Christianity without first conquering and colonizing, and those were the orders issued by King Charles III through his minister of state, Marquis de Grimaldi; to the viceroy, Marquis de Croix; and to the inspector general, José de Gálvez. Because of the influence of these three personalities and the next viceroy, Antonio Bucarelli, the great venture of settling and evangelizing California was undertaken with the aid of

countless eminent Spaniards who would play a role in North American history. To protect the Manila galleon, Spanish ships maintaining the trading link between Mexico and the Philippines, and to foil the Russian attempts to settle in California, the best solution, it had been decided, was to establish a number of missions to preach Christianity to the Indians of the region, thus turning them into allies of the Spanish policy. Military *presidios* would protect the missions at San Diego, Monterey, Santa Barbara and San Francisco. The chief task of the missionaries was to spread the faith, but at the same time they would teach the Indians their language and skills at farming, arts and crafts. The missions were to be maintained to a great extent by the king, and the expenditure eventually exceeded that of the military and civil government of New Mexico and California together.

Little by little, in the course of about 50 years, 23 missions sprang up throughout the territory lying between San Diego and Sonoma (north of San Francisco). (Some

Santo of Our Lady of Mount Carmel. Denver Art Museum.

attained veritable prosperity, the causes and reasons for which were sometimes called in question, if not opposed, by the civil authorities.) Their influence is seen in the letters of General Alfred Sully, in 1849, written from Monterey, in which he relates the comments of the local people about the days when the fathers summoned their faithful by ringing a bell, and when their convents were a refuge for good or bad alike (the right of asylum, maintained by the Franciscans, gave rise to more than one conflict), rich or poor, white men or Indians, Spaniards or foreigners. The names of Serra's helpers, Fathers Juan Crespi, Francisco Palou (the author of the Junípero's biography, Fermín Lasuen, Julián López and the other numerous missionaries who followed them, deserve an exceptional place in the history of California.

The missions were reestablished in stages, so that the distance lying between them was equivalent to one day's journey on horseback; in this way, tired travellers could seek accommodation within the welcoming walls of the mission and enjoy good food from their well-stocked kitchens. The route linking the missions was called El Camino Real. (This is now Highway 101. In 1904 the El Camino Real Association came into being for the purpose of reviving this exceptional route and promoting the restoration of the missions scattered along it. It fully achieved its objectives, for most of the missions have been superbly rebuilt and are a testimony visitors of this piece of common Spanish-U.S. history. A string of 125 bells, replicas of those existing at the missions, are placed along El Camino Real 10 miles apart and invite travelers today to remember the Spanish missionaries. In 1995, the prince of the Asturias (the eldest son of the king of Spain) honored the Spanish past by traveling along the Camino Real.

Reconstructing California's Spanish past is far from difficult, for the occupation of this territory is one of the most well documented colonizing efforts: the number of registers, accounts, censuses and diaries kept in the course of the first 50 years of the existence of California is astonishing. The legalistic training of the government authorities and missionaries, and their often divergent viewpoints when reporting to their respective superiors, contributed to producing these exceptional archives.

San Diego

Spanish History

The Spanish colonizers entered California from the south and worked their way northward. California's European discoverer was the Portuguese Juan Rodríguez Cabrillo, in the service of the Emperor Charles V, with the assistance of his pilot, a Valencian, Bartolomé Ferrelo. (The historian Harry Kelsey has argued persuasively that Cabrillo was born in Spain at Sevilla o Cuéllar.) Their ships were the *San Salvador* and the *Victoria*, funded by Pedro de Alvarado. They arrived on September 28, 1542, at San Miguel. They had set sail from the harbor at Navidad on June 27, 1542. At the 27th parallel they had passed the bay they called Magdalena, and at the 32nd parallel, they named a headland Cabo del Engaño.

On Point Loma peninsula, at the entrance to San Diego Bay, the Cabrillo National Monument covers an area of 80 acres today. This is believed to have been the spot where the navigator disembarked on a tongue of land that he called La Punta de los Guijarros (Pebbles Point), today, Ballast Point. The fort built there was called Fuerte Guijarro. Documents discovered recently in Mexico show that the original name was Real Fuerte de San Joaquín de Punta de Guijarros. In 1949 the Portuguese presented the city with a statue of Cabrillo by sculptor Alvaro de Bree. In 1988, a new statue by Joao Charters de Almeida e Silva replaced the original, which had deteriorated.

On November 11, 1602, Sebastián Vizcaíno spotted a haven that at first sight struck him as very safe for vessels sailing to and from the Philippines: he called it San Diego because it was the feast day of that saint. "This harbor of San Diego is very good and large," states the "Relación resumida," or short account, written by one of the historians of the expedition, Friar Antonio de la Ascensión, who mentioned, among other things, that the Indians reported the proximity of other white people (one wonders where and who). The captain entered the haven with three ships: the *San Diego*, in which sailed Vizcaíno himself, the pilot major (Francisco de Bolaños), the master (Baltasar de Armas) and the cosmographer (Jerónimo Martín Palacios); the *Santo Tomás* commanded by Toribio Gómez de Corbán, with Juan Pascual as pilot, and Friar Antonio de la Ascensión as cosmographer; and the frigate *Tres Reyes*, commanded by Ensign Sebastián Meléndez, with Antonio Flores as the pilot.

This was the second expedition attempted by Vizcaíno to explore California. The first had brought him as far as the haven at Zalagua, the Mazatlán Islands off Mexico and the entrance to the Gulf of California. He had landed in another haven, which he called San Felipe, and took possession of the territory, which he named Nueva Andalucía. He called a bay in the northwest La Paz, but he had not had the chance to explore land lying farther north.

On this second occasion, the expedition had been prepared thoroughly with plenty of time, and the ships had sailed from Acapulco on May 5. Having followed the same route as before and after passing Cape San Lucas, they called at a number of places, to which they gave Spanish names, and drew up maps of the area. On November 19, the expeditionaries held a meeting and decided on a system of signals to communicate the discoveries along the coast from one ship to another. They dropped anchor off Santa Catalina island 10 days later.

The basic history of the city of San Diego begins in 1769. On July 1, two expeditions, one by sea and the other over land, met at this spot. The maritime expedition was initially composed of three ships transporting troops and four missionaries; the *San Carlos, San Antonio,* and *San José* had sailed from La Paz on January 9, February 15, and June 16, 1769, respectively. The *San Carlos* reached the rendezvous three weeks after the *San Antonio,* while the *San José* was never heard of again. The overland expedition consisted of two groups: the main party commanded by Captain Fernando de Rivera y Moncada, while the second party came under the command of Gaspar de Portolá, the leader of the expedition that included Father Junípero Serra. On the way, the Franciscan founded the mission of San Fernando de Vellicatá. Of the 219 men who had set out two months earlier, little more than 100 arrived at the rendezvous, and not all in good health as they had to endure many hardships on the way.

After two weeks' rest, Governor Portolá and a party of those who were fit to travel set off northward to Monterey Bay, one of the goals of the expedition; he was accompanied by Lieutenant Pedro Fagés, Sergeant José Francisco Ortega, and Father Crespi. Owing to the painful state of his ulcered leg, Junípero Serra stayed behind. Six months would pass before Portolá and his men returned without reaching their goal. On the second day of their travels some Indians appeared and, wishing to accompany the expeditionaries, hampered their advance. Portolá estimated a population of some 6,000 Indians in five townships. The captain endeavored to follow the coastline, but when this did not prove possible, had to cross deep canyons, in one of which the party encountered a pack of bears (whence the name Cañón de los Osos), and ate bear meat.

They had great difficulty in finding a pass through the Santa Lucía Mountains (named by Vizcaíno) until Ortega came up with the only solution, a hazardous climb. Following a difficult ascent, on September 26 the expeditionaries caught sight of a large expanse of water. Portolá unsuccessfully despatched Rivera to ascertain whether it was Monterey Bay. Continuing their march, the advance guard under Ortega brought encouraging news to the effect that they had seen San Francisco Bay, to judge by the description given in 1732 by Cabrera Bueno, the pilot of the Manila galleons. A few days later, the whole party pitched camp on the shore of the bay. Realizing that Monterey lay farther south, Portolá gave orders to return to San Diego in the belief that he had not achieved his objective. In fact, he had done so, for he stopped at Monterey without realizing it.

During their absence, on July 16, only two days after their departure, Fray Junípero Serra founded the mission of San Diego de Alcalá. Shortly afterward Indians attacked, causing some damage and killing one boy and wounding two. Portolá spent several months supervising the construction of the *presidio* and houses to accommodate those who remained at San Diego. Faced with a desperate situation at this first Spanish foundation in California when the ship *San Antonio,* which had been sent to San Blas to fetch provisions and assistance, failed to return, Portolá even considered withdrawing from San Diego and returning to New Spain. Fray Junípero Serra opposed this decision. Their doubts and distress were overcome when the *San Antonio* appeared bringing relief from their hardships on March 19, 1770.

Consequently, Portolá set out for Monterey by land in April; Fray Junípero embarked on the *San Antonio* bound for the same destination. Portolá and his men found the journey much easier and quicker, for most of the route was already familiar. One sunny morning they reached a beach and were delighted to find that one of the crosses that they had set up on their previous visit was still standing. The overawed natives told them how the cross lighted up on moonlit nights. After some debate, they concluded that this spot was precisely Monterey.

When Gaspar de Portolá withdrew to New Spain according to plan, the *presidio* at San Diego was left under the command of Captain Fernando de Rivera y Moncada, until he was transferred to Monterey in 1774. He was replaced at San Diego by Lieutenant José Francisco de Ortega, who brought with him his wife María Antonia Carrillo, who had been living at Loreto until then. She and the wives of other soldiers were the first Western women to live in California. In February 1775, Antonia gave birth to a son, the first European child born in the territory.

In the course of the following year, Ortega received orders to found the mission of San Juan de Capistrano, about 69 miles from San Diego, for the purpose of providing support on the northward route to offset the frequent Indian raids in the area. In his absence, the San Diego mission suffered a fierce Indian attack on November 4, 1775. While Father Fermín Lasuén was in charge of the Franciscans (during Father Serra's journey to Mexico), the mission had been moved to a spot some five and a half miles from the *presidio;* so, when the assault took place the soldiers at the *presidio* were unaware of its location and unable to defend the inhabitants. Father Jaume, a blacksmith named Romero and a carpenter, Urselino, were killed and many of the Indians on the mission were wounded. Ortega returned as soon as he heard what had happened but found that no harm had come to the people at the *presidio* and that his family was safe.

Captain Rivera came to San Diego the following January, accompanied by Juan Bautista de Anza, who had just led an expedition of colonists as far as Monterey on their way to settle at San Francisco Bay. The Indians taken prisoner during the previous raid were interrogated, but it was hard to locate the leaders, Carlos and Francisco. Carlos was eventually captured and brought to the *presidio,* but succeeded in escaping and seeking refuge and the right of asylum at the church. When Rivera demanded that he be handed over and then took him by force, Father Serra, who had warned against violence, excommunicated him. The friction between the civil and religious authorities caused by this incident was smoothed out when Captain Felipe de Neve was appointed and took up his post as the new governor. Captain Rivera received a commission to escort a party of colonists from Sonora to the San Gabriel Mission, but a Yuma Indian attack put an end to the expedition and almost all its members perished, including their leader.

Ortega stayed at San Diego until 1782, when he received orders to found a *presidio* at Santa Barbara. His place was taken by Captain José de Zúñiga. In 1787, Juan Pablo Grijalva took command; over the next eight years he organized 15 expeditions against the Indians. In 1795, he was ordered to found a *presidio* halfway between San Diego and Santa Barbara and he chose the San Jose valley as the site. In 1796, Grijalva obtained from the Crown a grant of land which shortly afterward formed the Santiago de Santa Ana ranch, at the foot of the Santiago Mountains, some 75 miles north of San Diego. His partner in this venture was José Antonio Yorba, his son-in-law, who was also a member of the *presidio* garrison. In time this ranch was to become very popular and, lying only four miles off El Camino Real, became a regular halt for people traveling via this route. Grijalva received the ship *Discovery* with Captain George Vancouver aboard, just as his successor, Major Juan Rodríguez Cabrillo welcomed the American ship *Betsey,* skippered by William Shaler, in 1803.

Throughout this period, the San Diego Mission progressed and, by the beginning of the 19th century, had 20,000 sheep, 10,000 head of cattle and 1,250 horses; it covered an area of 50,000 acres and was renowned for its wines. The mission declined when the government of California came into Mexican hands. In 1846 it was sold to Santiago Argüello. Twenty-two acres were returned to the Catholic Church in 1862; renovation of the church began in 1931, and it was reopened for worship a few months later.

The City Today

The sector of the city of San Diego called the Old Town occupies the spot on which the first Spanish mission stood in 1769, southeast of the crossing of Highways 101 and 80. El Presidio Real, which collapsed in 1835, used to stand on Presidio Hill. The San Diego Historical Society rebuilt it in 1969 to celebrate the 200th anniversary of its foundation—the oldest *presidio* in the American West. The society itself has its headquarters in the nearby Junipero Serra Museum. Also nearby is the old square or plaza (on the corner of Calhoun and Wallace Streets), likewise rebuilt with a Spanish character. Closeby is the Casa de Estudillo, known as "Ramona's Marriage Place," which became popular as a result of the novel *Ramona* by Helen Hunt Jackson, which is set in the Spanish days of California.

The city spreads along the shores of San Diego Bay, and from the *embarcadero,* visits can be made to many places in the area, including nearby Coronado peninsula, with the town of the same name called after the Spanish *conquistador.* Balboa Park has a number of surprising Spanish Renaissance–style buildings, which were used for two international exhibitions in 1915 and 1935: El Prado, with the Cabrillo Bridge; the Alcazar Garden, inspired by the Alcázar at Seville, with a statue of El Cid by Anna Hyatt Huntington; La Laguna de las Flores; the Spanish Village Art Center; the Old Globe Theater; the Fine Arts Gallery; the Organ Pavilion; Balboa Park Bowl (for concerts); Balboa Stadium; and the Zoological Gardens.

The Casa de España is very active in San Diego and the Institute for Hispanic Media and Culture at the University of Southern California sponsored a literary contest in 1984 on "The Contribution of Spain to the Independence of the United States."

North of San Diego, the Mission Bay Park area is being developed not far from the town of La Jolla, with one of the campuses of the University of California. South of San Diego lies the municipal area of Chula Vista, which holds an annual Fiesta de la Luna, where traditional costumes are worn. The review *Toros* (an English-language publication on bullfighting) was also published here. Inland from San Diego lies a predominantly mountainous area with the Pechanga, Pauma, La Jolla, Santa

Mission de Alcalá in San Diego, California.

Ysabel and Viejas Indian reservations. The Pala Mission, founded in 1816, still serves the Indians for whom it was founded. Townships nearby bear such names as La Mesa, El Cajon, Ramona, Julian and Mesa Grande.

On the eastern side of these mountains can be found, to the north, the Borrego State Park, and to the south, the Anza Desert State Park, named after Juan Bautista de Anza, the founder of San Francisco. Its highest point, Font's Point, was named after the chaplain Pedro Font, who accompanied the settlers led by Anza.

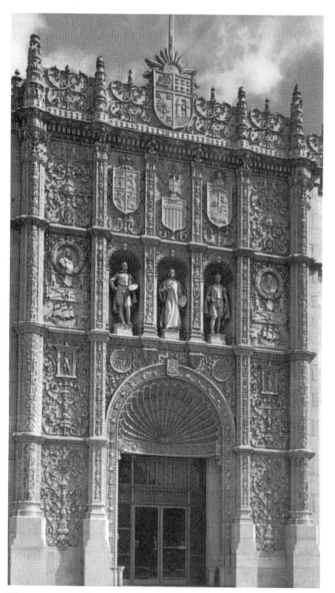

The entrance to the Fine Arts Gallery, Balboa Park, San Diego, California.

San Francisco Solano de Sonoma Mission in California.

Missions South of Los Angeles

On the Camino Real from San Diego, the second mission encountered is San Luis Rey, near Oceanside. (This mission was not the second to be founded, an honor that fell to the mission of Carmel at Monterey.) San Luis Rey Mission was the 18th of the Californian missions. It was consecrated on June 13, 1798, by Father Fermín Lasuén, the successor of Serra as head of the Franciscans in the area. He stayed there for six weeks until the new foundation had got under way. In time, San Luis

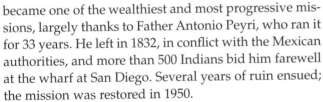

The mission of Santa Barbara (left) and the mission of San Juan de Capistrano (right), in California. Carlos M. Fernández-Shaw.

became one of the wealthiest and most progressive missions, largely thanks to Father Antonio Peyri, who ran it for 33 years. He left in 1832, in conflict with the Mexican authorities, and more than 500 Indians bid him farewell at the wharf at San Diego. Several years of ruin ensued; the mission was restored in 1950.

Farther up the highway lies San Juan de Capistrano Mission (whose swallows are celebrated in the popular song) founded by Father Serra on November 1, 1775. A previous mission had been established a year earlier on the present site of San Luis Rey, after Father Junípero had succeeded in convincing Captain Rivera of the need to build a mission between San Diego and San Gabriel; the Indian assault on San Diego, just when the evangelization work was beginning, made it necessary to withdraw, and the bells were buried. The mission bells were placed in the belfry of the new mission in 1797, but the size of the mission community in that same year led to the construction of a larger church. Isidoro Aguilar, an expert builder, began the construction but died before the building was completed. This explains the

existence of six cupolas and a style that differs from the other missions of simpler design.

The earthquake in 1812 caused the deaths of 40 neophytes, who were buried by the collapsing walls of the church; it was never rebuilt, and worship continued in the original church. At this very romantic and beautifully restored mission, set amid gardens full of birds, and known as "the gem of the missions," visitors can see the mighty walls of the big church, the peaceful early chapel where Father Serra said Mass (today presided over by a fine gilded altar brought from Spain in 1906 as a gift from Archbishop Cantwell of Los Angeles); the bells that rang the alarm during the attack by pirate Hipólito Bouchard (who plagued many of the local missions) in 1818; the statue of the founder; several fountains; and bougainvillea adorning the walls on all sides.

El Camino Real continues on its way through far-flung orange groves and localities bearing such names as El Toro and Santa Ana, while the coast road boasts such beaches as San Onofre, Laguna, Corona del Mar, Cabrillo, Palos Verdes, Redondo, Hermosa, Del Rey and Santa Monica. The highway also crosses the Santa Ana and San Gabriel Rivers, named by the Portolá expedition in 1769. It was on their banks that the Spanish expeditionaries experienced the first earth tremors, which caused them considerable alarm, for one tremor lasted as long as an Ave María.

Los Angeles

The foundation of Los Angeles was the work of the Spanish governor of California, Felipe de Neve, who named it El Pueblo de Nuestra Señora La Reina de Los Angeles (The Village of Our Lady the Queen of Angels) in 1781. It was founded in pursuit of the policy introduced by Felipe de Neve of setting up townships where Spaniards could settle apart from the Franciscan missions intended for the Indians; the purpose was to establish the presence of Spain firmly and render the best possible assistance in defending the territory against enemies and in aiding its economic development.

Another town, San José de Guadalupe, had been established here previously. De Neve entrusted Lieutenant José Francisco Ortega with the task of seeking a spot for the new town; accompanied by Sergeant Juan José Robles, Ortega explored the region until they decided on a site in the vicinity of the Porciúncula River. However, his plan was not implemented until two years later, when colonists received a plot of land on which they could each build a dwelling. No chapel was built, however, and the inhabitants of Los Angeles therefore had to travel over nine miles every Sunday to attend Mass at the San Gabriel Mission. Eventually, a chapel was erected under the advocation of Nuestra Señora de los Angeles, and can be visited to this day in the Old Spanish Plaza, standing on a spot slightly southwest of the original site: the present chapel was erected between 1800 and 1812.

Today, this church is run by the Claretians and tends the large Hispanic community of Los Angeles. An outer porch is decorated with murals depicting scenes from the days of its foundation. On the west side of the plaza, the first bishop of Los Angeles (then Los Angeles-Monterrey) Father Tadeo Amat, a native of Barcelona, set up his see at the end of 1859. It was thanks to his efforts that the Church of Santa Vibiana was built, and it is there that he is buried. The inaugural sermon was delivered by Archbishop Sadoc Alemany of San Francisco in Spanish. The church was modeled along the lines of that of San Miguel del Puerto, in Barcelona. Bishop Amat was succeeded by Bishop Francis Mora.

In the plaza, bullfights were held even after California became a part of the United States. (The last bullfight took place in 1860, practically at the same time that the first baseball team was formed!) Near the plaza is Olvera Street, with Mexican shops and other establishments, lending a touch of color to this sector of the city. Here, too, is the Avila Adobe, named after its owner and builder in 1818, Mayor Francisco Avila. Various statues around the city depict King Charles III, Governor Felipe de Neve and Father Junípero Serra, and a memorial tablet is inscribed with the names of the first settlers in

1771. (A large municipal building, at Broadway and First Streets, was named after Father Serra as well.) The Casa de España elects a "Reina de la Hispanidad" annually.

In one of the quarters of the coat of arms of the city of Los Angeles appears the ensigns of Castilla and León, and at City Hall, three Spanish flags fly: a white one with a burgundy cross, brought by Juan Rodríguez Cabrilla; another white one with the royal arms, for many years the flag of Spain; and a red and yellow banner with the shield of Carlos III.

It was at Los Angeles that the most influential ranchers and dons in California met when news arrived of the invasion of Spain by Napoléon and the accesion of his brother Joseph to the Spanish throne. Furious at this outrage, they swore loyalty to the Junta, and at the suggestion of Antonio María Lugo, owner of the Rancho San Antonio, lying east of Los Angeles toward the San Bernardino Mountains, they studied steps to overcome the awkward situation caused for the territory and *presidios* by the lack of ships from New Spain, since they no longer received provisions or funds to pay their garrisons.

Many streets and squares in greater Los Angeles are named for the founders, such as Junipero Avenue, De Neve Square, Crespi Street and Portola Avenue. There are the names of writers, such as Cervantes Place, Don Quixote Drive, Lorca Road and Unamuno Avenue (built at the time of the recent centenary of his birth). The *conquistadores* are also honored, with De Soto Street, Alvarado Street, Balboa Boulevard and Pizarro Street. Many other regions, cities and towns bear the names of Spanish saints and artists, and more general Spanish names.

Nearby Hollywood has seen many popular Spaniards in the film and entertainment industry. Some of these include Antonio Moreno, Catalina Bárcenas, Enrique Jardiel Poncela, Edgar Neville, José López Rubio, Antonio Banderas and Sara Montiel.

In northeast Los Angeles is Elysian Park; on the left of the entrance a block of granite records the fact that Gaspar de Portolá and Father Juan Crespi pitched camp there on their way to Monterey, and in the same sector, the Casa de Adobe houses furniture and utensils from the Spanish period. The nearby Southwestern Museum houses an Indian collection. El Alisal, now a state monument, was formerly the home of the historian Charles F. Lummis, who built it himself. Much of what we know about Spanish California is due to his work *The Spanish Pioneers and the California Missions,* and his efforts to restore these missions.

Other buildings in Spanish style include the Pasadena Community Playhouse and the Los Angeles County Arboretum, near the old Rancho Santa Anita. At San Marino, the Art Gallery is housed in the former residence of millionaire Henry E. Huntington, whose name was given to the famous adjacent library, which houses a magnificent collection of manuscripts, letters and documents of all types concerning the Spanish colonization of the Southwest. The Teatro Campesino in Los Angeles founded by Luis Valdes in 1965, produces works of Chicano literature.

The University of California at Los Angeles has its campus (as well as a department of Spanish) here, as do Loyola and Southern California Universities. The dean of the University of Southern California Law School was at one time an eminent Hispanic scholar, James Brown Scott.

The Del Amo Foundation, established by Gregorio del Amo, in 1929, is of great cultural importance, providing grants for exchange students from Spain and California. King Juan Carlos of Spain visited Los Angeles in 1987 and recalled, "This is the first time that a king of Spain has visited California, although it was during the reign of a Spanish monarch, Charles III, that Spain's links with this land first began . . . California is a beacon and hive of activity with which Spain is attempting to maintain and develop a very special relationship."

Lying off Los Angeles in the open sea are the islands of Santa Catalina, named by Vizcaíno on November 25, 1602, and San Clemente and Santa Barbara, discovered by Cabrillo and sighted by Vizcaíno.

Missions North of Los Angeles

Not far from Los Angeles stands the mission of San Gabriel, founded some time before the village. When 10 new Franciscans arrived from Baja California in 1771, Father Serra had enough missionaries to continue his work, and on September 8 of that same year, on the road linking the missions of Monterey and San Diego, he blessed the mission of San Gabriel. It prospered from the start and by March 22, 1774, was ready to welcome the expedition of settlers led by Juan Bautista Anza. In 1774, Anza received orders from the viceroy to find a route from Sonora to California through the Colorado River area. Then in command of the *presidio* at Tubac, Arizona, Anza, who was a local Creole, followed the Gila River accompanied by only a few soldiers. After much trial and error and getting lost in the desert, Anza

succeeded in leading his men to the San Gabriel Mission. On reporting his success to his superior in Mexico, he was commissioned to recruit settlers and lead them to San Francisco Bay. Each settler would receive wages from the time he enlisted for the expedition, and both he and his family would be entitled to daily rations of food, clothing and other essential commodities. The cost per settler amounted to roughly $800.

The party was to consist of 240 people. They were organized into three groups: the first commanded by Anza; the second, under Sergeant Juan Pablo Grijalva; and the third, commanded by Second Lieutenant Joaquín Moraga. The expeditionaries traveled together from Sonora to the Californian desert, in which they spent Christmas 1775. Each party traveled separately when crossing the desert for the sake of greater safety.

Bitterly cold weather accompanied by snow, scarcity of water and the loss of most of their horses, which were either stolen or frozen to death, were just a few of the hardships that the expedition experienced but were overcome thanks to the gifted leadership of Anza. However, since his plans to reach Monterey by a new route looked hazardous, Anza considered it wiser to take the already explored route via San Gabriel. After crossing the Santa Ana River and the Del Trabuco Sierras, the weary expeditionaries joyfully caught sight of the belfry of the San Gabriel Mission on January 4, 1776. They were housed there for many months while Captain Rivera made them bide their time until the foundation of San Francisco. The buildings to be seen today were built in 1796, when the priests moved the mission five miles northwest. When it passed into the hands of a civil administrator in 1834, as a result of the Mexican laws confiscating Church property, the mission farm had 16,500 cows. In 1908 Claretian fathers took over the mission.

Today, San Gabriel possesses one of the finest collections of missionary relics including, among other things, pictures of the Murillo school, copies of Raphael, Correggio and Andrea del Sarto, Spanish sculptures, and a baptismal font presented by King Charles III. The Fiesta de San Gabriel is held in September every year and includes the *tardeada*, a traditional reception given at the mission, begun in 1934. Since 1961 there has been a plaque in the cemetery dedicated to the victims of the massacre perpetrated by the Yuma Indians on the Colorado River in July 1781, and a wreath of flowers is placed before it every year by the Compadrinos de San Gabriel.

The mission of San Fernando, Rey de España (King of Spain) lies north of Los Angeles. It was founded by

Father Lasuén, on September 8, 1797. It was his fourth mission. Initially there was some difficulty about choosing the site, for the land belonged to the ranch of Francisco Reyes, mayor of Los Angeles; the controversy ended by Reyes sponsoring the mission and acting as godfather to the first child baptized in the church. The mission quickly progressed and by 1806, was producing considerable quantities of leather, soap, tallow and other materials; it came to have 13,000 head of cattle, 8,000 ewes and 2,300 horses. Although not on El Camino Real, it became an essential way station for travelers on this route, so the missionaries had to add a guesthouse to the existing mission buildings. At the time of the transfer of sovereignty to Mexico, it was run by Father Ibarra, who refused to renounce his loyalty to Spain; since there was nobody to succeed him, he was allowed to stay on at his beloved mission until 1835.

Years of abandon in the hands of private owners ensued. In 1896, Charles Lummis started a campaign for its reconstruction. These efforts progressed from 1923 onward, when the Oblate fathers took over the buildings. Today, visitors can still admire the old organ and the altar, the lower part of which is composed of mirrors. At the entrance to the park stands a statue of Fray Junípero.

Passing through the Santa Monica mountains, including four peaks rising to over 10,000 feet high (San Antonio, San Jacinto, San Bernardino and San Gorgonio) the mission of San Buenaventura is next encountered on El Camino Real heading north, in the city of Ventura. It was founded by Father Serra on March 31, 1782, at a spot claimed for Spain 240 years earlier by Juan Rodríguez Cabrillo. In early March 1782, Governor Felipe de Neve, Serra, three of his Franciscans and the commander of San Diego, José Francisco Ortega, had met at San Gabriel Mission. They had decided to found San Buenaventura and Santa Barbara, and also a *presidio* close to the latter. It was the first time that Neve, who favored the foundation of Spanish towns with European colonists rather than missions for the Indians, agreed to such foundations. He claimed that the townships were cheaper for the Spanish exchequer and more useful as a means of cooperating in the expansion of Spanish frontiers and in the defense of the territory. In accordance with the instructions given by Major de Croix, the new missions would not embark upon any industrial ventures, and their single missionary would confine himself to preaching the Gospels to the Indians. Neve had intended to supervise the foundation but was away on orders from his superiors. When he returned, he found San Buenaventura established along the old lines. From the outset the mission of San Buenaventura grew quickly and was visited by Captain George Vancouver in 1793. Among the early missionaries here was Friar José Senán. The earthquake of 1812 caused serious damage to the mission but did not affect it as much as others. The museum exhibits two wooden bells, which are among the oldest recovered.

Some nine miles from Ventura lies Rancho Cañada Larga, which encompasses the ruins of Santa Gertrudis Mission, thought to have been founded by Serra in 1790. Burned down shortly afterward, it was not rebuilt until 1809 and was destroyed once again in the earthquake of 1812. During the raid by pirate Hipólito Bouchard, Father Senán and his parishioners took refuge at Santa Gertrudis.

Santa Barbara

Santa Barbara also lies on El Camino Real. Discovered by Juan Cabrillo in 1542, it received its name from Sebastián Vizcaíno in 1602, who sighted it on December 4. In 1782, Governor Felipe de Neve commissioned José Francisco Ortega to construct a *presidio* on that spot; the Yuma Indians had recently slaughtered an expedition of colonists led by Fernando Rivera and it was therefore thought necessary to establish more garrisons at strategic points. With a large escort and accompanied by his brother-in-law, Corporal Mariano Carrillo, Ortega departed from San Diego, called at the mission of San Juan de Capistrano, rendezvoused at San Gabriel with Fray Serra and Governor Neve, and continued northward to take part in the foundation of San Buenaventura.

Proceeding to Santa Barbara, Ortega chose a small hill commanding a good view as a site for a *presidio*, only a mile from the beach. On April 21 a cross was set up within the palisade that had been built, and Governor Neve took possession of the place officially on behalf of King Charles III. Ortega stayed behind as commander, and with the help of the soldiers and sailors from the galleon *San Blas* succeeded in building a *presidio*, a sound stone and adobe wall, with accommodation for the officers and soldiers, a chapel and warehouses, among other things. Ortega was to remain at Santa Barbara until 1786, when he was transferred to Monterey. But, when he retired in 1795, he obtained a grant of land, not far from the city, called Rancho de Nuestra Señora del Refugio. This estate suffered serious damage at the time of the attack by the pirate Bouchard, but did not take long to recover.

The Santa Barbara Mission was not founded until 1787, during the governorship of Pedro Fagés. Consequently, Serra never saw it, and it was begun by Friar Fermín Lasuén. It soon progressed and a number of buildings sprang up around it; the last, completed in 1820, lasted until 1925, when an earth tremor caused considerable damage. When the Spanish friars were expelled by the Mexican government in 1833, they were replaced by Franciscans from the convent at Zacatecas. The first bishop of California, Francisco García Diego, moved his see to the mission in 1842. In this way the buildings have survived to the present day, and this is the only mission that has never left Franciscan hands since its foundation.

The facade of the mission has been preserved in amazingly good condition until the present time, and it has been called the "queen of missions." It is well worth seeing the chapel, cloisters, new buildings of the Franciscan novitiate and the gardens. On the esplanade before the entrance can be seen the remains of its original wash house. There is a fine collection of documents in the mission archives, such as the autographed letter of Serra urging that California not be abandoned, or an admirable synoptical chart with two entries, made in 1800, giving a summary of births on the mission and the movement of livestock and farm produce. In 1995, Don Felipe de Borbón visited the mission and was paid homage by the descendants of original Spanish settlers.

A stroll through the streets and plazas of the city Santa Barbara today recalls its Spanish past. There are so many Spanish names that a local author, Rosario Curletti, has devoted a book to them called *Pathways to Pavements*. Just a few of them include Alameda Padre Serra, Alvarado, Arguello, Arrellaga, Ayala, Calandria, Calle Crespis, Calle Granada, Calle Noguera, Canon Perdido, Carrillo, De La Guerra, Ferrelo, Figueroa, Goleta, Juana Maria, Las Palmas, Lasuen, Micheltorena, Ortega, Paseo del Descanso, Plaza Rubio, Salsipuedes and others, many of which bear the names of saints.

The history of the city is also evoked through events such as the Old Spanish Days Fiesta, which is held every August and lasts four days, including competitions, dances, shows of costumes and horses, and plays.

An area of the city has been reconstructed with a Spanish atmosphere. In one of its narrow alleyways, like those in Andalusia, two commemorative plaques composed of decorative tiles are set into the walls of the house that the commander of the *presidio*, José de la Guerra Noriega, had built for himself, now called Old De La Guerra House. (This was the setting for the popular novel by Richard H. Dana, *Two Years Before the Mast.*) It was during

Palace of Justice, Santa Barbara, California. Carlos M. Fernández-Shaw.

Dolores Mission, San Francisco, California. Carlos M. Fernández-Shaw.

the command of Guerra that the pirate Bouchard disembarked on the coast at Santa Barbara; however, the commander of the *presidio* had been warned in advance and succeeded in preparing the defenses. Fearing defeat, the pirate did not attempt to attack.

The post office and a government building stand on part of the land that originally belonged to the *presidio*. El Cuartel, which dates from 1782, is still standing and is the oldest building in the city. Not far away are the Lobero Theater (built in 1872 by José Lobero) and the Carrillo Adobe House. The Covarrubias Adobe House (built by Domingo Carrillo, but owned since 1847 by the Covarrubias family) and the Historic Adobe House now belong to the Rancheros Visitadores, a riding organization. The Historical Museum documents the Spanish period.

A building in markedly Spanish style is the courthouse, opened in 1929 to replace the previous building, which burned down. The architect, William Mooser, succeeded in giving the building a perfect Andalusian style, and it is a happy example of the possibility of adapting the historical spirit of the city to modern times. The patio is particularly beautiful, with the coffered ceilings inside showing Moorish overtones. The walls are white and the roofs are made of red tiles; the passageways inside are flanked by artistic tile panels and are lit by quaint lanterns. The main chambers are decorated with Hispanic motifs; the Supervisor's Hall or Room has some large paintings of Juan Rodríguez Cabrillo, Sebastián Vizcaíno, and Fathers Junípero Serra and Fermín Lasuén by artist Dan Sayre Groesbeck. A legend in Spanish on the walls reads "Dios Nos Dió el Campo; El Arte Humano Edificó las Ciudades" (God gave us the country; human art built the towns).

East Cabrillo Boulevard leads to Cabrillo State Park, a memorial to the mariner who died, on January 3, 1543, on the nearby island of San Miguel, or La Posesión: his remains are thought to have been buried there, and his companions called it Isla de Juan Rodríguez. Cabrillo died when he broke his arm falling from a rock and gangrene set in; he appointed Bartolomé Ferrelo to replace him as leader of the exploratory expedition.

Missions North of Santa Barbara

The west coast of Santa Barbara has some splendid beaches—Gaviota, Refugio, El Capitan, Goleta and Arroyo Puro—along the route taken by the Portolá expedition, which experienced difficulty in getting the animals to cross the sands. The coast is skirted by El Camino Real, which turns north sharply to reach the Santa Ines mountains via Gaviota Pass.

The mission of Santa Ines, in a perfect state of repair, has one of the finest historical museums to be found in the chain of missions. The mission was founded on September 17, 1804, and although it prospered in its early days, its hopes were not confirmed in later times. The earthquake in 1812 caused serious damage, and although rebuilt in 1817, it fell into the hands of the Indians during the uprising in 1824; only the church was saved, partly thanks to the attackers themselves, who helped to save it from the fire. A happy interlude in the history of this mission came between 1842 and 1845, in the days of the Mexican governor Micheltorena, who had a great liking for Spain and maintained very friendly relations with the missionary fathers.

The chapel was never abandoned. The missionary running it at the time of the enforced sale of Church properties arranged for the buildings and part of the land to be used as a school for religious instruction, firstly for Fran-

The mission where Fray Junípero Serra is buried, Carmel, California. Carlos M. Fernández-Shaw.

ciscans and afterward for Brothers of the Christian Doctrine. Later, when it was abandoned, the remaining priest persuaded a bricklayer to live there, who carried out small repairs and prevented the building's deterioration.

Further along the Camino Real lies the township of Lompoc, within whose municipal limits, about four miles from the town, stands the mission of La Purísima Concepción. Its original site coincides with the modern town, but the great gash left in the terrain by the earthquake in 1812 led the missionaries to rebuild it a short distance away. It takes its name from the date of its foundation by Father Lasuén: December 8, 1787 (the Holy Day of the Immaculate Conception). Its most outstanding missionary was Fray Mariano Payeras, who worked here for 20 years and put his heart and soul into the rebuilding of the mission after the earthquake before he died in 1823. The Indians took the mission during their uprising and built a fort; a contingent of 100 men sent from Monterey by the Mexican governor had difficulty in dislodging them. In 1934 accurate renovation work began, and today visitors can admire the convent, church, barracks and gardens where only the plants grown by the missionaries can be seen.

Before reaching the next mission, San Luis Obispo de Tolosa, El Camino Real passes through such towns as Los Alamos, Santa Maria, Arroyo Grande and Avila Beach. San Luis is set in La Cañada de los Osos, given this name by Gaspar de Portolá in 1769, when his expedition suddenly found the way blocked by a group of bears. A hunt immediately began, and two bears were shot down with muskets.

The mission was founded on September 1, 1772, by Father Serra while on his way to San Diego, where he was to collect the provisions brought for the Monterey mission by the ships San Carlos and San Antonio, whose captains were reluctant to go as far as the bay. Manned originally by a single priest, the mission grew rapidly in spite of three Indian attacks having occurred by 1774. When the thatched roofs caught fire, the missionaries were forced to make roof tiles of a sort that would thereafter be used at all the missions. In time, it came to have many buildings to accommodate the Indians, and the mission books recorded no fewer than 2,074 baptisms in 1804. The most outstanding figure in the history of the mission is Father Luis Martínez, who had frequent showdowns with the civilian authorities, who after

Mission of San Gabriel, California.

1810, when Mexico began her rebellion against Spain, sought revenues since funds were no longer received from Spain. He succeeded in bringing days of great prosperity to the mission and maintained direct trade with British and American ships that approached the coast surreptitiously. At the time of the Hipólito Bouchard attack (1818), Father Martínez courageously led a company of Indians at Santa Barbara and San Juan de Capistrano. After 34 years' service at the mission, he abandoned it in 1830 following orders from the Mexican government.

The backdrop to this whole region is formed by the Santa Lucia Mountains, so named by Sebastián Vizcaíno, because he saw them for the first time on that saint's feast day, December 13. Their difficult passes, considerable height and the depth of their gorges forced the Gaspar de Portolá expedition to carry out one of the most amazing feats in the history of these explorations. Sergeant José Francisco Ortega and a patrol were sent ahead and spent several days trying to find a pass; it proved elusive, but they eventually found it. After hacking their way through thick pine woods and climbing for two hours up a dangerous path above a deep abyss, the whole group succeeded in reaching the crest of the chain, where they admired the view lying before them to the north. The names Cuesta Pass and Paso Robles (the name of one of the corporals accompanying Ortega) commemorate this venture.

The San Miguel Arcangel Mission was established on July 25, 1797. San Simeón, or rather the ranch which once existed there, belonged to the mission, as did others such as Paso de Robles, La Asunción and Santa Isabel. This gives some idea of the size of the domains of the mission and the prosperity that it achieved. A devastating fire jeopardized its existence in 1806, but it was soon rebuilt and the church was enlarged in 1816 so

San Juan Bautista Mission, California.

that it recovered its prosperity and importance. Friar Juan Cabot was the most outstanding figure here from 1800 onward for 30 years. The last Franciscan disappeared in 1840, and shortly afterward the mission became one of the most popular saloons along El Camino Real. The Church of San Miguel, open for worship, is one of the few in which paintings and decorations have not needed restoration.

Highway 101, leading north, reaches from San Miguel to San Ardo and San Lucas. Nearby is a military area in which stands the mission of San Antonio de Padua, on the banks of the river of that same name. This was the third mission founded by Fray Junípero, preceded only by San Diego and San Carlos. On July 14, 1771, the mission was blessed, and the bells pealed for the first time, rung by a Franciscan friar as a call to the local Indians. The mission prospered from the outset, as indicated in accounts by Governor Pedro Fagés (who was not on particularly good terms with Fray Junípero) in 1782 and by Father Font in 1776 when Juan Bautista de Anza called at the mission on his second journey. As early as 1779 a church almost 150 feet long was built here, and building continued in the ensuing years, including a water tank and an aqueduct. San Antonio had a resident priest until 1882. In June 1950 restoration was begun, and the surroundings of the mission have been kept intact, just as they were two centuries ago.

The next mission along El Camino Real is Nuestra Señora de la Soledad. The name Soledad was given by Portolá: when the expeditionaries encountered an Indian, he replied with sounds and gestures that suggested the word *soledad*, or "solitude." When Father Lasuén began the building's foundation on October 9, 1791, he did not hesitate to accept the name found on the maps. From the start this choice was inauspicious. Indian neophytes were scarce, particularly at first, and for lack of prosperity the early buildings made of brushwood and brambles could only be replaced by adobe after six years. Eventually, in 1805, the mission experienced a rapid decline, aided by the outbreak of an epidemic, which took a heavy toll among the Indians.

Two missionaries made a special mark here: Fray Florencio Ibáñez, who died in 1818 and is buried there (near the tomb of Governor José Arrillaga, who retired to the mission to die in 1814); and Friar Vicente Sarria, the last Franciscan at Soledad, who was president of the order at the time of its secularization. Found dead before the altar in May 1835, he was carried in his coffin by his faithful Indians to the mission of San Antonio.

Monterey

Monterey played a key role in the Spanish colonization of California. Discovered by Rodríguez Cabrillo in 1542, it was given its name by Sebastián Vizcaíno, in honor of the governing viceroy. On December 16, 1602, a group of captains, pilots and cosmographers decided to explore it further, and consequently Enrico Martínez made two drawings, which were often used thereafter. A thorough inspection was made of the port, the river flowing into it was discovered (and named Carmelo), woods were found nearby (of good use if it became necessary to repair the ships) and the bay was found to be a good haven for ships from the Orient seeking a refuge. But for many years afterward, the discovery brought no

tangible results; it was only when King Charles III finally decided to colonize California that Monterey assumed greater significance.

Monterey was the goal that Gaspar de Portolá established during his exploratory expedition in 1769. It was also the objective given to the patrol under Captain Fernando Rivera after crossing the Santa Lucia massif that same year. But Rivera failed to find it and Portolá himself, with Pedro Fagés, José Francisco Ortega, Father Juan Crespi and the other members of the expedition proved unable to identify it when they camped on its shores on November 28, returning disappointed after reaching San Francisco Bay. When Portolá decided to persist in his search, organizing a simultaneous expedition by sea on

Mission of San Carlos in Monterey, California, founded in 1770 by Spanish Franciscans. U.S.I.S.
Photo Lab, Madrid.

the ship *San Antonio,* on which Fray Junípero had embarked, they found the bay, together with the cross that they had driven into the beach months earlier, and that shone so that the natives had attributed miraculous properties to it. The overland expedition reached the spot a week earlier than the maritime party. On June 1, 1770, after a ceremonial raising of the Spanish flag, taking possession of the site in the name of the king and blessing it, work began on the *presidio* and the mission church. (In July 1970, Monterey commemorated the bicentenniel of its foundation, while Lérida, Spain, organized events in honor of Portolá. Two statues by sculptor Enrique Monjó were erected at Balaguer, Spain, and Monterey.)

After the township was founded and Portolá was succeeded in his command by Pedro Fagés (as had been decided from the outset), days of friction ensued between Fray Junípero and the new leader, resulting in the decision of the Franciscan to move the mission five miles south to the banks of the Carmelo River. The chapel at the *presidio* remained, however, for use by the garrison. The original mission was consecrated under the name of San Carlos (St. Charles) Borromeo, but in its new location it became known as Carmel. A major part in the missions affairs was played by the builder Esteban Ruíz. The rivalry between Serra and Fagís continued and resulted in the Franciscan traveling to Mexico, where he succeeded in persuading the viceroy to dismiss his rival. Captain Rivera y Moncada was appointed in his stead, but Fray Junípero did not enjoy better relations with him either.

In 1776 the Spanish colonists arrived at Monterey, led by Juan Bautista de Anza, for the purpose of founding a settlement on San Francisco Bay. Their plans had been delayed by their enforced stay at San Gabriel Mission to the south, as a result of Rivera's demand that Anza should accompany him and his men to San Diego, where an Indian uprising had taken place. Anza decided, after much delay, to proceed with the establishment of the mission entrusted to him by the viceroy, even at the risk of upsetting governor Rivera, who was after all the territorial superior of all concerned. The colonists were received jubilantly at Monterey by Serra and three other missionaries, and the pealing of the bells seemed to the expeditionaries to presage the early achievement of their dreams.

In order to prepare the way, Anza wished to explore the future site personally with a few of his men; in spite of his precarious state of health and high fever, he ordered his men to help him mount on his horse and set off northward. On his return, Anza left specific instructions for his deputy, Joaquín Moraga, to proceed with the mission's foundation. He decided to try for the last time to gain Rivera's approval or, otherwise, to appeal to the viceroy himself in Mexico. He did not succeed in speaking to the governor, and was forced to set out. The governor reconsidered the matter shortly afterward, however, and granted permission for the establishment of the *presidio,* but not the mission. Father Serra was not deterred by this command, and when the ship *San Carlos* arrived to transport the supplies that the colonists needed, he convinced the captain, Fernando Quirós, to include the materials needed for the future mission. The march of the Franciscan founders overland began on June 17, at Monterey, with Grijalva in command of the main party. Fathers Francisco Palou and Pedro Benito Cambón joined the group (Serra stayed behind at San Carlos) with a considerable number of Indians, as well as cattle.

When Rivera was replaced by Governor Felipe de Neve in 1775, the capital was transferred from Baja California to Monterey, coinciding with the creation of the new post of general commander in the person of Teodoro de Croix. These two men brought with them a new approach to colonizing these new lands, emphasizing the importance of Spanish territory in a defensive role against raids by Russians, British and pirates in general. The territory would, therefore, be populated with Spanish colonists who would cooperate in fighting against the Indians and against foreign dangers. To Neve, the purpose of the missions was strictly spiritual, and they would play no further part in economy or rule of the territory. Although he did not succeed in modifying the existing missions during his rule between 1777 and 1784 (and even in the next administration until

San Miguel Mission, California.

1786) only the San Buenaventura Mission was founded. Neve was replaced by Pedro Fagés in 1784, but his foreseeable clash with Serra, who had influenced his dismissal during his earlier reign as governor, was avoided by the missionary's death.

Fray Junípero Serra died on August 28, 1786, at his mission of San Carlos Borromeo, where his remains lie today at the high altar, together with those of his companions, Juan Crespi (who died in 1782), Fermín Lasuén and Julián López. Before his death, Serra had visited the beloved missions founded under his leadership in California. At his deathbed he was attended by Father Francisco Palou, who, on his retirement to Mexico in 1785, would write Serra's biography. Serra was buried in a solemn funeral, attended by fathers from several missions, the colonists at Monterey, hundreds of Indians and the crew of a ship lying in the harbor. The guns aboard the ship were fired in a salute every half hour, and answered by the *presidio* batteries. A week later a major memorial service took place, presided over by the commander of the *presidio*.

From that day onward, the fame of Fray Junípero and his work has spread widely, and his memory has been honored publicly in many different ways: statues of him were erected in many places in California, and in 1910 a large cross was raised on the summit of Mount Robidoux, California, recalling the most memorable dates of his life as a founder missionary. In the Capitol in Washington, D.C., one of the two statues representing California is of Serra, unveiled on August 28, 1959. (He had been proclaimed an American citizen by an act passed on August 28, 1934.) At his inauguration as governor of California, in December 1966, Ronald Reagan took his oath on the Bible used by the Franciscan. The Serra International Club, a Catholic organization of laypeople devoted to promoting vocations for the priesthood, has chapters around the world. Serra's birthplace, in the town of Petra, Majorca, was turned into a museum and was presented as a gift to the city of San Francisco. In Spain, an association of Friends of Fray Junipero Serra (Asociación de Amigos de Fray Junípero Serra) was founded and in 1963 helped commemorate the 250th anniversary of his birth, attended by Chief Justice of the United States Supreme Court (and former governor of California) Earl Warren and the mayors of San Francisco and Carmel and Father Moholy. Gold, silver and copper medals were struck, and a plaque containing the names of the Majorcan Franciscans who served on the Californian missions was presented at Petra by the deputy governor. In 1984,

to commemorate the bicentenary of his death, events were organized at Monterey and Petra, and stamps were issued with a portrait of the missionary in Spain.

In 1987, Pope John Paul II visited Monterey and the tomb of Father Junípero. The pope beatified him at the Vatican on September 25, 1988.

It was during the term of government of Pedro Fagés that Monterey was visited by the French mariner Comte de la Perouse, at the invitation of King Charles III. Orders had been given to permit him to anchor—his was the first foreign ship to obtain permission to do so—and resupply, and he was to be shown every possible courtesy. This visit was seen as a sign that trade relations with other countries had begun.

Fagés was replaced as governor by José Francisco Ortega in 1791; his departure was due to the continual pleadings of his wife who did not appreciate the assignment as much as her husband did and whose attitude had caused him embarrassment on more than one occasion. The next few governors, in quick succession owing to illness, were Antonio Romeu and José Joaquín de Arrillaga; the post was taken up in October 1794 by Diego Borica.

At the time of the attack on Monterey by pirate Hipólito Bouchard in 1818, the governor was Pablo Vicente Sola. Although warned that an attack was imminent by the commander at Santa Barbara, he was unable to prevent 80 pirates from sacking and setting fire to the *presidio* and the surroundings.

Sola was still governor when the transfer of sovereignty from Spain to Mexico took place. He was succeeded by the commander of the *presidio* at San Francisco during the Spanish period, Luis Antonio Argüello, who, as the first Mexican governor, disembarked and was received ceremoniously at Monterey in November 1822. Sola received a courteous farewell, and the transfer took place peacefully. While the territory had remained loyal to Spain, it accepted its new political prospects optimistically. Monterey continued to be the capital, even when California passed into the hands of the United States. An account of how California preserved its Spanish characteristics, even in 1849, is told in some curious letters by General Alfredo Sully, who married Manuela de la Guerra, a member of one of the leading families in the region.

Today, Monterey (it was spelled "Monterrey" in Spanish times) retains many relics of its Spanish past. The *presidio*, called the Old Custom House, stands on the shores of the bay. A statue of Fray Junípero stands in front, and the old *presidio* chapel, with one of the most elaborate mission facades and the only *presidio* chapel surviving in California, has been in use since 1795: fishermen visit it in September and carry the statue of St. Rosalia in procession for the blessing of the fishing boats. Other buildings include Casa Sobranes, Casa del Oro, Casa Gutiérrez and Casa Estrada. Casa Munras is a splendid motel situated on the former Rancho San Vicente, owned by Esteban Munras.

There are plenty of streets in Monterey bearing Spanish names. It is not unusual when strolling along the streets to find signs such as "El Estero" (flower shop), "El Patio" (restaurant) or "El Adobe" (motel). Along the coast are many capes, some of them with Spanish names: Cabrillo, Lucas, Pinos, Pescadero and Lobos (which, was originally called Punta de los Lobos Marinos, or "Point of the Sea Wolves").

The Carmel Mission is not far from Monterey. Elected to preside over the California missions, Father Fermín Lasuén ran them for 20 years; his was the golden age of the missions. Carmel, which declined following the laws confiscating Church property in 1836, began to be rebuilt in 1882 and became a parish church in 1933, when a new period of splendor began thanks to the enthusiasm of its pastor, Father Michael D. O'Connell, and architect Harry W. Downie. Today, visitors can see it fully restored, its patio full of flowers. Many Hispanic names can be found on the gravestones in the cemetery, and a memorial presented on behalf of the Instituto de Cultura Hispánica stands nearby. The front courtyard or patio is large, even by present-day standards. Its belfry, outbuildings, the cell occupied by Fray Junípero and his tomb sculpted by Joe Mora are still to be seen. Around the mission today lies the city of Carmel, a place with picturesque streets, art galleries and a beach festooned with trees.

Missions South of San Francisco

The mission of San Juan Bautista stands beside El Camino Real. It was founded by Father Fermín Lasuén on June 24, 1797, and within six months had a chapel, a convent, a granary, barracks and even living quarters for the neophytes. Father Arroyo de la Cuesta served here from 1808 until 1833. He built a church with a nave and two side aisles in 1812, the largest in the province. In 1820, he engaged carpenter Thomas Doak (the first United States resident in California) to decorate the walls of the church. Father Arroyo produced two substantial works, one a compendium of Indian sayings, the other, an exhaustive study of the Mutsumi language; he spoke a dozen Indian languages and preached in seven

of them. The mission was known for the musical training of the new converts thanks to the efforts of Father Esteban Tapia, and in 1828, Father Custa bought the organ that can still be seen in the museum.

From 1839 onward a township began to form around the mission and is now also known as San Juan Bautista. The cemetery was in use until 1930, when the last of the mission Indians, Ascensión Solórzano, died. Long arcades form one side of the main square and several buildings have been declared monuments by the state: the Plaza Hotel (built on the first story of the Spanish barracks), the Castro House (named after Mexican general José de Castro), Plaza Stable, Zanetta house (built by an Italian specialist in the culinary arts) and Zanetta Cottage. Today San Juan Bautista hosts popular rodeos.

Santa Cruz Mission lies to the north of Monterey Bay. Founded on September 25, 1791, on the banks of the San Lorenzo River, the church was not completed until 1794; its presence is now recalled by a new church, an accurate copy of the style of the original, but half its size. The present city of Santa Cruz had its origins in the Spanish period. In 1797, Governor Diego Borica founded a township—the third—in the vicinity, called Branciforte (in honor of the viceroy, Marqués de Branciforte). The project was planned thoroughly, and every hardworking colonist in good health was to receive a home, furniture, tools, clothing and a payment of $116 a year for the first two years, and $66 a year for the ensuing three years. Indians would live among the European colonists, since it was thought that this would speed up the process of assimilating the natives into Western civilization. Branciforte did not prosper, however, during the Spanish period though later it would develop into the locality of Santa Cruz, a summer resort. All that now remains of Branciforte is a street bearing its name.

El Camino Real next leads to the Santa Clara Mission, situated near the city of San Jose. Once the foundation of San Francisco had been authorized by Governor Fernando Rivera, he had no objection to Lieutenant Joaquín Moraga and Fathers Tomás de la Peña and José Murguía proceeding to start work on a new settlement, which they began on January 18, 1777. The area was fertile along the banks of the river San José de Guadalupe, and from the outset, the Indians were receptive. Following a devastating flood in 1784, the mission had to be moved to a higher site, until its destruction by an earthquake in 1818. Later buildings have lasted until the present day thanks to the care lavished on them by the Jesuits, who in 1851, began to use them as a school that is still open today.

The history of the mission runs parallel to that of one of the first townships of Spanish colonists in California, San José de Guadalupe, the work of Governor Felipe de Neve. Neve was pursuing a policy of secular colonization in California and charged Lieutenant Moraga with the task. Accompanied by some colonists from San Francisco, Moraga started the community in June 1777; in a very short time it was to become very prosperous and by November there was already a town council. The conditions there made it possible to produce cash crops and breed livestock. Despite its distance from the mission about two and a half miles away, there were times when friction arose concerning jurisdiction, until an official demarcation fixed the respective boundaries in 1801.

Some 14 miles north of the city of San Jose, on the east shore of San Francisco Bay, the mission of San José de Guadalupe once stood; it is now the town of Fremont. It came into existence 20 years after the village of San José de Guadalupe, following a request that Governor Diego Borica made on behalf of Father Lasuén to Viceroy Branciforte to start another mission. Permission was given and the father, accompanied by Sergeant Pedro Amador and five soldiers, proceeded to found the mission on June 11, 1797. Life was not easy however for the new settlement, because the Indians in the valley were reluctant to be converted and often opposed the missionaries. Amador himself led an expedition in which much blood was shed and many prisoners were taken. Later, in 1826, under Mexican rule, a force commanded by Mariano Vallejo fought a pitched battle against 1,000 rebel Indians led by Estanislao, a neophyte from San Jose. When the Indians were defeated, their leader could not be found, for he had sought asylum in the church.

Father Narciso Durán is the most closely associated with this mission, where he served from 1806 until 1833, when he was replaced by a Franciscan of Mexican nationality from the friary at Zacatecas. Durán acted as president for two periods, (1825–1827 and 1831–1838), and his efforts have been compared to those of Father Lasuén.

From San Jose a peninsula forms and ends at the northern tip in the city of San Francisco, with the peninsula bathed by the waters of the Pacific Ocean on one side, and San Francisco Bay on the other. Its spinal cord is Highway 5, along which there are several sights: Portola State Park; San Lorenzo valley; Los Gatos City; La Honda Road, leading to the locality of San Gregorio and to San Mateo County; Cañada Road, which leads to the Pulgas Water Temple at the Crystal Springs Reservoir;

and others. Not far from San Jose, on the bay, is Palo Alto and the university of Stanford. The name Palo Alto is said to have derived from the nickname of a Basque, Pedro Altube, who looked tall and upright like an oak tree and had a ranch in this region. The university campus is well laid out, and several streets bear names such as Alvarado, Alameda and Salvatierra. At Stanford University, the residents of Bolivar House and Alvarado House (where for many years Professor Ronald Hilton produced the monthly publication *Hispanic American Report*) maintain an interest in Hispanic culture, as does an excellent Spanish department. Also, Stanford University's Research Institute has been the base for José Meseguer, a well-known expert in computer languages, and his research for the past 15 years.

A little farther north, the Allied Arts Guild, at Menlo Park, assists in the preservation of El Rancho de las Pulgas, originally owned by the Argüello family, who played a significant role in the state's early history; the remaining buildings include the granary and outhouses, which now house art galleries and stores.

Also found along El Camino Real are the cities of San Carlos and San Mateo.

San Francisco

The first Spaniard to see the San Francisco Bay was Sergeant José Francisco Ortega, who, leading an eight-man patrol, had been sent ahead by Gaspar de Portolá in search of Monterey Bay. It was November 1 or 2, 1769. Standing on a hilltop, for some time he could see nothing of the scenery stretching at its feet owing to the (now famous) fog enshrouding the harbor, until the horizon cleared and in the distance he spied a large mass of water surrounded by wooded coasts and scattered with a number of islands. On receiving such an optimistic report, Portolá ordered the expedition to advance, and after covering difficult terrain on November 4 and 5, at last he and his party descended to the bay, which appeared to be an arm of the Pacific Ocean. Ortega was again entrusted with the exploration of the surroundings and, after several nonhostile encounters with the local Indians, returned four days later to report that this terrain was indeed the bay called San Francisco on the map drawn by Cabrera Bueno, and not Monterey Bay. In view of his report, Portolá decided to turn back southward in search of elusive Monterey Bay. In 1984, San Mateo County acquired the hill known as Sweeney Ridge in the city of Pacifica; it was from this vantage point that the bay was sighted in 1769. It was eventually made a national park.

The next Spaniard to visit the area was Juan Bautista de Anza with a small party of men. He had left at Monterey the expedition of colonists sent on orders from the viceroy of New Spain to set up a *presidio,* a colony and a mission, and was in search of a suitable place for the future foundation. It must have taken a great force of will to conduct the exploration. The fever that had seized him at Monterey left him barely able to move, and he had to be lifted to the saddle of his horse by his soldiers.

Anza selected for his purpose a rocky point on the southern shore of the bay, with Punta Reyes opposite at some distance and a view of the islands at the entrance. Having inspected the area and established friendly relations with the local Indians, to whom he made a number of gifts, he departed with his men, determined to start building the future city of San Francisco immediately. If Governor Rivera interfered with his plans to establish the settlement, despite superior orders, Anza would have to convince him or, otherwise, would depart for Mexico to place the matter in the hands of the viceroy; unfortunately he found himself forced to resort to the latter course.

The expeditionary party at Monterey commanded by Lieutenant Joaquín Moraga was impatiently awaiting news, when Juan Pablo Grijalva, one of the commanders of the Anza expedition who had been delayed at San Gabriel by Rivera, at last received permission from the governor, who had convinced himself belatedly to proceed with the foundation of the *presidio* at San Francisco. The arrival of the messenger bearing these good tidings at Monterey on May 28, led to great rejoicing. With him came a small group of soldiers, in addition to all their families. Preparations for the expedition started immediately. Despite Rivera's refusal to allow the foundation of the mission, Fray Junípero was prepared to send two missionary fathers with the travelers and attempt to found the mission by every possible means. The packet-boat *San Carlos,* which brought provisions, was laden with the materials needed for the new settlement and two cannons for the fort. Serra took the opportunity of including everything necessary for the mission.

The first party to leave overland departed on June 17 under the command of Grijalva and was joined by the expedition leader, Moraga, after he had supervised the loading of the *San Carlos.* Accompanying the party were Fathers Francisco Palou and Pedro Benito Cambón. They passed through very beautiful scenery—following the route taken by Anza—and the advance guard under Grijalva caught sight of the bay on June 27.

After resting, they measured out an area 92 meters square on which to build the *presidio* and the quarters for soldiers and colonists alike. The work happened to begin, quite by chance, on July 4, 1776, the very day on which a group of settlers on the East Coast of the great continent declared their independence from Great Britain and laid the foundations for the United States of America.

The ship *San Carlos* took a long time to arrive when, one day in August, her sails were sighted. On August 18, she cast anchor in the bay amid general rejoicing. Work pressed ahead, and on September 17—the Feast of the Wounds of Saint Francis—they took possession of the living quarters and government buildings; a solemn "Te Deum" was sung, the scriveners recorded the event and the guns fired salvos.

The order to found the mission had not arrived, however, and since the captain of the ship was in a hurry to weigh anchor, it was decided, on the responsibility of the sailors, to inaugurate the mission of San Francisco on October 4, 1776, by blessing the spot, raising a cross and celebrating Mass. The mission was set up on the shores of a lagoon that Anza had called Nuestra Señora de los Dolores (Our Lady of the Sorrows), which is why it was known henceforth as Dolores rather than by its real name. Approval on the part of Rivera for what had already been done without his consent, although on orders from the viceroy, was not long in arriving.

The Dolores Mission soon became popular among the coastal Indians, who came to it in search of protection and food; but just as they came, so too, they departed, and this proved to be a serious problem for the mission because the desertion of the neophytes threatened its existence. The size of the peninsula and the continual mists also hampered farming, while the mission felt the pressure from the expanding colony to the north around the *presidio,* and to the south, from the missions of San José and Santa Clara. Therefore, Dolores never achieved the same degree of agricultural prosperity as its sister missions. Moreover, the epidemics that broke out prevented the settlement of a substantial Indian population. There was even thought of moving the mission farther north, but although the new foundation took place, Dolores persevered. In 1834 it was allowed to fall into ruin, until it was eventually returned to the Catholic Church.

Its distance from the nearby town saved it from the famous earthquake in 1906. Today it stands within the city limits, on Dolores Street, and literature published by the U.S. Department of Commerce includes it among the works of American architecture of great interest. All that remains is the chapel and a peaceful cemetery where a statue of Father Serra stands amid many tombs bearing Spanish names, among others the first *presidio* commander, Joaquín Moraga, another *presidio* commander, José Darío Argüello, and the first mayor of San Francisco, Francisco de Haro. Beside the little chapel stands a large modern Catholic basilica in a contrasting style, whose very size emphasizes the humility of its Franciscan founders.

The story of the *presidio* of Yerba Buena as it was known in the early days, is particularly colorful. José Darío Argüello was the second commander in 1786 and married a niece of Moraga. In 1805, his son, Luis Antonio Argüello, was appointed to the same post at the time the first Mexican governor of California was. In 1806, the ship *Juno* anchored in the bay; on board was Count Nicolai Petrovich Rezanov, sent by Czar Alexander of Russia on a mission to seek supplies for the Russian settlements at Sitka and other northern territories. He hoped to open up trade with California and sought permission to hunt otters and seal in the coastal waters. His attractive personality, refined education and dashing figure became widely popular. With regard to trade, he succeeded in getting a request sent to the viceroy, but as for obtaining concessions in the territory, the commander rejected his suggestions outright: Spain could not permit the presence of another power in her dominions.

In the course of the days that ensued, Rezanov took part in the daily life of the Argüello family and fell in love with the commander's sister, Conchita, a feeling she reciprocated. He was invited to visit El Rancho de las Pulgas, and at age 45, Rezanov asked her parents for the hand of their daughter, aged 15. The request was granted gracefully on condition that he should obtain permission from the pope and from King Charles IV. Rezanov prepared to depart at once, to see the czar and request his influence at the court in Madrid, visit the capital of Spain and within the year return to California.

No more was heard of Rezanov. Conchita waited many years in vain, until it was known that he had died on the steppes of Siberia in March 1807. The unfortunate girl decided to enter a convent as a nun and died there in 1857. This love story has inspired several authors, for example the novel *Rezanov* by Gertrude Atherton. Russian Hill in San Francisco remains as a memorial to this romantic story.

The sojourn of the Russian count would have other consequences, however. In 1812, the Russians built Fort Ross, north of San Francisco, and engaged in otter and seal hunting on the Farallon Islands and along the coast; the forces at the *presidio* were not strong enough to prevent encroachment, and the commander had to turn a blind eye to these breaches of sovereignty. The Russians stayed at the settlement until 1842, when they abandoned it voluntarily.

From Telegraph Hill can be seen lying in the bay the islands of Alcatraz (named by Juan Manuel de Ayala after a pelican living there), Angel, Yerba Buena and Treasure. On Telegraph Hill stand the Coit Memorial Tower and a huge statue of Christopher Columbus. Commanding the famous Golden Gate Bridge is the site of the Old Spanish Presidio mentioned earlier. Today this is the headquarters of the Sixth Corps of the U.S. Army. In the Officers' Club, which occupies the site of the old Spanish fortress, various rooms recall the early Spanish officers, such as Anza, Argüello, Moraga, Ortega and Portolá. Frescoes recall episodes from the Spanish history of the *presidio,* as does the Spanish coat of arms.

In the west of the city lies the Golden Gate Park, with the M.H. De Young Museum, which houses a fine collection of paintings, including works by El Greco and other Spanish painters, and a popular walk along which statues of Father Junípero Serra and Cervantes can be found. There is also a monument to El Cid in front of the Palace of the Legion of Honor, in Lincoln Park, the work of the Hispanist Anna H. Huntington. Local societies that promote Hispanic culture include the Unión Española de California, comprised of some 600 members, and the Centro Cultural Vasco. On October 12 every year, the Festival de la Raza y de la Hispanidad is held.

The first archbishop of San Francisco was a Spaniard, Monsignor José Sadoc Alemany, born at Vich in 1814 and a resident in the United States since 1840, when his Dominican superiors sent him to San Jose, Tennessee, owing to the anti-clerical policy of the Spanish government of the day and the confiscation of the properties of the religious orders. Ten years later, Pope Pius IX appointed him bishop of Monterey and, three years later, first archbishop of San Francisco. For 35 years Monsignor Sadoc remained in his diocese, where he promoted the construction of the cathedral, 150 other churches, six colleges, 18 schools, five homes, four hospitals and 12 orphanages. When he set foot in the city for the first time, there were 500 Catholics and three priests; when he left to attend Vatican Council I—from which he did not return—his flock amounted to 250,000 people and 250 priests. He died in Catalonia in 1887, but his remains were brought back to San Francisco in February 1965. A memorial service was sung in old St. Mary's Church (where there is a fine reproduction of Bartolomé Esteban Murillo's *Immaculate Conception* above the high altar), and his remains were buried in the Archbishop's Chapel in the mausoleum at Holy Cross Cemetery.

Another Spaniard, Enrique Jordá, spent many years conducting the San Francisco Symphony Orchestra.

Streets in San Francisco bearing Spanish names include among others, Anza Street, Arguello Boulevard, Balboa Street, Cardenas Avenue, Cervantes Boulevard, Galvez Avenue, Garces Drive, Magellan Avenue, Mendosa Avenue, Ortega Street, Pizarro Way, Portola Drive, Rivera Street, Valdez Avenue, Velasco Avenue, Avila Street, Barcelona Avenue, Granada Avenue, Mallorca Way, Valencia Street, El Camino del Mar, and the streets bearing the names of as many as three dozen Spanish saints.

North of San Francisco

One is lucky to get a view of the famous Golden Gate Bridge with good visibility. Guarding the entrance to the bay out to sea are the Farallon Islands, the name by which the bay itself was called originally. The highway north leads to Sausalito and to the towns of Tiburon and San Rafael, named after the mission established there.

The San Rafael Arcangel Mission is near the end of the chain founded by the Spanish Franciscans. At the Dolores Mission in San Francisco, consideration was given for some time to the advisability of moving to another spot as many neophytes at the mission fell prey to epidemics on account of the humidity and mist. The Franciscan president, Father Vincente Sarriá was doubtful about a new mission, but when Friar Luis Gil volunteered, the decision was made to proceed. On December 14, 1817, work on the new mission started; since this was not intended from the outset to be more than an offshoot of Dolores Mission, the buildings are not as large as most of the other missions. Since health was one of the prime reasons for its foundation, the fact that Father Gil was a skilled physician proved important, and he spent two years working in this capacity among the Indians. He was followed by Father Juan Amorós, a dynamic man who greatly boosted the mission and even won its independence. Attempts to shut down the San Rafael and Dolores Missions and establish another one farther north were cut short by Father Amorós, who devoted 13 years of his life, until his death, to his parishioners. The mission was then taken over by a Franciscan from Zacatecas, Father José Mercado, who was eventually expelled owing to his conflicts with General Mariano Vallejo; the mission was then secularized, the first of all the missions to be so.

A few miles farther along Highway 101 lies Sonoma, where the chain of missions ends. In the square is the old mission of San Francisco Solano, now a museum housing, among other mementos, 62 oil paintings of the missions by Chris Jorgensen. Used as the parish church of the town—which sprang up in 1834— until 1880, the mission properties were sold and the proceeds used to build a modern church. Now restored, it stands as a reminder that this was the last of the bastions built by Spain to defend her sphere of influence in California and evangelize among the Indians.

San Francisco Solano was the inspiration of Father José Altimira, from Dolores Mission, who wanted a more fertile field for his apostolic zeal and proposed a new mission to the commander of the *presidio*, Argüello. The president of the Franciscans, Father José Senan, and the missionary at San Rafael, Father Juan Amorós, opposed abandoning San Rafael and Dolores in order to build the new mission. The conflict was resolved by both maintaining the old missions and founding the new one of San Francisco Solano. Father Altimira set up a cross on the site on July 4, 1823, and the wooden church was consecrated in April the following year. Spain had withdrawn from California by then, and the influence of the missions had waned, so the enthusiastic missionary did not obtain the necessary supplies. By a quirk of fate, the Russians provided him with bells to call the faithful to worship and other items. (One reason to establish the new mission was the threat the Russian presence held to Spain.) In 1833 the mission was taken over by the Franciscans from Zacatecas. As occurred at San Rafael, they frequently clashed with the Mexican commander.

Today, Sonoma is known for its wines. Spanish vines had been imported by José Vallejo as early as 1527.

North of San Francisco are Alameda and San Leandro, the location of the Spanish organizations Club Ibérico and Sociedad Agustina de Aragón. The University of California at Berkeley, has an excellent Spanish department and has also been the affiliation of several prominent Hispanic scholars, including Hubert Howe Bancroft, George P. Hammond, James F. King and more recently Herbert Eugene Bolton.

Hubert Howe Bancroft had tremendous influence on the awakening interest in the history of the Hispanic peoples and their influence in the United States. Criticized by scholarly historians because of the bureaucratic way in which he organized historical research—he had the cooperation of 600 assistants who helped him compile his 39 volumes—his work and the importance of the manuscripts and books collected by him undoubtedly made a remarkable impact, and were made available to future researchers. His library, comprising 50,000 volumes by 1890, became the property of the University of California in 1907 and formed the exceptional Bancroft Library, directed by another Hispanist historian, George P. Hammond.

Yet another exceptional figure in American historiography is Herbert Eugene Bolton, the author of definitive works on the Spanish presence in the United States. His determination to highlight Spain's role in the history of the country and his theory about approaching United States events within the general context of the Americas had far-reaching repercussions; his specific contributions, such as the diary of Father Kino, have proved to be invaluable contributions to the clarification of historical truth. Awarded a gold medal from the university on October 2, 1987, Juan Carlos I recalled the names of Bancroft, Hammond and King as "blazers of new cultural trails who have illuminated, with documentary accuracy, the true outlines of our common past . . . California is for Spaniards an essential piece of the history of Spain in America."

On leaving Berkeley the mist enshrouding the bay usually disappears, and the San Joaquin valley appears, dazzling and flourishing, leading to Sacramento. The Capitol is flanked by impressive buildings—one of them bears the legend in Spanish "Dadme Hombres Parejos A Mis Montañas" (Give to me men matching my mountains)—and a well-laid-out park. Inside the Capitol a red and gold Spanish flag can be seen in the upper rotunda and a fine piece of sculpture stands in the vestibule presided over by Queen Isabella with Columbus and son Diego. A number of frescoes on the walls of the entrance chamber depict scenes from the Spanish history of California. In Sacramento there is a Círculo Hispano, or Spanish Club.

Grain was for a time the predominant crop in the San Joaquin valley but has now been practically replaced by irrigated produce: beetroot, onions (at Vacaville), cotton (from Pacheco Pass to Los Baños), asparagus (in Contra Costa County), almonds (at Chico), pears (at Placerville) and fruit in general (at Manteca and Merced). Gallo (at Modesto) and Petri (at Escalon) are the leading wineries. The Spanish names of these and other towns recall their Spanish history.

Also in this area, one can follow the route of the gold miners, who streamed into California after James Marshall discovered gold nuggets in 1848. As the historian Charles Lummis reminds us, the Spaniards had discovered gold centuries earlier and had started mining 10 years before Marshall's find. San Francisco then became the capital of California, snatching prominence away from Monterey. Other bustling townships sprang up, many to be virtually abandoned. The courthouse at Mariposa, built in 1854, is the oldest in the state. Hornitos, with its Spanish-style town square, was frequented by the famous bandit Joaquín Murrieta (immortalized in the work *Fulgor y muerte de Joaquín Murrieta* [*Splendor and Death of Joaquin Murrieta*] by Pablo Neruda), who avenged the Hispanic miners whom the Anglo-Saxon settlers prevented from taking part in the search for gold. Jacksonville, Columbia, Angels Camp (in Calaveras County), San Andreas, Mokelumne Hill, Amador City (with a museum of local history), Placerville, Grass Valley and Nevada City date from this colorful period.

The Sierra Nevada lies east of the Central Valley and the region described above. It is a huge massif running from north to south, with peaks such as Mount Whitney, more than 15,000 feet high. The Feather River country, north of the gold area, takes its name from the Spanish Río de las Plumas, the name given to it by the commander Luis Argüello, in 1820. Next to Nevada lies the small town of Portola, named after the colonizer of California. Farther north lie the Trinity Alps, which sometimes become more compact than Sierra Nevada. It is here that the Shasta region lies, where settlers from the north began to arrive from 1849 onward. In the northeast lies the town of Alturas, among the Warner Mountains, which are crossed from the east through the Fandango Pass, called after the dance held by some immigrants in 1855, when they considered that they had arrived safe and sound in California; in fact, their arrival was not so fortunate, for the Indians surprised them in midst of their rejoicings, and many were killed.

The Northern Coast

Along the coastline north of San Francisco, Point Reyes is a reminder of the nearby shipwreck of the *San Agustín*, commanded by Sebastián Rodríguez Cermeñón, in 1595. On one side lies Drake Bay, called after the English pirate, who visited this coast at the end of the 16th century. Beyond the headland lies Bodega Bay, near the town called Bodega after the Spanish navigator.

Sixteen miles farther on lies Fort Ross, where the Russians set up a post in 1812 to trade for pelts with the local Indians. Beyond Point Arena lies Mendocino, a name given to a small village and a county; and many miles farther north, the same name is born by the cape discovered by the Ferrelo expedition in 1542, past Point Cabrillo, Point Delgada and Punta Gorda, as well as the Mendocino National Forest.

Cape Mendocino was given this name by Bartolomé Ferrelo in 1543 in honor of Viceroy Antonio de Mendoza, who sponsored the expedition; Ferrelo had taken charge after the death of Cabrillo. Sebastián Vizcaíno also moored off this same tongue of land with the flagship and frigate on his expedition on January 12, 1603, when the council of captains and pilots advised the general to return and not proceed on the second part of his mission, since winter was setting in and many of the crew were sick. However, the wind drove them farther north involuntarily.

The largest town along the coast is Eureka, on the Oregon border named by the expedition led by Bruno de Heceta, who moored offshore on June 9, 1775. Two days later, he took possession of the territory in the name of the king. Juan Francisco de la Bodega y Cuadra and Francisco A. Mourelle remained there until June 19 and drew up a map of the area.

Spanish Place-Names

A veritable multitude of Spanish names have been used in California for cities, counties, rivers and mountains. Mention is made here of only a few. Counties bearing Spanish names include Alameda, Amador, Calaveras, Contra Costa, Del Norte, El Dorado, Fresno, Imperial, Los Angeles, Madera, Marin, Mariposa, Mendocino, Merced, Mono, Monterey, Nevada, Placer, Plumas, Sacramento, San Benito, San Bernardino, San Diego, San Francisco, San Joaquin, San Luis Obispo, San Mateo, Santa Barbara, Santa Clara, Santa Cruz, Sierra, Solano, and Ventura—altogether, four-fifths of the counties in California. Then there are towns of varying size: Adelanto, Alameda, Alamo, Alhambra, Alisal, Alta Loma, Altaville, Alturas, Amador City, Aptos, Arlanza Vil, Arroyo Grande, Atascadero, Bodega, Borrego Springs, Buena Park, Cabezon, Cadiz, Camarillo, Camino, Campo, Carpinteria, Casita, Castro Valley, Castroville, Chico, China, Chula Vista, Columbia, Corona, Coronado, Corte Madera, Costa Mesa, Del Dios, Del Mar, Del Paso, Esperanza, Famoso, Indio, La Jolla, La Mesa, La Mirada, La Puente, La Quinta, La Sierra, Loma Linda, Lomita, Los Alamitos, Los Alamos, Los Angeles, Los Banos, Los Gatos, Los Molinos, Los Nietos, Los Olivos, Madera, Malaga, Marina, Mariposa, Martinez, Mendocino, Merced, Mira Loma, Miramar, Modesto, Montecito, Monterey, Monterey Park, Monte Rio, Moraga, Moreno, Morro Bay, Murrieta, Nevada City, North Sacramento, Novato, Nuevo, Oro Grande, Oroville, Pacifica, Pala, Palo Alto, Palos Verdes Estates, Palo Verde, Paso Robles, Pescadero, Pico Rivera, Planada, Portola, Pulga, Punta Arena, Ramona, Rancho Santa Fe, Redondo Beach, Rio Linda, Rio Oso, Rio Vista, Sacramento, Salida, Salinas, Sierra Madre, Sierraville, Solano Beach, Soledad, Sonora, South Dos Palos, South Laguna Sultana, Tiburon, Tres Pinos, Trinidad, Vacaville, Vallecitos, Vallejo, Ventura, Vidal, Vina, Vista, Yermo, Yerba Linda, Zamora and 41 towns bearing the names of saints, notably San Francisco and San Diego.

◆ OREGON AND WASHINGTON ◆

Oregon

The state of Oregon bears the name of a vast territory that became the subject of international rivalry and diplomatic wrangling in the first half of the 19th century. Claimed by Spain as a result of her maritime explorations from the 16th century onward, Great Britain nevertheless considered it hers owing to the physical presence of her explorers and fur traders, and it was occupied by successive waves of American colonists from the East. In 1819, under the treaty transferring

Florida, differences between Spain and the United States were settled with regard to sovereign rights north of the 42nd parallel, which became the northern frontier of the dominions of King Ferdinand VII of Spain.

The name Oregon dates only from the l9th century. Many theories have attempted to explain the name, but most experts agree with the opinion given by Archbishop Blanchet. According to his theory, Jonathan Carver crossed the continent from Boston, departing in 1766 and not returning until 1768. Six years later, he published his impressions of his transcontinental journey and the lands along the Pacific seaboard. It is in these memoirs that the name "Oregon" appears for the first time: Archbishop Blanchet explains that the Spaniards were the first to explore the region, where they encountered Indians with large ears, whom they called *orejones*, meaning "big ears." When transcribing the word in the singular in English, Carver and those who followed him changed the letter *j* to a *g*. André Maurois provides the same explanation in his *History of the United States.*

Explorations by Sea

For centuries, Spanish seamen had sailed up and down the coast of Oregon naming capes, bays, rivers and dozens of geographical landmarks. As a result of the explorations by Hernán Cortés in Baja California and the reports brought back by Friar Marcos de Niza about the existence of the Seven Cities of Cibola to the north, Viceroy Antonio de Mendoza considered it advisable to make a further effort to bring those northern lands, which sounded so promising, within the Spanish sphere of influence. He reached an agreement with Pedro de Alvarado to outfit 12 ships; the death of the *conquistador* of Guatemala on the expedition to bring relief to the governor of Jalisco did not prevent the project from going ahead, for the viceroy gave his authorization for two of the ships that had been prepared, the *San Salvador* and the *Victoria*, to be entrusted to an expert sailor, Juan Rodríguez Cabrillo, and his pilot, Bartolomé Ferrelo. The expedition set sail from Navidad on June 27, 1542. Cabrillo was to get no farther than 38° 41', for he died on San Miguel Island. However, in his will, he requested that Ferrelo continue his voyage of discovery. In January 1543, Ferrelo crossed 40° north latitude and, on March 10, reached 44° latitude (about halfway up the coast of Oregon); here they suffered severely from the bitter cold and were tossed about by dangerous gales. Ferrelo apparently disembarked near present-day Port Orford. Farther south, near 42° latitude, Cape Ferrelo

recalls the pioneering spirit of this Spaniard, who was the first European to come into contact with that part of the continent.

During the mandate of Viceroy Luis de Velasco in New Spain, the ship *San Agustín* commanded by Sebastián Rodríguez Cermeñón was sent to resume the voyages of discovery and find a well-sheltered haven for the ships arriving from the Philippine Islands. However, she sank in a storm, and nothing is known about their explorations.

In the early 17th century, Sebastián Vizcaíno would subdue the territory. The viceroy, the count of Monterrey, had received orders from King Philip II to continue his attempts at discovery and penetration in Upper California for the purposes of missionary expansion and control over the pearl fishing industry, as well as to seek suitable harbors for trade with Asia. Vizcaíno's second voyage was particularly significant. On January 13, 1603, near Cape Mendocino, Vizcaíno convened a council of captains and pilots aboard the ships *San Diego* and *Tres Reyes* to negotiate the advisability of continuing the explorations entrusted to them by the viceroy: to reach the 44th parallel. After eight days' sailing they reached the 43rd parallel. The chronicler of the expedition, Friar Antonio de la Ascensión writes, "Here is the top and end of the kingdom and mainland of California and the beginning and entranceway to the Strait of Anian."

In the course of this mission, one of the headlands was called Point San Sebastián, after the patron of the captain of the expedition; this is one of the few cases in which the name for a place discovered was not linked to the saint on whose feast the discovery was made. There is a plaque on the spot recalling the event, set between two masts, with the text: "Spanish navigators were the first to explore the North American Pacific coast, beginning fifty years after Columbus discovered the Western Continents. Sebastian Vizcaíno saw this Cape in 1603 and named it after the Patron Saint of the day of his discovery. Other navigators, Spanish, British and American followed a century and a half later." The plaque is erroneous concerning the reason for the name. Vizcaíno also called the nearby river Santa Ynes. Farther north Cape Blanco was the name chosen by Martín de Aguilar, one of the lieutenants serving under Vizcaíno, who was in command of the first known exploration of the Umpqua River. On January 20, 1603, Vizcaíno ordered the expedition to return to New Spain.

In the second half of the 18th century, when the Spanish Court received news from its ambassador at St. Petersburg about Russian attempts to expand along the

Pacific coast of North America, King Charles III, through his first prime minister, the count of Floridablanca, instructed the viceroy of New Spain to investigate the matter and ordered the occupation of the northern lands along the Pacific coast of America. The viceroy appointed Juan Pérez to carry out an exploratory mission along the coast as far as the 60th parallel, without occupying it for the time being, since this could entail a conflict with the Russians, who might well have already settled there. The ship *Santiago* sailed from San Blas, Mexico, on January 24, 1774, passed by Oregon in May, reached what is now called Prince of Wales Island and then returned in July skirting the coast again. Pérez was therefore the first to explore the coast of British Columbia, Queen Charlotte Islands, Prince of Wales Island, Vancouver Island and Washington and Oregon, and the first to draw up a chart of the seaboard, although he did not disembark anywhere. He made contact with the natives of the area but did not set foot on their territory.

The reports made by Pérez were kept secret, but as a result, in 1775, the viceroy dispatched Lieutenant Bruno Heceta, with Pérez acting as second-in-command, aboard the *Santiago* (the same ship commanded by Pérez during his first voyage), accompanied by the schooner *Sonora*, commanded by Lieutenant Juan Francisco de Bodega y Cuadra. Having sailed on March 16, they made landfall off the Pacific shores of Washington. As a consequence of a number of vicissitudes, the council convened by Heceta decided that the *Sonora* should return, but Bodega persuaded Heceta to reconsider. Following a tremendous storm, the two ships separated. Bodega sailed along the coast as far as the 57th parallel, where he turned back and sailed down the southern part of Oregon exploring as he went. Heceta, however, sailed on as far as the Nootka estuary, although he overlooked the Juan de Fuca Strait and, on returning southward, anchored in the bay into which the Columbia River flows.

Heceta was the first European to provide a description of the Columbia River, one of the major features of Oregon's geography. He called it the San Roque, the same name he also gave to what was later to be called Cape Disappointment. He named what is now Cape Adams, Cabo Frondoso (Luxuriant Cape). The bay was called Asunción. The day after his arrival, Heceta wished to go ashore and determine if it was an island or the mainland. He realized there was a fast-flowing river nearby when he saw that a large mass of fresh water was driving the ship southwest and prevented her from approaching the shore as planned. The descriptions given by Heceta of the bay, capes and nearby mountains clearly reveal that he had discovered the mouth of the Columbia. At Monterey Bay, the *Santiago* and the *Sonora* were reunited and together proceeded to San Blas, the port from which they had departed in Mexico. After this expedition, the Spaniards had a clear portrait of the Northwest coastline and were the first to know of the existence of this great river.

Three years later, the British captain James Cook sighted the coast of Oregon but did not disembark. However, the names of some of the landmarks he spotted such as Cape Perpetua and Arago, have survived. The incidents that, a few years later, were to be known as the Nootka Controversy, caused by British claims to the regions now belonging to Canada around Vancouver Island and the neighboring mainland, gave rise to the organization of further Spanish expeditions up the Oregon coastline. Spain maintained her sovereign rights on the grounds that she had been present in the area before Cook, the first Englishman. The circumstances of Spanish home policy eventually resulted in a weakening of the Spanish position and recognition of the fact that she was unable to maintain the new territories by force of arms. Under the Nootka agreements of 1790, 1793 and 1794, Spain renounced her claims in the U.S. Pacific Northwest.

Later, Basque shepherds immigrated to the eastern mountains of Oregon, as they had in California, Nevada, Idaho and Montana. The first Basque to set foot in Oregon, in 1889, is thought to have been Antonio Azcuénaga, who settled in the Jordan valley. Later he was joined by Agustín Azcuénaga, Juan Acarregui (who had 5,000 sheep) and Luis Yturraspe (with 7,000 sheep). Today, natives of the Spanish Basque provinces still come to Oregon, as well as Nevada and Idaho. One of the senators of the state was Antonio Iturri, who is of Basque descent.

Spanish Place-Names

As a record of the Spanish presence in these parts, along the coast of Oregon there are such places as Cape Falcon, the town of Manzanita, Tierra Del Mar, Heceta Head at Florence and Heceta Point, as well as those already described, such as Cape Ferrelo, Cape Blanco and Cape Sebastian, and the memorial to Sebastian Vizcaíno. Towns in the rest of the state bearing Spanish names include Alfalfa, Bonanza, Camas Valley, Chico, Columbia City, Cornucopia, Estacada, Flora, Galena, La Grande, Leona, Moro, Paulina, Salado, Toledo, Vida and Wasco, in addition to Columbia County. In the mountains there are Cape Sebastian Summit, Camas Moutains, El Dorado Pass, Juniper Mountain and others with Spanish names.

Washington: Explorations by Sea

The ships of Spaniards Ferrelo and Vizcaíno did not sail in waters off the coast of Washington during the 16th and 17th centuries, but the expedition chartered in 1560 by the viceroy of Mexico did; it appears that the Greek navigator Apostolos Valerianos, better known as Juan de Fuca, took part in the expedition. According to the information that Juan de Fuca gave in 1596 to Michael Lok, English consul at Aleppo, he had spent 40 years in the service of Spain and acted as pilot on this voyage of discovery, which set out to find a hypothetical passage (the Anian Strait) connecting the Atlantic and Pacific Oceans via the north of America. In 1592, the expedition departed northward bound with two small ships, and at the 47th parallel, found a long arm of the sea, which, so Fuca reported, he followed and sailed as far as the Atlantic, whence he returned via the same route to Mexico. Subsequent investigations proved that this was untrue, but Juan de Fuca undoubtedly visited the coastline, and his name has been given to the strait separating Vancouver Island from the mainland.

When the Spanish Crown decided to occupy California along the northwest Pacific seaboard to prevent Russian penetration on the American continent, several maritime expeditions were dispatched to explore various points along the coast as far as Alaska. They visited the coast and waters of Oregon and Washington, as well as those near British Columbia.

As we have seen, in 1774, the viceroy of Mexico dispatched the ship *Santiago* commanded by Juan Pérez, with Esteban Martínez as his second-in-command. They approached the mouth of the Queets River, on the coast of Washington, and later reached the Queen Charlotte Islands in the far north, where they replenished their supply of freshwater; farther north still, they sighted Prince of Wales Island, in Alaska. On July 22, the ship headed south, skirted the same islands and dropped anchor on August 2, in Nootka Bay, which Pérez called San Lorenzo, on what was later to be called Vancouver Island. (One of the capes nearby today bears the name Esteban Point, in honor of Esteban Martínez.) Attempts to replenish their supply of drinking water failed, because a tremendous storm burst, and after recovering the boat put ashore for the purpose, the ship made out to

sea. On August 10, Pérez named the mountains, including Mt. Olympus and Sierra Nevada de Santa Rosalía. Practically the whole of the coastline of the state of Washington was skirted, although no other attempts were made to disembark. Pérez returned to his base and drew the first chart of this part of the American Pacific coast. He was first to discover Queen Charlotte Islands, Prince of Wales Island and Vancouver Island, as well as the coast of Washington and part of Oregon.

As noted, a second expedition was organized in 1775, commanded by Bruno Heceta in the *Santiago*, with Pérez acting as second-in-command, and accompanied by the schooner *Sonora*, commanded by Lieutenant Bodega. The first landfall in the state of Washington, after a hard slow voyage, was the Olympic Peninsula separating the Pacific from Puget Sound, the bay on which Seattle lies. Sailing before a gentle breeze, they searched along the coast for a safe haven, and the *Santiago* found one at what is now Point Grenville, while the schooner found another a few miles north. On July 14, 1775, Heceta ordered a boat to be lowered, and accompanied by Father Sierra, Cristóbal Revilla, Dr. Dávalos and a party of sailors, he rowed ashore. A cross was erected, and Heceta took possession of the territory in the name of the king of Spain and called the place Rada de Bucarelli (Bucarelli Roads) after the viceroy Antonio de Bucarelli y Ursa. Groups of Indians watched the ceremony and afterward traded for the trinkets the Spaniards offered them.

Meanwhile, the *Sonora* had encountered difficulties when endeavoring to avoid the reefs along the coast. The crew was received by a large crowd of Indians who began by singing and throwing feathers at them. Needing freshwater and encouraged by this welcome, Bodega ordered the boatswain, Pedro Santa Ana, and five men to row ashore in a boat. They had hardly disembarked when a horde of 300 Indians slaughtered them. The Indians then made for the *Sonora*, which was defended with great difficulty by Bodega, his orderly and the pilot Francisco Mourelle, who succeeded in making out to sea and meeting up with the *Santiago*. Once his crew had been reinforced, Bodega obtained permission from Heceta to continue his explorations northward, and reached the 58th parallel. On his return voyage he anchored off Vancouver Island and disembarked several times on the way to trade with the Indians. However, he did not see the Juan de Fuca Strait on account of the fog. On his way south, as we have seen, he discovered the Columbia River.

On March 7, 1778, the ships *Resolution* and *Discovery* under the command of the British captain James Cook, sighted land off Oregon but did not drop anchor until they reached the bay that Cook called Nootka, on Vancouver Island. In later years this was to become a fur trading center and a bone of contention with Spain. The Indians showed themselves willing to trade from the outset, but those along the coast attempted to prevent others farther inland from taking part in this trade. One thing in particular surprised the British: the discovery of two silver spoons in the possession of an Indian, unquestionable proof of the earlier presence of Westerners in the area. Seven years later, Nootka was visited by Captain James Hanna, from China; but it was from 1786 onward that the British began to visit the region frequently, from outposts in Asia.

Manuel Antonio Flores, the viceroy of New Spain received news of the numerous British calls along the north Pacific coast and, following instructions from Madrid based on the reports by the count La Pérouse, dispatched the frigates *Princesa* and *San Carlos* under Esteban José Martínez—the old companion of Pérez carrying Gonzalo López de Haro aboard as a pilot. They had orders to build a fort at Nootka and occupy the bay in the name of the king of Spain, in view of the sovereign rights of Spain over the American Pacific Coast, where she had been the first to explore and take possession. Sailing on March 8, 1788, Martínez found the American ships *Lady Washington* and *Columbia* at Nootka commanded by Captain Robert Gray (who had named the Columbia River) and Captain John Kendrick, respectively. While he did not obstruct their passage (they were on a voyage around the world), he at once began to seize a number of British ships (*Iphigenia, Northwest America, Princess Royal* and *Argonaut*), built barracks, living quarters, a cookhouse and a repair depot. He built Fort San Miguel with a battery of 10 guns on a height commanding the bay. Taking some of his prizes with him, he returned to the port at San Blas, Mexico.

At the same time, the anniversary of the independence of the United States was celebrated at Nootka on July 4, 1789: the frigate *Columbia* fired a 13 gun salute (for 13 years of freedom). The *Columbia*'s skipper invited Martínez, officers from the Spanish ships and from the *Argonaut* (their prisoners), chaplains and missionaries on board to a splendid banquet at which the health of King Charles III was toasted. The *San Carlos* and the fort responded to the salute in honor of the friendly nation.

The Nootka Controversy

When John Meares, in China, heard that the British ships had been seized, he sailed on the first ship for London. Shortly after his arrival, in April 1790, he submitted a memorandum to the government. Three months earlier the British chargé d'affaires in Madrid, Anthony Merry, had sent a secret report received from Mexico about Esteban José Martínez taking a British ship at Nootka. The reply given by the Spanish ambassador, Marqués del Campo, to the British complaint indicated that if the harmony happily existing between the two crowns was to be maintained, Great Britain must admit the sovereign right of Spain, by reason of discovery and exploration, along the north Pacific coast. Great Britain answered with an ultimatum.

Merry reported to his government in April that the Spanish government had ordered an inventory of their armaments. A few days later, Spain sent Great Britain a note undertaking to return the property confiscated and considering the incident closed, but at the same time reasserting her rights of sovereignty. It was at this juncture that Meares arrived. In the light of his report, the British cabinet demanded satisfaction from the Spanish government and, apart from restitution and indemnities, requested recognition of free trading and navigation of fishing rights, as well as the right to take possession of settlements in those parts not previously occupied by other European nations, with the consent of the natives.

The negotiations lasted for two months, in the course of which Great Britain, in case of war, secured the friendship of Prussia and alliance with Holland, while Spain obtained promises of aid from Louis XVI of France, who was virtually a prisoner of the revolutionaries in the Bastille. The beheading of the French king and the growing tension led the king of Spain to follow the advice of the count of Floridablanca and agree to sign the treaty proposed by the British, whereby they were allowed to trade in north Pacific waters. Another agreement, dated October 28, 1790, admitted the return to British subjects of the land of which they had been dispossessed by the Spaniards.

To enforce the agreement, Great Britain appointed Captain G. Vancouver, while Juan Francisco Bodega y Cuadra represented Spain. Bodega arrived at Nootka before his colleague, and therefore welcomed him with a 13 gun salute fired by the fort batteries and invited him to a five-course supper. Bodega used his abundant qualities, intelligence, pleasant manner and diplomacy to win Vancouver and his fellow countrymen over. (Vancouver Island appeared as "Quadra and Vancouver's Island," on the map that the British sailor made of the region shortly afterward.) When Bodega left, the Spaniards were sorry to see him go, in spite of the fact that he had not effected the transfer of powers for which he had been sent.

The governments of Spain and Britain had to sign additional agreements on February 12, 1793, and January 11, 1794, authorizing new agents to carry out the transfer of the territories from Spain to Britain. On March 23, 1795, Sir Thomas Pierce and Manuel de Alava exchanged the pertinent declarations at Nootka. To commemorate this treaty, a cape on the north coast of the state of Washington was given Alava's name: this was the United States' Finisterre, west of Cape Blanco, at longitude 124°4'10".

So the Spanish presence in the Northwest came to an end, though they were remembered on Vancouver Island with the names of Canal de Haro (Channel), San Gonzalo Point, San Juan Point, Alberni Channel, Carasco Bay, Boca de Ganavera, Ysla de Feran, Boca de Saavedra, San Rafael Point, Ysla de Galiano, Valdes (to the north), and Nuestra Señora del Rosario Channel, as shown on the map drawn up by Vancouver and published in 1798. A hill near the future capital of British Columbia, Victoria, was to retain the name Gonsales Hill, the name given to it by Manuel Quimper in 1790.

Basque shepherds populate the eastern area of the state, though fewer in number than in Oregon and Nevada.

Spanish Place-Names

Several Spanish geographical names remain from the Spanish settlement in Washington, which existed in 1792 on the westernmost tip of the Olympic Peninsula, between the Pacific and the Juan de Fuca Strait, now included in the Makah Indian Reservation. The islands comprising San Juan County in the Strait of Georgia, explored in 1791 by Spaniard Francisco Eliza, namely Patos, Sucia, San Juan, Lopez and Moran, have Spanish names. In Island County, there are Camanos Island, Fidalgo Island, with the town Anacortes, and Orcas Island. There are towns near Seattle called Redondo, Medina and Chico. There is Port Angeles, on the Juan de Fuca Strait. Localities in the rest of the state include Ayer, Bandera, Buena, Camas, Covada, La Mona, Malaga, Mesa, Montesano, Orondo, Oroville, Plaza, Rosalia, Sumas, Toledo and Trinidad. Mountain peaks with Spanish names include Eldorada, Bonanza and Monte Cristo. Finally, Columbia and San Juan Counties have Spanish names.

THE DISTANT STATES: ALASKA AND HAWAII

Alaska

It may seem unusual that the 24th district of Alaska, Alakanuk, has been represented in the state house of representatives by a Jesuit priest named Segundo Llorente, but in fact, Spanish explorers and missionaries have had a role in the history of this far-flung state. The Spanish Franciscan fathers Juan Riobo and Matías Nogueira were the first Europeans to set foot in this territory and celebrated Mass on May 13, 1779, as chaplains of the Spanish frigates *Favorita* and *Princesa*.

Exploration by Sea

The maritime expansion of Spain in the North Pacific can be divided into two periods. The first, from 1774 to 1779, includes the expeditions of Juan Pérez, Bruno Heceta, Ignacio de Arteaga and Juan Francisco de la Bodega y Cuadra, while the second, from 1788 to 1792, covers the activity of Esteban Martínez, Francisco de Eliza, Salvador Fidalgo, Manuel Quimper, Antonio de Valdés, Dionisio Alcalá Galiano, Alejandro Malaspina and Jacinto Caamaño. The second period of exploration arose in response to British expansion. The early explorers sought to offset Russian exploratory activities, about which due warning had been given by the Spanish ambassador at the court of the czars, Count de Lacy, in letters sent to the Spanish secretary of state, Marqués de Grimaldi, in 1773.

The first expedition was led by a midshipman, Juan Pérez, chosen by the viceroy of New Spain, Antonio de Bucarelli y Ursúa, because he was the pilot with most

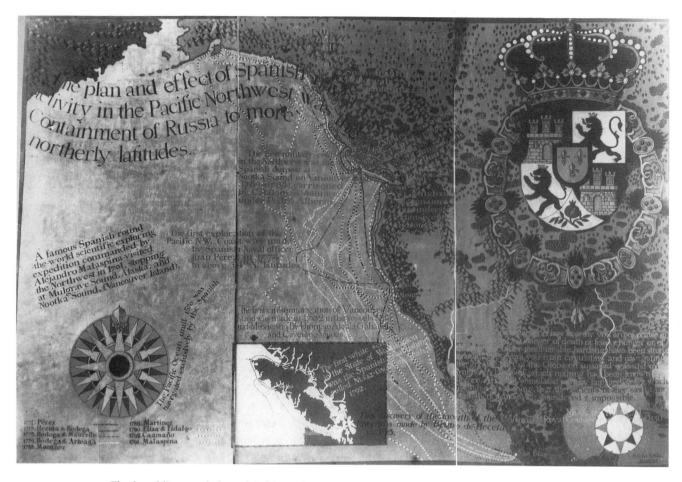

The dotted lines mark the paths of Spanish explorers, 1774–1791. Spanish expansion in the Pacific Northwest served to contain Russian settlements to more northerly latitudes.

experience in the seas in which the expedition was to sail. On January 25,1774, he sailed on the frigate *Santiago* with instructions to sail to 60° north latitude. He was not to undertake any settlements, but rather take possession of suitable sites for townships in the name of the king, and to dispossess any foreigners in the neighborhood. Primarily, he was ordered to obtain as much geographical information as possible about the local Indians, their customs and their encounters with earlier visitors. According to the diary of Father Juan Crespi, who served as chaplain to the expedition, accompanied by Friar Tomás de la Peña, on July 18, 1774, they reached three islands—called the Prince of Wales Islands today—and named them Santa Margarita, it being the feast of St. Margaret. Situated at 55°41', these islands lay to the south of Alaska. Here the Spaniards saw the Indians perhaps belonging to the Haida tribe, for the first time. They had light complexions and long hair, and were covered in skins. They approached the *Santiago*

singing and throwing plumes into the water in welcome. Of the 200 Indians who approached the vessel in 21 canoes, only two ventured aboard, and the rest collected the trinkets and shawls thrown to them over the side. This voyage led to the discovery of several important points along the west coast (among others, Nootka). It also revealed that the Russians had not yet organized a settlement in the area. It was the first Spanish contact with Alaska, well before the arrival of the British.

The second expedition sent by Viceroy Bucarelli was entrusted to Lieutenant Bruno Heceta on the frigate *Santiago,* with Juan Pérez as second-in-command. The schooner *Sonora* was commanded by Juan Manuel de Ayala, with Juan Francisco de la Bodega y Cuadra as second officer, and Francisco Mourelle acting as pilot. The packet boat *San Carlos* was commanded by Lieutenant Miguel Manrique, with José Cañizares as his pilot. With a course set for 65° latitude their purpose was similar to that of the previous voyage. They raised anchor at the port of San Blas, Mexico, on March 16, 1775, but the command changed hands when Manrique fell ill; Ayala was placed in command of the *San Carlos,* and Bodega, of the *Sonora.* The vessels parted for separate courses on July 30.

The *Sonora* reached the 57th parallel on August 15, and the crew sighted Alaska the following day; they saw some very high mountains, one of which they called San Jacinto, now Mt. Edgecumbe, situated on a cape that they called Cape Engaño, now Cape Cook. After discovering Port Mary on August 17 (they called it Guadalupe), on August 18, accompanied by 14 armed men, Juan Francisco Bodega y Cuadra disembarked at another smaller haven with a fair-sized beach, in order to establish possession and obtain water and firewood. They called the haven Nuestra Señora de los Remedios (Our Lady of Hope), and made contact with the Indians, whose reception was not reassuring. On August 21 they set sail once more and reached the 58th parallel on August 22. However, in view of the ill-health among the crew and the bitterly cold weather, Bodega gave orders to set a southerly course, and they skirted the coast, which they observed in detail, naming a number of places: Puerto de Bucarelli, San Carlos Island, Cape San Agustín and Ensenada del Príncipe (Prince Bay).

On August 30, 1775, with the entire crew suffering from scurvy, Bodega decided to abandon Alaskan waters and set course for Monterey, where he arrived on October 7, after a voyage fraught with hardship during which Bodega and Mourelle also fell ill. There they met up with the *Santiago* and the *San Carlos.* These two navigators had recorded abundant information in their respective logbooks, which greatly advanced knowledge of the northwest American coast. Mourelle's log was circulated in Europe and proved of great help to the British captain James Cook in his subsequent explorations. The accomplishments of Bodega and Mourelle are extraordinary, given the size of their little schooner and small crew.

Although the viceroys of New Spain planned to organize annual exploratory expeditions in the North Pacific, none could be undertaken until 1779, due to changing world politics, particularly in North America. But, with the news of the gradually increasing Russian presence in the area, Lieutenant Ignacio de Arteaga and Juan Francisco de la Bodega y Cuadra were placed in command of the frigates *Princesa* (built at San Blas) and *Favorita* (purchased by Bodega in Peru, and with Mourelle as second officer). Some time elapsed before

anchors were raised on February 11, 1779. Their orders were, among others, to reach 70° north latitude.

After 82 days' sailing they called at Port Bucarelli, at 55°17'north latitude and dropped anchor in an adjacent haven on May 3; they celebrated their discovery with a Mass sung onshore on May 13. They named the location Santa Cruz. Due to the size of Port Bucarelli, which comprised 11 other harbors, which could safely take "all the vessels that daily ply the seas in the four corners of the earth," as Ignacio de Arteaga put it, the expeditionaries made a thorough inspection of its shores and drew up a chart of Prince of Wales Island. It took them 26 days to complete the task and resulted in harbors named San Antonio de Padua, Nuestra Señora de la Asunción, Mayoral, la Caldera, la Estrella, del Refugio and de los Dolores; inlets names San Alberto and del Almirante; bays named Esquivel and Juan de Arriaga; islands named San Fernando, San Juan Bautista and Madre de Dios; canals named Portillo, Trocadero and Punta de la Arboleda; and many others.

Finally, on July 2, the two frigates continued on their way north. On July 9, they reached latitude 58°6', and on July 15, reconnoitered Cape San Elías and saw some very high snow-covered peaks (which they called Mt. St. Elías) at latitude 59°52'. Then came a number of discoveries that were shown on maps with the names Puerto de Santiago (later, Nuchik Bay) and Magdalena Island. After passing the 61st parallel, they sailed on skirting the coast in a westerly direction and took refuge in a well-protected inlet. On August 2, Juan Francisco de la Bodega and the second officer on the *Princesa,* Fernando de Quirós, went ashore (Arteaga was sick and unable to go), accompanied by the chaplains and the army, where they set up a cross and took possession of the largest of the islands and of the inlet, which they named Nuestra Señora de Regla. Iliamna Volcano was named Miranda Volcano by them.

Having ascertained that the famous passage connecting the Pacific and Atlantic Oceans was nonexistent, the explorers decided to return to Monterey and dropped anchor at San Francisco Bay on September 14. There the expeditionaries learned that Spain was at war with Britain. They also were to hear about Captain James Cook's voyage the previous year, to the area that they themselves had covered. Bucarelli had died in the meanwhile, and the new viceroy, Martín de Mayorga, congratulated the expeditionaries, rewarding them with promotions and other distinctions.

Almost 10 years passed before the Spaniards returned to the region. In the meanwhile, the British made great progress, which prompted Spain to organize a fourth expedition. The commander at San Blas, who was now Francisco de la Bodega y Cuadra himself, put Esteban José Martínez, a veteran who had accompanied Juan Pérez on his first expedition, in charge of this new endeavor, in command of the frigate *Princesa*; Gonzalo López de Haro would command the packetboat *San Carlos*. The purpose of the expedition lies in the reports made by the French navigator, Comte de la Pérouse, in February 1786, at Santiago, Chile, about the presence of the British and Russians in North Pacific waters. The expedition sailed on March 8, 1788, and the ships called at Prince William Sound on May 17; Martínez took possession of the harbor of Flores (named in honor of the viceroy who had sponsored the expedition). They reached latitude 60°7′ and found an excellent harbor that they called Floridablanca, and then proceeded to the Aleutian Islands, where on the northern side of one of the islands, they disembarked and took possession of the island in the name of the king of Spain. On Trinidad Island they encountered Russian settlements and established friendly relations with the head of the post, Delarof.

The fifth expedition, under Esteban José Martínez, was intended to occupy San Lorenzo de Nutka (Spanish for Nootka), not reaching as far as Alaska. The sixth expedition, commanded by Francisco de Eliza, sent to relieve the previous expeditionary party, also did not reach Alaska. It was from that point that the seventh expedition set out on May 4, 1790, aboard the packetboat *San Carlos* and under the command of Lieutenant Salvador Fidalgo. On May 23 they approached Prince William Sound and moored in Santiago before skirting the wide gulf with its many inlets, which they claimed and named Méndez. With the expert guidance of two Indians, they continued their discoveries: Port Revillagigedo, Conde Island, the Fidalgo Volcano and Valdés Inlet. On July 4, they landed at Unalaska Island, where they had a cordial meeting with the Russians.

The Spaniards returned to Alaska in 1791 with the corvettes *Descubierta* and *Atrevida,* commanded by Alejandro Malaspina and José de Bustamante, respectively. Their primary purpose was to undertake a scientific expedition, and they traveled as far north as Cape Edgecumbe. In measuring the distance from the cape to Nootka, they discovered that the famous Strait of Anian, claimed by Ferrer de Maldonado, did not exist. Malaspina continued his voyage in the Pacific, circumnavigating the globe and gathering important scientific information.

In 1792, Jacinto Caamaño explored the northern sector of the Pacific aboard the frigate *Aránzazu,* and reached Prince of Wales and Queen Charlotte Islands, as well as the islands of Revillagigedo and Aristizabal, which still bear these names. This expedition brought Spanish explorations in this area to a close.

Spanish Place-Names

The period of Spanish exploration is remembered in such local place-names as Valdez and Cordoba. Though neither Luis de Córdoba, who was captain general of the Spanish navy, nor Antonio de Valdés, who was secretary of state of the Indies, ever saw the coast of Alaska, it was at their urging that some of the Spanish maritime expeditions were undertaken. As a consequence of these voyages, the coast of Alaska has been sprinkled with Spanish names, though few have survived to the present day. Even so, it is astonishing to see the number that the historian Luis Bolin found on local maps:

On the map of the Craig region, which encompasses Prince of Wales Island and its surroundings—covering from 132° to 134° longitude west, and from the 55th to the 56th Parallels—I have found the following islands: Españolas, Heceta, Anguilas, Esquivel, San Lorenzo, San José, De La Culebra, San Felipe, Las Animas, Suémez, San Ignacio, San Fernando, Catalina, De La Cruz, San Alberto, La Ballena, La Balandra, San Juan Bautista, Las Cabras, Arboleda, Los Ladrones, Madre de Dios, Coronado, Ranchería, and Culebrinas; points: Desconocida, Bocas, Encarnación, Santa Teresa, Lontana, San Antonio, Cocos, San Rafael, San Roque, Arrecife, Maravilla, Santa Gertrudis, Santo Tomás, Crucero, Milflores, Azucenas, Arboleda, Quesada, San José del Rosaria, Refugio, Cangrejo, Providencia, Amargura, Tranquila, Batán, Lomas, Perlas, San Sebastián, Miravalles, and Blanquizal; the mouth Fines; Derrumba Mountains; the bays of Anguilas, Aguirre, Veta, Fortaleza, and San Alberto; Gulf of Esquivel; Sonora Passage; San Cristobal Channel; García, Pedro and Arena Inlets; Portillo Channel; Gaviota, Granito and Arcada Rocks; Fortaleza Lake and Heights; Cape and Mount Bartolomé; the havens of San Antonio, Alonso, Asunción, Carocal, Mayoral, Real, Real Marina, Dolores, Santa Cruz, and Estrella; Mount Pimienta; San Nicolás Channel; Las Palmas Passage and La Cruz Passage; Mount Juan; Ulloa Channel; Cape Félix; Adrian Inlet, Farallón Bay, Mount Madre, Decision Passage, Parida Island, and Point Cayman.

At Prince Rupert there is Las Vegas Island; in the region of Kechikan can be seen the inlet and township of Santa Ana and Point Caamaño; on Gravina Island, which incidentally is a long way from the harbor and island of Gravina, near Cordova, there are Vallemar Bay, Point and Rock; the deep bight of Cuadra has the North Quadra and South Quadra Mountains nearby, together with the Revillagigedo Channel. Cape Decisión and Port Toledo appear on the map of Port Alexander and on that of Dixon Entrance can be seen Agustín Cape and Bay; the map of Cordova shows Cape Magdalena, Bazán Port and Point, Cape Muzón, Port Nuñez and Nuñez Rock and Cape Chacôn. Near Sitka are Fortuna Point and Shallows, Port Mar; Islas Bay, on the map of Chicagof, is one of the largest in Alaska, and also Point Engaño, near Mount Edgecumbe, which for some time was known as Cape Cook.

In the Mount Fairweather region lies Point Villaluenga, and Palma Bay; near Valdez, which bears the name of the former Spanish Minister of the Navy, Antonio de Valdés y Bazán, there is Valdez Arm and Harbor; the Malaspina Glacier and Point Muñoz are close to Yukatat Bay and Mount Diablo can be found on the Kenai Peninsula, north of the bay, island and passage of Nutka. In the vicinity of Cordova, called after Captain Luis de Córdoba y Córdoba, is Cordova Airfield and Airport, San Mateo Bay, the Port and Island of Gravina and Port Fidalgo.

Hawaii: Explorations by Sea

Most histories attribute the discovery of the Hawaii Islands to Captain James Cook in 1778; he called Hawaii the "Sandwich Islands," in honor of his protector, the earl of Sandwich. In truth, however, the Spanish were the first to arrive. From the 16th through part of the 18th centuries, the Pacific Ocean was plied almost exclusively by Spanish ships sailing from the East, with the exception of the occasional British or Dutch pirate. Spain competed in the market for spices with the Portuguese, who came from the West. In spite of the vastness of the Pacific and Spain's efforts to explore other parts of the world, Spanish navigators were the first in the South Seas from the time of Magellan's voyage—when he named the Pacific Ocean—onward, for the greater glory of the Emperor Charles V, and Diego de Ribeiro used that name for the vast ocean on his map in 1529.

When five ships with 276 men aboard, under the command of a Portuguese man, Ferdinand Magellan, sailed from Sanlúcar de Barrameda, in Spain, on Sep-

tember 20, 1519, Spain was setting out on one of the most hazardous and important enterprises since the discovery of the New World by Columbus. The circumnavigation of the globe was accomplished successfully by only one of the ships, the *Victoria,* commanded by Juan Sebastián Elcano, Magellan's second officer. He arrived at Cadiz, Spain, on September 6, 1522, with 31 men, after a voyage lasting almost three years. In March 1521 they had discovered the archipelago of San Lázaro (later renamed in honor of King Philip II of Spain) where Magellan suffered a violent death on one of the islands, on April 27, 1521.

The voyage caused a great commotion in Portugal, which under the papal bull (1493) of Alexander VI, and later under the Treaty of Tordesillas, had carved up new territories of the world with Spain. Needing to establish a border between the two spheres of influence in the Far East, the king of Spain authorized an expedition under the command of García Jofre de Loaysa. In July 1525, seven ships set sail from La Coruña in Spain, and were in the Pacific by May 25 the following year. Dysentery took a heavy toll, and Loaysa, Elcano (the pilot major) and the third-in-command (Alonso de Salazar) all died in quick succession. By the time the expedition reached the Islas de las Especias (Spice Islands), now the Moluccas, in November 1526, only one ship was left, commanded by Martín de Iñiguez, who also died shortly afterward and was succeeded in his command by Hernando de la Torre.

Hernán Cortés decided to send Alvaro de Saavedra in search of the missing expedition. He departed from Zacatula, Mexico on October 31, 1527. In December, south of Kauai Island, a terrible storm wrecked the *San Diego,* commanded by Luis de Cardoza, and the corvette *Espíritu Santo,* under Pedro Fuentes. The flagship, the galleon *Florida,* weathered the storm, and Saavedra managed to continue toward Guam and the Moluccas, which he left in June 1528, bound for New Spain. Despite several attempts, severe winds prevented him from reaching his destination. He died on the north coast of New Guinea, on October 9, 1529. The *Florida,* however, succeeded in reaching Spain by rounding the Cape of Good Hope in 1536.

The expedition led by Alvaro de Saavedra also encountered the Hawaiian Islands; some Spaniards on the expedition were washed ashore after they were shipwrecked. Hawaiian oral tradition recounts the appearance of a sailing ship battered by the storm, and how the captain sought refuge ashore (his Hawaiian name is Kukanaloa), with his sister (Kamalau) and other companions. He knelt on the beach in thanksgiving, and today this spot is still known as Kulou. The natives gave them a cordial welcome and offered them food and accommodation. In time they married Hawaiian women and became the forebears of some of the leading families, such as that of Kaikioewa, one of the governors of Kauai. Some of the closest advisors of Emperor Kamehamea I were also of Spanish ancestry. On a British map of the North Pacific dated 1687, itself a copy of a Spanish map, next to a group of islands at the same latitude as the Hawaiian Islands is the date 1527, the year of Saavedra's voyage.

The Grijalva expedition, sent to the Pacific by Hernán Cortés, is not thought to have reached the Hawaiian Islands before its leader was murdered on the Moluccas, in 1539. On the other hand, a 1542 expedition led by Ruy Lôpez de Villalobos discovered a group of islands surrounded by coral reefs and coconut palms. He called them Islas del Rey (King's Islands), but many historians have identified them as Hawaii. They later called at another archipelago, which became known as the Carolinas, in honor of King Charles II of Spain. The discovery of Hawaii can therefore be credited to Villalobos, Juan Gaetano (the pilot major) and Gaspar Rico (the first pilot).

It was Alvaro de Mendaña and Pedro Sarmiento de Gamboa who discovered the Solomon Islands on February 9, 1568, three years after the first successful voyage from the Philippine Islands to the coasts of America by Father Andrés de Urdaneta, which opened up the route for what was to be the famous Manila galleon. Sarmiento had informed the governor of Peru, Lope García de Castro, of the Inca legend concerning the visit of Tupac to the distant islands in the ocean; the viceroy therefore placed the expedition under the command of García and his nephew, Alvaro de Mendaña. They departed from the port of Callao, Peru, on November 19, 1567, and sighted the island, which they called Ulloa, on December 27; this island was none other than Kauai. Since they had changed course so often, they did not reach Australia but instead sighted the Solomon Islands, so named because they were assumed to be the biblical Kingdom of Ophir. On one of the islands, Isabel, the pilot Hernán Gallego and Pedro Ortega built a brigantine with which they discovered, among other places, Guadalcanal, which played such a major part in the Pacific campaign in World War II. In September 1964, the Spanish and U.S.'s naval forces at Rota Base paid a tribute to Ortega at the town of Guadalcanal in the Spanish province of Cádiz.

The Solomon Islands were visited again by the second Mendaña expedition, which left Callao on April 9, 1595, with Pedro Fernández de Quirós as his pilot major, together with 378 people, many of them women, aboard six ships. On July 21, they sighted an archipelago for the first time and called it the Marquesas de Mendoza Islands in honor of the viceroy of Peru. In the course of this expedition Mendaña himself died on October 18, 1595, on Santa Cruz Island, which he had discovered; his widow, Doña Isabel Barreto took command of the expedition as adelantada del mar océano (adelantada of the ocean sea), jointly with Quirós. The Solomon Islands were not to be explored again for 200 years.

On December 21,1605, Pedro Fernández de Quirós set sail from Callao, with Luis Báez de Torres as his pilot. On May 14, 1604, they came upon one of the islands in the New Hebrides. On that date, by order of King Philip III, he took possession of all the islands and land discovered and to be discovered by him thereafter as far as the Pole, which he called Australia del Espíritu Santo, thus honoring the reigning dynasty in Spain. Scholar Carlos Sanz argues convincingly that this was the origin of the present name of the first continent: "While it is perhaps impossible to claim that the Spaniards were the first to set foot in Australia, on the other hand it is clear that it is to them that the world owes it awareness of the existence of a vast territory in the southern part of the Pacific Ocean." Quirós submitted to the king no fewer the 50 reports on his discoveries, and the eighth of those reports, estimating the size of Australia to be equivalent to Europe and Asia Minor, including the Mediterranean and Atlantic islands, became widely known throughout Europe. It is hardly surprising that Abel Janssen Tasman and James Cook used Quirós's report when undertaking their own exploratory adventures in the mid- and late 17th century. Báez de Torres, for his part, was separated from his leader following a storm and skirted the southern coast of New Guinea (Torres Strait), sighting the opposite shore of the Australian continent. He and his men were the first Europeans to embark on the new continent.

French historian Elysée Reclus attributes the discovery of the Hawaiian Islands, Santa Cruz, the Marquesas and the Solomon Islands to Mendaña. William Harvey, who accompanied Cook in 1778, called Hawaii "Mendaña Islands" in his diary. Some recent research indicates that the central Hawaiian island was Columbus's Cipango.

British Expeditions

In June 1743, the British ship *Centurion*, commanded by Lord George Anson, captured the Manila galleon after a fierce combat. On the galleon was a map containing all the Spanish discoveries made in the Pacific; apparently the Spanish rulers endeavored to keep these discoveries secret. The map included a group of islands situated at the same latitude as the Hawaii Islands but some 17° to the east. The southernmost island is shown on the map as La Mesa (Hawaii); farther north is La Desgraciada (Maui) and the trio called Los Monjes, or "The Monks" (Kahoolawe, Lanai and Molokai).

Captain James Cook disembarked on January 18, 1778, at Waimea, on Kauai; a monument marks the spot today. Another, in Kealakekua Bay, on Hawaii, recalls the siege in which Cook died at the hands of native warriors a year later. When he arrived, he was told of white men who had arrived in earlier times and saw various pieces of Spanish ironwork. Moreover, he undoubtedly knew about the map captured by Lord Anson and identified the islands of Mesa and Monjes with those that he had just located himself. The same conclusion was reached by French navigator Count La Pérouse in his scientific voyage in 1786.

The extent of British navigation in the Pacific and the increasing value of this ocean for trade resulted in friction with Spain. There were a number of incidents, most notably the Nootka Controversy, that almost led to an outbreak of war between Spain and Britain. This was avoided by the signing of the Nooka Treaty, in which Spain withdrew her claims to a monopoly.

In 1789, the Hawaiian Islands were visited by a Spanish officer, Esteban J. Martínez. His letters to the viceroy of New Spain advising Spanish settlement of the islands due to their advantageous strategic position led the viceroy to dispatch Lieutenant Manuel Quimper, who explored the islands in the spring of 1791 and drew up a report about their inhabitants, resources and opportunities for trade. But the domestic political situation in Spain prevented the fulfillment of Quimper's ideas.

The first livestock imported to the islands came from Santa Barbara, California, in 1794, sent by George Vancouver; the first horses were brought by Captain Stephen Grover Cleveland from Cape San Lucas.

The curious figure of the Andalusian Francisco de Paula Marín, known as "Manini," arrived in Hawaii in 1791 and remained there until his death in 1837. He enjoyed the trust of Kamehamea I, serving him as interpreter and tending to him during his fatal illness. Marín was responsible for introducing the cultivation of many fruits and flowers in Hawaii, such as oranges, figs, grapes and roses. By 1809 he was making butter, salting meat for ships and producing wine. A devout Catholic,

it appears that he secretly baptized more than 300 natives. His diary is an invaluable document of early Hawaiian culture.

Another Spaniard, Juan Elio de Castro, came in 1814, after he was freed by Captain Kotzebue from California authorities, who had imprisoned him for working with the Russians in the fur trade; he became private secretary to Kamehamea I. Luis Fernández Alvarez, a prominent Spanish doctor from California, practiced in Hawaii from 1887 until 1896. Asked to help fight leprosy, he left the islands to study at John Hopkins University before returning and spending several years in this work. During that time he held the post of honorary vice-consul of Spain in Honolulu.

As a result of Spanish voyages and shipwrecks throughout the area, there were undoubtedly many Spaniards who settled in the islands and, like their predecessors on the Saavedra expedition, mingled with the native populations. In 1825, Minister Henry August Pierce reported the existence in Hawaii of "Ehus," a people with fair skin and European features. Pierce maintained that the word *ehu* was a derivation of the Spanish word *hijo,* or "child." A bust at the Bishop Museum in Honolulu bears testimony to this group. Unearthed during construction at the turn of the century, the caption reads: "Captain of a Spanish ship sculpted by a local artist." The statue has long hair, a mustache, a goatee, a ruff and broad features.

Throughout the 19th and even the early 20th centuries, there were groups of Spaniards who settled on the Hawaiian Islands, either coming from the Philippines, California, Mexico or Puerto Rico, or directly from Spain. They introduced several crops and established herds of livestock. The name *paniolos,* which is now synonymous with horsemen in the islands, originally referred to these cowboys, or *españoles.* They introduced methods of breeding and training horses, the lasso, spurs, ponchos and sombreros, which can still be seen in Hawaii today.

Moreover, Spanish currency circulated for a long time on the islands, particularly the Spanish piece of eight, or dollar. Some Spaniards immigrated to California following the discovery of gold, but about 8,000 Andalusians settled in the islands between 1907 and 1913. Farmers from Puerto Rico also immigrated at that time.

The Territory of Guam

Guam has had a long and colorful association with Spain. The island lies about 1,450 miles from Manila and is some 4,700 miles from San Francisco. The center of the capital, Agaña, is still made up of the Plaza de España and the cathedral of La Dulce Nombre de María. Its busy San Luis de Apra Harbor has been known to Europeans from the arrival of the first Spanish ships almost 500 years ago. Today residents of Guam are United States citizens, although because Guam is a territory rather than a state they do not have voting privileges.

Ferdinand Magellan discovered the island on March 6, 1521, in the course of his famous voyage circumnavigating the globe. Magellan and his men remained in Umatac Bay until the morning of March 9 and had various contacts, both friendly and otherwise, with the natives, whom they called *chamorros*. An expedition led by García Jofre de Loaysa was the second from Spain to visit Guam. On September 4, 1526, while his ship was preparing to drop anchor, a party of natives, accompanied by Gonazalo de Vigo, a Spaniard from the Magellan crew who had spent four years with the *chamorros* until he was rescued by the Loaysa expedition, welcomed them.

The third Spanish contact with the island was led by General Miguel López de Legazpi on January 22, 1565. Father Urdaneta, a member of the expedition, liked the place so much that he proposed settling there. The general would not consent to this proposal, giving priority to colonization of the Philippine Islands. In spite of orders given by the general to avoid the natives, after several incidents the commander of the soldiery, Mateo del Saúz, disembarked at the head of a hundred men. Fathers Grijalva and Gaspar explored the island, describing its characteristics in a written report.

In 1600, the ship *Santa Margarita* was wrecked near Rota Island in a typhoon, and her cargo was plundered by the natives. The following year, six survivors succeeded in reaching the Spanish galleon *Santo Tomás*, sailing in nearby waters. When he heard that there were another 26 Spanish castaways on the island, Father Antonio de Morga disembarked to join the group. Three years earlier, an anonymous Franciscan living on another of the islands with the natives following a shipwreck had succeeded in informing Lope de Ulloa, in command of a fleet passing nearby, of the need for missionaries. This message was conveyed to the governor of the Philippines, Francisco Tello, and the news reached King Philip III, who ordered that a Spanish settlement be established. The settlement was begun with the arrival of Father Diego Luis de Sanvitores on Guam in 1668.

A Castilian Jesuit, Diego Luis de Sanvitores had secured his role by petitioning Queen Mariana, who took great interest in the venture, first as the wife of King Philip IV and then as queen regent following his death in 1665. Sanvitores was accompanied by five other Jesuits and some Filipino laymen. By 1669, the natives had already helped to build a church at Agaña. But, starting with the martyrdom of Brother Laurent during his visit to Anatjan, the situation gradually deteriorated, coinciding with rivalry between two local factions, and resulting in the use of military force on Tinian Island, where Father Luis Medina and a Filipino, Hipólito de la Cruz, were killed. With the outbreak of open rebellion by the natives, the Spaniards built a fort, Santa Soledad, armed with several cannons. In June 1671, the arrival of four priests coincided with a fresh uprising encouraged by the *makahnas,* or tribal witch doctors. Father Sanvitores and his Filipino assistant were murdered on April 2, 1672. The military garrison was reinforced and the uprising was put down. (Sanvitores was beatified by Pope John Paul II in October 1985.)

With peace restored, Christianity took root among the *chamorros,* and many chapels and churches were built. To this day Catholicism remains the predominant religion on the island. The Jesuits also introduced grape vines to the island; a small variety of banana, coffee, cocoa, corn, sweet potato and other plants; as well as cows and pigs, the Filipino carabao, dogs, cats, deer and chickens. The College of San Juan de Letrán was established, endowed with 3,000 pesos a year by Queen Mariana. The Augustinians replaced the Jesuits on November 2, 1769, following an edict issued by King Charles III.

During the 17th and 18th centuries additional forts were built: Santa María de Guadalupe (1683), Santiago (1721), Merizo battery (1724), San Luis (1737), Nuestra Señora del Carmen (1742), Santo Angel (1742), San Fernando (1772) and San Rafael (1799). In the 19th century, forts were built at: Santa Agueda (1800), Nuestra Señora de los Dolores y la Santa Cruz (1801) and San José (1803); Soledad was rebuilt in 1803. The forts at Santa Agueda, Santiago, Santo Angel, Soledad and San José are still standing.

Guam was visited by the scientific expedition sent by King Charles IV under Alejandro Malaspina, in February 1792. On board were botanists Thaddaeus Haenke and Louis Née, geologist Antonio Pineda, and a draftsman, Juan Ravenet, all of whom spent 12 days on the island. The plants and information collected were deposited at the Botanical Gardens at Madrid in 1794. Some 23 years later, in 1817, the sergeant major of the Spanish garrison, Luis de Torres, cooperated in scientific finds made by the expedition of Pedro Alexandrovich, count of Romanzoff, chancellor of the Russian Empire, accompanied by the botanist Adalbert von Chamisso. Letters written by the Spanish lieutenant Tomás Crozet, who visited Guam with a French expedition led by Nicolas Marion-Dufresne, influenced the famous *History* written by Abbé Reynal.

Throughout its history, Guam has been led by a number of outstanding Spanish governors. In 1681, Antonio de Saravia was appointed (notably, with powers entirely independent of the viceroy of Mexico and the governor of the Philippines). His first action was to convene a general assembly of the islanders, who rendered obeisance to the king of Spain and were given equal status with other Spanish subjects. Later Governors Damián Esplaña, Antonio Pimentel and Enrique de Olavide succeeded in preventing pirate raids. In the 19th century, Governors Francisco Ramón de Villalobos, Pablo Pérez, Felipe de la Corte and Francisco Moscoso strove to improve the economy of the island, fight leprosy and other diseases, and condition foreign immigrants for agricultural work.

Spanish rule ended with the Spanish-American War in 1898. Without warning, the cruiser *Charleston* entered San Luis de Apra Bay on June 20; Forts Santiago and Santa Cruz did not oppose her. After his troops disembarked, Captain Henry Glass succeeded in taking possession of the island without firing a shot, to the surprise of the garrison and the population, who did not realize that a war had broken out. The Spaniards were taken prisoner with their governor, Juan Marina, and shipped to Manila. Under the Treaty of Paris, signed on December 10, 1898, Spain transferred the islands of Puerto Rico, the Philippines and Guam to the United States.

Throughout its history, Guam and neighboring islands have been known by various names Magellan called them the Islas de las Velas Latinas (Islands of the Lateen Sails), when he saw the light, fast-moving boats from which the natives greeted their Spanish visitors. For a long time they were known as the Islas de los Ladrones (Islands of Thieves), because the natives had succeeded in capturing a ship during one Spanish expedition. They are also still called the Mariana Islands, after Queen Mariana. Today, the excavation of the wrecked galleon *Nuestra Señora del Pilar* off the coast of Guam by Australian divers may help to reveal more about Guam's Spanish past.

APPENDIXES

Significant Dates of the Spanish Presence in Colonial America

1493

Columbus lands in what is today U.S. Virgin Islands, naming the area Once Mil Vírgenes. Three of these islands (St. Thomas, St. John and St. Croix) are now U.S. possessions.

1513

Juan Ponce de León explores the east and west coasts of what is now Florida.

1517

Francisco Hernández de Córdoba leads an expedition into Florida.

1519

Alonso Alvarez de Pineda explores the west coast of Florida and the Gulf of Mexico. He is the first European to reach the Mississippi River.

1524

Esteban Gómez discovers the Hudson River (years before Henry Hudson) and names it Río San Antonio.

1526

Lucas Vázquez de Ayllón becomes *adelantado* of Florida.

1528–1536

Pánfilo de Narváez lands in Tampa Bay, Florida, and moves his soldiers north to present-day Tallahassee. Attacked by Indians, Narváez builds ships on Florida's Gulf coast and sails toward Mexico.

Alvar Núñez Cabeza de Vaca, the treasurer of the expedition, and 80 others are shipwrecked on the Gulf coast of Texas. On his return to Spain, Cabeza de Vaca writes a book entitled *La relación*, recounting his adventures in Florida and the Southwest. Cabeza de Vaca and his men explored more than a thousand miles in seven years.

1539

Father Marcos de Niza, with Estebanico the African, explores Arizona and New Mexico.

Hernando de Soto lands in Tampa Bay and explores 10 southern states. He celebrates the first Christmas in North America.

1540

Hernando de Alarcón sails from Acapulco into the Gulf of California, sighting the Colorado River as it empties into the gulf.

García López de Cárdenas is the first European to see the Grand Canyon in Arizona.

1540–1542

Francisco Vázquez de Coronado explores the Southwest in search of the Seven Cities of Cibola, encountering the Hopi, Apache, Pawnee, Zuñi and Wichita tribes.

1541

Hernando de Soto reaches the Mississippi River.

1543

Juan Rodríguez Cabrillo explores the coast of Oregon.

Appendixes have been updated by Gerardo Piña Rosales except where otherwise indicated.

1559

Tristán de Luna, governor of Florida, establishes settlement near present-day Pensacola and explores territory that is now Georgia.

1556

Spaniards arrive in Virginia.

1565

Pedro Menéndez de Avilés founds San Agustín, in Florida, on September 8 as the first permanent European settlement in the United States. He also founds the first mission in the United States, Nombre de Dios. Menéndez governs Florida, which extends from the present-day state of Florida up to Canada, for almost 10 years. During this time he founds six other settlements and missions: San Mateo (Fort Caroline), Santa Lucía (Saint Lucie County, Florida), Tequesta (now Miami), San Antón (Charlotte Harbor area), Tocobaga (Tampa Bay area) and Santa Elena (Parris Island, South Carolina).

1566

Juan Pardo and Hernando Boyano cross Georgia, both Carolinas and Alabama.

1581

Spanish missionaries travel along the Rio Grande, from Santa Bárbara (Chihuahua) to Bernalillo (New Mexico).

1582

Antonio de Espejo travels from Santa Bárbara to Arizona and on his return, reaches Pecos and Texas.

1598

Juan de Oñate and more than 100 Spanish colonists establish the colony of San Gabriel del Yunque, known today as the San Juan pueblo in New Mexico.

1603

Martín de Aguilar explores the coast of Oregon.

1604

Oñate crosses the desert from San Gabriel to the Gulf of California.

1610

Pedro de Peralta founds the city of Santa Fe (New Mexico).

1620

The chapel of Nuestra Señora de la Leche y del Buen Parto is dedicated at the Nombre de Dios Mission near St. Augustine. The chapel is the first shrine established in the first mission in the United States.

1633

Construction begins on the Camino Real between St. Augustine on the Atlantic coast of Florida and Florida's Gulf of Mexico coast. The road is completed at the end of the century and a chain of missions is established along it.

1654

A group of 23 Sephardic Jews, coming from Brazil, arrive in New Amsterdam (New York City). There they found the first synagogue in the U.S.

1672

Construction begins on Castillo de San Marcos in St. Augustine.

1687

Jesuit priest Eusebio Francisco Kino arrives in New Mexico. Over the next several years, Father Kino sets up a chain of missions in Arizona, among them San Xavier del Bac, south of Tucson.

1693

The king of Spain frees all slaves who have escaped from the British colonists in North America and are living in Florida.

1698

The viceroy of Mexico sends Andrés de Arriola of Veracruz with three ships and 200 men to Florida. Arriola lands in the bay of Pensacola and constructs Fort San Carlos, beginning the settlement of Pensacola.

1706

The Spanish found Albuquerque.

1738

Governor Manuel de Montiano of Florida establishes the first free black town in the present-day United States.

1747

José de Escandón surveys Texas. Over the next seven years Escandón distributes large parcels of land, called ranchos, to settlers. This marks the beginning of the cattle industry in Texas.

1763

When Spain joins France in the war against England, France secretly gives the Louisiana territory to its new ally. From 1766 to 1803, 10 governors rule over Spanish Louisiana, a territory that encompasses 13 states in whole or part, extending from the Gulf of Mexico to Canada and from the Mississippi River to the Rocky Mountains. Americans take over in New Orleans in 1803, and in St. Louis in 1804.

Spain cedes Florida to Great Britain by the Treaty of Paris.

1765

Under the direction of José de Gálvez, Spain and its colonies in the New World give military and financial aid to the thirteen colonies during the American Revolution.

1769

Fray Junípero Serra founds his first mission, San Diego de Alcalá (California).

Gaspar de Portolá discovers the bay of San Francisco.

1774

Juan Pérez, Bruno de Heceta and Juan Francisco de la Bodega y Cuadra begin their numerous expeditions by sea, exploring the lands of present-day Oregon, Washington and Alaska.

1776

Juan Bautista de Anza founds the city of San Francisco.

1777

Bernardo de Gálvez, governor of Louisiana, sends money, supplies and arms to the American generals George Rogers Clark in the Ohio valley and George Washington in Virginia.

1779

Gálvez raises an army in New Orleans, captures five British forts in the Mississippi valley and takes Mobile and Pensacola.

1781

Felipe de Neve founds Los Angeles.

1783

Spain regains Florida from England in the Treaty of Paris. Spain's rule in Florida continues until 1821.

Spanish Governors in the United States

Governors of Florida

FIRST PERIOD 1565–1763

Pedro Menéndez de Avilés, 1565–1574
Hernando de Miranda, 1575–1577
Pedro Menéndez Marqués (interim governor), 1577–1578
Pedro Menéndez Marqués, 1578–1589
Gutierre de Miranda, 1589–1592
Rodrigo de Junco, 1592
Domingo Martínez de Avandaño, 1594–1595
Gonzalo Méndez de Canzo, 1596–1603

Pedro de Ybarra, 1603–1609
Juan de Salinas, 1618–1623
Luis de Rojas y Borja, 1624–1629
Andrés Rodríguez de Villegas, 1630–1631
Luis Horruytiner, 1633–1638
Damián de Vega Castro y Pardo, 1639–1645
Benito Ruiz de Salazar Ballecilla, 1645–1650
Nicolás Ponce de León (interim governor)
Pedro Benedit Horruytiner (interim governor)
Diego de Rebolledo, 1655–1659
Alonso de Aranguiz y Cortés, 1659–1663
Francisco de la Guerra y de la Vega, 1664–1670
Manuel de Cendoya, 1670–1673
Nicolás Ponce de León (interim governor), 1674
Pablo de Hita y Salazar, 1675–1680
Juan Marqués Cabrera, 1680–1687
Diego de Quiroga y Losada, 1687–1693
Laureano de Torres y Ayala, 1693–1699
José de Zúñiga y Cerda, 1699–1706
Francisco de Córcoles y Martínez, 1706–1716
Juan de Ayala Escobar (interim governor), 1717–1718
Antonio de Benavides, 1718–1734
Francisco del Moral Sánchez, 1734–1737
Manuel José de Justis (interim governor), 1737
Manuel de Montiano, 1737–1749
Melchor de Navarrete, 1749–1752
Fulgencio García de Solís (interim governor), 1752–1755
Alonso Fernández de Heredia, 1755–1758
Lucas de Palacio, 1758–1761
Melchor Felíu, 1762–1763

SECOND PERIOD

EAST FLORIDA

Manuel de Zéspedes, 1783–1790
Juan Quesada, 1790–1795
Bartolomé Morales, 1795
Enrique White, 1795–1811
Juan de Estrada, 1811–1812
Sebastián Kindelan, 1812–1815
Juan de Estrada, 1815–1816
José Coppinger, 1816–1821

WEST FLORIDA

Arturo O'Neill, 1781–1793
Enrique White, 1793–1795
Francisco de Paula Gelabert, 1795–1796
Juan Folch, 1796–1811
Francisco St. Maxent, 1811–1812

Mauricio de Zúñiga, 1812–1813
Mateo González Manrique, 1813–1815
José Masot, 1816–1819
José Callava, 1819–1821

Manuel Salcedo, 1811–1813
Cristóbal Domínguez, 1814–1817
Ignacio Pérez, 1817
Manuel Pardo, 1817
Antonio Martínez, 1817–1822

Governors of Louisiana

Antonio de Ulloa, 1766–1768
Phillippe Aubry (interim governor), 1768–1769
Alejandro O'Reilly, 1769–1770
Luis de Unzaga y Amézaga, 1770–1777
Bernardo de Gálvez, 1777–1785
Esteban Rodríguez Miró, 1785–1791
Francisco Luis Héctor, baron of Carondelet, 1791–1797
Manuel Gayoso de Lemos, 1797–1799
Marqués de Casa Calvo, 1799–1801
Juan Manuel Salcedo, 1801–1803

Governors of Texas

Domingo Terán de los Ríos, 1691–1692
Gregorio de Salinas, 1692–1697
Francisco Cuervo y Valdés, 1698–1702
Mathias de Aguirre, 1703–1705
Martín de Alarcón, 1705–1708
Simón Padilla y Córdova, 1708–1712
Pedro Fermín de Echevers y Subisa, 1712–1714
Juan Valdéz, 1714–1716
Martín de Alarcón, 1716–1719
Marqués de San Miguel de Aguayo, 1719–1722
Fernando Pérez de Almazán, 1722–1727
Melchor Media Villa y Ascona, 1727–1730
Juan Bustillo Zevallos, 1730–1734
Manuel de Sandoval, 1734–1736
Carlos Benítez Franquis de Lugo, 1736–1737
Prudencio de Orobio Basterra, 1737–1741
Tomás Felipe Wintuisen, 1741–1743
Justo Boneo y Morales, 1743–1744
Francisco García Larios y Jáuregui, 1751–1759
Angel Martos y Navarrete, 1759–1766
Hugo O'Conor, 1767–1770
Barón de Riperdá, 1770–1778
Domingo Cabello, 1778–1786
Bernardo Bonavia, 1786
Rafael Martínez Pacheco, 1787–1788
Manuel Muñoz, 1790–1798
José Irigoyen, 1798–1800
Juan Bautista de Elguezabal, 1800–1805
Antonio Cordero y Bustamante, 1805–1810

Governors of New Mexico

Juan de Oñate, 1608
Cristóbal de Oñate, 1608–1610
Pedro de Peralta, 1610–1614
Bernardino de Ceballos, 1614–1618
Juan de Eulate, 1618–1625
Felipe Sotelo Ossorio, 1625–1630
Francisco Manuel de Silva Nieto, 1630–1632
Francisco de la Mora y Ceballos, 1632–1635
Francisco Martínez de Baeza, 1635–1637
Luis de Rosas, 1637–1641
Juan Flores de Sierra y Valdéz, 1641
Francisco Gómez, 1641–1642
Alonso Pacheco de Heredia, 1642–1644
Fernando de Argüello Carvajal, 1644–1647
Luis de Guzmán y Figueroa, 1647–1649
Hernando de Ugarte y la Concha, 1649–1653
Juan de Samaniego y Jaca, 1653–1656
Juan Manso de Contreras, 1656–1659
Bernardo López de Mendizábal, 1659–1661
Diego Dionisio de Peñalosa Briceño y Verdugo, 1661–1664
Juan Miranda, 1664–1665
Fernando de Villanueva, 1665–1668
Juan de Medrano y Mesía, 1668–1671
Juan Durán de Miranda, 1671–1675
Juan Francisco de Treviño, 1675–1677
Antonio de Otermín, 1677–1683
Domingo Jironza Petri de Cruzate, 1683–1686
Pedro Reneros de Posada, 1686–1689
Domingo Jironza Petri de Cruzate, 1689–1691
Diego de Vargas Zapata Luján Ponce de León, 1691–1697
Pedro Rodríguez Cubero, 1697–1703
Diego de Vargas Zapata Luján Ponce de León, 1703–1704
Juan Páez Hurtado, 1704–1705
Francisco Cuervo y Valdés, 1705–1707
José Chacón Medina Salazar, Marqués de las Peñuelas, 1707–1712
Juan Ignacio Flores Mogollón, 1712–1715
Felipe Martínez, 1715–1717

Juan Páez Urtado, 1717
Antonio Valverde y Cossío, 1717–1722
Juan Domingo de Bustamante, 1722–1731
Gervasio Cruzat y Góngoza, 1731–1736
Enrique de Olavide y Michelena, 1736–1739
Gaspar Domingo de Mendoza, 1739–1743
Joaquín Codallos y Rabal, 1743–1749
Tomás Vélez Cachupín, 1749–1754
Francisco Antonio Marín del Valle, 1754–1760
Mateo Antonio de Mendoza, 1760
Manuel de Portillo y Urrisola, 1760–1762
Tomás Vélez Cachupín, 1762–1767
Pedro Fermín de Mendinueta, 1767–1778
Francisco Trébol Navarro, 1778
Juan Bautista de Anza, 1778–1788
Fernando de la Concha, 1788–1794
Fernando Chacón, 1794–1805
Joaquín del Real Alencaster, 1805–1808
Alberto Maynez, 1808
José Manrique, 1808–1814
Alberto Maynez, 1814–1816
Pedro María de Allende, 1816–1818
Facundo Melgares, 1818–1822

Governors of California

Gaspar de Portolá, 1768–1770
Felipe de Barri, 1770–1775
Felipe de Neve, 1775–1782
Pedro Fagés, 1782–1791
José Antonio Romeu, 1791–1792
José Joaquín de Arrillaga, 1792–1794
Diego de Borica, 1794–1800
José Joaquín de Arrillaga, 1800–1814
José Argüello, 1814–1815
Pablo Vicente Sola, 1815–1822

Spanish Missions in the United States

Arizona

Arivaca
Jamac
Kisakobi
San Agustín y San José del Tucson
San Bartolomé de Shongopovi
San Bernardino

San Bernardino de Awatobi
San Buenaventura de Mishongnovi
San Cayetano de Calabazas
San Cosme del Tucson
San Francisco de Ati
San Francisco de Oraibi
San Gabriel de Guevavi
San José de Tumacacori
San Luis Bacuancos
San Marcelo de Sonoita
Santa Gertrudis de Tubac
San Xavier del Bac
Yuma

California

La Purísima Concepción
Nuestra Señora de la Soledad
Pala
San Antonio de Padua
San Buenaventura
San Carlos Borromeo (Carmel)
San Diego de Alcalá
San Fernando, Rey de España
San Francisco de Asís
San Francisco Solano
San Gabriel Arcángel
San José de Guadalupe
San Juan Bautista
San Juan Capistrano
San Luis Obispo de Tolosa
San Luis, Rey de Francia
San Miguel Arcángel
San Rafael Arcángel
Santa Bárbara
Santa Clara de Asís
Santa Cruz
Santa Gertrudis
Santa Inés

Florida

Afuyca
Asunción del Puerto
Nombre de Dios
Nuestra Señora de Guadalupe de Tolomato
Nuestra Señora de la Purísima Concepción de Ayubale
Purificación de Tama
Río Dulce

San Agustín de Urica
San Antonio de Bacuqua
San Antonio de Ecanape
San Carlos de Chacatos
San Carlos de los Calus
San Cosme y San Damián de Escambé
San Diego de Laca
San Diego de Salamototo
San Francisco de Chuaquín
San Francisco de Ocone
San Francisco Potano
San Ildefonso de Chamino
San José de Ocuia
San Juan de Aspalaga
San Juan de Guácara
San Juan del Puerto
San Lorenzo de Ivitachuco
San Luis de Acuera
San Luis de Tamalí
San Martín de Ayaocuto
San Martín de Tomole
San Mateo de Tolapatafi
San Miguel de Asile
San Pedro de los Chines
San Pedro de Potohiriba
San Pedro y San Pablo de Patale
San Salvador de Macaya
San Sebastián
Santa Catalina de Afuyca
Santa Cruz
Santa Cruz de Cachipile
Santa Cruz de Capola
Santa Cruz de Tarihica
Santa Elena de Machava
Santa Fe de Toluco
Santa Lucía
Santa María
Santa María de los Angeles de Arapaja
Santo Tomás de Santa Fe
Tequesta
Tocobaga

Georgia

Chatuache
Coweta
Nuestra Señora de la Candelaria de Tama
Ocotonico de Asao
San Buenaventura de Guadalquini
San Felipe

San José de Zapala
San Pedro de Mocamo
San Pedro y San Pablo de Porturibato
Santa Catalina de Guale
Santa María de Sena
Santiago de Ocone
Santo Domingo de Asao
Santo Domingo de Talaje
Tolomato (Espogache)
Tupique

Louisiana

San Miguel de los Adaes

New Mexico

Cebolleta
Ciénaga
Gran Quivira
Halona
La Concepción de Hawikuh
La Inmaculada Concepción de Quarai
Nambé
Nuestra Señora de Belén
Nuestra Señora de Guadalupe de Pojoaque
Nuestra Señora de la Asunción de Sía
Nuestra Señora del Socorro
Nuestra Señora de Navidad de Chililí
Pecos
San Agustin de Isleta
San Antonio de Isleta
San Antonio de Senecú
San Bartolomé
San Buenaventura de Cochití
San Cristóbal
San Diego de los Jémez
San Esteban Rey de Acoma
San Felipe
San Francisco de Asís de los Ranchos de Taos
San Francisco de Pojoaque
San Francisco de Sandía
San Gabriel
San Gregorio de Abó
San Ildefonso
San Jerónimo de Taos
San José de Laguna
San José de los Jémez
San Juan
San Juan de los Jémez

San Lázaro
San Lorenzo de Picuris
San Luis Obispo de Sevilleta
San Marcos
San Miguel
San Miguel (Santa Fe)
San Miguel de Tajique
San Pascual
San Pedro del Cuchillo
Santa Ana de Alameda
Santa Ana de Alamillo
Santa Ana de Tamayo
Santa Clara
Santa Cruz
Santa Cruz de Galisteo
Santo Domingo
Tesuque
Zuñi

North Carolina

Guatari

Texas

Corpus Christi de Isleta
Dolores
Nuestra Señora de Guadalupe de El Paso
Nuestra Señora de Guadalupe de los Nacogdoches
Nuestra Señora de la Candelaria
Nuestra Señora de la Candelaria del Cañón
Nuestra Señora de la Luz del Orocoquisac
Nuestra Señora de la Purísima Concepción de los Aynais
Nuestra Señora de la Purísima Concepción de María de
    Acuña
Nuestra Señora del Espíritu Santo de Zúñiga
Nuestra Señora de los Dolores de los Ais
Nuestra Señora del Pilar de Bucareli y de Nacogdoches
Nuestra Señora del Refugio
Nuestra Señora del Rosario
Nuestro Padre San Francisco de las Tejas
Penitas
San Agustín de Laredo
San Antonio de la Isleta del Sur
San Antonio de los Puliques
San Antonio de Senecú
San Antonio de Valero (El Alamo)
San Clemente
San Cristóbal

San Elizario
San Francisco de la Espada
San Francisco de los Julimes
San Francisco de los Tejas
San Francisco de los Neches
San Francisco del Socorro
San Francisco Solano de Ampuer
San Francisco Xavier de Horcasitas
San Ildefonso
San Joaquín del Monte
San José de los Nazones
San José y San Miguel de Aguayo
San Juan Bautista
San Juan Capistrano
San Lorenzo de la Santa Cruz
San Lorenzo el Real
San Miguel de Linares de los Adaes
San Pedro de Alcántara de los Tapalcomes
Santa Cruz de San Saba
Santa María de Navidad
Santa María la Redonda de las Cíbolas
Santiago

Virginia

Axacán

Spanish Forts and *Presidios* in the United States

Alabama

Carlota
Confederación
Esteban
Holy Trinity
Spanish Fort (Mobile)

Arizona

San Agustín del Tucson
Tubac
Yuma

Arkansas

Arkansas Post
Esperanza

California
Guijarros
Monterey
San Diego
San Francisco (Yerba Buena)
Santa Bárbara

Colorado
Sangre de Cristo Pass

Florida
Diego
Matanzas
Mosa
Picolata
San Bernardo de Pensacola
San Carlos de Austria
San Carlos de los Calus
San Carlos (Fernandina Beach)
San Luis de Apalache
San Marcos de Apalache
San Marcos de San Agustín
San Mateo
San Miguel
Santa Lucía
Sombrero
Tequesta
Tocobaga

Georgia
Chiaha
Coweta
Espogache
San Pedro
Santa Catalina de Guale
Zapala

Louisiana
Baton Rouge
Galvestown
Manchac
Miró
Nuestra Señora del Pilar de los Adaes
Spanish Fort (New Orleans)

Michigan
San José (conquered by the Spaniards)

Mississippi
Nogales
Panmure

Missouri
Don Carlos el Señor Príncipe de Asturias
Don Carlos Tercero el Rey
San Carlos

North Carolina
Cauchi
Guatari
San Juan de Xualla

South Carolina
San Felipe
San Marcos

Tennessee
Manchester (built by de Soto)
San Fernando de las Barrancas

Texas
Del Norte
Nuestra Señora de Loreto de la Bahía
Nuestra Señora de los Dolores
Old Stone Fort (Nacogdoches)
Sacramento
San Agustín de Ahumada
San Elizario
San Fernando de Béjar (later San Antonio)
San Francisco Xavier de los Horcasitas
San Luis de las Amarillas
Santa Cruz de San Saba

Events in Which the Spanish Were Forerunners in the United States

The first European to set foot on mainland North America was Juan Ponce de León. He explored the east and west coasts of what is now Florida. He dropped anchor on April 2, 1513. The first European woman was a member of the 1526 expedition of Lucas Vázquez de Ayllón.

The Spaniards were the first Europeans in the following states: Virginia, North Carolina, South Carolina, Georgia,

Florida, Tennessee, Alabama, Mississippi, Louisiana, Arkansas, Texas, Oklahoma, Kansas, Nebraska, Colorado, New Mexico, Utah, Arizona, Nevada, California, Oregon, Washington and Hawaii.

The first European male born on the North American continent may have been from one of the women on Vázquez de Coronado's expedition of 1540; in any case, Martín de Argüelles, who grew up to be sergeant mayor, was born in St. Augustine, Florida in 1566, 21 years before Virginia Dare was born in the English colony of Roanoke, Virginia.

The first European attempt to establish a permanent colony was made in 1526 by Lucas Vázquez de Ayllón in San Miguel de Gualdape in what is now Georgia or the Carolinas. Among those in the expedition were three Dominican missionaries, enslaved Africans and women. The colony of San Miguel de Gualdape was abandoned after six months. (European colonization of North America began in 1494 when the city of Isabela was established on the island La Española [Hispaniola] in Santo Domingo.)

The Solana family of St. Augustine, Florida, has the oldest North American antecedents in the National Archives; Vincente Solana and María Viscente were married on July 4, 1594.

Alvar Núñez Cabeza de Vaca traveled the breadth of the United States between 1528 and 1536, the first European to do so. Cabeza de Vaca was also the first United States historian.

Mexico's warm Gulf Stream was discovered during the expedition to Florida (1512–1513) by Juan Ponce de León, and was named after him. The pilot of the expedition was Antón de Alominos.

The first road was constructed around 1565 between St. Augustine and Fort Carolina, in St. John's River.

The oldest city in the country is St. Augustine, Florida, founded by Pedro Menéndez de Avilés on September 8, 1565.

The oldest public building standing today is the Governor's Palace in Santa Fe. Construction of the palace began in 1610.

The oldest public square in the United States is the Plaza de la Constitución in St. Augustine, Florida.

The colonists of San Miguel de Gualdape constructed the first ship built by Europeans in North America in 1526. Two years later the expeditionaries of Pánfilo de Narvaéz built three more crafts, with scarce materials, which they launched from Apalache Bay.

The first parish Mass was said at the Nombre de Dios Mission, on September 8, 1565. (The first one prayed on the continent was on January 6, 1494.) Father Juan Larios sang the first Mass at the Texas border on May 16, 1675, and in California it was celebrated for the first time on July 1, 1769.

The oldest church in the United States is San Francisco, in St. Augustine, Florida.

The oldest church still in use, the original walls of which are still standing, is the San Miguel Mission in Santa Fe, New Mexico, built in 1610.

The San Luis (St. Louis) Cathedral in New Orleans, built in 1794 by the Spaniard Andrés Almonester, is the oldest cathedral in the United States.

The first bishop to enter the territory of what is now the United States was Juan de las Cabezas Altamirano, bishop of Cuba. He visited Florida and the missions of Georgia in 1606.

The first Catholic bishop to reside in the United States was Luis de Pañalver y Cárdenas, who took over his see in New Orleans in 1795.

The oldest religious image in the United States is that of the Virgin La Conquistadora, which is worshiped in the cathedral in Santa Fe. It was brought from Spain by Friar Alonso de Benavides in 1625.

North America's first Christian martyr, Father Juan de Padilla, was killed by Indians in Kansas in 1542.

Hernando de Soto and his companions became the first to celebrate Christmas on the North American continent in 1539 near what is now Tallahassee, Florida.

Alvar Núñez Cabeza de Vaca published the first description of the territory of the United States, *Naufragios (Shipwrecks),* in 1542.

The first book written in the country was by Brother Báez, a Jesuit in Georgia's missions, in 1569.

The oldest school of technical education was located in the mission of San Agustín (approximately two miles from Tucson, Arizona) at the end of the 18th and beginning of the 19th centuries.

The first theatrical work performed in the United States was near El Paso, Texas, when Juan de Oñate and his expedition took over the "kingdom" of New Mexico on April 30, 1598. The comedy was written by Captain Marcos Farfán de los Godos for the occasion and rehearsed in great hurry. It was about the arrival of the Franciscans in the region, their long walks, their encounters with the natives, their preaching of the Gospel and their success in achieving the Indians' conversion. The second comedy—whose author is unknown—was performed by actors from the same expedition. It was staged on September 8 of the same year in San Juan, New Mexico.

The oldest city festival, is the Santa Fe Fiesta, which first began in September 1712 and is still celebrated today.

The first bullfight in North America took place during the course of Oñate's expedition in San Juan, New Mexico, on September 8, 1598.

The first legal process was held in St. Augustine from August 31 to September 23, 1602. It was an inquiry ordered by the king into the governance of Florida and its capital.

The first Thanksgiving was celebrated by Friar Juan de Padilla at the Canyon of Palo Duro, Texas during the expedition of Vázquez de Coronado in 1541.

Historical Societies

Revised by Pamela W. Zayer

National Societies

American Association for State and Local History
530 Church Street, Suite 600
Nashville, TN 37219

American Catholic Historical Association
Catholic University of America
Washington, DC 20064

American Catholic Historical Society
263 South Fourth Street
PO Box 84
Philadelphia, PA 19105

American Historical Association
400 A Street SE
Washington, DC 20003

Hispanic Foundation
Library of Congress
Washington, DC 20540

Historic House Association of America
1600 H Street NW
Washington, DC 22314

National Archives
Eighth Street and Constitution Avenue
Washington, DC 20408

National Endowment for the Humanities
806 15th Street NW
Washington, DC 20506

National Historical Publications and Records
  Commission
National Archives Building
Washington, DC 20408

National Trust for Historic Preservation
1785 Massachusetts Avenue NW
Washington, DC 20036

Naval Historical Center
Building 220, Navy Yard
Washington, DC 20374

Organization of American Historians
112 North Bryan Street
Bloomington, IN 47408-4199

Organization of American States
Columbus Memorial Library
19th Street at Constitution Avenue NW
Washington, DC 20408

Smithsonian Institution
1000 Jefferson Drive
Washington, DC 20560

The Society of Hispanic Historical and Ancestral
  Research
PO Box 490
Midway City, CA 92655-0490

U.S. Army Center of Military History
Washington, DC 20314-0200

U.S. Department of State
Bureau of Public Affairs
Washington, DC 20520

State Societies

ALABAMA

Alabama Historical Association
c/o James F. Sulzby Jr.
3121 Carlisle Rd.
Birmingham, AL 35213

Alabama State Department of Archives and History
624 Washington Avenue
Montgomery, AL 36130

Historic Mobile Preservation Society Inc.
350 Oakleigh Place
Mobile, AL 36604

Mobile Historic Development Commission
Box 1827
Mobile, AL 36633

Museums of the City of Mobile
355 Government Street
Mobile, AL 36602

ALASKA

Alaska Archives
165 East 56th Avenue, No. 1
Anchorage, AK 99518

Alaska Historical Library and Museum
Capitol
Juneau, AK 99811

Alaska Historical Society
Box 10-355
Anchorage, AK 99511

Kodiak Historical Society
101 Marine Way
Kodiak, AK 99615

ARIZONA

Arizona Historical Foundation
Hayden Library
Arizona State University
Tempe, AZ 85281

Arizona Historical Society
949 East Second Street
Tucson, AZ 85719

Arizona State Department of Library and Archives
Capitol, Third Floor
Phoenix, AZ 85007

Coronado National Memorial
RR2, Box 126
Hereford, AZ 85615

Primeria Alta Historical Society
Box 2281
Nogales, AZ 85621-2281

Tubac Presidian State Historic Park
River Road and Broadway
Tubac, AZ 85640

ARKANSAS

Arkansas Historical Association
History Department, University of Arkansas
12 Ozark Hall
Fayetteville, AR 72701

Arkansas History Commission
One Capitol Mall
Little Rock, AR 72201

CALIFORNIA

Amador County Historical Society
PO Box 761
Jackson, CA 93940

Cabrillo Historical Association/National Monument
Box 6670
San Diego, CA 92106

California Committee for the Promotion of History
6000 J Street
Sacramento, CA 70884-2060

California Historical Society
678 Mission Street
San Francisco, CA 91405

California History Center Foundation
21250 Stevens Creek Boulevard
Cupertino, CA 95014

California History Foundation
University of the Pacific
Stockton, CA 95211

California Mission Studies Association
PO Box 3357
Bakersfield, CA 93358-3357

California Mission Trails Association, Ltd.
25 West Anapamu Street
Santa Barbara, CA 93104

California Sesquicentennial Commission
914 Capitol Mall, Room 217
Sacramento, CA 95814

Colton Hall Museum and Old Monterey
Pacific Street between Madison and Jefferson
Monterey, CA 93940

Committee for El Camino Real
25 West Anapamu Street
Santa Barbara, CA 93104

Conference of California Historical Societies
University of the Pacific
Stockton, CA 95211

Coronado Historical Association
PO Box 761
Corona del Mar, CA 92625

El Pueblo de Los Angeles State
Historic Park/Historic Monument
845 North Alameda
Los Angeles, CA 90012

Encino Historical Society
16756 Moorpark Street
Encino, CA 91436

Friends of the Adobes
South Mission Street
San Miguel, CA 93451

Governor Pico Mansion Society
14216 Meargrove Road
La Mirada, CA 90638

Historical Society of Southern California
200 East Avenue, No. 43
Los Angeles, CA 90031

Huntington Library
1151 Oxford Road
San Marino, CA 91108

Las Vírgenes Historical Society
PO Box 124
Ajoura, CA 91301

Los Angeles City Historical Society
PO Box 41046
Los Angeles, CA 90041

Los Angeles Public Library
Mexican-American Collection
307 West Seventh Street
Los Angeles, CA 90014

Monterey History and Art Association
Box 805
Monterey, CA 93942

National Hispanic Museum
Box 985377
Los Angeles, CA 90087

National Hispanic Research Center
2727 West Sixth Street
Los Angeles, CA 90057

Office of Historic Preservation
PO Box 2390
Sacramento, CA 95811

Presidio of Monterey Museum
Monterey, CA 93940

San Diego Historical Society
PO Box 81825
San Diego, CA 92138-1825

San Gabriel Historical Society
Los Compadrinos Museum
807 Montecito Drive
San Gabriel, CA 91776

San Juan Bautista Historical Society
PO Box 1
San Juan Bautista, CA 95045

San Ramon Valley Historical Society
Box 521
Danville, CA 94526

Santa Cruz Historical Society
PO Box 246
Santa Cruz, CA 95061

Sierra Madre Historical Society
PO Box 202
Sierra Madre, CA 91024

Spanishtown Historical Society
PO Box 62
Half Moon Bay, CA 94019

Vista Rancho Historical Society
651 East Vista Way, Street A
PO Box 1032
Vista, CA 92085-1032

COLORADO

Huerfano County Historical Society
Box 3
La Vela, CO 81089

Pueblo County Historical Society
217 South Grand Street
Vail, CO 81003

The State Historical Society of Colorado
1300 Broadway
Denver, CO 80203

CONNECTICUT

Connecticut Historical Commission
59 South Prospect Street
Hartford, CT 06106

Connecticut Historical Society
1 Elizabeth Street
Hartford, CT 06105

Connecticut League of Historical Societies, Inc.
114 Whitney Avenue
New Haven, CT 06510

DELAWARE

Historical Society of Delaware
505 Market Street Hall
Wilmington, DE 19801

FLORIDA

Castillo de San Marcos and Fort Matanzas National
  Monuments
1 Castillo Drive
St. Augustine, FL 32084

Cuban Exile History and Archives Project
Center for Multilingual and Multicultural Studies
Florida International University
University Park
Miami, FL 33199

Florida Historical Research Foundation
2301 East 148th Avenue
Lutz, FL 33549

Florida Historical Society
435 Brevard Avenue
Cocoa, FL 32922

Florida Historical Society
University of South Florida Library
Tampa, FL 33620

Florida State Bureau of Historic Preservation
RA Gray Building
500 South Bronough Street
Tallahassee, FL 32399-0250

Florida Trust for Historic Preservation
PO Box 10368
Tampa, FL 33679

Historical Association of Southern Florida
3280 South Miami Avenue, Building B
Miami, FL 33129

Historic St. Augustine Preservation Board
48 King Street
PO Box 1987
St. Augustine, FL 32084

Historic Services Florida National Guard
PO Box 1008 State Arsenal
St. Augustine, FL 32085-1008

Institute for Early Contact Period Studies
2121 Turlington Hall
University of Florida
Gainesville, FL 32611

Manatee County Historical Society
8012 First Avenue West
Bradenton, FL 33529

Miami Dade Public Library System
The Hispanic Library
101 West Flagler Street
Miami, FL 33130–1504

Pensacola Historical Society
405 South Adams at Zaragossa
Pensacola, FL 32501

Pensacola Historic Preservation Society
204 South Alcaniz Street
Pensacola, FL 32582

P.K. Yonge Library of Florida History
404 Library West
University of Florida Libraries
Gainesville, FL 32611

St. Augustine Historical Society
271 Charlotte Street
St. Augustine, FL, 32084

University of Miami
Cuban Archives
Box 248214
Coral Gables, FL 33124

GEORGIA

Coastal Georgia Historical Society
600 Beachview
St. Simons Island, GA 31522

Coastal Heritage Society
1 Fort Jackson Road
Savannah, GA 31402

Department of Archives and History
330 Capitol Avenue SE
Atlanta, GA 30334

Georgia Historical Society
501 Whitaker Street
Savannah, GA 31401

Georgia Trust for Historic Preservation
11 Baltimore Place NW
Atlanta, GA 30388

Guale Historical Society, Inc.
PO Box 398
St. Marys, GA 31558

Historic Columbus Foundation, Inc.
700 Broadway
Columbus, GA 31901

GUAM

The Maritime Historical Association of the Western
  Pacific
The Guam Maritime Museum
Marine Dr., Asan
Agaña, GU 96910

HAWAII

Bernice Bishop Museum
1525 Bernice Street
Honolulu, HI 96817-0916

Hawaiian Historical Society
560 Kawaiahao Street
Honolulu, HI 96813

IDAHO

Idaho State Historical Society
610 North Julia Davis Drive
Boise, ID 83702

ILLINOIS

Chicago Historical Society
Clark at North Avenue
Chicago, IL 60614

Illinois State Historical Society
Old State Capitol
Springfield, IL 62706

Newberry Library
60 West Walton Street
Chicago, IL 60610

Society of American Archivists
330 South Wells, Suite 810
Chicago, IL 60606

INDIANA

Charles and Margaret Hall
Cushwa Center for the Study of American Catholicism
614 Hesburgh Library
University of Notre Dame
Notre Dame, IN 46556

Indiana Historical Bureau
140 North Senate Avenue, Room 408
Indianapolis, IN 46204

Indiana Historical Society
315 West Ohio Street
Indianapolis, IN 46202

Indiana Junior Historical Society
315 West Ohio Street
Indianapolis, IN 46202

Northern Indiana Historical Society
808 West Washington Street
South Bend, IN 48601

Organization of American Historians
112 North Bryan Street
Bloomington, IN 47408

Special Collections Department
Vigo County Public Library
One Library Square
Terre Haute, IN 47807

IOWA

Foundation for Historic Conservation
216 Davidson Building
Des Moines, IA 50309

Iowa State Department of History and Archives
600 East Locust
Des Moines, IA 50319-0290

State Historical Society of Iowa
402 Iowa Avenue
Iowa City, IA 52240

KANSAS

Kansas State Historical Society
6425 SW Sixth Avenue
Topeka, KS 66615-1099

Santa Fe Trail Center
Route 3
Larned, KS 67550

KENTUCKY

The Filson Club Historical Society
1310 South Third Street
Louisville, KY 40208

Kentucky Genealogical Society
Box 153
Frankfort, KY 40602

Kentucky Historical Society
300 West Broadway
Frankfort, KY 41601

LOUISIANA

De Soto Historical Society
Box 523
Mansfield, LA 71052

Foundation for Historical Louisiana
900 North Boulevard
Baton Rouge, LA 70802

The Historical Association of Central Louisiana
Box 843
Alexandria, LA 71301

Imperial Calcasieu Museum Inc.
204 West Sallier Street
Lake Charles, LA 70601

Louisiana Genealogical and Historical Society
PO Box 82060
Baton Rouge, LA 70884-2060-60

Louisiana Historical Association
PO Box 42808
University of Southwestern Louisiana
Lafayette, LA 70504-2808

Louisiana Historical Society
5801 St. Charles Avenue
New Orleans, LA 70115

Southeast Louisiana Historical Association
Box 1088, SLU
Hammond, LA 70402

Spanish Public Library
219 Loyola Avenue
New Orleans, LA 70140

MAINE

Maine Historical Society
485 Congress Street
Portland, ME 04101

MARYLAND

Academy of America Franciscan History
9800 Kentsdale Drive
Bethesda, MD 20817

Maryland Historical Society
201 West Monument Street
Baltimore, MD 21201

United States Naval Academy Museum
United States Naval Academy
Annapolis, MD 21402

MASSACHUSETTS

American Antiquarian Society
185 Salisbury Street
Worcester, MA 01609

Boston Athenaeum
$10^1/_2$ Beacon Street
Boston, MA 02108

Massachusetts Historical Society
1154 Boylston Street
Boston, MA 02215

MICHIGAN

Fort St. Joseph Historical Association
508 East Main Street
Niles, MI 49120

Historical Society of Michigan
2117 Washtenaw Avenue
Ann Arbor, MI 48104

MINNESOTA

Catholic Historical Society of St. Paul
2260 Osceok Street
St. Paul, MN 55105

Minnesota Historical Society
345 West Kellogg Boulevard
St. Paul, MN 55102-1906

MISSISSIPPI

Mississippi Coast Historical and Genealogical Society
Box 513
Biloxi, MS 39533

Mississippi Historical Society
PO Box 571
Jackson, MS 39205-0571

Mississippi State Department of Archives and History
100 South State Street
Jackson, MS 39201

Old Capitol Museum of Mississippi History
100 State
Jackson, MS 39201

MISSOURI

Missouri Heritage Trust
Box 895
Jefferson City, MO 65102

Missouri Historical Society
Jefferson Memorial Building
Forest Park
St. Louis, MO 63112-1099

Missouri State Archives
State Information Center
PO Box 778
Jefferson City, MO 65102

State Historical Society of Missouri
1020 Lowry Street
Columbia, MO 65201

MONTANA

Montana Historical Society
225 North Roberts
Helena, MT 59620

NEBRASKA

El Museo Latino
Livestock Exchange Building
2900 O Street, Suite 124
Omaha, NE 68107

Mari Sandoz High Plains Heritage Center
Chadron State College
Chadron, NE 69337

Mexican American Historical Society
Pioneer Park
27th and Broadway
PO Box 1662
Scottsbluff, NE 69631

Museum Association of American Frontiers
Route 2, Box 18
Chadron, NE 69337

Nebraska Historical Center
PO Box 82554
1500 R Street
Lincoln, NE 68501

Nebraska History Network
1997 280th Street
Seward, NE 68434-7823

Nebraska State Historical Society
1500 R Street
Lincoln, NE 68508

University Archives
University Library
University of Nebraska
60th and Dodge Streets
Omaha, NE 68182

Yutan Historical Society
214 Rose Avenue
Yuton, NE 68073

NEVADA

Nevada Historical Society
1650 North Virginia Street
Reno, NV 89503

Northeastern Nevada Museum
1515 Idaho Street
Elko, NV 89801

NEW HAMPSHIRE

New Hampshire Historical Society
30 Park Street
Concord, NH 03301

NEW JERSEY

New Jersey Historical Commission
113 West State Street, CN 520
Trenton, NJ 08625

New Jersey Historical Society
230 Broadway
Newark, NJ 07104

New Jersey State Archives
185 West State Street
Trenton, NJ 08625-0307

The Newark Museum
49 Washington Street
Newark, NJ 08101

NEW MEXICO

The Albuquerque Historical Society
1611 Bayita Lane NW
Albuquerque, NM 87107

Colonial New Mexico Historical Foundation
135 Camino Escondido
Santa Fe, NM 87501

Historical Center for Southeastern New Mexico
200 North Lea Avenue
Roswell, NM 88201

Historical Society of New Mexico
PO Box 5819
Santa Fe, NM 87502

The Historic Santa Fe Foundation
136 Griffin
Santa Fe, NM 87501

Museum of New Mexico
Division of History
Palace of the Governors
Santa Fe, NM 87501

New Mexico State Records Center and Archives
1209 Camino Carlos Rey
Santa Fe, NM 87505

Society for Historical Archaeology
c/o National Park Service
5000 Marble NE, Room 211
Albuquerque, NM 87110

Spanish History Museum
2221 Lead SE
Albuquerque, NM 87106

NEW YORK

The Hispanic Society of America
613 West 155 Street
New York, NY 10032

New-York Historical Society
2 West 77th Street
New York, NY 10024

New York State Historical Association
Route 80
Lake Road
Cooperstown, NY 13326

Society of American Historians
Fayerweather Hall
Columbia University
New York, NY 10027

United States Catholic Historical Society
1011 First Avenue
New York, NY 10022

NORTH CAROLINA

Federation of North Carolina Historical Societies
109 East Jones Street, Suite 305
Raleigh, NC 27601

NORTH DAKOTA

State Historical Society of North Dakota
612 East Boulevard Avenue
Bismarck, ND 58505-0830

OHIO

American Society for Legal History
Toledo College of Law
Toledo, OH 43606

Ohio Academy of History
Department of History
University of Cincinnati
Cincinnati, OH 45221

The Ohio Historical Society
1982 Velma Avenue
Columbus, OH 43211-2497

OKLAHOMA

Oklahoma Historical Society
2100 North Lincoln Boulevard
Oklahoma City, OK 73105

Thomas Gilcrease Institute of American History and Art
1400 North 25th West Avenue
Tulsa, OK 74127

OREGON

Columbia River Maritime Museum
1618 Exchange Street
Astoria, OR 97103

Oregon Historical Society
1230 SW Park Avenue
Portland, OR 97205

Southern Oregon Historical Society
106 North Central Avenue
Medford, OR 97501

PENNSYLVANIA

Historical Society of Pennsylvania
1300 Locust Street
Philadelphia, PA 19107

National Historical Society
Cameron and Kelker Streets
Harrisburg, PA 17105

The Pennsylvania Federation of Museums
Historical Organizations
PO Box 1026
Harrisburg, PA 17108-1026

Pennsylvania Historical Association
806 New Liberal Arts Building
University Park, PA 16802

U.S. Army Military History Institute
Carlisle Barracks, PA 17013-5008

RHODE ISLAND

John Carter Brown Library
Box 1894
Providence, RI 02912

Rhode Island Historical Society
110 Benevolent Street
Providence, RI 02906

SOUTH CAROLINA

Archeological Society of South Carolina
Institute of Archeology and Anthropology
University of South Carolina
Columbia, SC 29208

South Carolina Department of Archives and History
8301 Parklane Road
Columbia, SC 29223

South Carolina Historical Society
100 Meeting Street
Charleston, SC 29401

SOUTH DAKOTA

South Dakota Historical Society
900 Governors Drive
Pierre, SD 57501-2217

TENNESSEE

American Association for State and Local History
708 Berry Road
Nashville, TN 37204

Mississippi Valley Collection
Memphis State University Libraries
Brister Library
Memphis, TN 38152

Tennessee Historical Commission
2941 Lebanon Road
Nashville, TN 37243-0442

TEXAS

Dallas Historical Society
Hall of State, Fair Park
3539 Grand Avenue
Dallas, TX 75226-9990

East Texas Historical Association
Box 6223, S.F.A. Station
Nacogdoches, TX 75962

Historical Society of Denton County
PO Box 50503
Denton, TX 76206-0503

The Institute of Texan Cultures
Hemisfair Plaza
San Antonio, TX 78294

San Antonio Conservation Society
107 King William
San Antonio, TX 78209

Southeast Texas Genealogical and Historical Society
c/o Tyrrel Historical Library
695 Pearl Street
Beaumont, TX 77704

Spanish Governor's Plaza
105 Plaza de Armas
San Antonio, TX 78205

Texas Catholic Historical Society
1625 Rutherford Lane, Building D
Austin, TX 78754-5105

Texas Historical Commission
1511 Colorado
Austin, TX 78711-2276

Texas Historical Foundation
305 West 9th Street
Austin, TX 78711

Texas Old Missions Restoration Association
524 North 22nd Street
Waco, TX 76707

Texas State Historical Association
SRH2-306 University Station
Austin, TX 78712

UTAH

Utah State Historical Society
603 East South Temple
Salt Lake City, UT 84101

VERMONT

Vermont Historical Society
109 State Street
Montpelier, VT 05609-0901

VIRGINIA

Institute of Early American History and Culture
Box 220
Williamsburg, VA 23185

The Mariner's Museum
Museum Drive
Newport News, VA 23606

Virginia Historical Society
428 North Boulevard
Richmond, VA 23220

WASHINGTON

Lopez Island Historical Society
Lopez, WA 98261

Washington State Historical Society
315 North Stadium Way
Tacoma, WA 98403

WEST VIRGINIA

West Virginia Historical Society
PO Box 5220
Charleston, WV 25361-0220

WISCONSIN

State Historical Society of Wisconsin
816 State Street
Madison, WI 53706

WYOMING

Wyoming State Archives Museum
2301 Central Avenue
Cheyenne, WY 82002

National Parks, Monuments and Other Sites of Historic Interest

Alabama

* Marker separating the territories of Charles IV and the United States, latitude 31° on the banks of the Mobile River
* Spanish Fort, Mobile
* Plaza de España, Mobile

Arizona

* Bell's Spanish Mission, Grand Canyon
* Marcos Niza Rock, 8 miles southeast of Phoenix
* San Xavier del Bac Mission, 9 miles south of Tucson, Pima County
* Tumacacori Mission, Tumacacori
* Coronado National Memorial Park, Hereford

Arkansas

* Arkansas Post, near Gillett, Arkansas County

California

* Monument to the missionaries (erected by the Hispanic Cultural Institute), Carmel Mission
* Rancho La Brea, Hancock Park, Los Angeles

* Statue of Gaspar de Portolá with a plaque commemorating the visit of the king of Spain in 1987, Monterey
* Royal Presidio Chapel, Monterey
* Old Mission Dam (Padre Dam), San Diego
* Presidio, Presidio Park, San Diego
* Statue of Juan Rodríguez Cabrillo, San Diego
* Presidio of San Francisco, San Francisco
* Statue of Father Junípero Serra, San Juan de Capistrano Mission
* Santa Barbara Mission, Santa Barbara
* Sonoma Plaza, Sonoma
* Missionary bells along El Camino Real, throughout the state
* Monument to Queen Isabella, the Capitol, Sacramento
* Chain of 23 missions

Colorado

* Monument commemorating the victory of Juan Bautista de Anza over the Comanche "Cuerno Verde," Pueblo County, near road 85

District of Columbia

* Statues of Father Junípero Serra and Eusebio Kino, the Capitol
* The Columbus coat of arms and Spanish artworks in the Hispanic Room, Library of Congress

Florida

* De Soto National Memorial Park, Bradenton
* Plaza Hernando de Soto, with the reproduction of Extremadura Chapel, De Soto's home and other examples of Spanish architecture, Bradenton
* Milestones of De Soto's Floridian trail, throughout Florida highway system
* Marker commemorating the site of San Carlos Fort, Fernandina Beach
* Large map of the Spanish presence in Florida, Warm Mineral Springs, Fort Myers
* San Luis de Apalache, 2 miles west of Tallahassee, Leon County
* Monastery of San Bernardo de Sacramenia, North Miami
* Fort San Carlos de Barrancas, U.S. Naval Air Station, Pensacola
* Plaza Ferdinand VII, Palafox Street, Pensacola

- Plaza de la Evangelización, Miami
- Plate commemorating the crossing of Hernando de Soto, University of Tampa, Tampa

Saint Augustine
- Altar commemorating the first Mass, Nombre de Dios Mission
- Castle of San Marcos
- City gate
- Fort Matanzas
- Obelisk of the Constitution of Cádiz 1812, in the square
- Old San Agustín
- Steel cross, measuring 231 feet, commemorating the birth of Catholicism in North America, Nombre de Dios Mission

Georgia
- Marker of the visit of Spanish commissioners in 1736, Jekyll Island
- Fort Federica, St. Simons Island
- Marker of the Battle of Bloody Marsh, St. Simons Island

Kansas
- Obelisk of Juan de Padilla, Herington
- El Cuartelejo, Scott County State Park, 12 miles north of Scott City

Louisiana
- Plate commemorating the first Mass, Natchitoches
- The Cabildo, Jackson Square, New Orleans
- Jackson Square, New Orleans
- Spanish Fort, New Orleans
- Pontalba Apartments, New Orleans
- Plaza de España, New Orleans
- Vieux Carré district, New Orleans
- Presidio de Nuestra Señora del Pilar de los Adaes, Robeline
- Museo de los Isleños, Saint Bernard

Massachusetts
- Spanish Cloister in The Fenway Court, Boston

Michigan
- Stone detailing the history of Fort St. Joseph, Niles

Mississippi
- Spanish Fort, Pascagoula

Missouri
- Spanish Pavilion of the New York World's Fair, St. Louis
- Casa Alvarez, Florissant
- Giralda Tower (reconstruction), Kansas City

New Mexico
- Plate commemorating the crossing of the expedition of Coronado, near Bernalillo
- Manuelito Complex, McKinley County
- Mesilla Plaza, Mesilla
- Gran Quivira Mission Ruins, Route 1, Mountainair
- Rocks with inscriptions, El Morro, Ramah
- Palace of the Governors, Santa Fe
- Santa Fe Plaza, Sante Fe

New York
- Apse of San Martín of Fuentidueña, the Cloisters, New York
- Patio of the Palace of Vélez Blanco, the Metropolitan Museum of Art, New York
- Statue of El Cid and many other Spanish artworks, Hispanic Society of America

Oregon
- Commemorative plaque of the discovery of the western coast by Sebastián de Vizcaíno, Cape San Sebastian

Pennsylvania
- Medieval cloister, the Museum of Fine Arts, Philadelphia

Rhode Island
- Touro Synagogue, Newport

Tennessee
- Granite block commemorating the crossing of Hernando de Soto, Memphis Park, Memphis

Texas

* Plate commemorating the first Thanksgiving by Father Juan de Padilla, Cañón de Palo Duro
* Presidio de la Bahía, Goliad
* Monument to Cabeza de Vaca, Houston
* Presidio de San Luis de las Amarillas, Menard
* Old Stone Fort, Nacogdoches
* The Alamo Mission, San Antonio
* Governor's Palace, San Antonio
* San José Mission, San Antonio
* Espada Aqueduc, Espada Road, south San Antonio

Utah

* Granite Rock, with bronze plate, in memory of Father Silvestre de Escalante and Francisco Atanasio

Domínguez, Provo; other monuments in Spanish Fork, Cedar City, Lee's Ferry, Jensen

Virginia

* Marker of the Martyrs of Axacán, Aquia Creek, Quantico

Washington

* Memorial stone of the discovery of Mt. Olympus by Juan Pérez, Olympic National Park

---

◆ LANGUAGE AND CULTURE ◆

North American Universities and Colleges with Chapters of Sigma Delta Pi, the National Collegiate Hispanic Honor Society

Alabama

Auburn University
(Theta Delta)
Department of Foreign Languages
Auburn University, AL 36849

Judson College
(Beta Delta)
Department of Foreign Languages
Marion, AL 36756

Samford University
(Delta Nu)
Department of Foreign Languages
Birmingham, AL 35229

Spring Hill College
(Kappa Beta)
Department of Foreign Languages
Mobile, AL 36608

Troy State University
(Sigma Upsilon)
Department of Foreign Languages
Troy, AL 36082

University of Alabama
(Beta Alpha)
Department of Foreign Languages
Tuscaloosa, AL 35294

University of Alabama–Birmingham
(Omicron Mu)
Department of Foreign Languages
Birmingham, AL 35294

University of Montevallo
(Epsilon Eta)
Department of Foreign Languages
Montevallo, AL 35115

University of South Alabama
(Lambda Pi)
Department of Foreign Languages
Mobile, AL 36688

Arizona

Arizona State University
(Theta Epsilon)
Department of Foreign Languages
Tempe, AZ 85287

Northern Arizona University
(Iota Upsilon)
Department of Foreign Languages
Flagstaff, AZ 86011

University of Arizona
(Pi)
Department of Foreign Languages
Tucson, AZ 85721

Arkansas

Arkansas State University
(Pi Theta)
Department of Foreign Languages
State University, AR 72467

Ouachita Baptist University
(Xi Lambda)
Department of Foreign Languages
Arkadelphia, AR 71923

Southern Arkansas University at Magnolia
(Theta Phi)
Department of Foreign Languages
Magnolia, AR 71753

University of Arkansas
(Gamma Epsilon)
Department of Foreign Languages
Fayetteville, AR 72701

University of Arkansas–Little Rock
(Zeta Sigma)
Department of Foreign Languages
Little Rock, AR 72204

California

California State University–Bakersfield
(Omicron Theta)
Department of Foreign Languages
Bakersfield, CA 93311

California State University–Dominguez Hills
(Nu Psi)
Department of Foreign Languages
Carson, CA 90747

California State University–Fresno
(Alpha Gamma)
Department of Foreign Languages
Fresno, CA 93740

California State University–Los Angeles
(Gamma Psi)
Department of Foreign Languages
Los Angeles, CA 90032

California State University–Sacramento
(Iota Kappa)
Department of Foreign Languages
Sacramento, CA 95819

California State University–San Bernardino
(Zeta Pi)
Department of Foreign Languages
San Bernardino, CA 92407

California State University–Stanislaus
(Nu Alpha)
Department of Foreign Languages
Turlock, CA 95380

Chapman University
(Iota Theta)
Department of Foreign Languages
Orange, CA 92666

Dominican College
(Upsilon)
Department of Foreign Languages
San Rafael, CA 94901

Holy Names College
(Epsilon Rho)
Department of Foreign Languages
Oakland, CA 94619

Humboldt State University
(Pi Eta)
Department of Foreign Languages
Arcata, CA 95521

Loyola Marymount College
(Iota Rho)
Department of Foreign Languages
Los Angeles, CA 90045

Mills College
(Zeta Beta)
Department of Foreign Languages
Oakland, CA 94613

Mount St. Mary's College
(Delta Omicron)
Department of Foreign Languages
Los Angeles, CA 90049

Pepperdine University
(Omicron Alpha)
Department of Foreign Languages
Malibu, CA 90265

San Diego State University
(Eta Beta)
Department of Foreign Languages
San Diego, CA 92182

San Francisco College for Women
(Alpha Mu)
Department of Foreign Languages
San Francisco, CA 94117

San Jose State University
(Alpha Epsilon)
Department of Foreign Languages
San Jose, CA 95192

Scripps College
(Epsilon Zeta)
Department of Foreign Languages
Claremont, CA 91711

Sonoma State University
(Tau Kappa)
Department of Foreign Languages
Rohnert Park, CA 94928

Stanford University
(Kappa)
Department of Foreign Languages
Stanford, CA 94305

University of California–Berkeley
(Alpha)
Department of Foreign Languages
Berkeley, CA 94720

University of California–Davis
(Rho Chi)
Department of Foreign Languages
Davis, CA 95616

University of California–Irvine
(Xi Tau)
Department of Foreign Languages
Irvine, CA 92717

University of California–Los Angeles
(Iota)
Department of Foreign Languages
Los Angeles, CA 90024

University of California–Riverside
(Zeta Omega)
Department of Foreign Languages
Riverside, CA 92521

University of California–Santa Barbara
(Zi Pi)
Department of Foreign Languages
Santa Barbara, CA 93106

University of La Verne
(Omicron Xi)
Department of Foreign Languages
La Verne, CA 91750

University of Redlands
(Mu Iota)
Department of Foreign Languages
Redlands, CA 92373

University of San Diego
(Eta Zeta)
Department of Foreign Languages
San Diego, CA 92110

University of San Francisco
(Nu Tau)
Department of Foreign Languages
San Francisco, CA 94117

University of Southern California
(Eta)
Department of Foreign Languages
Los Angeles, CA 90089

University of the Pacific
(Zeta Delta)
Department of Foreign Languages
Stockton, CA 95211

Westmont College
(Tau Xi)
Department of Foreign Languages
Santa Barbara, CA 93108

Colorado

Colorado College
(Rho Gamma)
Department of Foreign Languages
Colorado Springs, CO 80903

Fort Lewis College
(Kappa Tau)
Department of Foreign Languages
Durango, CO 81301

University of Colorado
(Theta Nu)
Department of Foreign Languages
Colorado Springs, CO 80933

University of Colorado–Denver
(Sigma Omicron)
Department of Foreign Languages
Denver, CO 80204

University of Denver
(Nu Sigma)
Department of Foreign Languages
Denver, CO 80208

University of Northern Colorado
(Pi Zeta)
Department of Foreign Languages
Greeley, CO 80639

University of Southern Colorado
(Upsilon Zeta)
Department of Foreign Languages
Pueblo, CO 81001

Western State College
(Alpha Zeta)
Department of Foreign Languages
Gunnison, CO 81231

Connecticut

Albertus Magnus College
(Kappa Sigma)
Department of Foreign Languages
New Haven, CT 06511

Eastern Connecticut State College
(Nu Chi)
Department of Foreign Languages
Willimantic, CT 06226

Fairfield University
(Zeta Tau)
Department of Foreign Languages
Fairfield, CT 06430

Quinnipiac College
(Upsilon Epsilon)
Department of Foreign Languages
Hamden, CT 06518

Trinity College
(Mu Gamma)
Department of Foreign Languages
Hartford, CT 06106

University of Connecticut
(Gamma Omega)
Department of Foreign Languages
Storrs, CT 06269

Delaware

University of Delaware
(Kappa Upsilon)
Department of Foreign Languages
Newark, DE 19716

District of Columbia

Catholic University of America
(Kappa Alpha)
Department of Foreign Languages
Washington, DC 20064

Georgetown University
(Lambda Beta)
Department of Foreign Languages
Washington, DC 20057

George Washington University
(Delta Eta)
Department of Foreign Languages
Washington, DC 20052

Howard University
(Theta Xi)
Department of Foreign Languages
Washington, DC 20059

Florida

Eckerd College
(Zeta Mu)
Department of Foreign Languages
St. Petersburg, FL 33733

Florida Atlantic University
(Rho Omicron)
Department of Foreign Languages
Boca Raton, FL 33431

Florida Southern College
(Kappa Iota)
Department of Foreign Languages
Lakeland, FL 33801

Florida State University
(Alpha Delta)
Department of Foreign Languages
Tallahassee, FL 32306

Rollins College
(Omicron Nu)
Department of Foreign Languages
Winter Park, FL 32789

Stetson University
(Alpha Kappa)
Department of Foreign Languages
De Land, FL 32720

University of Central Florida
(Tau Delta)
Department of Foreign Languages
Orlando, FL 32816

University of Florida
(Beta Rho)
Department of Foreign Languages
Gainesville, FL 32611

University of Miami
(Alpha Chi)
Department of Foreign Languages
Coral Gables, FL 33124

University of Tampa
(Pi Sigma)
Department of Foreign Languages
Tampa, FL 33606

Georgia

Agnes Scott College
(Sigma Chi)
Department of Foreign Languages
Decatur, GA 30030

Armstrong State College
(Sigma Mu)
Department of Foreign Languages
Savannah, GA 31419

Berry College
(Omicron Sigma)
Department of Foreign Languages
Mt. Berry, GA 30149

Emory University
(Sigma Alpha)
Department of Foreign Languages
Atlanta, GA 30322

Georgia College
(Kappa Psi)
Department of Foreign Languages
Milledgeville, GA 31061

Georgia Southern University
(Zeta Phi)
Department of Foreign Languages
Statesboro, GA 30460

Georgia Southwestern College
(Kappa Gamma)
Department of Foreign Languages
Americus, GA 31709

Georgia State University
(Eta Omega)
Department of Foreign Languages
Atlanta, GA 30303

Kennesaw State College
(Tau Theta)
Department of Foreign Languages
Marietta, GA 30061

Morehouse College
(Omicron Beta)
Department of Foreign Languages
Atlanta, GA 30314

Spelman College
(Lambda Nu)
Department of Foreign Languages
Atlanta, GA 30314

University of Georgia
(Delta Gamma)
Department of Foreign Languages
Athens, GA 30602

Valdosta State College
(Nu Xi)
Department of Foreign Languages
Valdosta, GA 31698

Hawaii

University of Hawaii–Manoa
(Theta Tau)
Department of Foreign Languages
Honolulu, HI 96822

Idaho

University of Idaho
(Theta)
Department of Foreign Languages
Moscow, ID 83843

Illinois

Augustana College
(Epsilon Chi)
Department of Foreign Languages
Rock Island, IL 61201

Barat College
(Beta Tau)
Department of Foreign Languages
Lake Forest, IL 60045

College of St. Francis
(Mu Omega)
Department of Foreign Languages
Joliet, IL 60435

DePaul University
(Delta Epsilon)
Department of Foreign Languages
Chicago, IL 60614

Eastern Illinois University
(Zeta Eta)
Department of Foreign Languages
Charleston, IL 61920

Illinois Benedictine College
(Nu Kappa)
Department of Foreign Languages
Lisle, IL 60532

Illinois State University
(Eta Upsilon)
Department of Foreign Languages
Normal, IL 61761

Knox College
(Lambda Eta)
Department of Foreign Languages
Galesburg, IL 61401

Loyola University of Chicago
(Iota Sigma)
Department of Foreign Languages
Chicago, IL 60626

Monmouth College
(Delta Zeta)
Department of Foreign Languages
Monmouth, IL 61462

Northeastern Illinois University
(Mu Xi)
Department of Foreign Languages
Chicago, IL 60625

Northern Illinois University
(Beta Upsilon)
Department of Foreign Languages
De Kalb, IL 60115

North Park College
(Pi Mu)
Department of Foreign Languages
Chicago, IL 60625

Rosary College
(Beta Xi)
Department of Foreign Languages
River Forest, IL 60305

Southern Illinois University
(Sigma Eta)
Department of Foreign Languages
Carbondale, IL 62901

University of Illinois–Chicago
(Rho Psi)
Department of Foreign Languages
Chicago, IL 60680

University of Illinois–Urbana-Champaign
(Lambda)
Department of Foreign Languages
Urbana, IL 61801

Indiana

Butler University
(Delta Upsilon)
Department of Foreign Languages
Indianapolis, IN 46208

DePauw University
(Tau Upsilon)
Department of Foreign Languages
Greencastle, IN 46135

Indiana University–Purdue University
(Sigma Epsilon)
Department of Foreign Languages
Fort Wayne, IN 46805

Purdue University
(Delta Sigma)
Department of Foreign Languages
West Lafayette, IN 47907

Rose-Hulman Institute of Technology
(Upsilon Delta)
Department of Foreign Languages
Terre Haute, IN 47803

St. Mary-of-the-Woods College
(Xi Eta)
Department of Foreign Languages
St. Mary-of-the-Woods, IN 47876

University of Southern Indiana
(Iota Nu)
Department of Foreign Languages
Evansville, IN 47712

Valparaiso University
(Lambda Zeta)
Department of Foreign Languages
Valparaiso, IN 46383

Iowa

Cornell College
(Tau Omicron)
Department of Foreign Languages
Mt. Vernon, IA 52314

Iowa State University
(Sigma Psi)
Department of Foreign Languages
Ames, IA 50011

University of Iowa
(Gamma Alpha)
Department of Foreign Languages
Iowa City, IA 52242

University of Northern Iowa
(Theta Eta)
Department of Foreign Languages
Cedar Falls, IA 50614

Kansas

Baker University
(Nu Beta)
Department of Foreign Languages
Baldwin City, KS 66006

Emporia State University
(Delta Theta)
Department of Foreign Languages
Emporia, KS 66801

Friends University
(Kappa Phi)
Department of Foreign Languages
Wichita, KS 67213

Kansas State University
(Epsilon Xi)
Department of Foreign Languages
Manhattan, KS 66506

University of Kansas
(Beta Pi)
Department of Foreign Languages
Lawrence, KS 66045

Wichita State University
(Gamma Nu)
Department of Foreign Languages
Wichita, KS 67208

Kentucky

Asbury College
(Nu Pi)
Department of Foreign Languages
Wilmore, KY 40390

Berea College
(Omicron Omicron)
Department of Foreign Languages
Berea, KY 40404

Centre College
(Zeta Epsilon)
Department of Foreign Languages
Danville, KY 40422

Cumberland College
(Sigma Rho)
Department of Foreign Languages
Williamsburg, KY 40769

Eastern Kentucky University
(Eta Mu)
Department of Foreign Languages
Richmond, KY 40475

Georgetown College
(Gamma Sigma)
Department of Foreign Languages
Georgetown, KY 40324

Moorehead State University
(Rho Alpha)
Department of Foreign Languages
Moorehead, KY 40351

Murray State University
(Zeta Upsilon)
Department of Foreign Languages
Murray, KY 42071

Transylvania University
(Eta Epsilon)
Department of Foreign Languages
Lexington, KY 40508

University of Louisville
(Mu Epsilon)
Department of Foreign Languages
Louisville, KY 40292

University of Kentucky
(Epsilon Upsilon)
Department of Foreign Languages
Lexington, KY 40506

Western Kentucky University
(Epsilon Mu)
Department of Foreign Languages
Bowling Green, KY 42101

Louisiana

Dillard University
(Kappa Nu)
Department of Foreign Languages
New Orleans, LA 70122

Louisiana College
(Alpha Omicron)
Department of Foreign Languages
Pineville, LA 71359

Louisiana State University
(Alpha Lambda)
Department of Foreign Languages
Shreveport, LA 71115

Louisiana Tech University
(Alpha Omega)
Department of Foreign Languages
Ruston, LA 71272

Loyola University
(Mu Kappa)
Department of Foreign Languages
New Orleans, LA 70118

McNeese State University
(Sigma Tau)
Department of Foreign Languages
Lake Charles, LA 70609

Northeast Louisiana University
(Lambda Sigma)
Department of Foreign Languages
Monroe, LA 71209

Northwestern State University
(Lambda Kappa)
Department of Foreign Languages
Natchitoches, LA 71497

Southeastern Louisiana University
(Mu Chi)
Department of Foreign Languages
Hammond, LA 70402

Tulane University
(Theta of Louisiana)
Department of Foreign Languages
New Orleans, LA 70118

University of New Orleans
(Pi Kappa)
Department of Foreign Languages
New Orleans, LA 70148

University of Southwestern Louisiana
(Alpha Rho)
Department of Foreign Languages
Lafayette, LA 70504

Xavier University of Louisiana
(Mu Nu)
Department of Foreign Languages
New Orleans, LA 70125

Maine

Bates College
(Kappa Mu)
Department of Foreign Languages
Lewiston, ME 04240

Colby College
(Iota Eta)
Department of Foreign Languages
Waterville, ME 04901

University of Maine–Augusta
(Zeta Kappa)
Department of Foreign Languages
Augusta, ME 04330

University of Maine–Farmington
(Zeta Kappa)
Department of Foreign Languages
Farmington, ME 04938

University of Maine–Orono
(Zeta Kappa)
Department of Foreign Languages
Orono, ME 04469

Maryland

College of Notre Dame of Maryland
(Kappa Pi)
Department of Foreign Languages
Baltimore, MD 21210

Frostburg State University
(Iota Psi)
Department of Foreign Languages
Frostburg, MD 21532

Hood College
(Lambda Delta)
Department of Foreign Languages
Frederick, MD 21701

Loyola College
(Rho Theta)
Department of Foreign Languages
Baltimore, MD 21210

Morgan State University
(Xi Xi)
Department of Foreign Languages
Baltimore, MD 21239

Mount St. Mary's College
(Xi Theta)
Department of Foreign Languages
Emmitsburg, MD 21727

St. Mary's College of Maryland
(Pi Alpha)
Department of Foreign Languages
St. Mary's, MD 20686

Salisbury State University
(Omicron Iota)
Department of Foreign Languages
Salisbury, MD 21801

Towson State University
(Eta Gamma)
Department of Foreign Languages
Baltimore, MD 21204

University of Maryland
(Delta)
Department of Foreign Languages
Baltimore, MD 21228

Washington College
(Sigma Zeta)
Department of Foreign Languages
Chestertown, MD 21620

Massachusetts

College of the Holy Cross
(Omicron Epsilon)
Department of Foreign Languages
Worcester, MA 01610

Framingham State College
(Nu Theta)
Department of Foreign Languages
Framingham, MA 01701

Gordon College
(Eta Omicron)
Department of Foreign Languages
Wenham, MA 01984

Stonehill College
(Lambda Rho)
Department of Foreign Languages
North Easton, MA 02357

University of Massachusetts
(Omicron Tau)
Department of Foreign Languages
Amherst, MA 01003

University of Massachusetts–Dartmouth
(Mu Phi)
Department of Foreign Languages
North Dartmouth, MA 02747

Wellesley College
(Pi Upsilon)
Department of Foreign Languages
Wellesley, MA 02181

Westfield State College
(Rho Delta)
Department of Foreign Languages
Westfield, MA 01086

Wheaton College
(Lambda Lambda)
Department of Foreign Languages
Norton, MA 02766

Worcester State College
(Kappa Kappa)
Department of Foreign Languages
Worcester, MA 01602

Michigan

Adrian College
(Omicron Delta)
Department of Foreign Languages
Adrian, MI 49221

Calvin College
(Xi Mu)
Department of Foreign Languages
Grand Rapids, MI 49546

Central Michigan University
(Theta Theta)
Department of Foreign Languages
Mt. Pleasant, MI 48859

Grand Valley State University
(Sigma Xi)
Department of Foreign Languages
Allendale, MI 49401

Hillsdale College
(Xi Beta)
Department of Foreign Languages
Hillsdale, MI 49242

Hope College
(Epsilon Pi)
Department of Foreign Languages
Holland, MI 49423

Marygrove College
Delta Phi
Department of Foreign Languages
Detroit, MI 48221

Michigan State University
(Beta Beta)
Department of Foreign Languages
East Lansing, MI 48824

Oakland University
(Theta Psi)
Department of Foreign Languages
Rochester, MI 48309

Siena Heights College
(Pi Omega)
Department of Foreign Languages
Adrian, MI 49221

University of Michigan
(Beta Omicron)
Department of Foreign Languages
Ann Arbor, MI 48109

Minnesota

College of St. Benedict/St. John's University
(Sigma Pi)
Department of Foreign Languages
St. Joseph, MN 56374

College of St. Catherine
(Theta Lambda)
Department of Foreign Languages
St. Paul, MN 55105

Concordia College
(Theta Kappa)
Department of Foreign Languages
Moorhead, MN 56562

Gustavus Adolphus College
(Nu Upsilon)
Department of Foreign Languages
St. Peter, MN 56082

Hamline University
(Lambda Omicron)
Department of Foreign Languages
St. Paul, MN 55104

Macalester College
(Rho Epsilon)
Department of Foreign Languages
St. Paul, MN 55105

St. Cloud State University
(Pi Gamma)
Department of Foreign Languages
St. Cloud, MN 56301

Mississippi

Delta State University
(Omicron Eta)
Department of Foreign Languages
Cleveland, MS 38733

Millsaps College
(Zeta Rho)
Department of Foreign Languages
Jackson, MS 39210

Mississippi State University
(Epsilon Gamma)
Department of Foreign Languages
Mississippi State, MS 39762

Mississippi University for Women
(Delta Xi)
Department of Foreign Languages
Columbus, MS 39701

University of Mississippi
(Delta Iota)
Department of Foreign Languages
University, MS 38677

University of Southern Mississippi
(Beta Phi)
Department of Foreign Languages
Hattiesburg, MS 39406

Missouri

College of the Ozarks
(Eta Chi)
Department of Foreign Languages
Point Lookout, MO 65726

Drury College
(Gamma Iota)
Department of Foreign Languages
Springfield, MO 65802

Evangel College
(Xi Gamma)
Department of Foreign Languages
Springfield, MO 65802

Fontbonne College
(Zeta Chi)
Department of Foreign Languages
St. Louis, MO 63105

Lindenwood College
(Iota Xi)
Department of Foreign Languages
St. Charles, MO 63301

Northeast Missouri State University
(Rho Rho)
Department of Foreign Languages
Kirksville, MO 63501

Park College
(Iota Gamma)
Department of Foreign Languages
Parkville, MO 64152

Rockhurst College
(Upsilon Alpha)
Department of Foreign Languages
Kansas City, MO 64110

St. Louis University
(Kappa Omega)
Department of Foreign Languages
St. Louis, MO 63103

Southwest Missouri State University
(Eta Lambda)
Department of Foreign Languages
Springfield, MO 65804

University of Missouri–Columbia
(Beta)
Department of Foreign Languages
Columbia, MO 65211

University of Missouri–Kansas City
(Pi Delta)
Department of Foreign Languages
Kansas City, MO 64110

University of Missouri–St. Louis
(Omicron Psi)
Department of Foreign Languages
St. Louis, MO 63121

Washington University
(Beta Omega)
Department of Foreign Languages
St. Louis, MO 63130

William Jewell College
(Sigma Omega)
Department of Foreign Languages
Liberty, MO 64068

Montana

Montana State University
(Lambda Pi)
Department of Foreign Languages
Bozeman, MT 59717

University of Montana
(Zeta Xi)
Department of Foreign Languages
Missoula, MT 59812

Nebraska

University of Nebraska–Kearney
(Xi Phi)
Department of Foreign Languages
Kearney, NE 68849

University of Nebraska–Lincoln
(Rho Mu)
Department of Foreign Languages
Lincoln, NE 68588

University of Nebraska–Omaha
(Omicron Lambda)
Department of Foreign Languages
Omaha, NE 68182

Wayne State College
(Sigma Kappa)
Department of Foreign Languages
Wayne, NE 68787

Nevada

University of Nevada
(Zeta Omicron)
Department of Foreign Languages
Las Vegas, NV 89154

New Hampshire

Keene State College
(Xi Chi)
Department of Foreign Languages
Keene, NH 03435

St. Anselm College
(Omicron Rho)
Department of Foreign Languages
Manchester, NH 03102

University of New Hampshire
(Theta Gamma)
Department of Foreign Languages
Durham, NH 03824

New Jersey

Drew University
(Omicron Gamma)
Department of Foreign Languages
Madison, NJ 07940

Georgian Court College
(Epsilon Lambda)
Department of Foreign Languages
Lakewood, NJ 08701

Jersey City State College
(Tau Tau)
Department of Foreign Languages
Jersey City, NJ 07305

Monmouth College
(Eta Pi)
Department of Foreign Languages
West Long Branch, NJ 07764

Montclair State University
(Delta Chi)
Department of Foreign Languages
Upper Montclair, NJ 07043

Rider University
(Zeta Nu)
Department of Foreign Languages
Lawrenceville, NJ 08648

Rutgers University–Camden College of Arts and
   Sciences
(Eta Xi)
Department of Foreign Languages
Camden, NJ 08102

Rutgers University–New Brunswick
(Alpha Beta)
Department of Foreign Languages
New Brunswick, NJ 08903

Seton Hall University
(Theta Rho)
Department of Foreign Languages
South Orange, NJ 07079

New Mexico

New Mexico State University
(Beta Eta)
Department of Foreign Languages
Las Cruces, NM 88003

University of Albuquerque
(Xi Alpha)
Department of Foreign Languages
Albuquerque, NM 87131

University of New Mexico
(Mu Alpha)
Department of Foreign Languages
Albuquerque, NM 87131

Western New Mexico University
(Delta Delta)
Department of Foreign Languages
Silver City, NM 88061

New York

Adelphi University
(Tau)
Department of Foreign Languages
Garden City, NY 11530

Alfred University
(Mu Beta)
Department of Foreign Languages
Alfred, NY 14802

Baruch College, City University of New York
(Kappa Chi)
Department of Foreign Languages
New York, NY 10010

City College, City University of New York
(Omicron)
Department of Foreign Languages
New York, NY 10031

Colgate University
(Lambda Xi)
Department of Foreign Languages
Hamilton, NY 13346

College of New Rochelle
(Iota Lambda)
Department of Foreign Languages
New Rochelle, NY 10805

College of St. Rose
(Sigma Delta)
Department of Foreign Languages
Albany, NY 12003

Columbia University
(Gamma Zeta)
Department of Foreign Languages
New York, NY 10027

Cornell University
(Lambda Theta)
Department of Foreign Languages
Ithaca, NY 14853

D'Youville College
(Delta Rho)
Department of Foreign Languages
Buffalo, NY 14201

Fordham University
(Nu Delta)
Department of Foreign Languages
Bronx, NY 10458

Hartwick College
(Nu Gamma)
Department of Foreign Languages
Oneonta, NY 13820

Hofstra University
(Alpha Sigma)
Department of Foreign Languages
Hempstead, NY 11550

Hunter College, City University of New York
(Xi)
Department of Foreign Languages
New York, NY 10021

Iona College
(Iota Alpha)
Department of Foreign Languages
New York, NY 10021

Ithaca College
(Iota Pi)
Department of Foreign Languages
Ithaca, NY 14850

Lehman College, City University of New York
(Theta Alpha)
Department of Foreign Languages
Bronx, NY 10468

Long Island University–Brooklyn
(Beta Gamma)
Department of Foreign Languages
Brooklyn, NY 11201

Long Island University–C.W. Post
(Eta Phi)
Department of Foreign Languages
Greenvale, NY 11548

Manhattan College
(Mu Tau)
Department of Foreign Languages
Riverdale, NY 10471

Nazareth College of Rochester
(Mu Delta)
Department of Foreign Languages
Rochester, NY 14618

New York University
(Beta Theta)
Department of Foreign Languages
New York, NY 10003

Queens College, City University of New York
(Delta Alpha)
Department of Foreign Languages
Flushing, NY 11367

St. Bonaventure University
(Xi Delta)
Department of Foreign Languages
St. Bonaventure, NY 14778

St. Francis College
(Zeta Theta)
Department of Foreign Languages
Brooklyn, NY 11201

St. John's University
(Epsilon Kappa)
Department of Foreign Languages
Jamaica, NY 11439

St. Lawrence University
(Theta Mu)
Department of Foreign Languages
Canton, NY 13617

Skidmore College
(Rho Beta)
Department of Foreign Languages
Saratoga Springs, NY 12866

State University of New York–Albany
(Eta Psi)
Department of Foreign Languages
Albany, NY 12222

State University of New York–Binghamton
(Rho Nu)
Department of Foreign Languages
Binghamton, NY 13901

State University of New York–Buffalo
(Beta Nu)
Department of Foreign Languages
Buffalo, NY 14260

State University of New York–College at Buffalo
(Nu Iota)
Department of Foreign Languages
Buffalo, NY 14260

State University of New York–College at Cortland
(Mu Rho)
Department of Foreign Languages
Cortland, NY 13405

State University of New York–College at Fredonia
(Eta Alpha)
Department of Foreign Languages
Fredonia, NY 14063

State University of New York–College at Geneseo
(Tau Zeta)
Department of Foreign Languages
Geneseo, NY 14454

State University of New York–College at New Paltz
(Rho Zeta)
Department of Foreign Languages
New Paltz, NY 12561

State University of New York–College at Oswego
(Iota Zeta)
Department of Foreign Languages
Oswego, NY 13126

State University of New York–College at Plattsburg
(Iota Chi)
Department of Foreign Languages
Plattsburg, NY 12901

State University of New York–College at Potsdam
(Xi Omega)
Department of Foreign Languages
Postdam, NY 13676

Union College
(Tau Mu)
Department of Foreign Languages
Schenectady, NY 12308

Vassar College
(Nu Phi)
Department of Foreign Languages
Poughkeepsie, NY 12601

Wagner College
(Kappa Delta)
Department of Foreign Languages
Staten Island, NY 10301

York College, City University of New York
(Iota Iota)
Department of Foreign Languages
Jamaica, NY 11451

North Carolina

Appalachian State University
(Epsilon Omicron)
Department of Foreign Languages
Boone, NC 28608

Davidson College
(Omega)
Department of Foreign Languages
Davidson, NC 28936

Duke University
(Alpha Theta)
Department of Foreign Languages
Durham, NC 27706

Elon College
(Rho Eta)
Department of Foreign Languages
Elon, NC 27244

Fayetteville State University
(Upsilon Theta)
Department of Foreign Languages
Fayetteville, NC 28301

Gardner-Webb University
(Upsilon Theta)
Department of Foreign Languages
Boiling Springs, NC 28017

Greensboro College
(Tau Omega)
Department of Foreign Languages
Greensboro, NC 27401

High Point University
(Nu Mu)
Department of Foreign Languages
High Point, NC 27262

Mars Hill College
(Theat Sigma)
Department of Foreign Languages
Mars Hill, NC 28754

Meredith College
(Pi Epsilon)
Department of Foreign Languages
Raleigh, NC 27607

North Carolina A&T State University
(Upsilon Gamma)
Department of Foreign Languages
Greensboro, NC 27411

North Carolina State University
(Xi Omicron)
Department of Foreign Languages
Raleigh, NC 27695

Peace College
(Upsilon Gamma)
Department of Foreign Languages
Raleigh, NC 27604

Pembroke State University
(Iota Epsilon)
Department of Foreign Languages
Pembroke, NC 28372

University of North Carolina–Asheville
(Lambda Gamma)
Department of Foreign Languages
Asheville, NC 28804

University of North Carolina–Chapel Hill
(Zeta Psi)
Department of Foreign Languages
Chapel Hill, NC 27599

University of North Carolina–Charlotte
(Rho Sigma)
Department of Foreign Languages
Charlotte, NC 28223

University of North Carolina–Greensboro
(Alpa Tau)
Department of Foreign Languages
Greensboro, NC 27412

University of North Carolina–Wilmington
(Rho Lambda)
Department of Foreign Languages
Wilmington, NC 28403

Wake Forest University
(Tau Lambda)
Department of Foreign Languages
Winston-Salem, NC 27109

North Dakota

University of North Dakota
(Tau Rho)
Department of Foreign Languages
Fargo, ND 58105

Ohio

Ashland College
(Pi Tau)
Department of Foreign Languages
Ashland, OH 44805

Baldwin-Wallace College
(Alpha Nu)
Department of Foreign Languages
Berea, OH 44017

Bowling Green State University
(Beta Mu)
Department of Foreign Languages
Bowling Green, OH 43403

Cleveland State University
(Iota Omicron)
Department of Foreign Languages
Cleveland, OH 44115

College of Wooster
(Epsilon)
Department of Foreign Languages
Wooster, OH 44691

Denison University
(Phi)
Department of Foreign Languages
Danville, OH 43023

Heidelberg College
(Xi Psi)
Department of Foreign Languages
Tiffin, OH 44883

John Carroll University
(Pi Lambda)
Department of Foreign Languages
Cleveland, OH 44118

Kent State University
(Beta Lambda)
Department of Foreign Languages
Kent, OH 44242

Lake Erie College
(Rho Tau)
Department of Foreign Languages
Painesville, OH 44077

Marietta College
(Gamma Phi)
Department of Foreign Languages
Marietta, OH 45750

Miami University
(Alpha Alpha)
Department of Foreign Languages
Oxford, OH 45056

Ohio Northern University
(Eta Eta)
Department of Foreign Languages
Ada, OH 45810

Ohio State University
(Mu Lambda)
Department of Foreign Languages
Columbus, OH 43210

Ohio University
(Pi Rho/Tau of OH)
Department of Foreign Languages
Athens, OH 45701

University of Akron
(Eta Kappa)
Department of Foreign Languages
Akron, OH 44325

University of Cincinnati
(Gamma Tau)
Department of Foreign Languages
Cincinnati, OH 45221

University of Dayton
(Eta Tau)
Department of Foreign Languages
Dayton, OH 45469

University of Toledo
(Beta Epsilon)
Department of Foreign Languages
Toledo, OH 43606

Wilmington College
(Sigma Nu)
Department of Foreign Languages
Wilmington, OH 45177

Wittenburg University
(Lambda Iota)
Department of Foreign Languages
Springfield, OH 45501

Wright State University
(Iota Omega)
Department of Foreign Languages
Dayton, OH 45435

Xavier University
(Rho Upsilon)
Department of Foreign Languages
Cincinnati, OH 45207

Youngstown State University
(Nu Epsilon)
Department of Foreign Languages
Youngstown, OH 44555

Oklahoma

East Central University
(Xi Sigma)
Department of Foreign Languages
Ada, OK 74820

Northeastern State University
(Tau Epsilon)
Department of Foreign Languages
Tahlequah, OK 74464

Oklahoma State University
(Mu Upsilon)
Department of Foreign Languages
Stillwater, OK 74078

Oral Roberts University
(Kappa Rho)
Department of Foreign Languages
Tulsa, OK 74171

Southern Nazarene University
(Lambda Upsilon)
Department of Foreign Languages
Bethany, OK 73008

University of Central Oklahoma
(Eta Rho)
Department of Foreign Languages
Edmond, OK 73034

University of Oklahoma
(Gamma Theta)
Department of Foreign Languages
Norman, OK 73019

University of Tulsa
(Pi Iota)
Department of Foreign Languages
Tulsa, OK 74104

Oregon

Eastern Oregon State College
(Tau Sigma)
Department of Foreign Languages
La Grande, OR 97850

Oregon State University
(Delta Lambda)
Department of Foreign Languages
Corvallis, OR 97331

University of Oregon
(Gamma)
Department of Foreign Languages
Eugene, OR 97403

University of Portland
(Delta Mu)
Department of Foreign Languages
Portland, OR 97203

Willamette University
(Beta Zeta)
Department of Foreign Languages
Salem, OR 97301

Pennsylvania

Albright College
(Xi Zeta)
Department of Foreign Languages
Reading, PA 19612

Beaver College
(Sigma Iota)
Department of Foreign Languages
Glenside, PA 19038

Bucknell University
(Alpha Upsilon)
Department of Foreign Languages
Lewisburg, PA 17837

Dickinson College
(Epsilon Delta)
Department of Foreign Languages
Carlisle, PA 17013

Eastern College
(Omicron Omega)
Department of Foreign Languages
St. Davids, PA 19087

Edinboro University of Pennsylvania
(Theta Omicron)
Department of Foreign Languages
Edinboro, PA 16444

Franklin and Marshall College
(Rho Iota)
Department of Foreign Languages
Lancaster, PA 17604

Gannon University
(Mu Eta)
Department of Foreign Languages
Erie, PA 16541

Immaculata College
(Nu Omega)
Department of Foreign Languages
Immaculata, PA 19345

Indiana University of Pennsylvania
(Iota Mu)
Department of Foreign Languages
Indiana, PA 15705

Lafayette College
(Sigma Phi)
Department of Foreign Languages
Easton, PA 18042

LaSalle University
(Pi Beta)
Department of Foreign Languages
Philadelphia, PA 19141

Mansfield University
(Eta Theta)
Department of Foreign Languages
Mansfield, PA 16933

Rosemont College
(Omicron Chi)
Department of Foreign Languages
Rosemont, PA 19010

St. Joseph's University
(Omicron Phi)
Department of Foreign Languages
Philadelphia, PA 19131

Shippensburg University
(Tau Phi)
Department of Foreign Languages
Shippensburg, PA 17257

Slippery Rock University
(Epsilon Nu)
Department of Foreign Languages
Slippery Rock, PA 16057

Susquehanna University
(Xi Kappa)
Department of Foreign Languages
Selinsgrove, PA 17870

Temple University
(Delta Kappa)
Department of Foreign Languages
Philadelphia, PA 19122

Thiel College
(Epsilon Alpha)
Department of Foreign Languages
Greenville, PA 16125

University of Pennsylvania
(Gamma Omicron)
Department of Foreign Languages
Philadelphia, PA 19104

Villanova University
(Rho Pi)
Department of Foreign Languages
Villanova, PA 19085

Washington and Jefferson College
(Gamma Mu)
Department of Foreign Languages
Washington, PA 15301

West Chester University
(Pi Xi)
Department of Foreign Languages
West Chester, PA 19383

Westminster College
(Epsilon Tau)
Department of Foreign Languages
New Wilmington, PA 16172

Rhode Island

Brown University
(Rho Phi)
Department of Foreign Languages
Providence, RI 02912

Providence College
(Nu Rho)
Department of Foreign Languages
Providence, RI 02918

Salve Regina University
(Epsilon Sigma)
Department of Foreign Languages
Newport, RI 02840

University of Rhode Island
(Theta Beta)
Department of Foreign Languages
Kingston, RI 02881

South Carolina

Charleston Southern University
(Tau Nu)
Department of Foreign Languages
Charleston, SC 29423

Citadel
(Tau Iota)
Department of Foreign Languages
Charleston, SC 29409

Clemson University
(Iota Phi)
Department of Foreign Languages
Clemson, SC 29634

College of Charleston
(Nu Zeta)
Department of Foreign Languages
Charleston, SC 29424

Columbia College
(Lambda Mu)
Department of Foreign Languages
Columbia, SC 29203

Erskine College
(Omicron Pi)
Department of Foreign Languages
Due West, SC 29639

Furman University
(Rho Kappa)
Department of Foreign Languages
Greenville, SC 29613

Newberry College
(Theta Upsilon)
Department of Foreign Languages
Newberry, SC 29108

University of South Carolina
(Chi)
Department of Foreign Languages
Spartanburg, SC 29303

Winthrop College
(Epsilon Epsilon)
Department of Foreign Languages
Rock Hill, SC 29733

Wofford College
(Gamma Xi)
Department of Foreign Languages
Spartanburg, SC 29303

South Dakota

South Dakota State University
(Rho Xi)
Department of Foreign Languages
Brookings, SD 57007

University of South Dakota
(Nu Omicron)
Department of Foreign Languages
Vermillion, SD 57069

Tennessee

Austin Peay State University
(Pi Nu)
Department of Foreign Languages
Clarksville, TN 37044

Carson-Newman College
(Gamma Chi)
Department of Foreign Languages
Jefferson City, TN 37760

David Lipscomb College
(Mu Sigma)
Department of Foreign Languages
Nashville, TN 37204

East Tennessee State University
(Theta Pi)
Department of Foreign Languages
Johnson City, TN 37614

Lee College
(Nu Eta)
Department of Foreign Languages
Cleveland, TN 37311

Lincoln Memorial University
(Beta Psi)
Department of Foreign Languages
Harrogate, TN 37752

Maryville College
(Zeta Iota)
Department of Foreign Languages
Maryville, TN 37801

Memphis State University
(Gamma Delta)
Department of Foreign Languages
Memphis, TN 38152

Middle Tennessee State University
(Pi Omicron)
Department of Foreign Languages
Murfreesboro, TN 37132

Tennessee State University
(Gamma Eta)
Department of Foreign Languages
Nashville, TN 37209

University of Tennessee
(Alpha Psi)
Department of Foreign Languages
Knoxville, TN 37996

University of Tennessee–Chattanooga
(Rho)
Department of Foreign Languages
Chattanooga, TN 37403

University of Tennessee–Martin
(Mu Theta)
Department of Foreign Languages
Martin, TN 38238

University of the South
(Kappa of TN)
Department of Foreign Languages
Sewanee, TN 37383

Vanderbilt University
(Alpha Xi)
Department of Foreign Languages
Nashville, TN 37235

Texas

Angelo State University
(Eta Nu)
Department of Foreign Languages
San Angelo, TX 76909

Austin College
(Delta Omega)
Department of Foreign Languages
Sherman, TX 75090

Baylor University
(Nu)
Department of Foreign Languages
Waco, TX 76798

East Texas Baptist University
(Kappa Lambda)
Department of Foreign Languages
Marshall, TX 75670

East Texas State University
(Theta Zeta)
Department of Foreign Languages
Commerce, TX 75429

Hardin-Simmons University
(Beta Sigma)
Department of Foreign Languages
Abilene, TX 79698

Howard Payne University
(Tau Pi)
Department of Foreign Languages
Brownwood, TX 76801

Lamar University
(Eta Iota)
Department of Foreign Languages
Orange, TX 77630

Lubbock Christian University
(Nu Lambda)
Department of Foreign Languages
Lubbock, TX 79407

McMurry University
(Lambda Epsilon)
Department of Foreign Languages
Abilene, TX 79697

Midwestern University
(Delta Beta)
Department of Foreign Languages
Wichita Falls, TX 76308

Our Lady of the Lake University
(Xi Upsilon)
Department of Foreign Languages
San Antonio, TX 78207

Prairie View A&M University
(Theta Iota)
Department of Foreign Languages
Prairie View, TX 77446

Rice University
(Gamma Upsilon)
Department of Foreign Languages
Houston, TX 77251

Sam Houston State University
(Kappa Zeta)
Department of Foreign Languages
Huntsville, TX 77341

Southern Methodist University
(Alpha Eta)
Department of Foreign Languages
Dallas, TX 75275

Southwestern University
(Iota Delta)
Department of Foreign Languages
Georgetown, TX 78626

Southwest Texas State University
(Epsilon Beta)
Department of Foreign Languages
San Marcos, TX 78666

Stephen F. Austin State University
(Epsilon Psi)
Department of Foreign Languages
Nacogdoches, TX 75962

Sul Ross State University
(Sigma Sigma)
Department of Foreign Languages
Alpine, TX 79832

Texas A&M University
(Lambda Tau)
Department of Foreign Languages
College Station, TX 77843

Texas A&M University–Kingsville
(Gamma Lambda)
Department of Foreign Languages
Kingsville, TX 78363

Texas Christian University
(Lambda Alpha)
Department of Foreign Languages
Fort Worth, TX 76129

Texas Southern University
(Epsilon Phi)
Department of Foreign Languages
Houston, TX 77004

Texas Tech University
(Alpha Phi)
Department of Foreign Languages
Lubbock, TX 79409

Texas Wesleyan University
(Eta Delta)
Department of Foreign Languages
Fort Worth, TX 76105

Texas Women's University
(Xi Epsilon)
Department of Foreign Languages
Denton, TX 76204

Trinity University
(Epsilon Omega)
Department of Foreign Languages
San Antonio, TX 78212

University of Houston
(Gamma Rho)
Department of Foreign Languages
Houston, TX 77204

University of Mary Hardin-Baylor
(Sigma)
Department of Foreign Languages
Belton, TX 76513

University of North Texas
(Alpha Pi)
Department of Foreign Languages
Denton, TX 76203

University of St. Thomas
(Theta Omega)
Department of Foreign Languages
Houston, TX 77006

University of Texas–Arlington
(Zeta Alpha)
Department of Foreign Languages
Arlington, TX 76019

University of Texas–Austin
(Zeta)
Department of Foreign Languages
Austin, TX 78712

University of Texas–Brownsville
(Tau Chi)
Department of Foreign Languages
Brownsville, TX 78520

University of Texas–El Paso
(Alpha Iota)
Department of Foreign Languages
El Paso, TX 79968

University of Texas–Pan American
(Xi Rho)
Department of Foreign Languages
Edinburg, TX 78539

University of Texas–San Antonio
(Omicron Zeta)
Department of Foreign Languages
San Antonio, TX 78249

University of Texas–Tyler
(Mu Omicron)
Department of Foreign Languages
Tyler, TX 75799

West Texas A&M University
(Gamma Kappa)
Department of Foreign Languages
Canyon, TX 79016

Utah

Brigham Young University
(Delta Pi)
Department of Foreign Languages
Provo, UT 84602

University of Utah
(Zeta Gamma)
Department of Foreign Languages
Salt Lake City, UT 84112

Utah State University
(Tau Eta)
Department of Foreign Languages
Logan, UT 84322

Vermont

Castleton State College
(Tau Beta)
Department of Foreign Languages
Castleton, VT 05735

Middlebury College
(Mu)
Department of Foreign Languages
Middlebury, VT 05753

Virginia

College of William and Mary
(Gamma Pi)
Department of Foreign Languages
Williamsburg, VA 23187

Emory & Henry College
(Lambda Omega)
Department of Foreign Languages
Emory, VA 24327

George Mason University
(Mu Pi)
Department of Foreign Languages
Fairfax, VA 22030

Hollins College
(Upsilon Eta)
Department of Foreign Languages
Roanoke, VA 24020

James Madison University
(Mu Psi)
Department of Foreign Languages
Harrisonburg, VA 22807

Liberty University
(Pi Chi)
Department of Foreign Languages
Lynchburg, VA 24506

Longwood College
(Pi Phi)
Department of Foreign Languages
Farmville, VA 23909

Old Dominion University
(Lambda Chi)
Department of Foreign Languages
Norfolk, VA 23529

Radford University
(Xi Iota)
Department of Foreign Languages
Radford, VA 24142

Randolph-Macon College
(Sigma Theta)
Department of Foreign Languages
Ashland, VA 23005

Roanoke College
(Kappa Eta)
Department of Foreign Languages
Salem, VA 24153

Sweet Briar College
(Rho Omega)
Department of Foreign Languages
Sweet Briar, VA 24595

University of Richmond
(Sigma Gamma)
Department of Foreign Languages
Richmond, VA 23173

University of Virginia
(Zeta Zeta)
Department of Foreign Languages
Charlottesville, VA 22903

Virginia Commonwealth University
(Pi Psi)
Department of Foreign Languages
Richmond, VA 23284

Virginia Military Institute
(Omicron Kappa)
Department of Foreign Languages
Lexington, VA 24450

Virginia Tech
(Lambda Psi)
Department of Foreign Languages
Blacksburg, VA 24061

Virginia Wesleyan College
(Sigma Beta)
Department of Foreign Languages
Norfolk, VA 23502

Washington

University of Puget Sound
(Tau Alpha)
Department of Foreign Languages
Tacoma, WA 98416

Whitman College
(Xi Nu)
Department of Foreign Languages
Walla Walla, WA 99362

West Virginia

Bethany College
(Kappa Xi)
Department of Foreign Languages
Bethany, WV 26032

Davis & Elkins College
(Iota Beta)
Department of Foreign Languages
Elkins, WV 26241

Marshall University
(Beta Kappa)
Department of Foreign Languages
Huntington, WV 25755

University of West Virginia
(Delta Tau)
Department of Foreign Languages
Morgantown, WV 26506

West Virginia State College
(Beta Chi)
Department of Foreign Languages
Institute, WV 25112

Wisconsin

Carroll College
(Mu Zeta)
Department of Foreign Languages
Waukesha, WI 53186

Marquette University
(Gamma Gamma)
Department of Foreign Languages
Milwaukee, WI 53233

University of Wisconsin–Eau Claire
(Delta Psi)
Department of Foreign Languages
Eau Claire, WI 54702

University of Wisconsin–Green Bay
(Omicron Upsilon)
Department of Foreign Languages
Green Bay, WI 54311

University of Wisconsin–LaCrosse
(Epsilon Theta)
Department of Foreign Languages
LaCrosse, WI 54601

University of Wisconsin–Madison
(Psi)
Department of Foreign Languages
Madison, WI 53706

University of Wisconsin–Milwaukee
(Epsilon Iota)
Department of Foreign Languages
Milwaukee, WI 53201

University of Wisconsin–Oshkosh
(Eta Sigma)
Department of Foreign Languages
Oshkosh, WI 54901

University of Wisconsin–Whitewater
(Zeta Lambda)
Department of Foreign Languages
Whitewater, WI 53190

State Chapters of the American Association of Teachers of Spanish and Portuguese (AATSP)

Alabama

Attn: Peter Bernstein
721 12th Street NE
Jacksonville, AL 36265

Arizona

Attn: Lucy Linder
2229 N. 87th Way
Scottsdale, AZ 85257

Arkansas

De Soto Chapter
Attn: Dorothy Bell
Cabot High School
504 East Locust Street
Cabot, AR 72023

California

Northern California Chapter
Attn: Carol E. Feige
967 H La Mesa Terrace
Sunnyvale, CA 94086

Roger C. Antón Chapter
Attn: Raymond González
2501 Horace Street
Riverside, CA 92506

San Diego Chapter
Attn: Jesse Lomeli
1315 Vista Colina Drive
San Marcos, CA 92069-4957

Southern California Chapter
Attn: Lynne LaFleur
2500 Via Anacapa
Palos Verdes Estates, CA 90274

Canada

Atlantic Provinces Chapter
Attn: Carol Hartzman
Department of Modern Languages
Mount St. Vincent University
Halifax, Nova Scotia B34 2J6
Canada

Ontario Chapter
Attn: Mercedes Rowinsky
Wilfrid Laurier University
Department of Modern Languages and Literatures
Waterloo, Ontario N2L 3GS
Canada

Colorado

Attn: Jane Scott Chamberlain
2946 Kalmia Avenue, No. 53
Boulder, CO 80301

Connecticut

Attn: Alicia Almagro
45 Slater Road
Glastonbury, CT 06033

Delaware

Attn: Linnea Raffaele
50 South Fourth Street
Oxford, PA 19363

District of Columbia

Attn: Haydee Magro
3401 38th Street NW, No. 327
Washington, DC 20016

Florida

Attn: Olga Vasseur
8865 SW 16th Street
Miami, FL 33165

Georgia

Attn: Anita Picas
250 Ansley Drive
Athens, GA 30605

Hawaii

Attn: Raylice Wong
99-1440 Aiea Heights Drive, No. 59
Aiea, HI 96701

Idaho

Attn: Annette Wiggins
3492 North 900 East
Castleford, ID 83321

Illinois

Chicago Area Chapter
Attn: Jeanette Wanner
12 Country Oaks Lane
Barrington Hills, IL 60010-9620

Downstate Illinois Chapter
Attn: Dolores Decaroli
409 Clark St.
Oglesby, IL 61348

Northern Illinois Chapter
Attn: Linda Noshay
6702 Concord Trail
Crystal Lake, IL 60012

Indiana

Attn: Alan Garfinkel
2229 Carberry Drive
West Lafayette, IN 47906-1943

Iowa

Attn: Mary Stimmel
2014 44th Street
Des Moines, IA 50310

Kansas

Kansas/Sunflower Chapter
Attn: Connie Kopsa
Beloit High School
1712 North Walnut
Beloit, KS 67420

Kentucky

Attn: Daniel P. Kinnell
PO Box 2
Vancleve, KY 41385

Louisiana

Louisiana Chapter
Attn: Margaret Mary Friesenhahn
307 Florida Boulevard
New Orleans, LA 70124-1805

Antonio Margil Chapter
Attn: Lydia B. Keyser
335 Keegan Drive
Natchitoches, LA 71457

Maine

García Lorca Chapter
Attn: Eugenia Wheelwright
299 Durham Road
Brunswick, ME 04011

Maryland

Attn: Loretta Prevas
129-E Versailles Circle
Towson, MD 21204

Massachusetts

Massachusetts Bay Chapter
Attn: Mary-Anne Vetterling
35 Turning Mill Road
Lexington, MA 02173-1319

Michigan

Attn: Charles A. Ahnert
509 Claremont
Buchanan, MI 48107-1711

Minnesota

Attn: Francis Cutter
1169 Veronica Lane
Mendoza Heights, MN 55118

Mississippi

Attn: Felice Coles
1740 Jackson Avenue, No. E1
Oxford, MS 38655

Missouri

San Luis Rey Chapter
Attn: Sandra Mabrey
Northeast Middle School
181 Coeur De Ville Drive
St. Louis, MO 63141

Nebraska

Omaha Chapter
Attn: Debra Johnson
5626 South 148th Plaza
Omaha, NE 68137-2514

New Hampshire

Attn: Frederick S. Fernald
Box 1805
Wolfeboro, NH 03894-1805

New Jersey

Attn: Martin Smith
10 Twin Oaks Drive
Edison, NJ 08820

New Mexico

Cíbola Chapter
Attn: Thomasina Hannum
508 Golden Meadow NW
Albuquerque, NM 87114

New York

Dos Ríos Chapter
Attn: Maire E. Chianese
21 Lincoln Street
Waverly, NY 14892

Fronteras del Norte Chapter
Attn: Don King
Box 261
Waddington, NY 13694

Long Island Chapter
Attn: Margaret Fernández
67 Chestut Avenue
Larchmont, NY 10538

Metropolitan New York Chapter
Attn: Glen Nadelbach
64 East St. Marks Place
Valley Stream, NY 11580

North Carolina

Attn: María J. Fraser-Molina
Durham Technical County College
1637 Lawson Street
Durham, NC 27703

North Dakota

Attn: Jeanne House
900 Fourth Avenue
Mandan, ND 58554

Ohio

Buckeye Chapter
Attn: Betty Croswell
601 North Breiel Boulevard
Middeltown, OH 45042

Northern Ohio Chapter
Attn: William Kelley
3911 Bridge Avenue
Cleveland, OH 44113

Oklahoma

Attn: Charlotte Lovett
1420 Magonolia
Norman, OK 73072-6826

Oregon
Attn: Matt Courtney
828 South Fifth Avenue
Cornelius, OR 97113

Pennsylvania
Delaware Valley Chapter
Attn: Michèle S. De Cruz-Sáenz
739 Windsor Place
Wallingford, PA 19086

Greater Philadelphia Area Chapter
Attn: Thomasina I. White
1403 72nd Avenue
Philadelphia, PA 19126

Northeastern Pennsylvania Chapter
Attn: Molly Hayes
231 West Sherman Street, Apartment 4
McAdoo, PA 18237-1109

Río Arriba Chapter
Attn: Michelle Smith
439 West Park Avenue
State College, PA 16803

Western Pennsylvania Chapter
Attn: Kathleen Boykin
165 Bradman Estates
Slippery Rock, PA 16057-3207

Puerto Rico
Attn: José Rodríguez Valentín
Calle Amapola T-7
Lomas Verdes, Bayamón, PR 00956

Rhode Island
Attn: Alice M. McNaught
5 Melody Lane
Cumberland, RI 02864

South Carolina
Attn: Barbara B. Melver
Claflin College
Orangeburg, SC 29115

South Dakota
Attn: LaRee Mayes
3203 Meadowbrook Drive
Rapid City, SD 57702

Tennessee
Attn: Juanita Shettlesworth
Department of Foreign Languages, TTU
Box 5061
Cookeville, TN 38505

Texas
Brazos Chapter
Attn: Benjamin F. Griffith
229 Westmoreland, No. 11
Houston, TX 77006

Costa del Sol Chapter
Attn: Judy Kelso
5013 Denver
Galveston, TX 77551

Llano Estacado Chapter
Attn: Mary Alice González
4804 41st Street
Lubbock, TX 79414-3009

Lone Star Chapter
Attn: Phillip Johnson
Department of Modern Languages
Box 97393
Baylor University
Waco, TX 76798

Río Grande Chapter
Attn: Martín Rede
10919 Artwall Drive
El Paso, TX 79936

San Antonio de Béjar Chapter
Attn: Johnnie Eng
531 West Mariposa Drive
San Antonio, TX 78212

Texas Chapter
Attn: Amy Jo Lasker
1114 East Liberty Avenue
Round Rock, TX 78664

Utah

Attn: A. Tracy Rush
Butler Middle School
7530 South 2700 East
Salt Lake City, UT 84121

Virginia

Potomac Chapter
Attn: Mary Goldin
Department of Foreign Languages
George Mason University
Mail Stop 3E5
Fairfax, VA 22030

West Virginia

Attn: Kelly S. Moore
RD 1, Box 183
Triadelphia, WV 26059

Wisconsin

Attn: E. Alan Magnuson
Stevens Point Area High School
1201 North Point Drive
Stevens Point, WI 54481

Wyoming

Attn: Paul Mandell
University of Wyoming
Department of Modern and Classical Languages
222 Hoyt
Laramie, WY 82071

Hispanic Associations

Alabama

Latin American Club
1060 Government Street
Mobile, AL 36604

Nuestra Raza/Hispanic/Latino Students of UAH
University of Alabama–Huntsville
13019 Astalot Drive
Huntsville, AL 35803

Alaska

Image
Anchorage Chapter
PO Box 100051
Anchorage, AK 99510-0051

Latinos Unidos del Norte
PO Box 74795
Fairbanks, AK 99707

Arizona

Alianza Hispano-Americana
133 West Congress Street
Tucson, AZ 85701

Arizona Hispanic Chamber of Commerce Foundation
2400 North Central Avenue, No. 303
Phoenix, AZ 85004

Center for Bilingual and Bicultural Education
Arizona State University
College of Education
Tempe, AZ 85287-1511

Chicano Research Collection
PO Box 871006
Arizona State University
Hayden Library
Tempe, AZ 85287-1006

Hispanic Research Center
Arizona State University
PO Box 2702
Tempe, AZ 85287-2702

Arkansas

League of United Latin American Citizens
7922 West 28th Street
Little Rock, AR 72204

California

Academia Iberoamericana de Poesía
California Chapter
31 East Carson Street
Carson, CA 90745

Asociación de Intelectuales Hispanos
(Association of Hispanic Intellectuals)
3460 Division Street
Los Angeles, CA 90065

Asociación de Periodistas de los Medios en Español
7356 Dinwiddie Street
Downey, CA 90241

Asociación Espannñola de California
La Peña
515 North Altura Road
Arcada, CA 91006

Basque American Foundation
PO Box 13212
Fresno, CA 93705

Basque Cultural Center
599 Railroad Street
South San Francisco, CA 94080

Casa de España
PO Box 2924
San Diego, CA 92112

Casa de España, Inc.
5456 Barton Avenue
Hollywood, CA 90038

Casa de España, Inc.
PO Box 2498
Pasadena, CA 91102-2498

Casa de los Catalanes
1705 Mission Street
South Pasadena, CA 91030

Casa dels Catalans de California
PO Box 91142
Los Angeles, CA 90009

Casa Social Española de Fontana
255 South Glendora Avenue
Glendora, CA 91740

Centro Boeckman para los Estudios
Ibéricos e Iberoamericanos
Doheny Memorial Library
DML Basement
University of Southern California
University Park
Los Angeles, CA 90089-0182

Centro de la Raza
302 West Seventh Street
Long Beach, CA 90813-4206

Chicano Studies Department
Loyola Marymount University
Loyola Boulevard at West 80th Street
Los Angeles, CA 90045

Chicano Studies Program Center
University of California–Berkeley
3404 Dwinelle Hall
Berkeley, CA 94720

Chicano Studies Program Center
University of California–Davis
T.B. 101
Davis, CA 95616

Chicano Studies Research Center
University of California–Los Angeles
3121 Campbell Hall
Los Angeles, CA 90024

Chino Basque Club
PO Box 1080
Chino, CA 91710

Círculo Artístico y Literario de España
5006 Snow Drive
San Jose, CA 95111

Círculo Español de Stockton
PO Box 7802
Stockton, CA 95202

Círculo Español Orange
821 Chicago Avenue
Placentia, CA 92670

Círculo Hispano
7055 Elder Way
Sacramento, CA 95831

Club Español
PO Box 15
Rocklin, CA 95677

Club Español de Fontana
8904 Locust Street
Fontana, CA 92335

Club Hispano del Pueblo
(People's Hispanic Club)
2323 Workman Street
Los Angeles, CA 90031

Club Ibérico Benéfico
1349 Hayes Street
San Leandro, CA 94577

Club Ibérico de España
PO Box 765
Winters, CA 95694

Comité para Fiestas Hispánicas
(Hispanic Festivities Committee)
1200 North State Street, No. 1103
Los Angeles, CA 90033

Cuadratura del Círculo Poético
Iberoamericano
PO Box 54
Santa Monica, CA 90406-0054

Ethnic Studies Center
California State University–Humboldt
Wagner House 73
Arcata, CA 95521

Federación de Asociaciones y Sociedades
Españolas de California
6720 Stonegate Drive
Chino, CA 91710

Fundación de la Familia Hispano-Americana del Año
(Hispanic-American Family of the Year)
10654 Woodbridge Street
North Hollywood, CA 91602

Fundación Gregorio del Amo
1162 Union Bank Building
742 South Hill
Los Angeles, CA 90014

Hispanic Studies Program Center
West Coast Christina College
North Maple Avenue
Fresno, CA 93710

Instituto Literario y Cultural Hispánico
Hispanic Literary and Cultural Institute)
8452 Furman Avenue
Westminster, CA 92683

Instituto para Estudios de la Cultura Hispánica
(Institute for Hispanic Cultural Studies)
2050 Colorado Avenue, Suite 103
Santa Monica, CA 90404-3416

La Sociedad de las Américas
2235 47th Avenue
San Francisco, CA 94116

Latin American Studies Center
California State College–Bakersfield
Bakersfield, CA 93309

Los Fundadores (The Founders)
1053 South White Road
San Jose, CA 95127

Los Pobladores 200 (The Settlers 200)
1200 South Atlantic Boulevard
Monterey Park, CA 91754

Movimiento Estudiantil Chicano de Aztlán
900 Varsity Road
Arvin, CA 93203

National Concilio of America
41 Sutter Street, Suite 1067
San Francisco, CA 94104

National Network of Hispanic Women
12021 Wilshire Boulevard, Suite 353
Los Angeles, CA 90025

Pena Cultural "El Ateneo"
(Cultural Club "The Atheneum")
10977 Santa Monica Boulevard
Los Angeles, CA 90025

Public Affairs Office
Presidio of San Francisco Headquarters
Presidio, CA 94129

Public Affairs Office
Defense Language Institute
Presidio of Monterey, CA 93940

Public Affairs Office
Mission Dolores Basilica
3321 16th Street
San Francisco, CA 94114

San Joaquin Valley Military Historical Society
1408 H Street
PO Box 932
Fresno, CA 93714

Sociedad Agustina de Aragón
1349 Hayes Street
San Leandro, CA 94577

Sociedad Cultural Hispánica de California
(California Hispanic Cultural Society)
PO Box 41345
Los Angeles, CA 90041

Sociedad de Señoras Isabel La Católica
PO Box 60848
Sunnyvale, CA 94088

Sociedad Española Cervantes
627 East Tylor Street
Sunnyvale, CA 94086

Sociedad Española de Beneficencia Mutua
(Spanish Association for Mutual Assistance)
113 South 22 Street
Montebello, CA 90640

Sociedad Iberoamericana de Escritores
de los Estados Unidos de América, SIADE
(Society of Iberoamerican Writers of the United States)
453 South Spring Street, Suite 1202
Los Angeles, CA 90013

Society of California Pioneers
456 McAllister Street
San Francisco, CA 94102

Spanish American Heritage Association
1008 Larkin Circle
Salinas, CA 93907

Teatro Campesino
Box 1240
San Juan Bautista, CA 95045

Unidad Española de California "La Peña"
515 North Altura Road
Arcadia, CA 91006

Unión Española Benéfica
PO Box 1063
Hollister, CA 95023

Unión Española de California
2850 Alameny Boulevard
San Francisco, CA 94112

Colorado

Genealogical Society of Hispanic America
PO Box 9060
Denver, CO 80209-0606

Hispanic Cultural Center
University of Northern Colorado
1410 20th Street
Greeley, CO 80639

Hispanics of Colorado
1029 Sante Fe Drive
Colorado Springs, CO 80910

Museo de las Américas
861 Santa Fe Drive
Denver, CO 80204

El Parnaso
ES Building 220
Adams State College
Alamosa, CO 81102

St. Thomas Seminary Library
1300 South Steele
Denver, CO 80210

Connecticut

Daughters of Isabella
375 Whitney Avenue
New Haven, CT 06511

Hispanic Cultural Society
87 West Street
Danbury, CT 06810

Knights of Columbus
Columbus Plaza
New Haven, CT 06507

Spanish Action Council
629 South Main Street
Waterbury, CT 06706

Spanish Community
37 Hall Avenue
Wellingford, CT 06492

Spanish Cultural Association
153 Howard Avenue
New Haven, CT 06519

Spanish Speaking Center
83 Cherry Street
Waterbury, CT 06702

Delaware

Foundation "The Good Samaritan"
9034 DuPont Building
Wilmington, DE 19098

Governor's Council on Hispanic Affairs
Carvel State Office Building
820 North French Street, Fourth Floor
Wilmington, DE 19801

District of Columbia

Afro-Hispanic Institute
3306 Ross Place NW
Washington, DC 20008

Asociació de Catalans de l'Area de Washington
PO Box 9481
Washington, DC 20016-9481

Aspira of America
1112 16th Street NW, Suite 340
Washington, DC 20036

Centro Anglo-Español
2022 Hillyer Place NW
Washington, DC 20009

Centro Español de Washington, D.C.
PO Box 9485
Washington, DC 20016

Centro Vasco
2915 Arizona Avenue
Washington, DC 20016

Christopher Columbus Quincentenary Jubilee
   Commission
1801 F Street NW
Washington, DC 20006

Club de las Américas
PO Box 11095
Washington, DC 20008

Congressional Hispanic Caucus Institute
504 C Street NE
Washington, DC 20002

Fernando Rielo Foundation
3636 16th Street NW
B. 1133
Washington, DC 20010

Foundation for the Advancement of Hispanic
   Americans
Box 66012
Washington, DC 20035

Hispanic Higher Education Coalition
20 F Street NW, Suite 200
Washington, DC 20001

Hispanic Institute for the Performing Arts
1629 K Street NW, Suite 800
Washington, DC 20006

Latin American Institute
3713 Macomb Street NW
Washington, DC 20016

National Association for Bilingual Education (NABE)
1201 16th Street NW, Room 408
Washington, DC 20036

National Association of Hispanic Journalists (NAHJ)
National Press Building, Suite 634
Washington, DC 20045

National Association of Latino Elected and Appointed
   Officials (NALEO)
708 G Street SE
Washington, DC 20003

National Council of La Raza
810 First Street NE
Washington, DC 20002

Secretariat for Hispanic Affairs
(National Conference of Catholic Bishops)
1312 Massachusetts Avenue NW
Washington, DC 20005

Spanish Club
The Catholic University
208 McMahon Hall
Washington, DC 20064

Florida

Amigos de Madrid
2845 Coral Way
Miami, FL 33145

Asociación de Graduados de Universidades Españolas
   (AGUE)
(Attn: Dr. Ramiro Marrero)
1221 SW 27th Avenue
Miami, FL 33135

Cámara de Comercio Latina de los Estados Unidos
   (CAMACOL)
1417 West Flagler Street
Miami, FL 33135

Casa de España del Este de la Florida Central
PO Box 14148 B
Orlando, FL 33857

Casal Català
c/o Professor Joaquín Roy
Center for Advanced International Studies
University of Miami
PO Box 248123
Coral Gables, FL 33124

Casa Sta. Marta de Ortigueira
1815 NW North River Drive
Miami, FL 33125

Casino Español de la Habana
110 20th Street
Miami Beach, FL 33139

Centro Asturiano de Miami
4315 NW 7th Street
Miami, FL 33126

Centro Asturiano de Tampa
1913 Nebraska Avenue and Palm Avenue
Tampa, FL 33602

Club Ibérico Español
PO Box 261841
Tampa, FL 33685

Club Vasco
"Txoko Alai"
4315 NW 7th Street
Miami, FL 33126

Cuban American National Council
300 SW 12th Avenue
Miami, FL 33130-2038

Discovery of America Quincentennial Committee, Inc.
4011 West Flagler Street, Suite 505
Miami, FL 33134

Fiesta of Five Flags
(Order of Don Tristán de Luna)
2121 West Intendencia Street
PO Box 1943
Pensacola, FL 32589-1943

Florida's Columbus Hemispheric Commission
2701 Le Jeune Road, Suite 330
Coral Gables, FL 33134

Hernando de Soto Historical Society
The Spanish Manor House
910 Third Avenue West
Bradenton, FL 34205

Hispanic Heritage Festival
4011 Flagler Street, Suite 503
Miami, Fl 33134

Koubek Center for Continuing Education
University of Miami
2705 SW Third Street
Miami, FL 33135

Men of Menendez
New World Garrison of the Spanish Marine Corps
ORDEN DEL MAR, an Honorary Living History
    Organization

Historic Florida Militia
42 Spanish Street
St. Augustine, FL 32084

Orden del Buen Vino (Order of Good Wine)
(Attn: Milton Lehr)
c/o American Travel Club
2351 West Flagler Street
Miami, FL 33135

Real Club Social Deportivo Español
7401B NW Eighth Street
Miami, FL 33126

Royal Order of the Ponce de León Conquistadors
PO Box 0664
Punta Gorda Port
Charlotte, FL 33950-0664

Salvador Dali Foundation
Dali Museum
1000 Third Street South
St. Petersburg, FL 33701

Spain U.S. Chamber of Commerce in Florida
2655 Le Jeune Road, No. 906
Coral Cables, FL 33134

Tourist Office of Spain
1221 Brickell Avenue, No. 1850
Miami, FL 33131

Georgia

Asociación Cultural Hispano-Americana
de la CSRA "Miguel de Cervantes"
PO Box 1083
Augusta, GA 30903

Latin American Association
2665 Buford Highway
Atlanta, GA 30324

Spanish Speaking Organization
Georgia Tech
Service Building, 123 ISSP Office
Atlanta, GA 30332-0284

Hawaii

Hispanic Cultural Association
91-95 Kuhina Street
Ewa Beach, HI 96706

Hispano-American Cultural Exchange and Rediscovery
Society
720 Unelei Road, No. 303
Honolulu, HI 96817

Idaho

Basque Club
1421 Warm Spring Avenue
Boise, Idaho 83702

Idaho Commissions on Hispanic Affairs
5460 West Franklin Road, Suite B
Boise, ID 83705

Illinois

American Spanish Institute
2619 West Armitage Avenue
Chicago, IL 60606

Asociación de Periodistas y Locutores Interamericanos
PO Box 608305
Chicago, IL 60660

Ensemble Español
5500 North St. Louis Avenue
Chicago, IL 60605

Hispanic Alliance for Cultural Expression and
Recognition
University of Chicago
5801 South Ellis Avenue, No. 230
Chicago, IL 60637

Hispanic Heritage Club
3801 South Central
Morton College
Cicero, IL 60650

Hispanic Image
PO Box 11100
Chicago, IL 60611

Mosaico
280 Illini Union
140 West Green Street
University of Illinois–Urbana-Champaign
Urbana, IL 61801

Sociedad Española de Medio Oeste
5255 Carpenter Street
Downers Grove, IL 60515

Spanish and Portuguese Translators Association
79 West Monroe
Chicago, IL 60603

Spanish Association of the Midwest
1448 Elm Avenue
Northbrook, IL 60062

Indiana

Center for the Study of Contemporary Society
Memorial Library
University of Notre Dame
Notre Dame, IN 46656

Hispanic Society
1400 Western Hills Drive
Evansville, IN 47712

Indiana Hispanic Chamber of Commerce
342 North Senate Avenue
Indianapolis, IN 46204

Indiana University
Office of Latino Affairs
Memorial Hall W108
Bloomington, IN 47405

Latinos Unidos, Latino Cultural Center
Indiana University
715 East Seventh Street
Bloomington, IN 47405

Sociedad Española Inc.
PO Box 10037
Merrillville, IN 46411

Iowa

Spanish Club
Iowa State University
300 Pearson Hall
Ames, IA 50011

Kansas

Kansas Advisory Committee On Hispanic Affairs
117 SW 10th Avenue
Topeka, KS 66612-2201

Kentucky

National Association of Hispanic and Latino Studies
Morehead State University
212 Rader Hall
Morehead, KY 40351-1689

Louisiana

Cámara de Comercio Hispana de Louisiana
1221 Elmwood Park, Suite 401
Harahan, LA 70123

Centro Social Español de Beneficiencia
PO Box 13562
New Orleans, LA 70176

Cervantes
Fundación Hispanoamericana de Arte
5519 Elysians Fields Avenue
New Orleans, LA 70122

Hispanidad
7111 St. Charles Avenue
New Orleans, LA 70118

League of United Latin American Citizens
2216 Landay Avenue
Bossier City, LA 71111

Sociedad Española
7111 St. Charles Avenue
New Orleans, LA 70118

Maryland

Asociación Cultural Hispana de Maryland
1840 York Road, No. G
Timonium, MD 21093

Casa de España
2508 Old North Point Road
Baltimore, MD 21222

Centro Español de Maryland
10927 Summit Avenue
Baltimore, MD 20715

Círculo Cultural Hispánico
PO Box 910
Mitchell Road
La Plata, MD 20646-0910

Fundación Biblioteca Hispana de Maryland
Towson University
Cook Library
Towson, MD 21252

The Hispanics in History Cultural Organization
9659 Basket Ring Road, No. 2
Columbia, MD 21045

Los Peñeros Españoles
4707 Ebenezer Road
Baltimore, MD 21236

Maryland Hispanic Chamber of Commerce
PO Box 11286
Baltimore, MD 21239

National Clearing House for Bilingual Education (NCBE)
8737 Colesville Road
Silver Spring, MD 20902

Sister Cities Committee of Cádiz-Baltimore
8402 Kellog Court
Baltimore, MD 21093

Massachusetts

Boston-Barcelona Sister City Association
Head, University Professors Program
Boston University
Boston, MA 02215

Cardinal Cushing Spanish Center
26 Union Park Street
Boston, MA 02110

Centro Las Américas
11 Sycamore Street
Worcester, MA 01608

Centro Panamericano
1 Parker Street
Lawrence, MA 01841

Club Hispano-Americano International House
470 Atlantic House
Boston, MA 02110

Hispanic Chamber of Commerce
PO Box 16542
Worcester, MA 01601

Spanish Cultural Institute of New England
152 North Street
Boston, MA 02109

Michigan

Hispanic Center
1537 South Washington
Saginaw, MI 48601

Hispanic Cultural Center
1145 Ballard
Lansing, MI 48906

Hispanos Unidos de Detroit
3564 West Vernon Highway
Detroit, MI 48216

Michigan Hispanic Chamber of Commerce
32450 North Abis
Madison Heights, MI 48071

Minnesota

Amigos de las Américas
17825 Sixth Avenue North
Minneapolis, MN 55447

Instituto de Arte y Cultura
3501 Chicago Avenue
Minneapolis, MN 55407

Society for Spanish and Portuguese Historical Studies
Department of History
614 Social Sciences Building
University of Minnesota
Minneapolis, MN 55455

Mississippi

American Association of Teachers of Spanish and
    Portuguese
PO Box 6349
Mississippi University
(Executive Director: James R. Chatham)
State College, MS 39762

Sociedad Honoraria Hispánica
PO Box 330
Crump Building
Armory, MS 38821

Missouri

Centro Hispano
Box 2032
St. Louis, MO 63158

Hispanic Chamber of Commerce of Greater Kansas City
1828 Walnut Street, No. 200
Kansas City, MO 64108

Sociedad Española de St. Louis
7107 Michigan Avenue
St. Louis, MO 63111

Montana

Montana Migrant Legal Services
2442 First Avenue North
Billings, MT 59101

Nebraska

Hispanic Community Center
2300 O Street
Lincoln, NE 68510

Institute for Ethnic Studies
University of Nebraska
141 Andrews Hall
Lincoln, NE 68512

Society of Spanish and Spanish-American Studies
Department of Modern Languages and Literatures
Oldfather Hall
University of Nebraska
Lincoln, NE 68538

Nevada

Club Euzkaldunak
PO Box 1321
Elko, NE 89801

Latin Chamber of Commerce of Nevada
PO Box 7500
829 South Sixth Street, No. 3
Las Vegas, NV 89125-7500

Nevada Association of Latin Americans
323 North Maryland Parkway
Las Vegas, NV 89101-3130

Sociedad Cultural Hispana
PO Box 11174
Las Vegas, NE 89111

New Hampshire

La Alianza Latina
Dartmouth College
PO Box HB 6072
Hanover, NH 03755

New Jersey

Aula de Bayonne
"Calderón de la Barca"
767 Avenue A
Bayonne, NJ 07002

Aula de Manhattan
"Rosalia de Castro"
11-18 Floral Avenue
Fair Lawn, NJ 07410

Aula de Paterson
"García Lorca"
136 Franklin Avenue
Wyckoff, NJ 07481

Aula de Union City
"Camilo José Cela"
4916 Murphy Place
West New York, NJ 08093

Casa de España
2310 Summit Avenue
Union City, NJ 07087

Centro Español
88 Roosevelt Avenue
Carteret, NJ 07008

Centro Orensano, Inc.
148 Lafayette Street
Newark, NJ 07105

Círculo de Cultura Panamericano
16 Malvern Place
Verona, NJ 07044

Club España, Inc.
180-2 New York Avenue
Newark, NJ 07105

Club Español de Paterson
60 Butler Street
Paterson, NJ 07524

Federación de Asociaciones Españolas de EE.UU.
"Fase EE.UU."
PO Box 1363
Fair Lawn, NJ 07410-8363

Hispanic American Chamber of Commerce of New Jersey
221 Rector Street
Perth Amboy, NJ 08861

Hispanic Culture Club
2641 Kennedy Boulevard
Saint Peter's College
Jersey City, NJ 07306

Hispanic Institute for Research and Development
182 Main Street
Ridgefield Park, NJ 07660

Spanish American Citizens Club
382 Broadway
Bayonne, NJ 07002

Spanish American Social and Cultural Association of New Jersey
PO Box 2248
Levitt Parkway and Charleston Road
Willingboro, NJ 08046

New Mexico

Hispanic Culture Foundation
PO Box 7279
Albuquerque, NM 87194-7279

The Hispano Chamber of Commerce
PO Box 6389
Santa Fe, NM 87502

Latin American Institute
801 Yale NE
Albuquerque, NM 87131

New York

Academia Iberoamericana de Poesía
(Chapter of New York)
PO Box 7, FDR Station
New York, NY 10022

Academia Norteamericana
de la Lengua Española
GPO 349
New York, NY 10116

Agrupación Martínez
PO Box 48
East Norwich
Long Island, NY 11732

ALDEEU (Asociación de Licenciados y Doctores
    Españoles en Estados Unidos)
33 West 42nd Street
Graduate School and University Center
New York, NY 10036

American Friends of Spain
667 Madison Avenue
New York, NY 10021

American Spanish Committee
80 Box 119, Canal Street Station
New York, NY 10013

Amigos de la Zarzuela
241 West 97th Street, Suite 4M
New York, NY 10025

Asociación Pro-Zarzuela en América
Box 992, FDR Station
334 58th Street, Room 30
New York, NY 10150

Aspira of New York
470 Seventh Avenue, Third Floor
New York, NY 10018

Association of Hispanic Arts
200 East 87th Street
New York, NY 10028

Aula de Queens
"Miguel de Cervantes"
236 West 10th Street
New York, NY 10014

Ballet Hispánico of New York
167 West 89th Street
New York, NY 10024

Bergondo y Sus Contornos
Centro Español
239 W 14th Street
New York, NY 10011

Bronx Council for the Arts
1738 Hone Avenue, Corner Morris Park
Bronx, NY 10461

Casa de España de I.E.E.
314 East 39th Street
New York, NY 10016

Casa Galicia, Unidad Gallega
125 East 11th Street
New York, NY 10003

Catalan Institute, Inc.
173 Argonne Drive
Buffalo, NY 14217

Center for Cuban Studies
124 West 23rd Street
New York, NY 10011

Centro de Estudios Puertorriqueños
Hunter College
695 Park Avenue
New York, NY 10021

Centro Español de Staten Island, Inc.
147 Union Avenue
Staten Island, NY 10303

Centro Rey Juan Carlos I
New York University
53 Washington Square, Suite 201
New York, NY 10012-1098

Centro Vasco-Americano
"Zorionak"
307 Eckford Street
Brooklyn, NY 11222

Cervantes Cultural Association
1000 Clove Road
New York, NY 10301

Círculo de Escritores y Poetas Iberoamericanos de
    Nueva York (CEPI)
PO Box 831, GPO Station
New York, NY 10016

Círculo Español
41-01 Broadway
Astoria, NY 11103

Círculo Español de Nueva York, Inc.
PO Box 2889
New York, NY 10001

Club Acacia
71 West 23rd Street
New York, NY 10010

Club España
244 West 14th Street
New York, NY 10011

Comité del Desfile de la Raza
174-76 Fifth Avenue, Suite 401
New York, NY 10010

Council of the Americas
680 Park Avenue
New York, NY 10021

Fundación Cultura Hispánica de Estados Unidos
PO Box 7
New York, NY 10022

Hispanic Institute in the United States
612 West 116th Street
New York, NY 10027

Hispanic Society of America
613 West 155th Street
New York, NY 10032

Hostos Center for the Arts and Culture
Hostos Community College
500 Grand Concourse Avenue, No. C141
Bronx, NY 10451

Instituto Cervantes
122 East 42nd Street, No. 807
New York, NY 10168

Instituto de Escritores Latinoamericanos
(Latin American Writers Institute)
Hostos Community College
500 Grand Concourse Avenue, No. C141
Bronx, NY 10451

Intar (Hispanic-American Arts Center)
420 West 42nd Street, Second Floor
New York, NY 10036

Latin American and Caribbean Studies
Hostos Community College
500 Grand Concourse
Bronx, NY 10451

National Hispanic Business Group
960 Southern Boulevard
New York, NY 10459

National Hispanic Historical Committee
150 Ash Street
Floral Park, NY 11001

North American Catalan Society
Peter Cocozzella, Secretary
Department of Romance Languages
State University of New York–Binghamton
Binghamton, NY 13901

Ollantay Center for the Arts
PO Box 720636
Jackson Heights, NY 11372-0636

Sociedad Española de Socorros Mutuos
239 West 14th Street
New York, NY 10011

Society of Spanish Engineers, Planners and Architects
PO Box 75, Church Street Station
New York, NY 10007

Spain-U.S. Chamber of Commerce
350 Fifth Avenue, No. 2029
New York, NY 10118

Spanish American Citizens Club Queens
23/09/31 Street Astoria
Long Island, NY 11105

Spanish American Institute
215 West 43rd Street
New York, NY 10036

Spanish Benevolent Society "La Nacional"
239 West 14th Street
New York, NY 10011

Spanish Institute
684 Park Avenue
New York, NY 10021

State University of New York–Albany
Department of Puerto Rican, Latin American and
    Caribbean Studies
1400 Washington Avenue
Albany, NY 12222

Unidad Gallega de U.S., Inc.
Casa Galicia
119-125 East 11th Street
New York, NY 10003

Veterans of the Abraham Lincoln Brigade
799 Broadway, Room 227
New York, NY 10003

North Carolina

Carolina Hispanic Association
210 Steele Building, No. CB 3110
University of North Carolina–Chapel Hill
Chapel Hill, NC 27599-3110

El Centro Hispano
1852 Liberty Street
Durham, NC 27703

Institute of Latin American Studies
University of North Carolina
215 Murphey Hall
Chapel Hill, NC 27599

North Dakota

Migrant Legal Services
118 Broadway, No. 305
Fargo, ND 58102

Ohio

Amistad
5635 Glenview Avenue
Cincinnati, OH 45224

Committee on Relations with Toledo
245 Summit Street
Toledo, OH 43604

El Encuentro Cultural de Ohio
PO Box 09369
Bexley, OH 43209-0369

Hispanic Advisory Panel
14223 Detroit Avenue, Second Floor
Lakewood, OH 44107

La Alianza Iberoamericana
Case Western Reserve University
10900 Euclid Avenue
Cleveland, OH 44106-7062

La Mesa Española de Cleveland
286 Sheri Lane
Brunswick, OH 44212

Mesa Española
2550 Kemper Road
Cleveland, OH 44120

Pan American Society of Cincinnati
8633 Mockingbird Lane
Cincinnati, OH 45231

Spanish-American Cultural Club
3264 Sundale Drive
Columbus, OH 43232

University Council of Hispanic Organizations
2070 Neil Avenue
Ohio State University
Columbus, OH 43210

Oklahoma

Hispanic-American Foundation
PO Box 580266
Tulsa, OK 74158-0266

Hispanic Center
308 SW 25th Street
Oklahoma City, OK 73109

Oklahoma Hispanic Heritage Association
3828 SW 37th Street
Oklahoma, OK 73119

Oregon

Centro Cultural
Box 708
Cornelius, OR 97113

Hispanic Metropolitan Chamber of Commerce
2402 NE Oregon Street
Portland, OR 97232-2329

Oregon Commission on Hispanic Affairs
255 Capitol Street, NE
Salem, OR 97310

Pennsylvania

Asociación de Músicos Latinoamericanos
PO Box 50296
2757 North Fifth Street
Philadelphia, PA 19132

Círculo Español
6564 Germantown Avenue
Philadelphia, PA 19119

Círculo Español
320 Wellington Road
West Chester, PA 19380

Instituto Internacional de Literatura Iberoamericana
University of Pittsburgh
312 Cathedral of Learning
Pittsburgh, PA 15260

Spanish Speaking Center
301 13th Street
Harrisburg, PA 17104

Rhode Island

Governor's Commission on Hispanic Affairs
421 Elmwood Avenue
Providence, RI 02907

Instituto Internacional
645 Elmwood Avenue
Providence, RI 02907

South Carolina

Sociedad Honoraria Hispánica
Porter-Gaud School
Albernale Point
Charlestown, SC 29407

Spanish Club
Clemson University
201 Strode Tower
Clemson, SC 27634

South Dakota

Proteus
121 West Dakota Avenue
Pierre, SD 57501

Tennessee

Pan American Association of Tennessee
PO Box 2751, Arcade Station
Nashville, TN 37219

Sociedad Honoraria Hispánica
Christian Brothers High School
5900 Walnut Grove Road
Memphis, TN 38120

Texas

American Institute for Catalana Studies
(Instituto de Estudios Catalanes)
14314 Cindywood
Houston, TX 77079

Amigos de las Américas
5618 Star Lane
Houston, TX 77057

Arte Público Press
University of Houston
MD Anderson Library
4800 Calhoun, No. 2L
Houston, TX 77204-2090

Asociació d'Amics de Gaspar de Portolá
c/o Dr. Joan Oró
University of Houston
Department of Biophysical Science
4800 Calhoun Road
Houston, TX 77004

Benson Latin American Collection
University of Texas
Sid Richardson Hall, 1.109
Austin, TX 78713-7330

Casa de España
PO Box 1667
Brownsville, TX 78520

Casa de España
2501 Oak Lawn Avenue, Suite 201
Dallas, TX 75219

Casa de España
PO Box 20511
Houston, TX 77225

Casa de España
PO Box 790734
San Antonio, TX 78279-0734

Center for Inter-American and Border Studies
University of Texas
Miner Hall
El Paso, TX 79968-0605

Club de España Paso el Norte
PO Box 220295
El Paso, TX 79913

Club Patronato de la Cultura Hispano-Americana
232 Meadowbrook
San Antonio, TX 78232

Committee for Hispanic Arts and Research
PO Box 12865
Austin, TX 78711

El Patronato
620 Terrell Road
San Antonio, TX 78209

Hispanic Association of Colleges and Universities
411 SW 24th Street
San Antonio, TX 78285

Houston Hispanic Chamber of Commerce
2900 Woodridge Drive, No. 312
Houston, TX 77087-2506

Instituto de Cultura Hispánica
5 Chelsea Place
Houston, TX 77006

Instituto de Cultura Hispánica en Corpus Christi
PO Box 7201
Corpus Christi, TX 78415

La Sociedad Hispana Cultural
411 SW 24th Street, No. FH 214
San Antonio, TX 78207-4666

League for United Latin American Citizens (LULAC)
262 Losoya, Suite 320
San Antonio, TX 78205

San Antonio Hispanic Chamber of Commerce
South Texas Building
603 Navarro, No. 100
San Antonio, TX 78205

SER/Jobs for Progress
1355 River Bend Drive, Suite 240
Dallas, TX 75247

Utah

La Antorcha
2747 South State Street
Salt Lake City, UT 84115

Asociación Latinoamericana de Utah
1900 South Berkeley Street
Salt Lake City, UT 84108

Hispanic Affairs Office
27 C Street
Salt Lake City, UT 84103

Somos
250 Bell Plaza
Salt Lake City, UT 84130

Utah Governor's Office on Hispanic Affairs
324 South State 500
Salt Lake City, UT 84111

Utah Hispanic Chamber of Commerce
56 East 800 South
Salt Lake City, UT 84111

Virginia

Círculo Hispánico
11300 Foxtrail Lane
Blacksburg, VA 24060

Club España
2756 Hyson Lane
Falls Church, VA 22043

Club Hispano Americano de Tidewater
507 Earl Street
Norfolk, VA 23503

Hispanic Committee of Virginia
5827 Columbia Pike, Second Floor
Falls Church, VA 22041

Hispanic Cultural Society of Virginia
6705 West Scott Road
Falls Church, VA 22042

Hogar Hispano
915 South Wakefield Street
Arlington, VA 22204

Rincón de España
PO Box 9895
Virginia Beach, VA 23452

La Sociedad Hispánica
Randall Hall
University of Virginia
Charlottesville, VA 22903

Washington

America's Institute of Art, History and Culture
PO Box 80114
Seattle, WA 98108

National Hispanic Coalition
1601 Lind Avenue SW
Renton, WA 98055

Organización de Latinoamericanos
Washington State University
Pullman, WA 99164-4011

Spanish Club of WA
PO Box 214
Hamilton Hill, WA 98225

Wisconsin

Centro Hispano
1321 East Mifflin Street, No. 200
Madison, WI 53703

Club Español
2810 West Highland Avenue
Milwaukee, WI 53208

Hispanic Chamber of Commerce of Wisconsin
816 West National Avenue
Milwaukee, WI 53204

Ibero-American Studies Center
University of Wisconsin
Van Hise Hall
Madison, WI 53706

Milwaukee Council for the Spanish Speaking
614 West National Avenue
Milwaukee, WI 53204

Spanish Center
1212 57th Street
Kenosha, WI 53140

Wyoming

Latin American Club
265 Dillon Avenue
Cheyenne, WY 82007

Holidays and Festivals

January

ARIZONA

Tucson: Baile de las Flores, on the 30th.

NEW MEXICO

San Ildefonso: San Ildefonso Fiesta, on the 23rd.

February

ARIZONA

Apache Junction: Burro Derby, on the 21st.
Phoenix: Dons Club Travelcade (horse tour to different state towns), during February and March.

Prescott: Official raising of the Avenue of Flags, on the 14th.
Scottsdale: Parada del Sol, during the first 10 days.
Tucson: Fiesta de los Vaqueros, on the third weekend.

CALIFORNIA

Monterey: Baile de los Cascarones, at the Civic Club.

FLORIDA

Boca Raton: Fiesta de Boca Raton, last 10 days of the month.
Punta Gorda: Commemoration of the landing of Ponce de León, during the first fortnight.
Tampa: Gasparilla Pirate Festival, first fortnight of the month.

TEXAS

Brownsville: Charro Days, end of the month
Harlingen: Fiesta Turista, end of the month.
Mission: Texas Citrus Fiesta, first 10 days of the month.

March

ARIZONA

Phoenix: World's Championship Rodeo of Rodeos, second week of the month.

CALIFORNIA

El Cajon: El Cajon Rodeo, last week of the month.
Hemet: De Anza Cavalcade, first week of the month.
San Juan Capistrano Mission: Fiesta de las Golondrinas, in the middle of the month, usually on St. Joseph's Day.

FLORIDA

Bradenton. De Soto Celebrations, in the middle of the month.
Hollywood: Tropical Fiesta, last week of the month.
Miami: Carnival Miami/Calle Ocho.
New Port Richey: Chasco.
Tampa: Latin American Fiesta, in Ybor City, second week of the month.

MISSISSIPPI

Gulfport: Heritage Parade, during the month.

TEXAS

McAllen: Spring Fiesta, second week of the month.

April

ARIZONA

Bullhead City: Burro Days, last Saturday of the month.
Tucson: Fiesta de la Placita, during the month.
Tucson (San Xavier del Bac Mission): San Xavier Fiesta, on the Friday after Easter Sunday.

CALIFORNIA

Lakewood: Pan-American Week, around the 14th.
Los Angeles: Blessing of the Animals in the Old Plaza, on the 19th.
San Francisco: Día de las Américas.

FLORIDA

Bradenton: Florida Heritage Festival.
St. Augustine: Easter Week Festival, Easter Week.

GEORGIA

Columbus: Miss Columbus Pageant, on the 24th and 25th.

IOWA

Des Moines: Mexico Week, April 7–11.

LOUISIANA

New Orleans: Pan-American Days, around the 14th.

NEW MEXICO

Santa Fe: Performance in Spanish of the play *La Pasión*, Holy Week.

OREGON

Portland: Cinco de Mayo Festival, April 30–May 3.

RHODE ISLAND

Providence: New England Latin American Film Festival.

TEXAS

Corpus Christi: Holy Week Celebrations, Holy Week.
El Paso: "First Thanksgiving Ever Held by Explorer Juan de Oñate," end of the month.
Raymondsville: Onion Fiesta and Rio Grande Music Festival, during the month.
San Antonio: Fiesta San Antonio, third week of the month.
San Antonio: Performance in Spanish of the play *La Pasión*, in San José Mission, Holy Week.

May

ARIZONA

Nogales: Fiestas de Mayo Celebrations, first week of the month.
Phoenix: Fiestas de Mayo Celebrations, first week of the month.

CALIFORNIA

King City: Corpus Christi Fiesta, on Corpus Christi Day.
Lompoc: La Purísima "Fiesta Pequeña," on the 17th.
Monterey: Adobe Tour of Monterey, first week of the month.
San Antonio de Padua Mission: Corpus Christi Fiesta, on Corpus Christi Day.
San Francisco: Cinco de Mayo Celebration, first days of the month.
Santa Barbara: Rancheros Visitadores Trek (horse tour to the valley of Santa Inez), during the month.
Vacaville: Fiesta Days, second fortnight.

FLORIDA

Crestview: Old Spanish Trail Festival.
Immokalle: Cinco de Mayo.
New Smyrna Beach: Seaside Fiesta, during the month.

ILLINOIS

Chicago: Cinco de Mayo Festival, first days of the month.

LOUISIANA

Gonzales: East Ascension Strawberry Festival, on the 11th and 12th.

MISSISSIPPI

D'Iberville: Gulf Coast Hispanic Cultural Society Dance, the 10th.

NEW MEXICO

Albuquerque: Corpus Christi Procession, on Corpus Christi Day.
Taos (Los Cordovas): San Isidro Fiesta, on the 15th.

OHIO

Toledo: Day of the two Toledos, end of the month.

TEXAS

Dallas: Cinco de Mayo Fiesta, first days of the month.
Fort Worth: Casa Mañana Musicals, from the end of the month until the beginning of September.

June

ARIZONA
Tubac: San Juan Day Celebrations, on the 23rd and 24th.

CALIFORNIA
San Antonio de Padua Mission: Animal Fiesta, on the 14th.
San Fernando: Fiesta, first week of the month.
San Francisco: Celebration of the landing of the first settlers to the city on June 27, 1776.

FLORIDA
Fernandina Beach: Fiesta of Eight Flags, second week of the month.
Pensacola: Fiesta of Five Flags.
St. Augustine: Commemoration of the "Night Watch," on the 17th.

GEORGIA
Columbus: Festival Days, third week of the month.

IDAHO
Ketchum: Basque Festival, second fortnight.

MINNESOTA
Montevideo: Fiesta Days Celebration, 26th to 28th.

NEW MEXICO
Albuquerque: New Mexico Arts and Crafts Fair (exhibition and demonstrations by craftspeople showing the Spanish, Indian and North American cultures), end of the month.
Sandia Indian Pueblo: Fiesta in honor of San Antonio, on the 13th.
San Juan Pueblo: St. John's Festival, on the 24th.
Santa Fe: La Fiesta de la Reconquista. Procession to the Rosario Chapel, second fortnight.
Taos: Fiesta de la Loma, on the 12th.

NORTH CAROLINA
Beaufort: Reenactment of Spanish Invasion in 1747, on the 27th.
Cherokee: Theatrical performance of *Unto These Hills*, from the end of June until the beginning of September.

OHIO
Cleveland: Parade the Circle Celebration, the 13th.

TEXAS
Goliad (Presidio La Bahía): Gálvez Fiesta and Spanish Nightwatch, first days of the month.
Llano: Llano County Rodeo, first days of the month.
San Antonio: Fiesta Noche del Rio, from the beginning of the month until the end of August.

July

CALIFORNIA
Chula Vista: Fiesta de la Luna, first fortnight.
Monterey: Paisano El Toro Boat Races, first week.
Oceanside: Old Mission Fiesta, Mission San Luis Rey, on the 25th and 26th.
San Clemente: La Cristianita Fiesta (commemorating the first baptism in California), the closest weekend to the 21st.
San Diego: Trek to the Cross, honoring Father Junípero Serra, first fortnight (Festival of the Bells).
San Juan Bautista: Fiesta Rodeo, first fortnight.

COLORADO
Durango: Spanish Trails Fiesta, end of the month.
Leadville: World's Championship Pack Burro Race, end of the month.

DISTRICT OF COLUMBIA
Festival of American Folklife, first days of the month.

MICHIGAN
Detroit: Latin American Festival, last days of the month.

NEVADA
Ely: Basque Dance and Picnic, second fortnight.

NEW MEXICO
Cochiti Pueblo: Fiesta, on the 14th.
Las Vegas: Old Town Spanish Fiesta, on the 4th.
Taos: Spanish Colonial Fiesta, on the 25th and 26th.

TEXAS
El Paso: El Paso Festival, first days of the month.

August

CALIFORNIA
Aptos: Cabrillo Music Festival, second fortnight.

Lake Tahoe: Fun in the Sun Fiesta, from the 12th to the 15th.

Petaluma: Old Adobe Days, from the 15th to the 23rd.

San Antonio Mission: Junípero Serra Day, on the 23rd.

Santa Barbara: Old Spanish Days Fiesta, in the middle of the month.

COLORADO
Fort Collins: Historical Pageant, from the 6th to the 8th.

Norwood: San Miguel Fair and Rodeo, first fortnight.

IDAHO
Boise: Basque Festival, in the middle of the month.

MARYLAND
Salisbury: Salisbury Latino Festival, the 29th.

MASSACHUSETTS
Boston: Dominican Festival, August 14–16.

Worcester: Latin American Festival, August 16–17.

MINNESOTA
Minneapolis: Resource Fair for the Latino Family, the 22nd.

MISSOURI
Callao: Harvest Fiesta, second fortnight.

MONTANA
Red Lodge: Festival of Nations, third week.

NEVADA
Elko: Basque Festival, first fortnight.

NEW MEXICO
Isleta Pueblo: San Agustín Fiesta, on the 28th.

Santa Clara Pueblo: Fiesta, on the 12th.

Santo Domingo Pueblo: Corn Dance and Fiesta, on the 4th.

Zia Pueblo: Assumption Day Fiesta, on the 15th.

NORTH CAROLINA
Charlotte: Miss Reina Latina Cultural Gala, August 1.

September

CALIFORNIA
Aptos: Cabrillo National Monument, Cabrillo Festival, September 27–October 4

San Diego: San Diego Harbor Days, second fortnight.

San Diego: Taste of Old Town, the 19th.

San Francisco: Cine Latino! Film Festival, September 16–20 and 25–27.

San Francisco: A Mexican Presence, September 4–November 1.

Ventura: Fiesta de La Marina, first fortnight.

HAWAII
Honolulu: Hawaii International Latin Music Festival, Labor Day weekend.

MICHIGAN
Grand Rapids: Hispanic Festival, September 11–13.

NEVADA
Port Arthur: Mexican Heritage Fiesta.

Las Vegas: Festival de Diez y Seis de Septiembre, on the 16th.

NEW JERSEY
Atlantic City: Festival Latino Americano, September 12–13.

NEW MEXICO
Laguna Pueblo: Fiesta, on the 19th.

Santa Fe: Santa Fe Fiesta, first weekend.

Taos: Annual Taos Pueblo Fiesta, on the 29th and 30th.

NEW YORK
Syracuse: The Spanish Mosaic, September 19–20.

OKLAHOMA
Stillwater: National Hispanic Heritage Month, on the 20th.

TENNESSEE
Germantown: Grand National Championship Pino Fino Horse Show, September 24–28.

TEXAS
Austin: Salsa Music Festival, the 6th.

Eagle Pass: Fall Fiesta, in the middle of the month.

Port Arthur: Mexican Heritage Fiesta, September 12–13.

San Antonio: Diez y Seis de Septiembre, September 12–15.

San Antonio: Noche Mexicana, on the 12th.

October

CALIFORNIA

Bodega Bay: Discovery Day Celebration, 3rd and 4th.
Culver City: Fiesta La Ballona, first week of the month.
Larkspur: Latino Film Festival, October 28–November 1.
Los Angeles: Port of Los Angeles Fishermen's Fiesta, second fortnight.
San Francisco: Columbus Day, around the 12th.
San Francisco: Día de la Hispanidad, on the 12th.
Santa Clara: Columbus Celebration, first Sunday of the month.
Soledad Mission: Children's Festival, first week.

DISTRICT OF COLUMBIA

Discovery Day Celebrations, on the 12th.

FLORIDA

Miami: Hispanic Heritage Festival, during the month.

HAWAII

Honolulu: Hawaii Hispanic Festival, on the 12th.

KANSAS

Columbus: Miss Columbus Contest, on the 12th.

LOUISIANA

New Orleans: Hispanic Parade, Sunday prior to the 12th.

MONTANA

Columbus: Centennial Day Celebration, on the 12th.

NEW HAMPSHIRE

Manchester: Columbus Day Celebrations, on the 12th.

NEW JERSEY

Asbury Park: Columbus Day Celebration, on the 12th.

NEW MEXICO

Taos: Spanish Village Fiesta, on the 3rd.

NEW YORK

New York City: Columbus Day, around the 12th.
New York City: Spanish Week, week around the 12th. Día de la Hispanidad.

OKLAHOMA

Pawhuska: Heritage Week, beginning of the month.

RHODE ISLAND

Warren: Miss Columbus Day Pageant and Parade, 11th and 12th.

TEXAS

Del Rio: Fiesta de Amistad, closest weekend to the 24th.
San Antonio: Día de la Raza, Festival in the Park, around the 12th.

November

CALIFORNIA

San Diego: Fiesta de la Cuadrilla, first week.

MINNESOTA

St. Paul-Festival of Nations, first week.

NEVADA

Beatty: World's Championship Wild Burro Races, first week.

NEW MEXICO

Tesuque and Jemez Pueblos: St. James Day Fiesta, on the 12th.

TEXAS

Edinburg: Bronco Days, at the end of the month.
Weslaco: Fiesta de Amistad, in the middle of the month.

December

ARIZONA

Scottsdale: Miracle of the Roses Parade (tribute to Our Lady Guadalupe), on the 12th.

CALIFORNIA

Oceanside: "Las Posadas" in the San Miguel Mission, on the 15th.
San Diego (Mission of San Luis Rey): Festival of Our Lady Guadalupe, on the 12th.
San Diego: Old San Diego Posada in the Old Town Plaza, second fortnight.
Santa Barbara: "Las Posadas" in the Mission, on the 22nd.

COLORADO

Denver: Luminarias de Santa Fe, December 12–13.

Denver: Our Lady of Guadeloupe Feast Day, December 12–15.

FLORIDA
Tallahassee: Winter Festival.

IDAHO
Boise: Euzkaldunak's New Year's Dance (at the Basque Center) on the 31st.

NEW MEXICO
Santa Fe: Feast of Our Lady Guadalupe, on the 12th.

Santa Fe: Performance of the plays *Los Pastores* and *Los Tres Reyes Magos* in Spanish and in English, during Christmas time.

Taos: Feast of our Lady Guadalupe, on the 12th.

TEXAS
Laredo: Christmas Fiestas, starting on the 16th.

San Antonio: Performance of the play *Los Pastores* in Spanish, in San José Mission, during Christmas time.

NOTE: The Spanish names of the fiestas are the ones that are officially used.

MEDIA

Periodicals Published in Spanish
(NOTE: Some periodicals listed here are bilingual.)

Alaska
Hispanic Resource Directory
(biannually)
Denali Press
PO Box 021535
Juneau, AK 99802-1535

Arizona
Ave Fenix de Arizona
(bimonthly)
PO Box 398
Glendale, AZ 85311

Bahía del Sol
(quarterly)
1209 A First Avenue
Phoenix, AZ 85003

Buen Dinero
(weekly)
1730 North Tucson Boulevard
Tucson, AZ 85716

Novedades
(weekly)
111 South Church Avenue, No. 200
Tucson, AZ 85004

Revista Unidos
(weekly)
1715 East Washington
Phoenix, AZ 85034

Sin Fronteras
(weekly)
1690 North Stone Avenue, No. 108
Tucson, AZ 85021

El Sol
(weekly)
8986 North Central, Suite 206
Phoenix, AZ 85020

Arkansas
El Sol de Arkansas
(weekly)
1001 East Walnut, No. 5A
Rogers, AR 72756

California
Adelante!
(monthly)
125 Imperial Street
Oxnard, CA 93030

El Aguila
(weekly)
PO Box 42116
Los Angeles, CA 90042

Ahora Now Newspaper
(weekly)
675 East San Ysidro Boulevard
San Diego, CA 92173

El Americano
(monthly)
Society of Ibero American Writers of the USA
453 South Spring Street, Suite 1202
Los Angeles, CA 90013

El Avisador
(weekly)
1722 Junction Avenue East
San Jose, CA 95112

El Aviso
(weekly)
8101 Long Beach Boulevard, No. L
South Gate, CA 90280

El Bohemio News
(biweekly)
3133 22nd Street
San Francisco, CA 94110

Calendario
(monthly)
1317 North San Fernando Boulevard, No. 246
Burbank, CA 91504

Caminos Magazine
(monthly)
421 North Avenue 19, Fourth Floor
Los Angeles, CA 90031

El Chicano Newspaper
(weekly)
PO Box 827
Colton, CA 92324

Conquista
(monthly)
PO Box 80244
San Marino, CA 91108

El Diario de Los Angeles
(daily)
2300 South Broadway
Los Angeles, CA 90007

Directorio Hispanos de California
(biannually)
PO Box 8220
Santa Rosa, CA 95407-1220

Eastern Group Publications
(weekly)
PO Box 33803
Los Angeles, CA 90033

Eastside Journal
(weekly)
5420 North Figueroa Street
Los Angeles, CA 90041

Enfoque, In Focus
(weekly)
Park Plaza Hotel
607 South Park View Street
Los Angeles, CA 90057

Entre Nosotros
(three times per year)
Sigma Delta Pi
(attn: Professor I. R. M. Galbis)
PO Box 55125
Riverside, CA 92517

Excelsior
(weekly)
915 Katella Avenue
Anaheim, CA 92805

Familia Latina
(monthly)
421 North 19th Avenue, Fourth Floor
Los Angeles, CA 90031

La Gente de Aztlán
(bimonthly)
UCLA
308 Westwood Plaza
112-D Kerckhoff Hall
Los Angeles, CA 90024

La Guía de TV en Español
(weekly)
14654 Oxnard Street
Van Nuys, CA 91411

El Heraldo Católico
(five times per year)
5890 Newman Court
Sacramento, CA 95819

Hispanic Business
(monthly)
360 South Hope Avenue, Suite 300C
Santa Barbara, CA 93105

Hispanic Conventioneer
(annually)
421 North 19th Avenue, Fourth Floor
Los Angeles, CA 90031

Hispanic News de California
(weekly)
1436 South La Cienaga Boulevard
Los Angeles, CA 90035

El Hispano
(weekly)
PO Box 2856
Sacramento, CA 95812

Hispanos Unidos
(weekly)
411 West Ninth Avenue
Escondido, CA 92025-5034

Horizontes
(monthly)
466 Collingwood Street
San Francisco, CA 94114

Humanizarte
(quarterly)
2868 Mission Street
San Francisco, CA 94110

El Independiente
(weekly)
6045 Atlantic Boulevard
Maywood, CA 90270

El Informador
(monthly)
1701 Colgate Circle
La Jolla, CA 92037

El Latino
(weekly)
PO Box 550
San Diego, CA 92112

Latino Viewer
(monthly)
2929 19th Street
San Francisco, CA 94110

Legislative Bulletin
(quarterly)
National Hispanic Research Center
2727 West Sixth Street
Los Angeles, CA 90057

El Mensajero
(weekly)
385 Eighth Street, No. 203
San Francisco, CA 94103

El Mercado
(weekly)
1206 East 17th Street, Suite F
Santa Ana, CA 92701

Mr. Teve
(weekly)
3008 Belden Drive
Los Angeles, CA 90068

El Mundo
(weekly)
630 20th Street
Oakland, CA 94612

Mundo Artístico
(weekly)
217 East Alameda Avenue, Suite 211
Burbank, CA 91502

Nacional Guía Cine, Radio y TV
(weekly)
7700 State Street
Huntington Park, CA 90255

Noticias del Mundo
(daily)
1301 West Second Street
Los Angeles, CA 90026

Novedades
(weekly)
1241 South Soto, No. M 203
Los Angeles, CA 90023

Nuestra Gente
(daily)
16027 Ventura Boulevard, No. 340
Encino, CA 91432

Nuestro Tiempo
(special section of *Los Angeles Times*)
(monthly)
Times Mirror Square
Los Angeles, CA 90053

La Nueva Prensa
(bimonthly)
1170 Burnett Avenue, No. H
Concord, CA 94520

El Nuevo Tiempo
(weekly)
715 Anacapa Street, Drawer 1359
Santa Barbara, CA 93102

El Observador
(weekly)
PO Box 1990
777 North First Street, Suite 420
San Jose, CA 95112

La Oferta Review
(weekly)
3146 Bilbo Drive
San Jose, CA 95121

La Opinión
(daily)
411 West Fifth Street
Los Angeles, CA 90013

Los Padrinos
(monthly)
Los Padrinos of Southern California
Box 479
San Bernardino, CA 92402

Pesca y Marina
(bimonthly)
527 North Las Palmas Avenue
Los Angeles, CA 90004

El Popular Spanish Newspaper
(weekly)
5512 South Union Avenue
Bakersfield, CA 93307

La Prensa de Los Angeles
(weekly)
1505 Gardens Avenue
Glendale, CA 91204

La Prensa de San Diego
(weekly)
1950 Fifth Avenue
San Diego, CA 92101

La Prensa Hispana
(weekly)
730 South Central, No. 209
Glendale, CA 91204

La República
(weekly)
415 North Abbey Street
Fresno, CA 93721

La Revista
(monthly)
1436 South Main Street
Los Angeles, CA 90015

Saludos Hispanos
(six times per year)
19510 Ventura Boulevard, Suite 204
Tarzana, CA 91356

El Sol
(monthly)
727 West 27th Street
Los Angeles, CA 90007

El Sol
(weekly)
230 Capitol Street
PO Box 1610
Salinas, CA 93901

El Sol del Valle
(bimonthly)
718 N Street
Sanger, CA 93657

El Sol Latino
(weekly)
1015 West First Street, Suite B
Santa Ana, CA 92703

El Tiempo
(weekly)
3526 Stockton Boulevard
Sacramento, CA 95814

El Tiempo Latino
(weekly)
3288 21st Street, No. 9
San Francisco, CA 94110

Tiempo Latino
(weekly)
2595 Mission Street, Suite 300
San Francisco, CA 94110

30 de Mayo
(weekly)
1824 Sunset Boulevard, No. 202
Los Angeles, CA 90026

Vida
(weekly)
2520 Miramonte Drive
Oxnard, CA 93030

La Voz
(weekly)
685 West Mission Boulevard
Pomona, CA 91766

La Voz Libre
(weekly)
3107 West Beverly Boulevard, Suite 1
Los Angeles, CA 90057

Colorado

El Semanario
(weekly)
2865 West 44th Avenue
Denver, CO 80211

La Voz Hispana de Colorado
(weekly)
2885 West Third Avenue
Denver, CO 80219

Connecticut

Desarrollo Nacional
(monthly)
15 Ketchum Street
Westport, CT 06881

Qué Pasa
(monthly)
115 Bedford Street
Hartford, CT 06120

El Reportero
(monthly)
50 Fitch Street, Second Floor
New Haven, CT 06515

La Revista Aquino
(monthly)
PO Box 15760
Stamford, CT 06901

La Voz Hispana de Connecticut
(biweekly)
32 Elm Street
New Haven, CT 06510

Delaware

Hoy
(monthly)
PO Box 593
Georgetown, DE 19947

District of Columbia

Americas Magazine
(bimonthly)
Organization of American States (OAS)
Administration Building, Third Floor
19th Street and Constitution Avenue NW
Washington, DC 20850

Caminando
(quarterly)
Casa del Pueblo
1459 Columbia Road NW
Washington, DC 20009

Enlace
(quarterly)
400 C Street NW
Washington, DC 20002

Gaceta Iberoamericana
(quarterly)
PO Box 9762
Washington, DC 20016

Hispanic
(monthly)
111 Massachusetts Avenue NW, Suite 410
Washington, DC 20001

Hispanic Link
(weekly)
1420 N Street NW
Washington, DC 20005

Hispanic Review of Business
(10 times a year)
PO Box 75418
Washington, DC 20013

El Latino
(weekly)
PO Box 43284
Washington, DC 20010

The Reporter
(quarterly)
1030 15th Street NW
Washington, DC 20005

Florida

Aboard
(bimonthly)
777 41 Street
PO Box 40-2763
Miami Beach, FL 33140

Ahora
(monthly)
4048 SW 94 Street
Miami, FL 33156

Alerta
(monthly)
426 SW Eighth Street, Suite 6
Miami, FL 33130

Boletín de FESELA
(Federación Sefaradí Latinoamericana)
(monthly)
1200 Normandy Drive
Miami Beach, FL 33141

The Broward Latino
(bimonthly)
2613 West Davie Boulevard
Fort Lauderdale, FL 33312

Buenhogar
(biweekly)
6355 NW 36th Street
Virginia Gardens, FL 33166

El Clarín
(monthly)
8900 SW 107th Avenue, No. 306
Miami, FL 33176

Cosmopolitan en Español
(monthly)
6355 NW 36th Street
Virginia Gardens, FL 33166

4 Tiempos
(six times per year)
5600 SW 135 Avenue, Suite 110-A
Miami, FL 33183

Customs Business
(monthly)
170 NE 214th Street
North Miami Beach, FL 33172

Diario de la Mujer
(daily)
Box 14-5393
Coral Gables, FL 33114-5393

Diario Las Américas
(daily)
2900 NW 39th Street
Miami, FL 33142

Erotica
(monthly)
6360 NE Fourth Court
Miami, FL 33138

Espada de España Newsletter
(quarterly)
42 Spanish Street
St. Augustine, FL 32084

El Especial
(weekly)
175 Fontainebleau Boulevard
Miami, FL 33144

Estrella de Florida
(weekly)
2613 West Davie Boulevard
Fort Lauderdale, FL 33312

Exito
(weekly)
8323 NW 12th Street, No. 212
Miami, FL 33126

Foto-Pimienta
(monthly)
6360 NE Fourth Court
Miami, FL 33138

La Gaceta
(weekly)
PO Box 5536
Tampa, FL 33675

Geomundo
(monthly)
6355 NW 36th Street
Virginia Gardens, FL 33166

Golazo
(weekly)
2613 West Davie Boulevard
Fort Lauderdale, FL 33312

Harper's Bazaar en Español
(monthly)
6355 NW 36th Street
Virginia Gardens, FL 33166

El Heraldo de Broward
(biweekly)
2613 West Davie Boulevard
Fort Lauderdale, FL 33312

Hombre del Mundo
(monthly)
6355 NW 36th Street
Virginia Gardens, FL 33166

El Latino Semanal
(weekly)
4325 Georgia Avenue
West Palm Beach, FL 33405

Mecánica Popular
(monthly)
6355 NW 36th Street
Virginia Gardens, FL 33166

Miami Mensual
(monthly)
265 Sevilla Avenue
Coral Gables, FL 33134

Mi Casa
(weekly)
1800 W 49th Street, Suite 121
Hialeah, FL 33012

La Nación
(weekly)
1393 SW First Street, Suite 205
Miami, FL 33135

El Nuevo Herald
(daily)
3191 Coral Way
Miami, FL 33145

Nuevo Siglo
(weekly)
7137 North Armenia Avenue, No. B
Tampa, FL 33604-5250

Panorama Metropolitano
(bimonthly)
285 NW 27th Avenue, Suite 19
Miami, FL 33135

La Prensa
(weekly)
395 North Orange Avenue
Orlando, FL 32801

La Prensa Gráfica
(weekly)
293 SW 27th Avenue
Miami, FL 33135

Réplica
(monthly)
2994 NW Seventh Street
Miami, FL 33125

El Sol de Hialeah
(weekly)
436 Palm
Hialeah, FL 33012

Spanish Today
(monthly)
7751 SW 32 Court
Miami, FL 33165

Sweetwater Tribune
(weekly)
10702 SW Sixth Street, Apartment 1
Miami, Fl 33174

Tenis Mundo
(bimonthly)
PO Box 145456
Coral Gables, FL 33114

Tiles Newsletter
(quarterly)
635 Mariner Way
Altamonte Springs, FL 32701-5420

Tú
(monthly)
6355 NW 36th Street
Virginia Gardens, FL 33166

Turismo Latino
(six times a year)
PO Box 34-3106
Coral Gables, FL 33134

TV y Novelas
(biweekly)
6355 NW 36th Street
Virginia Gardens, FL 33166

Vanidades Continental
(monthly)
6355 NW 36th Street
Virginia Gardens, FL 33166

La Voz
(Catholic Archdiocese)
(bimonthly)
9401 Biscayne Boulevard
Miami Shores, FL 33138

La Voz Informativa (de Ecuador)
(quarterly)
585 East 49th Street, Suite 18-412
Hialeah, FL 33013

Georgia

Mundo Hispánico
(monthly)
1275 Goodwin Road NE
Atlanta, GA 30324

El Nuevo Día
(biweekly)
3754 Burford Highway, A-4
Atlanta, GA 30329

Hawaii

Hawaii Hispanic News
(biweekly)
500 University Avenue, No. 1803
Honolulu, HI 96826

Idaho

El Centinela
(monthly)
1350 Kings Road
Nampa, ID 83653

Informe
(quarterly)
417 North Curtis
Boise, ID 83706

La Voz de Idaho
(monthly)
PO Box 490
Caldwell, ID 83606

Illinois

Applause/Aplauso
(monthly)
3918 West North Avenue
Chicago, IL 60647

El Cometa
(bimonthly)
4744 South Loomis Boulevard
Chicago, IL 60602

El Día
(weekly)
4818 West 23rd Place
Chicago, IL 60650

Exito
(monthly)
820 North Orleans Street, No. 400
Chicago, IL 60610-3051

Extra Publications
(weekly)
3918 West North Avenue
Chicago, IL 60647

El Heraldo
(weekly)
3734 West 26th Street
Chicago, IL 60623

Industria Avícola
(monthly)
Sandstone Building
Mount Morris, IL 61054

Industrias Lácteas
(bimonthly)
5725 East River Road, Suite 825
Chicago, IL 60631

El Informador
La Voz
Impacto
El Imparcial
(weeklies)
3653 West 26th Street, Suite 3
Chicago, IL 60623

Latino
(quarterly)
Latino Institute
228 South Wabash, Sixth Floor
Chicago, IL 60604

El Mañana
(five times per week)
2700 South Harding Avenue
Chicago, IL 60623

Mundo Hispano
(weekly)
2350 South Cicero Avenue
Cicero, IL 69804

Panadero Latinoamericano
(bimonthly)
5725 East River Road
Chicago, IL 60631

La Raza Newspaper
(weekly)
3909 North Ashland Avenue
Chicago, IL 60613

Success/Exito
(annual)
3918 West North Avenue
Chicago, IL 60647

Tele Guía
(weekly)
PO Box 23133
Chicago, IL 60623

Indiana

Estrella Hispana
(monthly)
22 East Washington, Suite 316
Indianapolis, IN 46204

El Sol
(annually)
404 South Walnut Street, Second Floor
South Bend, IN 46619

La Voz
(quarterly)
2905 Calhoun Street
Fort Wayne, IN 46807

Iowa

El Nahuatzen
(quarterly)
University of Iowa
310 Calvin Hall
Iowa City, IA 55242

Kansas

Radio y Televisión
(six times yearly)
9221 Quvira Street
Shawnee Mission, KS 66215

Tinta e Hilo
(weekly)
9800 Metcalf
Overland Park, KS 66121-2215

Kentucky

Estrella de Esperanza
(monthly)
Highway 72
Crockett, KY 41413

Louisiana

Aquí New Orleans
(monthly)
4324 Veterans Boulevard, No. 205
Metairie, LA 70006

Mensaje
(monthly)
PO Box 1817
Kenneth, LA 70063

Qué Pasa New Orleans?
(bimonthly)
PO Box 8399
New Orleans, LA 70182

Revista Internacional
(monthly)
World Trade Center
2 Canal Street
New Orleans, LA 70130

Maryland

El Mensajero
(monthly)
205 East Joppa Road, No. 2502
Towson, MD 21204

El Pregonero
(weekly)
5001 Eastern Avenue
Hyattsville, MD 20782

Prensa Hispana
(monthly)
8519 Piney Branch Road
Silver Spring, MD 20901

La Tertulia
(bimonthly)
Casa de España
2508 Old North Point Road
Baltimore, MD 21229

Massachusetts

Mundo
(weekly)
20 Columbia Street
Cambridge, MA 02139

La Semana
(weekly)
911 Massachusetts Avenue
Boston, MA 02118

El Universal
(weekly)
1738 Washington Street
Boston, MA 02118

Michigan

El Central
(weekly)
4124 West Vernor
Detroit, MI 48209

El Renacimiento
(monthly)
1132 North Washington Avenue
Lansing, MI 48906

El Vocero Hispano
(every 10 days)
1119 Burton SE
Grand Rapids, MI 49509

La Voz
(bimonthly)
560 Hall South West
Grand Rapids, MI 49503

Minnesota

Visiones de la Raya
(monthly)
2025 Nicollet Avenue South
Minneapolis, MN 55408

El Xicano
(monthly)
340 East Lake Street, No. 7
Minneapolis, MN 55408

Mississippi

Enlace
(three times a year)
AATSP
Lee Hall 218, Box 6349
Mississippi State University
Mississippi State, MS 39762

Hispania
(quarterly)
AATSP
Mississippi State University
PO Box 6349
Mississippi State, MS 39762-6349

Missouri

Daily World/La Palabra Diaria
(monthly)
1901 NW Blue Parkway
Unity Village, MO 64065-0001

Dos Mundos Newspaper
824 Southwest Boulevard
Kansas City, MO 64108

Nebraska

El Hispano
(weekly)
PO Box 814
1110 North Adams Street
Lexington, NE 68850

Nevada

Ahora
(biweekly)
30 Mary Street, No. 2
PO Box 3582
Reno, NV 89509

Ahora Spanish News
(twice a year)
PO Box 3582
Reno, NV 89505

El Mundo
(weekly)
15 North Mojave
Las Vegas, NV 89101

New Jersey

Ahora
(weekly)
409 39th Street
Union City, NJ 07087

Avance
(weekly)
1803 Manhattan Avenue
Union City, NJ 07087

El Especial
(weekly)
510 Bergenline Avenue
Union City, NJ 07087

La Información
(weekly)
PO Box 587
Perth Amboy, NJ 08861

Mensaje
(weekly)
614 Franklin Street
Elizabeth, NJ 07206-1211

La Tribuna
(bimonthly)
PO Box 805
300 36th Street
Union City, NJ 07087

La Tribuna de North Jersey
(bimonthly)
PO Box 902
Newark, NJ 07101

La Voz
948 Elizabeth Avenue
Elizabeth, NJ 07201

New Mexico

El Crepúsculo News
(weekly)
PO Box U-11
Guadalupe Plaza
Taos, NM 87571

La Herencia del Norte
(monthly)
PO Box 22576
900 Park Avenue SW
Albuquerque, NM 87102

El Hispano News
(weekly)
PO Box 986
900 Park Avenue SW
Albuquerque, NM 87102

The Taos News
(weekly)
PO Box U
Taos, NM 87571

New York

Artes/Export Grafics USA
(quarterly)
399 Conklin Street, 306
Farmingdale, NY 11735

The Buniness Link
(quarterly)
350 Fifth Avenue, Suite 3514
New York, NY 10118

Canales
(monthly)
215 West 92nd Street, Suite 1E
New York, NY 10025

Deportista Hispano
(monthly)
PO Box 188
Jackson Heights, NY 11372

El Diario/La Prensa
(daily)
143 Varick Street
New York, NY 10013

Futbol en el Mundo
(monthly)
1212 37th Avenue
Long Island, NY 11101

Hola
(annually)
29-28 41st Avenue
Long Island City, NY 11101

Impacto, The Latin News
(weekly)
853 Broadway, Suite 811-E
New York, NY 10003

Latina Publications
(monthly)
1500 Broadway, No. 600
New York, NY 10036

Listín USA
(weekly)
250 West 100th Street, No. C-104
New York, NY 10025

Noticias del Mundo
(six days per week)
401 Fifth Avenue
New York, NY 10016

Qué pasa New York?
(weekly)
7201 Grand Avenue
Maspeth, NY 11378-1525

Reader's Digest en Español
(monthly)
200 Park Avenue
New York, NY 10166

Reportero Industrial
(monthly)
150 Great Neck Road
Great Neck, NY 10017

Revista Aérea Latinoamericana
(10 times yearly)
310 East 44th Street, Suite 1601
New York, NY 10017

Revista Maryknoll
(monthly)
Maryknoll Fathers
Maryknoll, NY 10520

Sugar y Azúcar
(biweekly)
25 West 45th Street
New York, NY 10036

El Tiempo
(weekly)
37-37 88 Street
Jackson Heights, NY 11372

Tiempos del Mundo
(weekly)
401 Fifth Avenue, Third Floor
New York, NY 10016

La Tribuna Hispana USA
(weekly)
PO Box 186
Hempstead, NY 11550

La Voz Hispana
(weekly)
159 East 116th Street
New York, NY 10029

North Carolina

El Informativo Latino
(monthly)
322 Hawthorne Lane
Charlotte, NC 28204

Ohio

Albricias
Reading Community High School
810 East Columbia
Cincinnati, OH 45215-4806

El Nuevo Día
(monthly)
6516 Deteroit Avenue, No. 4
Cleveland, OH 44102

Oklahoma

El Nacional
(monthly)
304 SW 25th Street
Oklahoma City, OK 73109

Oregon

El Hispanic News
(weekly)
2044 East Burnside
Portland, OR 97207

Pennsylvania

La Actualidad
(weekly)
4953 North Fifth Street
Philadelphia, PA 19120

El Directorio Hispano
(weekly)
850 Lancaster Avenue
Reading, PA 19607

El Hispano
(weekly)
8605 West Chester Park
Upper Darby, PA 19082

Rhode Island

La Nueva Visión
(monthly)
342 Veazle Street
Providence, RI 02904

Nuevos Horizontes
(weekly)
508 Dexter Street
Central Falls, RI 02863

Shoreline en Español
(weekly)
560 York Avenue
Pawtucket, RI 02861

South Carolina

La Bobina
(bimonthly)
PO Box 1986
Columbia, SC 29202

Tennessee

Información Punto Inicial
(quarterly)
5820 Labrador Lane
Antioch, TN 37013

Texas

La Buena Suerte
(weekly)
6065 Hillcroft, No. 400
Houston, TX 77081

El Continental
(daily)
2300 East Yandell
PO Box 1950
El Paso, TX 79903

Del Rio News-Herald
(daily)
321 South Main
Del Rio, TX 78840

El Editor
(weekly)
PO Box 1250
Lubbock, TX 79401

La Estrella
(weekly)
Box 1870
Ft. Worth, TX 76101

El Heraldo de Brownsville
(daily)
PO Box 351
Brownsville, TX 78520

The Hispanic News
(monthly)
349 St. Cloud
San Antonio, TX 78201

La Información
(weekly)
6065 Hillcroft, No. 400
Houston, TX 77081

La Información Mundial
4010 Blue Bonnet Boulevard
Houston, TX 77025

Laredo Morning Times
(daily)
111 Esperanza Drive
Laredo, TX 78041

Latin American Music Review
(biannually)
University of Texas Press
PO Box 7819
Austin, TX 78713

El Mundo
(bimonthly)
3201 East Cesar Chavez Street, No. B
Austin, TX 78702

El Mundo
(weekly)
3130 SW Freeway, Suite 508
Houston, TX 77098

La Prensa de San Antonio
(weekly)
13 Lexington Avenue
San Antonio, TX 78205-1312

El Sol de Houston
(weekly)
3130 Navigation Boulevard
Houston, TX 77003

El Sol de Texas
(weekly)
4260 Spring Valley Road
Dallas, TX 75244

La Verdad
(weekly)
910 Franscisca Street
Corpus Christi, TX 78405

La Voz de Houston
(weekly)
7819 Easton
Houston, TX 77017

Utah

Mundo Latino
(weekly)
840 West North Temple
Salt Lake City, UT 84116

La Voz Hispana de Utah
(quarterly)
324 State Street, No. 500
Salt Lake City, UT 84111

Virginia

Crónica
(weekly)
6231 Leesburg Pike, No. 416
Falls Church, VA 22044

El Eco de Virginia
(monthly)
101 West Plume Street, Fourth Floor
Norfolk, VA 23510

Washington

The Hispanic News
(weekly)
2318 Second Avenue
Seattle, WA 98121

El Mundo
(weekly)
PO Box 2231
Wenalchee, WA 98807

La Voz
(10 issues per year)
157 Yesler Way, No. 400
Seattle, WA 98104

Wisconsin

Nosotros
(monthly)
2430 Independence Lane, No. 103
Madison, WI 53704-3545

Spanish Journal
(weekly)
238 Wisconsin Avenue, No. 306
Milwaukee, WI 53203

Periodicals That Highlight Hispanic History and Culture

AHA! Hispanic Arts News
Association of Hispanic Arts
(monthly)
173 East 116 Street, Second Floor
New York, NY 10029
(Hispanic arts: painting, music, etc.)

Alaluz: Revista de Poesía, Narración y Ensayo
(2 times/year)
Department of Spanish and Portuguese
University of California
Riverside, CA 92521
(Contemporary Hispanic literature and poetry)

Alba de América: Revista Literaria
(2 times/year)
Instituto Literario y Cultural Hispánico
8452 Furman Avenue
Westminster, CA 92683
(Spanish and Latin American literature)

Albricias
(quarterly)
Sociedad Honoraria Hispánica
6328 North Troy Street
Chicago, IL 60659
(Literature)

America
(weekly)
106 West 56th Street
New York, NY 10014
(General subject, published by the Jesuits)

American Heritage
(bimonthly)
60 Fifth Avenue
New York, NY 10011
(Historical subject, published by the American Heritage
    Publication Company, in collaboration with the
    American Association for State and Local History)

The American Hispanist
(nine times per year)
Box 64
Clear Creek, IN 47426
(General subject)

The American Historical Review
(quarterly)
400 A Street SE
Washington, DC 20003
(Historical subject, published by the American Historical
    Association)

Américas
(6 times/year)
19th and Constitution Avenue NW
Washington, DC 20006
(Latin American culture, art, history)

Americas
(monthly)
Pan American Union
Washington, DC 20006
(General subject, published in English and in Spanish
    by the Organization of American States)

The Americas
(quarterly)
Academy of American Franciscan History
PO Box 5966
Washington, DC 20014
(Historical subject, published by Franciscan Friars)

The Americas Review
(3 times/year)
Arte Público Press
University of Houston
4800 Calhoun
Houston, TX 77204
(Create literature and art by Hispanic Americans)

Americas Society
(monthly)
680 Park Avenue
New York, NY 10029
(Latin American literature and art)

Anales de la Literatura Española Contemporánea
(1–3 times/year)
Department of Spanish and Portuguese
University of Colorado
McKenna Language Building, Box 278
Boulder, CO 80309-0278
(Literature of 20th-century Spain)

Anales Galdosianos
(annual)
645 Commonwealth Avenue
Boston University
Boston, MA 02215
(Literary subject)

Anuario Medieval
(annually)
Department of Modern Foreign Languages and Classical
    Studies
St. John's University
Grand Central and Utopia Parkways
Jamaica, NY 11439
(Medieval literature)

Apoyo
(6 times/year)
Asociación para la Conservación del Patrimonio Cultural
    de las Américas
PO Box 76932
Washington, DC 20013
(Latin American culture)

Archives of American Art Journal
(quarterly)
Archives of American Art
Smithsonian Institution
41 East 65th Street
New York, NY 10021
(Artistic subject)

Arkansas Historical Quarterly
(quarterly)
Arkansas Historical Association
History Department
University of Arkansas
Fayetteville, AR 72701
(Historical subject)

Aztlán: A Journal of Chicano Studies
Chicano Studies Research Center
(2 times/year)
University of California–Berkeley
405 Hilgard Avenue
Los Angeles, CA 90024
(On the Chicano experience)

Basque Studies Program Newsletter
(biannually)
Basque Studies Program
University of Nevada
Reno, NV 89557
(Basque culture and people)

The Bilingual Review/La Revista Bilingüe
(3 times/year)
Hispanic Research Center
Arizona State University
Tempe, AZ 85287-2702
(U.S. Hispanic literature)

Boletín de la Academia Iberoamericana des Poesía–Capítulo de Nueva York
(quarterly)
Box 183
Teachers College, Columbia University
New York, NY 10027
(Peninsular and Latin American literature)

Boletín de la Academia Norteamericana de la Lengua Española
GPO 349
New York, NY 10116
(Literary subject)

Boletín de Artes Visuales
(yearly)
Museum of Modern Art–Latin American
AOS 1889 F Street NW
Washington, DC 20006
(Latin American art)

Boletín del CEPI
(quarterly)
Círculo de Escritores y Poetas
Iberoamericanos de Nueva York
PO Box 831, GPO Station
New York, NY 10116
(Peninsular and Latin American literature)

Books Abroad
(quarterly)
Oklahoma University Press
Norman, OK 73069
(Literary subject)

Brújula/Compass
(quarterly)
Instituto de Escritores Latinoamericanos
Eugenio María de Hostos County College
Bronx, NY 10451
(Peninsular and Latin American literature; U.S. Hispanic literature)

Bulletin of the Cantigueiros de Santa María
(annually)
Department of Spanish and Italian
University of Kentucky
Lexington, KY 40506
(Medieval literature)

Bulletin of the Comediantes
(2 times/year)
Department of Spanish and Portuguese
University of California–Riverside
Riverside, CA 92521-0222
(Spanish Renaissance and Baroque drama)

The Business Link
(quarterly)
Spain-U.S. Chamber of Commerce
350 Fifth Avenue, Suite 3514
New York, NY 10118
(Commercial subject)

California History
(quarterly)
2090 Jackson Street
San Francisco, CA 94109
Historical subject, published by the California Historical Society)

Californian Historian
(quarterly)
University of the Pacific
Stockton, CA 95211
(Historical subject, published by the Conference of California Historical Society)

La Campana
(quarterly)
Santa Barbara Trust for Historic Preservation
123 East Cañon Perdido Street
Santa Barbara, CA 93102
(Historical subject)

El Campanario
(quarterly)
The Texas Old Mission and Forts Restoration Association
524 North 22nd Street
Waco, TX 76707
(Historical subject)

Catholic Historical Review
(quarterly)
Catholic University of America Press
Michigan Avenue, NE
Washington, DC 20017
(Historical subject, published by the American Catholic Historical Association)

Celestinesca
(biannually)
Attn: Professor Joseph Snow
Department of Romance Languages
University of Georgia
Athens, GA 30602
(Literary subject)

Cervantes: Bulletin of the Cervantes Society of America
ASB 170, University of Florida
Gainesville, FL 32611
(Literary subject)

Chasqui: Revista de Literatura Latinoamericana
(2 times/year)
4048 JKHB
Brigham Young University
Provo, UT 84602
(Latin American literature)

Chiricú
(annually)
Chicano-Riqueño Studies
Ballantine Hall 849
Indiana University
Bloomington, IN 47405
(Latin American literature and poetry)

Chronicles of Oklahoma
(quarterly)
Oklahoma Historical Society Building
2100 North Lincoln Boulevard
Oklahoma City, OK 73103
(Historical subject)

Cincinnati Romance Review
(annually)
Department of Romance Languages
University of Cincinnati
Cincinnati, OH 45221
(Romance literatures and languages)

Círculo, Revista de Cultura
(annually)
Círculo de Cultura Panamericano
16 Malvern Place
Verona, NJ 07044-2554
(Spanish American and Spanish literature)

Coloquio, Revista Cultural Hispana
(monthly)
PO Box 11572
Baltimore, MD 21229-0572
(Spanish and Latin American literature and culture)

The Colorado Heritage
(quarterly)
State Historical Society of Colorado
1300 Broadway
Denver, CO 80203
(Historical subject)

Comparative Literature Studies
(quarterly)
Illinois University
Urbana, IL 61801
(Literary subject)

Confluencia: Revista Hispánica de Cultura y Literatura
(2 times/year)
Department of Hispanic Studies
University of Northern Colorado
Greeley, CO 80639
(Spanish and Spanish American culture and literature)

Crítica Hispánica
(2 time/year)
Duquesne University
Department of Modern Languages
Pittsburgh, PA 15282
(Spanish and Spanish American literature and linguistics)

Crítica Hispánica
(several times per year)
Box 24302
East Tennessee State University
Johnson City, TN 37614
(Literary subject)

La Crónica
(quarterly)
Historical Society of New Mexico
PO Box 5819
Santa Fe, NM 87502
(Historical subject)

*La Crónica: Spanish Medieval Language and Literature Journal
and Newsletter*
(biannaully)
Department of Languages
153 OSH
University of Utah
Salt Lake City, UT 84112
(Literary subject)

Cuadernos de ALDEEU
(2 times/year)
Graduate School and University Center of the City
University of New York
Ph.D. Program in Hispanic and Luso-Brazilian Literatures
33 West 42 Street
New York, NY 10036
(Spanish and Spanish American literature and culture)

Cuban Heritage
(quarterly)
Cuban Exile History and Archives Project
Florida International University
University Park
Miami, FL 33199
(Dedicated to the Cuban heritage)

De Soto Plume
(quarterly)
De Soto Historical Society
Box 523
Mansfield, LA 71052
(Historical subject)

Despacho del Presidio de San Diego
(monthly)
The San Diego Historical Society
PO Box 10248
Old San Diego Station
San Diego, CA 92110
(Dedicated to the history of California)

*Dieciocho: Hispanic Enlightenment, Aesthetics, and Literary
Theory*
(2 times/year)
53 King Charles Lane
Newton, PA 18940-2312
(Hispanic Enlightenment)

Dispositio, Revista de Semiótica Literaria
(several times per year)
Attn: Professor Walter Mignolo
Department of Romance Languages
University of Michigan
Ann Arbor, MI 48109
(Literary subject)

The East Florida Gazette
(quarterly)
The St. Augustine Historical Society
271 Charlotte Street
St. Augustine, FL 32084
(Historical subject)

East Texas Historical Journal
(quarterly)
Box 6223, SFA Station
Nacogdoches, TX 75962
(Historical subject)

Encuentro
(2 times/year)
Latin American Institute
University of New Mexico
801 Yale NE
Albuquerque, NM 87131
(Latin American literature)

Los Ensayistas
(annually)
Department of Romance Languages
University of Georgia
Athens, GA 30602
(Art of the essay; Hispanic thought)

Entre nosotros
(annually)
Revista Oficial de la Sociedad Nacional
Honoraria Hispánica Sigma Delta Pi
The Citadel
171 Moultrie Street
Charleston, SC 29409
(Spanish and Latin American literature and culture)

Escandalar
(several times per year)
Hampton Street
Elmhurst, NY 11373
(Literary subject)

El Escribano
(annually)
The St. Augustine Historical Society
271 Charlotte Street
St. Augustine, FL 32084
(Historical subject)

Estreno: Cuadernos de Teatro Español Contemporáneo
(2 times/year)
Pennsylvania State University
350 North Burrowes Building
University Park, PA 16802
(20th-century Spanish theater)

Explicación de Textos Literarios
(periodically)
Department of Spanish and Portuguese
California State University
Sacramento, CA 95819
(Literary subject)

Five Hundred
(bimonthly)
Five Hundred Publishing Group
1550 Madruga Avenue, Suite 503
Coral Gables, FL 33146

Florida Historical Quarterly
(quarterly)
Florida Historical Society
University of Florida
Box 14045, University Station
Gainesville, FL 32604-2045
(Historical subject)

Florida State Museum Newsletter
(monthly)
University of Florida
Gainesville, FL 32611
(Historical subject)

García Lorca Review
(periodically)
Foreign Language Department
State University College
Brockport, NY 14420
(Literary subject)

Georgia Historical Quarterly
(quarterly)
Georgia Historical Society
501 Whitaker Street
Savannah, GA 31401
(Historical subject)

Gestos: Teoría y Práctica del Teatro Hispánico
(2 times/year)
Department of Spanish and Portuguese
University of California
Irvine, CA 92717
(Spanish, Latin American and Mexican American theater)

Glosas
Academia Norteamericana de la Lengua Española
606 Gateway Valley
Cottage, NY 10989

Gulf Coast Historical Review
(biannually)
History Department
Humanities Building
University of South Alabama
Mobile, AL 36688
(Historical subject)

Handbook of Latin American Studies
(annually)
University of Florida
Gainesville, FL 83611
(Bibliographic subject, containing all aspects of Latin America prepared by the Library of Congress, Washington, D.C.)

Harvard Studies in Romance Languages
(annually)
Department of Romance Languages and Literatures
Harvard University
Cambridge, MA 02138
(Romance languages)

Hemisphere
(three times per year)
Latin American and Caribbean Center
Florida International University
Miami, FL 33199
(American subjects)

Hispamérica: Revista de Literatura
(3 times/year)
5 Pueblo Court
Gaithersburg, MD 20878
(Spanish American literature)

Hispania
(4 times/year)
Editorial Office
Georgetown University
Box 571112
Washington, DC 20057
(Spanish, Spanish American, Portuguese, and Brazilian literature, language, linguistics, pedagogy)

The Hispanic American Historical Review
(quarterly)
Duke University Press
Box 5697, College Station
Durham, NC 27706
(Historical subject)

Hispanic American Report
(monthly)
Hispanic American Studies
Stanford University
Stanford, CA 94305
(General subject, particularly containing political aspects
    of the Hispanic countries)

Hispanic Journal
(biannually)
Department of Foreign Languages and Literatures
Sutton Hall
Indiana, PA 15705
(Literary subject)

Hispanic Linguistics
(2 times/year)
Department of Spanish and Portuguese
34 Folwell Hall
9 Pleasant Street SE
University of Minnesota
Minneapolis, MN 55455
(Interlinguistic studies that focus on Hispanic language)

Hispanic Review
(quarterly)
Department of Romance Language
University of Pennsylvania
Philadelphia, 14114
(Literary subject)

Hispanofilia
(three times a year)
Department of Romance Languages
University of North Carolina
Chapel Hill, NC 27514
(Literary subject)

Historic Preservation
(quarterly)
National Trust for Historic Preservation
1785 Massachusetts Avenue NW
Washington, DC 20036
(Historical subject)

Historical Archaeology
(quarterly)
Society for Historical Archaeology
5000 Marble NE, Room 211
Albuquerque, NM 87110
(Archaeological subject)

History News
(quarterly)
American Association for State and Local History
708 Berry Road
Nashville, TN 37204
(Historical subject)

Horizonte 21
(2 times/year)
Academia Iberoamericana de Poesía
PO Box 9007
McLean, VA 22102-0007
(Spanish and Latin American poetry)

Humanities
(quarterly)
National Endowment for the Humanities
806 15th Street NW
Washington, DC 20506
(Important cultural subjects)

Ideas '92
(quarterly)
Institute of Iberian Studies
Graduate School of International Studies
University of Miami
Coral Gables, FL 33124
(Subjects related with the anniversary of the fifth
    centennial of the discovery of America)

Ideologies and Literatures
(six times per year)
Folwell Hall
9 Pleasant Street
University of Minnesota
Minneapolis, MN 55455
(Literary subject)

Inter-American Review of Bibliography
(annually)
Organization of American States
1889 F Street NW
Washington, DC 20006
(Hispanic culture)

INTI
(biannually)
Department of Modern Languages
Providence College
Providence, RI 02918
(Literary subject)

The Journal of Arizona History
(quarterly)
Arizona Historical Society
949 East Second Street
Tucson, AZ 85719
(Historical subject)

Journal of Hispanic Philology
(three times per year)
Department of Modern Languages
Florida State University
Tallahassee, FL 32306
(Literary subject)

Journal of Interamerican Studies and World Affairs
(quarterly)
Institute of Interamerican Affairs
University of Miami
Box 248123
Coral Gables, FL 33124
(International political subject)

Journal of Interdisciplinary Literary Studies/Cuadernos Interdisciplinarios de Estudios Literarios
(2 times/year)
The Latino Review Books
University of Albany, SUNY
Albany, NY 12222
(Hispanic literature and culture)

Journal of Mississippi History
(quarterly)
Mississippi Historical Society
Mississippi State Department of Archives
100 South State Street
Jackson, MS 39201
(Historical subject)

Journal of Southern History
(quarterly)
Southern Historical Association
Department of History
University of Georgia
Athens, GA 30602
(Historical subject)

Journal of the Society of Basque Studies in America
(annually)
47 Stemway Road
Trumbull, CT 06601
(Basque scholarship, including literature, linguistics, ethnology, folklore and history)

Kansas History
(quarterly)
Kansas State Historical Society
120 West 10th Street
Topeka, KS 66612
(Historical subject)

Kentucky Heritage
(quarterly)
Kentucky Historical Society
300 West Broadway
Frankfort, KY 40601
(Historical subject)

Kentucky Romance Quarterly
(quarterly)
University of Kentucky
Lexington, KY 40506
(Literary subject)

Latin American Literary Review
(2 times/year)
2300 Palmer Street
Pittsburgh, PA 15218
(Latin American literature and the arts)

Latin American Theatre Review
(2 times/year)
Center of Latin American Studies
University of Kansas
Lawrence, KS 66045
(Theater and drama of Spanish and Portuguese America)

Lectura y vida
(annually)
International Reading Association
800 Barksdale Road
PO Box 8139
Newark, DE 19714-8139
(Spanish and Latin American culture)

Letras Femeninas
(biannually)
Box 10023
Lamar University
Beaumont, TX 77710
(Literary subject)

Letras Femeninas
(2 times/year)
Department of Modern Languages
University of Nebraska–Lincoln
111 Oldfather Hall
Lincoln, NE 68588-0315
(Hispanic feminism)

Letras Peninsulares
(3 times/year)
Department of Romance and Classical Languages
Michigan State University
East Lansing, MI 48824-1027
(Peninsular Spanish literature from the 18th century through the present)

Linden Lane Magazine
(3 times/year)
PO Box 331964
Fort Worth, TX 76163
(Spanish and Latin American literature)

Louisiana History
(quarterly)
Louisiana Historical Association
203 Carondolet Street
New Orleans, LA 70130
(Historical subject)

Lucero: A Journal of Iberian and Latin American Studies
(annually)
Department of Spanish and Portuguese
University of California–Berkeley
Berkeley, CA 94720
(Hispanic and Loso-Brazilian literature, linguistics and history)

Luz en arte y literatura
(2 times/year)
Luz Bilingual Publishing
PO Box 57062
Tarzana, CA 91357
(Spanish and Latin American literature)

Mester
(quarterly)
Department of Spanish and Portuguese
University of California
Los Angeles, CA 90024
(Literary subject, published by graduate students)

The Miami Jewish Tribune
(weekly)
3550 Biscayne Boulevard, Suite 600
Miami, FL 33137
(Referring to the Jews and the Sephardics)

Mississippi Valley Collection Bulletin
(quarterly)
Memphis State University
Memphis, TN 38152
(Historical subject)

Missouri Historical Review
(quarterly)
State Historical Society of Missouri
Hitt and Lowry Streets
Columbia, MO 65201
(Historical subject)

MLN (Modern Language Notes)
(Dedicating an issue each year to Spanish, Italian, French and German literature)
The Johns Hopkins University Press
Baltimore, MD 21218
(Literary subject)

Modern Drama
(quarterly)
University of Kansas
Lawrence, KS 66045
(Literary subject)

Modern International Drama
(biannually)
University of Pennsylvania
Philadelphia, PA 19104
(Literary subject)

Modern Language Studies
(4 times/year)
Department of English
Box 1852
Brown University
Providence, RI 02912
(Romance languages, literatures and linguistics)

Modern Philology: A Journal Devoted to Research in Medieval and Modern Literature
(4 times/year)
University of Chicago
1050 East 59th Street
Chicago, IL 60637
(Spanish and Latin American literature)

Modern Philosophy
(quarterly)
University of Chicago
Chicago, IL 60637
(Literary subject)

Monographic Review/Revista Monográfica
(annually)
Box 8401
University of Texas of the Permian Basin
Odessa, TX 79762-0001
(Spanish and Latin American literature and culture)

National Geographic Society
(monthly)
PO Box 2895
Washington, DC 20013
(Cultural subject with predominance of geographic
    attention)

Nebraska History
(quarterly)
Nebraska State Historical Society
1500 R Street
Lincoln, NE 68508
(Historical subject)

New Mexico Quarterly
(quarterly)
University of New Mexico
Albuquerque, NM 87131
(Literary subject)

New York History
(quarterly)
New York State Historical Association
Lake Road, Route 80
Cooperstown, NY 13326
(Historical subject)

The North Carolina Historical Review
(quarterly)
Division Archives and History
109 East Jones Street
Raleigh, NC 27611
(Historical subject)

*North Carolina Studies in the Romance Languages and
    Literatures*
(annually)
Department of Romance Languages
Campus Box 3170
University of North Carolina
Chapel Hill, NC 27599
(Spanish and Latin American literature)

Noticias Quarterly
(quarterly)
Santa Barbara Historical Society
Old Mission
136 East De La Guerra Street
Santa Barbara, CA 93101

Ojáncano: Revista de Literatura Española
(2 times/year)
Department of Romance Languages
University of Georgia
Athens, GA 30602
(18th-, 19th-, 20th-century Spanish literature)

Oklahoma Heritage
(quarterly)
Oklahoma Heritage Association
201 NW 14th Street
Oklahoma City, OK 73103
(Historical subject)

Ollantay Theater Magazine
(annually)
Ollantay Center for the Arts
PO Box 636
Jackson Heights, NY 11372
(Latin American Theater)

Oregon Historical Quarterly
(quarterly)
Oregon Historical Society
1230 SW Park Avenue
Portland, OR 97205
(Historical subject)

The Pacific Historian
(quarterly)
University of the Pacific
Stockton, CA 96211
(Historical subject, published by the Pacific Center for
    Western Studies)

Pacific Historical Review
(quarterly)
University of California
Los Angeles, CA 90007
(Historical subject, published by the Pacific Southern
    Coast Branch of the American Historical Association)

La Palabra: Revista de Literatura Chicana
(2 times/year)
1616 Westchester Drive
Tempe, AZ 85283
(Chicano literature)

El Palacio
(quarterly)
Museum of New Mexico
Palace of Governors
Santa Fe, NM 87501
(Archaeological subject)

PMLA
(five times per year)
10 Astor Place
New York, NY 10003
(Literary subject, published by the Modern Language Association of America)

Prologue: The Journal of the National Archives
Eighth and Constitution Avenue
Washington, DC 20408
(Historical subject, referring to the archives deposits)

Report on the Americas
(annually)
North American Congress on Latin America
475 Riverside Drive, No. 454
New York, NY 10115
(Latin American culture)

Review of Latin American Studies
(2 times/year)
Latin American Studies Center
Arizona State University
Tempe, AZ 85287-2401
(Latin American literature and history)

Revista de Estudios Hispánicos
(3 times/year)
Washington University
One Brookings Drive
St. Louis, MO 63130-4899
(Spanish and Spanish American language)

Revista Hispánica Moderna
(quarterly)
Hispanic Institute in the U.S.A.
Columbia University
612 West 116th Street
New York, NY 10027
(Literary subject in English and Spanish)

Revista Iberoamericana
(4 times/year)
312 Cathedral of Learning
University of Pittsburgh
Pittsburgh, PA 15260
(Iberoamerican literature and culture)

Revista Iberoamericana de Ciencias Sociales
(quarterly)
Pan American Union
Washington, DC 20006
(About social sciences, published in Spanish by the Organization of American States)

Revista Interamericana de Bibliografía
(quarterly)
Pan American Union
Washington, DC 20006
(Bibliographic subject, referring to all the branches of knowledge, published in Spanish by the Organization of the American States)

Revista Literaria Iberoamericana
(annually)
Department of Languages and Literatures
California State University
Los Angeles, CA 90032
(Latin American literature and history)

Romance Linguistics & Literature Review
(annually)
359 Royce Hall, UCLA
405 Hilgard Avenue
Los Angeles, CA 90024-1532
(Romance linguistics and literature)

Romance Notes
(biannual)
Department of Romance Language
North Carolina University
Chapel Hill, NC 27514
(Literary subject)

Romance Philology
(quarterly)
University of California Press
Berkeley, CA 94720
(Literary subject, dedicated to the Romance languages)

Romanic Review
(quarterly)
University of Columbia
New York, NY 10027
(Dedicated to subjects related to Romance literature)

The San Antonio Conservation Society Newsletter
(monthly)
San Antonio Conservation Society
107 King William
San Antonio, TX 78209
(Referring to Texas)

Sea History
(quarterly)
National Maritime Historical Society
2 Fulton Street
New York, NY 11201
(Historical maritime subject)

Selecta: Journal of the Pacific Northwest Council on Foreign Languages
(annually)
Department of Foreign Languages
Campus Box 8067
Idaho State University
Pocatello, ID 83209
(Spanish and Latin American literature, linguistics and culture)

La Semana
(weekly)
778 Dudley Street
Boston, MA 02125

Sephardic Bulletin Yeshiva University
(quarterly)
500 West 185th Street
New York, NY 10033
(Referring to Sephardics)

Sephardic Highlights
(monthly)
515 Park Avenue Suite 515
New York, NY 10022
(Referring to Sephardics)

The Sephardic Home News
(monthly)
2266 Cropsey Avenue
Brooklyn, NY 11214
(Referring to Sephardics)

Sephardic Views International
(monthly)
2667 Coney Island Avenue
Brooklyn, NY 11223
(Referring to Sephardics)

Siglo XX/20th Century
(2 times/year)
Department of Spanish and Portuguese
University of Colorado
McKenna Languages Building
Campus Box 278
Boulder, CO 80309-0278
(20th-century Spanish and Latin American literature)

Sister City News
(six times a year)
120 South Payne Street
Alexandria, VA 22314
(About sister cities)

Smithsonian
(monthly)
Smithsonian Institution
100 Jefferson Drive
Washington, DC 20560

South Carolina Historical Magazine
(quarterly)
South Carolina Historical Society
100 Meeting Street
Charleston, SC 29401
(Historical subject)

Southern California Quarterly
(quarterly)
Historical Society of Southern California
200 East 43 Avenue
Los Angeles, CA 90031
(Historical subject, with special reference to the southern area of California)

Southwestern Historical Quarterly
(quarterly)
SRH2-308 University Station
Austin, TX 78712
(Historical subject, published by the Texas State Historical Association)

Studies in Romance Languages
(annually)
Department of Spanish and Italian
University of Kentucky
Patterson Tower
Lexington, KY 40506-0027
(Romance languages and literatures)

Sunland Tribune, The Journal of Tampa Historical Society
(monthly)
245 Hyde Park Avenue
Tampa, FL 33606
(Historical subject)

Symposium: A Quarterly Journal in Modern Foreign Literatures
(4 times/year)
210 H. B. Crouse Hall
Syracuse University
Syracuse, NY 13244-1160
(Modern foreign literatures)

Tennessee Historical Quarterly
(quarterly)
Tennessee Historical Society
War Memorial Building
Nashville, TN 37219
(Historical subject)

Texas People
(quarterly)
The Institute of Texan Cultures
Hemisphere Plaza
San Antonio, TX 78294
(Referring to Texas)

The Texas Quarterly
(quarterly)
University of Texas
Austin, TX 78712
(General subject, especially regarding Texas)

Texas Studies in Literature and Language
(quarterly)
University of Texas
Austin, TX 78712
(Literary subject)

Times Gone By
(quarterly)
San Diego Historical Society
PO Box 10571
San Diego, CA 92110
(Historical subject, published in the place where
    California was born and dedicated to the state)

Tinta
(annually)
Department of Spanish and Portuguese
University of California at Santa Barbara
Santa Barbara, CA 93106
(Hispanic and Luso-Brazilian literature)

Tropos
(annually)
Michigan State University
East Lansing, MI 48824-1112
(Spanish and Latin American literature and history)

University of South Florida Language Quarterly
(quarterly)
University of South Florida
Tampa, FL 33620
(Literary subject)

U.S. Catholic Historian
(quarterly)
United States Catholic Historical Society
c/o Seminary of St. Joseph
Dunwoodie
Yonkers, NY 10704
(Historical subject)

Vista
(weekly)
999 Ponce de León Boulevard, Suite 600
Coral Gables, FL 33134
(Contemporary matters)

Radio and Television Stations That Broadcast in Spanish

NOTE: The following stations broadcast more than 100 hours per week. Some of these stations broadcast in Spanish and English.

Television Stations

ARIZONA

KDRX Channel 64
4001 East Broadway, No. B-11
Phoenix, AZ 85040

KHRR Channel 40
2921 East Broadway
Tucson, AZ 85716

KTVW Channel 33
3019 East Southern Avenue
Phoenix, AZ 85040

CALIFORNIA

Buena Visión Cable Televisión
912 North Eastern
Los Angeles, CA 90063

Eco/Galavisión
2121 Avenue of the Stars
Los Angeles, CA 90067

KBNT Channel 19
5764 Pacific Center Boulevard, No. 110
San Diego, CA 92121

KCBA Channel 35
PO Box 3560
Salinas, CA 93912

KCSO Channel 19
2942 Iowa Avenue
Modesto, CA 95351

KDTV 14
2200 Palou Avenue
San Francisco, CA 94124

KFTV Channel 21
3239 West Ashlan Avenue
Fresno, CA 93711

KFTV Hanford
3239 West Ashlan Avenue
Fresno, CA 93711

KMEX-TV Channel 34
6701 Center Drive West
Los Angeles, CA 90045

KNTV 11
645 Park Avenue
San Jose, CA 95110

KSCI Channel 18
1954 Cotner Avenue
Los Angeles, CA 92410
or
280 I Street
San Bernardino, CA 92410

KSTS-TV 48
2349 Bering Drive
San Jose, CA 95131

KVEA-TV Channel 52
1139 Grand Central Avenue
Glendale, CA 91201

XETV Channel 6
8253 Ronson Road
San Diego, CA 92111

XHAS Channel 13
6048 Cornerstone Court West, No. A
San Diego, CA 92121

COLORADO

K11SF Austin
Box 255
Evergreen, CO 80439

K54CQ Fort Collins
Box 255
Evergreen, CO 80439

KSBS Channel 24
2701 Alcott Street, No. 391
Denver, CO 80211

CONNECTICUT

WRDM Channel 13
886 Maple Avenue
Harford, CT 06114

DISTRICT OF COLUMBIA

W14AA Channel 14
5151 Wisconsin Avenue, NW, Suite 303
Washington, DC 20016

WZGS Channel 64
2000 North 14th Street, No. 480
Arlington, VA 22201

FLORIDA

WHRS Channel 42
505 South Congress Avenue
Boyton Beach, FL 33426

WINK Channel 11
2824 Palm Beach Boulevard
Ft. Myers, FL 33901

WLTV Channel 23
9405 NW 41 Street
Miami, FL 33178-2301

WSCV Channel 51
2100 Coral Way
Miami, FL 33145

W61BL
2942 West Columbus Drive, Suite 204
Tampa, FL 33607

GEORGIA

W67CI-TV Channel 67
5901 Goshen Springs Road
Norcross, GA 30070

ILLINOIS

W46AR Channel 46
26 North Halsted Street
Chicago, IL 60661

WCIU Channel 60
552 North Broadway
Chicago, IL 60604

WSNS-TV
430 West Grant Place
Chicago, IL 60614

MARYLAND

WMDO Channel 48
962 Wayne Avenue, No. 900
Silver Spring, MD 20910

MASSACHUSETTS

WUNI Channel 27
33 Fourth Avenue
Needhma, MA 02194

NEVADA

K47CO Channel 47
961 Matley Lane, No. 130
Reno, NV 89502

NEW JERSEY

WNJU Channel 47
47 Industrial Avenue
Teterboro, NJ 07608

WXTV Channel 41
Twinbridge Plaza
24 Meadowland Parkway
Secaucus, NJ 07094-2904

NEW MEXICO

KGSW Channel 14
2017 San Mateo NE
Albuquerque, NM 87110

KLUZ Channel 41
2725 F Broadbent Parkway NE
Albuquerque, NM 97107-1635

NEW YORK

WNJU Channel 47
1740 Broadway
New York, NY 10019

WXTV Channel 41
605 Third Avenue
New York, NY 10158-0118

OKLAHOMA

WPRV-TV
PO Box 1887
Muskogee, OK 74401

PENNSYLVANIA

WTGI TV Channel 61
520 North Columbus Boulevard
Philadelphia, PA 19123

TEXAS

KFWD-TV
1720 Regal Row
Dallas, TX 75235

KGBS Channel 65
3307 Northland Drive, No. 175
Austin, TX 78731

KINT Channel 26
5426 North Mesa
El Paso, TX 79912

KORO Channel 28
The 600 Building
Corpus Christi, TX 78401

KTMD-TV Galveston
3903 Stoney Brook
Houston, TX 77063

KUVN-TV
6015 Commerce Drive, Suite 440
Dallas, TX 75063

KWEX Channel 41
411 East Durango
San Antonio, TX 78204

SATV Channel 17
600 Augusta
San Antonio, TX 78215

WASHINGTON

KCTS Channel 9
401 Mercer
Seattle, WA 98901

WISCONSIN

K46AE TV
509 West Wisconsin Avenue
Milwaukee, WI 53203

Radio Stations

ARIZONA

KNOG-FM 91.1
PO Box 1614
150 West First Street
Nogales, AZ 85621

KPHX
824 East Washington Street
Phoenix, AZ 85034

KSUN
714 North Third Street
Phoenix, AZ 85004

KVVA
1641 East Osborne Road, Suite 8
Phoenix, AZ 85016

KVVA-FM
1641 East Osborne Road, Suite 8
Phoenix, AZ 85016

KXEW
889 El Puente Lane
Tucson, AZ 85713

KXMG-FM
889 El Puente Lane
Tucson, AZ 85713

ARKANSAS

KZRA-FM 1599
70 North East Street, No. 100
Fayetteville, AR 72701

CALIFORNIA

KAFY
1527 19th Street
Bakersfield, CA 93301

KALI
5723 Melrose Avenue
Hollywood, CA 90038

KBRG-FM
39111 Paseo Padre Parkway
Fremont, CA 94538

KCAL
29800 Greenspot Road
East Highlands, CA 92346

KCTY
190 Natividad Road
Salinas, CA 93906

KDIF
1465-A Spruce Street
Riverside, CA 92507

KGST
1900 Mariposa Mall, Suite 121
Fresno, CA 93721

KGZO-FM 90.9
PO Box 504
McFarland, CA 93250

KHOT
219 1/2 Yosemite Avenue
Madera, CA 93638

KIBG-FM 106.3
PO Box 2838
Merced, CA 95344-0838

KIQI
2601 Mission Street
San Francisco, CA 94110

KJOP
15279 Hanford-Armona Road
Lemoore, CA 93245

KLFA-FM
124 North Second Street
King City, CA 93930

KLOB-FM 94.7
41601 Corporate Way
Palm Desert, CA 92260-1986

KLOC
1303 10th Street
Modesto, CA 95353

KLOQ
705 West Main Street
Merced, CA 95340

KLVE-FM
1645 North Vine Street
Los Angeles, CA 90028

KNEZ
322 North H Street
Lompoc, CA 93436

KNSE
8720 East Ninth Street
Rancho Cucamonga, CA 91724

KNTO-FM
416 Third Street, Box 248
Livingston, CA 95334

KOXR
418 West Third Street
Oxnard, CA 93030

KQVO-FM
2300 Imperial Avenue, Suite 1
Box 232
Calexico, CA 92231

KRAY-FM
190 Natividad Road
Salinas, CA 93906

KRCX
8642 Quail Lane
Roseville, CA 95678

KSKQ
5700 Sunset Boulevard
Los Angeles, CA 90028

KSKQ-FM
5700 Sunset Boulevard
Los Angeles, CA 90028

KSTN-FM
2171 Ralph Avenue
Stockton, CA 95206

KTAP
104 West Chapel Street
Santa Maria, CA 93454

KTNQ
1645 North Vine Street, Suite 200
Los Angeles, CA 90028

KTRO
3434 Dodge Road
Oxnard, CA 93034

KWAC
5200 Standard Street
Bakersfield, CA 93308

KWKW
6777 Hollywood Boulevard, Suite 400
Hollywood, CA 90028

KXEM
Box 326
McFarland, CA 93250

KXEX
2247 West Church
Fresno, CA 93706

KXMX-FM
Security Pacific Bank Building
1060 Fulton Mall
Fresno, CA 93721

KXSP-AM 1590
6150 Olivas Park Drive
Ventura, CA 93003

KZMS-FM 97.1
1620 North Carpenter Road, No. C17
Modesto, CA 95351

KZSJ-AM 1120
2670 South White Road, No. 165
San Jose, CA 95148

COLORADO

KBNO
999 18th Street, Suite 305
North Tower
Denver, CO 80202

KNKN-FM 107.1
30 North Electric Drive
Pueblo West, CO 81007

CONNECTICUT

WDJZ-AM 1530
PO Box 1322
Naugatuck, CT 06770

DELAWARE

WYUS-AM 930
1666 Blairs Pond Road
Milford, DE 19963

FLORIDA

WAMA
5203 North Armenia Avenue
Tampa, FL 33603

WAQI
2960 Coral Way
Miami, FL 33145

WCMQ
1411 Coral Way
Miami, FL 33145

WCMQ-FM
1411 Coral Way
Miami, FL 33145

WOCN
1779 West Flagler
Miami, FL 33135

WONQ-AM 1030
1033 Semoran Boulevard, No. 243
Castleberry, FL 32707

WQBA
2828 Coral Way
Miami, FL 33145

WQBA-FM
2828 Coral Way
Miami, FL 33145

WQBN
3303 West Columbus Drive
Tampa, FL 33607

WRHC
330 SW 27th Avenue
Miami, FL 33184

WSKP-FM 107.9
1001 Ponce de Leon Boulevard
Coral Gables, FL 33134

WSUA
2100 Coral Way
Miami, FL 33145

GEORGIA

WKZD-AM 1330
1864 Thompson Bridge Road
Gainesville, GA 30501

IDAHO

KJHY-FM 101.0
PO Box 4489
Boise, ID 83711

ILLINOIS

WIND
625 North Michigan Avenue
Chicago, IL 60611

WLXX-AM 1200
625 Michigan Avenue
Chicago, IL 60611

WOJO-FM
625 North Michigan Avenue
Chicago, IL 60611

WONX
2100 Lee Street
Evanston, IL 60202

WTAQ
9355 West Joliet Road
La Grange, IL 60525

INDIANA

WRSW-FM 107.3
Box 1448, Times Building
Narsaw, IN 46581

IOWA

KDMI-AM 1460
2350 NE 44th Court
Delaware Township, IA 50317

KANSAS

KIBFN-FM 90.7
105 South Broadway Street, No. 70 S
Wichita, KS 67202-4225

LOUISIANA

WFNO-AM 830
111 Veterans Boulevard, No. 1850
Metarie, LA 70005

MASSACHUSETTS

WUNR-AM 1600
160 North Washington Street
Boston, MA 02114

MARYLAND

WILC
Box 42
Laurel, MD 20707

WMDO-AM 1540
962 Wayne Avenue
Silver Spring, MD 20910

MICHIGAN

WBYW-FM 89.9
Box 2892
3066 Three Mile Road
Grand Rapids, MI 49504

NEVADA

KXTO-AM 1550
101 Washington Street, No. 101
Reno, NV 89506

NEW HAMPSHIRE

WNNW-AM 1110
PO Box 1110
150 Main Street
Salem, NH 03079

NEW MEXICO

KABQ
1400 Central SE, Suite 22200
Albuquerque, NM 87196

KALI-AM 1240
2505 5th St. NW
Albuquerque, NM 87102

KALY
9100 Second Street, NW, Box 10267
Albuquerque, NM 87114

KDCE
403 West Pueblo Road
Española, NM 87533

KIDI
3800 Carlisle NE
Albuquerque, NM 87107

KLMA-FM 96.5
Box 457
108 South Willow
Hobbs, NM 88240

KNUM-FM 95.3
106 South Bullard Street
Silver City, NM 88061

KXKS
1923 San Mateo NE
Albuquerque, NM 87110

NEW YORK

WADO
666 Third Avenue
New York, NY 10017

WJIT
600 Madison Avenue
New York, NY 10021

WKDM
570 Seventh Avenue, Suite 1406
New York, NY 10036

WPAT-FM 93.1
26 West 56th Street
New York, NY 10019

WSKQ
1500 Broadway, 10th Floor
New York, NY 10036

NORTH CAROLINA

WETC-AM 540
1604 U.S. 64
Zebulon, NC 27597

OHIO

WNZN-FM 89.1
9712 State Route 113
Berlin Heights, OH 44814

OKLAHOMA

KTLV-AM 1220
1005 North Main
New Castle, OK 73065

OREGON

KNTA
5410 SW Macadam Avenue, Suite 240
Portland, OR 97201

KWBY-AM 940
1585 North Pacific Highway, No. H
Woodburn, OR 97071

PENNSYLVANIA

WLCH-FM 91.3
30 North Ann Street, Second Floor
Lancaster, PA 17602

RHODE ISLAND

WRCP-AM 1290
1110 Douglas Avenue, North Providence
Providence, RI 02904

SOUTH DAKOTA

KKQQ-FM 102.3
Box 790
111 Main Avenue
Brookings, SD 57006

TEXAS

KAMA
4150 Pinnacle
El Paso, TX 79902

KBDR-FM 100.5
815 Salinas Avenue, No. 1140
Laredo, TX 78040-8012

KBNA
5710 Trowbridge
El Paso, TX 79925

KBNA-FM
570 Trowbridge
El Paso, TX 79925

KBOP
215 North Main
Pleasanton, TX 78064

KBOR
1050 McIntosh
Brownsville, TX 78523

KCCT
701 Benys Road
Corpus Christi, TX 78408

KCOR
1115 West Martin
San Antonio, TX 78207

KCTM-FM
Route 2, Box 103 FM
Rio Grande City, TX 78582

KDSI
Highway 281 North, Box 731
Alice, TX 78333

KEDA
510 South Flores Street
San Antonio, TX 78204

KELG
7524 North Lamar Boulevard, Suite 200
Austin, TX 78752

KEPI-FM 88.7
PO Box 873
Eagle Pass, TX 78853

KEPS
127 Kilowatt Pass Drive
Eagle Pass, TX 78852

KESS
7700 Carpenter Freeway
Dallas, TX 75247

KFHM
501 West Quincy Street
San Antonio, TX 78212

KFLZ-FM
110 East Main Street
Bishop, TX 78343

KGBT
1519 West Harrison
Harlingen, TX 78550

KHER-FM
PO Box 743
Big Wells Highway
Crystal City, TX 78839

KIWW-FM
5621 South Expressway 83
Harlingen, TX 78552

KKHQ-FM
4718 Leopard
Corpus Christi, TX 78408

KKLB-FM 92.5
7524 North Lamar Boulevard, No. 200
Austin, TX 78752

KLAT
1415 North Loop West, Suite 400
Houston, TX 77008

KLFB
2700 Marshall
Lubbock, TX 79415

KLVL
111 North Ennis Street
Houston, TX 77003

KOND-FM 97.1
1980 Post Oak Road
Houston, TX 77056

KQLM-FM 107.9
Box 7319, 1100 Gant B
Odessa, TX 79763

KQQK-FM
5959 West Loop South, No. 444
Bellaire, TX 77401

KQXX-FM
608 South 10th Street
McAllen, TX 78501

KRGT-FM
Route 3, Box 390
Hutto, TX 78634

KRIA
3407 North East Parkway
San Antonio, TX 78218

KSAH
1777 NE Loop 410, Suite 803
San Antonio, TX 78217

KTXZ
3532 Bee Cave Road, Apartment 210
Austin, TX 78746

KUNO
Box 4722
Corpus Christi, TX 78469

KVIV
4180 North Mesa
El Paso, TX 79902

KVOZ
Box 1638
Laredo, TX 78041

KXYZ
2700 East Pasadena Freeway
Pasadena, TX 77506

XEMU
352 Rio Grande, Suite 107
Eagle Pass, TX 78852

XEROK
2100 Trawood Drive
El Paso, TX 79935

XHSG-FM
2100 Trawood Drive
El Paso, TX 79935

UTAH

KRCW-FM 96.3
Box 800, 121 Sunnyside Avenue
Granger, WA 98932

WISCONSIN

KBJX-AM 1460
2310 South Green Bay Road, No. C
Racine, WI 53406

◆ SELECTED READINGS ◆

Andrews, Charles M. *The Colonial Period of American History.* New Haven, Conn.: Yale University Press, 1989.

Angulo, Jaime de. *Cuentos Indios.* Madrid: Editorial Hiperion, 1992.

Armero, Alvaro. *Los españoles en Hollywood.* Madrid: Compañía Literaria, 1995.

Arnade, Charles W. "A Guide to Spanish Florida Source Material." *Florida Historical Quarterly* (1961): 320–325.

Avina, Rose H. *Spanish and Mexican Land Grants in California.* Salem, N.H.: Ayer Company Publishers, 1976.

Bancroft, Caroline. *Colorful Colorado.* Boulder, Colo.: Johnson Publishing Co., 1963.

Bancroft, Hubert Howe. *History of California.* San Francisco: Bancroft Press, 1967.

Bannon, John Francis. *Bolton and the Spanish Borderlands.* Norman: University of Oklahoma Press, 1964.

———. *The Spanish Borderlands Frontier 1513–1825.* New York: Holt, Reinhart & Winston, 1970.

Basque, Joseph. "Law and Order in Texas." *El Campanario* 19, no. 4 (December 1988).

Bauman, J. N. "The Names of the California Missions." *The Americas* XXI, no. 4 (April 1965): 363–374.

Berger, Joseph. *Discoveries of the New World.* New York: American Heritage Publishing Co., 1960.

Bethell, Leslie, ed. *Colonial Spanish America.* New York: Cambridge University Press, 1989.

———. *Spanish America After Independence, 1820–1870.* New York: Cambridge University Press, 1989.

Blackmar, F. *Spanish Colonization in the Southwest.* New York: Gordon Press, 1976.

Bolton, Herbert E. *Colonization of North America, 1492–1783.* New York: Hafner Press, 1971.

———. *The Padre on Horseback.* Chicago: Loyola University Press, 1963.

———. *The Spanish Borderlands.* New Haven, Conn.: Yale University Press, 1919.

Bolton, Herbert E., ed. *Spanish Exploration in the Southwest, 1542–1706.* New York: Barnes & Noble, 1963.

Boscana, Gerónimo. *Life in California During a Residence of Several Years in that Territory, Compromising a Description of the Country and the Missionary Establishments.* New York: Da Capo Press, 1969.

Bourne, Edward Gaylord. *Spain in America, 1450–1580.* New York: Barnes & Noble, 1962.

Boyd, E. *Popular Arts of Colonial New Mexico.* Santa Fe, N.M.: Museum of International Folk Art, 1959.

Boyd, Marke F., Hale G. Smith and John N. Griffin. *Here They Stood.* Gainesville: University of Florida Press, 1951.

Cabeza de Vaca, Alvar Núñez. *Adventures in the Unknown Interior of America.* Trans. and ed. by Cyclone Covey. New York: Collier Books, 1961.

Cardenas, Juan Francisco de. *Hispanic Culture and Language in the United States.* New York: Instituto de las Españas, 1933.

Carter, Hodding. *Doomed Road of Empire: The Spanish Trail of Conquest.* New York: McGraw-Hill, 1963.

Caruso, John Anthony. *The Southern Frontier.* New York: Bobbs-Merril, 1963.

Chadwick, French Ensor. *The Relations of the United States and Spain: The Spanish-American War.* New York: Russell & Russell, 1968.

Chapman, Charles E. *A History of California: The Spanish Period.* New York: Macmillan, 1939.

Cheyney, Edward Potts. *European Background of American History, 1300–1600.* New York: Collier Books, 1961.

Clisby, Arthur Stanley. *Old New Orleans.* New Orleans: Harmanson Publishing, 1962.

Conly, Robert L. "St. Augustine, Nation's Oldest City, Turns 400." *National Geographic* 129, no. 2 (February 1966): 196–229.

Cortes, Carlos E., ed. *Spanish and Mexican Land Grants.* Salem, N.H.: Ayer Company Publishing, 1974.

Crosby, Alfred W. *The Columbian Exchange: Biological and Cultural Consequences of 1492.* Westport, Conn.: Greenwood Press, 1973.

Cubeñas, José Antonio. *Spanish and Hispanic Presence in Florida. The Oliveros House. Two Essays on Florida's Spanish History.* Madrid: Editorial Mensaje, 1979.

Cummings, W. P., et. al. *The Exploration of North America, 1630–1776.* New York: G.P. Putnam's Sons, 1974.

Deakin, Edwin. *California Missions.* Los Angeles: National History Museum of Los Angeles County, 1973.

Deegan, Kathleen. *Spanish St. Augustine.* New York: Academic Press, 1983.

Delaney, Caldwell. *The Story of Mobile.* Mobile, Ala.: Gill Press, 1981.

Demarest, Donald. *The First Californian: The Story of Fray Junipero Serra.* New York: Hawthorn Books, 1963.

De Soto, Hernando. *Narratives of the Career of Hernando de Soto in the Conquest of Florida.* Trans. by Buckingham Smith. New York: Bradford Club, 1866.

De Voto, Bernard. *The Course of Empire.* Boston: Houghton Mifflin, 1960.

Diaz del Castillo, Bernal. *Conquest of New Spain.* New York: Penguin, 1963.

Doran, Barbara. "With De Soto to Tallahassee." *Cuban Heritage* 1, no. 2 (Fall 1987).

Duell, Prent. *Mission Architecture.* Tucson: Arizona Archaeological and Historical Society, 1919.

Dye, David H. "Death March of Hernando De Soto." *Archaelogy* 42, no. 3 (May–June 1989).

Ellis, Bruce T. *The Historic Palace of Governors.* Santa Fe: Museum of New Mexico Press, n.d.

Ellis, John Tracy. "Catholics in Colonial America." *The American Ecclesiastical Review* 136 (January 1957).

Espinosa, Juan Manuel. "Journal of the Vargas Expedition into Colorado, 1694." *Colorado Magazine* XVI, no. 3 (May 1939).

Fernández Florez, Dario. *The Spanish Heritage in the United States.* Madrid: Españolas, 1965.

Fernández-Shaw, Carlos M. "Quixotes North of the Rio Grande." *The Americas* 28, no. 9 (1976).

Fernández y Fernández, Enrique. *Spain's Contribution to the Independence of the United States.* Washington, D.C.: Embassy of Spain in the United States of America, 1985.

Fletcher, F. N. *Early Nevada: The Period of Exploration, 1776–1848.* Reno, Nev.: Carlisle & Co., 1929.

Forrest, Earle R. *Missions and Pueblos of the Old Southwest.* Chicago: Rio Grande Press, 1962.

Foster, George M. *Culture and Conquest: America's Spanish Heritage.* New York: Wenner-Gren Foundation for Anthropological Research, 1960.

Frank, Waldo. *America Hispana: Portrait and Prospect.* New York: Charles Scribner's Sons, 1931.

Fretwell, Jacqueline K. *Clash Between Cultures: Spanish East Florida, 1784–1821.* St. Augustine, Fla.: St. Augustine Historical Society, 1988.

Fuentes, Carlos. *The Buried Mirror: Reflections on Spain and the New World.* Boston: Houghton Mifflin, 1992.

Gann, L. H., and Peter J. Duigan. *The Hispanics in the United States: A History.* Boulder, Colo.: Westview Press, 1986.

Gannon, Michael V. *The Cross in the Sand.* Gainesville: University of Florida Press, 1965.

Garcilaso de la Vega. *The Florida of the Inca.* Trans. and ed. by John G. Varner and Jeanette J. Varner. Austin: University of Texas Press, 1951.

Gibson, Charles. *Spain in America.* New York: Harper & Row, 1968.

Gibson, Charles, ed. *The Black Legend: Anti-Spanish Attitudes in the Old World and the New.* New York: Knopf, 1971.

Gilbert, Charles E. *A Concise History of Early Texas.* Houston: n.p., 1964.

Gongora, M. *Studies in the Colonial History of Spanish America.* New York: Cambridge University Press, 1975.

Greenleaf, Cameron, and Andrew Wallace. "Tucson: Pueblo, Presidio and American City." *Arizoniana* 3, no. 2 (1962): 18–27.

Hafen, Leroy R. *Fort Vasquez.* Denver: State Historical Society of Colorado, 1964.

Hannan, Hans W. *The California Missions.* Garden City, N.Y.: Doubleday, 1953.

Haring, Clarence H. *The Spanish Empire in America.* New York: Harcourt Brace Jovanovich, 1963.

Harrod, Roy. *The Dollar.* London: Macmillan, 1953.

Hawthorne, Hildegarde. *California's Missions.* New York: Appleton-Century, 1942.

Henderson, Bruce E. "Florida and Spain: A Historical and Contemporary Relationship." *Aboard* 12, no. 6 (1988).

Hernández Sánchez-Barba, Mario. *Historia de Estados Unidos.* Madrid: Editorial Marcial Pons, 1998.

Hispanic Community of the County of Los Angeles. *Directory.* 4th ed. Los Angeles: University of Southern California, 1988.

Hispanic Society of America. *Handbook.* New York: n.p., 1938.

Hittell, Theodore H. *Brief History of California.* San Francisco: Stone Educational Co., 1898.

Hoberman, Louisa, ed. *Cities and Society in Colonial Latin America.* Albuquerque: University of New Mexico Press, 1986.

Hodge, F. W., and T. H. Lewis, eds. *Spanish Explorers in the Southern United States, 1528–1543.* New York: Barnes & Noble, 1959.

Hoffman, Paul E. *The Spanish Crown and the Defense of the Caribbean, 1535–1585.* Baton Rouge: Louisiana State University Press, 1980.

Horgan, Paul. *Conquistadores in North American History.* New York: Farrar, Straus & Co., 1963.

———. *Great River: The Rio Grande in North American History.* New York: Holt, Rinehart & Winston, 1954.

Hudson, Charles M. "Tracking the Elusive De Soto." *Archaelogy* 42, no. 3 (May–June 1989).

Jennings, Hohn. *The Golden Eagle: Hernando de Soto.* New York: Dell Publishing, 1958.

Kanellos, Nicolás. *Hispanic First: 500 Years of Extraordinary Achievement.* Detroit: Gale, 1995.

Kelsey, Harry. *Juan Rodriguez Cabrillo.* San Marino, Calif.: Huntington Library, 1906.

Kraus, Michael. *The United States to 1865.* Ann Arbor: University of Michigan Press, 1959.

Landa, Diego de. *Yucatan Before and After the Conquest.* New York: Dover, 1978.

Lanning, John Tate. *The Spanish Missions of Georgia.* Chapel Hill: University of North Carolina Press, 1935.

Laxalt, Robert. "Basque Shepherders: Lonely Sentinels

of the American West." *National Geographic* (June 1966): 870–888.

Lowery, Woodbury. *The Spanish Settlements Within the Present Limits of the United States, 1513–1561.* New York: Russell & Russell, 1959.

Lyon, Eugene. *The Enterprise of Florida: Pedro Menéndez de Avilés and the Spanish Conquest of 1565–1568.* Gainesville: University of Florida Press, 1976.

McAlister, Lyle N. *Spain & Portugal in the New World, 1492–1700.* Minneapolis: University of Minnesota Press, 1984.

MacCurdy, Raymond R. "A Tentative Bibliography of the Spanish-Language Press in Louisiana." *The Americas* X, no. 3 (January 1954).

McDermott, John F. *The Spanish in the Mississippi Valley, 1762–1804.* Chicago: University of Illinois Press, 1974.

MacNally, Michael J. "Florida Catholicism: 422 Years of History." *Miami Herald*, June 9, 1987.

Malagon, Javier. *A Hispanic Look at the Bicentennial.* [Houston?], Tex.: Institute of Hispanic Culture of Houston, 1976.

McKnight, Joseph W. "Law on the Anglo-Hispanic Frontier." *El Campanario* 16, no. 4 (December 1985).

McWilliams, Carey. *North from Mexico: The Spanish-Speaking People of the United States.* Rev. ed. New York: Greenwood Press, 1968.

Mestre, Jose A. *The Flag and the Cross.* Miami: 1988.

Milanich, Jerald T., and Susan Mulbrath, eds. *First Encounters: Spanish Exploration in the Caribbean and the United States.* Gainesville: University of Florida Press, 1990.

Moody, Ralph. *The Old Trails.* New York: Thomas Y. Crowell, 1963.

Moore, Joan W. and Harry Pachon. *Hispanics in the United States.* Englewood Cliffs, N.J.: Prentice Hall, 1985.

Morgan, H. Wayne. *America's Road to Empire: The War with Spain and Overseas Expansion.* New York: John Wiley & Sons, 1965.

Morison, Samuel Eliot. *The Oxford History of the American People.* New York: Oxford University Press, 1965.

Morris, Richard B., ed. *Encyclopedia of American History.* New York: Harper & Row, 1961.

Nasatir, Abraham P. "Juan Rodriguez Cabrillo." *The Western Explorer* III, no. 2 (December 1964): 3–12.

Natella, Arthur A. *Spanish in America, 1513–1979: A Chronology and Fact Book.* New York: Oceana, 1980.

Nelson, Edna Deu Pree. *The California Dons.* New York: Appleton Century Crofts, 1962.

Neuerburg, Norman. "Painting in the California Missions." *America Art Review* IV, no. 1 (July 1977).

Nussbaum, Arthur. *A History of the Dollar.* New York: Columbia University Press, 1957.

Operé, Fernando. "Españoles cautivos en Norteamérica," in *De la catedral al rascacielos. Actas de la XVII Assamblea General de ALDEEU.* Rafael Corbalán, Gerardo Pixa, Nicolás Toscano, eds. New York: ALDEUU, 1998, p. 235–244.

Ortega, Peter Ribera. "The Caballeros de Vargas and the 350th." *The Santa Fe Scene* III, no. 22 (June 18, 1960): 8–9.

———. *Christmas in Old Santa Fe.* Sante Fe, N.M.: Pinyon Publishing, 1961.

Pérez de Villagrá, Gaspar. *History of New Mexico.* Albuquerque: University of New Mexico Press, 1992.

Pomeroy, Earl. *The Pacific Slope: A History of California, Oregon, Washington, Idaho, Utah and Nevada.* New York: Alfred A. Knopf, 1965.

Powell, Philip Wayne. *Tree of Hate: Propaganda and Prejudices Affecting United States Relations with the Hispanic World.* Vallecito, Calif.: Ross House Books, 1985.

Proske, Beatrice Gilman. *Archer Milton Huntington.* New York: Hispanic Society of America, 1963.

Repplier, Agnes. *Junipero Serra.* New York: All Saints Press, 1962.

Riesenberg, Felix. *The Golden Road: The Story of California's Mission Trail.* New York: McGraw-Hill, 1962.

Ross, Mary. "With Pardo and Boyano on the Fringes of the Georgia Land." *The Georgia Historical Quarterly* XIV, no. 4 (December 1930).

Rueda, Germán. *La Emigración contemporánea de españoles a Estados Unidos.* Madrid: Colección MAPFRE, 1992.

Rule with French Intrusions, 1520–1670. Gainesville: University of Florida Press, 1956.

Saavedra, Santiago. *To the Totem Shore: The Spanish Presence on the Northwest Coast.* Madrid: Ediciones El Viso, 1986.

Saenz de Santa María, et al. *Las culturas hispánicas en los Estados Unidos.* Madrid: Asociación Cultural Hispano-Norteamericana, 1975.

Salmoral, Manuel Lucena. *America 1492: Portrait of a Continent 500 Years Ago.* New York: Facts On File, 1990.

Sandos, James A. "Junipero Serra's Canonization and the Historical Record." *The American Historical Review* 53, no. 5 (December 1988).

Santovi, Al. *New Americans.* New York: Viking, 1988.

Sastre, Alfonso. *Historias de California.* N.p.: MIRV Narrativa, 1996.

Sauer, Carl Ortwin. *Sixteenth Century North America.* Berkeley: University of California Press, 1971.

Sahagún, Bernardino de. *Florentine Codex: A General History of the Things of New Spain.* Salt Lake City: University of Utah Press, 1982.

———. *The Conquest of New Spain.* Salt Lake City: University of Utah Press, 1989.

Schorr, Alan Edward. *Hispanic Resource Directory.* Juneau, Alaska: Denali Press, 1988.

Shinn, Charles Howard. "Pioneer Spanish Families of California." *The Journal of San Diego History* XI, no. 3 (June 1965): 1–14.

Shorris, Earl. *Latinos: A Biography of the People.* New York: W.W. Norton, 1992.

Simmons, Marc. *Spanish Government in New Mexico.* Albuquerque: University of New Mexico Press, 1968.

Stavans, Ilán. *The Hispanic Condition: Reflections on Culture and Identity in America.* New York: HarperCollins, 1995.

Steen, Charlie R., and Rutherford J. Gettens. "Tumacacori Interior Decorations." *The Journal of Arizona History* III, no. 3 (Fall 1962): 7–33.

Stewart, George R. *The California Trail.* New York: McGraw-Hill, 1962.

———. *Names on the Land.* Boston: Houghton Mifflin, 1958.

Syme, Ronald. *Cabeza de Vaca: The First Man to Cross America.* William Morrow & Co., 1961.

Taylor, Ralph C. *Colorado, South of the Border.* Denver: Sage Books, 1963.

Tebeau, Charlton W. *A History of Florida.* Coral Gables, Fla.: University of Miami Press, 1971.

Tepaske, John Jay. *The Governorship of Spanish Florida, 1700–1763.* Durham, N.C.: Duke University Press, 1964.

Thomas, Alfred B. "Spanish Expeditions into Colorado." *The Golden Nugget* VI, no. 3 (May 1929): 79–91.

Thomas, Chauncey. "The Spanish Fort in Colorado, 1819." *The Colorado Magazine* XIV, no. 3 (May 1937): 81–85.

Thompson, Ray. "The Old Spanish Trail." *Down South* 4, no. 3 (May–June 1954): 3ff.

Thomson, Bailey. "Archaeologists on De Soto's Trail." *FEH Florida Forum Feature* XI, no. 3 (Fall 1988).

Thomson, Buchanan Parker. *Spain: Forgotten Ally of the American Revolution.* North Quincy, Mass.: Christopher Publishing House, 1976.

Todorov, Tzvetan. *The Conquest of America: The Question of the Other.* New York: Harper & Row, 1984.

Van Every, Dale. *A Company of Heroes: The American Frontier, 1775–1783.* New York: William Morrow & Co., 1962.

Varona, Frank de. *Hispanics in American History.* Englewood Cliffs, N.J.: Globe Book Company, 1989.

Varona, Frank de, ed. *Hispanic Presence in the United States.* Miami: National Hispanic Quincentennial Commission, 1993.

Vega, Garcilaso de las. *Florida of the Inca.* Austin: University of Texas Press, 1957.

Verdú, Vicente. *El planeta americano.* Barcelona: Editorial Anagrama, 1996.

Wallace, Andrew, ed. *Sources and Readings in Arizona History.* Tucson: Arizona Pioneer's Historical Society, 1965.

Warren, Nina Otero. *Old Spain in the Southwest.* New York: Harcourt, Brace, 1937.

Weber, David J. *New Spain's Far Northern Frontier: Essays on Spain in the American West, 1540–1821.* Dallas: Southern Methodist University Press, 1988.

Weber, Francis J. "Catholicism in Colonial America." *The Homiletic and Pastoral Review* (July 1965): 842–851.

Weddle, Robert S. *Spanish Sea: The Gulf of Mexico in North American Discovery, 1500–1684.* College Station: Texas A&M University Press, 1985.

Weyr, Thomas. *Hispanic U.S.A.: Breaking the Melting Pot.* New York: Harper & Row, 1988.

Williamson, René de Visme. *Culture and Policy: The United States and the Hispanic World.* Knoxville; University of Tennessee Press, 1949.

Worcester, Don. *From the Plains of Andalucia to the Prairies of Texas.* College Station: Texas A&M University Press, 1986.

Wriger, Ralph B., ed. *California's Missions.* Los Angeles: Sterling Press, 1962.

INDEX

Page numbers in *italics* indicate illustrations. Those followed by *m* indicate maps.